AUBREY BEARDSLEY

THE FIN-DE-SIÈCLE MAGICIAN
OF LIGHT AND DARKNESS

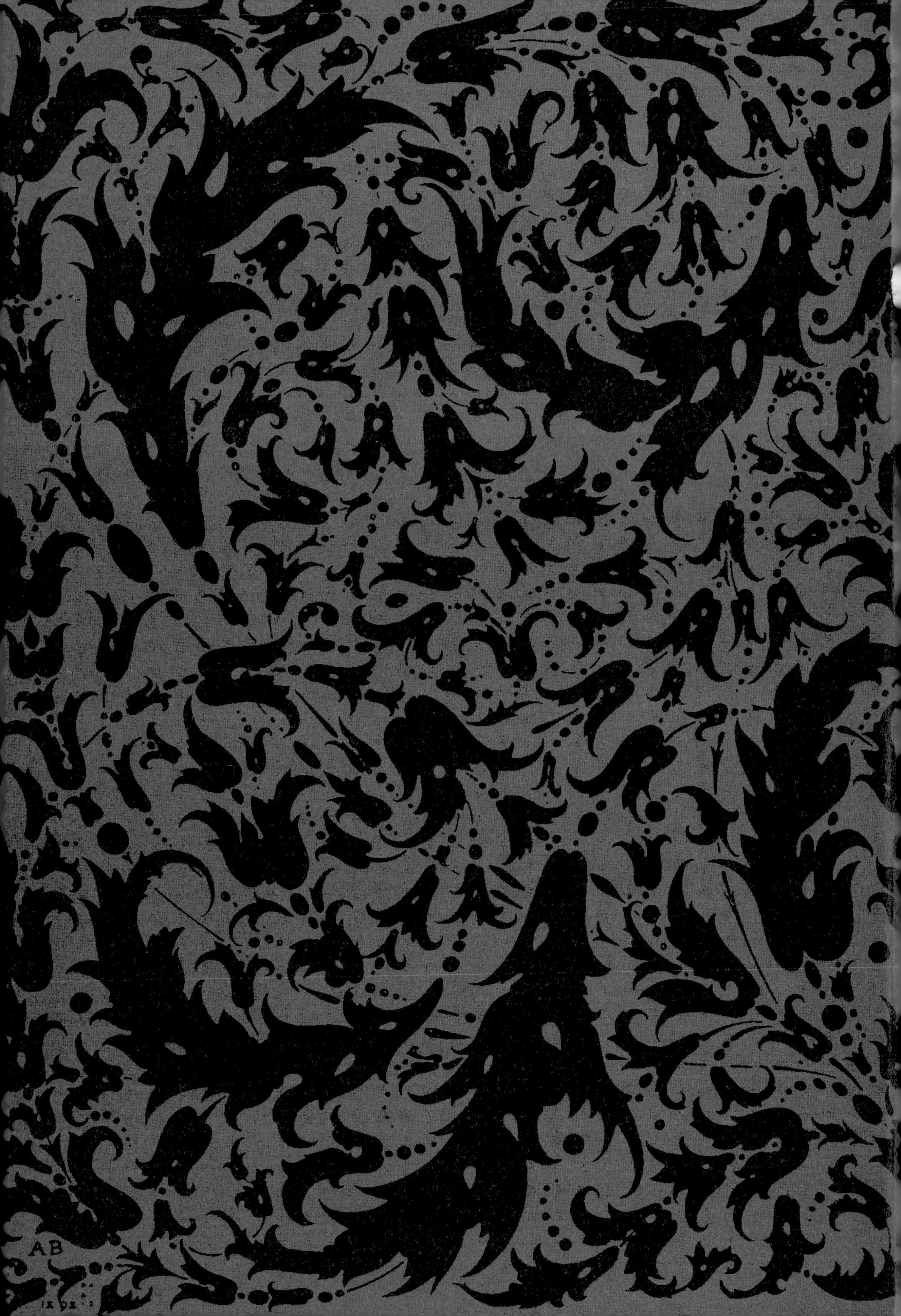

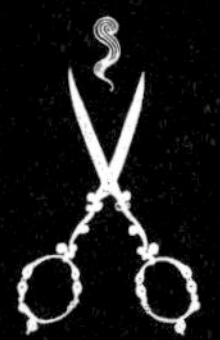

Aubrey Beardsley

The Fin-de-Siècle Magician of Light and Darkness

By Hiroshi Unno

PIE

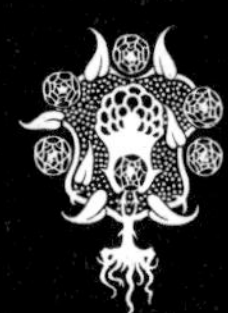

Table of Contents

Aubrey Beardsley

A Shooting Star Who Vanished into the Fin de Siècle Darkness

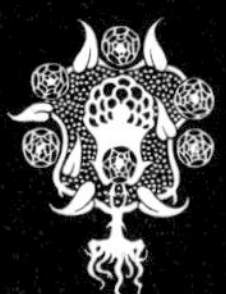

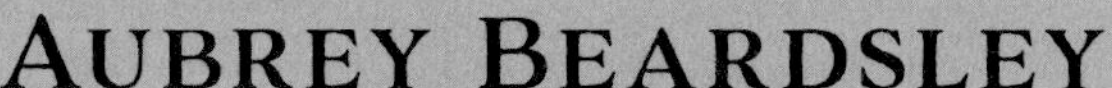

Aubrey Beardsley

A Shooting Star Who Vanished into the Fin de Siècle Darkness

By Hiroshi Unno

Beardsley's Magical Monochrome

Like a flash of light breaking open the night sky, Beardsley's light burned brightly for a brief moment and then was gone. His life was cut tragically short. Yet the works he left behind are, once seen, hard to erase from memory. Indeed, they sometimes return to haunt us like nightmares.

Beardsley's career as an artist spanned less than ten years, and its stage was the final decade of the nineteenth century—the so-called fin-de-siècle years. He appeared seemingly out of nowhere and instantly drew attention with artwork as groundbreaking as if it had fallen to earth from another galaxy. It was not just surprise that Beardsley's drawings induced in people, but fear also—there was something about them that seemed to imperil the stability of people's everyday world.

It is hard for us now to imagine why Beardsley caused such an uproar in British society— why he was branded the devil's apprentice, and his works criticized for offending public decency. To understand this better, we need to remember that the drama played out in the reign of Queen Victoria, which lasted for the majority of the nineteenth century. The Victorian era was defined by its ludicrously rigid and conservative sense of morality. A queen may have occupied the throne, but the society was intensely male-dominated and patriarchal in nature. The virtuous woman was seen as modest and humble, rarely venturing outside the home.

Moreover, anything related to sex was papered over at any cost. When women did go out, they were not allowed to reveal any skin; even their hands and feet had to be covered. Not only was anything of a sexual nature hidden, but its very existence was denied, and hence speaking about such matters was forbidden. A particularly comical example relates to furniture legs, which were regarded as obscene and thus clothed in skirts to conceal them. This stood in sharp contrast to the eighteenth-century attitude, where furniture was created with 'ball and claw' feet, explicitly designed to look like animal legs. In this way, sex in Victorian Britain was buried under layer upon layer of repression. Beardsley found this kind of concealment risible, and his work sought to tear away the hypocritical, moralistic wrapping that covered up the sensual world.

Yet if Beardsley was a rebel pushing back against the Victorian era, he was not only that; he was also a child of that era, and it is in the combination of these two aspects that his appeal lies. His works both clearly transgressed the boundaries of nineteenth-century art and foreshadowed modern art. Picasso, Kandinsky and Mondrian can all be tied to Beardsley. At the same time, Beardsley was a child of the end of the nineteenth century, whose artistic activity occurred during the eccentric fin-de-siècle years of the Victorian era. The rich allure of his work exudes the light and dark of that end-of-the-century period; his ghost is inseparable from it.

Beardsley's relationship with Art Nouveau can also be understood in light of that ambivalence. While Beardsley is regarded as one of the forerunning Art Nouveau artists, it is clear that he far transcended the movement, and cannot be understood purely within its terms. Yet his work shares that slightly risqué fin-de-siècle quality that made Art Nouveau so popular. We cannot speak of the fin de siècle without talking of Beardsley, and the better we understand that period of history, the more fascinating Beardsley becomes.

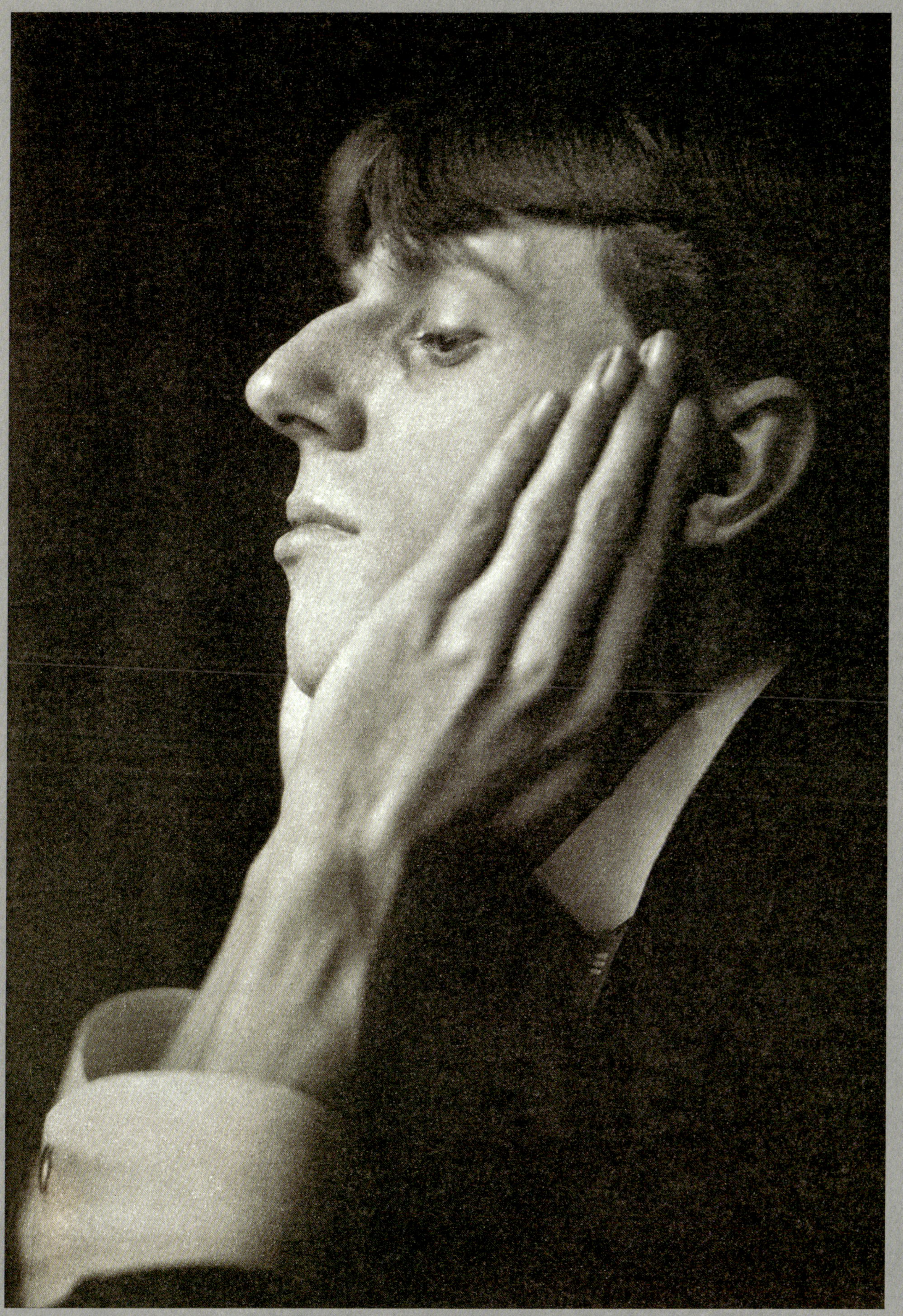

THE RAPE OF THE LOCK

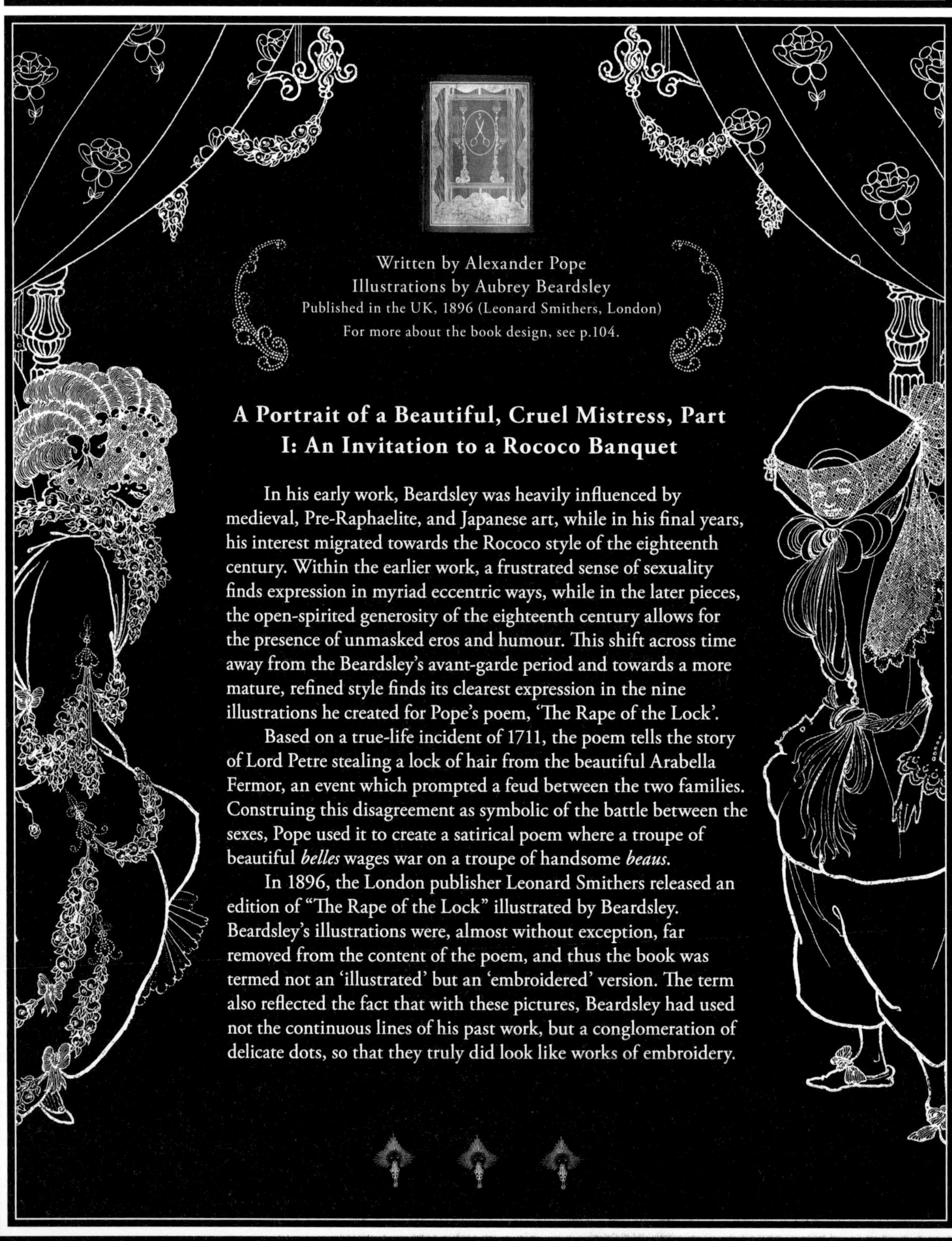

Written by Alexander Pope
Illustrations by Aubrey Beardsley
Published in the UK, 1896 (Leonard Smithers, London)
For more about the book design, see p.104.

A Portrait of a Beautiful, Cruel Mistress, Part I: An Invitation to a Rococo Banquet

In his early work, Beardsley was heavily influenced by medieval, Pre-Raphaelite, and Japanese art, while in his final years, his interest migrated towards the Rococo style of the eighteenth century. Within the earlier work, a frustrated sense of sexuality finds expression in myriad eccentric ways, while in the later pieces, the open-spirited generosity of the eighteenth century allows for the presence of unmasked eros and humour. This shift across time away from the Beardsley's avant-garde period and towards a more mature, refined style finds its clearest expression in the nine illustrations he created for Pope's poem, 'The Rape of the Lock'.

Based on a true-life incident of 1711, the poem tells the story of Lord Petre stealing a lock of hair from the beautiful Arabella Fermor, an event which prompted a feud between the two families. Construing this disagreement as symbolic of the battle between the sexes, Pope used it to create a satirical poem where a troupe of beautiful *belles* wages war on a troupe of handsome *beaus*.

In 1896, the London publisher Leonard Smithers released an edition of "The Rape of the Lock" illustrated by Beardsley. Beardsley's illustrations were, almost without exception, far removed from the content of the poem, and thus the book was termed not an 'illustrated' but an 'embroidered' version. The term also reflected the fact that with these pictures, Beardsley had used not the continuous lines of his past work, but a conglomeration of delicate dots, so that they truly did look like works of embroidery.

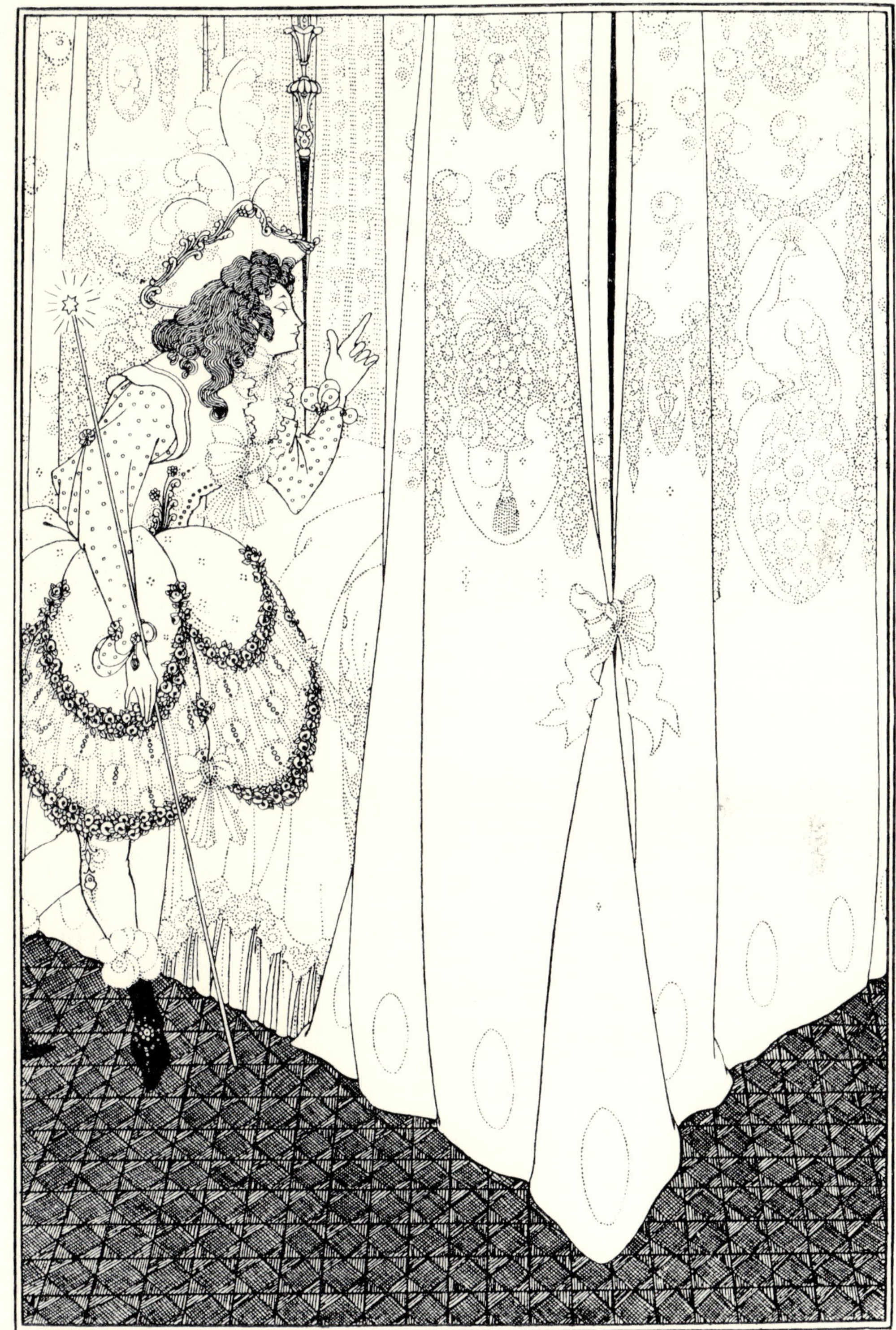

Frontispiece: 'The Dream'

The picture shows a sylph who has slightly parted the drapes of the four-poster bed in order to whisper to its inhabitant. In the bed is Belinda, a beautiful woman whom the sylph is protecting—in this case, bestowing her with a morning doze and pleasant dreams. The design of peacocks and floral bouquets embroidered on the curtains almost seems to be the content of Belinda's dreams. The sylph holds a magic cane with a shining star at its top. The picture seems suffused with the peaceful contentment of dreamtime. How different this illustrative style seems from Beardsley's bold early work, with its disregard for the laws of perspective.

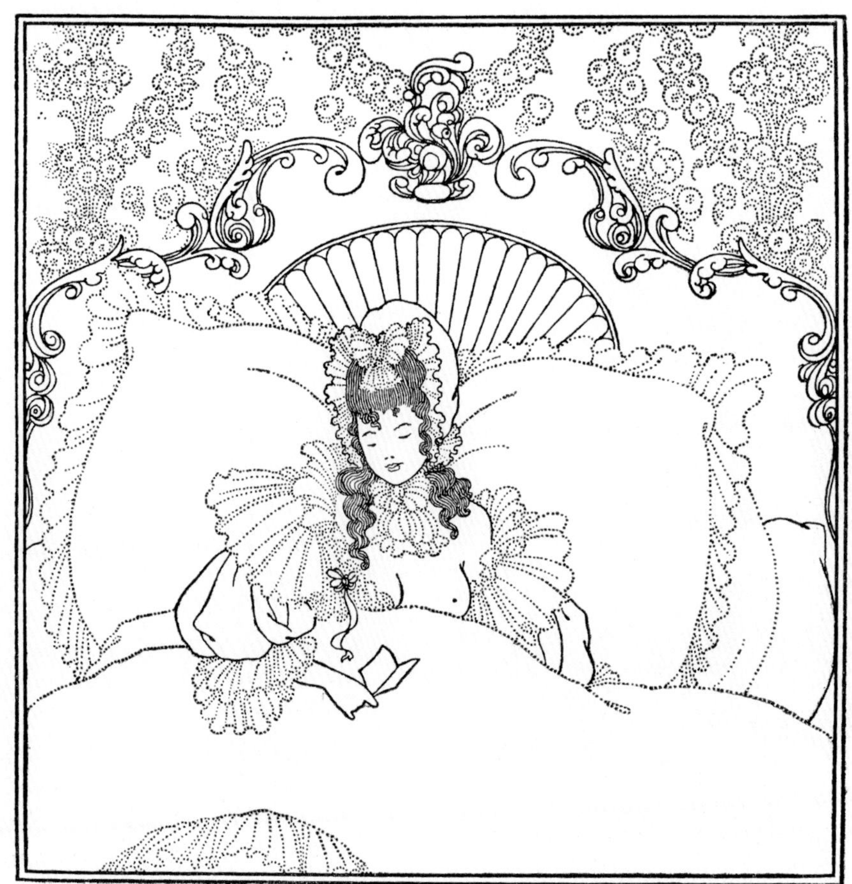

THE RAPE OF THE LOCK

CANTO I

WHAT dire Offence from am'rous Causes springs,
What mighty Contests rise from trivial Things,
I sing—This verse to CARYL, Muse! is due;
This, ev'n *Belinda* may vouchsafe to view:

B

Headpiece for the first canto: 'The Billet-Doux'

Here the reader discovers that inside the four-poster bed into which the sylph was peering is none other than the beautiful Belinda. On her bed is a radial pattern of flower petals, topped by swirling arabesque designs, while the wall behind is adorned by garlands of flowers. Belinda leans back on the pillows of that extravagant Rococo-style bed, wearing a frilled negligee from which one of her breasts has fallen fully out. Her luscious ringlets spill out from underneath her nightcap. What is she dreaming about?

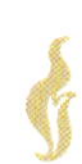

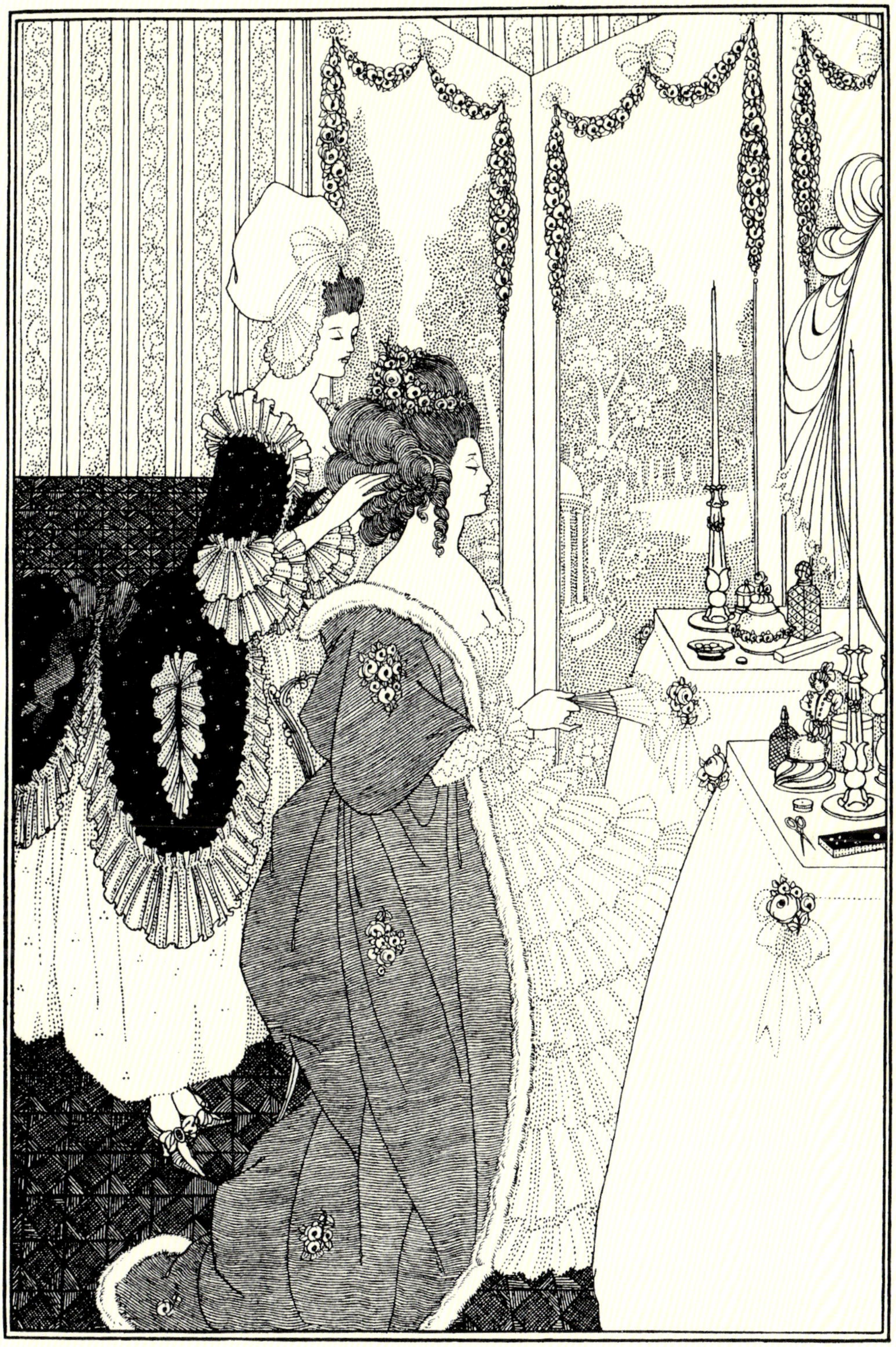

'The Toilet'

No story of a beautiful aristocratic woman is complete without a scene of her toilette—although Belinda's routine differs considerably from that of Salome. With these illustrations, we see that Beardsley has made the shift from a style suitable for woodblock printing to a more delicate pen and ink style. When creating wooden printing plates, the lines Beardsley had first drawn in pen or pencil would have to be engraved into wood. But with the appearance of photomechanical printmaking techniques, it became possible to print illustrations using pen drawing alone. This in turn made it possible to print drawings and sketches making use of pointillist and other more delicate artistic touches. Here, in the representation of the trees outside the window and the folds of the women's skirts, we see how clearly the intricate dots have been reproduced. Yet some might miss the suggestive shapes constructed of simple, bold lines from Beardsley's previous works.

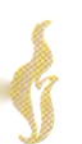

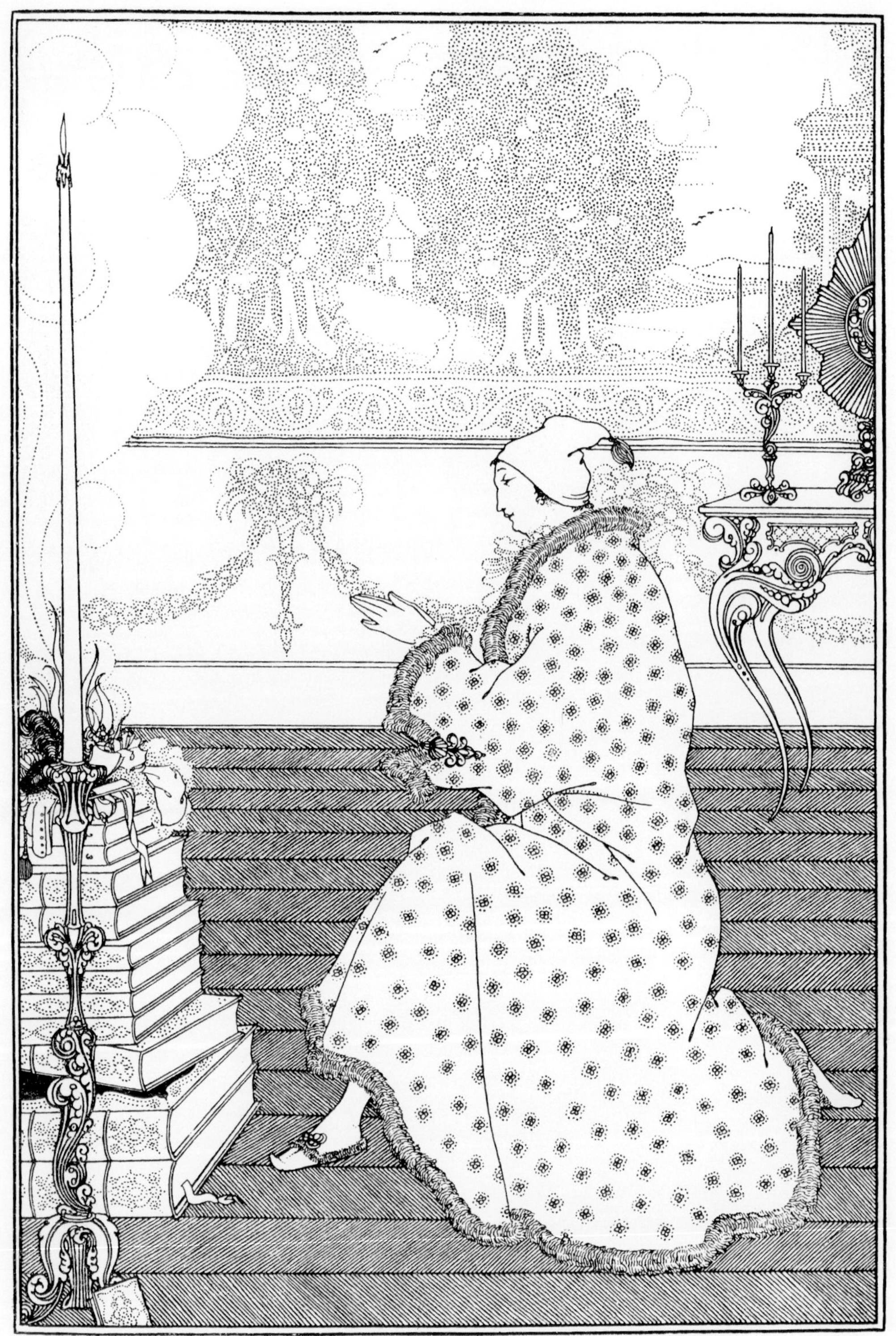

'The Baron's Prayer'

Belinda's glorious hair was the talk of the town, and eventually a certain Lord got wind of them. The Lord, who was something of an aesthetic connoisseur, collected works of art and books, and worshipped at the temple of beauty. Hearing the rumours of Belinda's beautiful locks, he decided he must get his hands on one of them, and install it in his own personal shrine. Here the Lord attired in a dressing gown is praying at an altar created on top of a stack of books. The trees and garden outside the window seem as if they have been embroidered. The Lord's hands clasped in prayer come together with the garland pattern on the wallpaper, which elsewhere appears to have grabbed hold of his hair. Rococo-style furniture is dotted about the room.

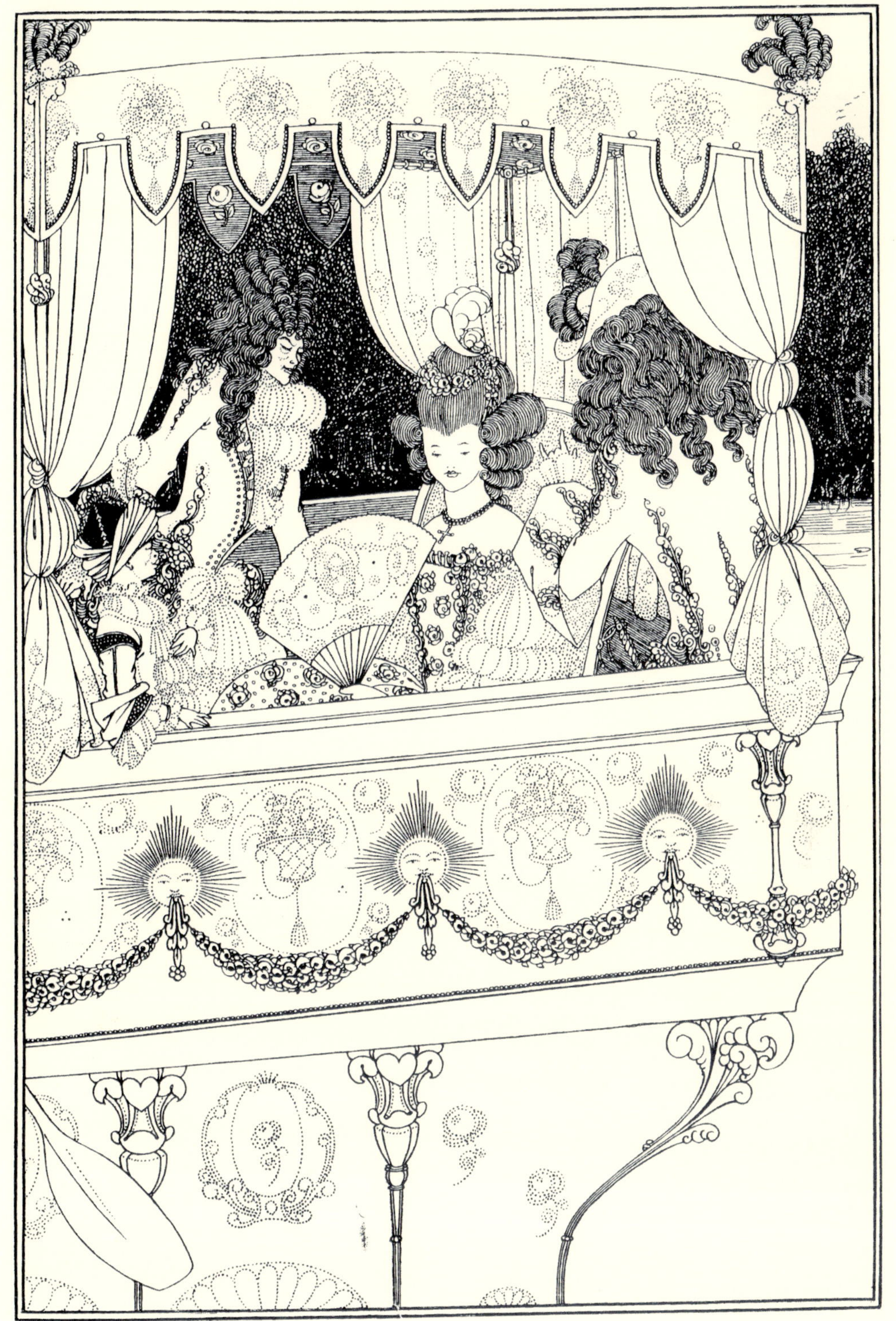

'The Barge'

A party held on a pleasure-boat offers the Lord the chance he has been waiting for, and he is able to approach Belinda as she is surrounded by fashionable gentlemen. Her notorious ringlets are swept up high on her head. The plate offers a catalogue of Rococo ornamentation, with the details of the side of the barge particularly enthralling.

After enjoying the journey down the river, Belinda and the gentlemen sit down to play at cards, and as the betting intensifies, so does the mood of gaiety. Wearing the hair swept up on the head in this way was the fashion in the late Baroque era, when hair served as a symbol of beauty and strength.

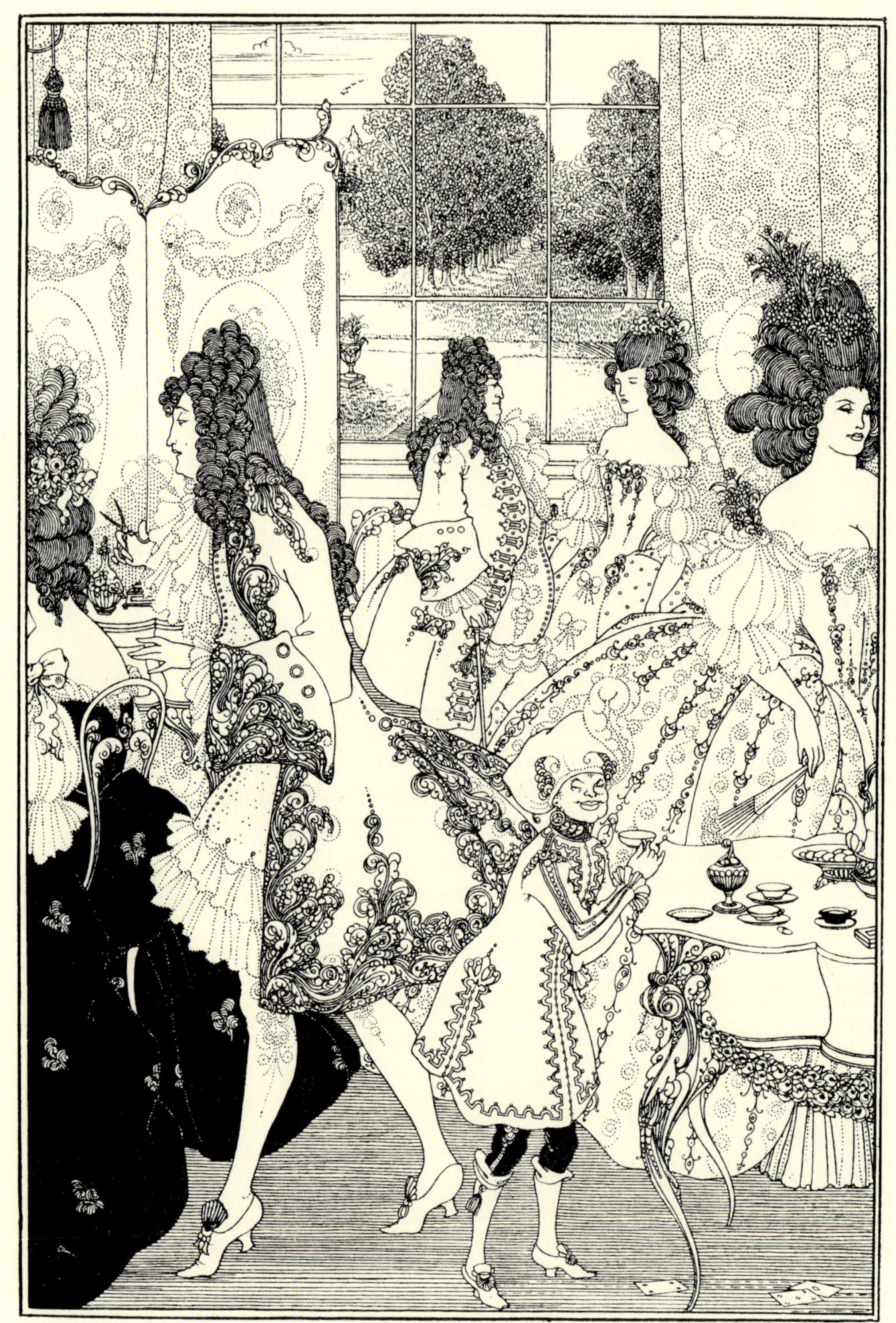

'The Rape of the Lock'

We finally reach the climactic scene where the lock of hair is stolen. The dwarf jester standing centrally is a kind of narrator, informing the audience of the theft. The interjection of this kind of narrator allegedly stems from Beardsley's memories of travelling shows and farce comedies, of which he was fond. To the left side of the picture, one can see Belinda, and the Lord approaching from behind with a pair of scissors. The woman to the right takes out a pair of scissors from her handbag and passes them to the Lord, while trying to make off unnoticed. The dwarf is laughing at their elaborate artistry. And thus, the lock is cut off…

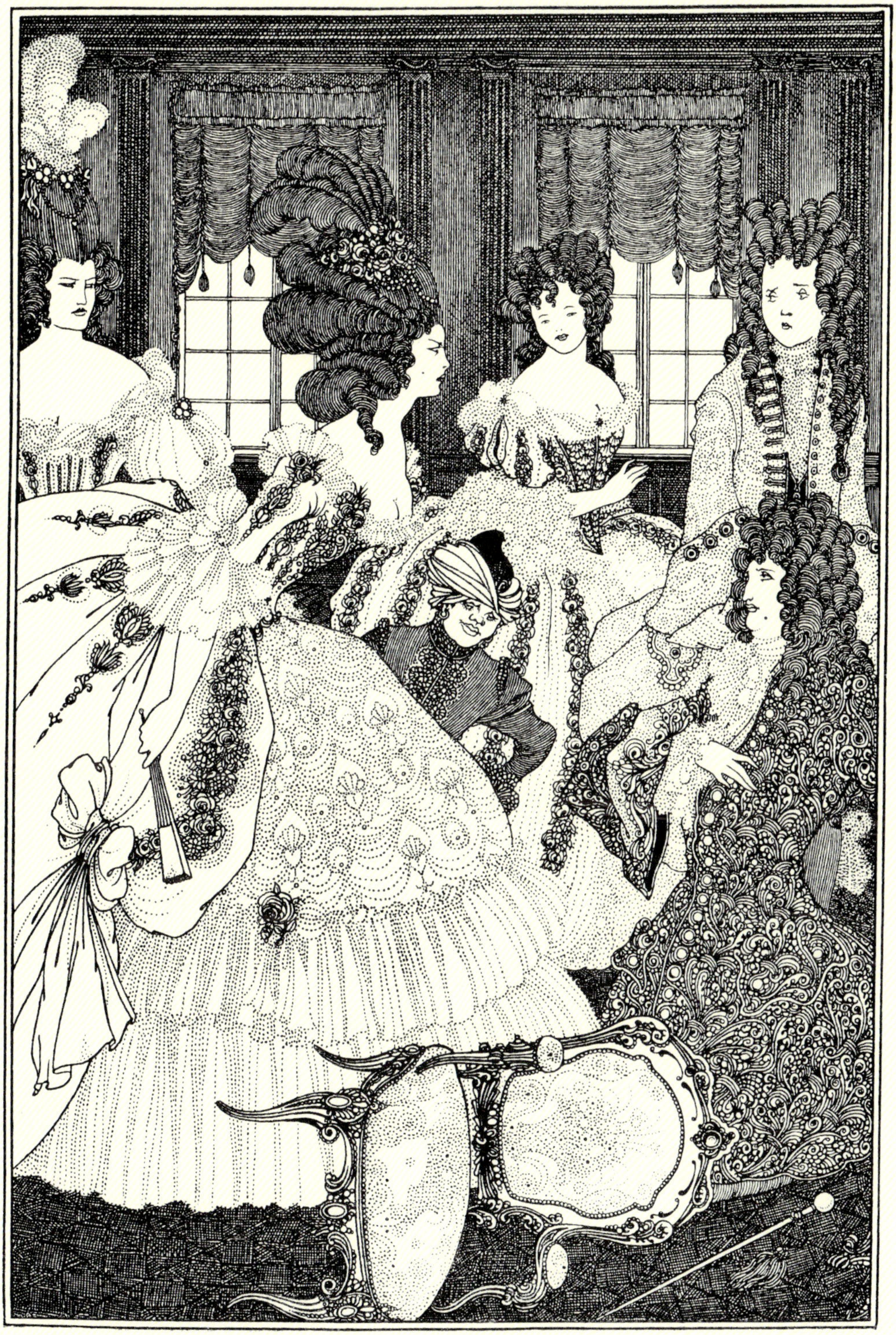

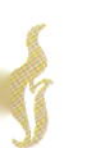

'The Battle of the Beaux and Belles'

Belinda rushes over to the Lord in a fury. The dwarf stands between them, cocking his head amusedly as he surveys the situation. Belinda's hair is still looking as abundant as ever, and it's impossible to tell which part has been snipped. Her flamboyant costume has been portrayed in the pointillist style. The men's attire is rendered in the style of the eighteenth century in which Pope was writing, but the women's costume seems mismatched. This discrepancy is explained by the fact that Beardsley dressed his characters in whichever costumes most appealed to him, regardless of the age they came from. The dense arabesque pattern on the Lord's coat is staggering.

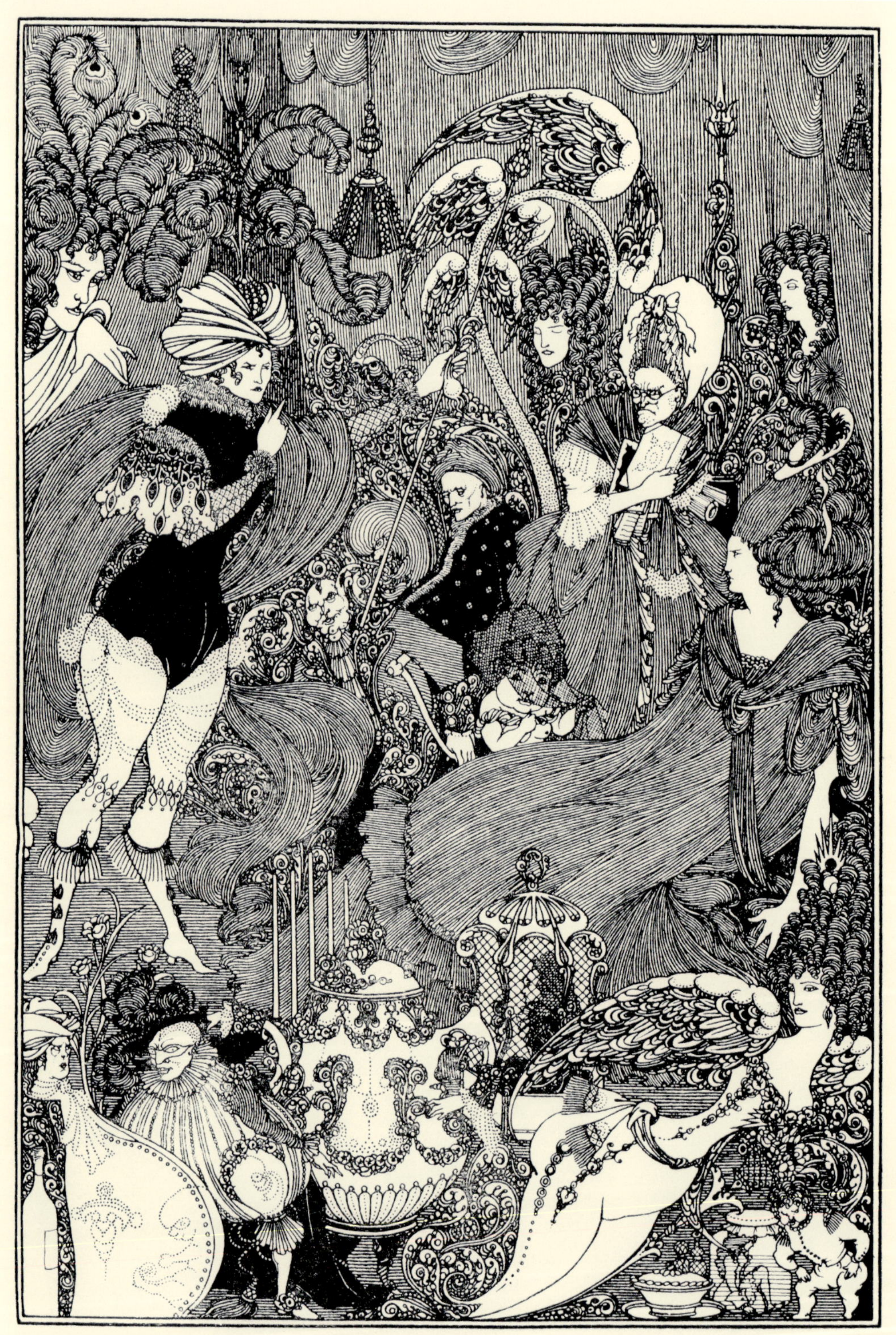

'The Cave of Spleen'

Divested of her lock of hair, Belinda wages war on the men. The world is divided into two factions, and the battle begins. Even the gods and the fairies take part in the conflict. In this illustration we see the eerie scene inside 'The Cave of Spleen' where the inhuman creatures—fairies, spirits and the like—gather. Beardsley's illustrations for *The Rape of the Lock* are generally people-pleasing and cheerful, with this rather grotesque plate alone hearking back to his Salome days. Holding a cane like that of Hermes and addressing the others is a sprite called Umbriel. At the bottom of the picture are what are known in Japanese as *kikai*—the spirits of containers or implements. From this we can conclude that Beardsley was most likely influenced by Japanese pictures of yōkai and other ghostly apparitions.

When those fair Suns shall set, as set they must,
And all those Tresses shall be laid in dust;
This *Lock*, the Muse shall consecrate to fame,
And 'midst the stars inscribe *Belinda's* Name!   150

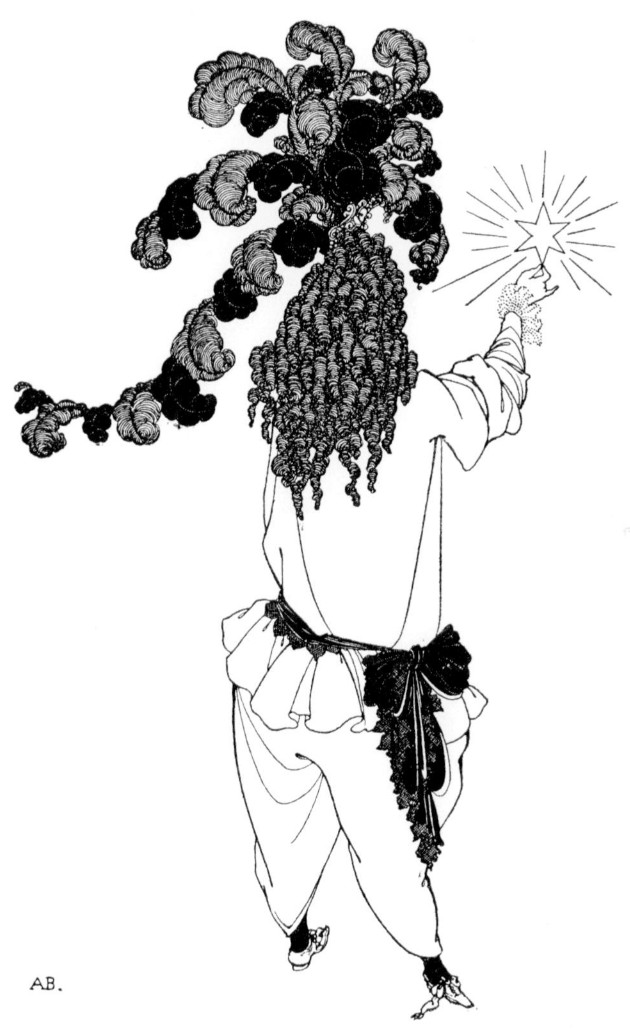

'The New Star'

In the final scene of 'The Rape of the Lock', Belinda wins the war. Her hair rises to the heavens and becomes a star, upon which Belinda's name is engraved. The figure appearing here with a star in hand wears the carnival costume for the court of Louis XIV—it was drawn by Beardsley after seeing 'The Rape of the Lock' performed on the occasion of such a carnival. It's possible that the costume parades he had observed in festivals in his hometown of Brighton were the source of this image. His pictures seem full of memories of such carnivals and shows.

1. A Brighton Boyhood

Aubrey Beardsley was born in Brighton in 1872. His father, Vincent Beardsley, was the son of a gem merchant from Clerkenwell, London, while his mother, Ellen Agnus Pitt, was the daughter of the Surgeon-Major in the Indian army. Born in India, Ellen moved to Brighton with her family after her father retired from service.

Beardsley's upbringing in Brighton hasn't been touched upon that much, but it seems worthy of note. Brighton is a seaside resort town on the south coast of England. From the late eighteenth century onwards, it became a place where members of the aristocracy had their second homes. George IV was a particular fan of the place during his time as Prince of Wales, and between 1787 and 1823, commissioned the architect John Nash to build a Royal Pavilion there, which looked like something lifted from the pages of the Arabian Nights.

Queen Victoria, who despised the excesses of the reign of her hedonistic uncle George, sold off the Royal Pavilion to the city of Brighton. The city created Brighton Pier, and with the royal pavilion as the central attraction, the entire town became much like an amusement park to which tourists began to flock. By the end of the nineteenth century, Brighton had become the liveliest seaside resort in Britain. Come summer, it would be spilling over with stalls, shows and the like, and the atmosphere was unrestrained and sordid. The Victorian age may have clamped down on morality, but Brighton was comparatively free from such constraints.

Brighton's carnivalesque atmosphere—varied, erotic and grotesque—surely cast a long shadow across the imagination of young Beardsley.

Beardsley's mother, Ellen Pitt, is also an intriguing figure. In her younger days, she was a slender beauty who had turned heads on the seaside road of Brighton, earning her the nickname 'the bottomless Pitt'—a name that in the strict Victorian age would have been very crass. The 'pitt' element also alluded to hell as well as holes, and we have to wonder whether it was intended to allude to her immorality, as well as her slim figure. In any case, Ellen was a free-spirited seaside girl. She met Vincent, who would go onto be her husband, close to the pier, and the two quickly married. Vincent may have been the son of a gem merchant, but he worked more or less as a peddler selling accessories and so on, and had probably come to Brighton for business. He had been seeing other girls too, and when he announced his wedding, another woman came forward to contest the marriage. Naturally, Ellen's parents were against the marriage, but she refused to heed their warnings.

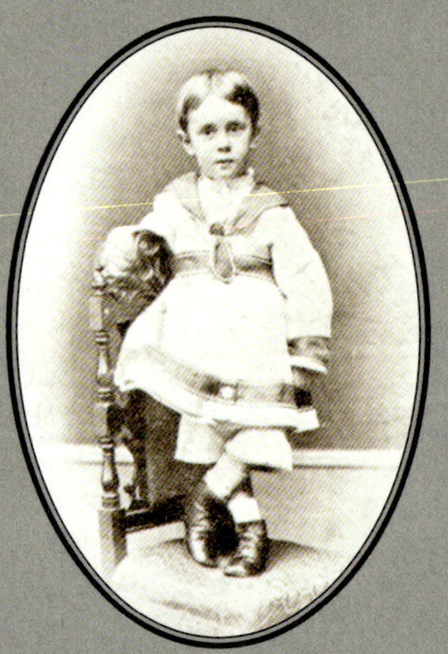

Beardsley at age 2

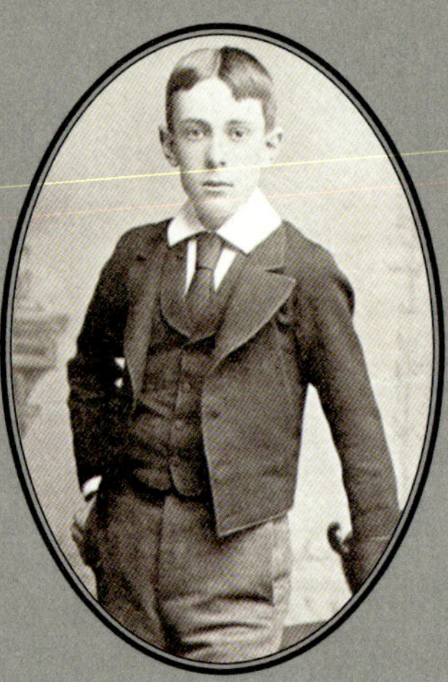

Beardsley at age 10

In 1871, their daughter Mabel was born. A year later, in 1872, came Aubrey, and not long after that, Vincent more or less disappeared. Ellen moved about here and there, working and raising her two children, with the help of her parents.

It seems to me clear that Ellen was no run-of-the-mill woman. As the epithet 'bottomless' perhaps suggests, she was daring, and able to accommodate reality for what it was. She remained unfazed by what the world said about her and, despite her financial struggles, taught her son literature, music and art, determined to bring him up as an artist. She also had an open-minded attitude towards sexuality, which was rare for a women of that era of history. What surprises me most is that she accepted everything that her son created, even when his sudden fame brought a torrent of criticism proclaiming his work obscene and immoral. The generous Ellen, who embraced the sexual, the extraordinary, the diseased, the lunatic, and everything else besides as part and parcel of her son's artistic world truly was, in some sense, bottomless.

Beardsley spent his short life cared for by two women: his mother Ellen and his older sister Mabel. Victorian society revolved around men, and was patriarchal in nature. The fact that Beardsley grew up in a household without a father figure surely holds great significance to understanding his art. Beardsley was able to search out a free form of expression, without being restricted by his actual father. He was also unconstrained by academicism, the 'father of the art world', meaning he was free to depict his fin-de-siècle vision just as he wished.

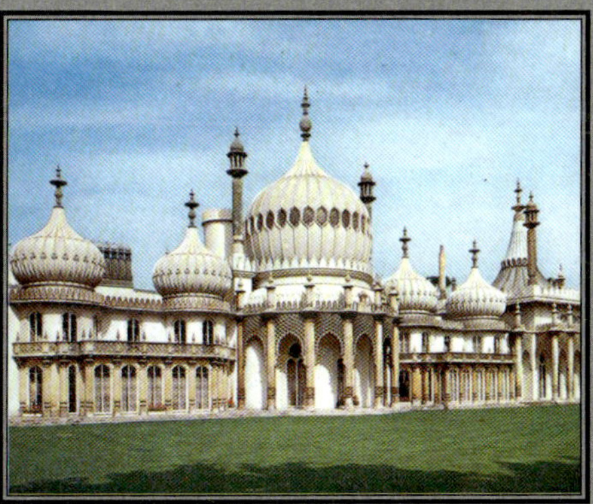

The Royal Pavilion, Brighton

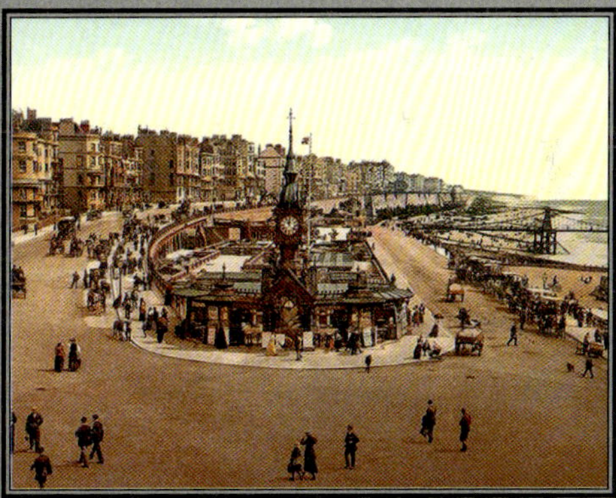

Brighton town centre, late 19th century

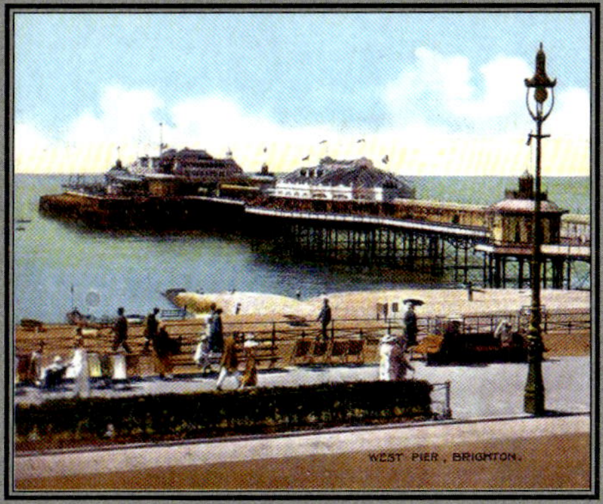

Brighton Pier

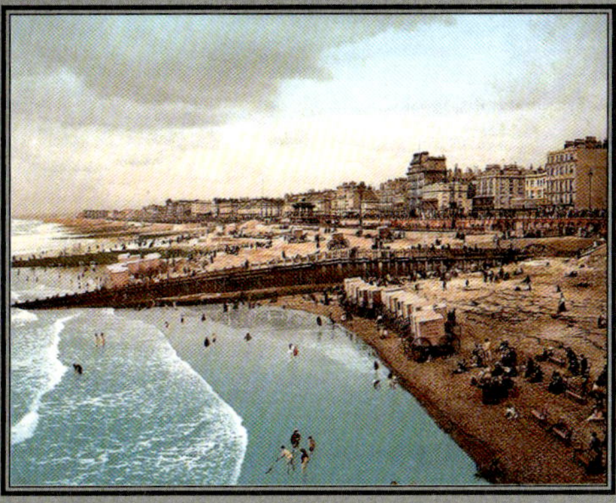

Brighton Beach, late 19th century

Beardsley was of a weak physical disposition from birth. His father suffered from tuberculosis, and in fact, one of the reasons he had come to Brighton was supposedly to recuperate from the condition. Tuberculosis was prevalent from the end of the nineteenth century on, and remained a significant problem until the mid-twentieth century—in a sense it was the fin-de-siècle disease. Beardsley inherited this unfortunate legacy from his father. At that time, there was still no known cure for it, and the only treatment was recuperation in the mountains or by the sea where the air was clear.

Beardsley lived in his mother's aunt's house, attending school in Brighton. He was classmates with Charles B. Cochran, who would later go on to be known as an impresario and manager of several theatres in the London theatre world, bringing success to the plays of Noël Coward and others. Cochran remembers well the gangly red-haired and fair-skinned boy with whom he was at school. The two of them were both passionate about theatre, and Beardsley would write scripts which Cochran would put on. This passion for the stage is evident in Beardsley's pictures too. Beardsley also played at putting on plays with his sister Mabel. During his childhood and adolescence in Brighton, he also wrote poems and stories and drew pictures.

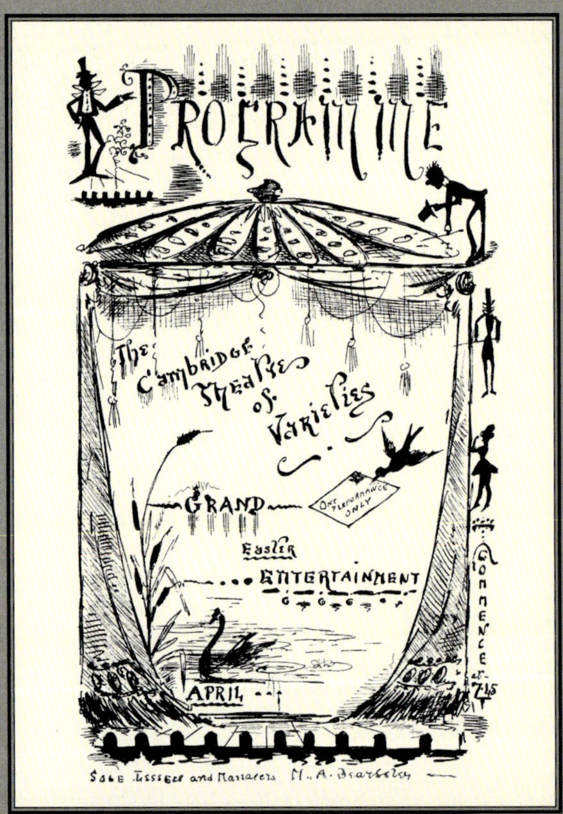

Program of Beardsley's own drawn for playing theatre, 1884-85

2. Fin-de-siècle London

In 1888, at the age of fifteen, Beardsley moved to London. He had to work, and he found himself jobs working at a surveyor's office, and as an office clerk in an insurance company. The smoke-filled London air, markedly different from Brighton's fresh-aired climate, exacerbated his illness. After returning home from the office, Beardsley would create stage sets and costumes, performing plays he'd written at home for his sister Mabel. Beardsley rented a house in Pimlico, near Victoria Station (1 on map), east of Chelsea, and close to the Tate Gallery.

What was London like back then, in the late nineteenth century? In what follows, we will try to build up an image. First, let's get off the train at Victoria Station (2). To the north, lies St. James' Park, where Buckingham Palace is located. To the south is the River Thames, coming in at a steep upward curve from the West. The area spanning from Victoria Station up until the Thames is Pimlico where the Beardsley family first moved to, subsequently moving again several times.

To the west of Pimlico lies Chelsea. Chelsea was once a tranquil area of open fields, but with the creation of the Chelsea Embankment in 1874, it began to flourish as a new riverside residential area. It was the artists who flocked there first to rent studios, creating an artists' colony. Notably, it was the base of the Pre-Raphaelites, with the artist Dante Gabriel Rossetti and his sister, poet Christina Rossetti, as well as Edward Burne-Jones and William Morris all living there.

In 1891, Beardsley visited Burne-Jones' studio, at the north end of West Kensington, together with his sister Mabel. Beardsley had great admiration for Burne-Jones, and he took along a portfolio of sketches he'd been working on.

Burne-Jones looked at Beardsley's sketches, and declared them to be 'full of thought, poetry and imagination'. Oscar Wilde also happened to be visiting the studio at the time. Burne-Jones recommended that Beardsley gave up his office job and devoted himself to his art.

That day, Oscar Wilde gave the Beardsleys a ride home in his Hansom cab. Wilde's lodgings (3) were in Tite Street, to the west of the Royal Hospital gardens in Chelsea, where he lived from 1884 up until his arrest in 1895. Many artists had studios in Tite Street, including James Abbott McNeill Whistler and John Singer Sergeant. Wilde and Whistler were good friends for a time.

Wilde also had a big influence on Beardsley. He was arrested in the Cadogan Hotel in Chelsea (4), carrying a yellow book (see p.114).

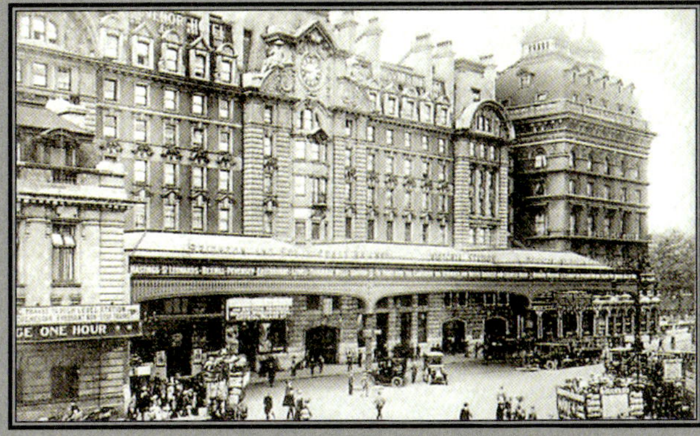

Victoria Station circa 1900 (2 on map)

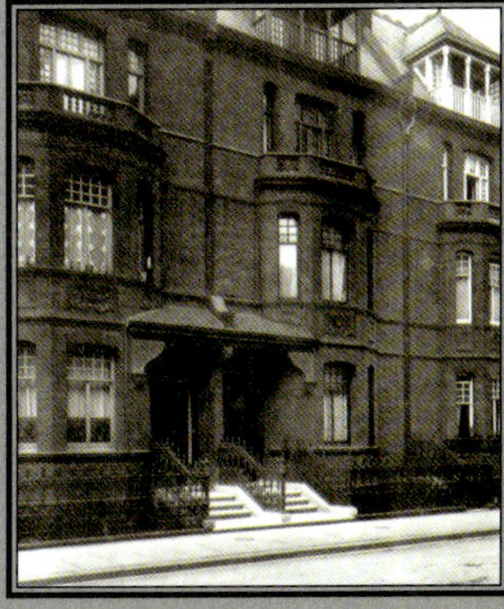

Oscar Wilde's house on Tite Street
(3 on map)

At the recommendation of Burne-Jones, Beardsley attended Westminster School of Art from autumn 1891. He quit after a year, and this year was his only formal education in art, making him largely self-educated, although Burne-Jones and Whistler proved to be big influences on his work. Beardsley went to see the Peacock Room (5) that Whistler had created at Frederick R. Leyland's mansion in Prince's Gate in Kensington. The blue and gold screen-painting speak to the influence of Japanese art on Whistler, although it was widely criticized as in bad taste, and Leyland himself was not keen on the room.

After Oscar Wilde sung the praises of The Peacock Room while visiting the USA on a lecture tour, the American industrialist and art collector Charles Lang Freer bought the entire room in 1904 and transported it to America. The room now belongs in the Freer Gallery of Art in Washington D.C.

As well as being entranced by The Peacock Room, Beardsley took an interest in *ukiyo-e* (woodblock prints) and other aspects of Japanese art, and these formed a key influence on the development of the Beardsley style. The insurance company where he worked was not far from The Peacock Room. Evans' bookshop on Queen Street was also close, and Beardsley was a frequent visitor. It was Frederick Evans, the proprietor of this shop, who introduced Beardsley to the publisher J. M. Dent, who in 1892 would commission Beardsley to produce the illustrations for Thomas Malory's *Le Morte d'Arthur*. This was Beardsley's first major commission, and he left his office job in order to work on it. The fee for the work was £250, and it took him over two years to produce the necessary illustrations, which numbered over 500.

Beardsley's career as an artist was finally underway. Yet before we explore this element of his life, let us first continue with our exploration of fin-de-siècle London.

Head northeast down Victoria Street from Victoria Station and you reach the Palace of Westminster (the Houses of Parliament). Go north, passing through Trafalgar Square, and head down Haymarket and you reach Piccadilly Circus (6), the epicentre of London's entertainment district, and of fin-de-siècle London. Unlike Paris, London has very little in the way of Art Nouveau architecture and sculptures, and Piccadilly Circus is a rarity in that respect. The figure of the angel towering above the fountain in its centre is the work of sculptor Alfred Gilbert. Created to commemorate philanthropist Lord Shaftesbury, the sculpture is intended to depict Anteros, 'the Angel of Christian Charity', but is known affectionately to Londoners as Eros, and in end-of-century London, served as a symbol of everything erotic. It also a strange coincidence that the Art Nouveau sculpture was created in 1892, which was the year that Beardsley's artistic career took off.

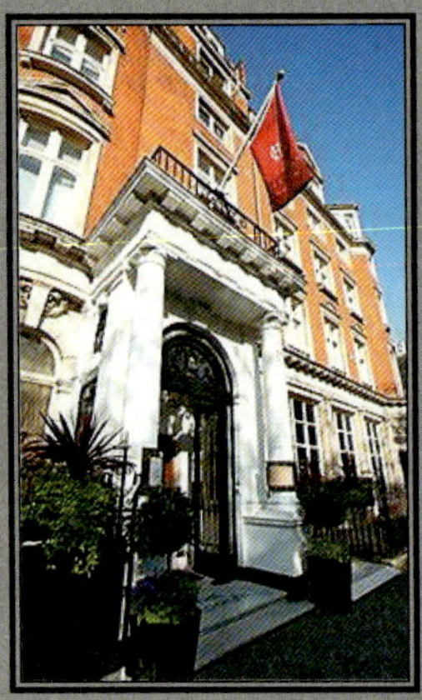

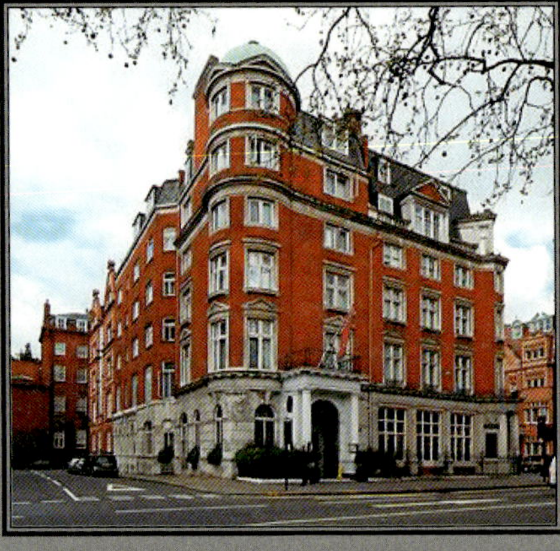

The entrance (left) and exterior (right) of Chelsea's Cadogan Hotel, which remains to the present day. (4 on map)

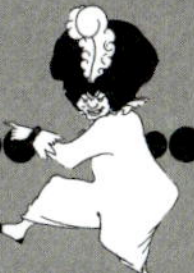

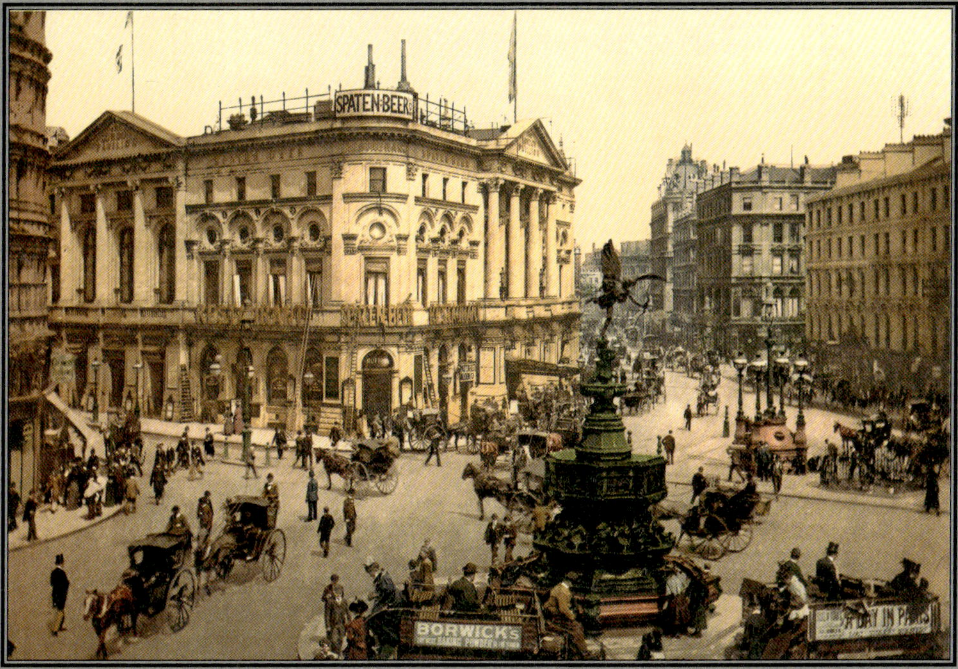

Piccadilly Circus, the epicentre of fin-de-siècle London, with Eros in the middle (6 on map)

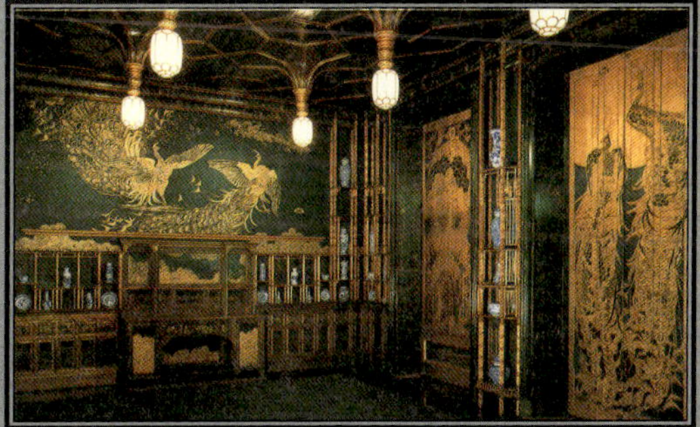

Whistler's Peacock Room 1876-7 (5 on map)

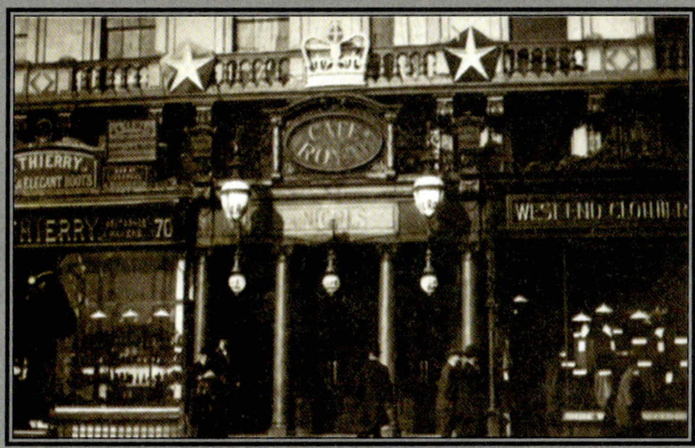

Exterior of the Café Royal at the end of the nineteenth century (7 on map)

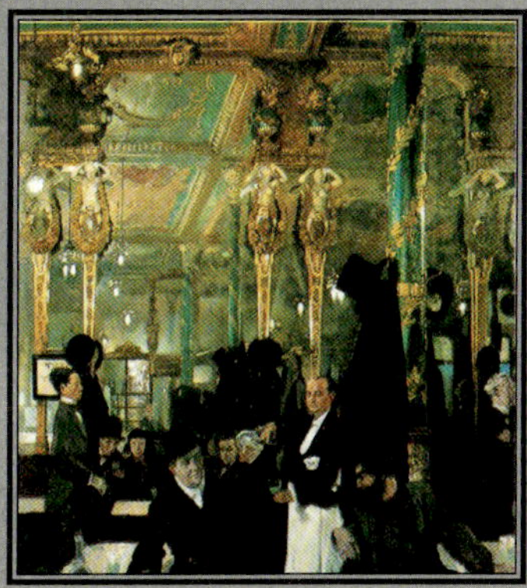

Café Royal, oil painting, 1912

In Victorian London, the area around Piccadilly Circus, from Haymarket through to Leicester Square, was known as the place where prostitutes gathered. Near to this were the theatres, and in the streets behind them, the sex trade was thriving.

This provides a neat display of the hypocritical two-tiered nature of Victorian society. There was a strict clampdown on sexuality on the surface, but behind the scenes much sexual decadence was to be found.

Facing out onto The Quadrant, where the road curving from Piccadilly Circus to Regent Street was sliced into neat quarters, was the Café Royal (7). It was such an institution that if one said the word 'café' to a Londoner at the time, they would know this was the place of which you were speaking.

Café Royal had started out its life in 1863 as a restaurant serving French food and wine, set up by French-born restaurateur Daniel Nicols. When it reopened as The Quadrant at the end of the century, it became a stylish café that proved a magnet for many of London's celebrities. Oscar Wilde would frequently come with his lover, Alfred Douglas. Other regular patrons included the artists Whistler and Augustus John, and the writers George Moore and Max Beerbohm, not to mention Aubrey Beardsley himself.

Daniel Nicols wrote a memoir called *Café Royal Days* (the date of publication is unknown, though it is believed to be around the early 1930s). According to this memoir, Beardsley took one look at the new interior and declared, 'This is real Rococo.' It is interesting to ponder the connection between this event and his Rococo-style illustrations for *The Rape of the Lock*.

Incidentally, Wilde's most frequent haunts were Café Royal and another restaurant called Kettner's (8). In Café Royal, he would get his friends and fans together and delight them with his witty conversation. Kettner's on the other hand, which lay in Romilly Street on the north side of Leicester Square, was a more discrete location. Here he would enjoy inviting students and budding actors, and drinking wine in the restaurant's private room.

Regent Street and Piccadilly Circus formed the borderline between the west side of Mayfair and the east side of Soho—the boundary line between the public face of fin-de-siècle London and its backstreets. Soho was London's underworld, full of 'establishments of ill repute'.

Covent Garden, to the east of Soho, was the theatre district. Until the mid-nineteenth century, London's theatre scene had been hugely limited, with only two theatres, in Drury Lane and Covent Garden, permitted to stage shows. With an amendment to the theatre law in

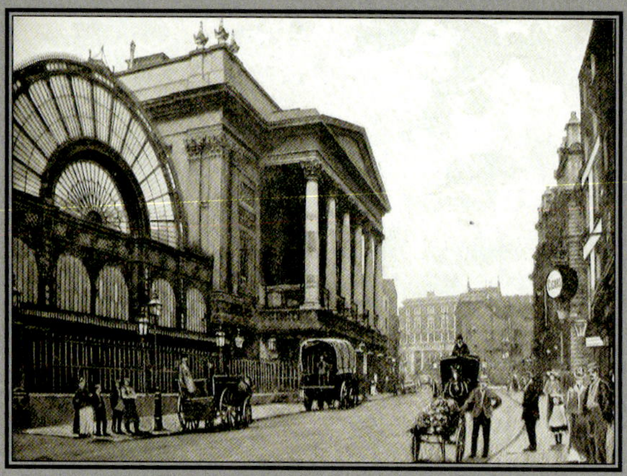

The Royal Opera House in Covent Garden, 1987 (9 on map)

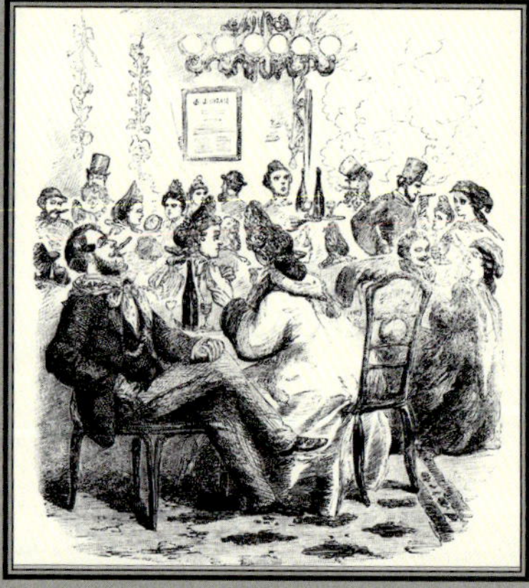

A nineteenth century night club on Haymarket

1843, suddenly all kinds of theatres were allowed. In the Victorian era, the main theatres were the Theatre Royal on Drury Lane, Her Majesty's Theatre and Haymarket Theatre on Haymarket, and the Royal Opera House (9) and the Lyceum in Covent Garden.

In 1881, the theatrical impresario Richard D'Oyly Carte opened the Savoy Theatre (10) on The Strand (see p.181), an event which signalled the start of the fin-de-siècle theatre boom. In the Royal Theatre on Dean Street, D'Oyly Carte found success putting on comic operas produced by W. S. Gilbert and Arthur Sullivan, and built the Savoy Theatre to stage their works.

As well as these theatres, late nineteenth century London also had many music halls and travelling shows. Here, aristocrats mingled with working men in the auditorium, and there would also be prostitutes as well. High-class courtesans came together in the promenades of music halls such as the Empire and Alhambra, bringing too the men in search of them. There was one notorious prostitute at the Empire who was very fat and decked out in lavish jewellery—as if she had risen out of one of Beardsley's illustrations. Needless to say, Beardsley had closely observed the scenes that unfolded in London's music halls and on its streets.

After his success with the Savoy Theatre, D'Oyly Carte opened the Savoy Hotel (11) in 1889. It was adjacent to the theatre district, east down The Strand from Trafalgar Square. The Savoy Hotel was furnished with all the latest amenities in the American style: an elevator and electrical lighting. Wilde, who was partial to anything new, was an early visitor, bringing attractive young men to stay with him.

If you pass the Savoy Hotel and head further east down the Strand, you come to a large building called Somerset House. In front of it, where the road turns in a semi-circular loop, is Aldwych, although this was only created in 1905 and is thus after Beardsley's time.

A little way further on, one could turn right down Arundel Street, which led onto the Thames Embankment, where Leonard Smithers had his bookshop. When he started working for the quarterly literary periodical, *The Yellow Book*, Beardsley would frequently pop into this bookshop, and became friendly with Smithers. After being dismissed from *The Yellow Book*, Beardsley joined forces with Smithers to produce *The Savoy*.

The Bodley Head (12), John Lane's publishing house which published *The Yellow Book*, was on Vigo Street, off to the west as Piccadilly Circus curves round into Regent Street.

Our tour of fin-de-siècle London has taken us from the streets of Chelsea to Piccadilly Circus with its statue of Eros, from the entertainment district of Soho to the theatre district heaving with theatres and music halls, all the way to The Strand. It was these underworld streets that Beardsley used to roam, avidly taking in the various wondrous and surprising scenes they had to offer.

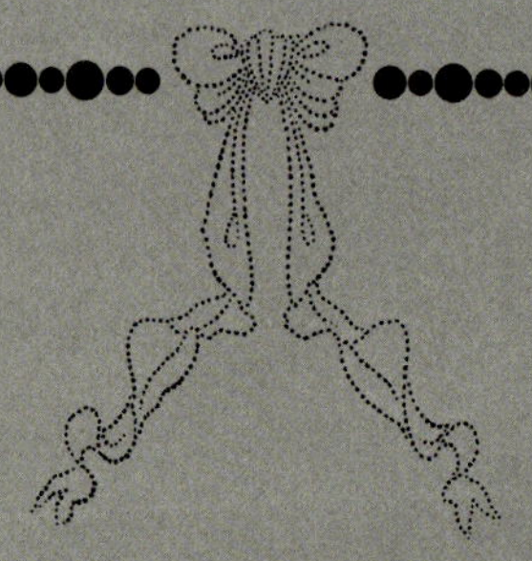

MAP OF BEARDSLEY'S LONDON

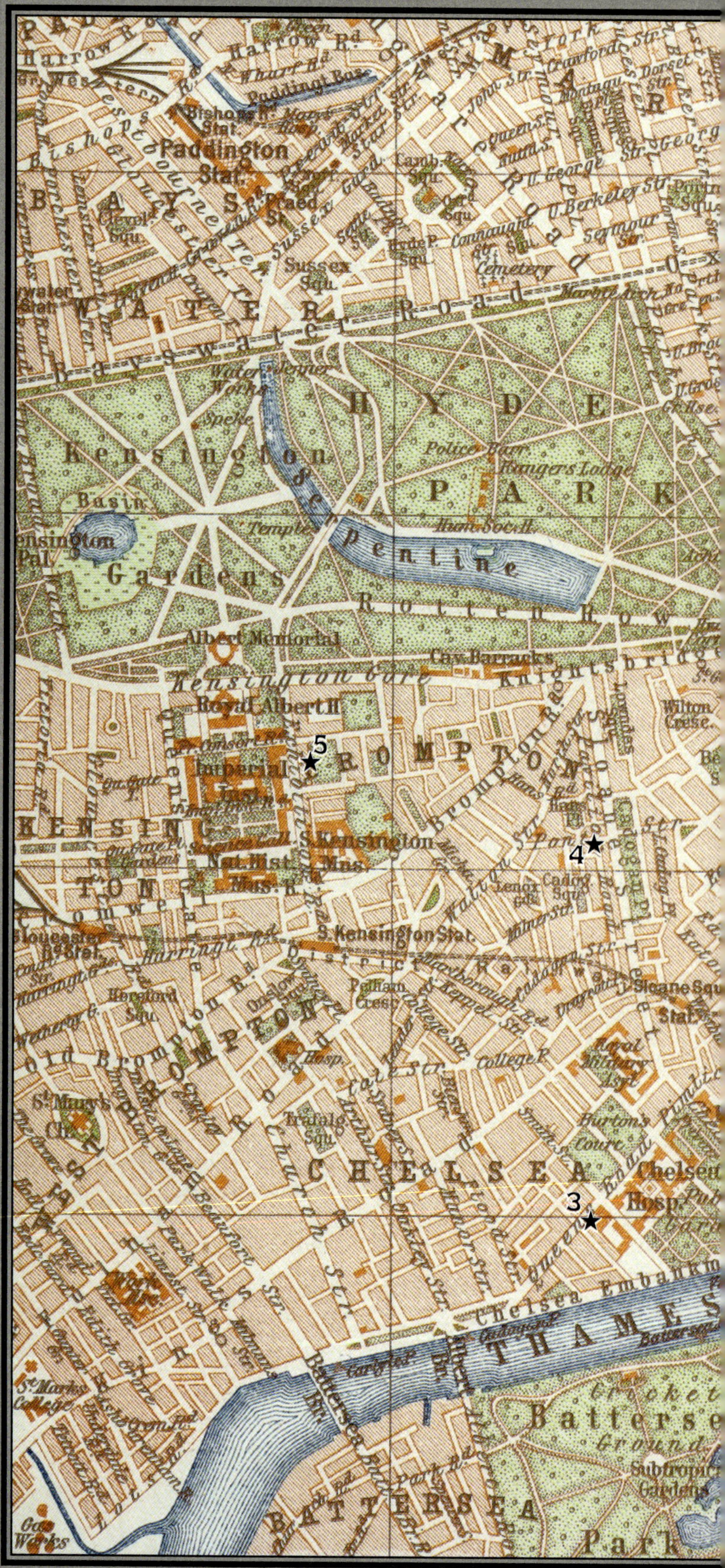

FROM A 1899 MAP OF LONDON

★1 BEARDSLEY'S HOUSE

★2 VICTORIA STATION

★3 OSCAR WILDE'S HOUSE

★4 CADOGAN HOTEL

★5 THE PEACOCK ROOM

★6 PICCADILLY CIRCUS

★7 CAFÉ ROYAL

★8 KETTNER'S

★9 ROYAL OPERA HOUSE

★10 SAVOY THEATRE

★11 SAVOY HOTEL

★12 THE BODLEY HEAD

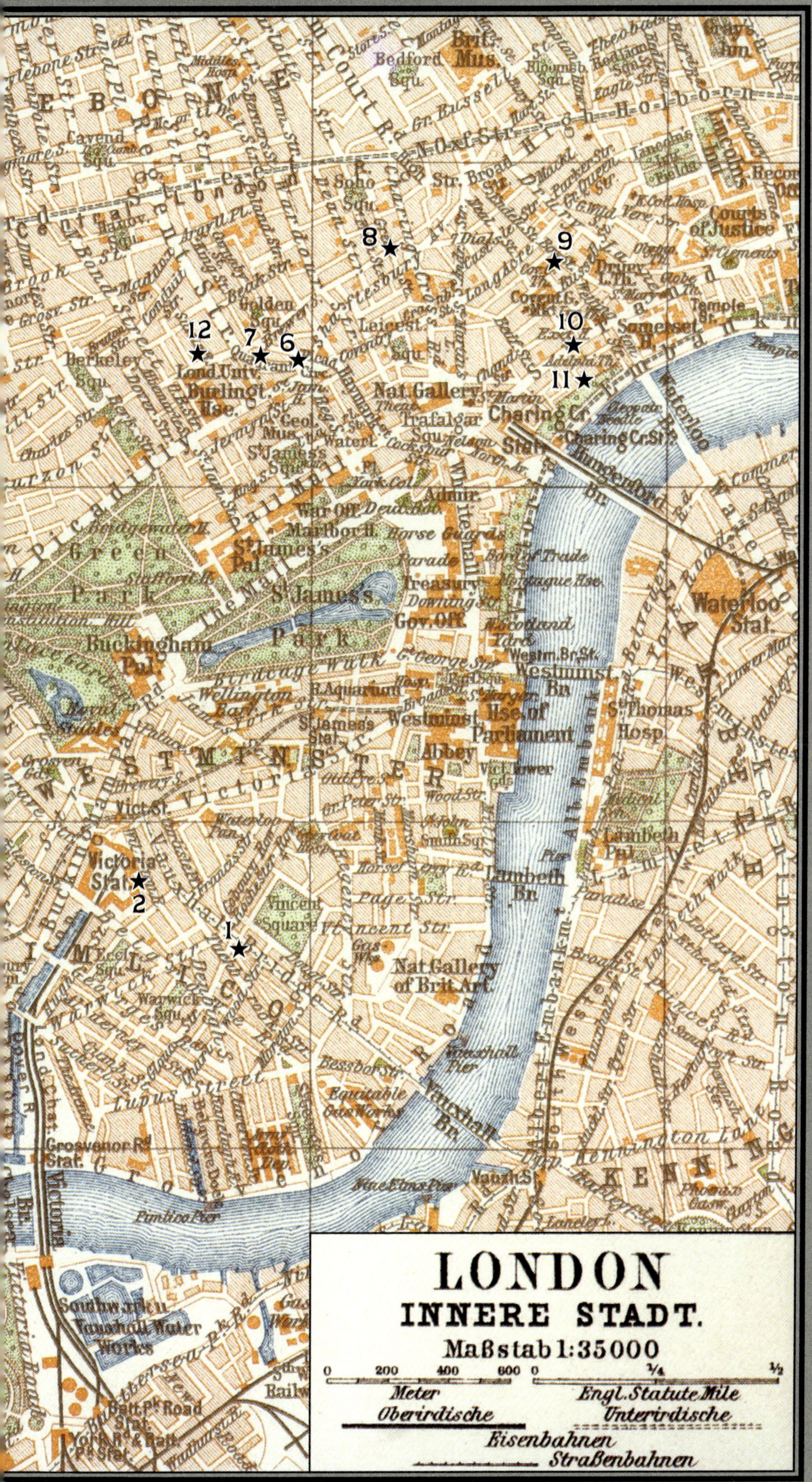

LONDON
INNERE STADT.
Maßstab 1:35000
0 200 400 600
Meter
0 1/4 1/2
Engl. Statute Mile
Oberirdische
Unterirdische
Eisenbahnen
Straßenbahnen

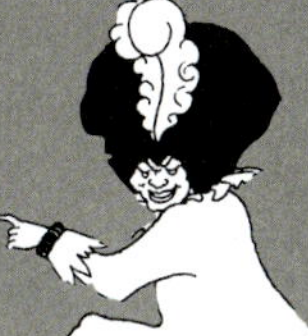

3. 1893: The Year of Salome

Beardsley's artistic destiny was swept up high in the air by the whirlwind that was Oscar Wilde, and then left suddenly to plummet. Beardsley's meeting with Wilde and his creation of the illustrations for Salome saw him becoming the darling of the age for a time, but after Wilde's arrest and fall from grace, Beardsley too was caught up in the maelstrom of the scandal.

Wilde became famous before he had produced any significant works of literature. He was a hero created by the scandal-loving journalism culture that existed at the end of the nineteenth century. Born in Dublin in 1856, Wilde studied at Oxford before moving to London. He wrote poetry, yet the real cause of his fame was less his artistic outpourings and more his extravagant fashion sense, scandalous lifestyle, and original witticisms and pronouncements. He became known for walking around the streets of Piccadilly carrying poppies or lilies.

When Gilbert and Sullivan took their hit comic opera 'Patience', based on the character of Oscar Wilde, to the U.S. on tour, Wilde suddenly became a phenomenon over the water too. He was invited to visit, and spent a whole year there, giving a travelling lecture tour and generally being shown star treatment. The American public tired of him soon enough, however, and Wilde returned to the UK rather demoralised. For a while it seemed that his days of glory were over, and he spent a few years of hardship, but into the 1890s his talents came into bud. With the staging of 'Lady Windemere's Fan' in 1892, Wilde was recognized as a playwright, and returned to the spotlight once again. His novel *The Picture of Dorian Grey* released in 1891 was also met with a positive reception.

One of the causes of Wilde's success this time around was his conversance with the French world of literature and art, through his frequent trips to Paris. At this time, there was a creativity to the ambience in Paris that wasn't found to be in Victorian London. Artistic expression was also freer. In the theatrical world, it was the age of Sarah Bernhardt. *Salomé* was first written while Wilde was in Paris in 1891, and performed in French. Beardsley read it in French, and decided to translate himself into English. In 1893, the Bodley Head decided to release an English edition, but selected Wilde's lover Alfred Douglas as the translator.

Instead, Beardsley's contribution took the form of creating the book's cover and ten full-page illustrations. At the time of his commission, he had already created some drawings inspired by his reading of the play. These were published in the new periodical *The Studio*, and were highly rated by those who had seen them. It was thus that Beardsley came to be commissioned to illustrate the book.

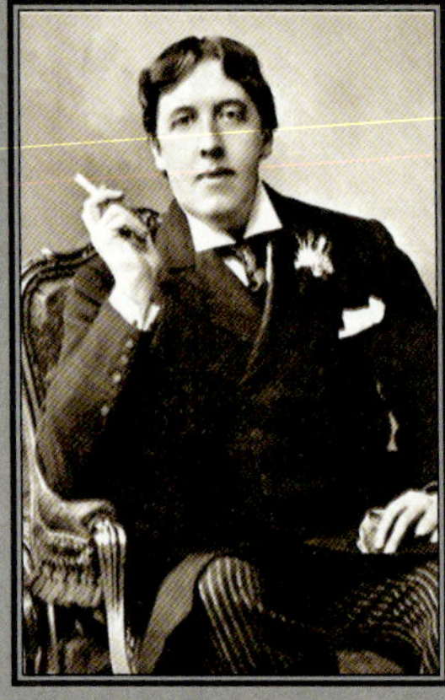

Oscar Wilde

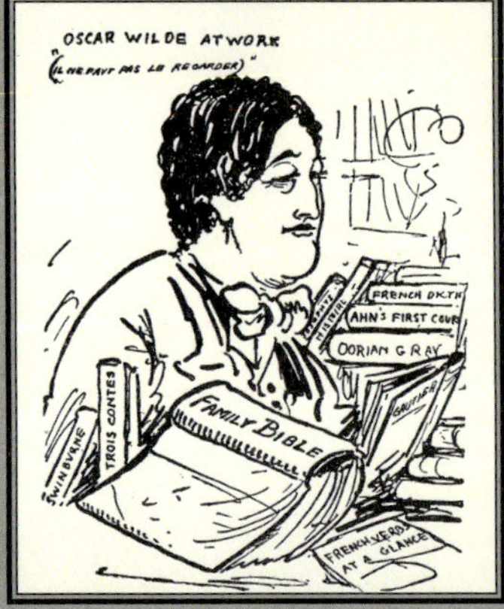

*Oscar Wilde at work
by Aubrey Beardsley*

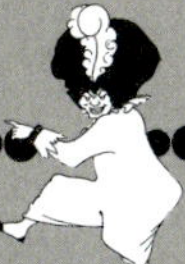

Beardsley would eventually come to dislike Wilde, but at this time he still had much respect for him, and looked forward to the idea of visiting Paris with him. For artists living in London at the end of the nineteenth century, of whom Wilde was just one example, having contact with the Parisian belle époque world and being stimulated by it was an important thing. It seems that for Beardsley too, it was his contact with fin-de-siècle Paris that enabled him to discover his own unique style, which was almost entirely unique in Britain. Without doubt it was Wilde who awakened Beardsley to the charms of France.

Le Morte d'Arthur was in a sense Beardsley's first proper illustration job, and we can still see the influence of the work of Pre-Raphaelite artist Burne-Jones on his work. With Salome, however, the trademark Beardsley style suddenly makes an appearance. It seems likely that this sudden transformation can be put down to his encounter with fin-de-siècle France, as well as Japanese influences in the form of woodblock prints and the like.

Beardsley's illustrations for *Salome* are not visual representations of Wilde's play, but rather his own free imaginings. They have a feeling of excess and mystery to them not present in the original script. 'Salome' was written in 1891, published in French in 1893 and in English in 1894. Yet it wasn't allowed to be performed until 1931, and so Wilde never saw it on stage. It makes one wonder what would have happened if it had been illustrated by someone else, for the original script is not that extreme or erotic. The imagery comes from Beardsley's illustrations. Perhaps without such illustrations, it might have been deemed performable. Beardsley's illustrations were sufficiently over the top and dramatic to worry Wilde and the publisher. Wilde feared that they might take over from the script, while John Lane feared that the book might be found indecent, and banned. Beardsley added various tricks and games into his illustrations, adding caricatures of Wilde's face and sneaking in erotic elements.

Salome turned out to be the battleground for Wilde and Beardsley's fight over aesthetics. Beardsley looked down Wilde's decadent dandyism for dragging the snobbery of the Victorian era with it, and preferred to pick a fight with the Victorian era itself. Yet despite this conflict, *Salome* provoked a ludicrous amount of public interest since before its publication, and Beardsley's risqué talents were highly esteemed. The most alarming aspect to the situation is that in 1893, Beardsley's artwork suddenly assumed that unmistakeable Beardsley quality. Quite as if he had sold his soul to the devil, the Pre-Raphaelite style amateur suddenly began to unveil work the likes of which nobody had ever seen before.

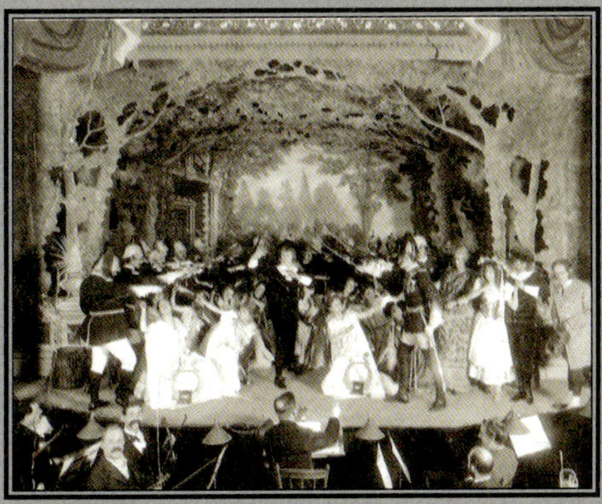

The Gilbert & Sullivan comic opera, 'Patience'

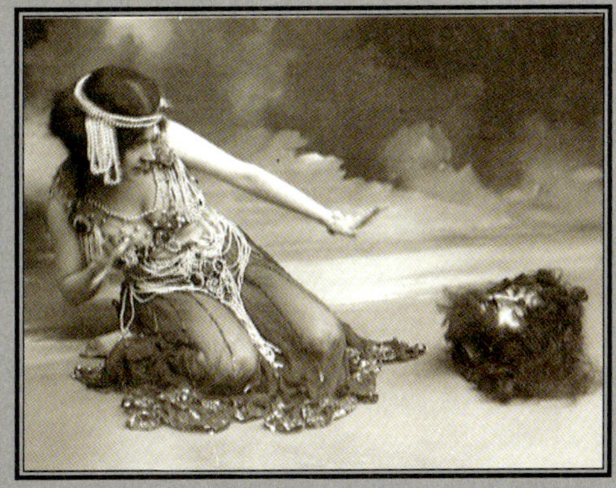

Maud Allan playing Salome, 19th century

SALOME

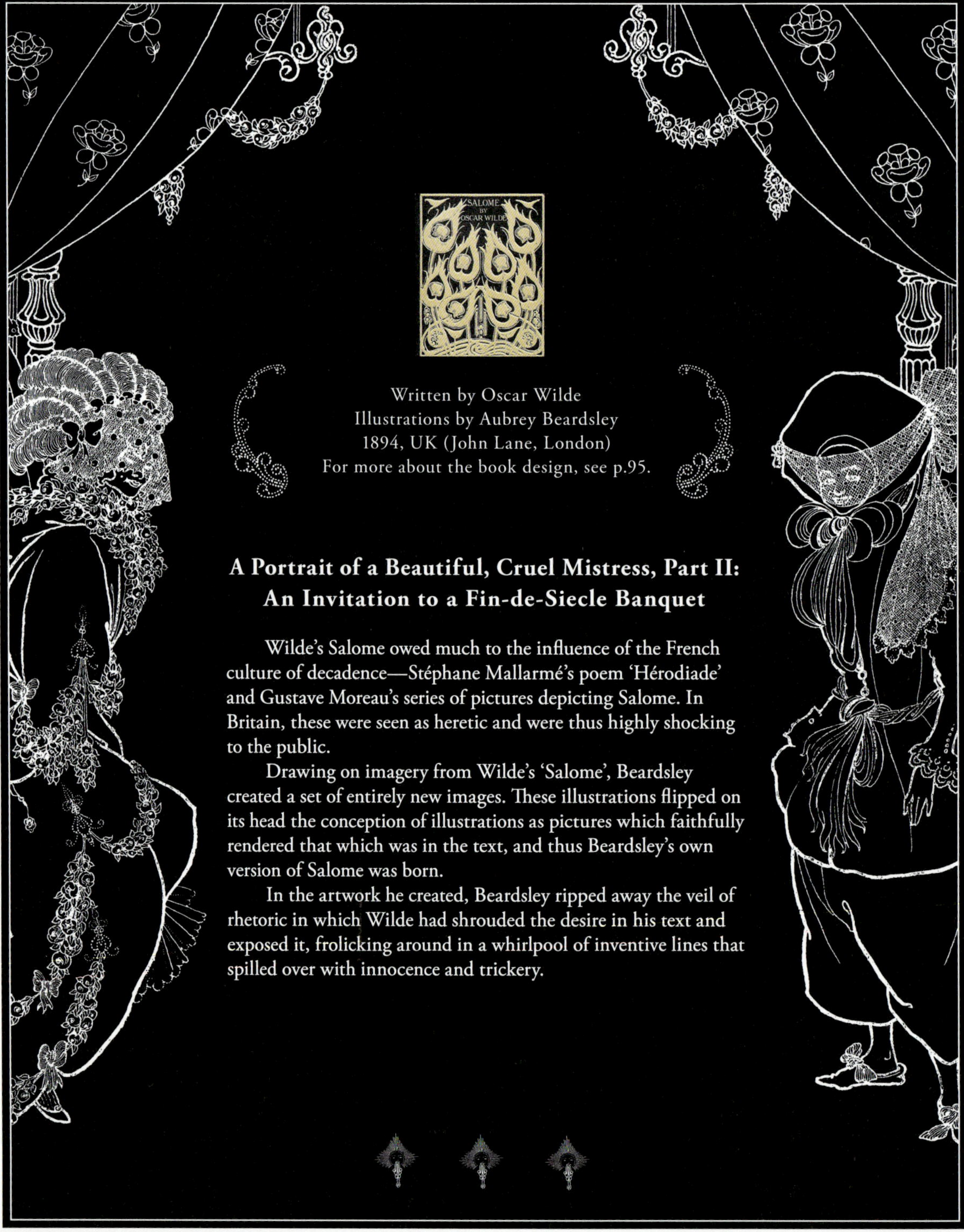

Written by Oscar Wilde
Illustrations by Aubrey Beardsley
1894, UK (John Lane, London)
For more about the book design, see p.95.

A Portrait of a Beautiful, Cruel Mistress, Part II: An Invitation to a Fin-de-Siecle Banquet

Wilde's Salome owed much to the influence of the French culture of decadence—Stéphane Mallarmé's poem 'Hérodiade' and Gustave Moreau's series of pictures depicting Salome. In Britain, these were seen as heretic and were thus highly shocking to the public.

Drawing on imagery from Wilde's 'Salome', Beardsley created a set of entirely new images. These illustrations flipped on its head the conception of illustrations as pictures which faithfully rendered that which was in the text, and thus Beardsley's own version of Salome was born.

In the artwork he created, Beardsley ripped away the veil of rhetoric in which Wilde had shrouded the desire in his text and exposed it, frolicking around in a whirlpool of inventive lines that spilled over with innocence and trickery.

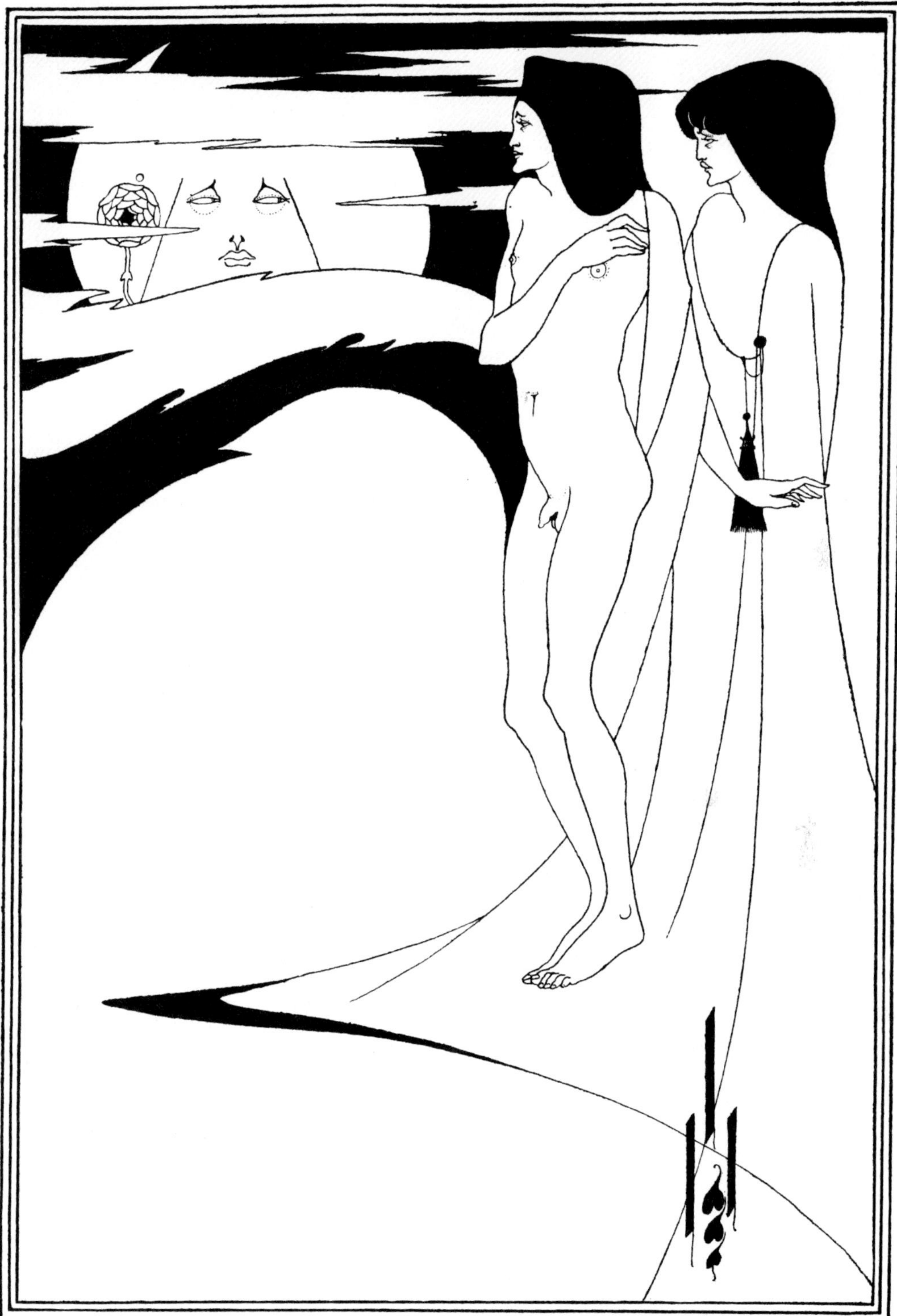

Frontispiece: 'The Woman in the Moon'

This is the standout illustration of all those Beardsley produced for *Salome*. It is hard to find drawings that rival this one in terms of the sparseness of its lines, and the masterfully arrangement of blank space. The picture is based on lines from the beginning of the play such as 'How beautiful is the Princess Salome to-night!' and 'Look at the moon. How strange the moon seems!' but uses these as a point of departure for creating an entirely freestanding image. The countenance of the woman in the moon is a caricature of Wilde's face. The fact that Beardsley has drawn the genitals of the naked boy on the right led the drawing to be deemed indecent at the time. The woman to the right could well be Salome. It is impossible to make out the lines of her body. The sweeping lines create mysterious white spaces, such as the peculiar round shape stretching in front of the two figures and the intersection of the lines below them. In the bottom right-hand corner is Beardsley's signature mark.

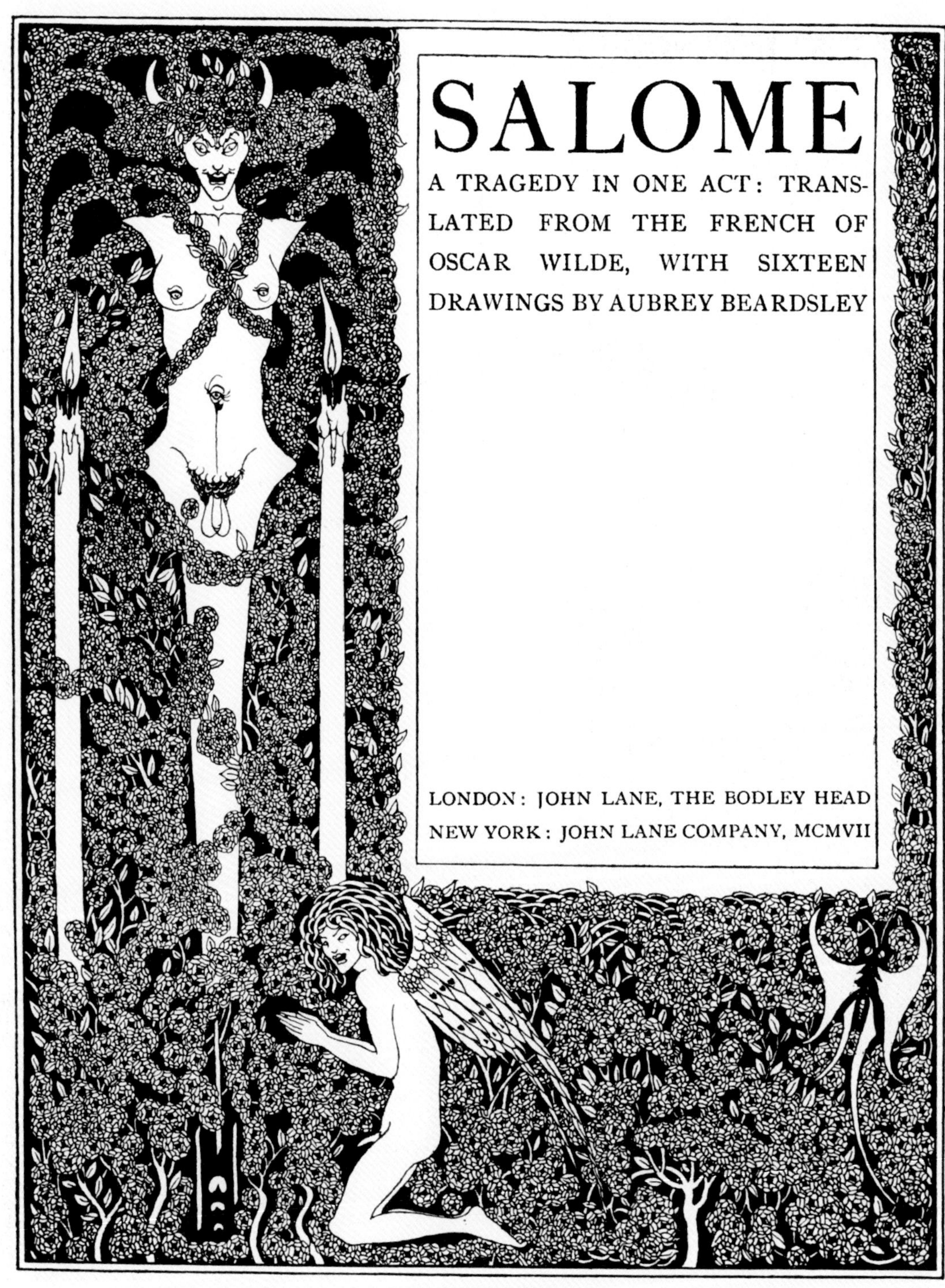

Title Page

An angel is worshipping a devil standing between two candles. This devil icon is an instantiation of Beardsley's signature mark (look closely and one can see the mark has been repeated underneath.) It barely seems thinkable that an artist would insert his own secret emblem into the title page, but Beardsley has done so. The devil seems to be a hermaphrodite, having both breasts and a penis, and its nipples have eyes. The figure seems to have borrowed inspiration from the herma, a form of sculpture with a head and genitals that originated in ancient Greece and was placed by the side of the road. The angel, who looks much like a young boy, is also showing his genitals. The butterflies to the right are possibly there as a dig at Whistler, whose emblem was a butterfly. Beardsley's mockery knew no bounds.

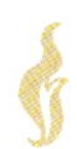

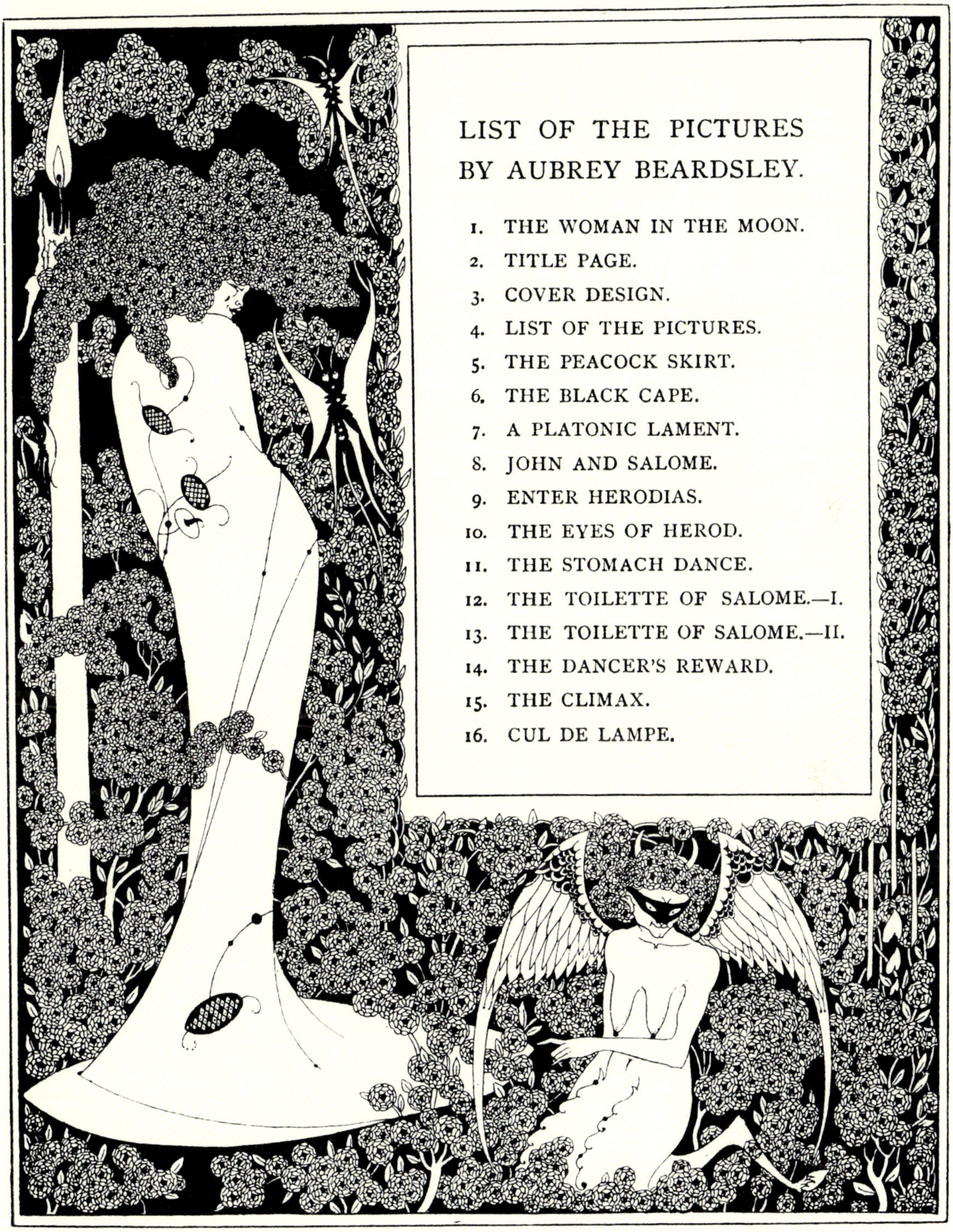

LIST OF THE PICTURES
BY AUBREY BEARDSLEY.

1. THE WOMAN IN THE MOON.
2. TITLE PAGE.
3. COVER DESIGN.
4. LIST OF THE PICTURES.
5. THE PEACOCK SKIRT.
6. THE BLACK CAPE.
7. A PLATONIC LAMENT.
8. JOHN AND SALOME.
9. ENTER HERODIAS.
10. THE EYES OF HEROD.
11. THE STOMACH DANCE.
12. THE TOILETTE OF SALOME.—I.
13. THE TOILETTE OF SALOME.—II.
14. THE DANCER'S REWARD.
15. THE CLIMAX.
16. CUL DE LAMPE.

Picture Index

A woman with her back to us stands next to a giant candle. The pose is reminiscent of the mikaeri-bijin—'beautiful woman turning around'—which is a common trope in Japanese prints. Her twisted back creates glorious curved lines, but a close examination reveals a somewhat unnatural shape, as if she didn't have hands. Beardsley would often ignore the principles of anatomy so as to give rise to his own unique forms. To the right is an evil-looking angel in a black mask with breasts, whose lower half is that of a goat. A rather eerie butterfly is flying through the dense foliage.

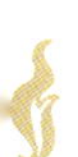
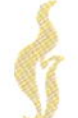

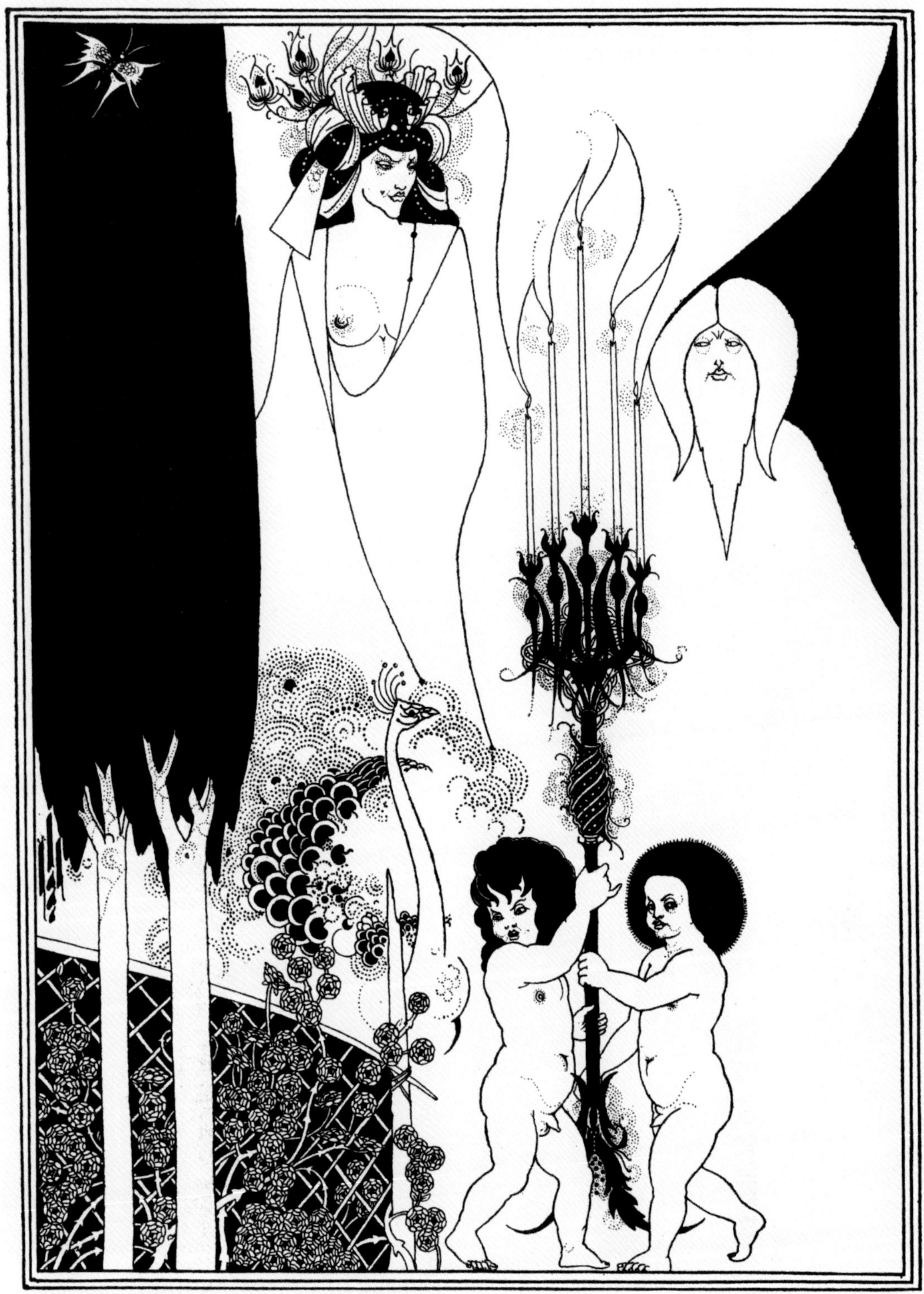

'The Eyes of Herod'

'Why does the Tetrarch look at me all the while with his mole's eyes under his shaking eyelids?' asks Salome. To the right is King Herod, bewitched by the sight of his daughter-in-law, Salome. On the left is Queen Herodias, who looks on disapprovingly. Between the two of them towers a candle stand supported by two putti, or naked children. The simple lines picking out the contours of the king and queen, and the curved lines above the king's head are extremely effective. They also form a wonderful contrast with the intricately detailed sections of the picture, such as the Queen's hair ornament and the peacock standing beside the furred candlestick. Beardsley's characteristic composition that combines abstract with erotic details is here seen in full force. The simple contours of the queen's body are particularly outstanding.

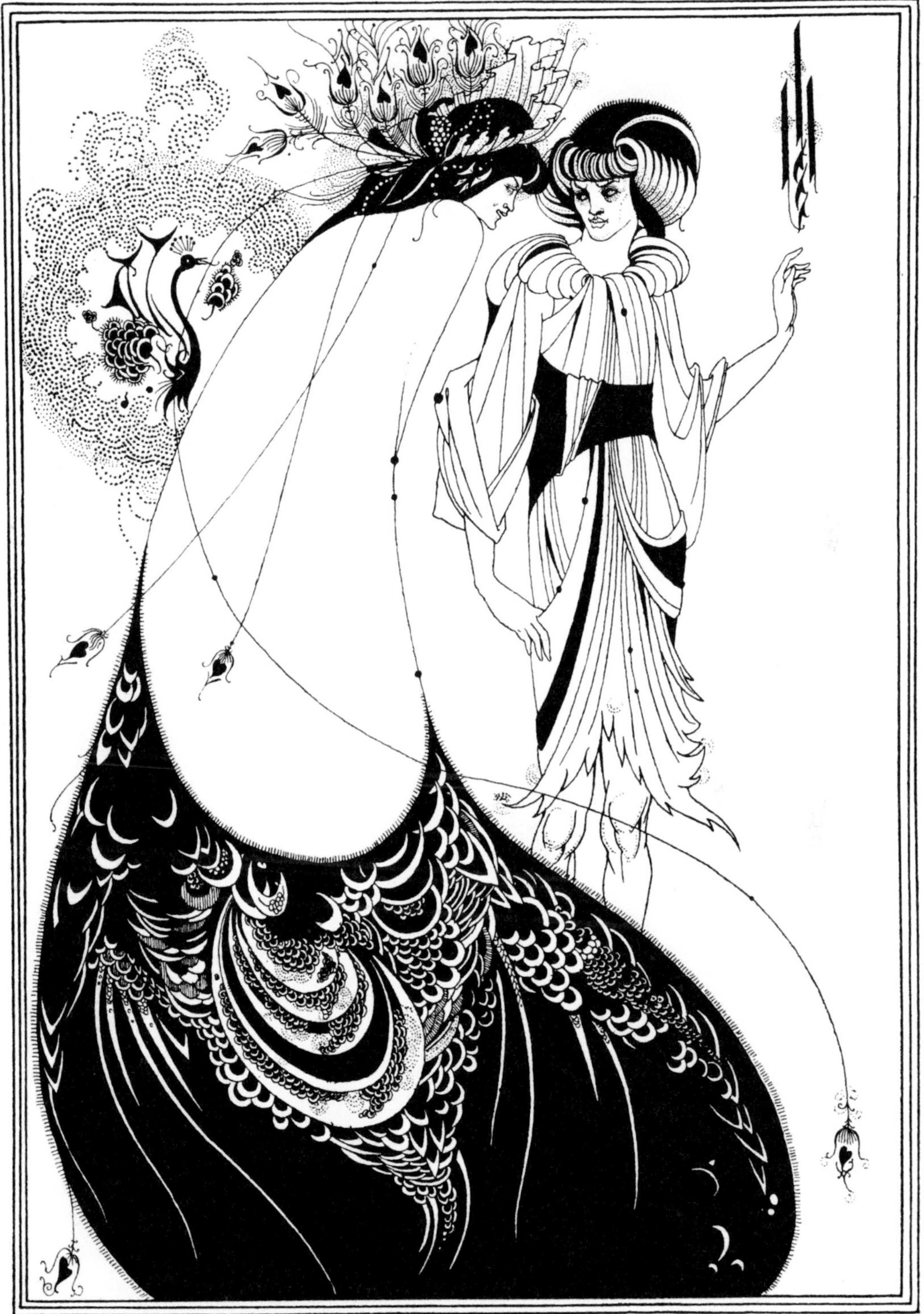

'The Peacock Skirt'

Because of the free nature of Beardsley's illustrations, it is hard to know what in Wilde's original they are depicting, and from which scene. Some see the woman on the left-hand side of this picture as Salome, but it seems more likely that it is intended to be Salome's mother, Herodias. The young man on her right is her slave. The text says of Queen Herodios that she 'wears a black mitre sewed with pearls, and whose hair is powdered with blue dust.' Beardsley adorns her entire figure with a peacock patterning from the crown of her head to the hem of her skirt, and adds in a real peacock standing beside her. The bizarre shape of her body seen from the back is said to have been influenced by the *oiran* courtesan depicted by Hiroshige, but also hints at the shape of the phallus.

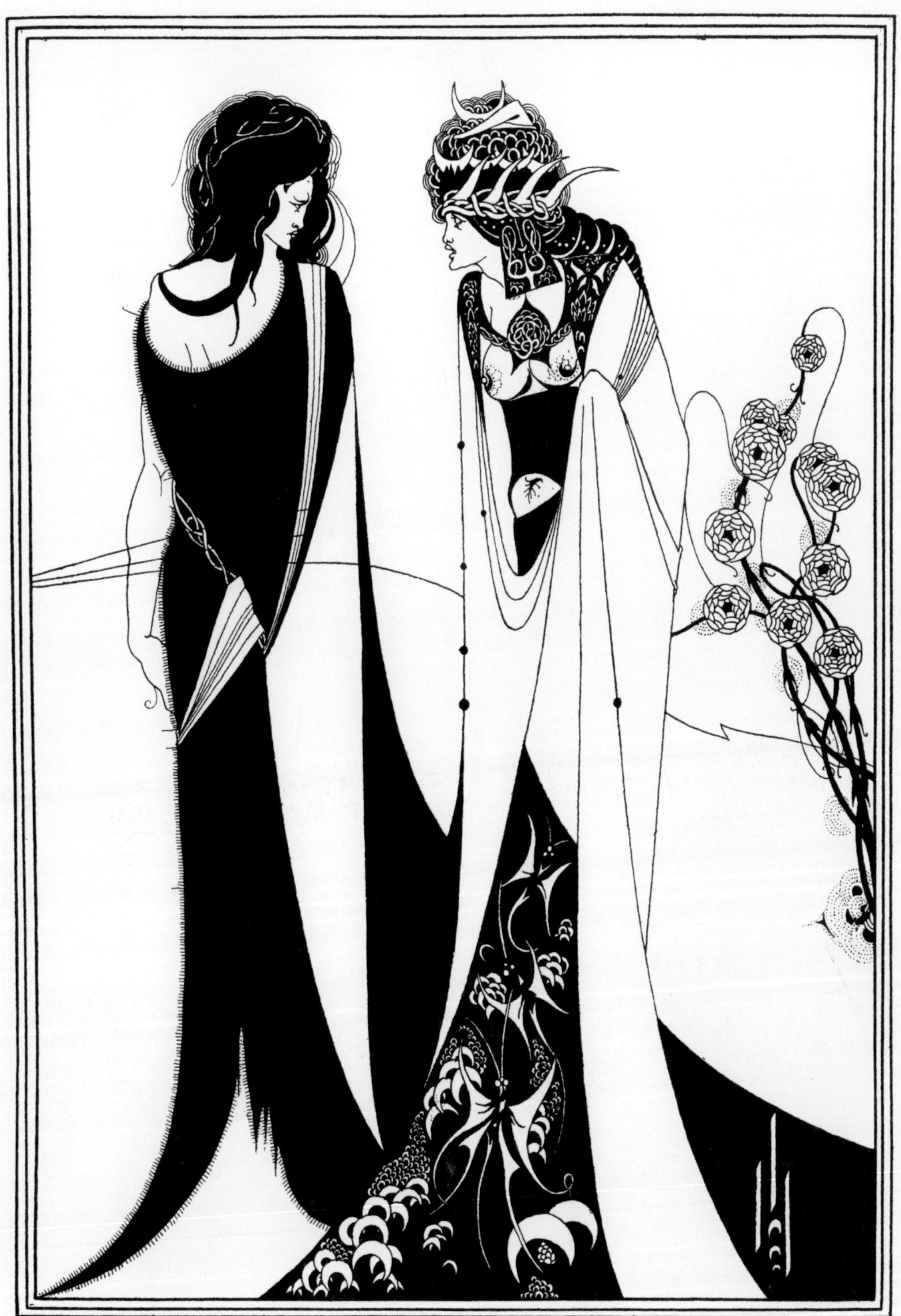

'John and Salome'

Salome has the captured prophet Iokanaan (John the Baptist) brought up from his cistern and attempts to approach him, but he rejects her, calling her 'daughter of Sodom'. Not used in the 1894 first edition, this illustration was first added in 1907. The depiction of John the Baptist is distinctive, with the lines in the background passing through him. The picture is scattered with Art Nouveau style ornamentation, such as the roses and thorns, Salome's Celtic-style headdress, and the fish-scale and butterfly patterns. The way that the space is divided up by the folds of the flat, abstract clothing seems something only Beardsley would have been capable of.

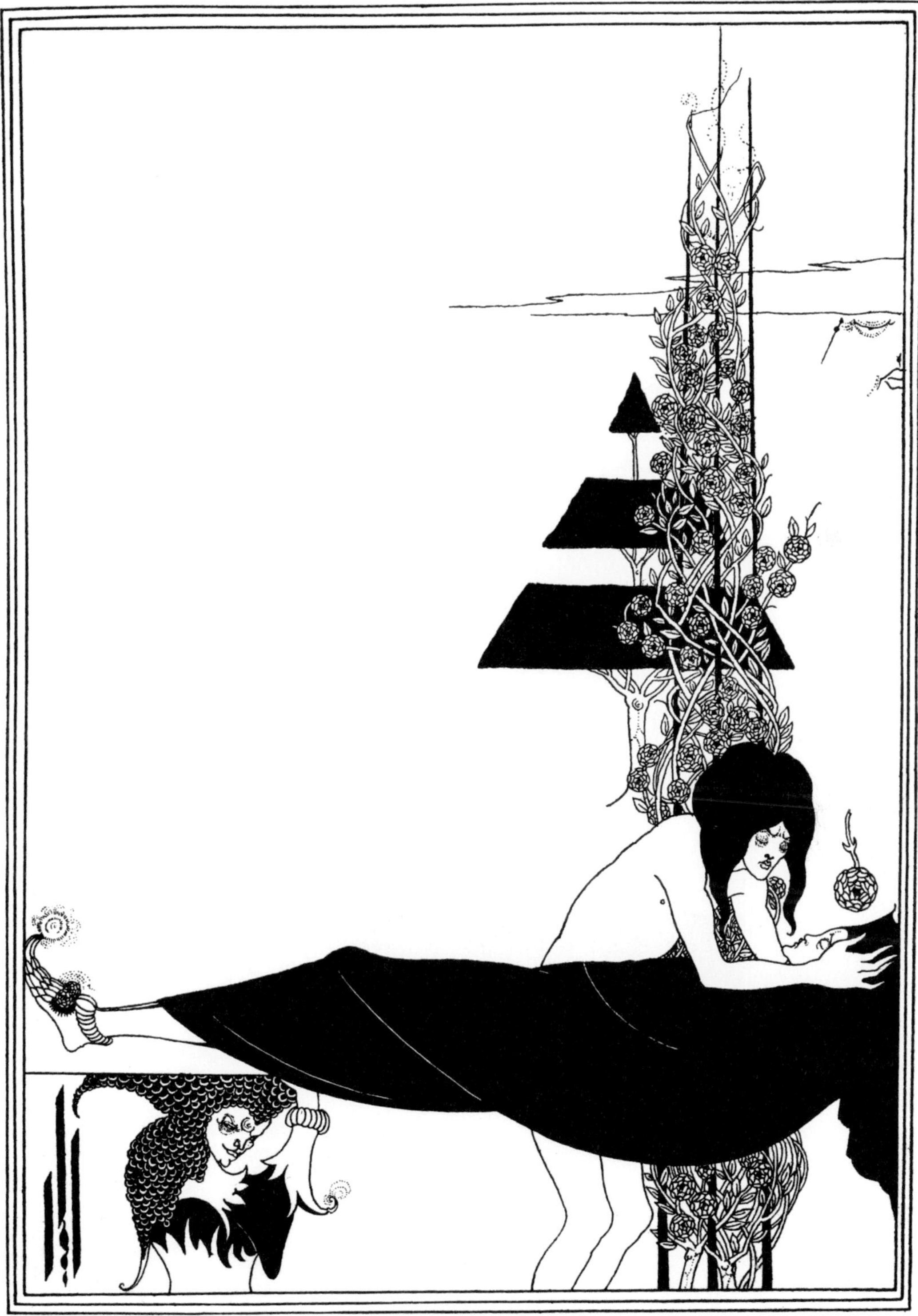

'A Platonic Lament'

Elaborate vines snake themselves around three columns, which seem to pass through the dead body lying horizontally across the illustration. These are, needless to say, an enlargement of Beardsley's mark, also found in the bottom left of the picture. Observing Salome's fixation on John the Baptist, the young Syrian captain was overcome by his love for her and took his own life. The figure sat beside him lamenting is Herodias' slave boy, who was himself enamoured with the Syrian—it is to homosexual love that the word 'Platonic' in the title refers. Below the cloud in the top right drifts Wilde's face, looking down protectively on the cross formed by of the plant piercing the dead body, which signifies homosexual love. Underneath the bed, a demon laughs cruelly.

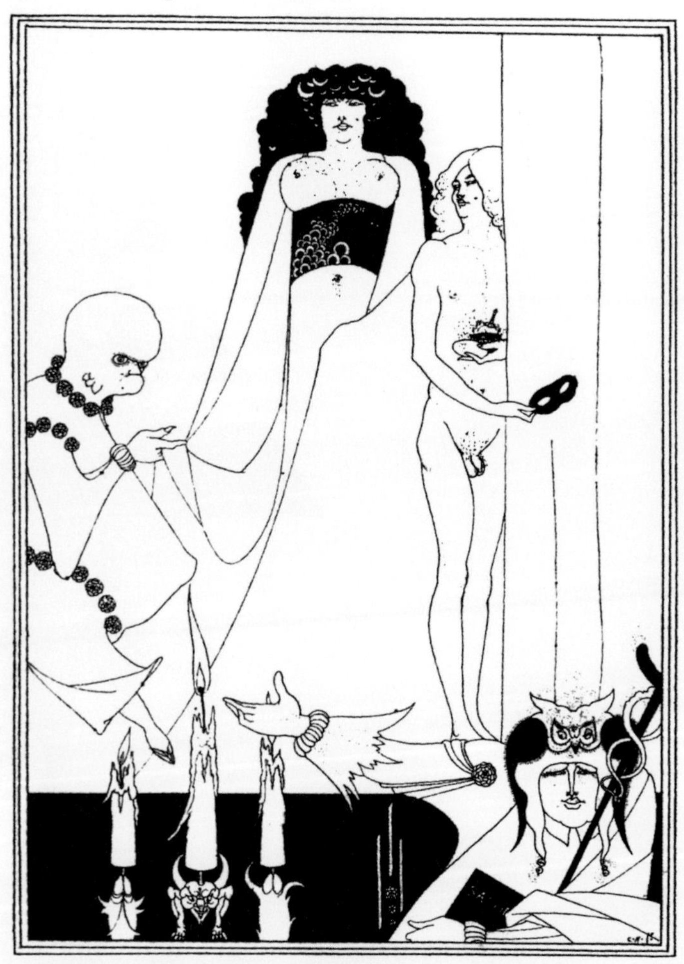

'Enter Herodias'

Queen Herodias enters with her slave. Here we see her as the image of the voluptuous courtesan who often appears in Beardsley's work. The slave was originally drawn naked, with his genitals exposed (p.36), but after this was rejected by John Lane a figleaf was added (p.37)—which in fact only served to make the image seem more obscene. Holding a powder-puff, he is a homosexual in love with the young Syrian. In the bottom right, Wilde in an owl hood and holding the Staff of Hermes with its intertwined snakes is explaining the action taking place on stage. The holders for the three candles are very explicit. To the left of the picture a grotesquely depicted dwarf is touching the queen's dress, the front of his costume jutting out unnaturally to indicate his sexual arousal.

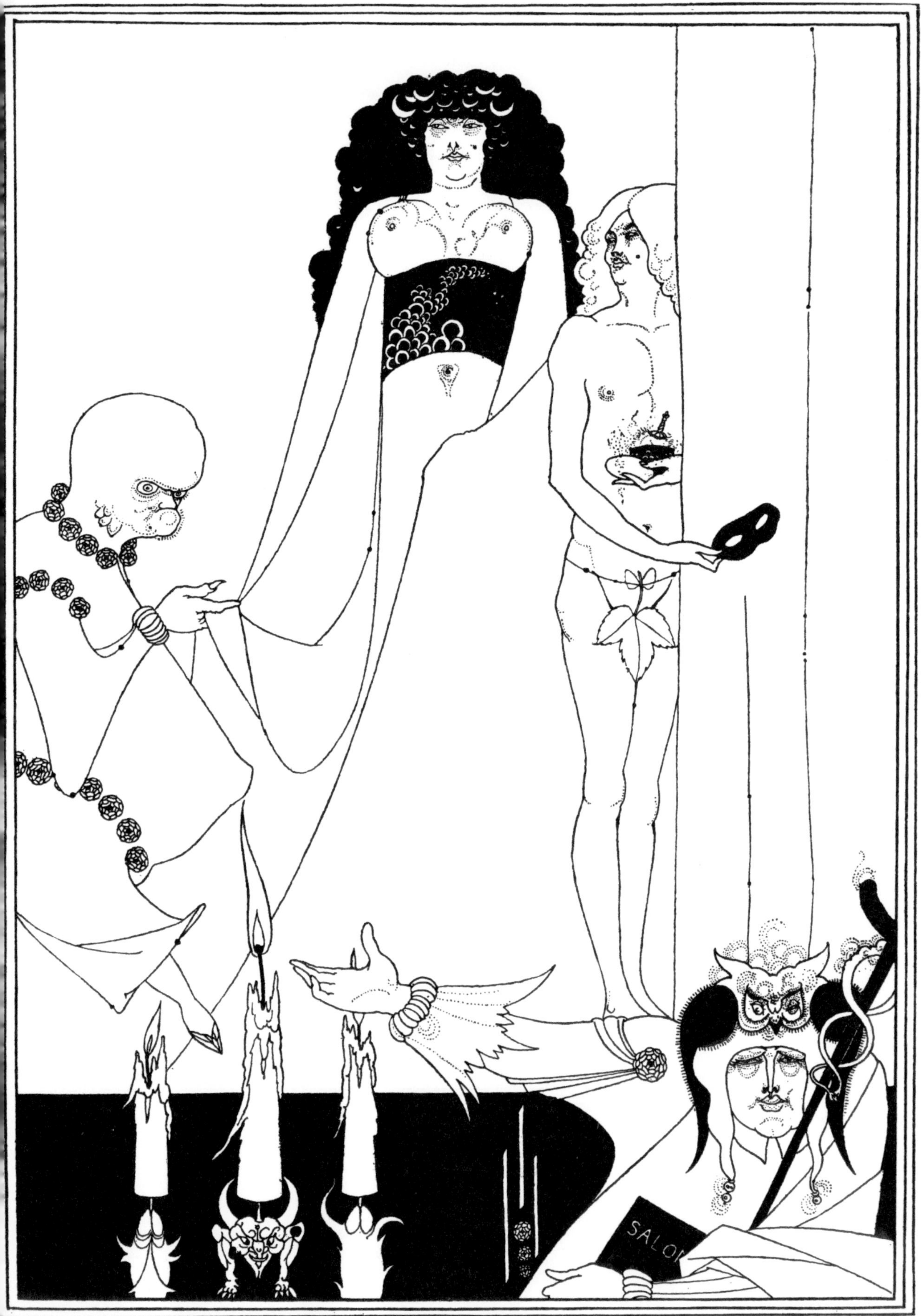

SALO

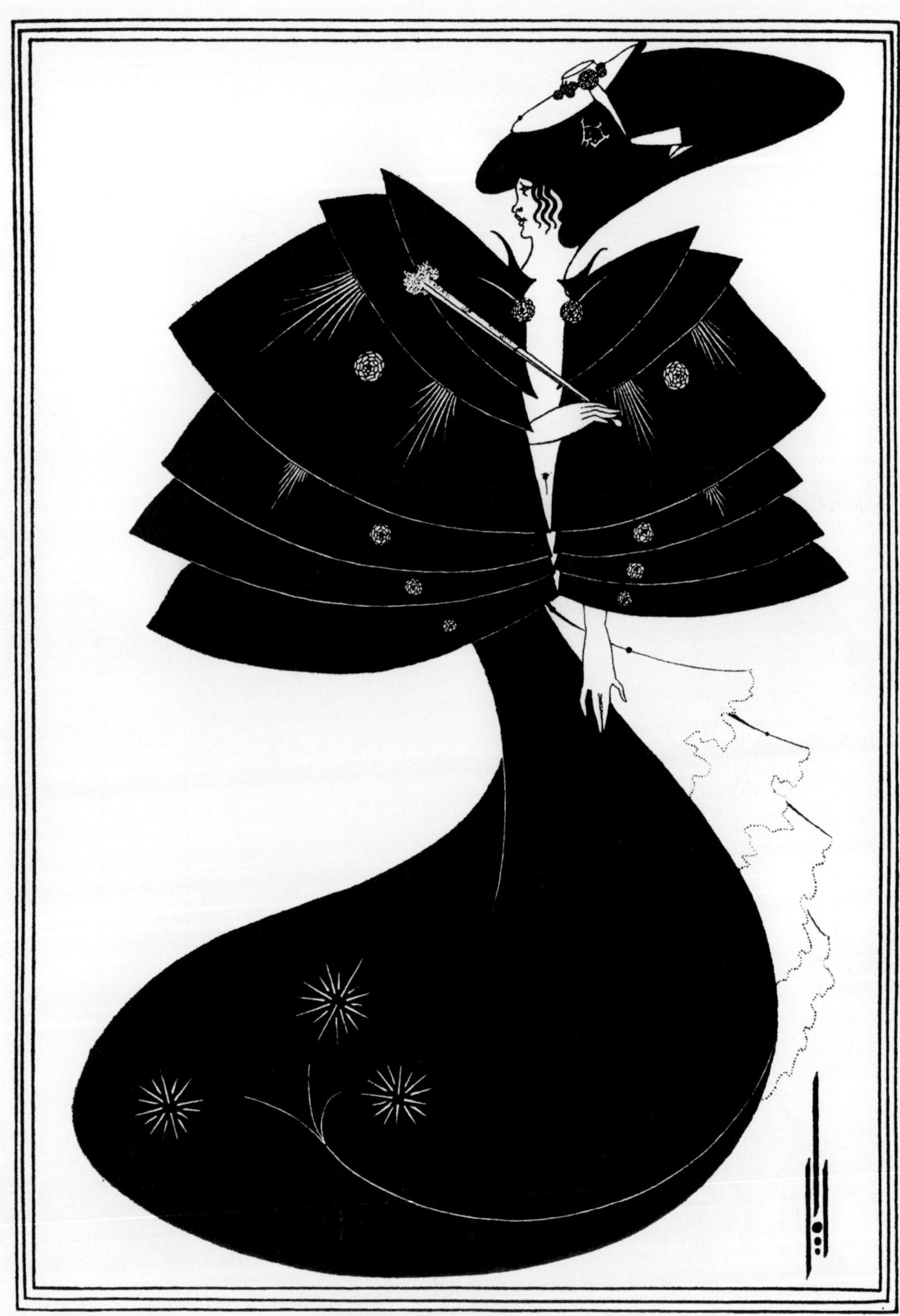

'The Black Cape'

This picture has no relation to anything in the play, and is rather a characterization of the fashions at the time. The shape of the model's body is entirely ignored, so that the upper and lower halves barely seem connected. Rather, Beardsley freely pursues the fascination that ensues from the abstract design of the dress. The bottom half echoes the shape of a giant tongue, and other suggestive shapes are secreted here and there across the picture. If we see the illustration not as a human form but rather as an abstract design, it appears as a distinctive sculptural object, and we can enjoy it simply for the allure of its formal properties.

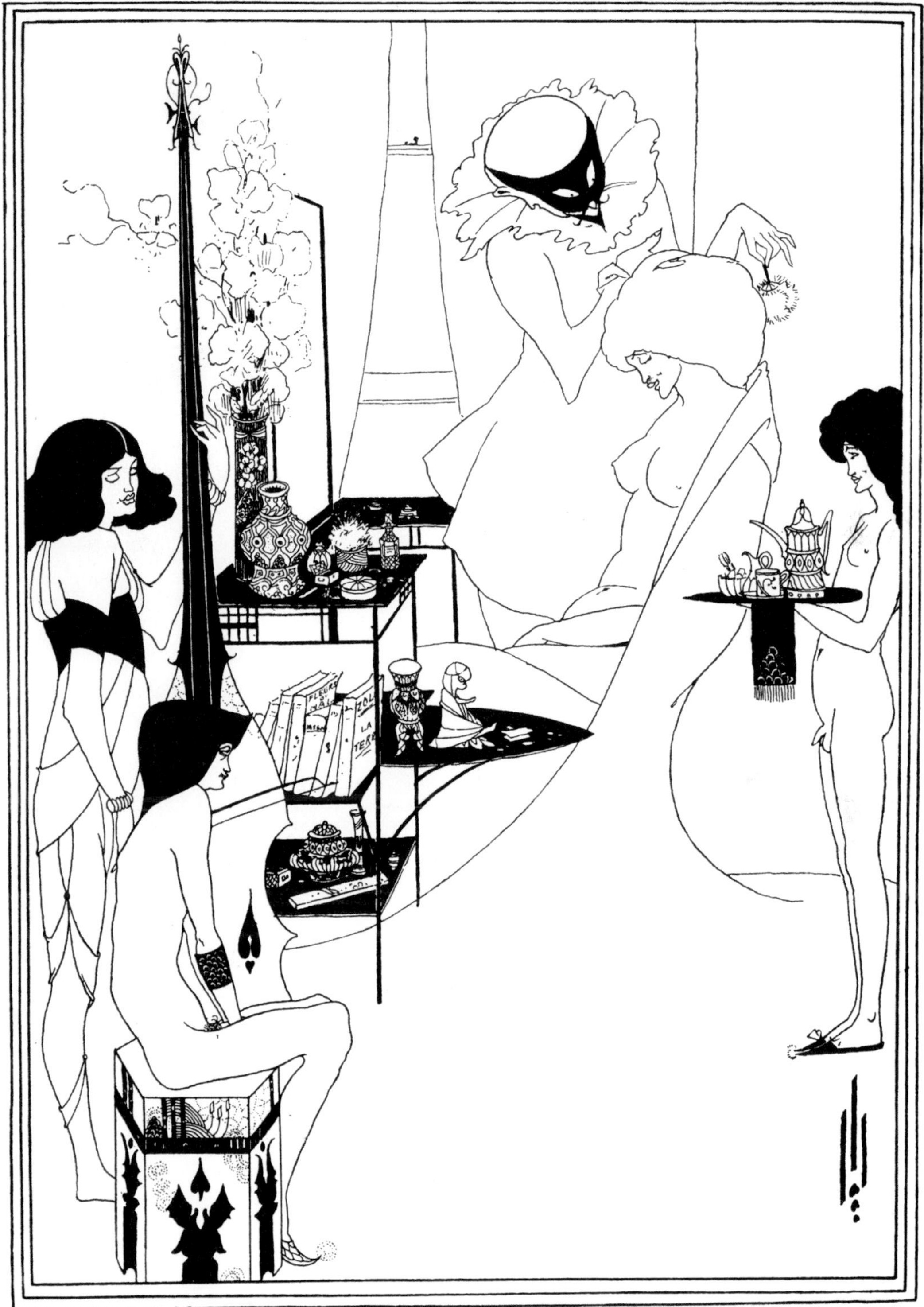

'The Toilette of Salome' I

Wilde's play includes nothing about the toilette of Salome. The idea likely came from the frequent images of women at their toilette found in Japanese woodblock prints. In giving a glimpse into women's private lives, the image of a woman's toilette stimulates hidden desires in the viewer. This picture was rejected for the first edition of Salome, and Beardsley produced another version, 'The Toilette of Salome' II. Why was this picture rejected? The reason would seem to lie in the naked young boy with his genitals on full view. The crisply designed furniture in the picture is that of the Arts and Crafts movement spearheaded by William Godwin and others.

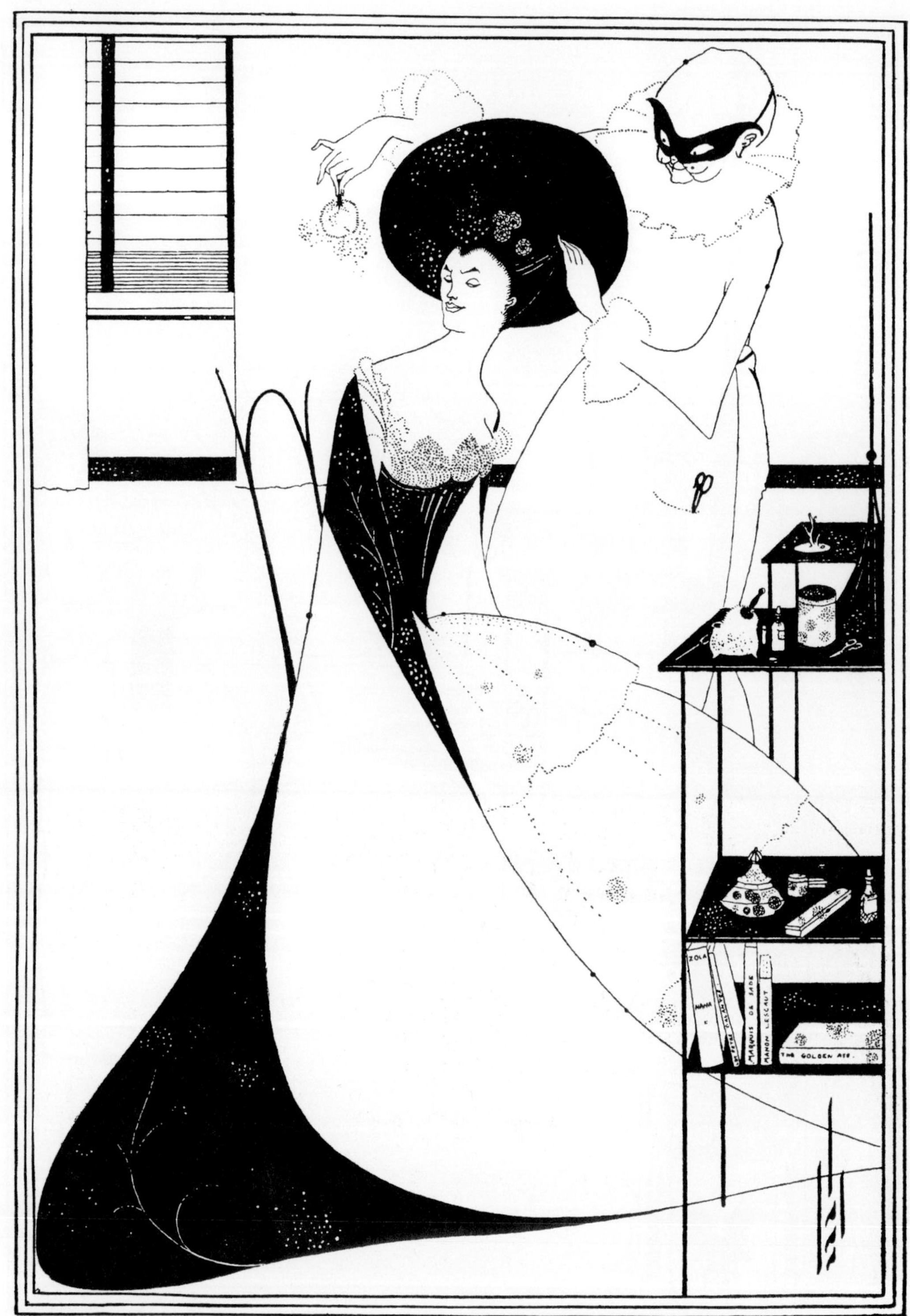

'The Toilette of Salome' II

Having grown bored with historical pictures in medieval and Pre-Raphaelite style, Beardsley created this illustration with clear gesturing towards the latest fashions of the time. The chair and the makeup table also feature a modern design. The freshness of the forms produced by the intersection of the white and black on Salome's dress are not lost on us even now. The nineteenth-century interior crammed busily full of furniture has been transformed into a bare, minimalist modern interior with its plethora of white. The lowest shelf features *The Golden Ass* by Apuleius, Abbé Prévost's *Manon Lescault*, Marquis de Sade, *Fêtes Galantes* by Paul Verlaine, and Émile Zola's *Nana*.

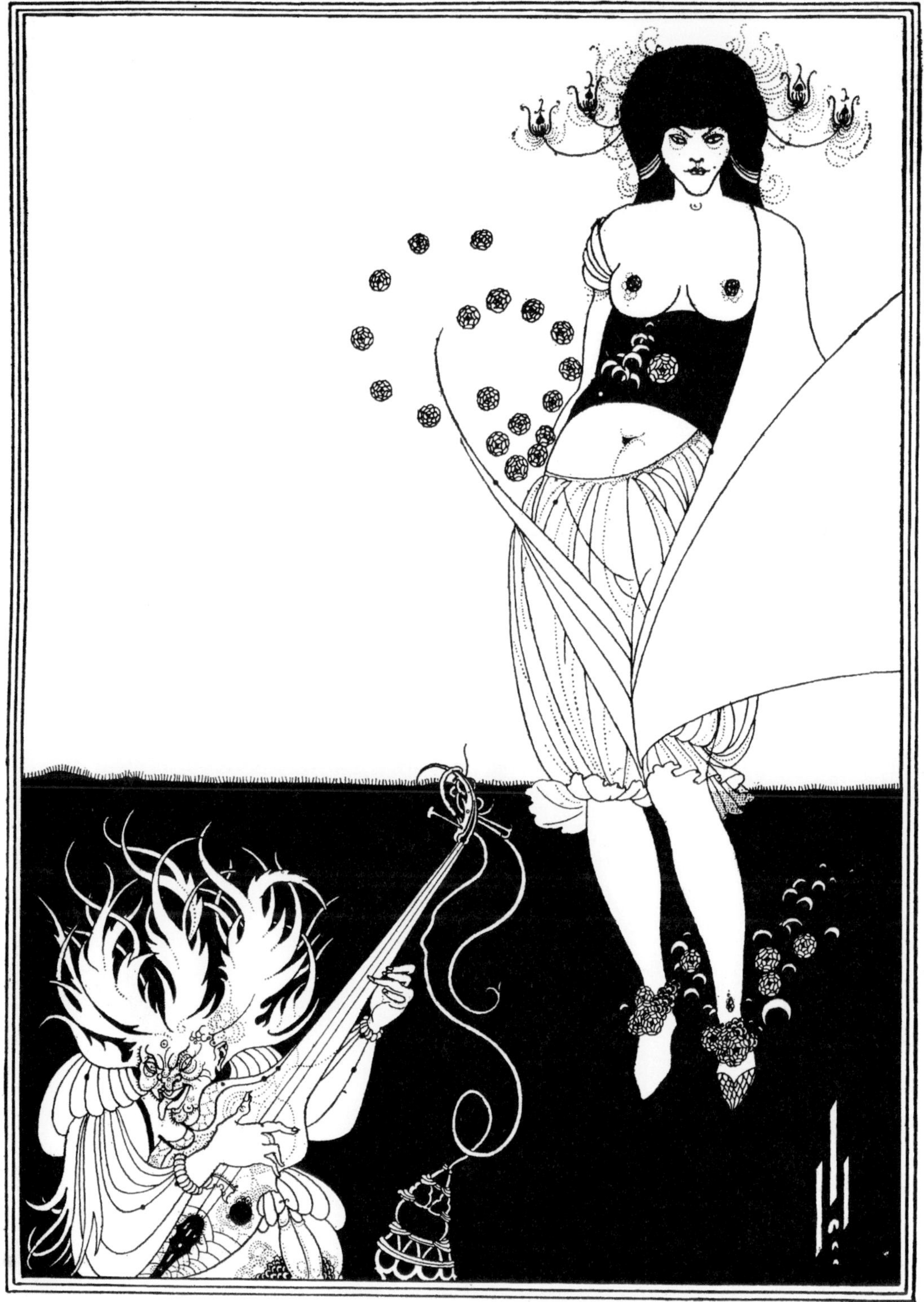

'The Stomach Dance'

Here we see Salome performing what we would these days term a belly dance. She is not keen on the idea, but is persuaded to do so by King Herod's promise that he will give her what she desires if she agrees. The picture is divided into sections of black and white, so that Salome's torso is cast against a white background, while the area beneath her knees is sunk in black. Against the black background, an eerie dwarf plays a musical instrument. The veil draped around Salome's shoulder flies off to the right, revealing her abdomen. From between her legs, the end of the veil reaches up, surrounded by roses, in a way that symbolizes the phallus and ejaculation. The dwarf below symbolizes Herod's murky desire for his stepdaughter. The dwarf's entire body is dotted with sexual organs.

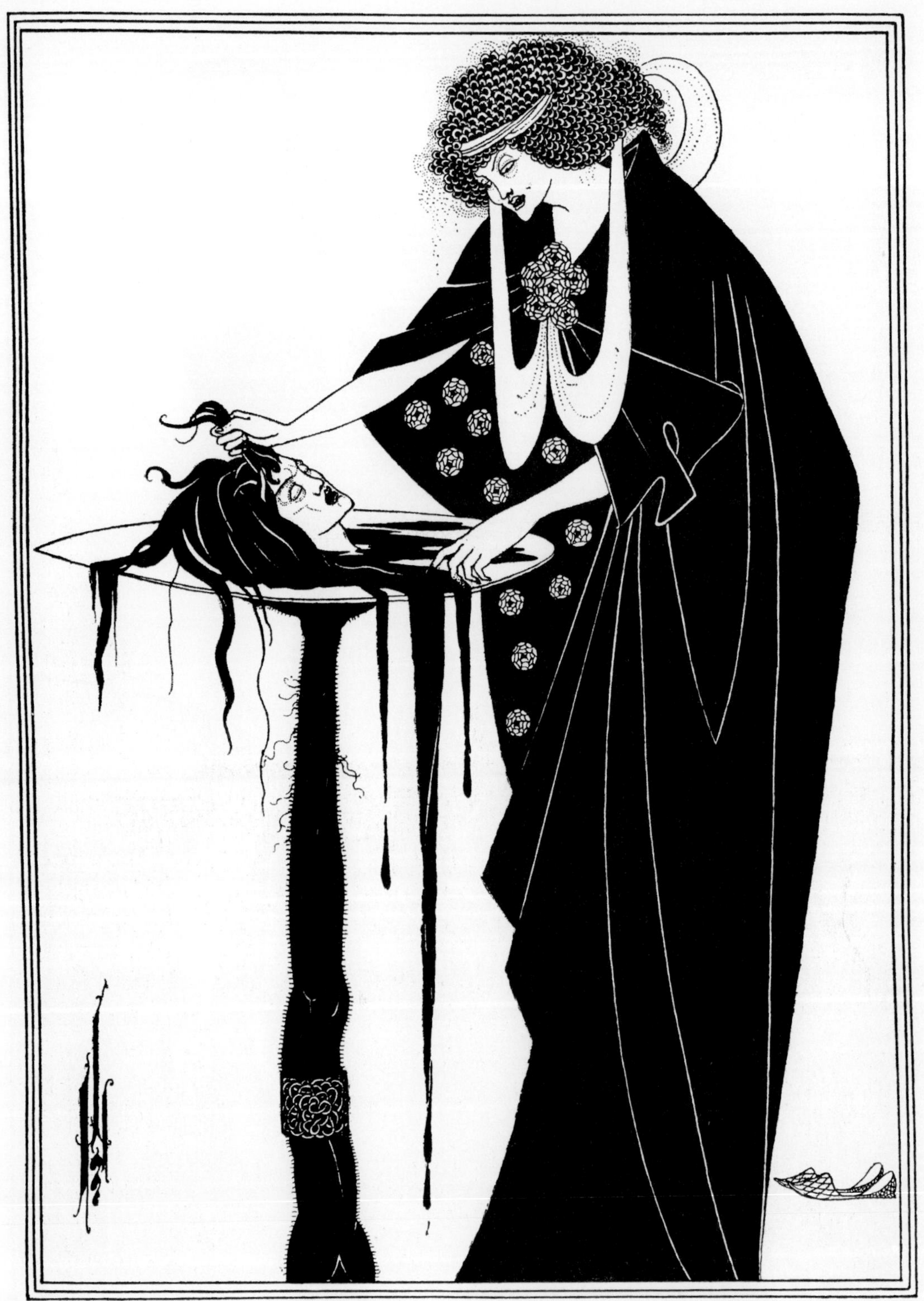

'The Dancer's Reward'

As a reward for dancing for King Herod, Salome requests John the Baptist's head. This immaculately balanced composition features not a single redundant element. Beardsley's rendering of the black arm holding up the silver plate bearing the severed head, and the sharp lines of the folds in Salome's gown are breath-taking. Behind Salome's head rests a hat—most likely the ascot hat which the pierrot is placing on her head in 'The Toilette of Salome' II. At the bottom right we can see her sandals, for predecessor to Isabella Duncan that she was, Salome had danced barefoot.

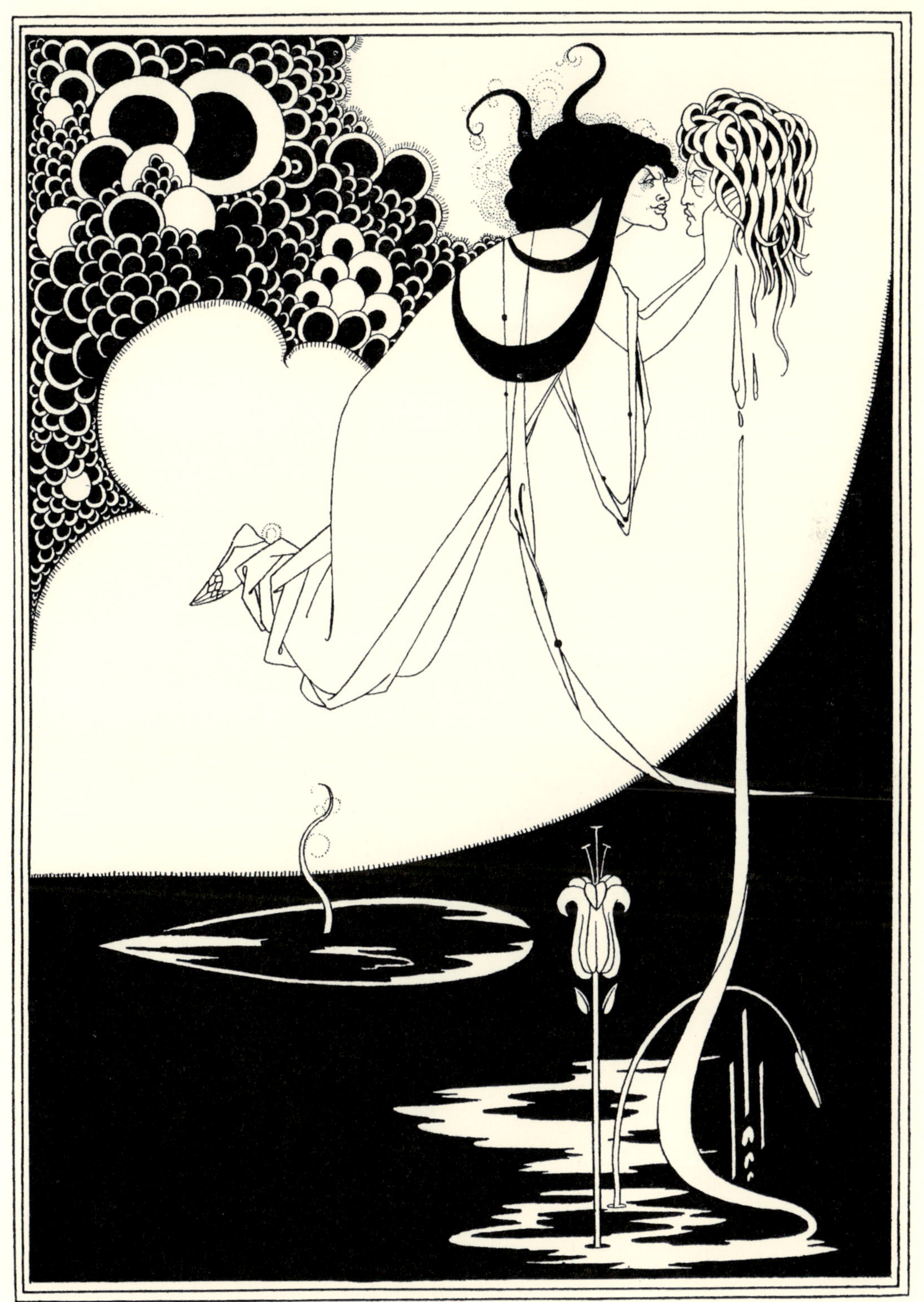

'The Climax'

This image was created by Beardsley after he saw *Salomé*, the French edition of Wilde's play, and was featured in the inaugural volume of *The Studio* in 1893. It was after seeing this that John Lane commissioned Beardsley to illustrate the English edition. The drawing featured in the magazine was drawn in pen. This picture, where the detailed sections from the original have been simplified, was used for the first edition of *Salome*. The wonderful of division of space, with the gently curving line that changes from horizontal to vertical dividing the black and white backgrounds, remains unchanged, but some miss the delicate tremors of the fine lines of the original. Personally, I like both versions.

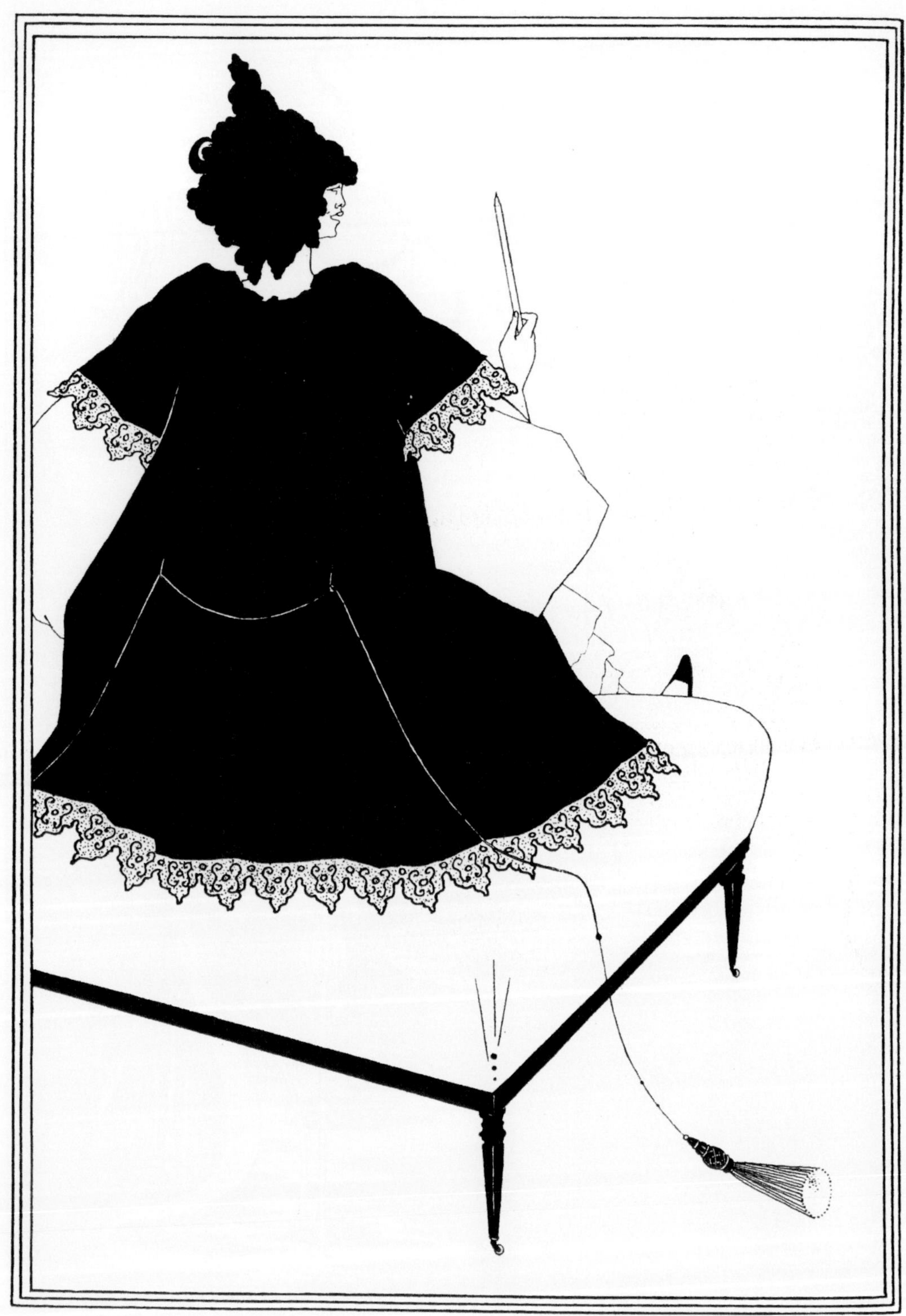

'Salome on a Settle'

This illustration wasn't used in the first edition of Salome, because it was deemed to have nothing to do with the original text, and because John Lane worried it might be obscene. The French title was *Maitresse d'Orchestre*, which has been translated as 'Female Conductor'. The conductor's baton held in her right hand was deemed to be a phallic symbol, and the tassel hanging down on the right was also supposed to represent the penis. There has also been the slightly confusing explanation that 'Maitresse' meant 'mistress', and so the picture was thought to imply that Salome was somehow the 'mistress' of the orchestra. However, as well as meaning the musical troupe, the word 'orchestra' also denotes the seats in the pit of the theatre, and so it seems possible that the title 'Maitresse d'Orchestre' in fact signified the overweight prostitute who sat surveying the scene around her. The folds in the corner of the chair are Beardsley's mark.

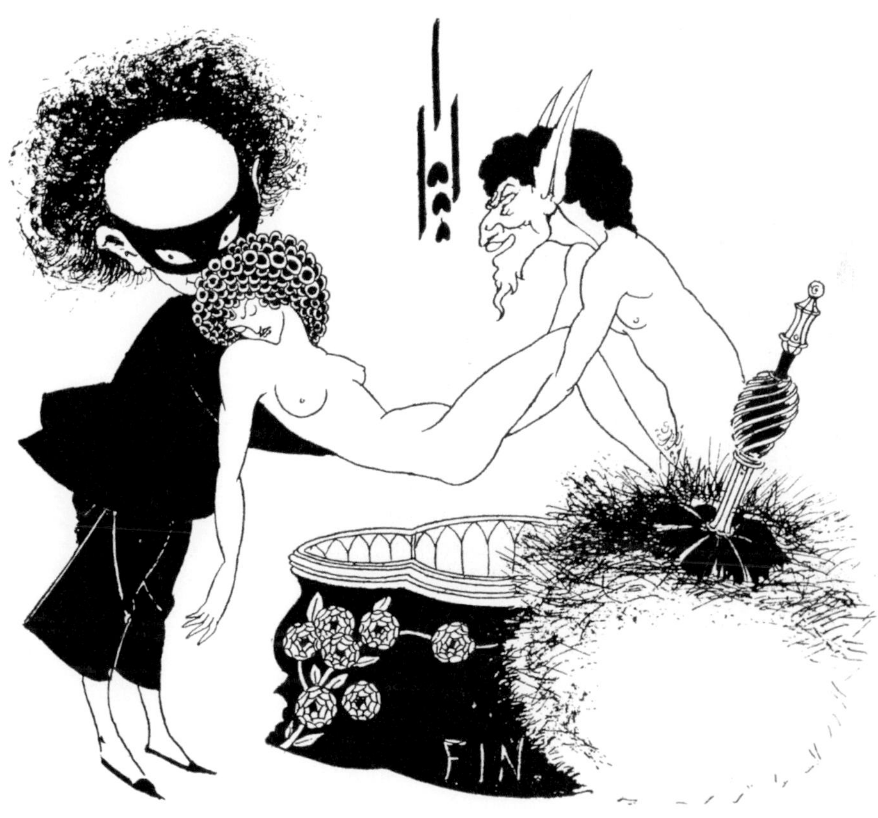

'Cul de Lampe'

Seeing Salome kissing John's severed head, King Herod orders her death. Wilde's play ends there, but Beardsley adds a burial scene for Salome. Her masked pierrot-beautician and the long-eared satyr are placing the naked Salome into a casket that looks like a powder case. The satyr's hairy hindquarters merge into the powder puff, whose handle rises up like a phallus. In the centre is Beardley's signature mark. The cruel Salome here appears somewhat delicate.

BEARDSLEY'S EARLY WORKS

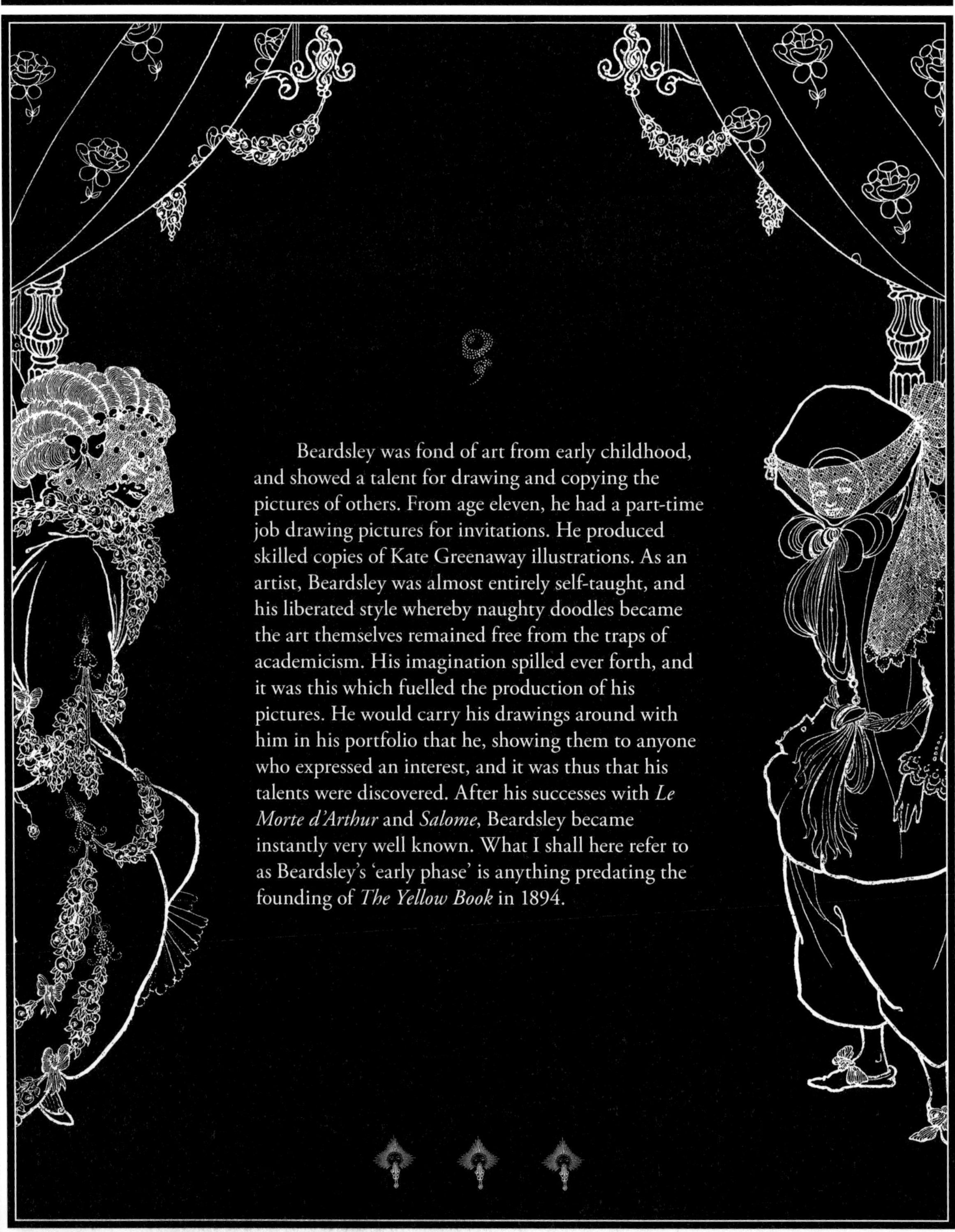

Beardsley was fond of art from early childhood, and showed a talent for drawing and copying the pictures of others. From age eleven, he had a part-time job drawing pictures for invitations. He produced skilled copies of Kate Greenaway illustrations. As an artist, Beardsley was almost entirely self-taught, and his liberated style whereby naughty doodles became the art themselves remained free from the traps of academicism. His imagination spilled ever forth, and it was this which fuelled the production of his pictures. He would carry his drawings around with him in his portfolio that he, showing them to anyone who expressed an interest, and it was thus that his talents were discovered. After his successes with *Le Morte d'Arthur* and *Salome*, Beardsley became instantly very well known. What I shall here refer to as Beardsley's 'early phase' is anything predating the founding of *The Yellow Book* in 1894.

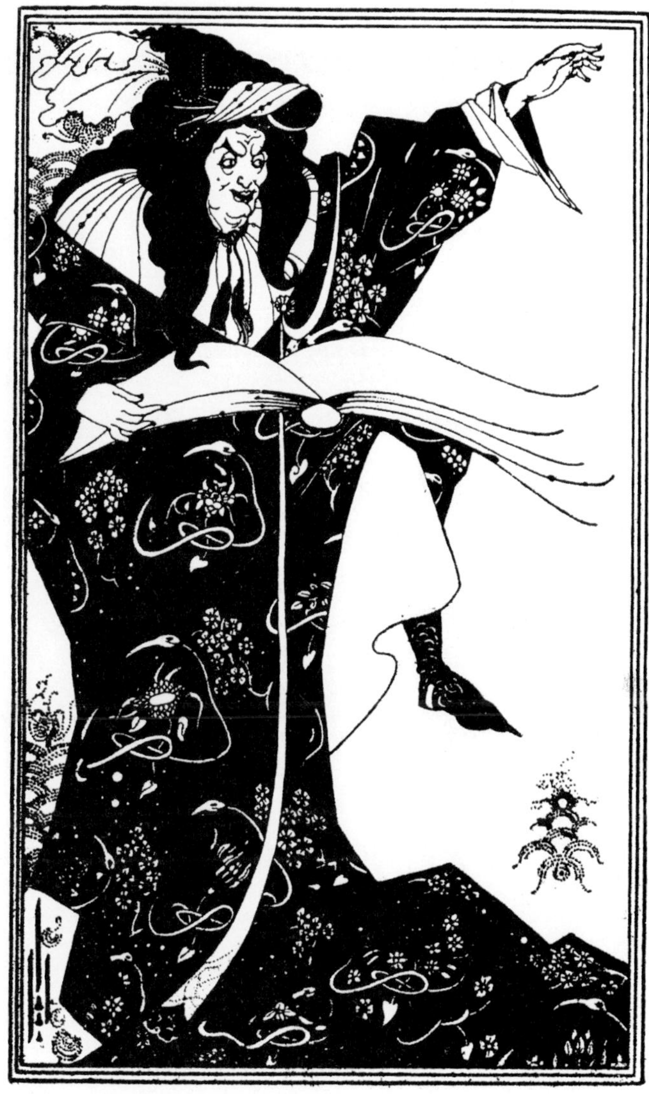

'Virgilius the Sorceror', 1894

This picture shows a strong influence from Japanese prints of kabuki actors. It was Beardsley's enthrallment with Japanese art which enabled him to break free from the stylistic influence of the Arts and Crafts movement. The grand, sweeping gestures are inspired by the poses of the kabuki stars and the portrayal of two-dimensional patterns on clothes were also techniques that he learned from *ukiyo-e*. The picture features a restless pattern resembling that of crested waves, while the bottom left features Beardsley's signature mark.

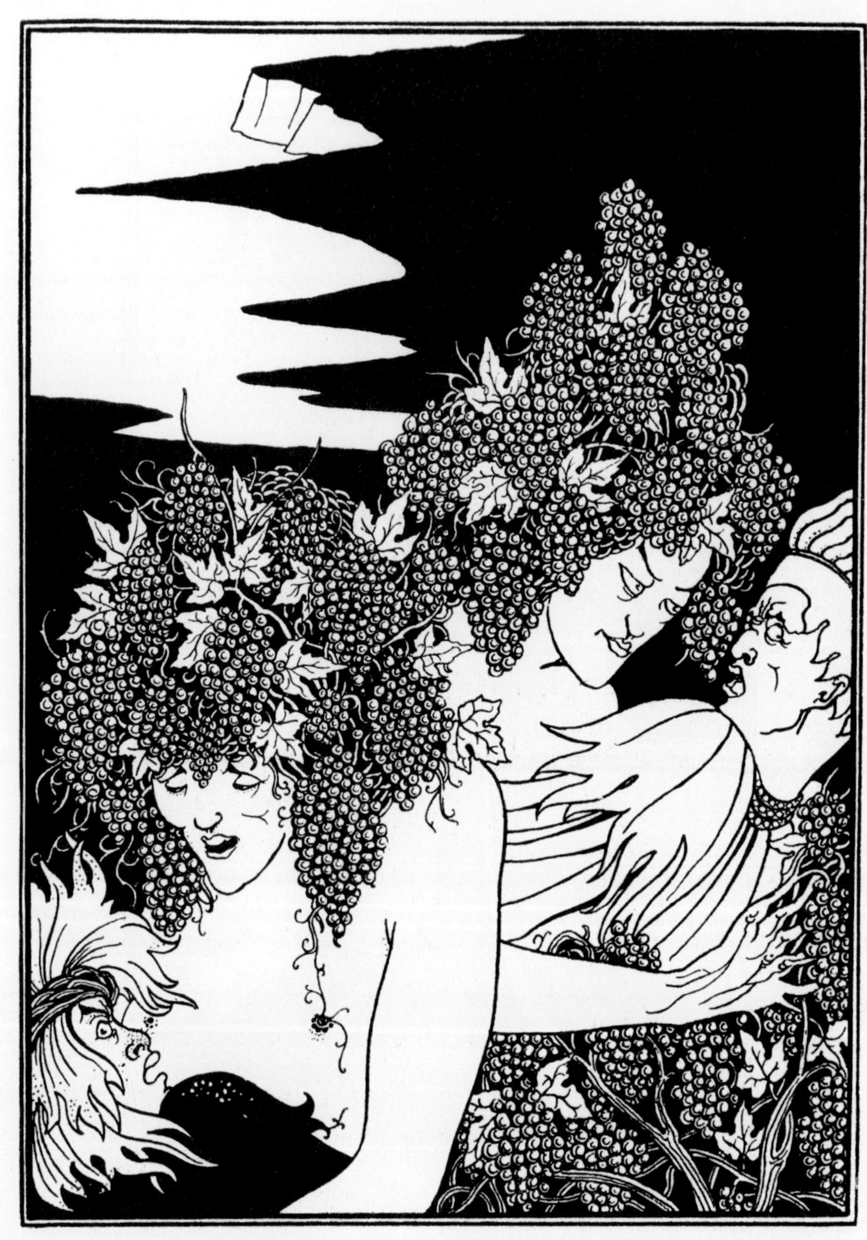

Illustration for Lucian's *True History*: 'A Snare of Vintage', 1893

Beardsley took on the job of illustrating Lucian's *True History* while he was creating the illustrations for *Le Morte d'Arthur*. He was supposed to draw around 30 pictures, but subsequently became busy with his illustrations for Salome. When the book was published in 1894, it featured only two pictures by Beardsley with the rest drawn by other artists. Lucian was a Roman satirist from the second century, and *True History* tells the tale of the author's travels through strange lands, taken as a precursor to *Gulliver's Travels*. 'A Snare of Vintage' tells the story of an island where women grow upon the vines, tempting the men who come to visit.

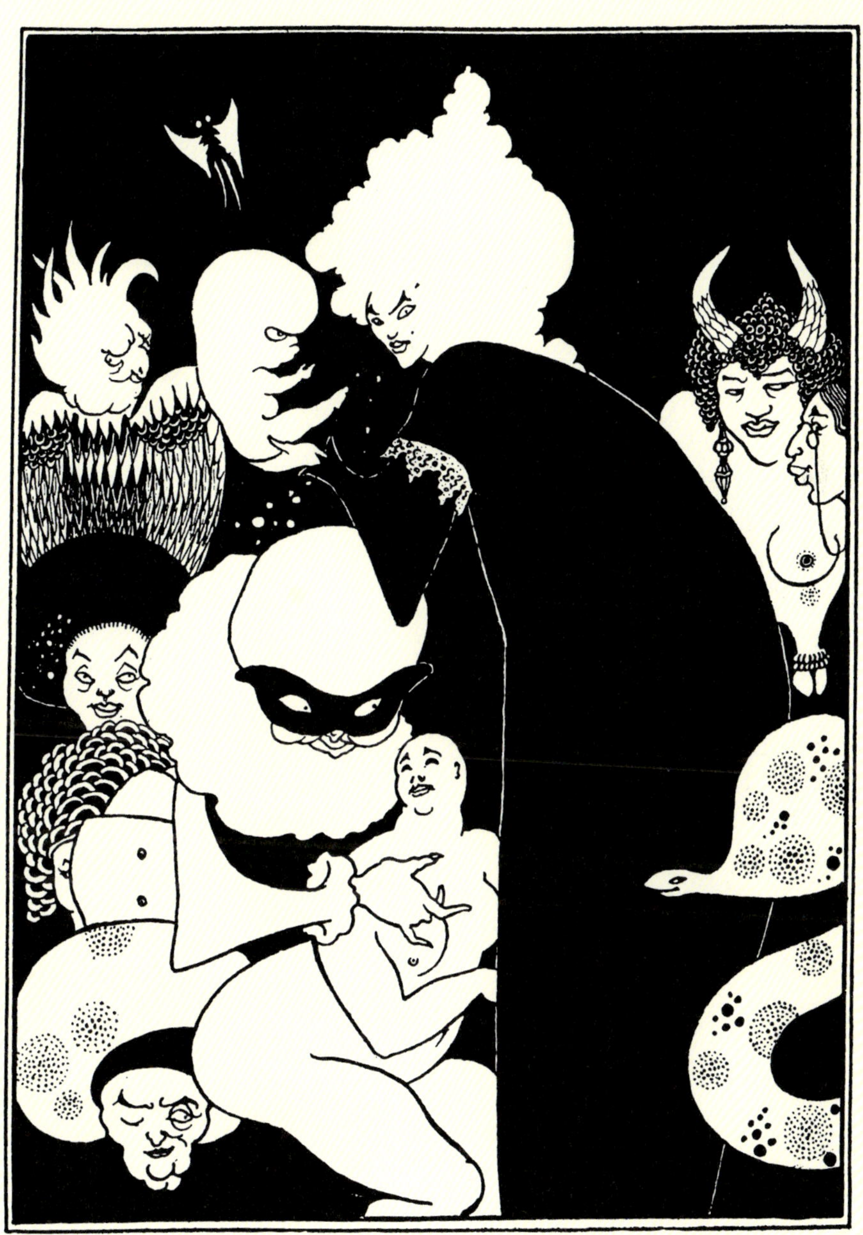

'Lucian's Strange Creatures', 1893

This illustration was created for Lucian's *True History*, but wasn't used in either the first edition in 1894 or the second in 1902. It was first put to use in the 1906 edition released by Smithers. Here, Beardsley has put his imaginative powers to the task of dreaming up the bizarre creatures that appear in Lucian's strange tales. The face of the hermaphrodite horned creature who appears in the top right appears to be that of Oscar Wilde. During this period, Beardsley was attracted to grotesque forms, and would often draw foetuses such as the one held by the witch in the centre. By this stage we can see that Beardsley has shifted from a style full of fine 'hairline' flourishes to a bolder, clearer style that prints better when made into woodblocks.

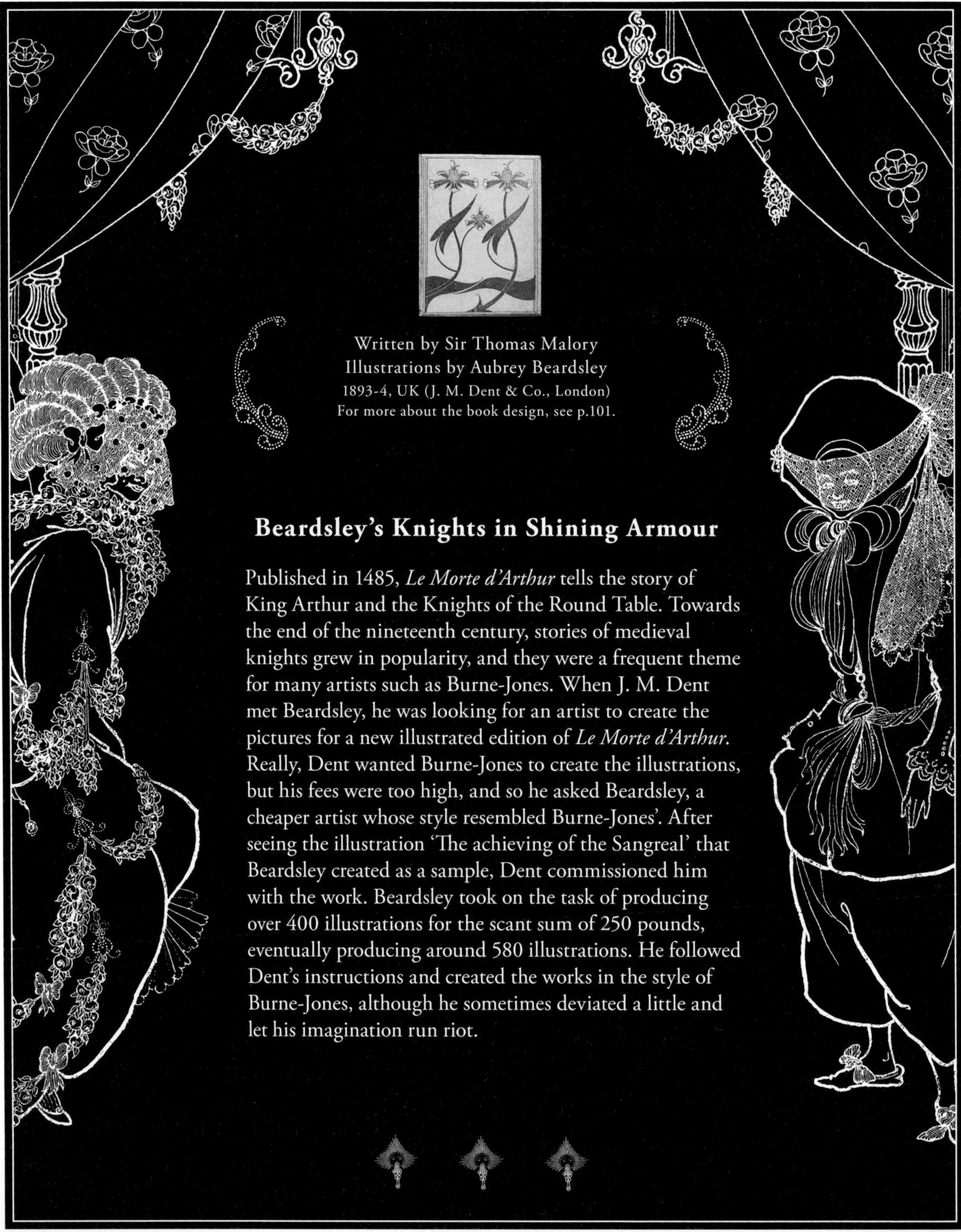

Written by Sir Thomas Malory
Illustrations by Aubrey Beardsley
1893-4, UK (J. M. Dent & Co., London)
For more about the book design, see p.101.

Beardsley's Knights in Shining Armour

Published in 1485, *Le Morte d'Arthur* tells the story of King Arthur and the Knights of the Round Table. Towards the end of the nineteenth century, stories of medieval knights grew in popularity, and they were a frequent theme for many artists such as Burne-Jones. When J. M. Dent met Beardsley, he was looking for an artist to create the pictures for a new illustrated edition of *Le Morte d'Arthur*. Really, Dent wanted Burne-Jones to create the illustrations, but his fees were too high, and so he asked Beardsley, a cheaper artist whose style resembled Burne-Jones'. After seeing the illustration 'The achieving of the Sangreal' that Beardsley created as a sample, Dent commissioned him with the work. Beardsley took on the task of producing over 400 illustrations for the scant sum of 250 pounds, eventually producing around 580 illustrations. He followed Dent's instructions and created the works in the style of Burne-Jones, although he sometimes deviated a little and let his imagination run riot.

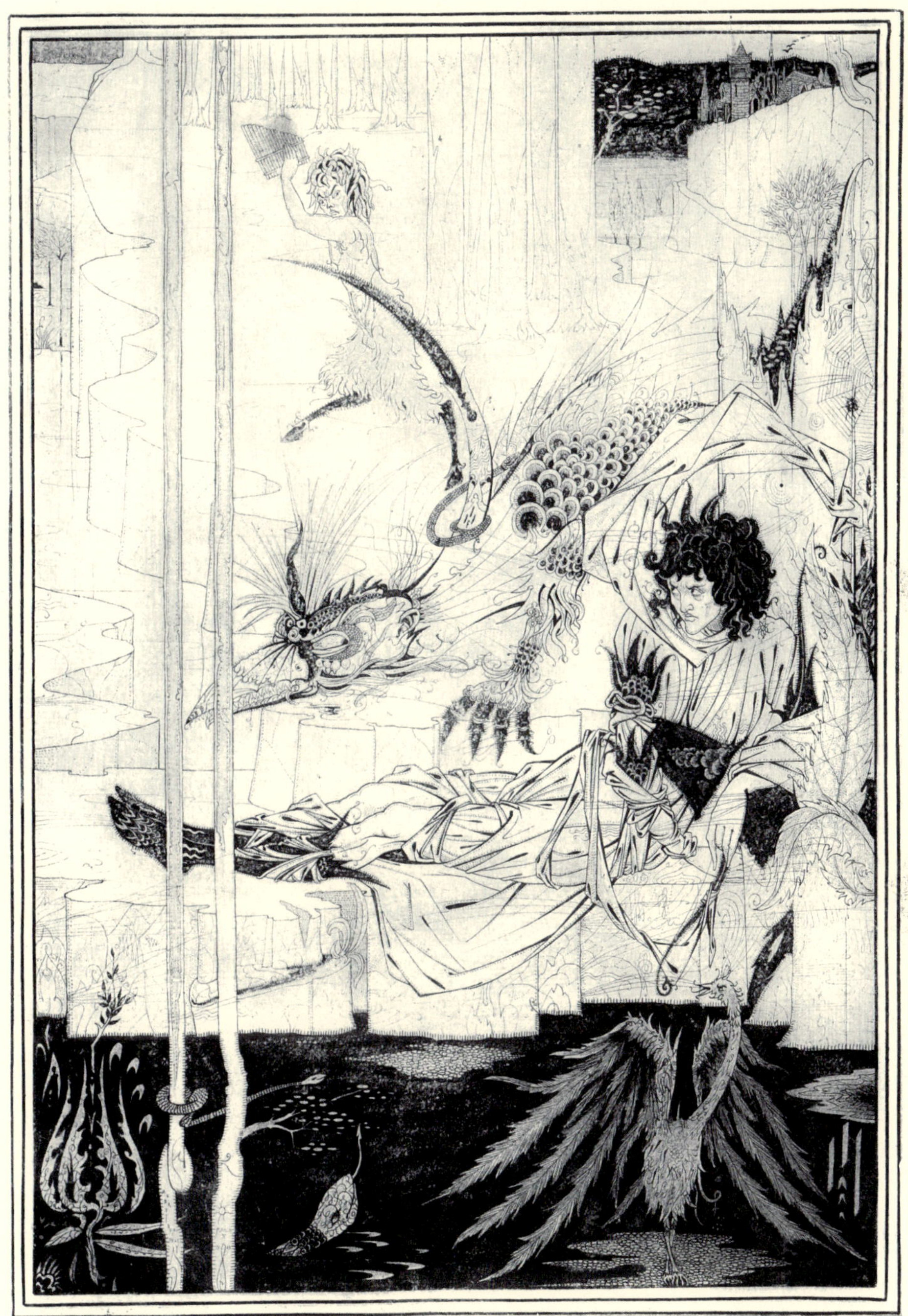

Frontispiece to Volume I:
'How King Arthur saw the Questing Beast, and thereof had great marvel'

Troubled by the mystery of his birth—which is to say, the identity of his father—King Arthur dreams of a strange creature called 'the questing beast'. This name references both the shroud of mystery enveloping the matter, and the fact that his father was in fact named 'Pendragon'. In Beardsley's illustration, a Japanese-style dragon appears by the side of a reclining Arthur. The illustrations for the main text use simple lines, but this frontispiece is rendered in a delicate hairline style, scattered with grotesque details.

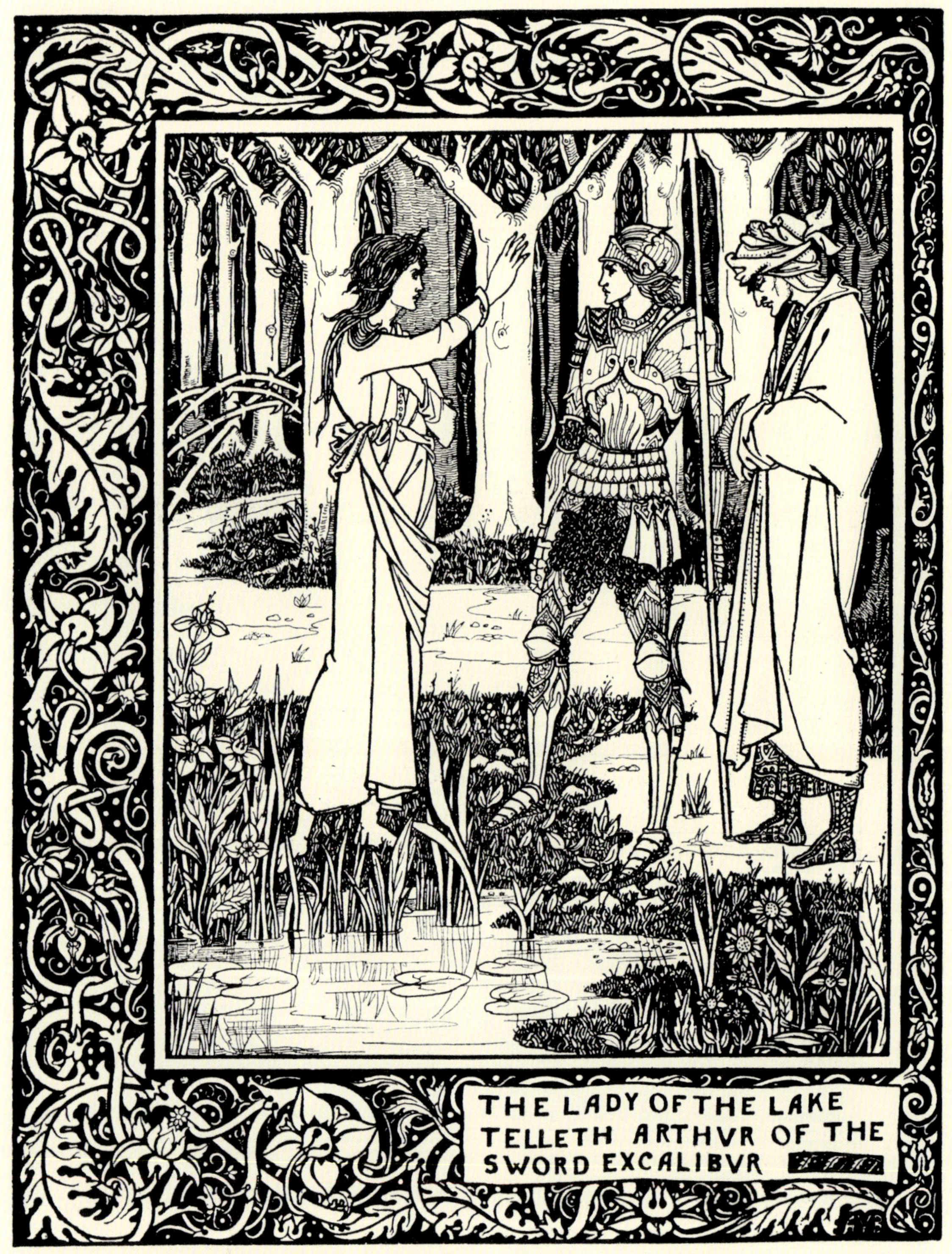

From Volume 1: 'The Lady of the Lake Telleth Arthur of the Sword Excalibur'

Led by the magician-knight Merlin (right), Arthur encounters the Lady of the Lake and thus comes upon the sword Excalibur. The illustrations accompanying the text are printed using the line block technique, a kind of mechanized descendant of the woodcut. This picture allegedly fuelled William Morris' dislike of Beardsley, who thought it was too similar to the works of Burne-Jones, and also resented that it was machine printed rather than hand-carved. Morris also felt that the arabesque patterning around the side was an imitation of Kelmscott Press, Morris' own printing press.

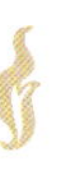

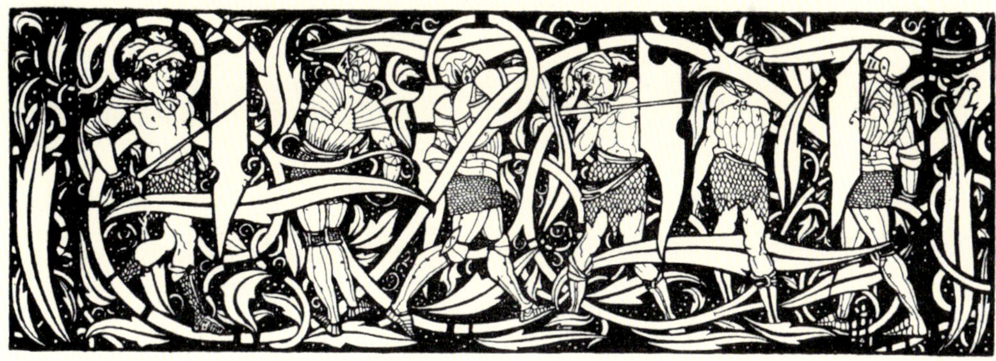

(a)

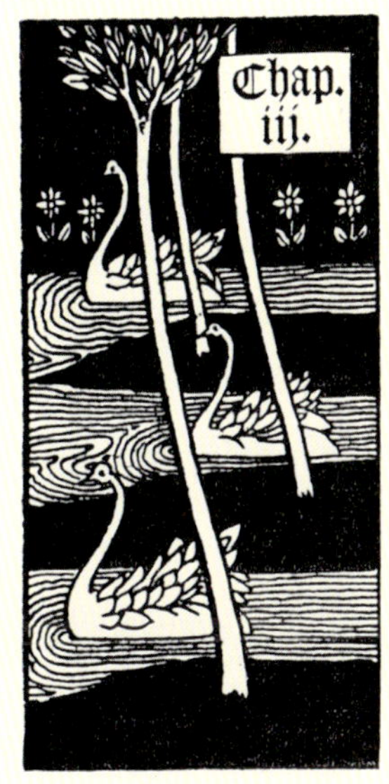

(b)

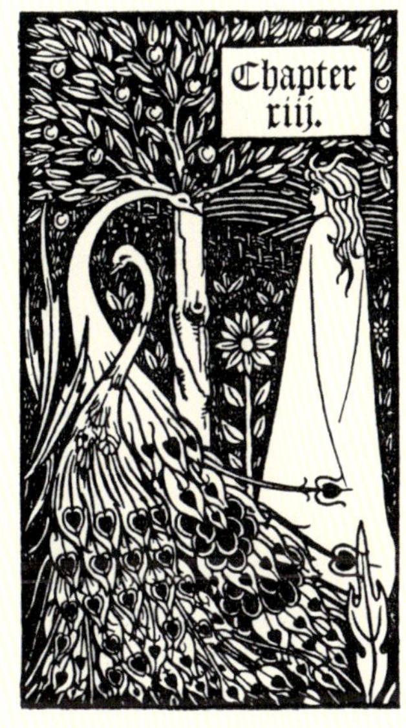

(c)

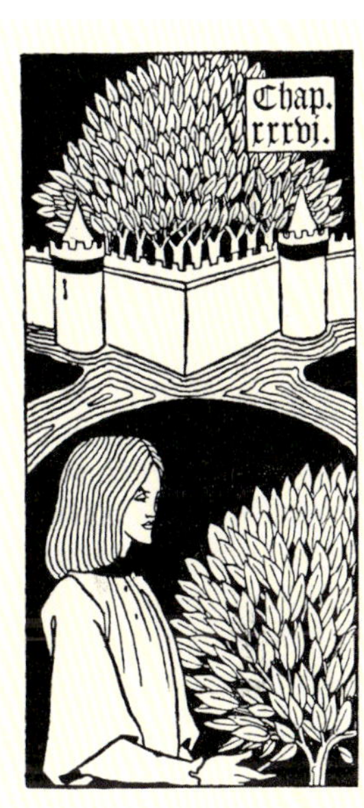

(d)

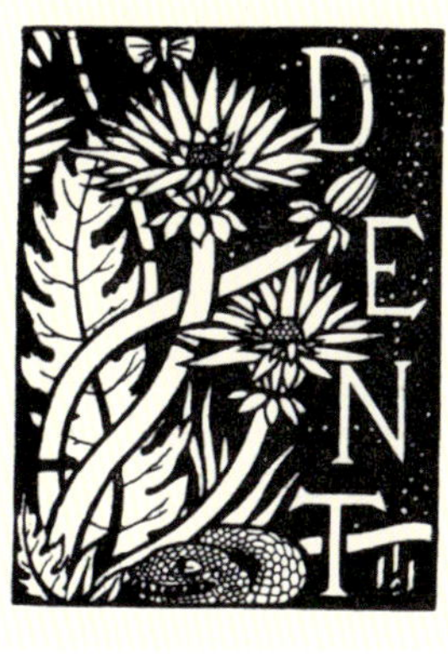

(e)

(f)

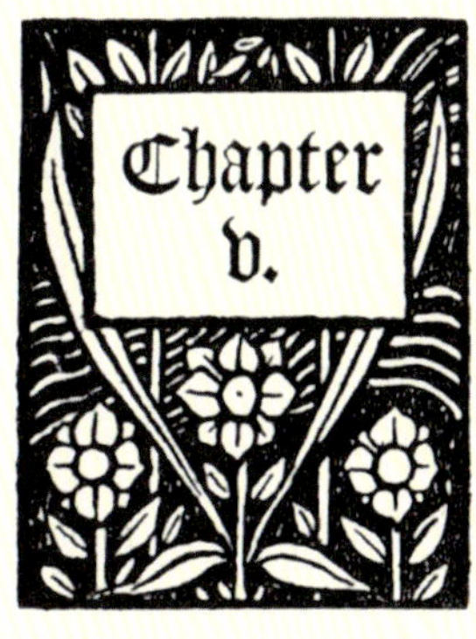

(g)

Small Illustrations I

The small illustrations scattered frequently throughout the text are good fun. The vertical frieze (a) that appears at the top of the title page for Volume One shows fighting knights entangled in winding vines. The inspiration for the vines here comes from Burne-Jones' *Briar Rose* series, but here the portrayal is more abstract. The Dent company logo that appears beneath them (e) also uses a dynamic plant design with thick stems. A square illustrative panel was included at the start of each chapter (b-d, f, g). The subject matter is very free, and Beardsley is clearly having fun experimenting with bold images.

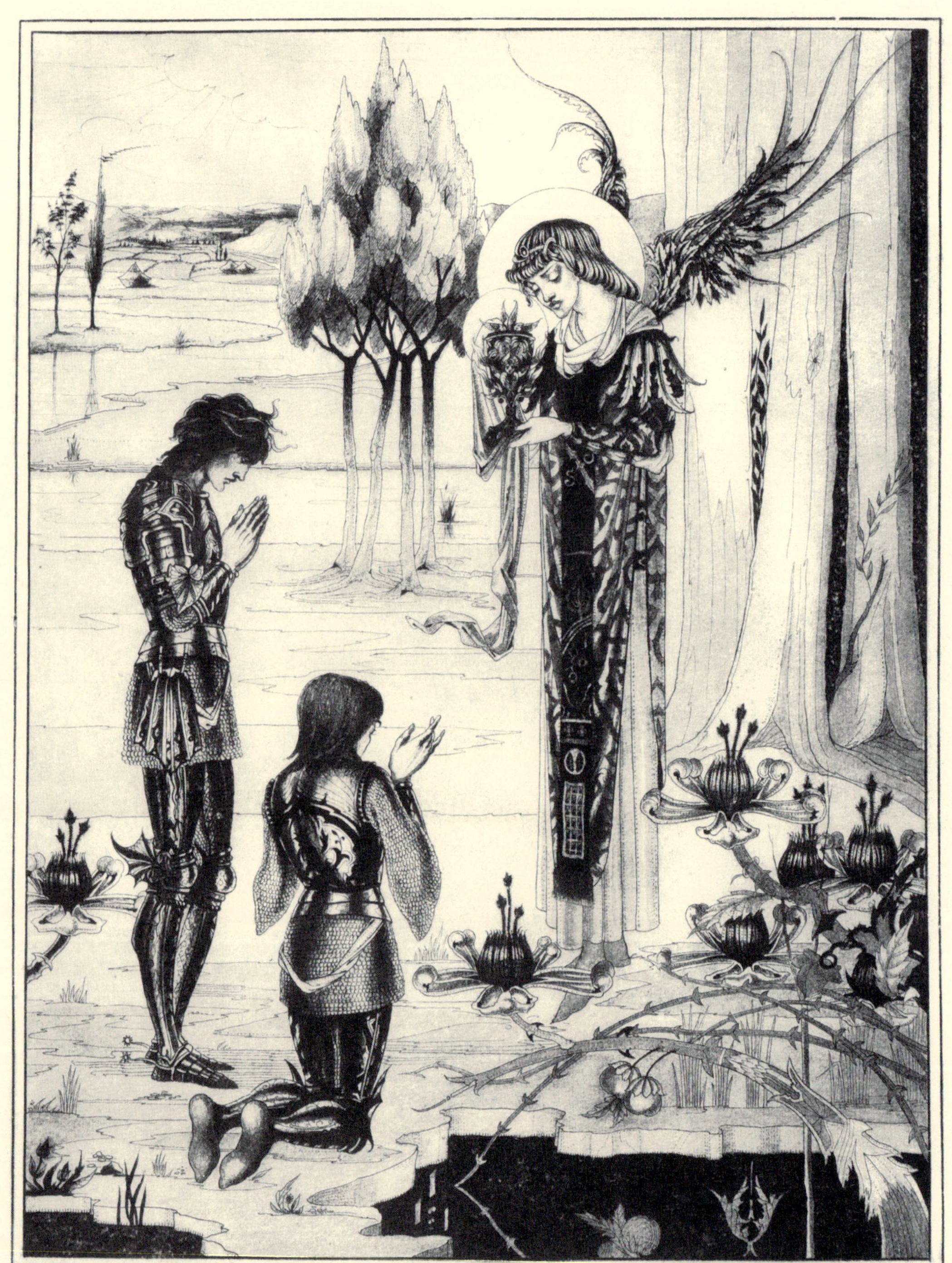

Frontispiece to Volume II: 'The achieving of the Sangreal'

This is the picture Beardsley produced as a sample, which was used as the frontispiece for the second volume. Percival battles with a knight he meets on his journey, and the two of them collapse injured on the floor. A maiden bearing the Sangreal, or Holy Grail, appears, healing the two and bowing to the the Holy Grail. The man kneeling is Percival. Along with 'How King Arthur saw the Questing Beast, and thereof had great marvel,' this is the only photogravure illustration, and is thus rendered in a delicate hairline style, in contrast to the bolder expression of the rest which are printed using the line block technique.

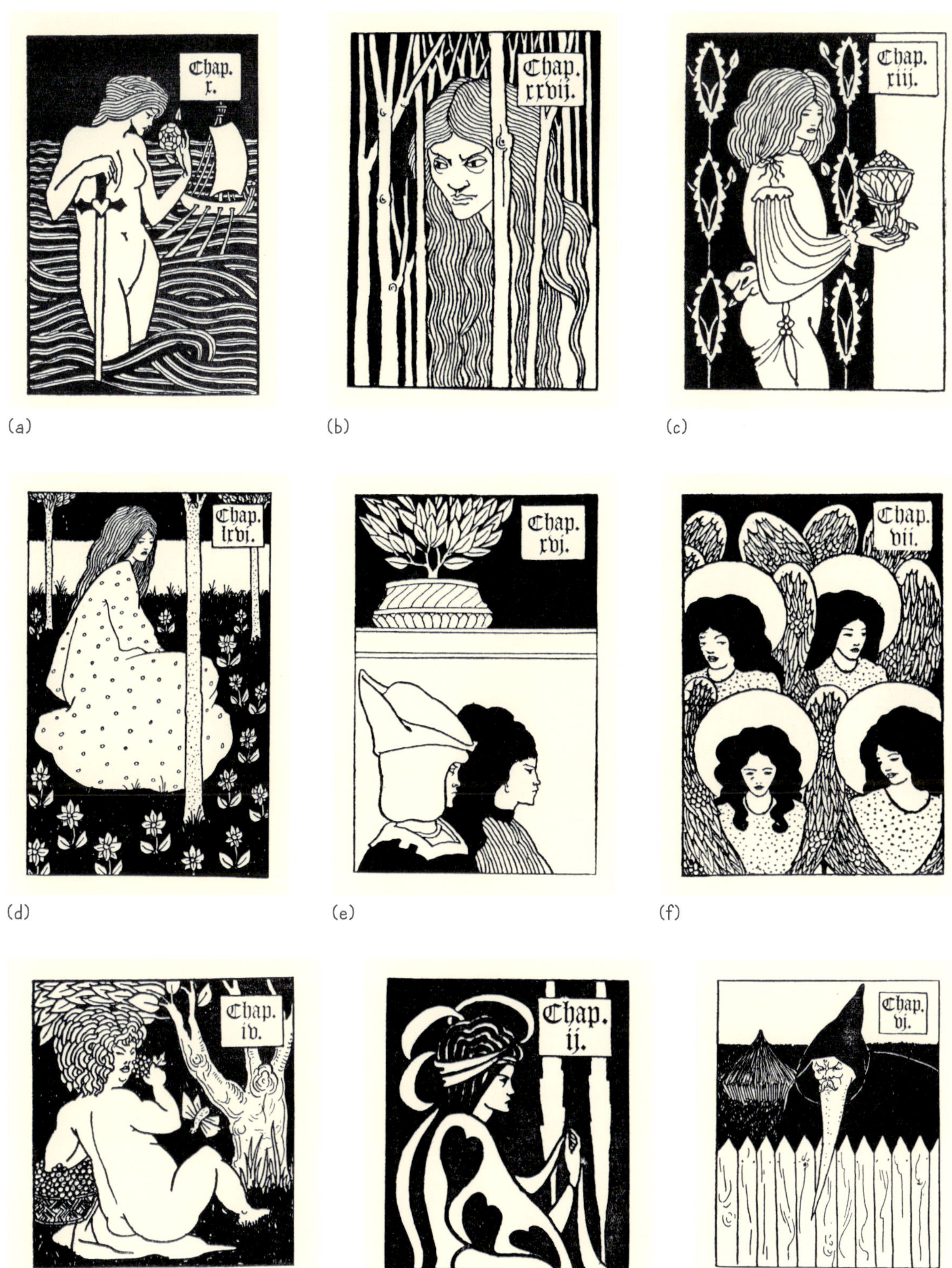

(a)　(b)　(c)

(d)　(e)　(f)

(g)　(h)　(i)

Small Illustrations II

Compared to the medieval times as they appear in the work of Morris and Burne-Jones, the medieval world of Beardsley's depiction is more erotic and contemporary in feel. There is something fresh and new about the Japanese-style winding lines used to portray the water from which the Lady of the Lake appears (a) and the bold patterns incorporated in fabrics and backgrounds. The unpolished description of the chubby, naked woman eating grapes (g) has a wild, naked eroticism to it, alongside a tangible lack of nostalgia for the past. Such a depiction would definitely not be found anywhere in the work of the Pre-Raphaelites.

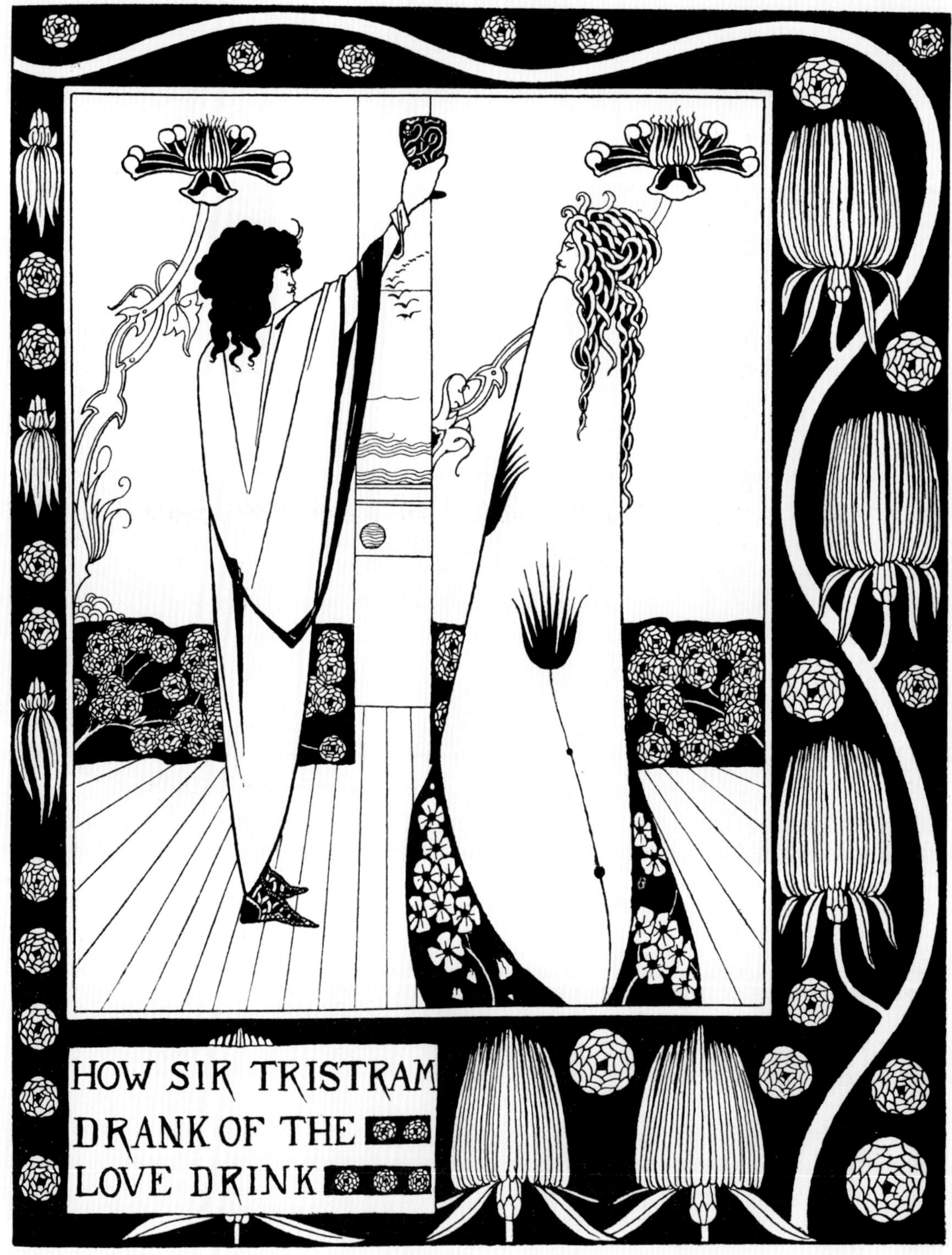

From Volume I: 'How Sir Tristram Drank of the Love Drink'

The story of Tristram and Iseult from Arthurian Legend was created into an opera by Wagner, which happened to be Beardsley's favourite opera of all time. Tristram (Tristan) drinks a love potion and falls in love with Iseult (Isolde). In this picture, the artist has shaken off the Burne-Jones style, and the trademark Beardsley-style figures come to the fore. The vine looping its way around the picture creates a distinctive, Art-Nouveau-style curve.

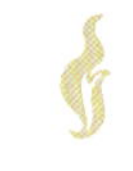

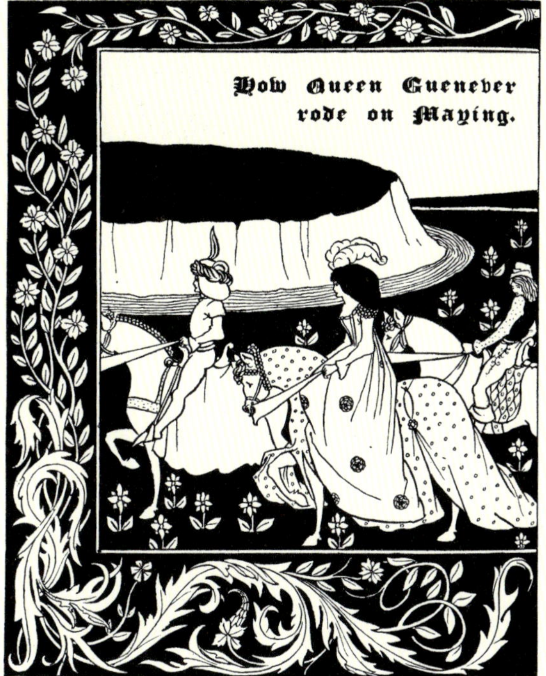

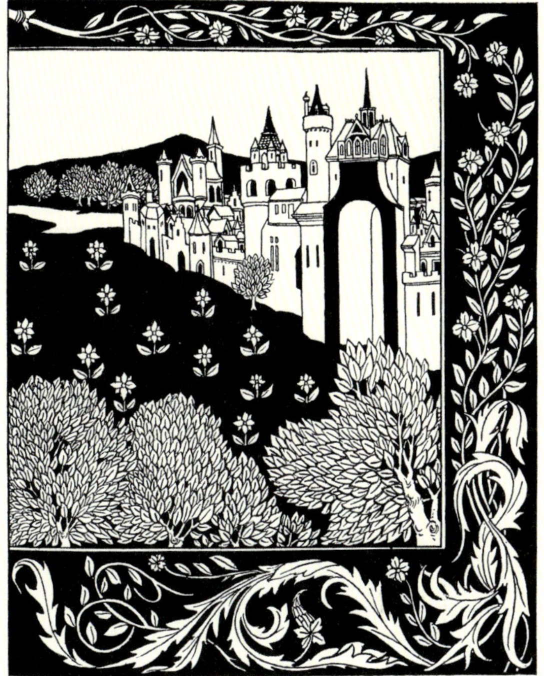

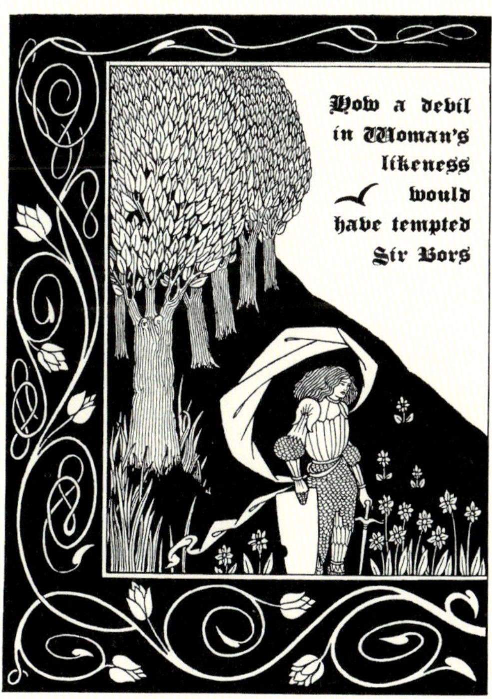

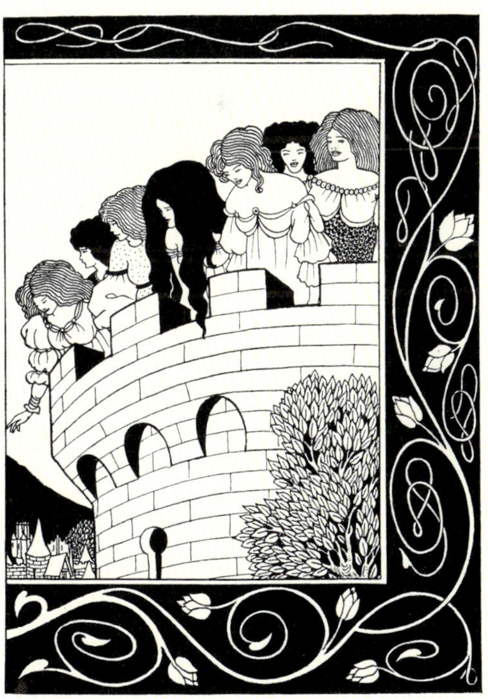

(Top) From Volume I: 'How Queen Guenever rode on Maying'

It is customary at Maying to pick flowers. The side-on depiction of the procession mimics the medieval style.

(Bottom) From Volume II: 'How a devil in Woman's likeness would have tempted Sir Bors'

Sir Bors was the son of King Bors of Gall, and cousin to Sir Lancelot. Into the second volume of the book, we find many large illustrations spread over two pages such as this one. On the left-hand page is Sir Bors in the forest, and on the right hand we find witches tempting him from the castle turret. The expressions of the women and the way their hair is rendered is often to be found in Beardsley's work from this point on. The frame is decorated with Art Nouveau-style branches.

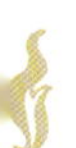

THE STUDIO

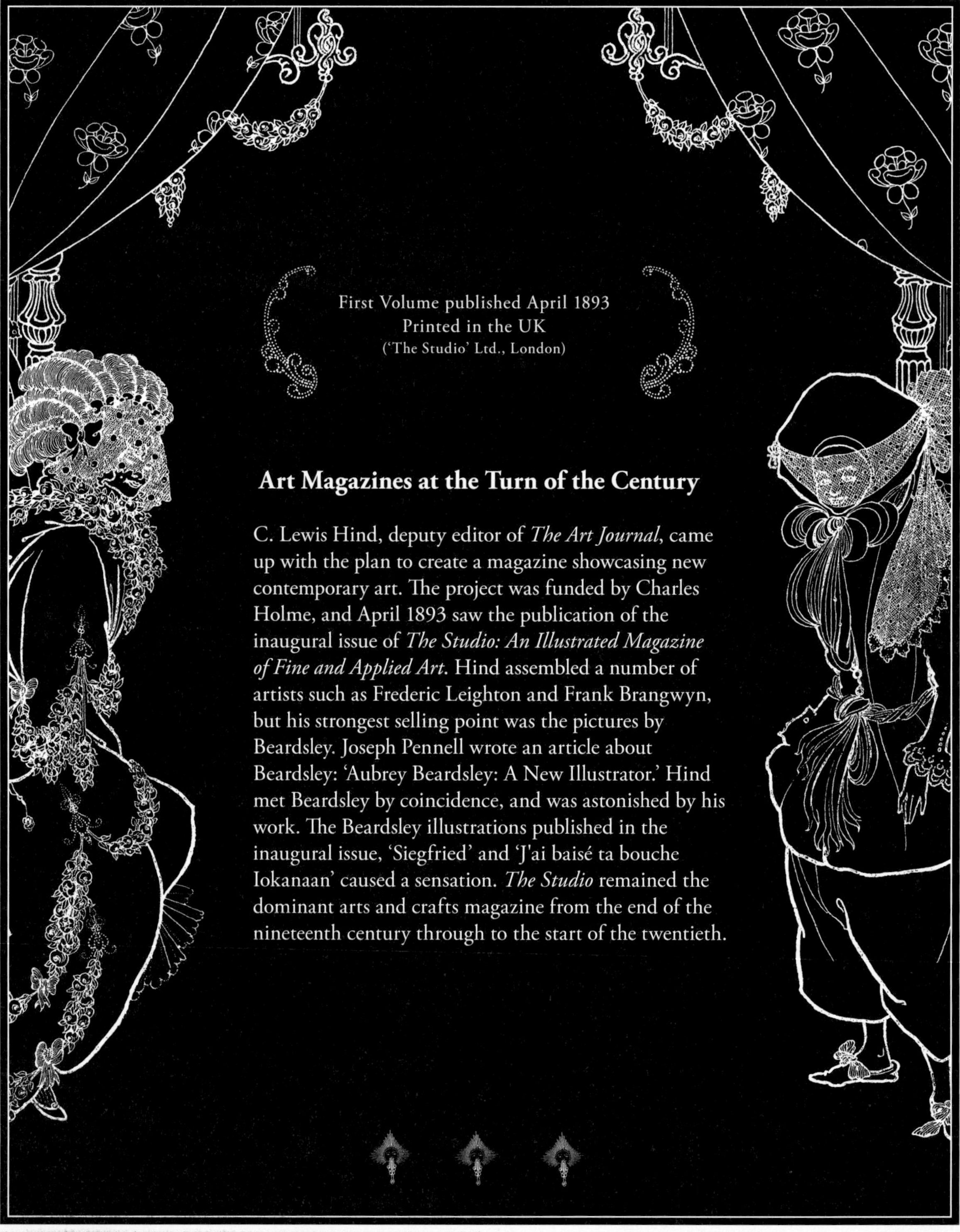

First Volume published April 1893
Printed in the UK
('The Studio' Ltd., London)

Art Magazines at the Turn of the Century

C. Lewis Hind, deputy editor of *The Art Journal*, came up with the plan to create a magazine showcasing new contemporary art. The project was funded by Charles Holme, and April 1893 saw the publication of the inaugural issue of *The Studio: An Illustrated Magazine of Fine and Applied Art*. Hind assembled a number of artists such as Frederic Leighton and Frank Brangwyn, but his strongest selling point was the pictures by Beardsley. Joseph Pennell wrote an article about Beardsley: 'Aubrey Beardsley: A New Illustrator.' Hind met Beardsley by coincidence, and was astonished by his work. The Beardsley illustrations published in the inaugural issue, 'Siegfried' and 'J'ai baisé ta bouche Iokanaan' caused a sensation. *The Studio* remained the dominant arts and crafts magazine from the end of the nineteenth century through to the start of the twentieth.

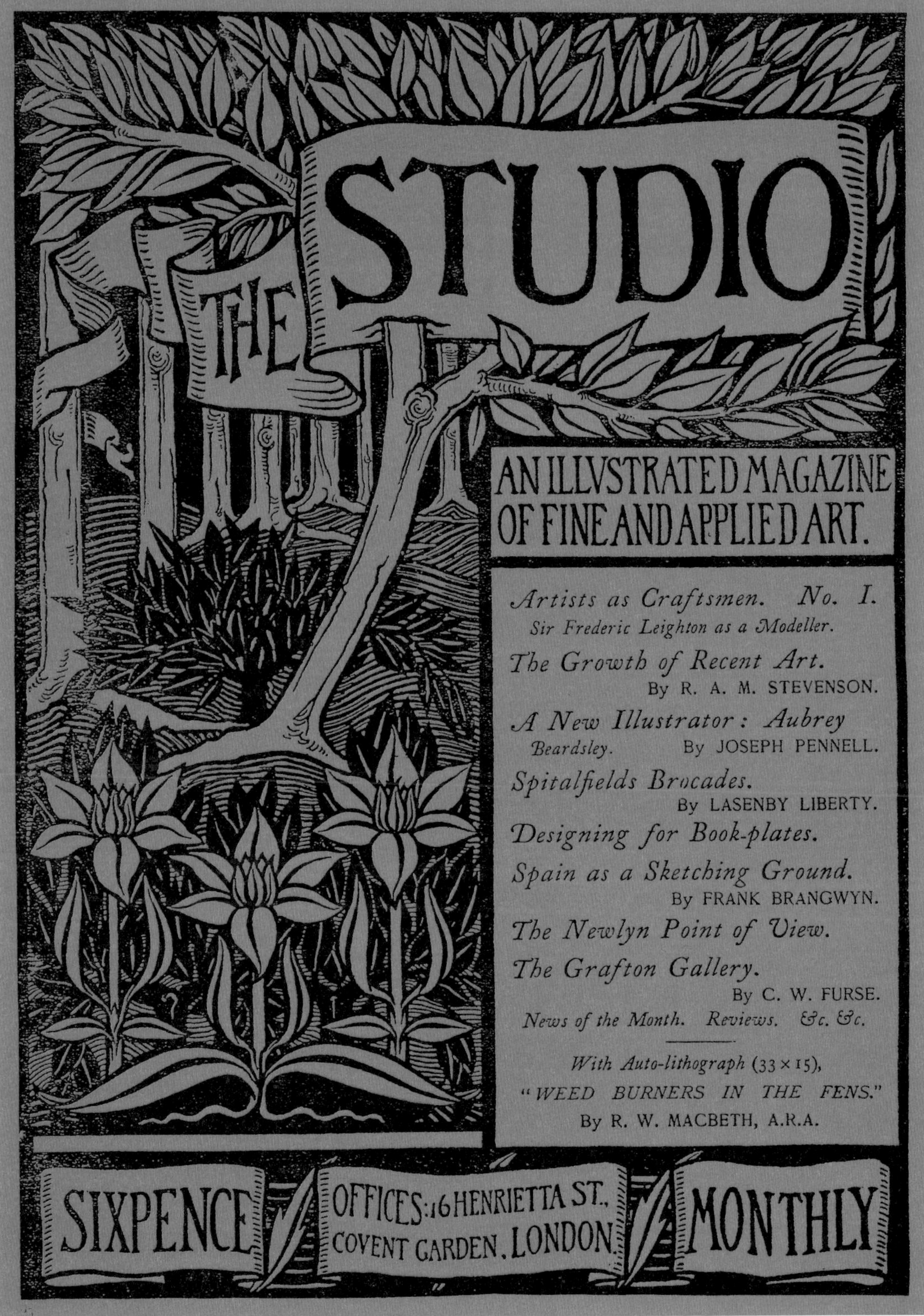

Cover to Volume I

This cover, featuring a banner bearing the magazine's name tangled up in the trees, owes a debt to Walter Klein. It is a relatively orthodox design, which adheres closely to the style of Morris and Klein's Arts and Crafts movement. As it happens, in the first version he created, Beardsley drew a faun to the left of the picture but it was deemed indecent and deleted. This goes to show how strictly his works were censored from the beginning.

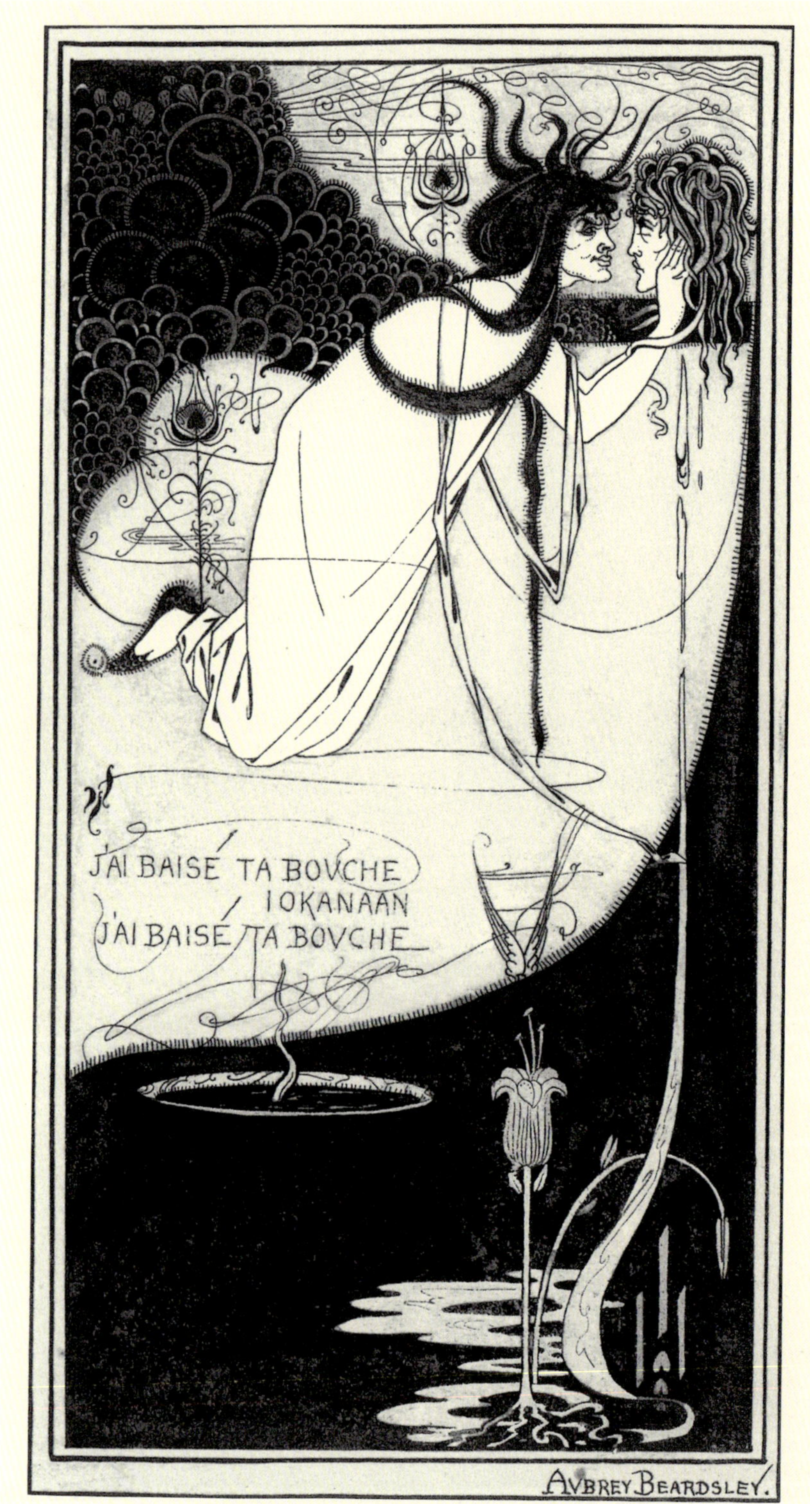

From Volume I: 'J'ai baisé ta bouche, Iokanaan'

This picture, whose title means 'I Kissed Your Mouth, Iokanaan,' was an image created by Beardsley after reading the French edition of Wilde's *Salomé*. It was this picture that inspired Wilde and John Lane to commission Beardsley to create the illustrations for the English edition of the play. This formed the basis for the illustration of 'The Climax' illustration that appeared in the published edition, but there the lines have been made simpler and more crisp. In these editions for *The Studio*, the staggeringly fine lines known as hairlines from Beardsley's first period are seen everywhere, filling the picture with delicate nervous vibrations. By the time of Salome, such delicacy of expression has disappeared, and black and white are used in stark contrast with one another.

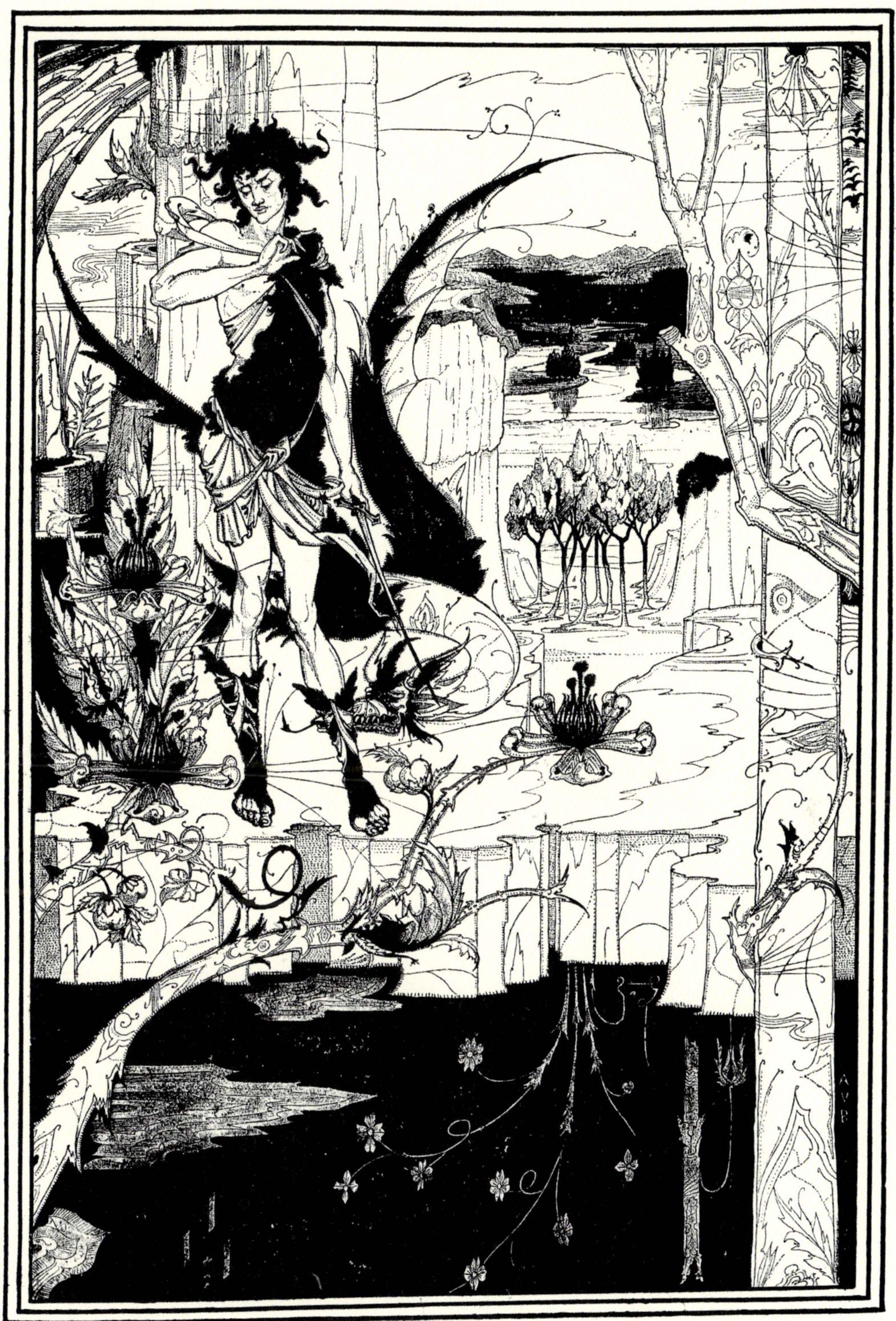

From Volume I: 'Siegfried, Act II'

This picture was included in the first edition of *The Studio*. Beardsley subsequently gave it to Burne-Jones. It is saturated by the sensitive, wispy lines characteristic of Beardsley's earlier hairline style. The picture depicts an image from the Wagnerian comedy, *Siegfried*, after Siegfried has slayed the dragon. The depiction of the hero as knock-kneed and somewhat feminine is a typically Beardsley-like touch. It is said that the background river scene comes from Pollaiolo's *The Martyrdom of Saint Sebastian*. Rather than a strong powerful hero, we see here a portrait of innocent, easily wounded youngster.

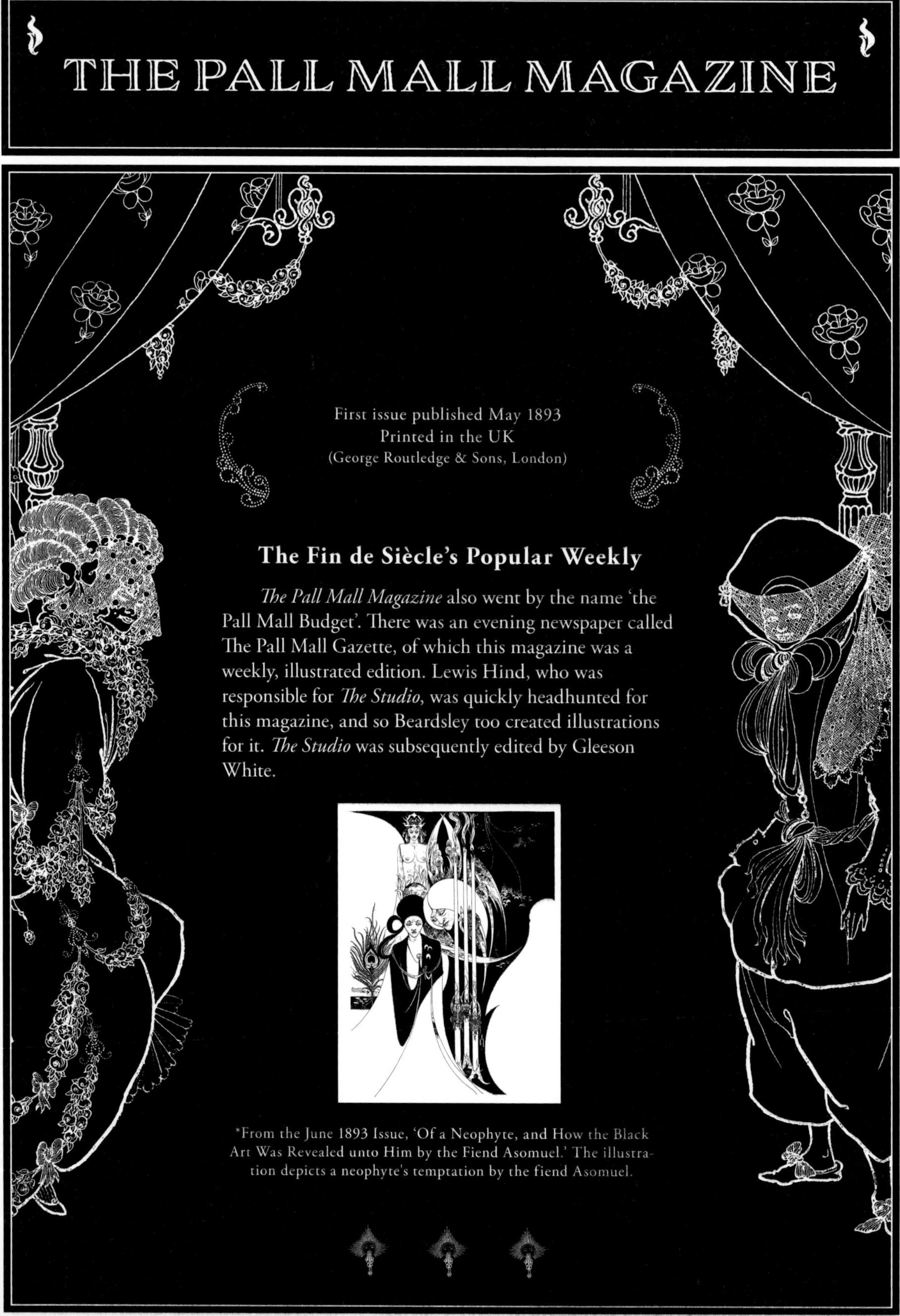

THE PALL MALL MAGAZINE

First issue published May 1893
Printed in the UK
(George Routledge & Sons, London)

The Fin de Siècle's Popular Weekly

The Pall Mall Magazine also went by the name 'the Pall Mall Budget'. There was an evening newspaper called The Pall Mall Gazette, of which this magazine was a weekly, illustrated edition. Lewis Hind, who was responsible for *The Studio*, was quickly headhunted for this magazine, and so Beardsley too created illustrations for it. *The Studio* was subsequently edited by Gleeson White.

*From the June 1893 Issue, 'Of a Neophyte, and How the Black Art Was Revealed unto Him by the Fiend Asomuel.' The illustration depicts a neophyte's temptation by the fiend Asomuel.

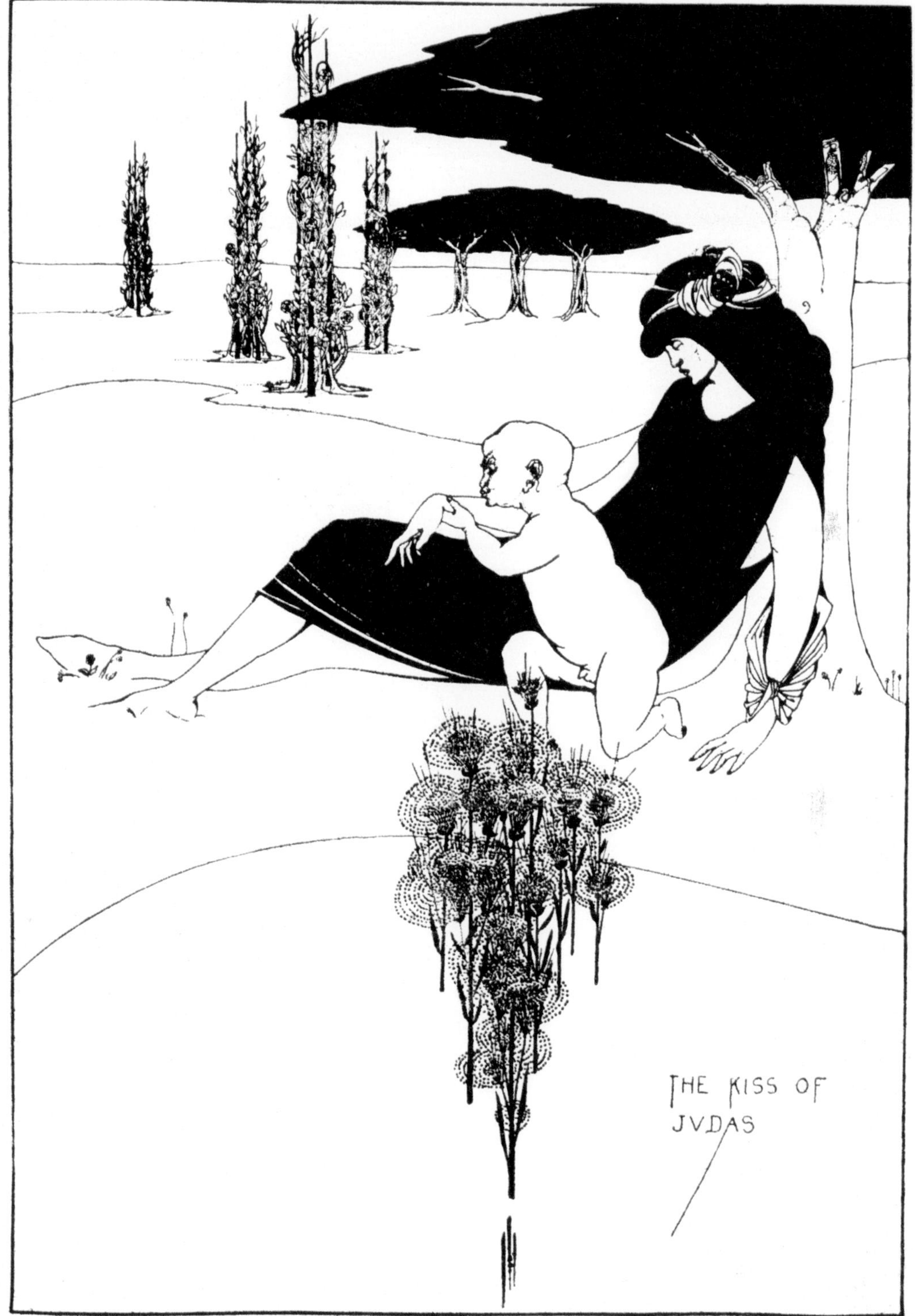

From August 1893 issue: 'The Kiss of Judas'

A Moldavian legend held that the descendants of Judas would plot to bring about the downfall of the human race, and anybody who kissed one of them would die. A marquise who heard of this apparently proclaimed, 'Oh, how wonderful!' Here, a naked boy kisses the hand of a beautiful woman leaning up against a tree. The boy's face has a mischievous, demonic cast. The focus of the picture lies in its upper section, with foliage filling its lower region. This foliage is an extended, enlarged version of Beardsley's signature mark that sits at the very bottom of the picture, and attempts to pierce the woman's flesh. Her arm is thrust through a piece of cloth whose knot takes the shape of a vagina. A risqué picture and no mistake.

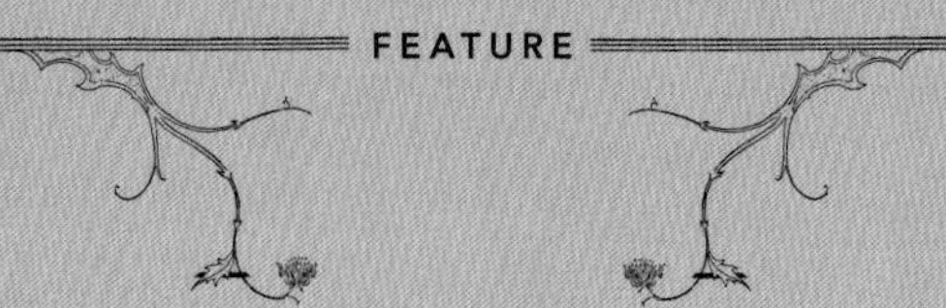

BEARDSLEY AND JAPONISM

In the late nineteenth century, the influence of all kinds of Japanese art, from *ukiyo-e* woodblock prints to the exquisite, gold-heavy natural landscapes of the Rinpa school, spread across Europe in a movement dubbed 'Japonism'. It originally found a reception with impressionist and symbolist artists in France, but eventually found its way to Britain as well. Beardsley was one of the most passionate imbibers of Japanese culture, and was regarded as something of a heretic in England as a result.

There were two aspects of Japanese art which particularly elicited Beardsley's fascination. The first was that of its forms. Beardsley avidly sought out the Japanese understanding of form, which was two-dimensional and lacking in depth, and where blank space was perceived not as a background or a gap between objects, but as an entity with its own significance. The other aspect was the approach to the erotic which he found in Japanese prints. The first aspect allowed Beardsley to destroy the preconceived notions around the space of the picture governed by academic rules of perspective, while the second allowed him to destroy hypocritical Victorian morality that sought to hide all sexuality. Thanks to this, Beardsley became the object of criticism for the good, decent people of Victorian Britain.

How did Beardsley come into contact with Japanese art? Apparently his encounter with Japan dated back to his boyhood in Brighton, when he was an avid reader of A. B. Mitford's *Tales of Old Japan* (fig.1). In London in 1890, there was a Hokusai exhibition at the London Art Association, which it is possible that Beardsley visited. Antique bookshops there would have stocked books such as *Hokusai Manga*. We also know that he received a collection of Japanese prints (including *shunga*, prints of an erotic nature) as gifts from his friend William Rothenstein. Beardsley was also collecting up such prints on a visit to France. Eventually, he met Leonard Smithers of *The Savoy* magazine. Smithers was also a collector of Japanese prints, and so many materials came to Beardsley via this channel. Around this time, the influence of Japonism came to be felt in London too. One example of this is The Peacock Room (fig.2) created by Whistler. In 1895, when Beardsley travelled to the French coast to recuperate from his tuberculosis, he asked Smithers to dispose of his collection of erotic prints that he kept in London. By the end of the century in London, the taste for all things Japanese was widespread enough that 'The Mikado' (fig. 4), which could fairly be described as 'a Japonist opera', was proving a huge hit, and prints of *Hokusai Manga* and similar could be acquired with relative ease in second-hand bookshops.

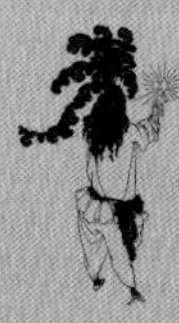

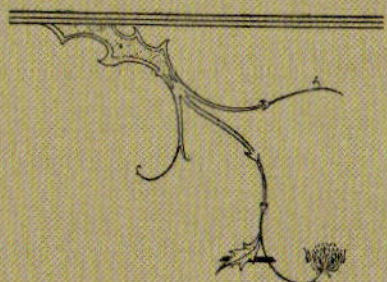
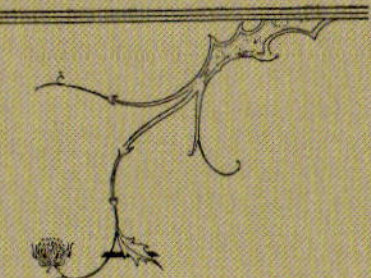

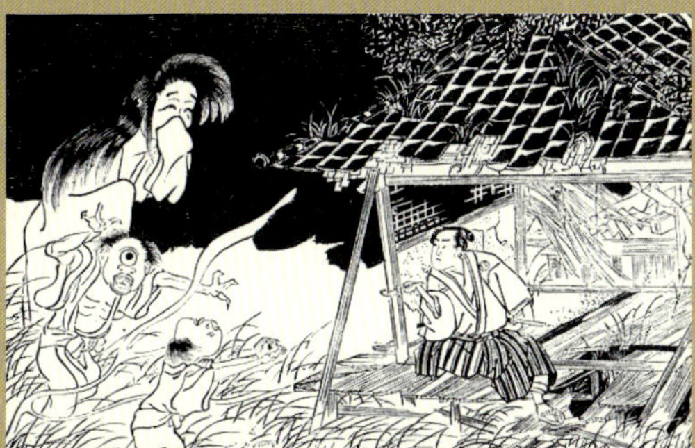

fig.1
Illustration from A. B. Mitford's *Tales of Old Japan*

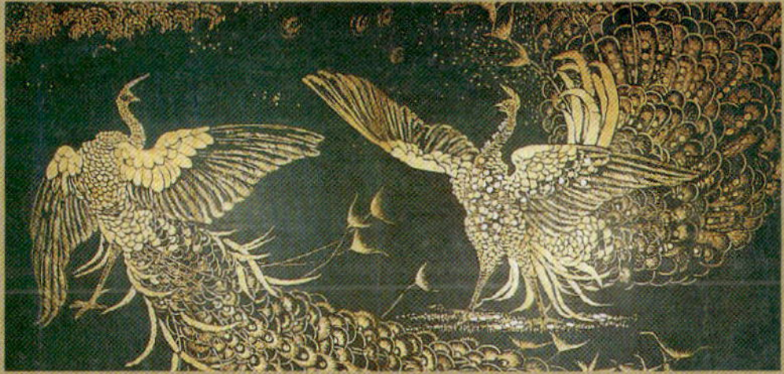

fig.2
Decoration from the wall of Whistler's Peacock Room, 1876-7

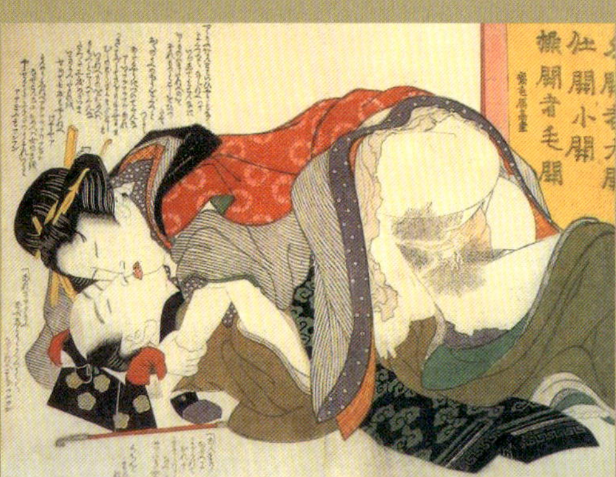

fig.3
Gōtekini onna ['The Luxurious Woman'] by Katsushige Hokusai
from *Tsui no Hinagata* [Patterns of Loving Couples],
19th Century

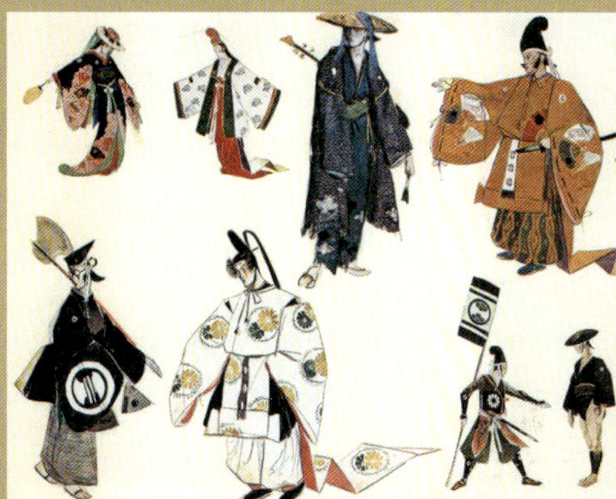

fig.4
Costume design for 'The Mikado' by Charles Ricketts

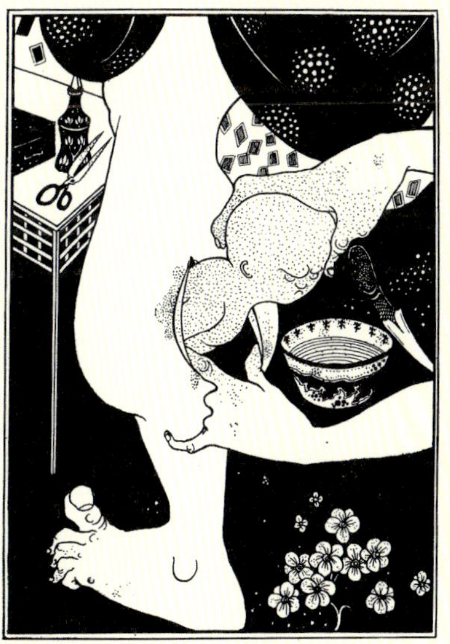

fig.5
'Birth from the Calf of the Leg' by Beardsley. In this work we
sense the strong influence of Japanese prints.

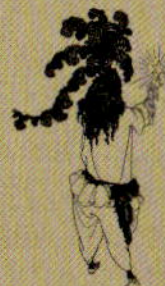

4. 1894: The Year of The Yellow Book

At the start of 1894, *Salome* was finally released. Then in April came the first volume of the quarterly periodical *The Yellow Book*, for which Beardsley was art editor. The year was to prove a very fruitful one for Beardsley.

The groundwork for this success was laid by the art magazine *The Studio*, which had been first published in 1893. The magazine was the brainchild of art journalist C. Lewis Hind, and he was looking for sensational new artists to appear in the first issue when he met Beardsley. Yet after no time Hind was headhunted to become chief editor of *The Pall Mall Magazine*, and Gleeson White took over as editor for *The Studio*. In the end, pictures by Beardsley were used in the debut issues of both, rocketing him to fame as a popular artist.

In *The Studio*, Beardsley was introduced as a young artistic genius. People were searching for a new generation of artists to take over from the Pre-Raphaelites, and *The Studio* became the magazine for this new wave of faces. The fin de siècle period saw a craze for art periodicals, and *The Studio* was very much the forerunner.

Amid this burgeoning demand for magazines, Beardsley decided that he wanted to release his own, where he could feature his own pictures as he wished. He met the young American artist Henry Harland and hit it off with him immediately, and the two decided to start a magazine together. They spoke with John Lane from the Bodley Head, and the matter was settled. The name, *The Yellow Book*, was apparently Beardsley's suggestion. Harland took care of the literary side of the magazine, while Beardsley was in charge of the artistic affairs. Yellow was said to be the colour which symbolised the 1890s. British society was in the process of moving from the grey of the Victorian age to an era of sensational, hedonistic yellow. Yellow was also associated with the French, as there were many French novels with yellow covers. Then, of course, there was Oscar Wilde's love of yellow sunflowers. These implications inherent in the magazine's title outraged decent Victorians, and *The Yellow Book* was deemed an immoral publication in bad taste. It was believed to be excessively French, where France represented hedonism and dissipation.

A pertinent question about *The Yellow Book* was what its relationship with Wilde was. Yellow was Wilde's colour, and the public viewed the new periodical as 'Wilde-like'. However, the editing department believed that having Wilde on board would generate prejudice towards the magazine, and believed he should be kept out. Beardsley, too, was attempting to free himself from the control of his former protector, and thus their ways parted.

Beardsley was over the moon about the prospect of releasing his own art magazine. He approached many artists he esteemed and asked them to produce pictures for it, including

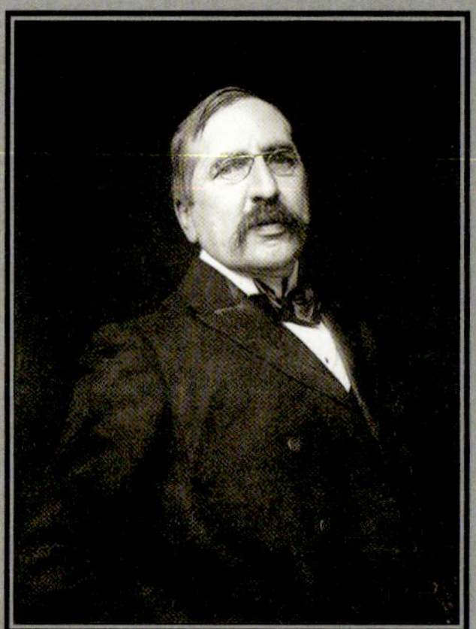

Gleeson White

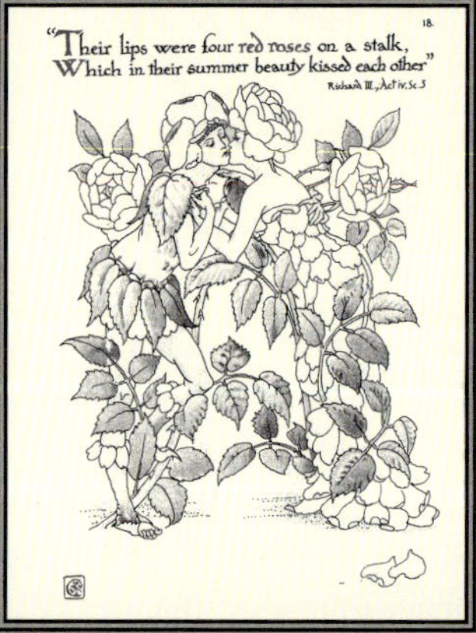

Flowers from Shakespeare's Garden, Walter Crane, 1906

Walter Klein. John Lane, meanwhile, worried about the more risqué elements of Beardsley's art. Since his experience with publishing *Salome*, he was constantly on guard to make sure Beardsley didn't try to sneak something outrageous past him.

In April 1894, the first issue of *The Yellow Book* was released into the world. It was the subject of much discussion even before its release, and once it was out, caused quite a stir in public. *The Times*, known as purveyors of good taste, denounced the new publication. With contributors such as Henry James to its inaugural edition, *The Yellow Book* had attempted to avoid creating an image for itself as a magazine with a particular bias. However, the doyen of academicism Frederic Leighton, who had given his permission for his work to be in the first edition was censured by those around him for appearing in the magazine, and consequently told the editors he didn't want his pictures to be featured any more. Criticism rained down on Beardsley's pictures for being obscene and in bad taste—and yet the first issue enjoyed multiple reprints.

One of the few literary critics who came out in favour of *The Yellow Book* was Edmund Gosse. Gosse liked supporting young artists and giving advice, and indeed, had been one of the first to praise Beardsley's works. As a scholar of seventeenth and eighteenth century literature, Gosse was well aware of the open-minded world of Eros that had existed before the moralism of the Victorian era took the reins. Indeed, it was him who had recommended Beardsley to create the illustrations for Pope's *The Rape of the Lock* and Ben Jonson's *Volpone*. It is thus to Gosse that we owe the existence of the illustrations for Beardsley's late-period masterpiece, *The Rape of the Lock*.

With its third volume published in October 1894, *The Yellow Book* reached a turning point. The issue featured a selection of works on somewhat risqué topics such as John Davidson's 'A Ballad of a Nun', Arthur Symonds' poem 'Credo', and Ernest Dowson's 'Apple Blossom in Brittany'. Beardsley himself contributed the pictures 'Self Portrait' and 'The Wagnerites'. The fourth volume was published in January 1895, as Beardsley was planning a lecture tour in America. Just as with Oscar Wilde before him, there was a lot of interest shown from across the pond to this figure who was the talk of the town in the UK. Such was the height that Beardsley's fame had reached. John Lane was planning to set up a branch of his publishing house in America, so the plan was that he would also go. However, in the end it didn't seem as if Beardsley's health could withstand a trip to America, and his lecture tour plans were abandoned, with Lane setting off alone. Beardsley was entrusted with producing the fifth issue of *The Yellow Book*, writing the story of Venus and Tannhauser, and creating illustrations to accompany it.

If only Beardsley had gone to America after all, people sometimes comment—or if Lane had remained in London. But as it was, Beardsley remained in London alone, and a fateful event befell *The Yellow Book*.

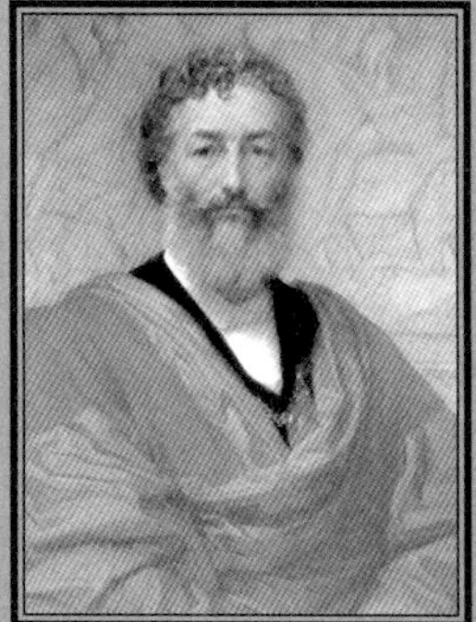

Self Portrait, Frederick Leighton, 1880

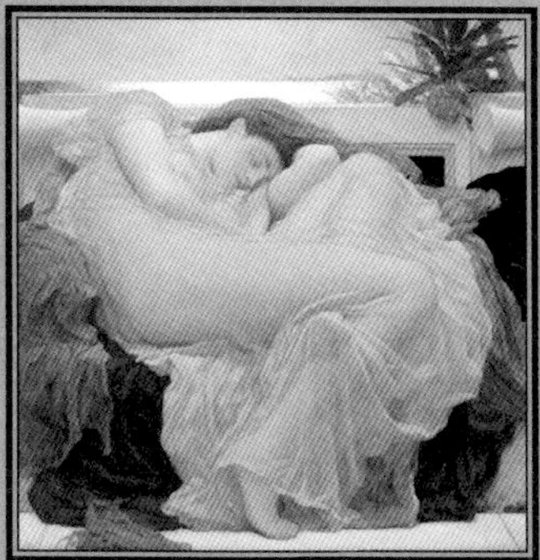

Flaming June, Frederic Leighton, 1895

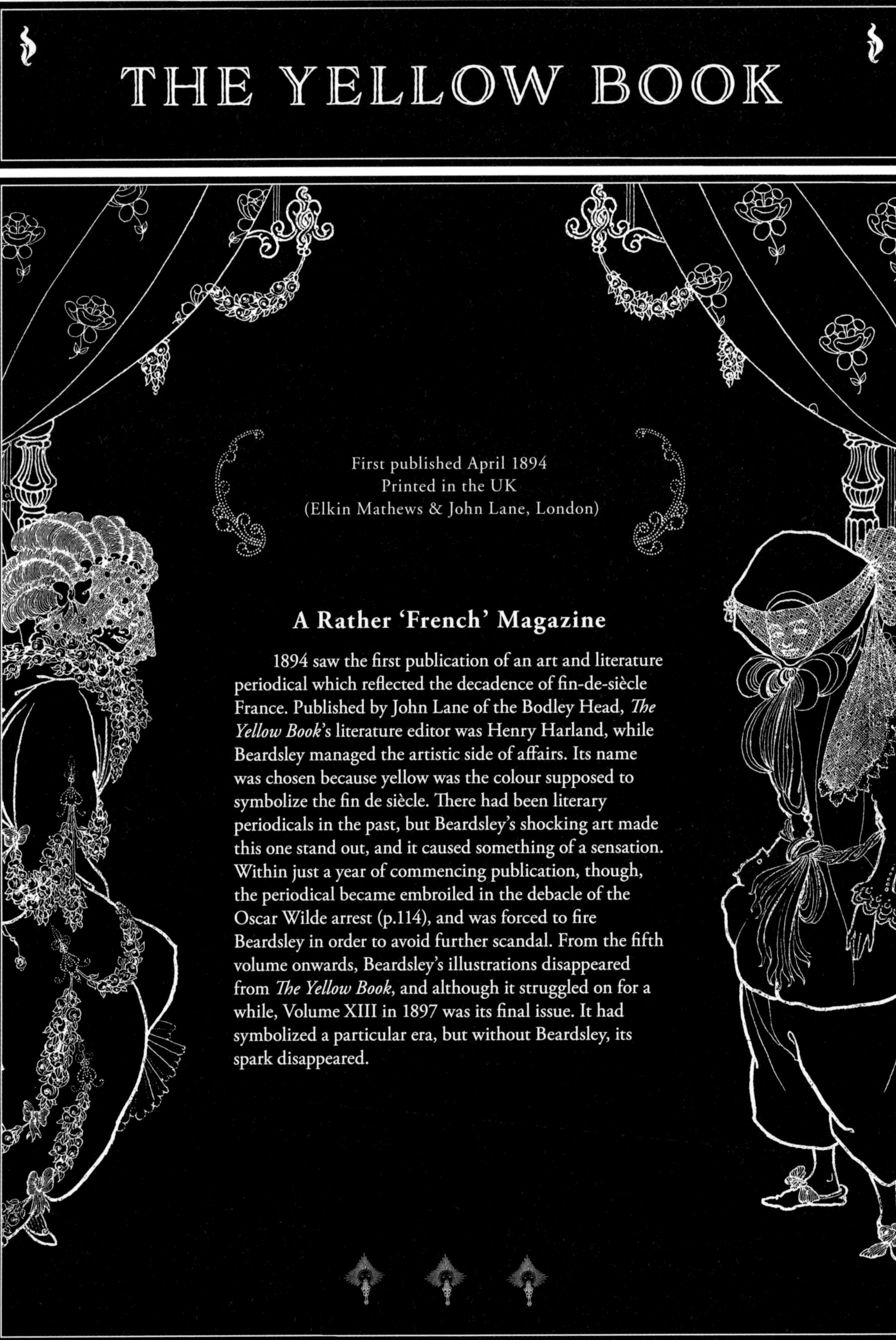

THE YELLOW BOOK

First published April 1894
Printed in the UK
(Elkin Mathews & John Lane, London)

A Rather 'French' Magazine

1894 saw the first publication of an art and literature periodical which reflected the decadence of fin-de-siècle France. Published by John Lane of the Bodley Head, *The Yellow Book*'s literature editor was Henry Harland, while Beardsley managed the artistic side of affairs. Its name was chosen because yellow was the colour supposed to symbolize the fin de siècle. There had been literary periodicals in the past, but Beardsley's shocking art made this one stand out, and it caused something of a sensation. Within just a year of commencing publication, though, the periodical became embroiled in the debacle of the Oscar Wilde arrest (p.114), and was forced to fire Beardsley in order to avoid further scandal. From the fifth volume onwards, Beardsley's illustrations disappeared from *The Yellow Book*, and although it struggled on for a while, Volume XIII in 1897 was its final issue. It had symbolized a particular era, but without Beardsley, its spark disappeared.

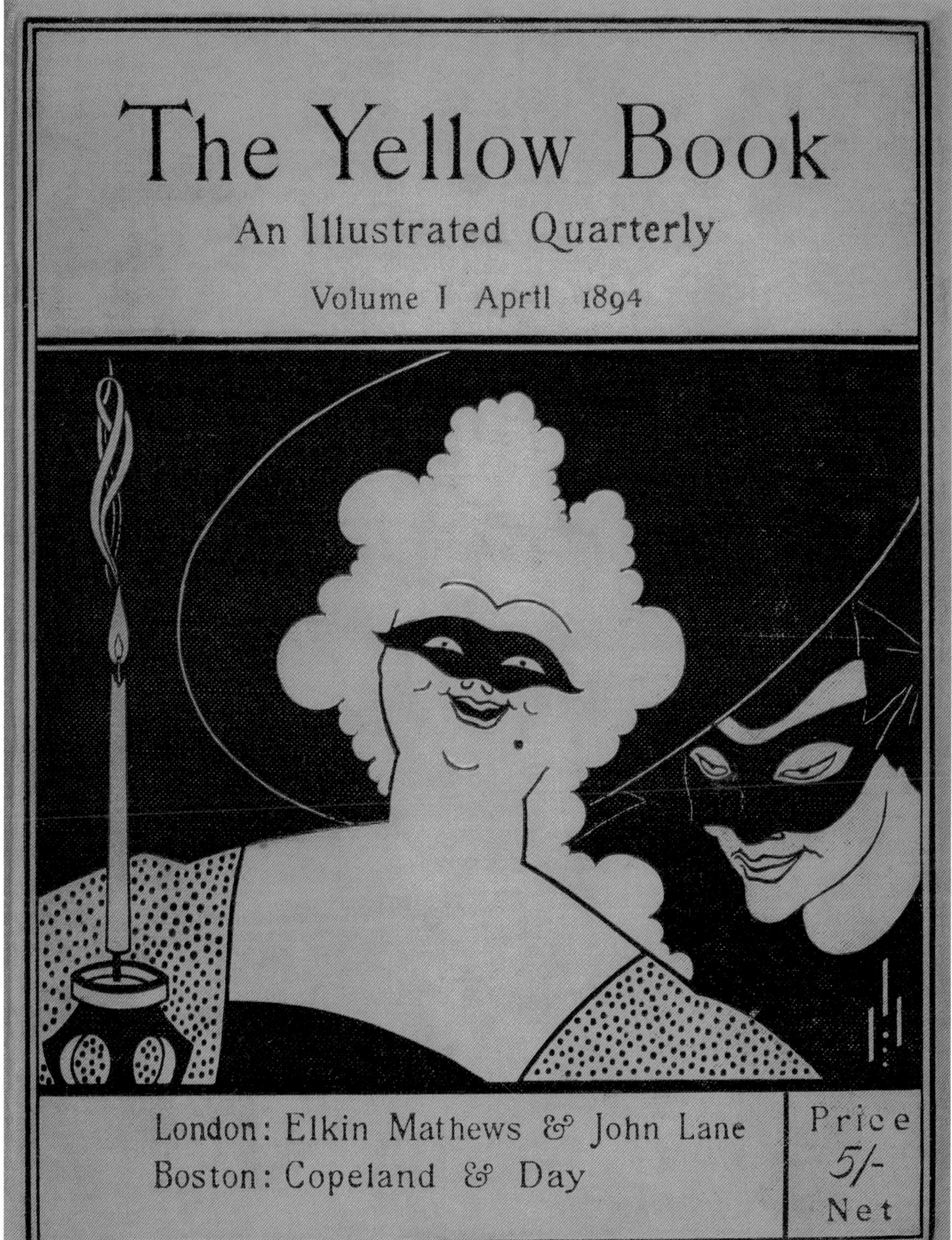

Cover to Volume I

This cover was deemed crass. A woman laughs heartily, while a suspicious-looking man in the background murmurs something to her. The scene has a seedy feel to it. This is the only of Beardsley's illustrations for *The Yellow Book* to feature such riotous laughter. Some critics have seen this as a representation of the Paris nightlife he had sampled on his visit the previous year. It should be remarked, though, that the composition with its contrast between dark and light is fantastic. The crisp lines have a remarkably exhilarating quality to them, such as the white line delineating the woman's hat, and the contour lines marking out her face and body. The phallic candle beside her and Beardsley's signature mark in the bottom right-hand corner echo one another.

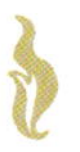

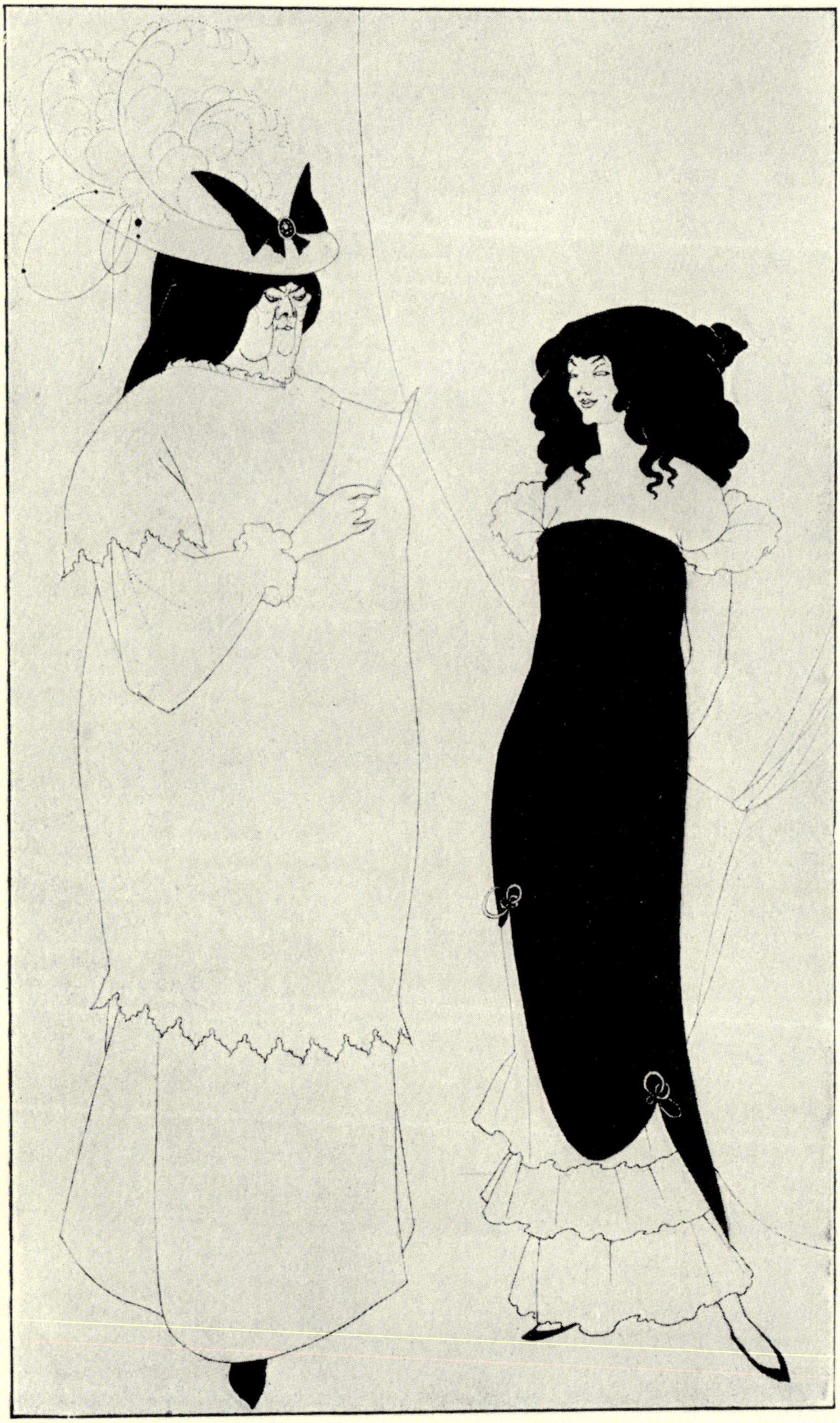

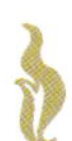

From Volume I: 'L'Education Sentimentale'

This is an illustration for Gustave Flaubert's novel of the same title. We see an older woman 'educating' a younger one. The difference between the two generations is vividly represented in the contrast between their black and white dresses. Here again, the sumptuousness of Beardsley's lines is worthy of marvel. There is something mesmerizing about the elegant lines forming the decorations on the older woman's hat, while the younger woman's attire seems stylish and new even now. Beardsley's skill as a fashion illustrator should also be acknowledged. Also noteworthy is the defiant stance of the two women, which seems likely to have been inspired by his study of Japanese prints.

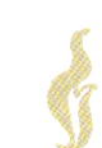

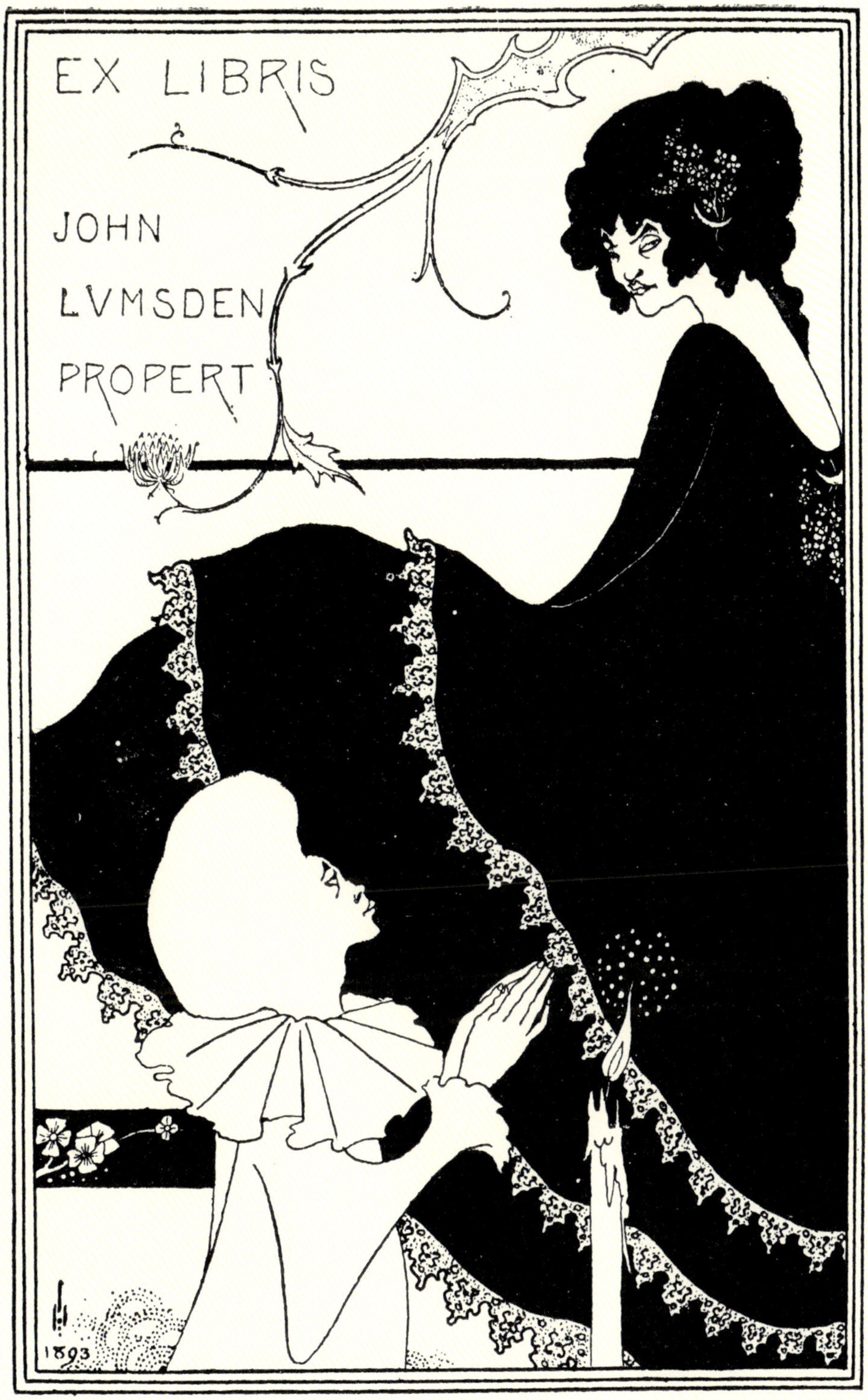

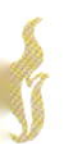

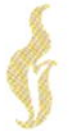

From Volume I: 'Ex Libris John Lumsden Propert'

This diagonally arranged composition is a frequent occurrence in Beardsley's works. The result is an off-balance, dynamic space. Here the woman and the pierrot—the black and the white segments, respectively—are arranged on a diagonal line. It is the detailed ornamentation in this picture that really sets it apart. With the branch tracing arabesque curves beside the woman's head, the floral pattern in her hair and at the back of her dress, the lace on the hem of her dress, the floral pattern to the left of the pierrot, and the pointillist wave pattern in the bottom left-hand corner, this is one of Beardsley's works where an Art Nouveau sensibility finds its fullest display.

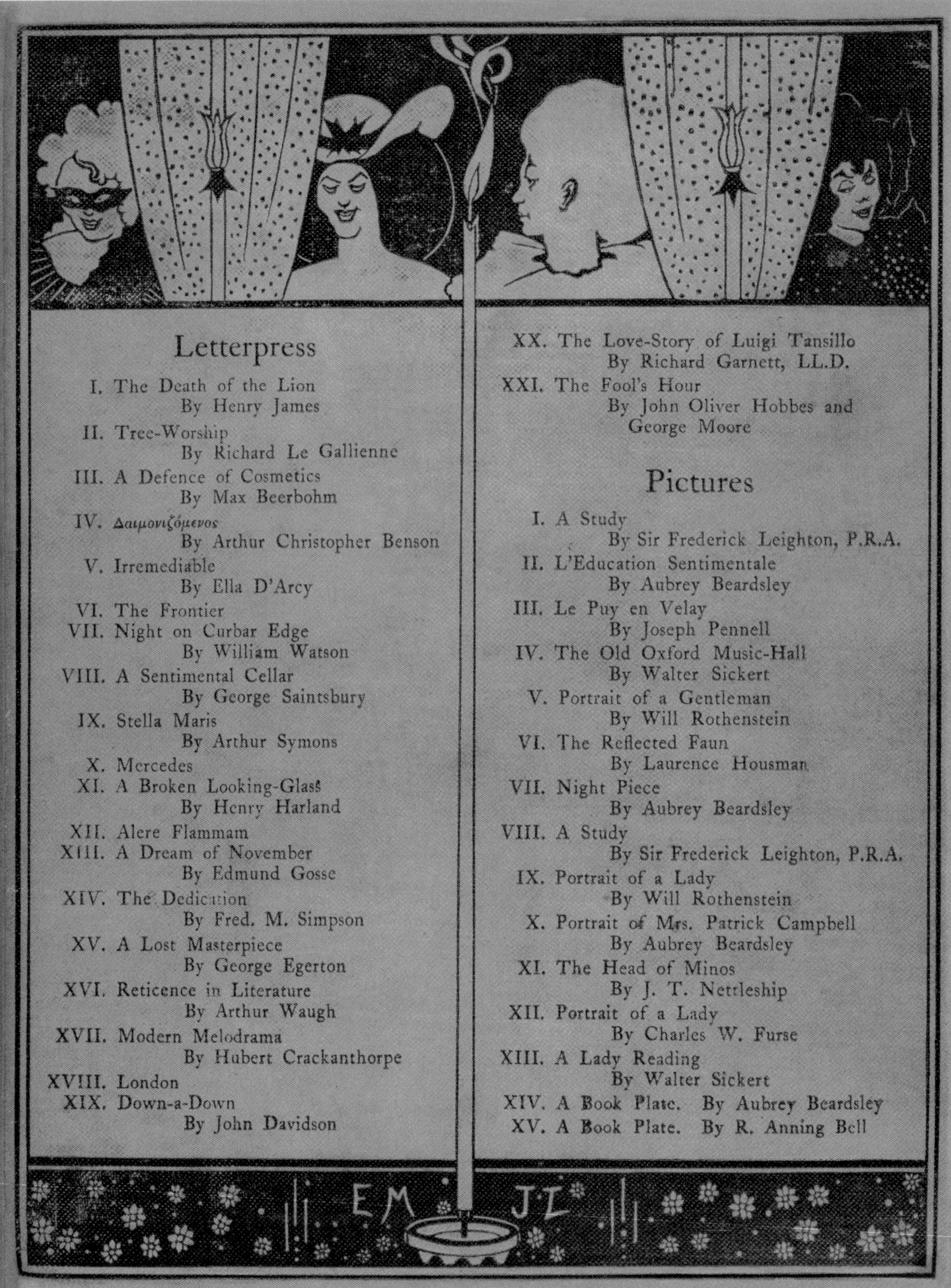

Back Cover to Volume I

This same design was used up until Volume V. Four rather quirky looking women are arranged in a row. Judging from the candle and the curtains, they are probably in some kind of theatre. Underneath is a list of the issue's contents. First on the list here is the esteemed author Henry James. Max Beerbohm's essay, 'A Defence of Cosmetics', caused something of a stir. Under the list of 'Pictures', the famous artist Sir Frederic Leighton's name is listed first, followed by Beardsley's 'L'Education Sentimentale'. By inviting the doyens of the literary and artistic worlds to contribute, *The Yellow Book* was attempting to establish itself as a respectable periodical, but there was no concealing Beardsley's true leanings.

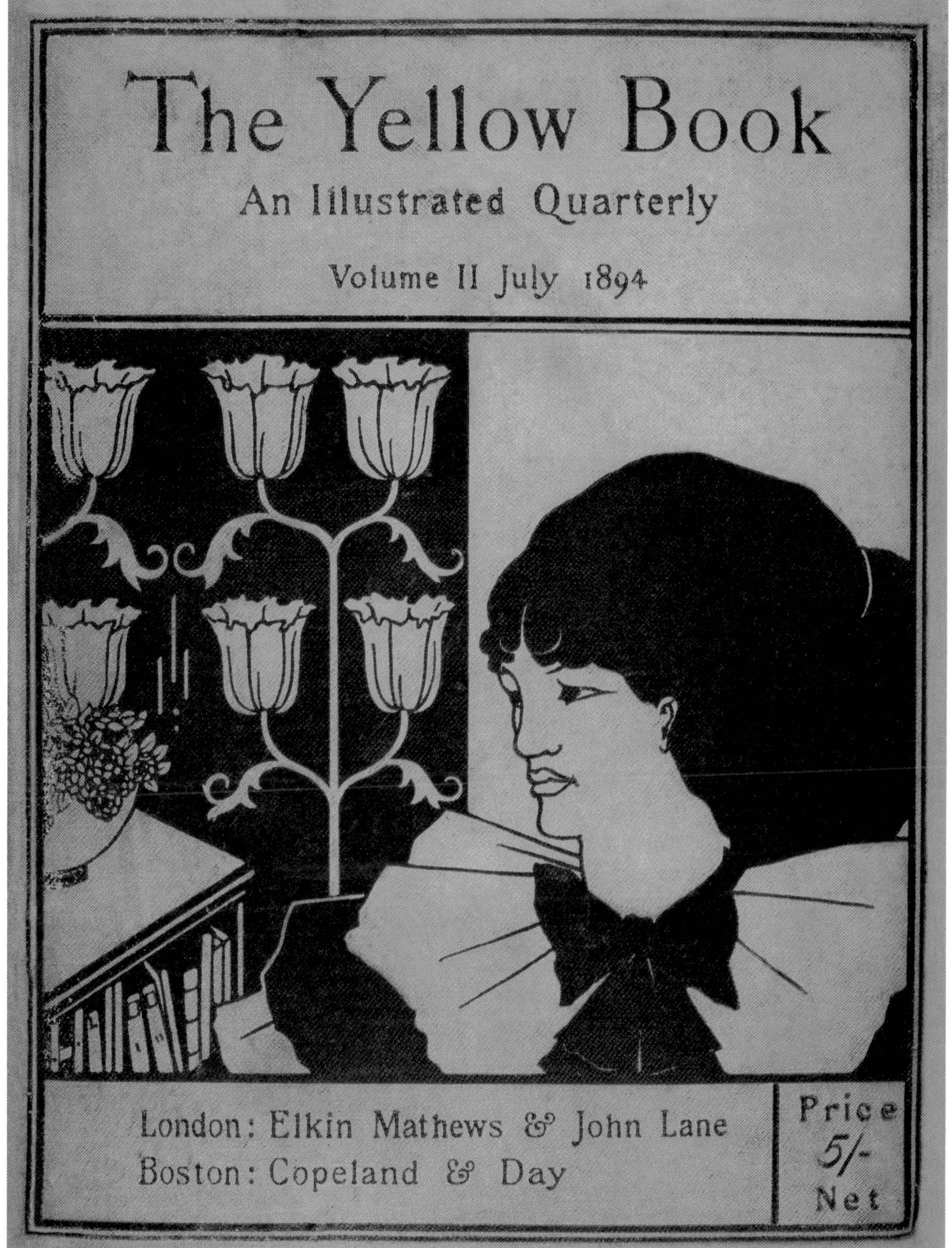

Cover to Volume II

A strong-looking woman with a well-defined nose and lips and voluminous hair poses a challenge to the Victorian era's ideal woman, who looked as though she might faint at any moment. This illustration angered British society at the time. The background features a stark division between black and white zones, with the woman occupying the white. In the black section on the left is a pattern of tulip-shaped flowers, along with Beardsley's signature mark. In the lower left is a book shelf, and a vase with flowers on top. The design nods to the Art Nouveau style, and also seems to look ahead to cubism.

The Yellow Book

An Illustrated Quarterly

Volume II   July, 1894

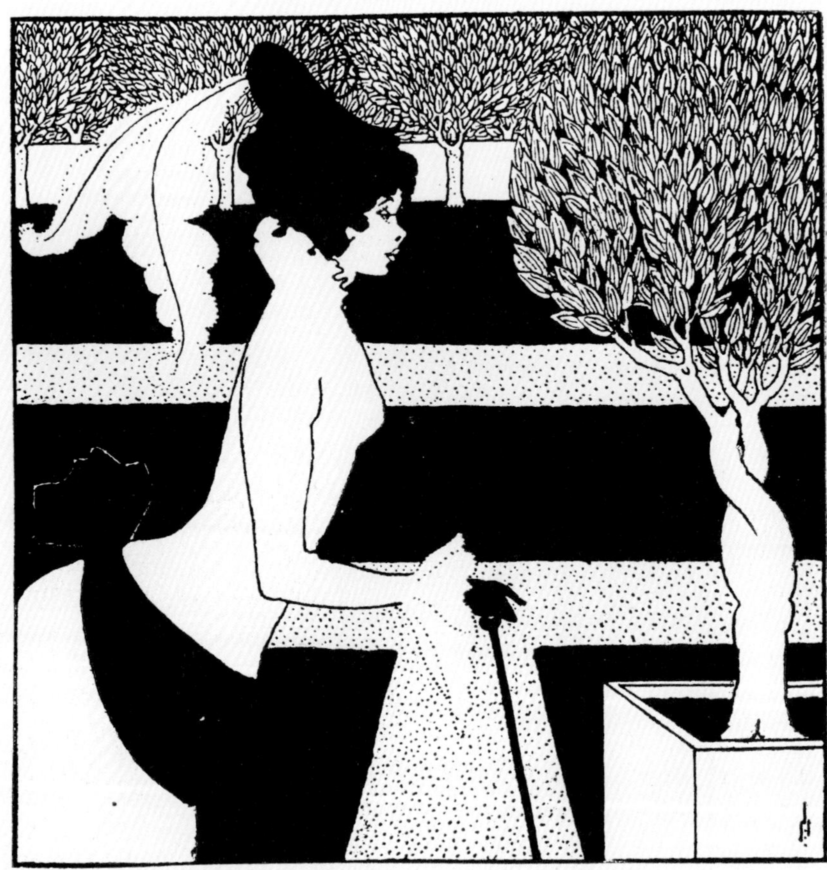

London : Elkin Mathews & John Lane
Boston : Copeland & Day
Agents for the Colonies : Robt. A. Thompson & Co.

Title Page to Volume II

The picture shows a lady strolling through a park, but the stark contrast between dark and light gives it the vibrancy of a Mondrian abstract. We have the vertical stripes and T-junctions created between the black lines of the grass and the gravelled path, and the outline of the woman falling diagonally over them. The longer one looks at the geometrical composition, the more one finds to fascinate within it. The curved lines scattered about the picture, as in the feathers trailing from the woman's hair and the twisted trunk of the tree on the right, accentuate the mysterious ambience of the picture. Beardsley is playing around with overlaying the simple fascination of shapes themselves with their various significances.

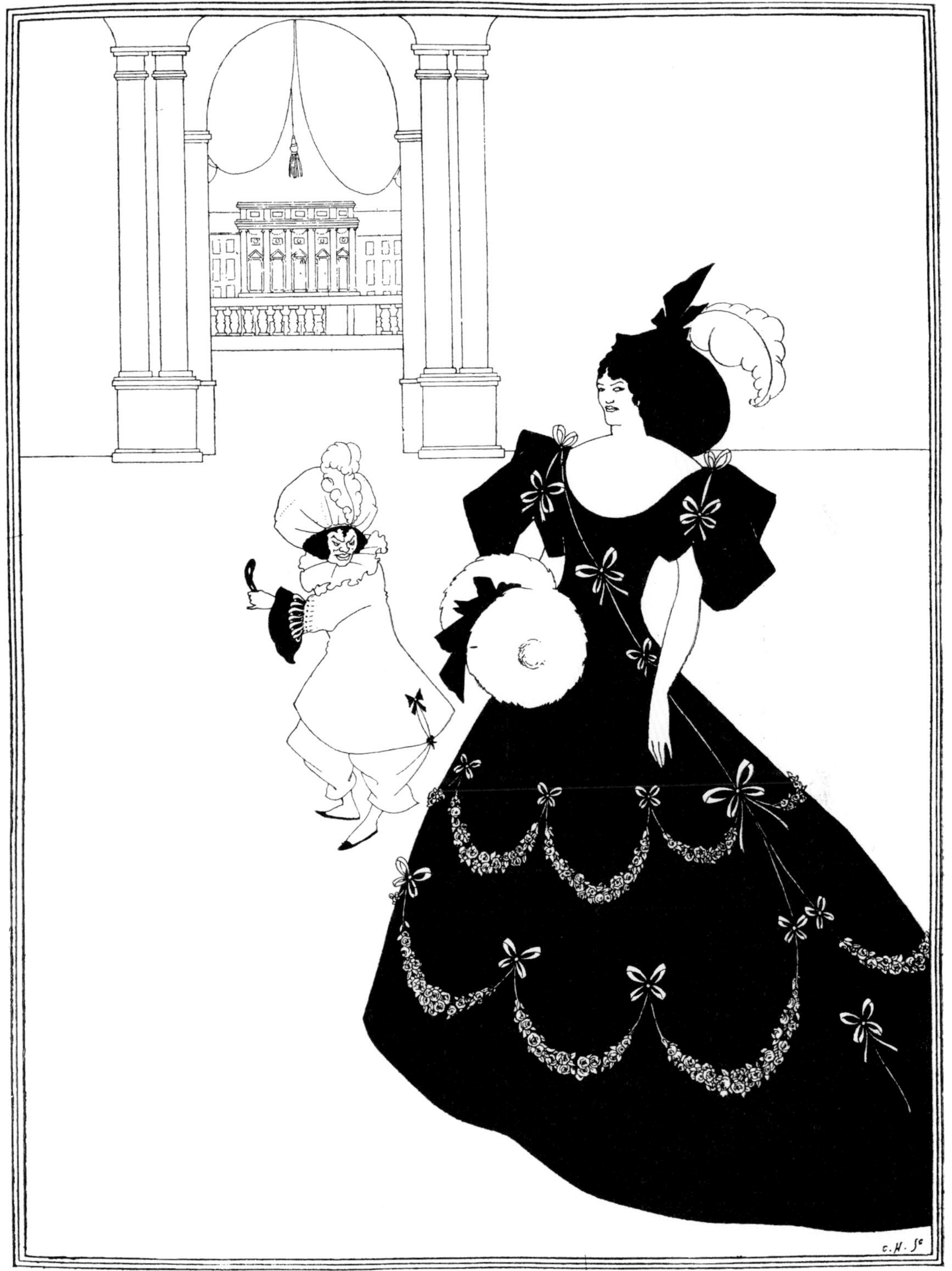

From Volume II: 'The Comedy Ballet of Marionettes I'

One in a series of three illustrations depicting a 'comedy ballet' staged by an impossible marionette troupe. The stage here is that of Beardsley's imagination. The dwarf clown is soliciting the woman to join a black mass taking place beyond the open doorway. The curtain hanging down at the entrance has a decidedly erotic shape. There are several versions of this picture, including a coloured one entitled *Caprice*.

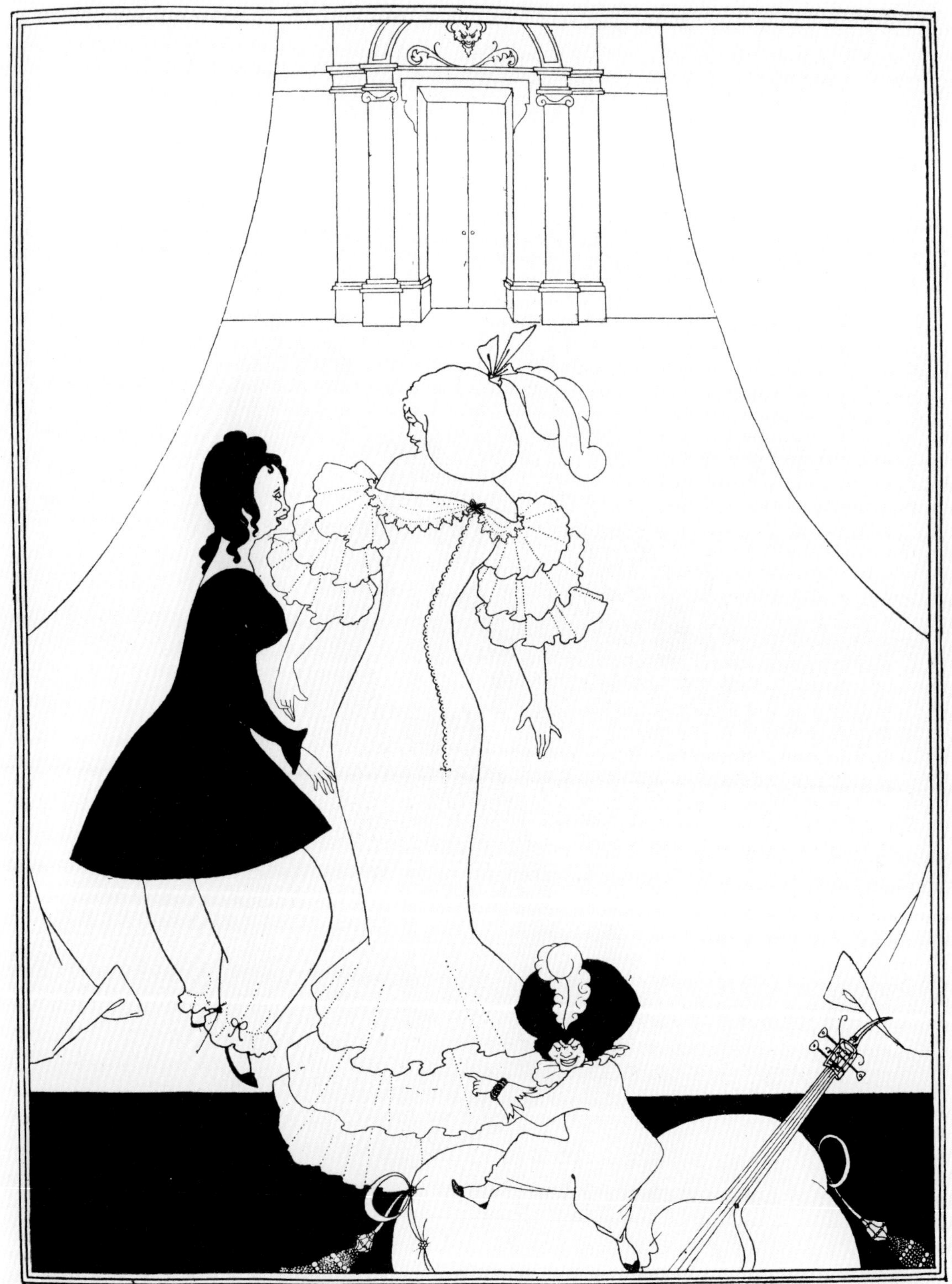

From Volume II: 'The Comedy Ballet of Marionettes I'

The second illustration in the series shows the woman from the first illustration being ushered inside the doorway. Her Rococo-style gown has morphed into a slimline dress, as was in fashion at the end of the nineteenth century. To her left is a woman in pantaloons and a black jacket. She has no chin—which, back in the nineteenth century, was visual code for a lesbian. Seeing the lesbian trying to tempt the woman, the dwarf is cackling in delight. The cane that the dwarf is straddling and even the outline of the woman's figure are highly phallic.

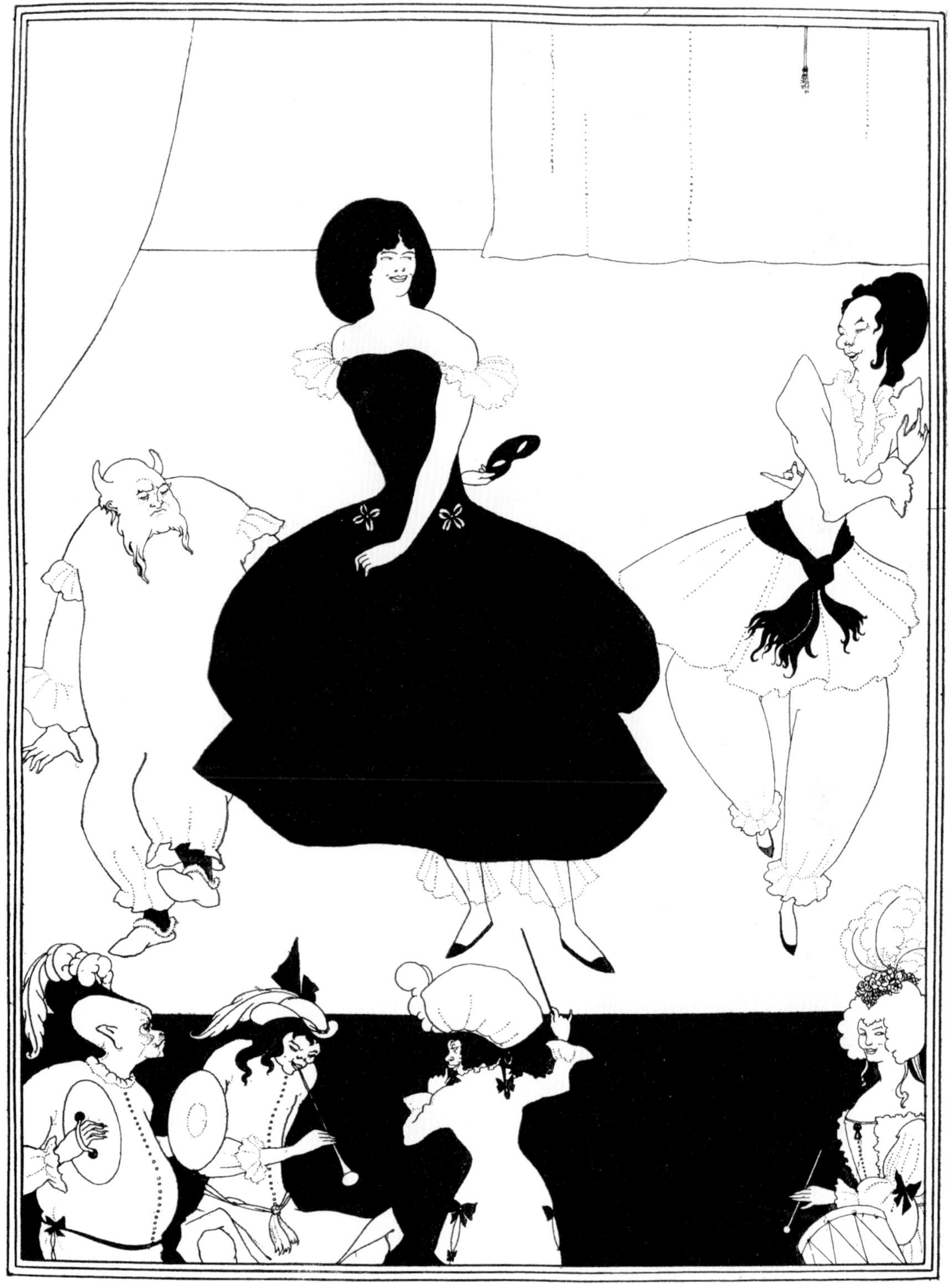

From Volume II: 'The Comedy Ballet of Marionettes III'

In the third and final picture in the series, the woman has assumed the attire of a short-skirted ballet dancer, and is frolicking with the lesbian. The hand holding her eye mask is thrust behind her back in a secret signal, to which the lesbian is answering with a pointed index finger behind her back. The entire scene is highly suggestive. On the left is the clown, now wearing the mask of a ram. In the orchestra box below the stage, a curious band are playing. Beardsley is afforded us the secret pleasure of peering in on this indecent play acted out on a plain white stage.

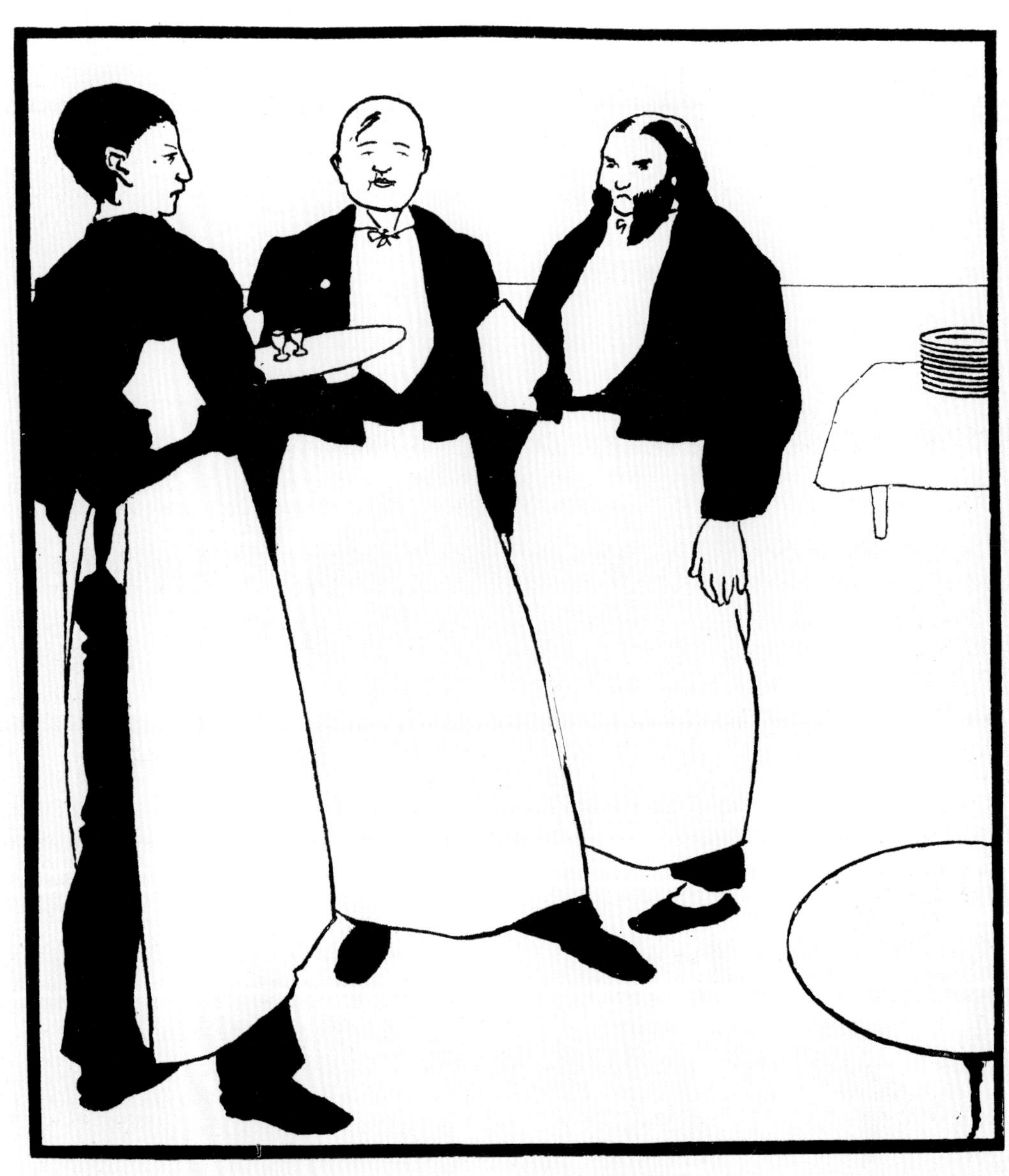

From Volume II: 'Garcons de Cafe'

    This picture depicts the garçons at Café Royal where the London literati gathered, and where Beardsley would sometimes go to meet Oscar Wilde. Unusually for Beardsley, the picture is a casual look into city life, which appears to have been influenced by the French printmaker Félix Vallotton. Vallotton is one of my favourite artists, and along with Pierre Bonnard and Edouard Vuillard, one of those painters referred to as intimists—those interested in the portrayal of quiet domestic scenes. His crisp, monochrome spaces must have piqued Beardsley's interest.

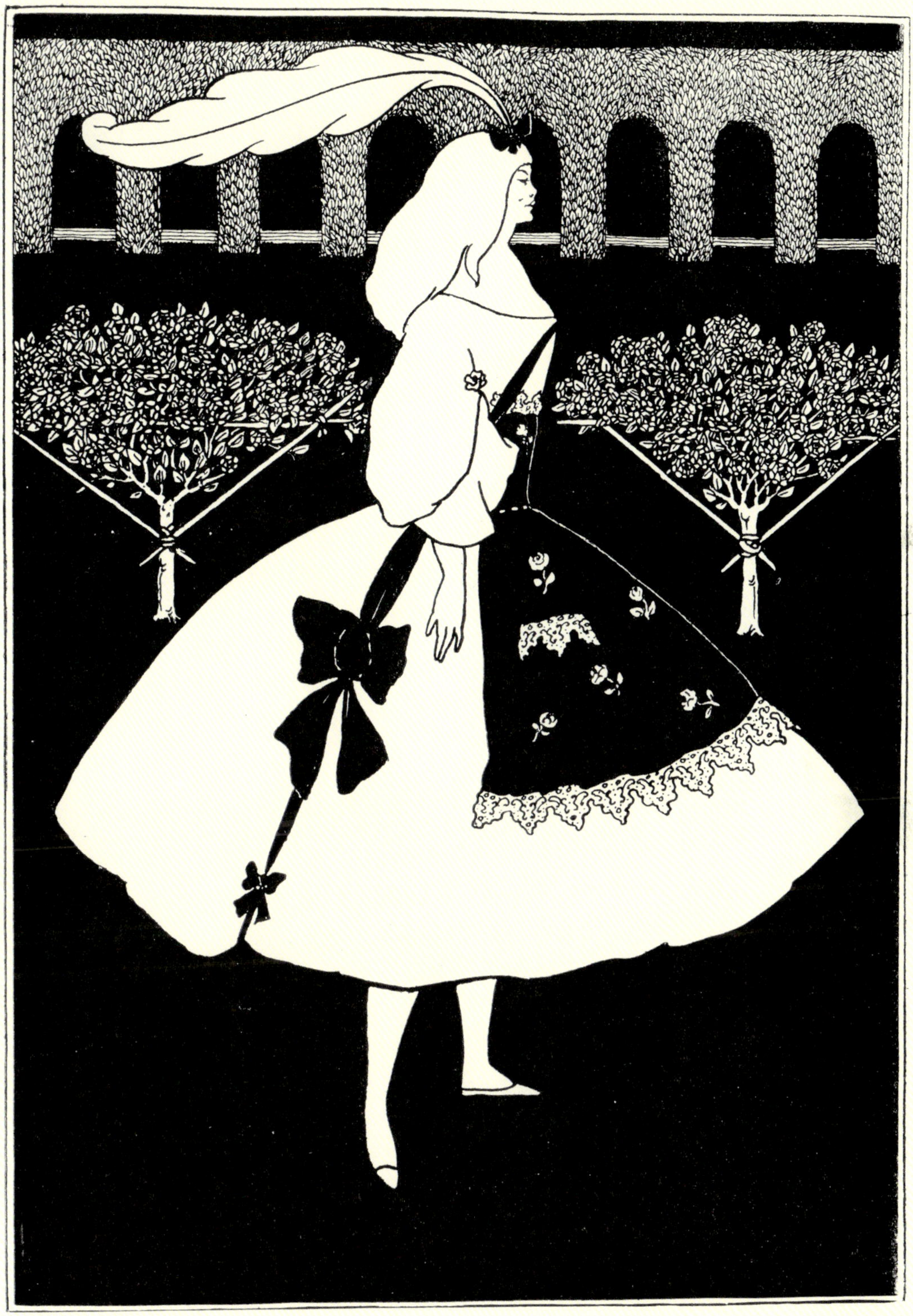

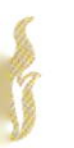

From Volume II: 'The Slippers of Cinderella'

The woman has been named Cinderella, but this illustration has little to do with the fairy tale. Rather, Beardsley has chosen to portray a young woman in profile, enjoying the diversion that the geometric composition supplies. The white shape of her body floats against a black background. The upside-down triangle shapes of the trees' canopies are contrasted with the triangle of the girls' skirt. The row of leaf-covered arches at the top form a high frame for the picture. The feather appearing from her head like a plume of smoke, the ribbon cutting her skirt into a diagonal, and the apron with its triangular trim and flower pattern—in the picture's details, Beardsley experiments with pattern.

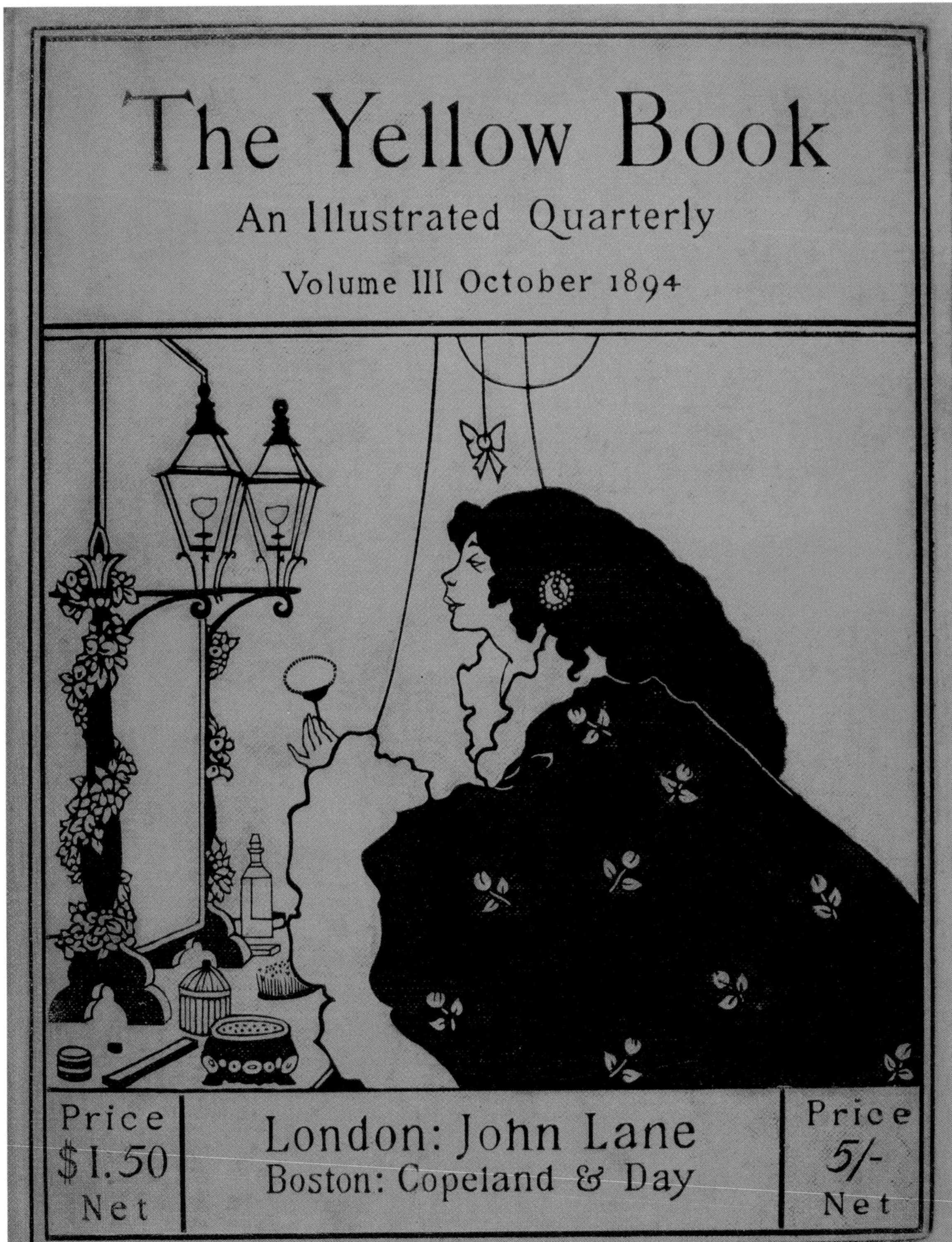

Cover to Volume III

Women at their toilette was a frequent motif for Beardsley. The black sections of the woman's hair and gown occupy most of the space to the right half of the picture. The collar and sleeves with their extravagant lace frills connote femininity, while the mirror to the left is decorated with garlands of flowers. The straight verticals and horizontals of its black frame and the candleholders capture the viewer's attention. The abstract, simple lines above the woman's head that apparently indicate the curtains are unmistakeably Beardsley. Note too the bizarre shape of the frill at the woman's collar which seems to be squirming as if it were alive.

The Yellow Book

An Illustrated Quarterly

Volume III   October, 1894

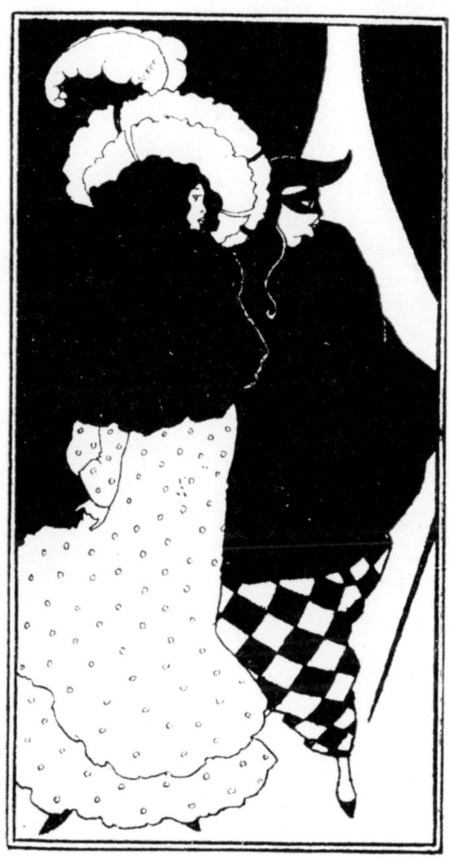

London : John Lane, The Bodley Head, Vigo Street
Boston : Copeland & Day
Agents for the Colonies : Robt. A. Thompson & Co.

Title Page to Volume III

At the end of the nineteenth century, harlequins, pierrots and other imagery from Italy's commedia dell'arte were all the rage. Everywhere one turned, one saw images of clowns in masks wearing checked pantaloons. Perhaps the dull, moralistic age had continued for so long that by the end of the century people wanted to let their hair down and have a bit of harmless fun. Beardsley, too, was attracted to images of pierrots. Doubtless they brought memories of the plays and circuses he saw at Brighton seaside as a boy flooding back to him.

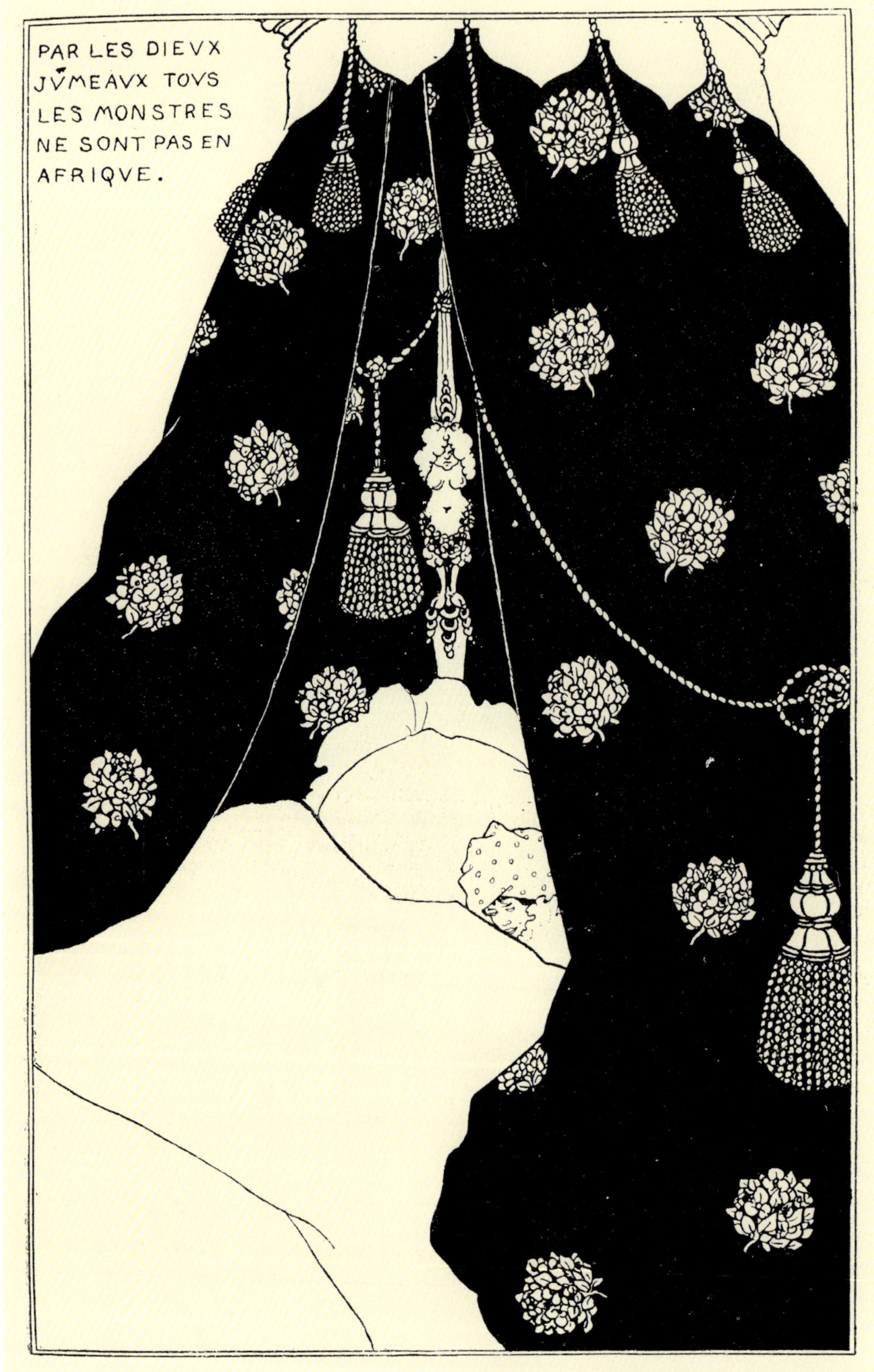

From Volume III: 'Self-Portrait'

On a bed swathed in gigantic curtains, apparently from the seventeenth century, the artist lies curled up wearing a nightcap. The curtains closely resemble the shape of women's ballooning skirts that Beardsley draws. Which is to say, Beardsley is portraying himself as a child hidden in a woman's skirts, i.e. the maternal womb. This much is made clear by the primordial mother goddess icon peeping out from between the curtains. The artist, the picture seems to say, is afraid to emerge from the womb. At the top left are written the words 'Pour les Dieux jumeaux tous les monstres ne sont pas en Afrique' ('For the twin gods, not all the monsters are in Africa'). Beardsley is proclaiming himself a monster, and the 'twin gods' references him and his sister Mabel.

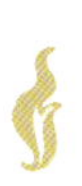

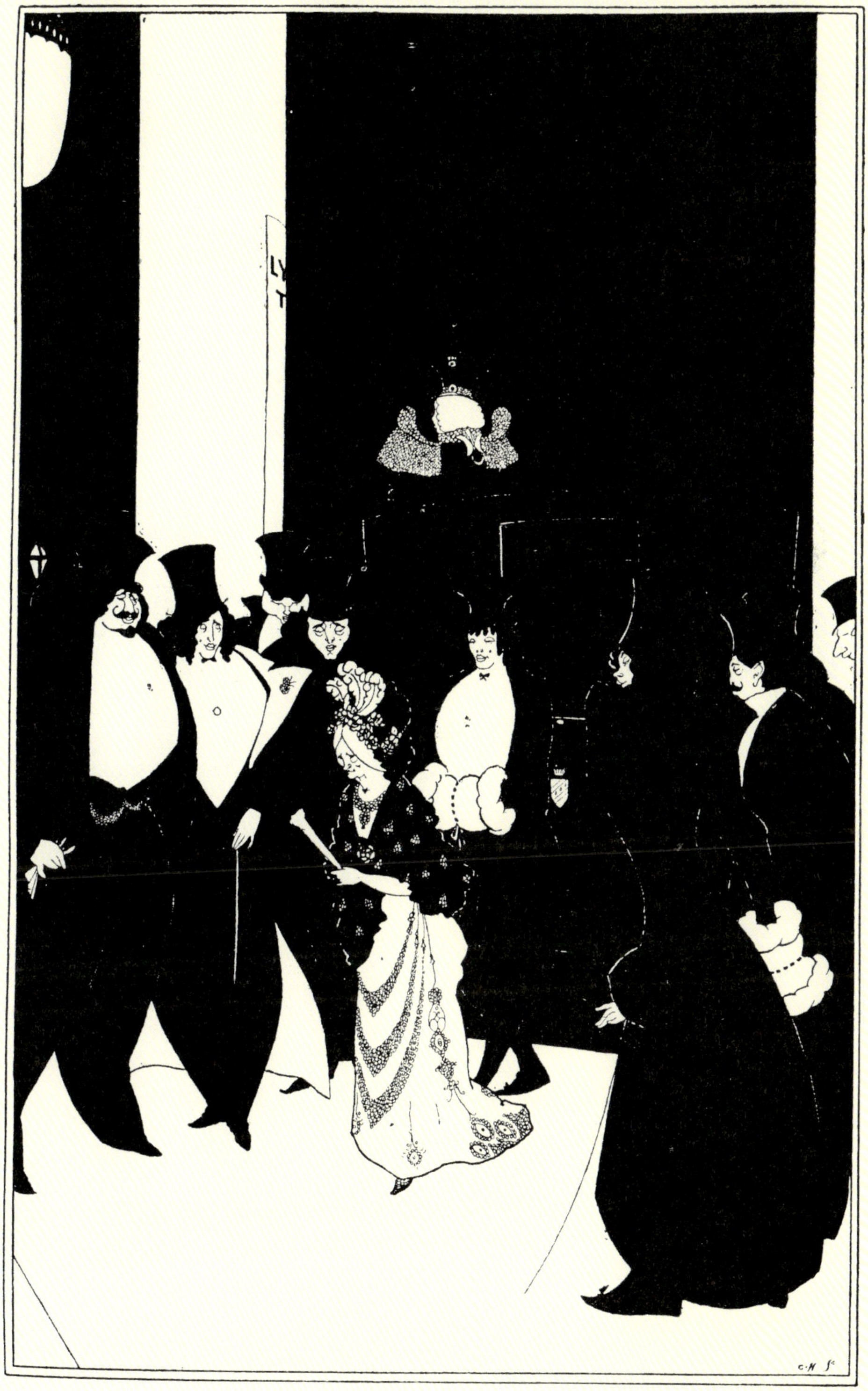

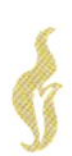

From Volume III: 'Lady Gold's Escort'

Given that the vast majority of Beardsley's oeuvre is monochrome, it seems possible to divide it into those pictures based in black and those based in white. This is one of the former pictures, originating from a period when Beardsley was particularly interested in nighttime scenes. In showing the figure of an old woman hideously dolled in formal attire and a silk hat receiving such an obsequious welcome, Beardsley provides a vivid depiction of the ostentation and decadent farcery of the social world. As Marcel Proust had done, Beardsley fiercely satirized society's ludicrous rituals while also being deeply entranced by them.

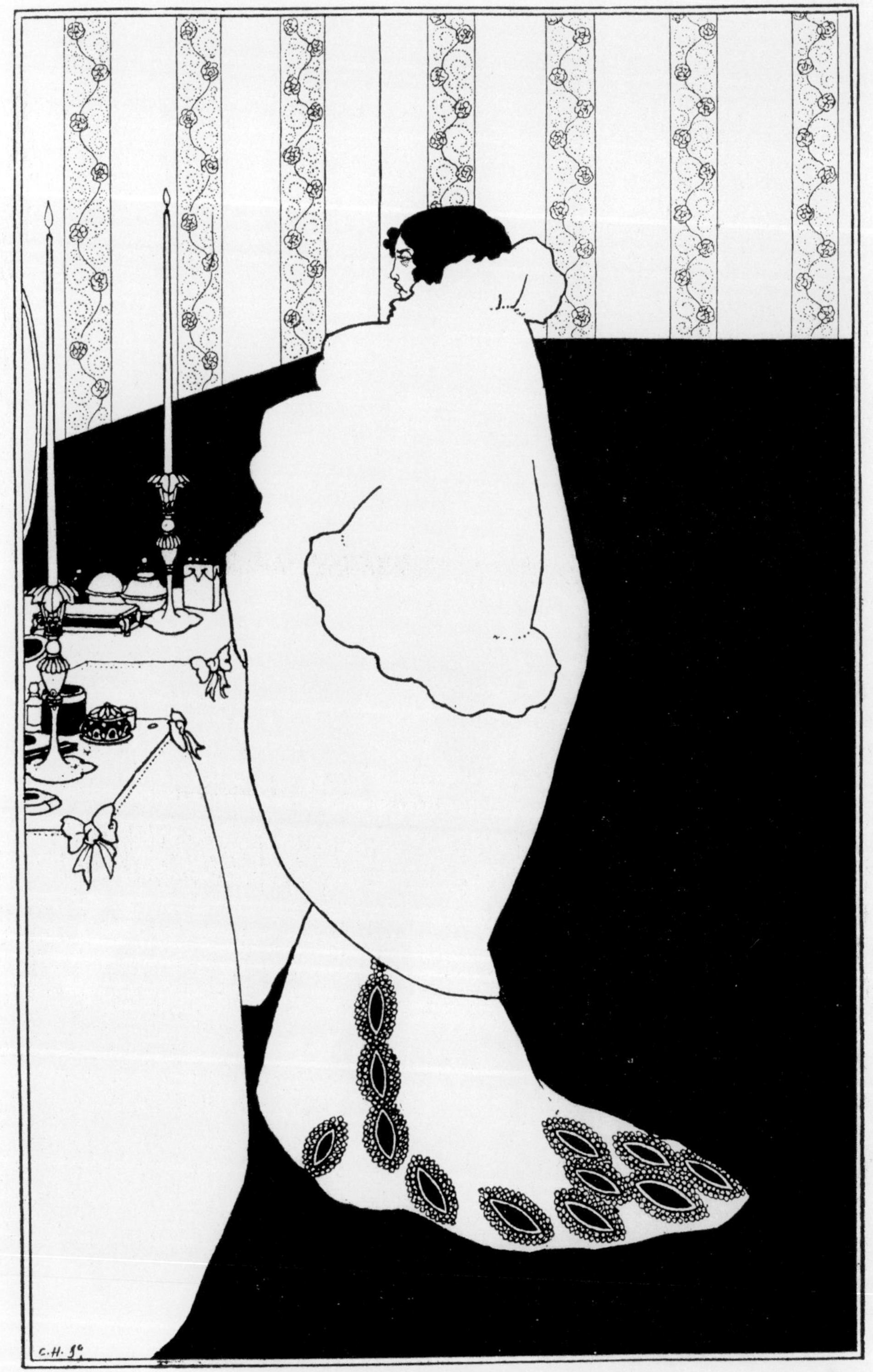

From Volume III: 'La Dame aux Camelias'

This picture was first featured in the April 1894 issue of *Saint Paul* magazine under the title 'Girl at her Toilet', before being featured again in Volume III of *The Yellow Book* in October, as an illustration for Dumas' novel, *The Lady of the Camellias*. The contours of the billowing white gown are splendidly rendered. In 1897, Beardsley created a coloured version of this picture. The expanse of black on the floor is particularly noticeable, while the shapes on the hem of the skirt which resemble both eyes and shells providing eye-catching detail. The camellia flowers buried in the stripes on the wallpaper hint at the themes of the novel.

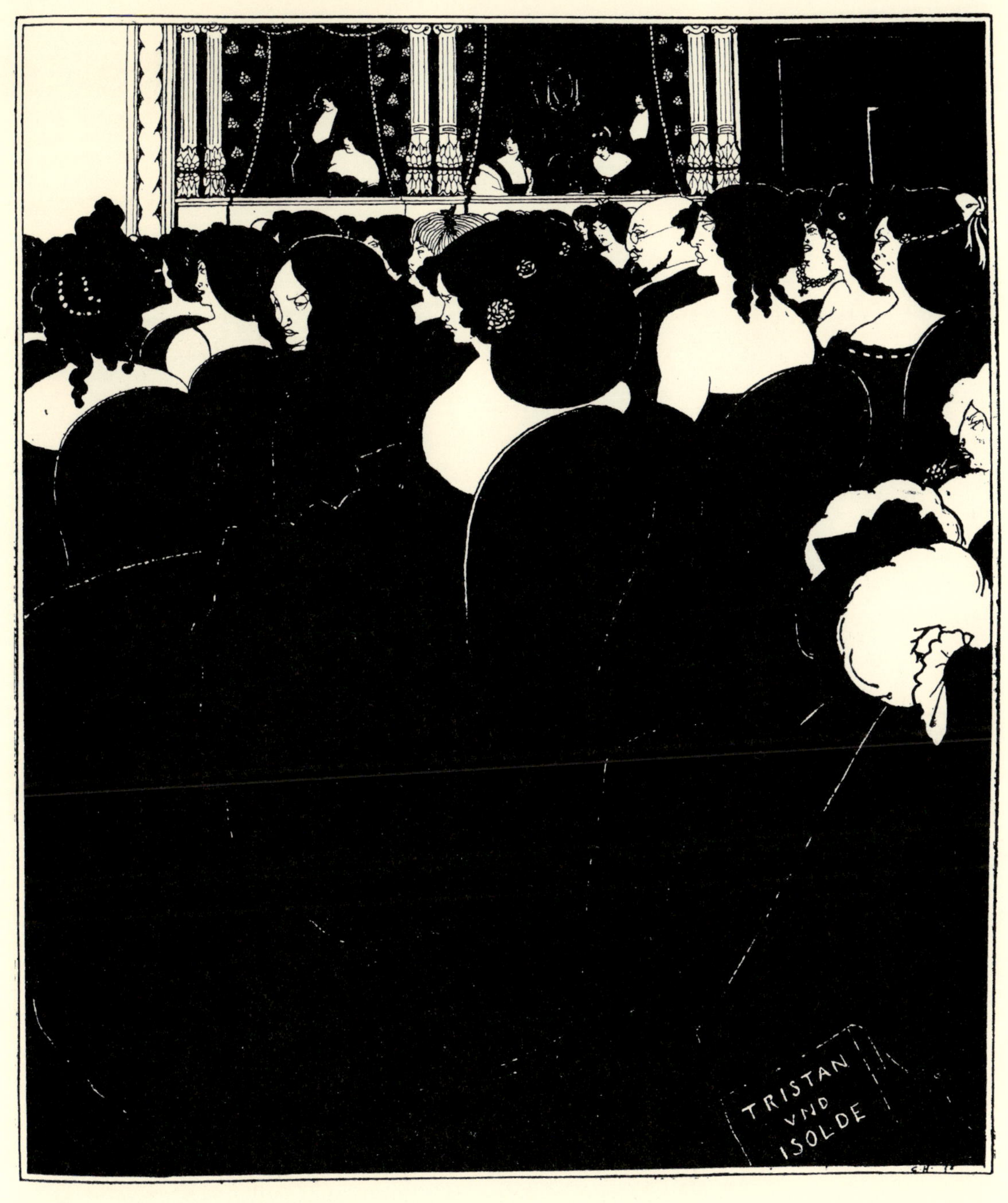

From Volume III: 'The Wagnerites'

This picture is Beardsley's black masterpiece. After the first performance of Wagner's *Götterdämmerung* (the Fourth Part of the Ring Cycle) at London's Her Majesty's Theatre in 1882, the late nineteenth century became the age of Wagner. The number of London Wagner fans steadily increased, and Beardsley counted himself as one of them. In the bottom right of the picture we can see a programme for *Tristan und Isolde*, Beardsley's personal favourite. In this picture, the ground floor seats are occupied almost entirely by women. The only man we can see, to the right of the woman in the centre, appears to be Jewish. Beardsley's depiction of the performance of this opera about pure love swarming with high-class prostitutes was somewhat ironic in tone.

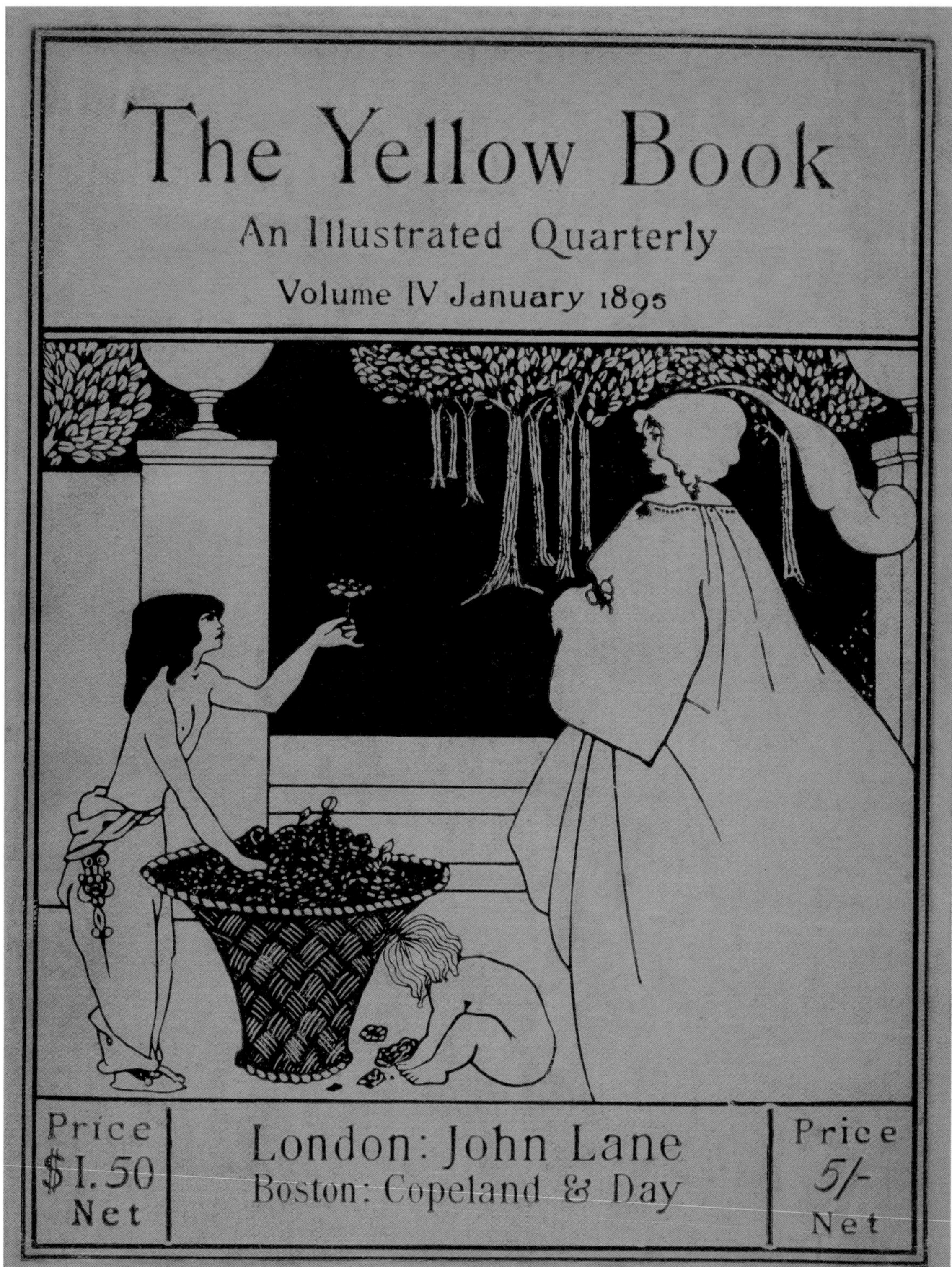

Cover to Volume IV

To the right of the picture is a woman trailing from her head a feather, depicted like a plume of smoke. On the left a young boy with a bare torso is offering a woman a flower from his basket. Besides the basket a naked baby plays around on the floor. In the background is a garden. The depiction of the boy has something of an ancient Grecian flavour to it. Unusually for Beardsley, the scene is a tranquil, idyllic one. The woman seems like she may be about to pass through the doors to paradise. Perhaps the young boy is inviting her through. In fact the scene seems so peaceful that we can't help feel a little concerned…

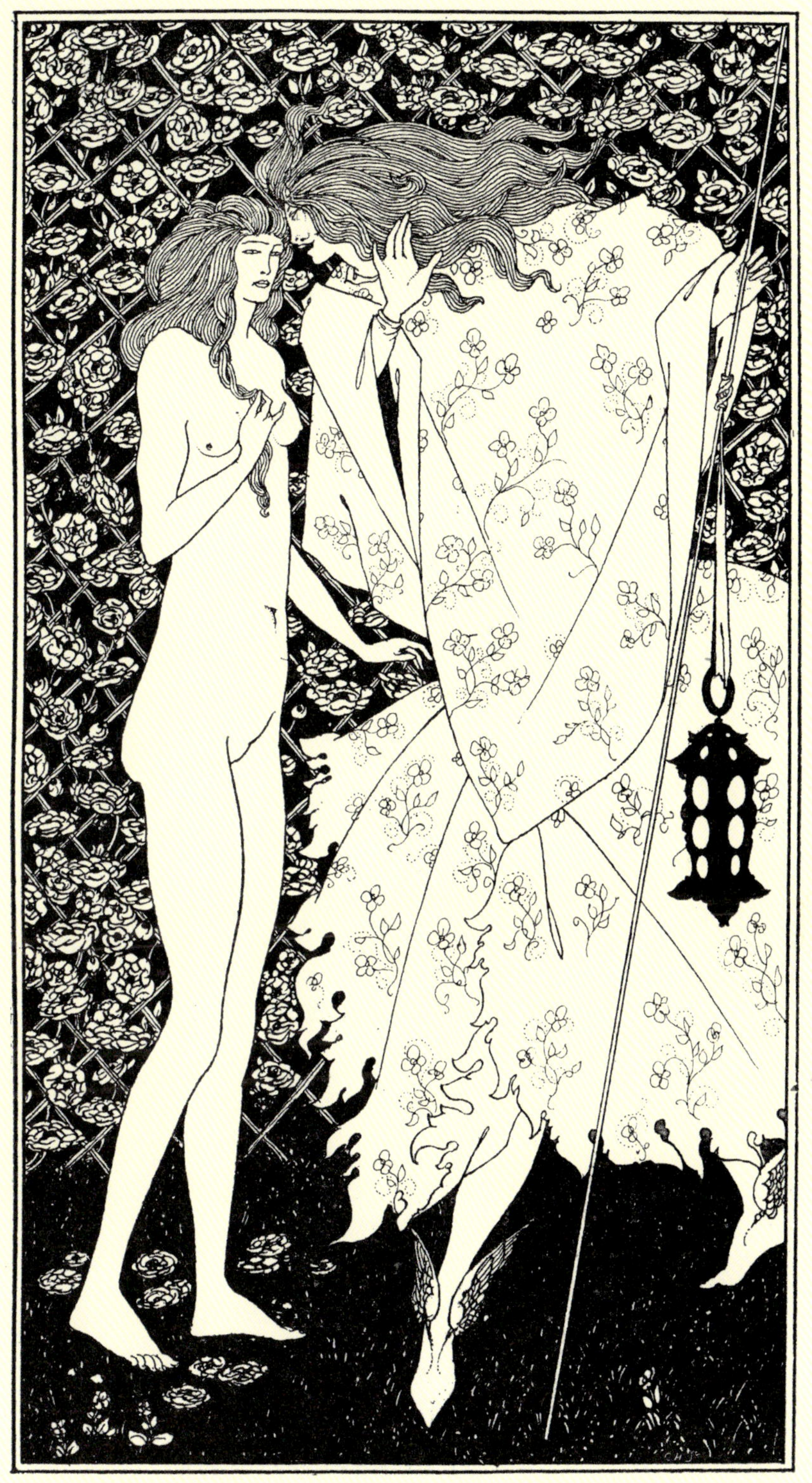

From Volume IV: 'The Mysterious Rose Garden'

This is one of the pieces where Beardsley's lines are at their most exquisite. The tranquil scene shown us on the cover was a deceitful veil; once we peel it back, Beardsley's black magic instantly launches an attack that leaves us reeling. There is such a plethora of interpretations of this picture that none really takes precedent. One reading suggests that here, Beardsley attempts to draw an annunciation scene for the first time—in other words, the woman is the Virgin Mary while the male figure is the angel Gabriel, telling Mary that she will give birth to Christ. Another contradictory interpretation suggests that the woman is Eve, and the man is a human incarnation of the snake, tempting Eve to eat the forbidden fruit. Is this woman holy or wicked? It seems hard to say for sure.

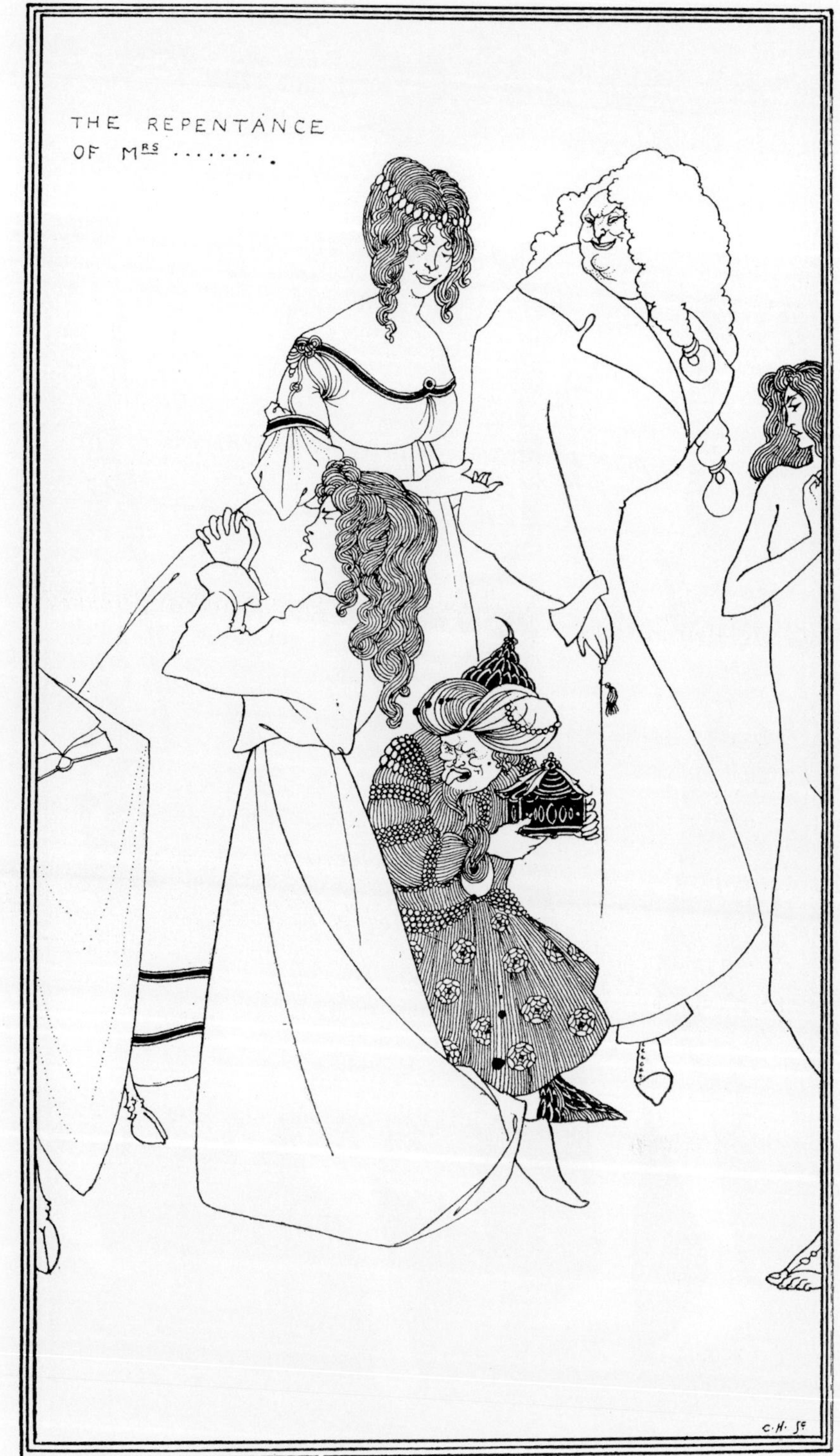

From Volume IV: 'The Repentance of Mrs ....'

The woman is kneeling, confessing her sins, while the man and woman standing beside her laugh derisively. At the far right stands a naked man, staring at her, while behind her a dwarf pokes her tongue out. This picture is based on the picture 'The Burial of St John' by Renaissance artist Andrea Mantegna of which Beardsley produced a copy in 1891. The kneeling figure is Mary Magdalene. Beardsley reimagines her story, a woman believed by nobody around her, as a portrayal of contemporary social relations, whereby a wicked woman confesses her sins. The laughing gentleman in the coat resembles Oscar Wilde. Not long after this issue had come out, Oscar Wilde was arrested and wrote his confessional work, *De Profundis*.

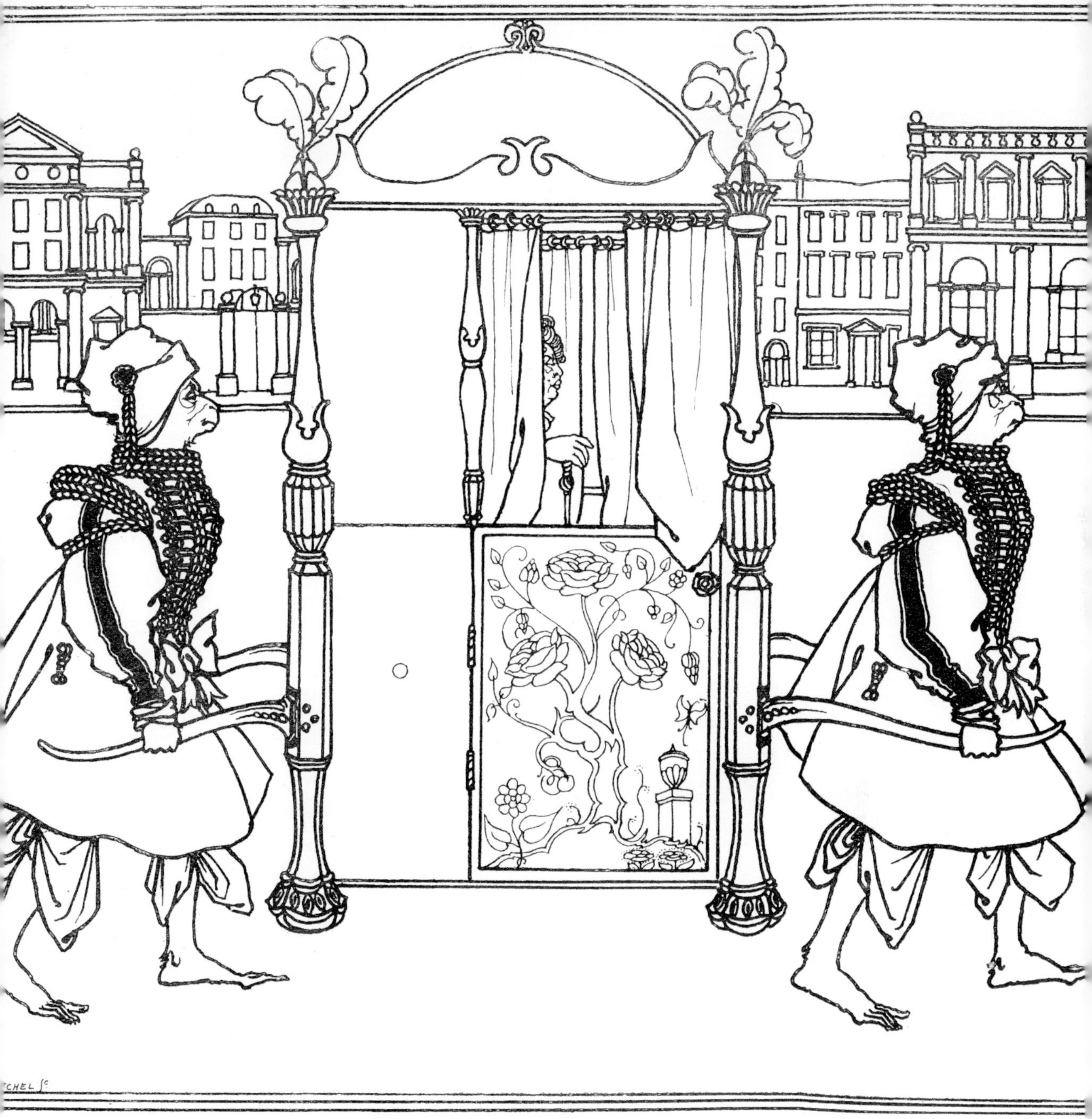

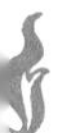

From Volume IV:
'Frontispiece for Juvenal'

Owing to Wilde's arrest, Beardsley's pictures vanished from *The Yellow Book* from Volume V on, and this was the last of his illustrations to appear in the magazine. Juvenal was a Roman satirical poet, and after this Beardsley produced more illustrations for his work, which were published by Smithers in 1906. In this plate, we see monkeys carrying a palanquin. Inside the luxurious box decorated with ornate roses sits a wealthy elderly person. The townscape in the background is not ancient Rome, but eighteenth century London. Yet we can't help but wonder if the palanquin is not actually a giant phallus, and the two monkeys are its testicles.

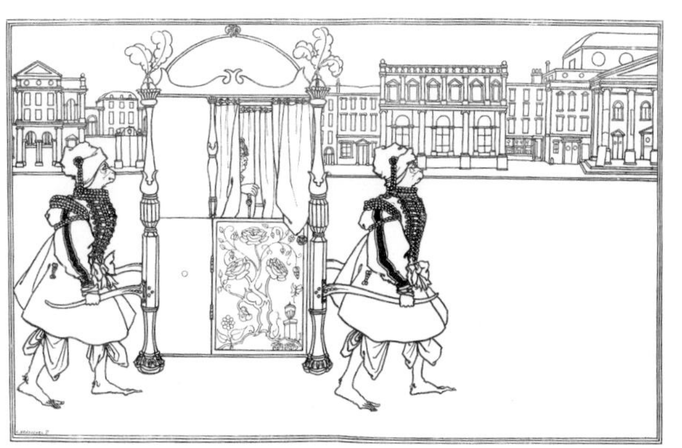

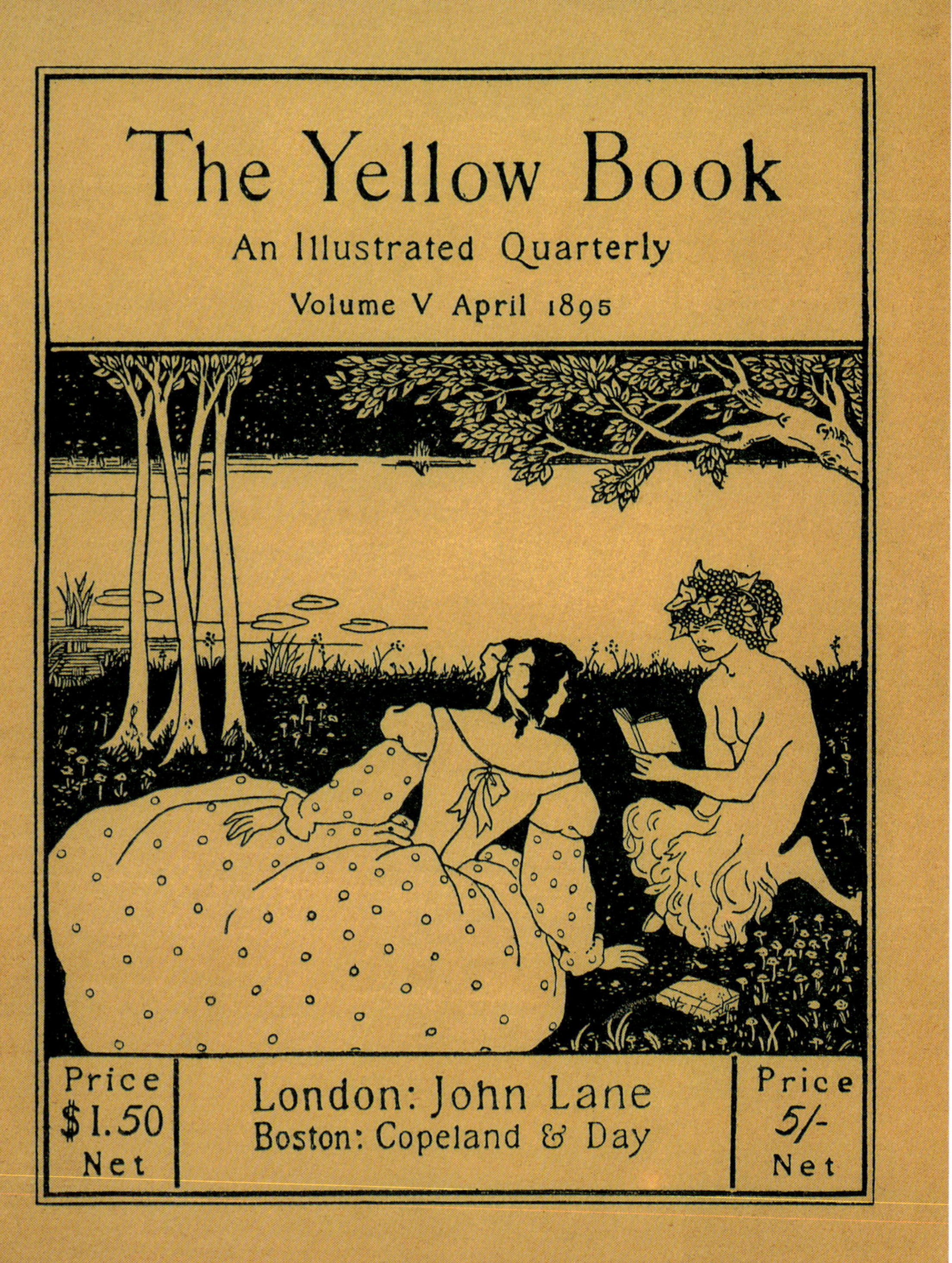

Cover Design for Volume V (not used), 1895

After Wilde's arrest, the works by Beardsley that had already been prepared for Volume V were replaced. They numbered five illustrations and this cover design, featuring a satyr reading to a woman. It is a peaceful pastoral scene. I can't help but notice that the satyr's lower half is somewhat unusually shaped, but that might be reading too much into it. This illustration was later repurposed as the front cover of a book published in a limited edition by Leonard Smithers.

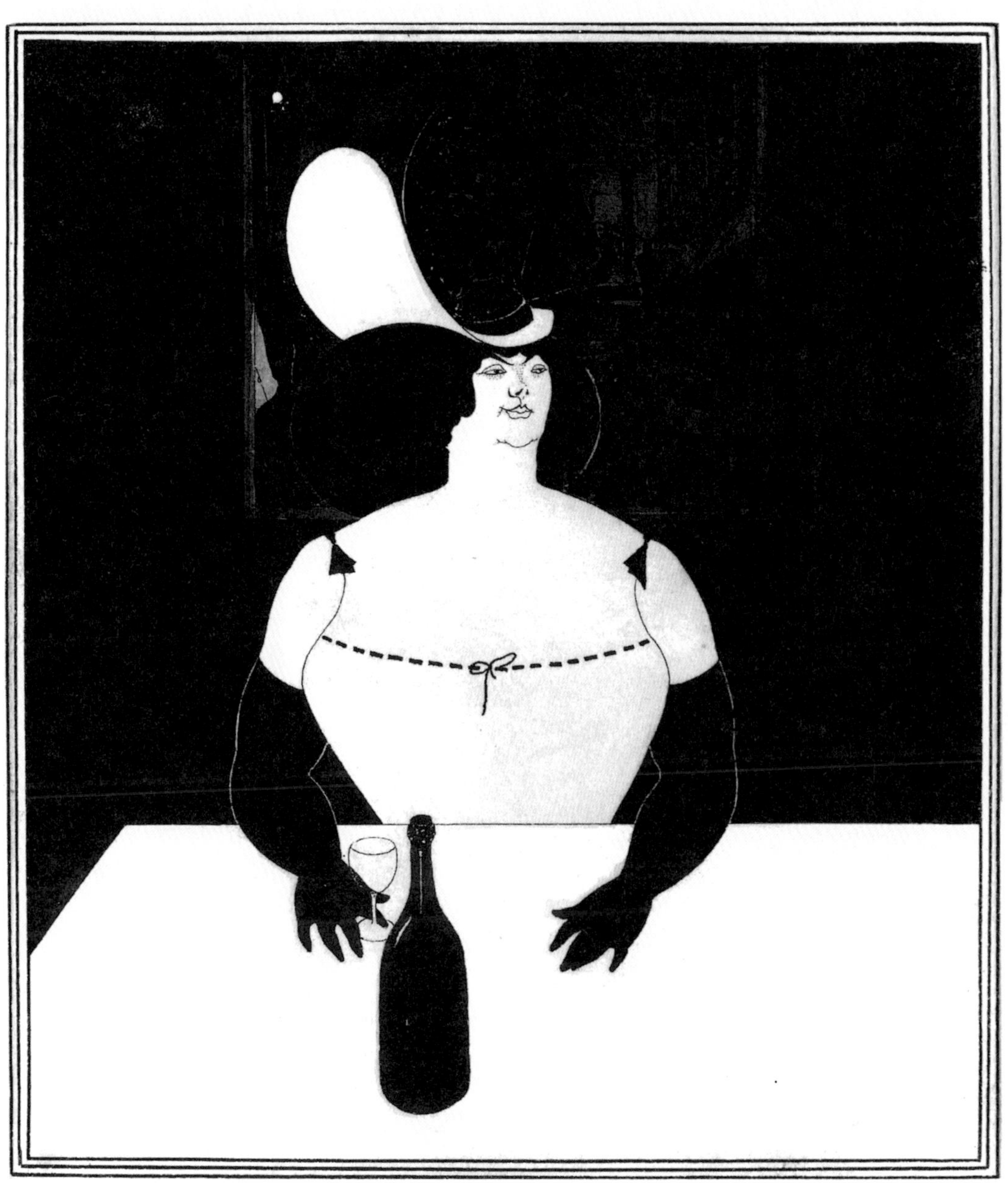

'The Fat Woman', 1894

This picture is said to be a caricature of the artist Whistler's wife. It was intended to be included in the first edition of *The Yellow Book*, but John Lane removed it. It was then published in the magazine *Today*, and apparently angered Whistler. However, I get the feeling that this is an amusing made-up anecdote, for in truth, this really is a fun, generous-spirited picture. One gets the sense that it is based on the image of women in cafes as drawn by Toulouse-Lautrec, and so on. Beardsley himself liked this picture. I consider it as one of Beardsley's greatest works.

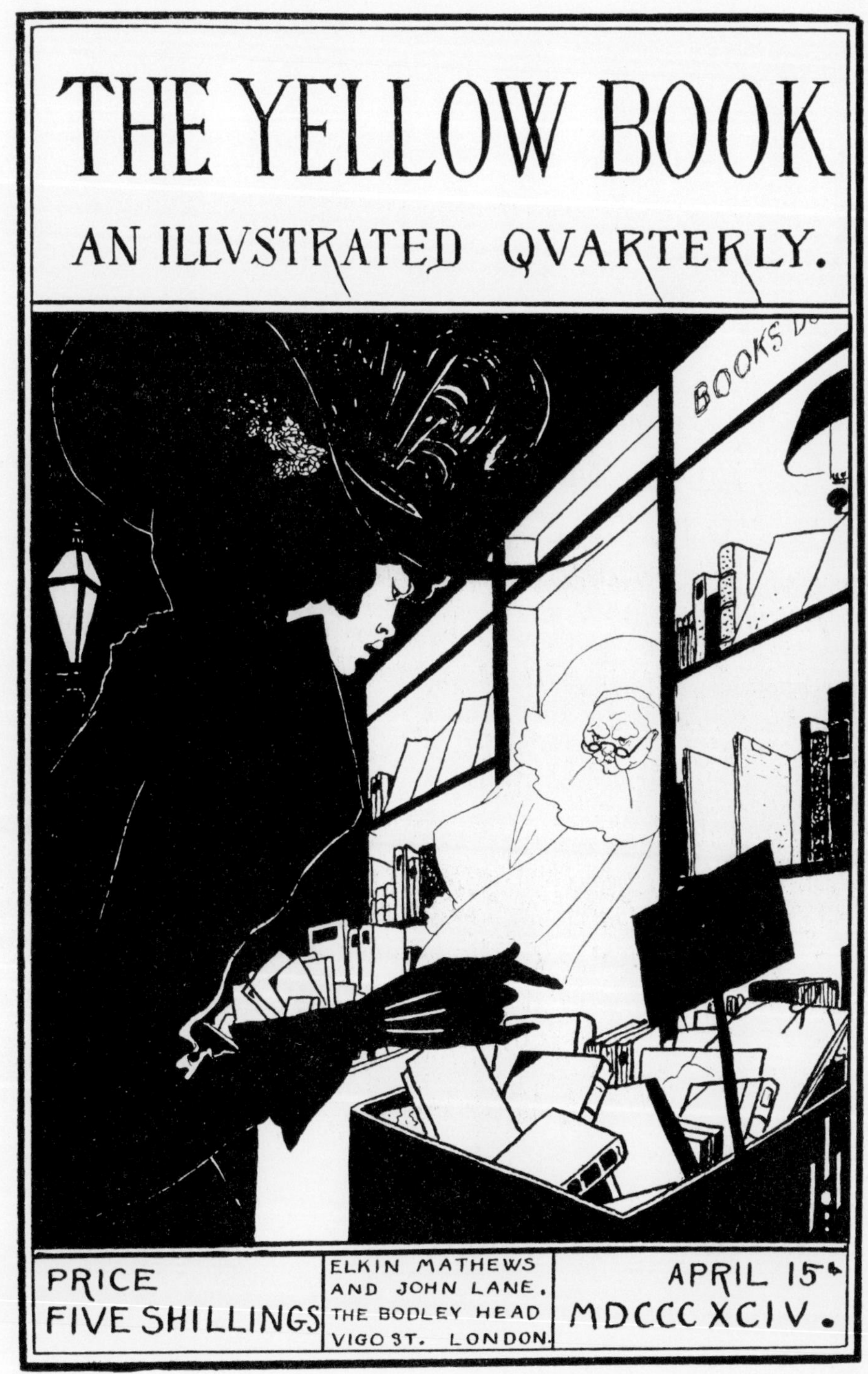

Prospectus for Volume I of _The Yellow Book_, 1894

A prospectus was an advertising flyer describing what a particular book was about. Here, we see a woman looking in a bookshop. Beardsley has dressed the bookshop owner in a pierrot outfit. This old man was Elkin Mathews, who ran the Bodley Head together with John Lane. The aim of this picture was to declare that that we now lived in an age where women could choose books for themselves in a bookshop, and that _The Yellow Book_ was an appropriate periodical for an intellectual woman of that kind.

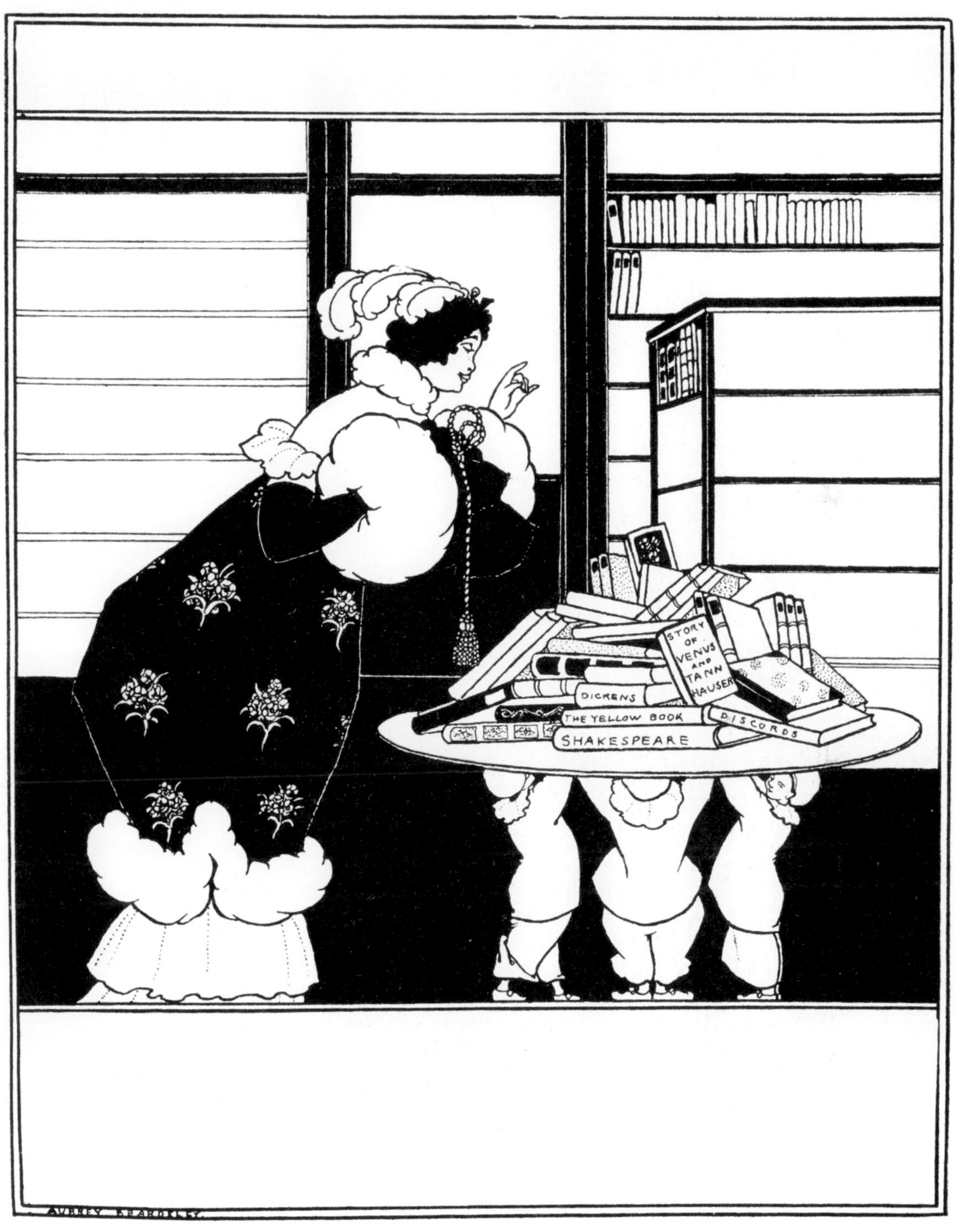

Cover design (not used), 1895

This cover that Beardsley prepared was not used in the end. On a platform supported by children lies a pile of books including *The Yellow Book* and *The Story of Venus and Tannhauser* that Beardsley was intending to publish. The black-bordered interior in the background is said to be deliberately rendered in a Japanese style. This picture was likely intended to be used for Volume VI. However, Beardsley was chased out of *The Yellow Book*, and *The Story of Venus and Tannhauser* was never completed.

BEARDSLEY'S BOOK DESIGNS

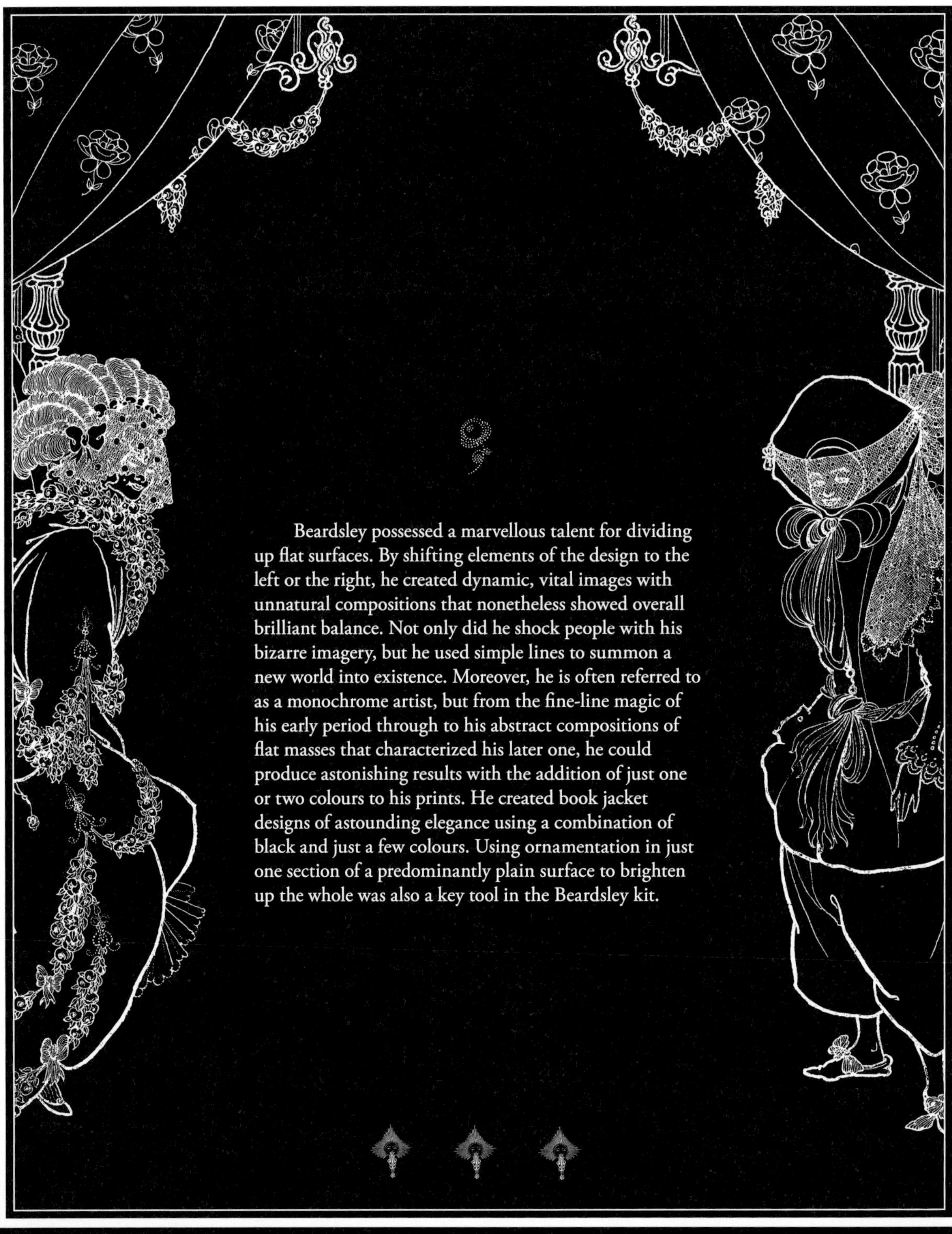

Beardsley possessed a marvellous talent for dividing up flat surfaces. By shifting elements of the design to the left or the right, he created dynamic, vital images with unnatural compositions that nonetheless showed overall brilliant balance. Not only did he shock people with his bizarre imagery, but he used simple lines to summon a new world into existence. Moreover, he is often referred to as a monochrome artist, but from the fine-line magic of his early period through to his abstract compositions of flat masses that characterized his later one, he could produce astonishing results with the addition of just one or two colours to his prints. He created book jacket designs of astounding elegance using a combination of black and just a few colours. Using ornamentation in just one section of a predominantly plain surface to brighten up the whole was also a key tool in the Beardsley kit.

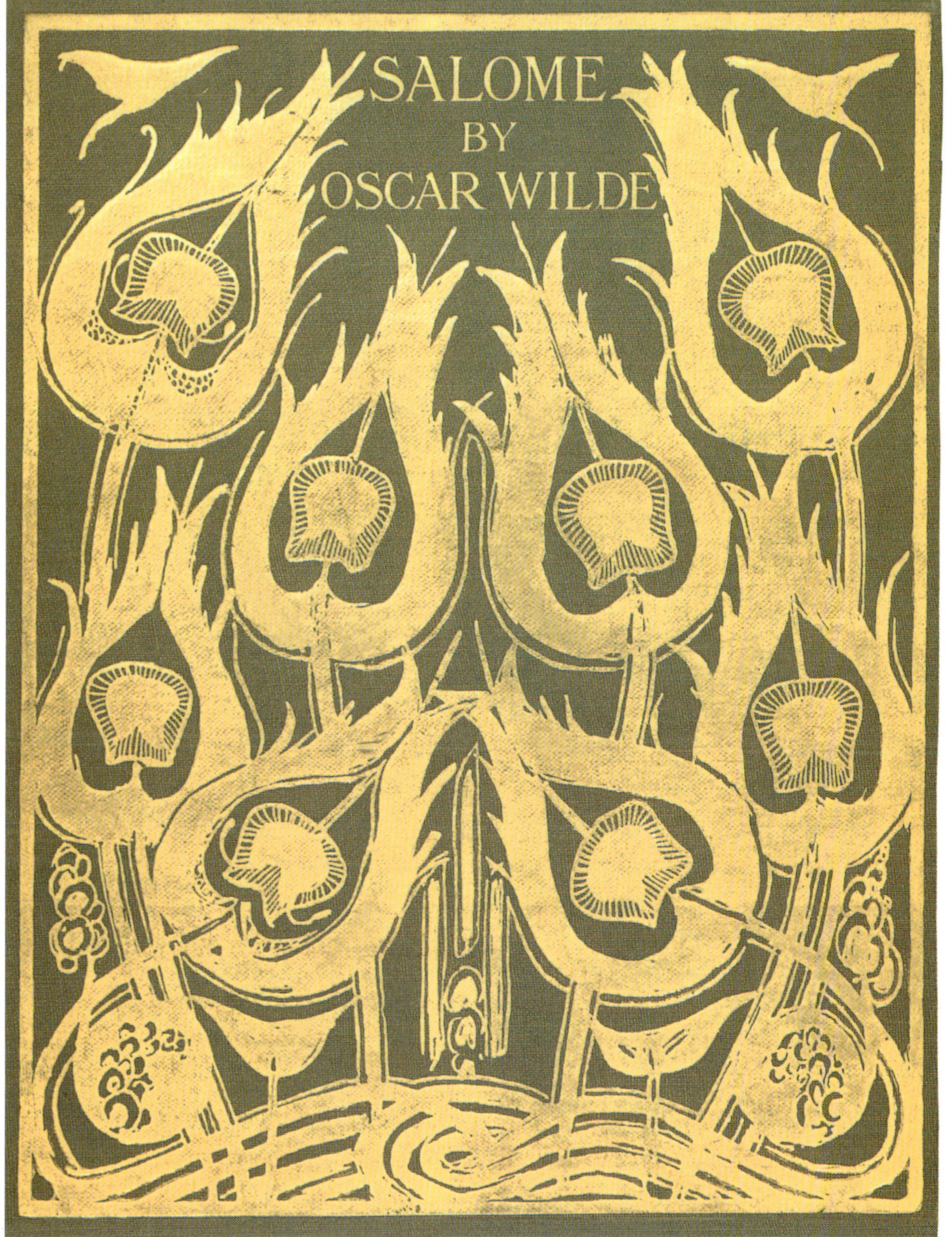

Cover to the second edition of *Salome*, 1907 / UK (John Lane, London)

This design wasn't used for the first edition in 1894. The peacock-feather pattern reveals the influence of Whistler's Peacock Room, and of Japanese art. This is the same pattern that is used for Salome's dress in Beardsley's illustrations, and it is thought he picked it up from Japanese painters such as Kōrin.

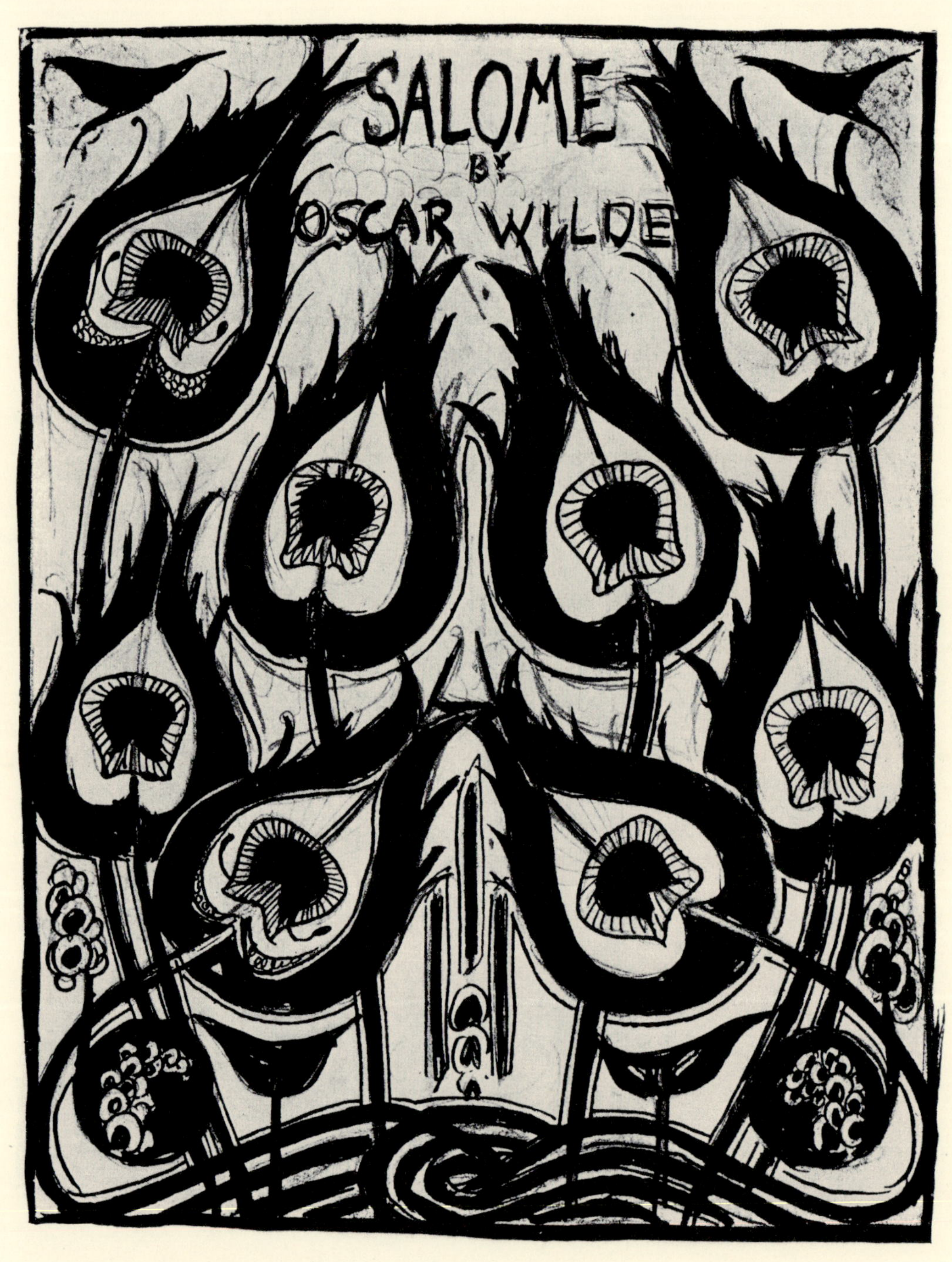

Sketch for the cover design of *Salome*, 1906

This sketch is notable for its dynamic black lines. Above the design reads the text 'Salome By Oscar Wilde', but directly below that is Beardsley's signature mark. This emblem of Beardsley features a rod (phallus) sandwiched between two lines, with drops of what appears to be liquid dripping down is a deliberate and utterly Beardsley-esque trick, which can be seen in many of his other works. It was thanks to his inclusion of this mark on the cover that the design wasn't used the first time.

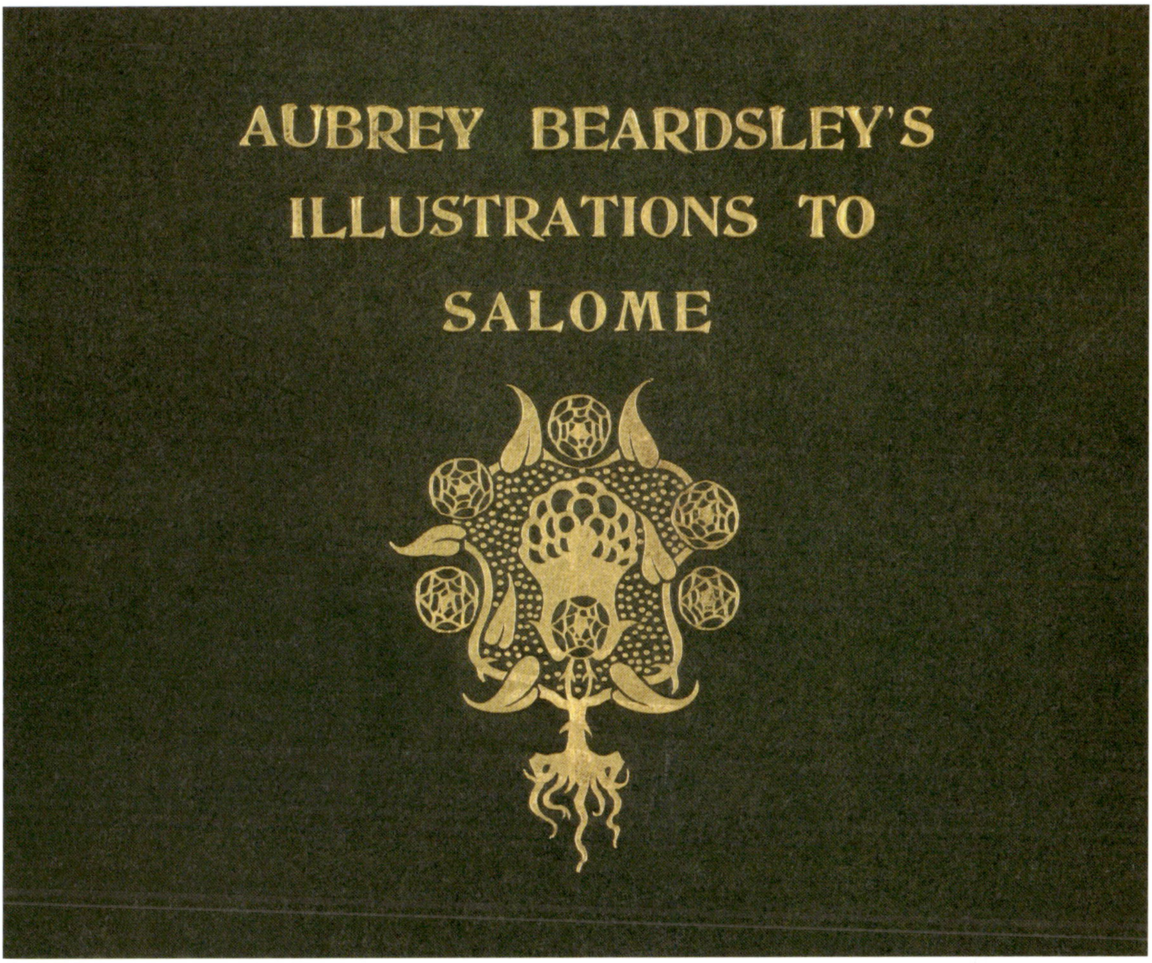

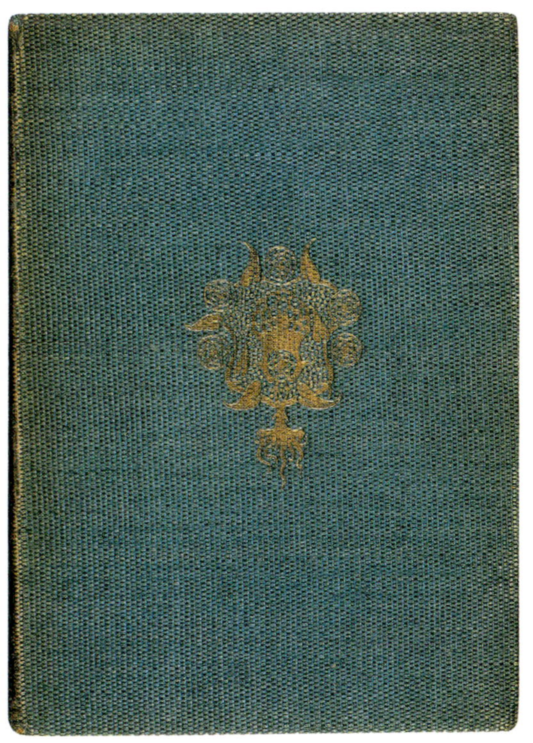

(Top)
**Aubrey Beardsley's Illustrations to *Salome*,
1906 UK (John Lane, London)**
(Bottom)
**Cover to the second edition of *Salome*, 1894
UK (Elkin Mathews & John Lane, London)**

The peacock-feather design was rejected for being obscene, and in the end, a simple design was settled on for the first edition of the book. The rose tree was designed by Beardsley himself, and was reused in subsequent publications. The book above is the cover for the collection of Beardsley's seventeen lithograph plates for *Salome*, sixteen of which had been used in the original book, plus one not yet released.

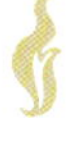

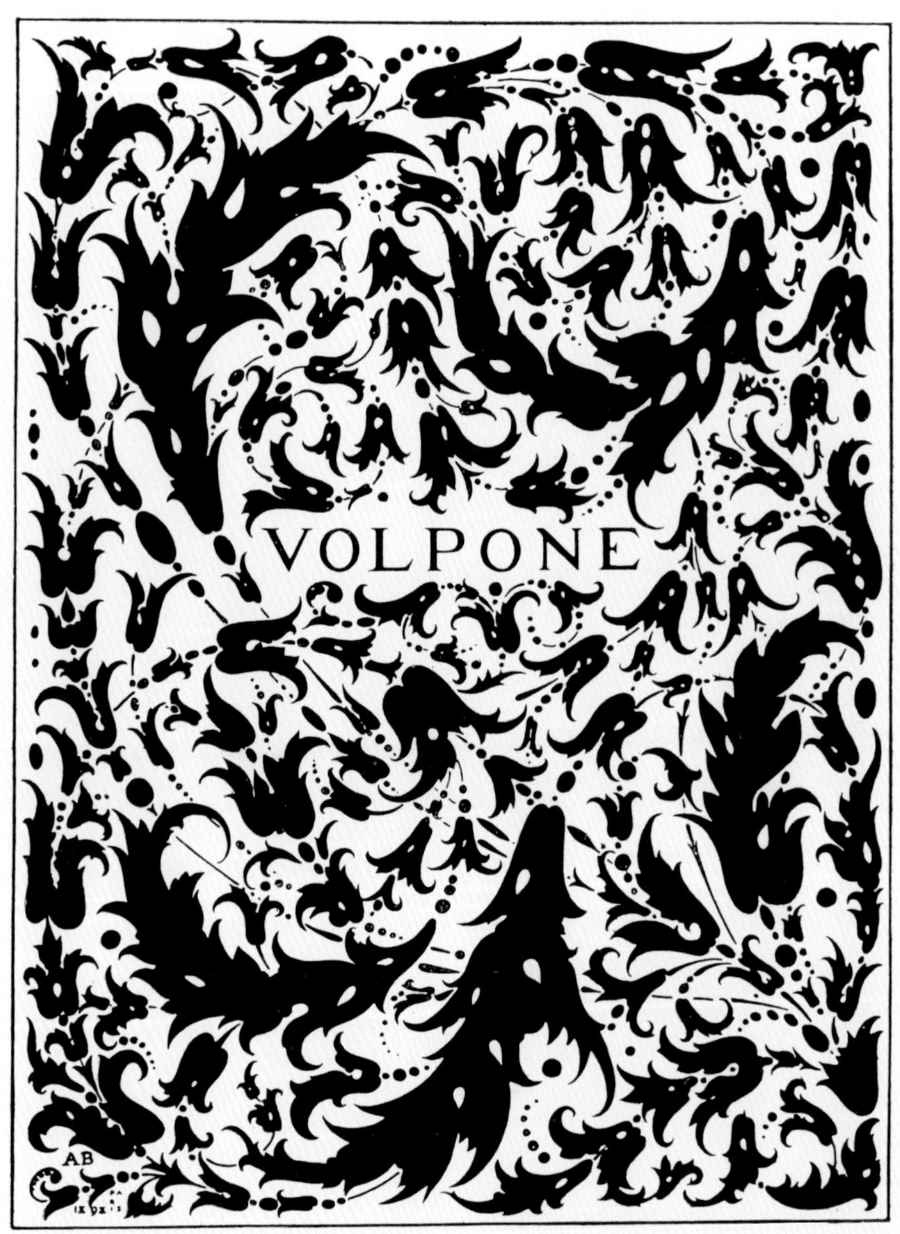

Cover to *Volpone*, 1898 UK (Leonard Smithers, London)

This design was initially conceived as the cover for *Ali Baba and the Forty Thieves*, but was used for this book instead. Indeed, it would otherwise seemed strange that Beardsley would have produced the cover design for *Volpone* but barely any of the illustrations, so the explanation that it was repurposed makes a lot of sense. The jacket design is printed in gold on a Turkish blue background. The intricate arabesques are said to be inspired by a seventeenth-century embroidery technique known as blackwork. Beardsley's late work with its fascination for detailed patterns should be re-evaluated for its contribution in the development of the art of William Morris and other members of the Arts and Crafts movement.

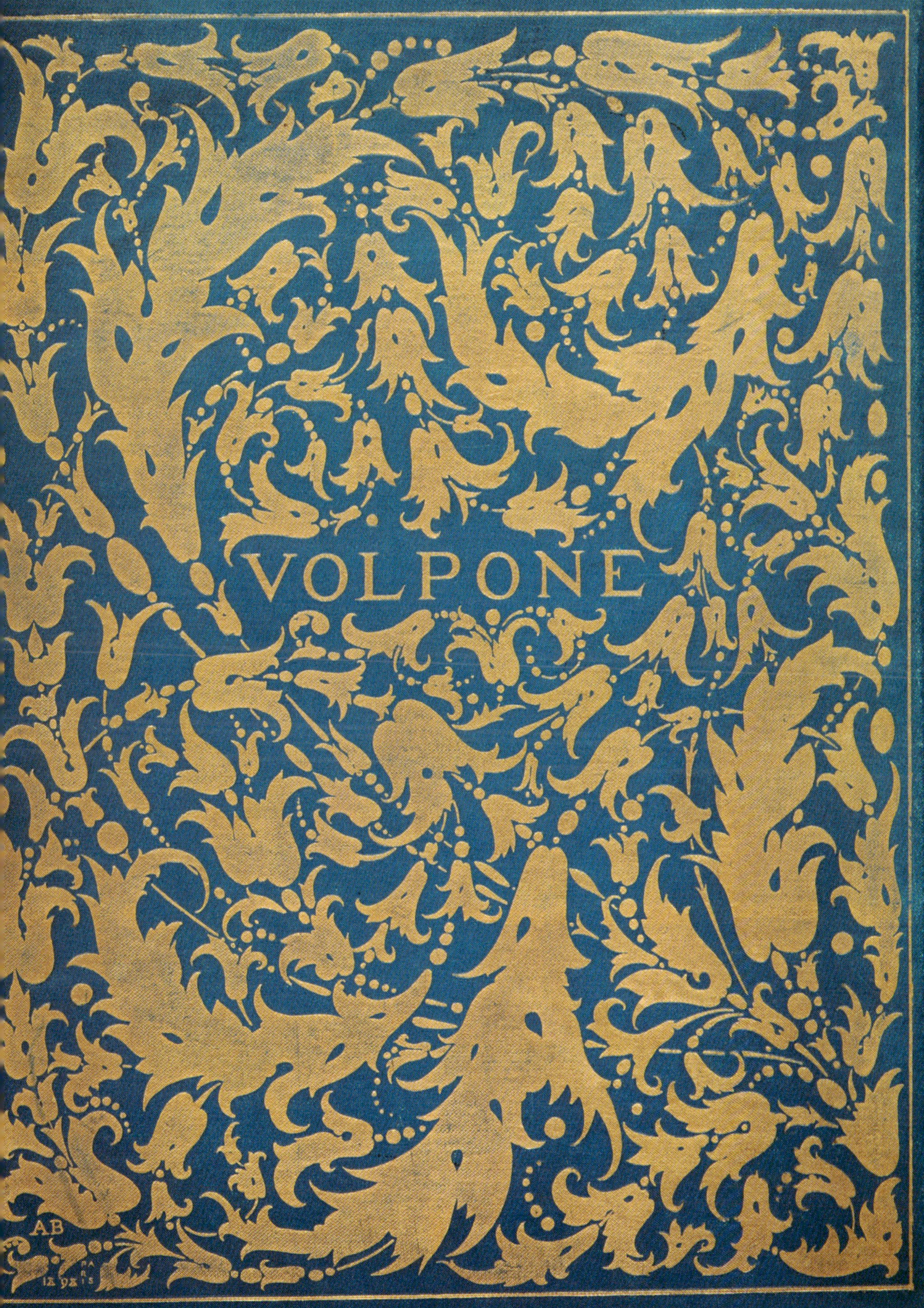

VOLPONE
AB
PA
RI
S
18 98

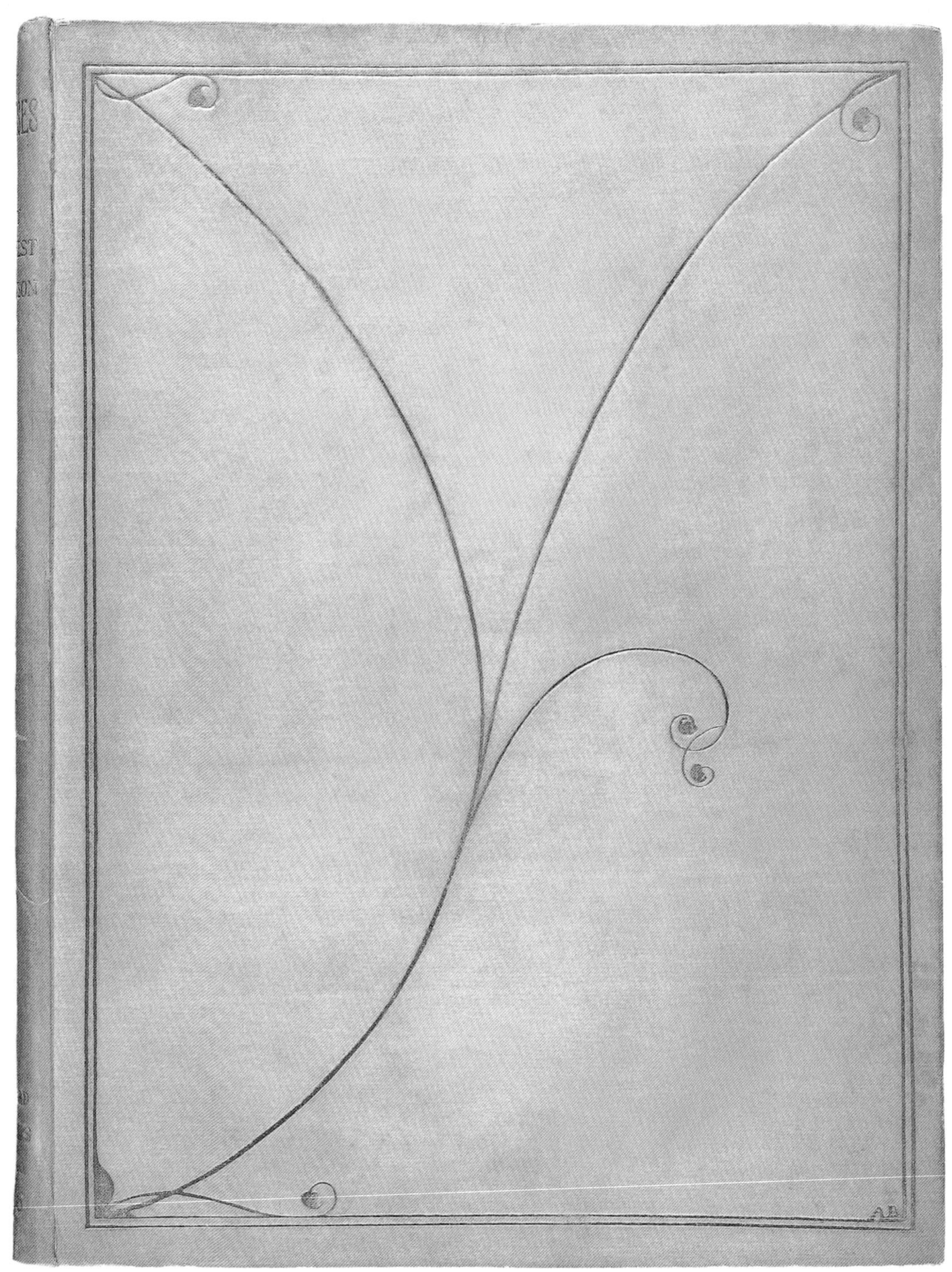

Cover to *Ernest Dowson Poems*, 1896
UK (Leonard Smithers, London)

It is believed that this design was derived by lifting the 'y' from the 'why' of the burning question on Beardsley's mind: 'Why do I have to do such a boring job?' Beardsley stated that he ended up producing such a simple design as a way of slacking off, but this supremely pared down arabesque design was received as a masterpiece, and the author Dowson was allegedly very fond of it.

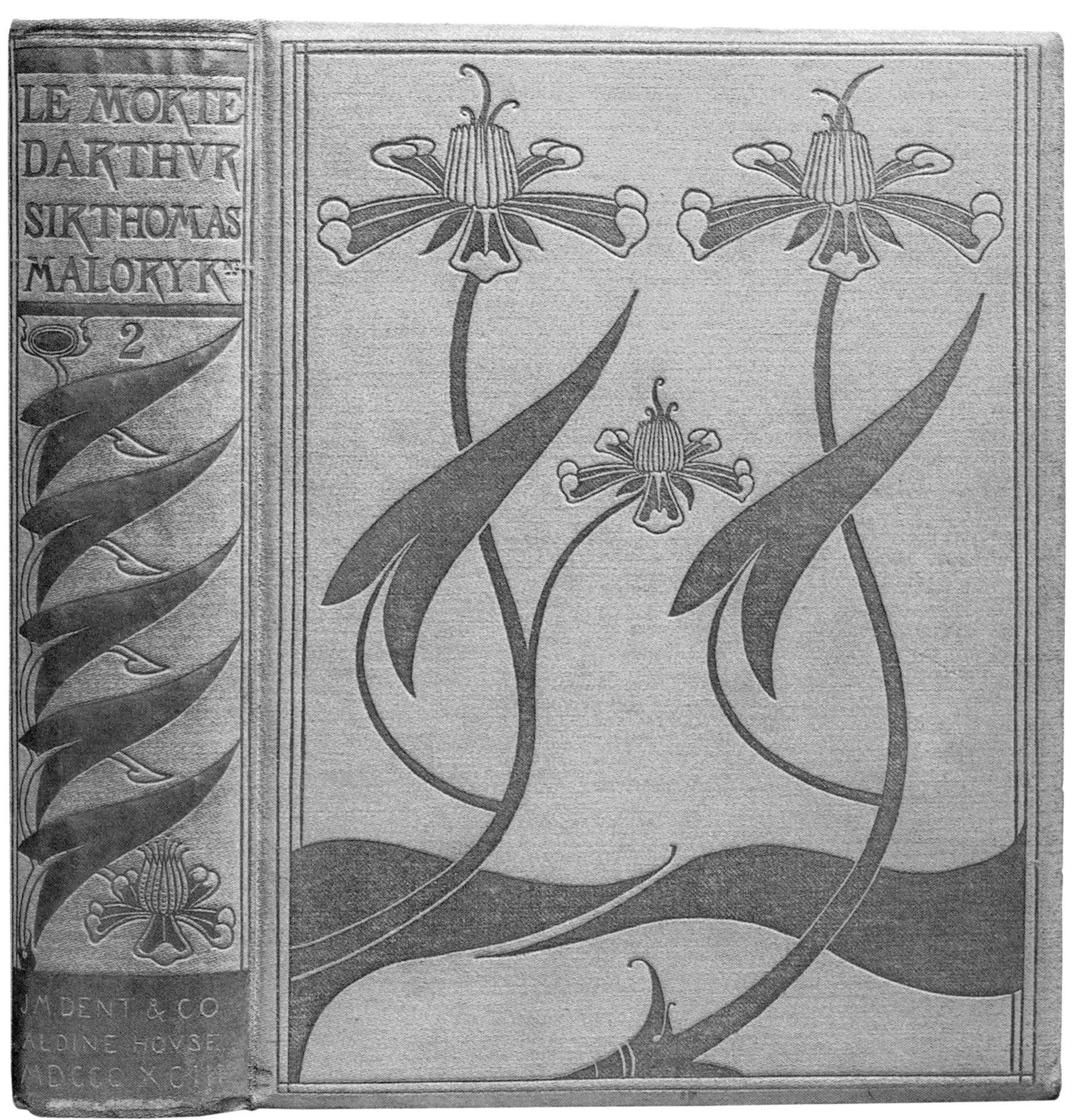

Cover to *La Morte d'Arthur*, 1893-4
UK (J. M. Dent & Company, London)

Between 1893 and 1894, this book was released in twelve parts, which were later combined into a three-volume book, of which a limited run of 300 copies, and a general run of 1500 copies were printed. For the illustrations, Beardsley emulated Burne-Jones' style, but with this cover he branched out and experimented with an utterly new design. The clematis and other flowers are made more abstract, with the use of lines pointing towards Art Nouveau. Along with the design for Ernest Dowson's poems, this cover is regarded as one of Beardsley's finest jacket designs.

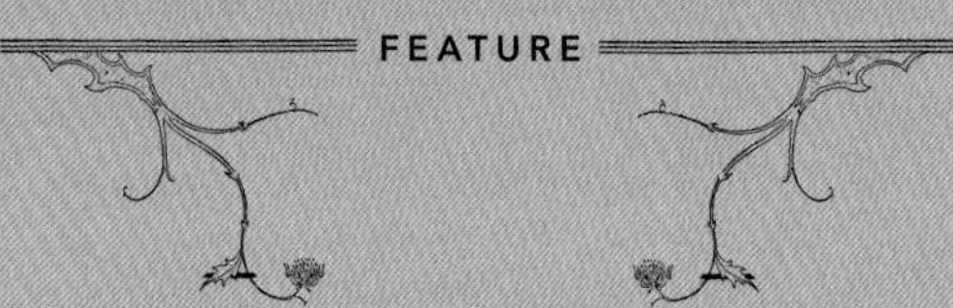

Beardsley and Floral Designs

Beardsley developed as an artist while surrounded by the Arts and Crafts movement of William Morris and Burne Jones, and it was from them that he learned to draw the gothic foliage scroll designs that enjoyed a revival with the movement (fig. 1). At the same time, he also was deeply affected by the plant patterns found in Japanese art (fig. 2). Beardsley's use of these foliage designs reached a peak with his jacket design for *Ernest Dowson Poems* in 1896 (see p.100). Beardsley states that asked by Smithers to do this job that he really wasn't enthused by, he slacked off and produced something very plain. Yet the simple, sweeping lines of the design of the utmost minimalism create an unforgettable impression.

In illustrations such as 'Three Musicians' (p.123) created for *The Savoy*, we also find trees, grasses and flowers rendered with great intricacy. Beardsley's floral and foliage designs vascillate between these two extremes. Broadly speaking, his earliest work such as *La Morte d'Arthur* (p.52-53) tends to include detailed plant motifs, referencing the Arts and Crafts movement (fig. 3), but very soon he begins to gravitate towards more abstract, simple designs (fig. 4.). Into his later work, he branches into a denser form of expression with Baroque and Rococo notes, where leaves are crowded together without any gaps (fig. 5). Even when creating these denser depictions, though, Beardsley is always conscious of the aesthetics of the blank space.

Between these two styles—abstract designs and dense descriptions—it is hard to say which is the more distinctively Beardsley. It seems like the most Beardsley-esque skill of all is being able to wield both skills freely. Beardsley's characteristic strength could be said to be his ability to create such wonderful lines as he comes and goes between nature and artifice.

We would also do well to think about Beardsley's relationship with Art Nouveau from the perspective of these two opposing poles. Art Nouveau never took off in Britain to the extent that it did in France or Belgium, and in being termed an Art Nouveau artist, Beardsley was a rarity in the UK. Yet even Beardsley didn't fit squarely into the Art Nouveau framework. Rather, he went beyond the movement to achieve a truly modern style. It would be hard to explain the abstract curves of the Dowson cover with reference only to Art Nouveau.

Yet if we conceive of the Art Nouveau curved lines not rigidly, but rather as a vital form of line-drawing that went beyond the fin-de-siècle period, then Beardsley without doubt shared these, as he showed those around him the forms that would be passed down to the next generation and live on.

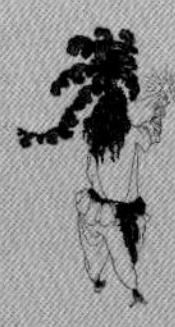

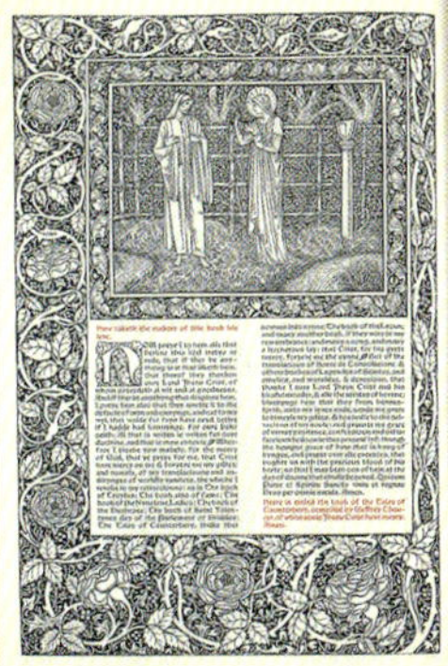 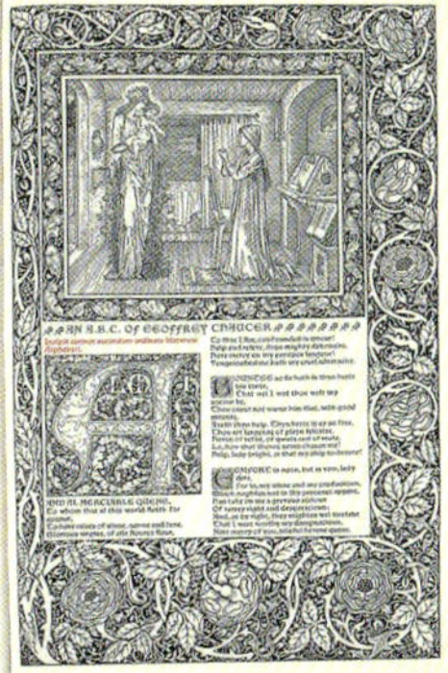

fig.1
The Works of Geoffrey Chaucer, illustrated by Burne-Jones and decorated by Morris, 1896

fig.2
Japanese paper stencil for dying paper with a chrysanthemum pattern. Along with *ukiyo-e* prints, these *katagami* or patterned papers were revered by craftsmen and artists in Europe.

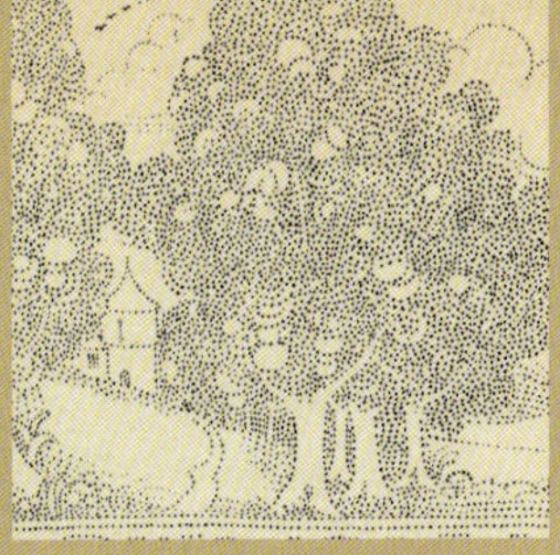

fig.5
Section from Beardsley's The *Rape of the Lock* (see p.10)

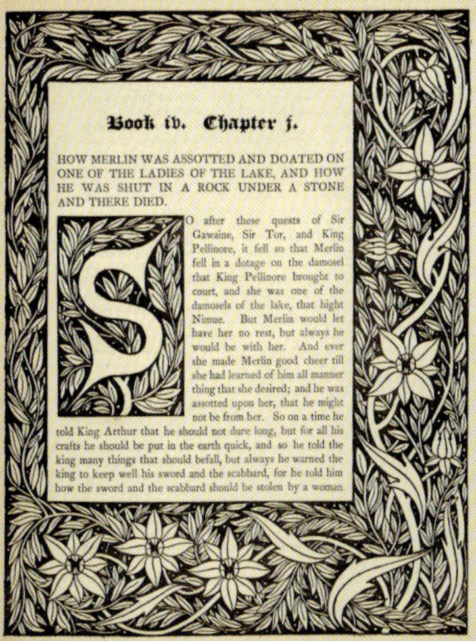

fig.3
When Beardsley's began work on *Le Morte d'Arthur* (see p.50), the influence from Morris and Burne-Jones was strong

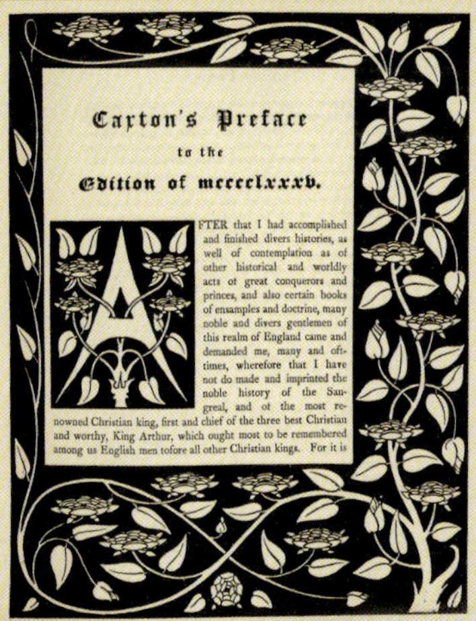

fig.4
Beardsley's work for *Le Morte d'Arthur* (see p.50); he gradually developed his own unique style, with its liberal use of blank space.

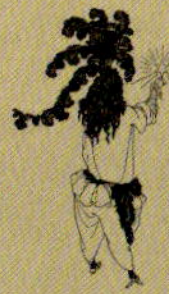

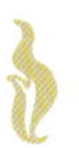

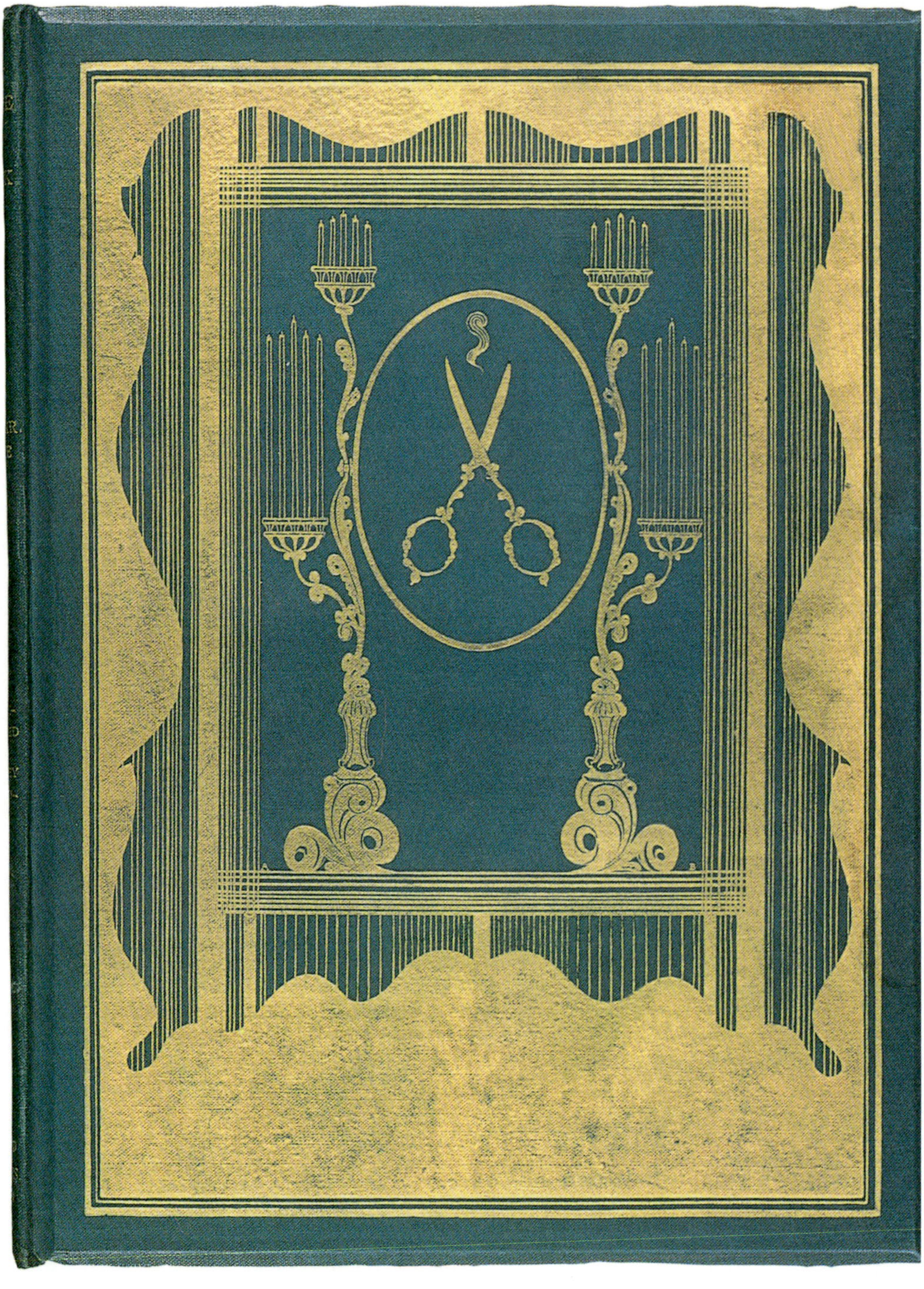

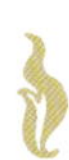

Cover to *The Rape of the Lock*, 1896 UK (Leonard Smithers, London)

This is a refined design of gold on a Turkish blue background, the straight lines forming a stark contrast with the soft curves. The cloudlike border pattern in gold is possibly inspired by images from Japanese folding screens. In the centre sits a pair of scissors and a lock of hair, alluding to the subject matter of the book. One could also see them as the masculine and feminine. If we're looking for typical Beardsley mischief, we could say that the clouds at the side of the frame take the form of a woman seen from the rear, her bottom jutting out.

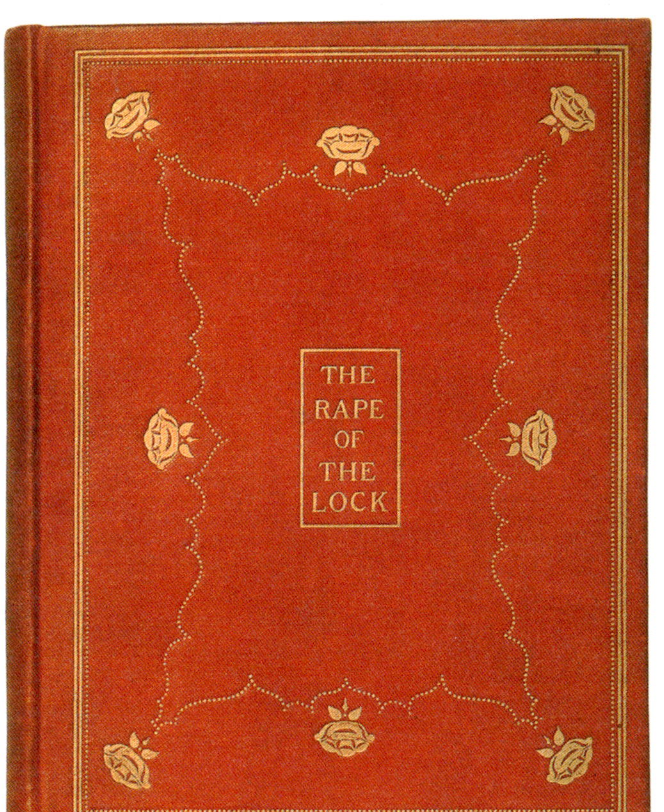

**Cover to *The Rape of the Lock*,
1897 UK (Leonard Smithers, London)**
Beardsley and Smithers created a condensed version of
The Rape of the Lock, which Beardsley referred to as 'the
rapette.' Beardsley created a new, simplified design for this
smaller edition, but it still exudes a Rococo daintiness.

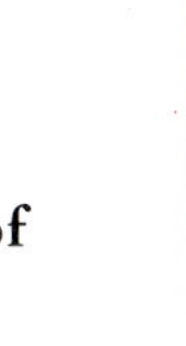

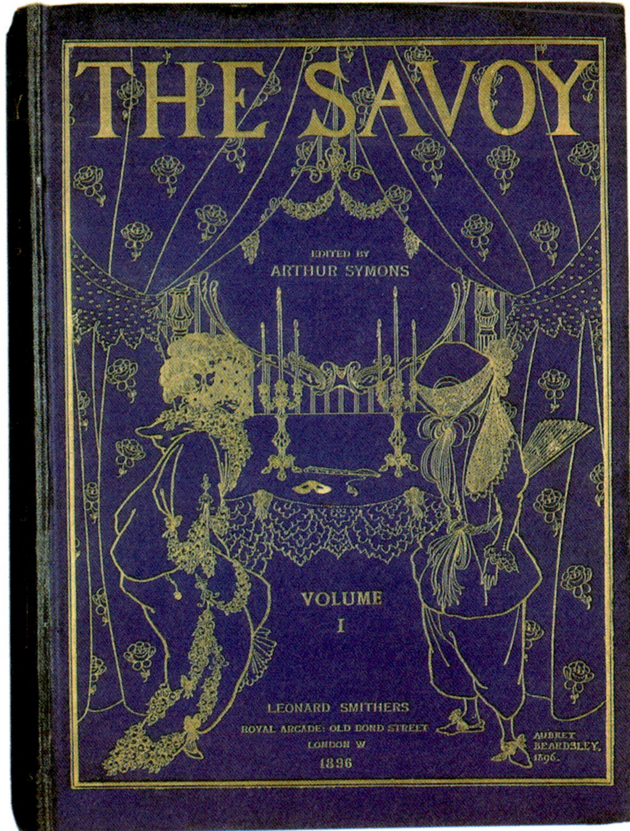

**Cover for collected edition of
The Savoy, 1896
UK (Leonard Smithers, London)**
The cover for the collectors' edition of the collected issues
of The Savoy, where all eight editions were featured in three
volumes. The illustrations Beardsley created for the title page
were embossed with gold leaf, creating a suitably luxurious
design for this collectors' edition.

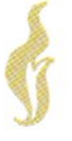

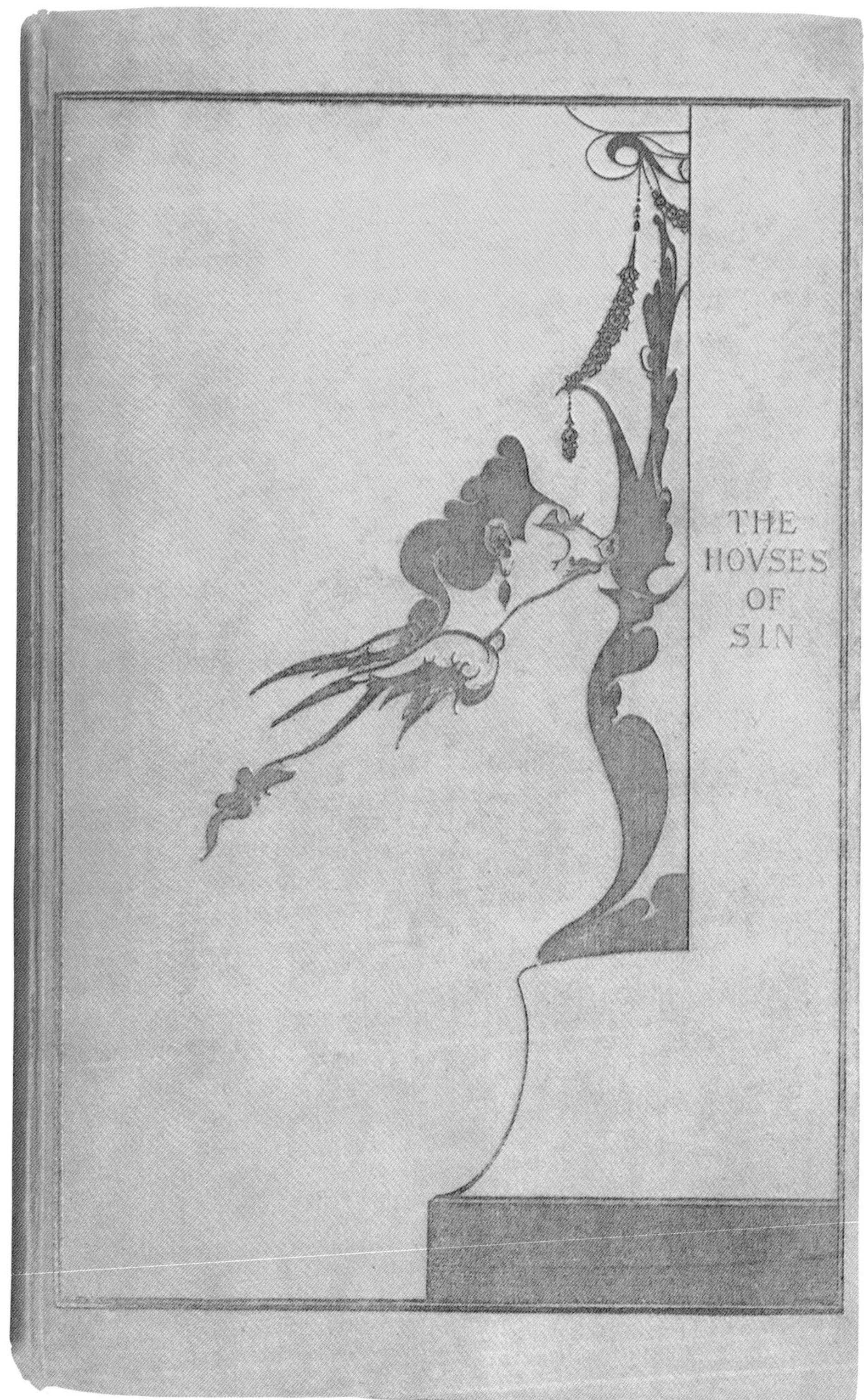

Cover for *House of Sin* by Vincent O'Sullivan, 1897 UK (Leonard Smithers, London)

O'Sullivan was a young modernist writer who was friends with Smithers. This cover to his collected short stories bears no relation to its contents, and the significance of the bizarre picture has not been unravelled. The design features a woman with a pig's snout burrowing her face into a bizarre amorphous plant like a cactus. From the waist down, her body resembles that of a bird. I can't help but wondering if Beardsley didn't first drip the ink randomly on the page, and subsequently decided to draw in the woman's face and the other decorations, in a way that presaged the automatic drawing of the surrealists and Pollock's dripping technique. Perhaps he had also been inspired by the *suminagashi* (ink swirls) found within Japanese painting.

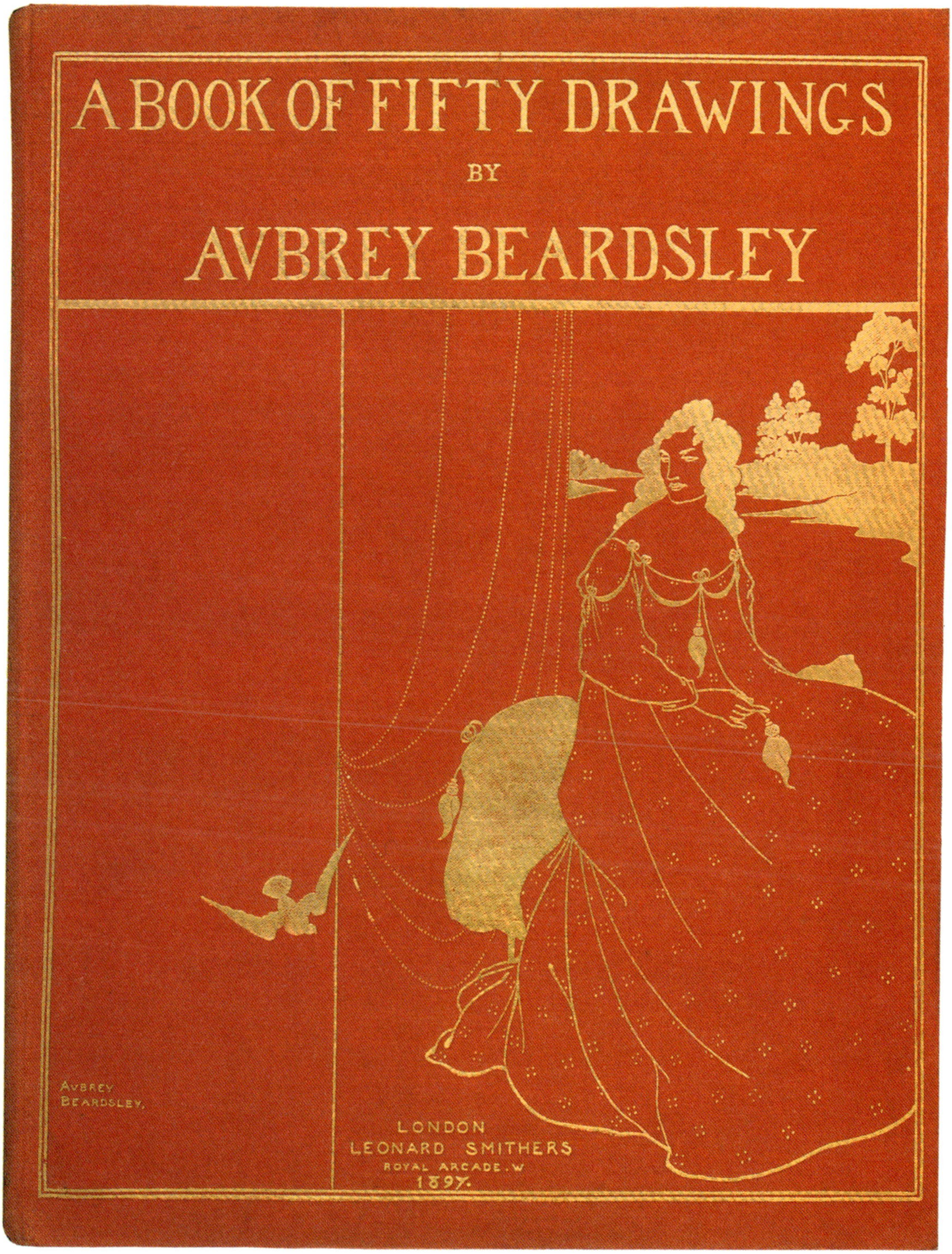

***A Book of Fifty Drawings by Aubrey Beardsley*, 1897 UK** (Leonard Smithers, London)

Sensing that he didn't have much time remaining, Beardsley submitted an urgent request to produce a book of his collected works, for which this is the design. This was drawn in black ink on a white background, but then flipped over, and rendered in gold on red. The image is split into two a third of the way across, with a picture taking up the larger two-thirds, and the remaining third drawn with just a bird that appears to be a swallow. The picture has a fierce intensity to it, as if Beardsley had drawn it in his own blood.

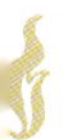
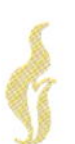

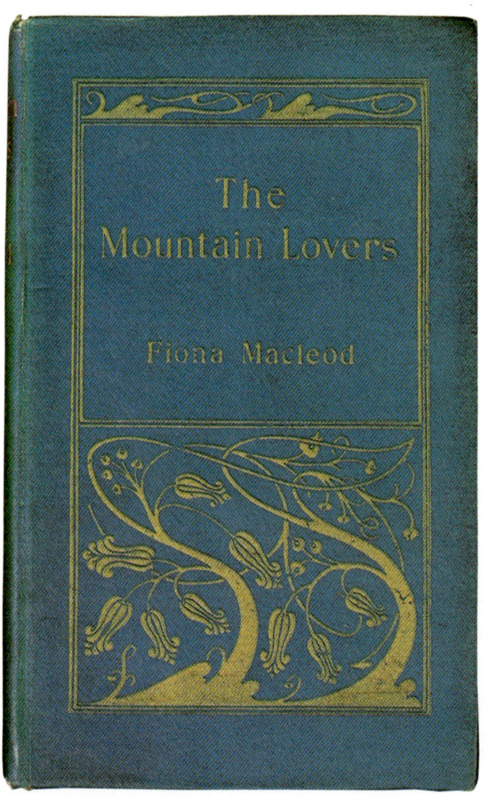

The Mountain Lovers, 1895

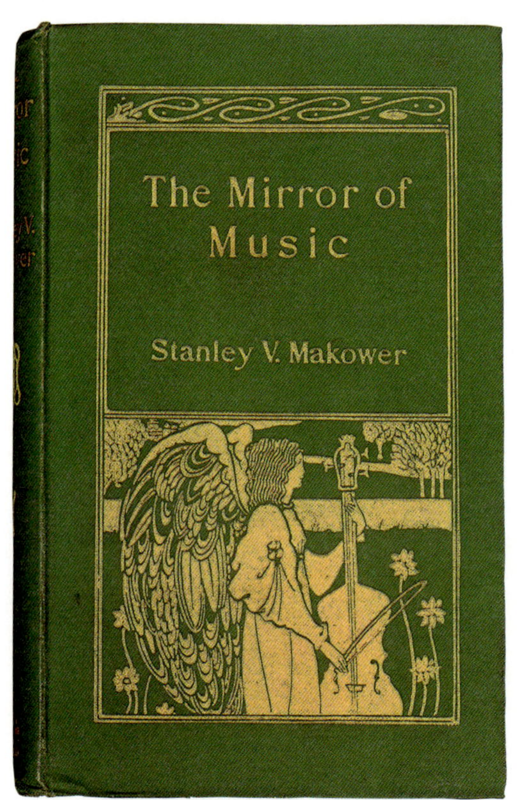

The Mirror of Music, 1895

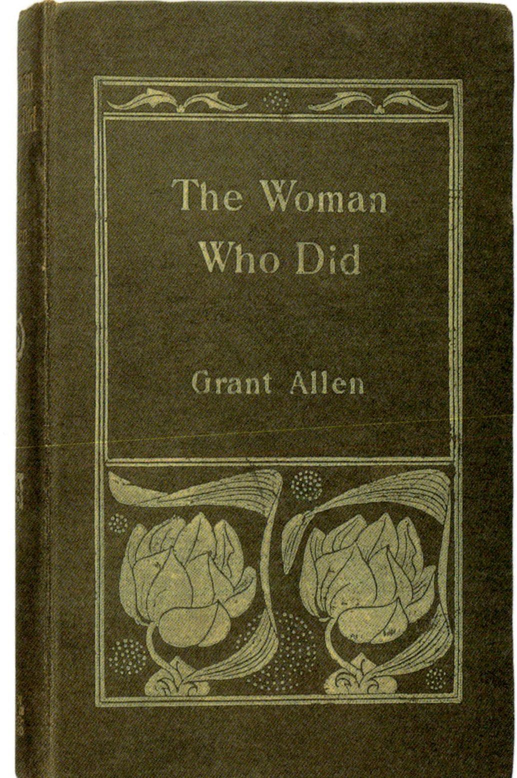

The Woman Who Did, 1895

Keynotes Series

The Keynotes Series was a collection of modern novels published by John Lane. Twenty volumes were released in the series between 1893 and 1896, whose jackets Beardsley was responsible for designing. The designs Beardsley created were simple and, reusing other patterns he'd used previously, didn't cost him much in the way of effort, but his use of colour, with black or gold printing upon a single colour, is splendid. Also borrowing from the series title, he created a range of stylish monograms in the form of keys (p.110).

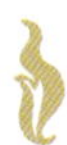

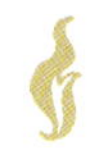

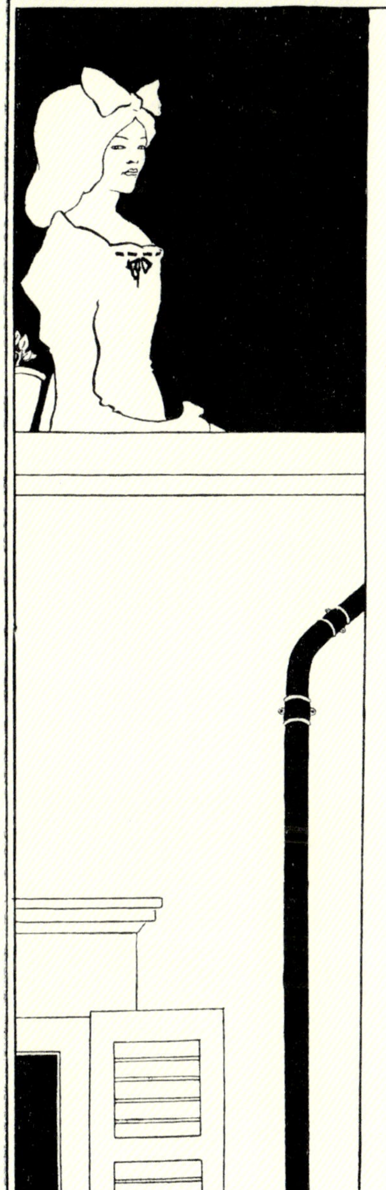

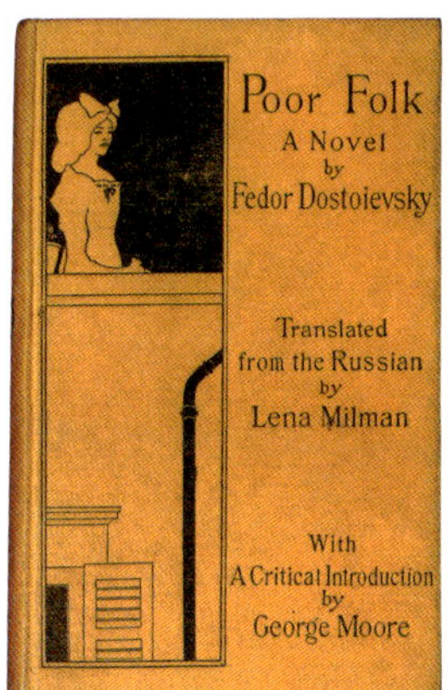

Poor Folk, 1894

This is the title page for Fyodor Dostoyevsky's *Poor Folk*. The woman at the top of the design resembles the woman in *Le Morte d'Arthur* (see p.55), but more worthy of attention are the water pipe and doorway, which have a truly modern simplicity to them. It feels almost alarming the extent to which Beardsley is foreshadowing modern design here, many years before its emergence. If we were to look just at this bottom section, we surely wouldn't know it from a contemporary illustration.

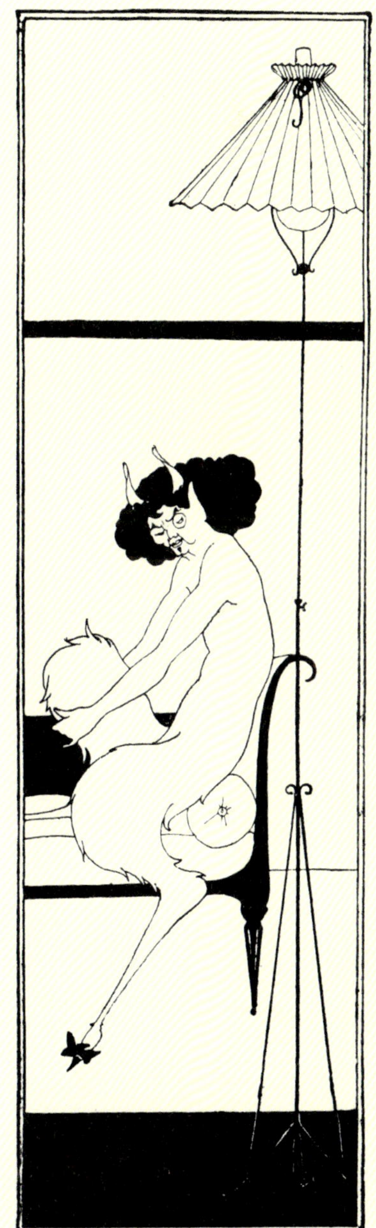

The Dancing Faun, 1894

This is the cover for *The Dancing Faun* by Florence Farr. The eye is first caught by the clean division of space, thanks to the structural composition with the lamp and black couch. In a way that has no relation with the plot of the book whatsoever, the faun appears to be a caricature of Whistler (p.234)—its hairstyle, monocle and are all distinguishing features of the artist. From a certain perspective, the faun's pose also appears somewhat lewd.

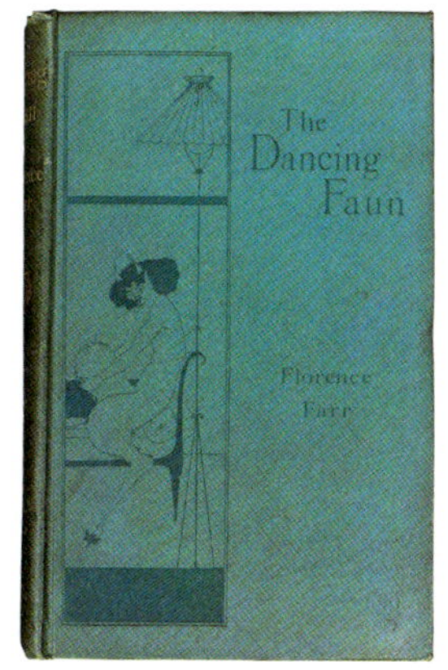

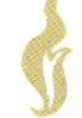

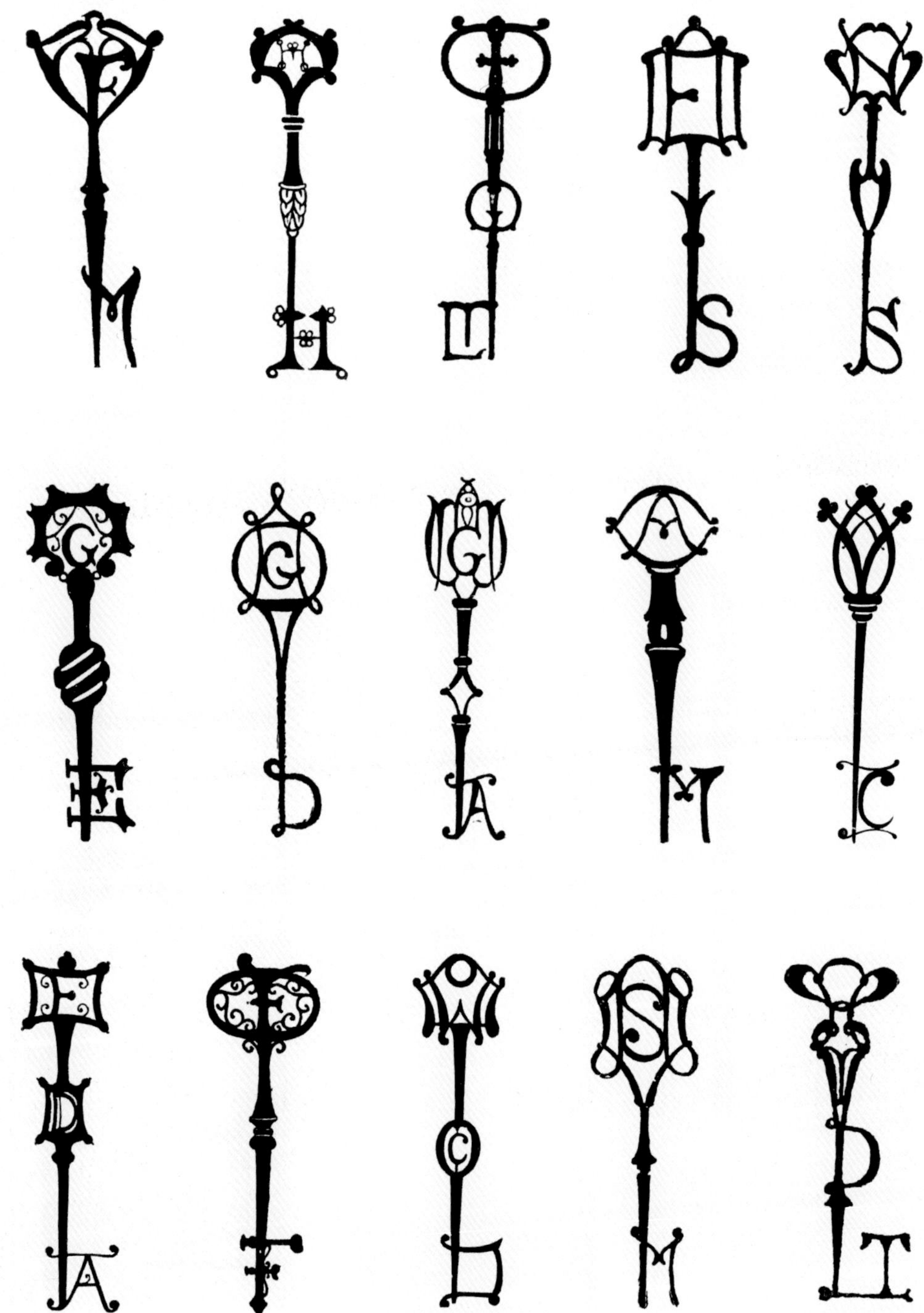

Monograms for the *Keynotes Series* (1893-96)

Beardsley designed monograms—designs bringing together the initials from a name into one design—for the authors of the Keynotes Series. The monogram on the top left, for instance, combines an F and an M of Fiona Macleod. On the right are the two H's of Henry Harland. The one right of that is slightly more complex. On top is Φ, which signifies 'F' in the Russian alphabet and in the middle is Д, or D—this is for Fyodor Dostoyevsky. The square at the bottom of the key brings together the L and the M of the translator Lena Milman.

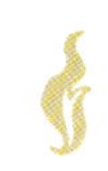

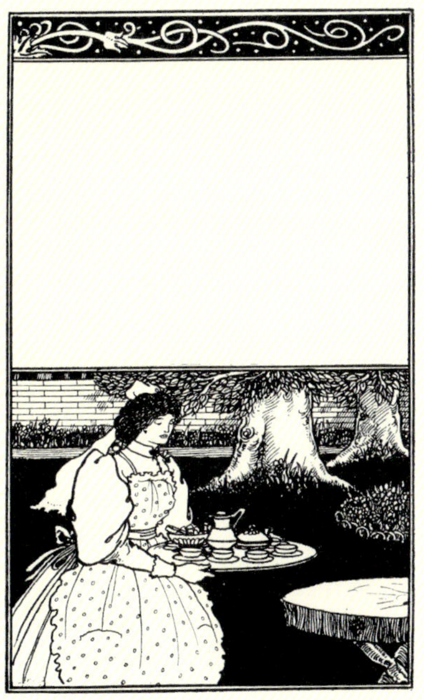

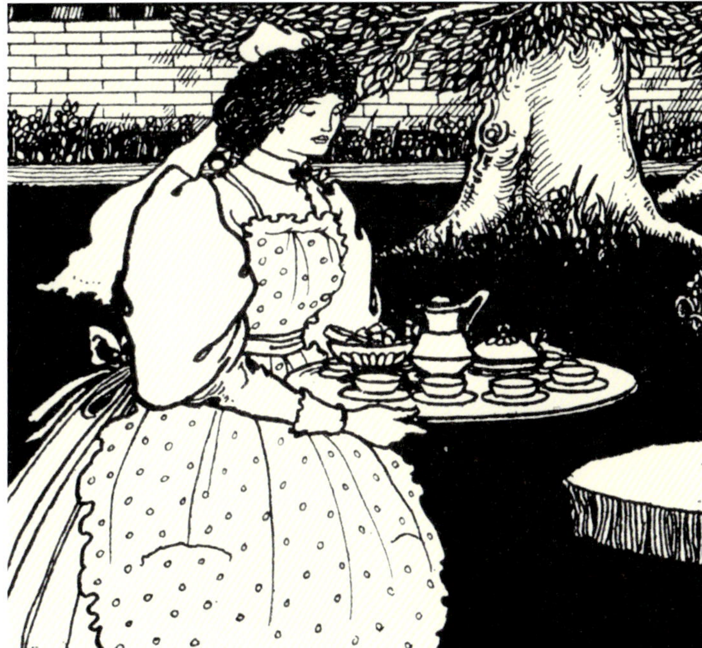

The British Barbarians, 1895

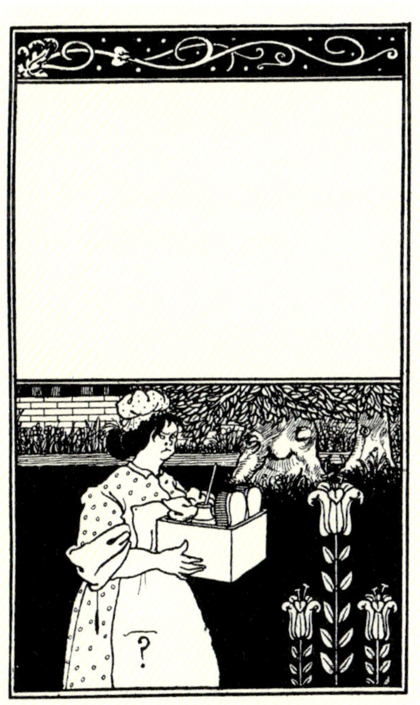

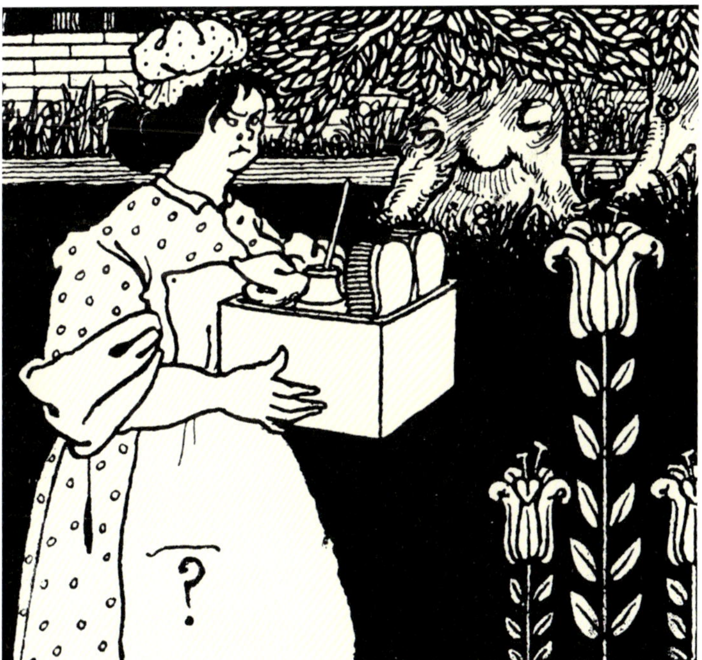

The Barbarous Britishers, 1895

Cover Design for the *Keynotes Series*

The upper design was released as the twenty-first volume in the Keynotes series, while the lower is Beardsley's parody of the first. In the top picture, a maid is placing a tea set out on a table, while in the lower one, a maid with a strange face is carrying instead a box. The tree has transformed into some kind of malevolent spirit, while the table has been replaced by suspicious-looking flowers (Beardsley's signature mark in floral form).

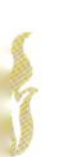

Platonic Affections, 1895

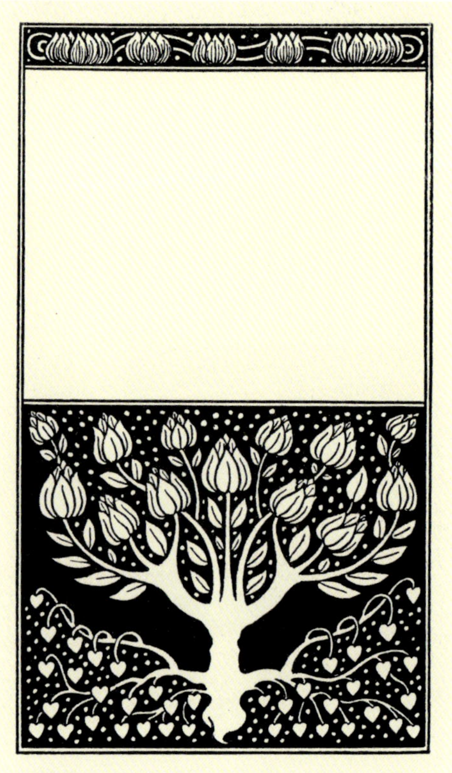

Yellow and White, 1895

The Three Impostors, 1895

The Girl From the Farm, 1895

At The First Corner, 1895

Women's Tragedies, 1894

Discords, 1894

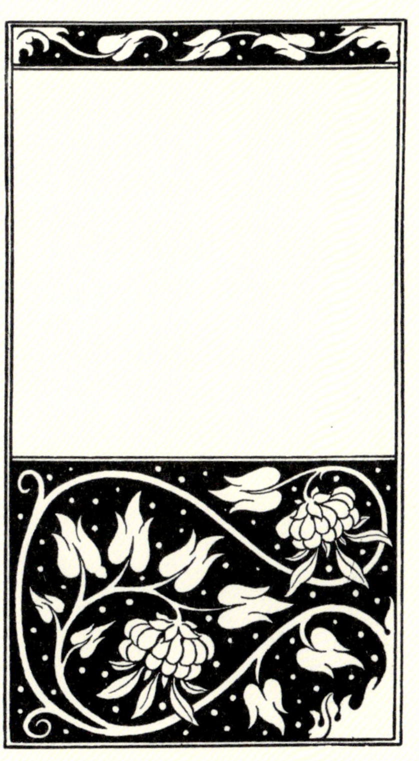

Monochromes, 1895

5. 1895: The Year of the Wilde Scandal

Having completed the editing work for Volume Five of *The Yellow Book*, Harland set out for Paris. It was just at that time that Oscar Wilde was arrested, with a yellow book under one arm.

Knowing of the scandal Wilde was embroiled in, John Lane attempted to sever ties with him. There were many rumours about the homosexual relationships that Wilde was having with young men, including Sir Alfred Douglas, or Bosie as he was often known.

Bosie's father, the Marquess of Queensberry, alleged that Wilde had seduced his son, while Wilde sued the Marquess for libel, and thus the affair was played out on a public stage and the trial widely reported. When Wilde lost, his friend, Robert Ross advised him to flee to France immediately, but instead Wilde loitered indecisively in the Cadogan Hotel with Bosie. It was there that he was arrested, and escorted off, yellow book still under one arm.

In this way, *The Yellow Book* came to be connected with the scandal, and the public came pouring into its editing department on Vigo Street, demanding that such an immoral magazine should be shut down immediately—although in fact the yellow book that Wilde was carrying was not the magazine, but a French novel with a yellow cover: Pierre Louÿs' *Aphrodite*.

Neither Lane nor Harland was around at the time, and Frederick Chapman from the Bodley Head made the decision to publish Volume Five of *The Yellow Book* without any of Beardsley's illustrations. Beardsley was subsequently expelled from the magazine. Ironically enough, although *The Yellow Book* had purportedly severed ties with Wilde, it was the Wilde scandal which sunk it. There were nine more issues published after Beardsley's expulsion before it folded. The only time that Beardsley had worked with Wilde was for *Salome*, but in the public mind, the two were indelibly linked, and there was no avoiding the downfall that was his destiny.

In despair, Beardsley wandered the streets of London. In spring 1895, immediately after being fired from *The Yellow Book*, he had visited a flat in Fountain Court near Temple Bar, close to the entrance to the City of London, where Irish poet William Butler Yeats lived with the critic Arthur Symons. Yeats had set up a society of poets in 1891. The members of said society were often to be found in The Cheshire Cheese, close to Temple Bar, with critic Edmund Gosse and poet Lionel Johnson often stopping by. Arthur Symons, who was studying the French symbolists, was attempting to set up a new magazine, and decided to try and involve Beardsley.

Owing to an amendment to British law in 1885, all homosexual acts between men had become illegal. Oscar Wilde was found guilty of sodomy and gross indecency, and sentenced to two years' hard labour. In other words, until 1885, homosexuality hadn't been clearly defined as illegal. This sudden change to the law is explained by the fact that during the 1870s and 1880s, homosexuality had become 'a social issue'.

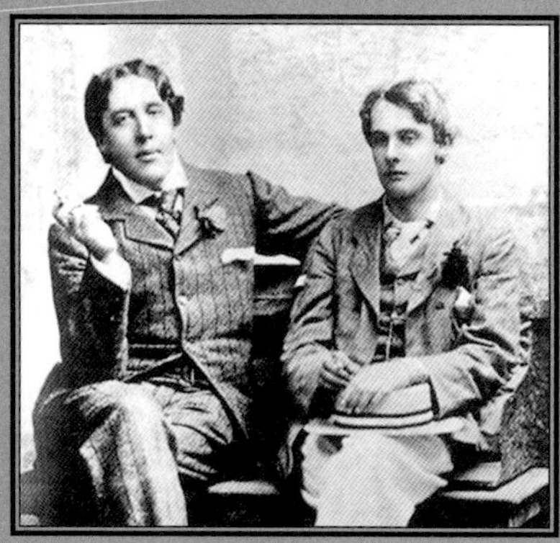

Oscar Wilde and Alfred Douglas

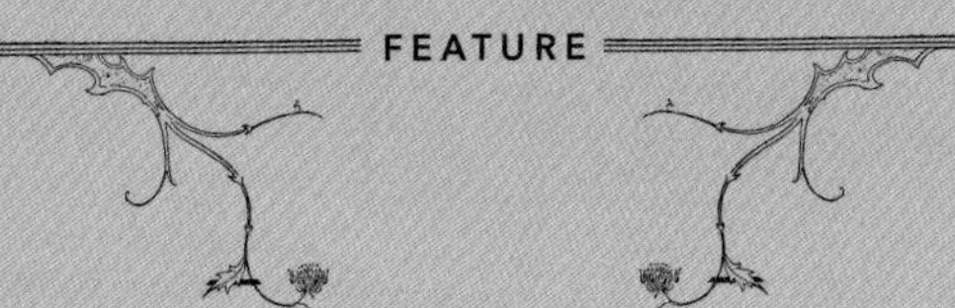

Homosexuality in Fin-de-Siècle Britain

Since Michel Foucault, it has become common to think of the homosexual as a fin-de-siècle invention. Needless to say, homosexuality had existed since antiquity, but criminalizing it caused public aversion towards homosexuality to grow, and also give birth to an underground homosexual culture. Which is to say, the more rigorously something is prohibited, the greater the interest in it grows, and it soon morphs into a forbidden pleasure.

The Victorian Age is seen as a Janus-faced society, where there were strict divisions between public and private, external and internal realms and selves. The external, public realm was male-dominated society, while the woman represented the private and internal. Women were denied entrance from clubs, which admitted only men. Thus the number of places where men lived together in close contact—public schools, universities, clubs and so on— grew, and many of these became hotbeds of homosexual acts. The higher the society, the greater the extent to which this double-sided aspect was protected. In the upper echelons of Victorian British society, one was permitted to lead a life where one maintained a moral public visage while acting in a licentious way behind closed doors, where homosexuality was also permitted.

This meant that although the Victorians were used to acting as though sexuality didn't exist, prostitution was in fact rife, and within high society, people didn't bat an eyelid at homosexuality. Oscar Wilde would take handsome young boys to stay at the Savoy Hotel, and his relationship with Alfred Douglas was there for anybody to see. He simply didn't believe that he would be punished for it.

Indeed, if Wilde hadn't decided to sue Douglas's father, the Marquess of Queensberry, he may well not have been convicted.

John Gray and Mark-André Raffalovich (p.258) who took care of the ailing Beardsley in his final days, were a gay couple, and Arthur Symons, the editor of *The Savoy*, was also homosexual. What about Beardsley, we might ask? It seems probable that he was not. But what we can say for certain was that he was fascinated by all kinds of all kinds of love and eros that defied normality, accepted all human mysteries, and was probably in some sense homosexual within the world of his painterly imagination.

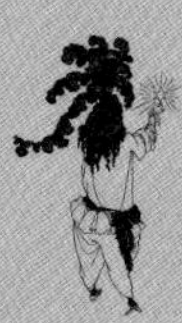

1896: The Year of The Savoy

Leonard Smithers, who ran a book shop on Arundel Street where he also sold pornography, decided to start a publishing company also. Planning a magazine to rival *The Yellow Book*, he enlisted Arthur Symons to help him. Symons, who had studied in France and been inspired by symbolists such as Paul Verlaine and Mallarmé, was part of a poets' society with Yeats, and close to the biologist Havelock Ellis, with whom he also shared a flat.

Smithers and Symons decided to invite Beardsley, who had just been kicked out of *The Yellow Book*, on board their new magazine project. Unlike the moralistic John Lane, Smithers had a taste for anything erotic and underground, and had been involved in releasing Richard Francis Burton's translation of *The Book of the Thousand Nights and a Night*.

Beardsley perked up with a new project on his hands, and set about creating illustrations both for the new magazine and for the book he had begun writing, *The Story of Venus and Tannhauser*. The new periodical's name, The Savoy, was Beardsley's idea, and was of course named after the stylish hotel that had been opened between The Strand and the Thames Embankment.

At this time Symonds was in Dieppe, on the Normandy coast, so Beardsley went out there to discuss the magazine. At the end of the nineteenth century, a lot of young bohemian artists and writers in search of a liberated lifestyle moved to the Normandy coast. Dieppe, in particular, was a resort town where young British authors congregated. Marcel Proust had also come to the Normandy coast. It seems worth mentioning a few points about the relationship between Beardsley and Proust on the coast at the end of the century.

During this visit, Beardsley drew a picture of three women on a Dieppe beach wearing frilly swimming costumes. The mood of the picture is light-hearted and fun, and rather unlike the pictures usually created by Beardsley, has a certain wholesomeness to it. Smithers would occasionally visit Dieppe also, causing problems for the people around him by bringing along obese courtesans in extravagant clothes.

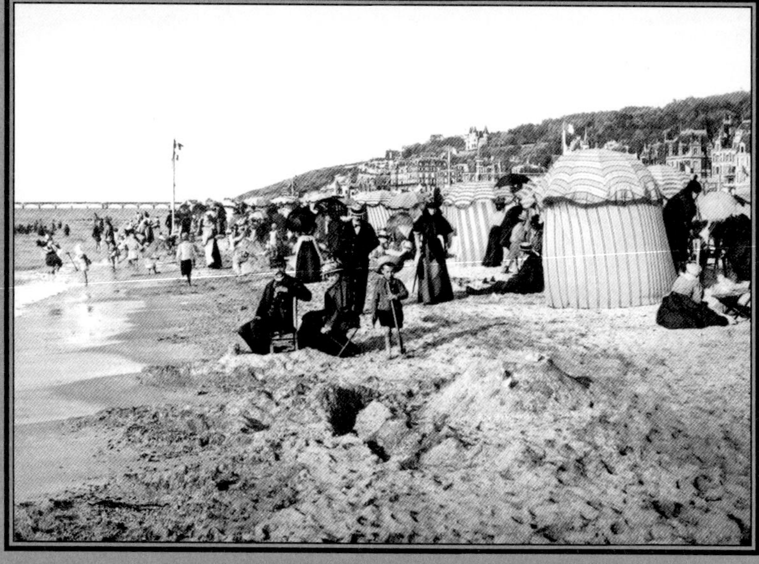

A Normandy beach at the end of the 19th century.

Come autumn, Beardsley began working in Paris, creating illustrations for *The Rape of The Lock* that Smithers was going to publish. In winter he returned to London, where he drew a sample image for the first issue of *The Savoy*, with pierrots on a stage announcing the magazine's release. However this cover illustration ended up having to be redrawn, when Smithers requested that he delete part where a cherubim was urinating on *The Yellow Book* (p.119). Beardsley's pictures always contained such kinds of mischief, and his publishers had to be constantly keeping a careful eye out.

Thanks to this revision, the magazine was delayed in going to print, and although the inaugural issue was slated for a Christmas release, it eventually made it into the world at the start of January 1896. To celebrate its launch, a party was held at the New Lyric Club. Beardsley attended, but seemed in ill spirits. It was clear that his condition was deteriorating, and his end was drawing near.

In the second issue of *The Savoy*, chapters one to three of Beardsley's book, *The Story of Venus and Tannhauser*, was published under the title 'Under the Hill'. The text for the fourth chapter was also published, but the illustrations weren't completed in time. Beardsley no longer had the strength to continue any further, and thus the story remained incomplete. After Beardsley's death, Smithers released a book featuring the sections that hadn't yet been published, but even so the work remained unfinished.

In April 1896, the second edition of *The Savoy* was released. The issue included a title page and list of contents by Beardsley, as well as one of the nine illustrations he had created for *The Rape of the Lock* which Smithers would be publishing. This had been created the previous year, and is one of Beardsley's late-period masterpieces. Even Whistler, who didn't rate Beardsley very highly, was said to have praised it.

When the second edition went to print, Beardsley left London and travelled to Brussels to recuperate. He planned at that time to create illustrations for Perrault's *Cinderella*, but unfortunately that plan never came to fruition. I would have much liked to have seen Beardsley's take on *Cinderella*.

While in Brussels, Beardsley created a poem and picture entitled 'The Ballad of a Barber' for Volume Three of *The Savoy*. However his illness subsequently got worse and he became unable to get out of bed.

It was at this time that Beardsley made friends with Marc-André Raffalovich (see p.258). Raffalovich was a close friend of John Gray, said to be the model for Wilde's *A Picture of Dorian Grey*. Gray was a passionate convert to the Catholic faith. Concerned about Beardsley's health, as was Raffalovich, he advised him to convert to Catholicism.

Beardsley created the pen drawing 'The Mirror of Love' for Raffalovich's poetry collection, *The Thread and the Path*. Raffalovich was the son of a Russian Jewish banker. He had come to London from Paris where he had become intimate with John Gray, and had converted to Catholicism at Gray's suggestion. He respected Beardsley, generously provided him with financial support, and recommended his conversion to Catholicism to guarantee him spiritual salvation.

Beardsley was affected by Raffalovich's suggestion, but felt he couldn't abandon the job of drawing the erotic illustrations for Aristophanes' *Lysistrata* which he'd been commissioned with by Smithers.

Despite the poor critical reviews of the first and second issues of *The Savoy*, it had sold well, and Smithers had decided to make the publication monthly, releasing the third edition in July. This was an ill-conceived plan, because not only was there insufficient time to collect manuscripts but also because Beardsley, on whom the magazine's reputation rested, was in such bad health that he was unable to create work for the magazine.

Beardsley left London once again, moving to Epsom, known for its horseracing track, and then to Bournemouth, a seaside resort town.

For the fourth edition of *The Savoy*, only the cover and the list of contents featured Beardsley's illustrations. Yet, despite his illness, he managed to create eight illustrations for *Lysistrata* inspired by the images on Grecian urns while in his hotel in the resort town of Bournemouth. These pictures were so lewd that Smithers was unable to publish them generally, and decided to publish them as a limited edition.

At the time, Beardsley was also trying to produce illustrations for *Ali Baba and the Forty Thieves*. I can't help but think how wonderful if would have been if Beardsley had had the time to draw his version of the world of the Arabian Nights.

Beardsley moved from Epson to Bournemouth. His hometown of Brighton would have fitted the bill as a seaside resort town, but it was already a very popular tourist destination, and so Beardsley chose Bournemouth, further to the West, which was quieter and whose air was clearer.

The fifth issue of *The Savoy* in September featured 'The Woman in White', a sketch drawn previously by Beardsley. The sixth issue in October featured a new work, 'The Death of a Pierrot'. The image seemed to foretell both Beardsley's death and that of the periodical.

The Savoy came to an end with its eighth edition in December. This issue took the form of an anthology of everything Beardsley had created so far, and featured fourteen of Beardsley's drawings.

Indeed, *The Savoy* was so much a periodical for Beardsley that one wonders if it wouldn't have been more appropriately named 'The Beardsley'. Of course it contained many intriguing works of fiction and non-fiction, but without Beardsley's pictures, it wouldn't have had anything like the allure that it did.

While lamenting the end of The Savoy, Beardsley began expressing the wish to publish a collection which brought together all the work he had produced up to that point, and began selecting the drawings it would contain. This was eventually released by Smithers as *A Book of Fifty Drawings*.

Beardsley feared that his death was imminent. When would he become able to stop creating work? He confessed his fear to Raffalovich, and sought refuge in Catholicism. He also felt anxious at being left alone in the lonely seaside resort of Bournemouth, far away from London. What was going on in London? What had become of the pictures he'd sent? How was the editing coming along for his collection? These were the thoughts that filled his mind.

He had been commissioned by Smithers to produce the cover and illustrations for a complication of Ernest Dowson's poems and his one-act play, *The Pierrot of the Minute*. Beardsley lamented that he had to work on such trifling projects, and produced a cover design comprising just two curved lines, tracing the 'Y' of an indignant 'why?' (see p.100). However, looking back on it now, we are stunned by the striking beauty of these simple lines.

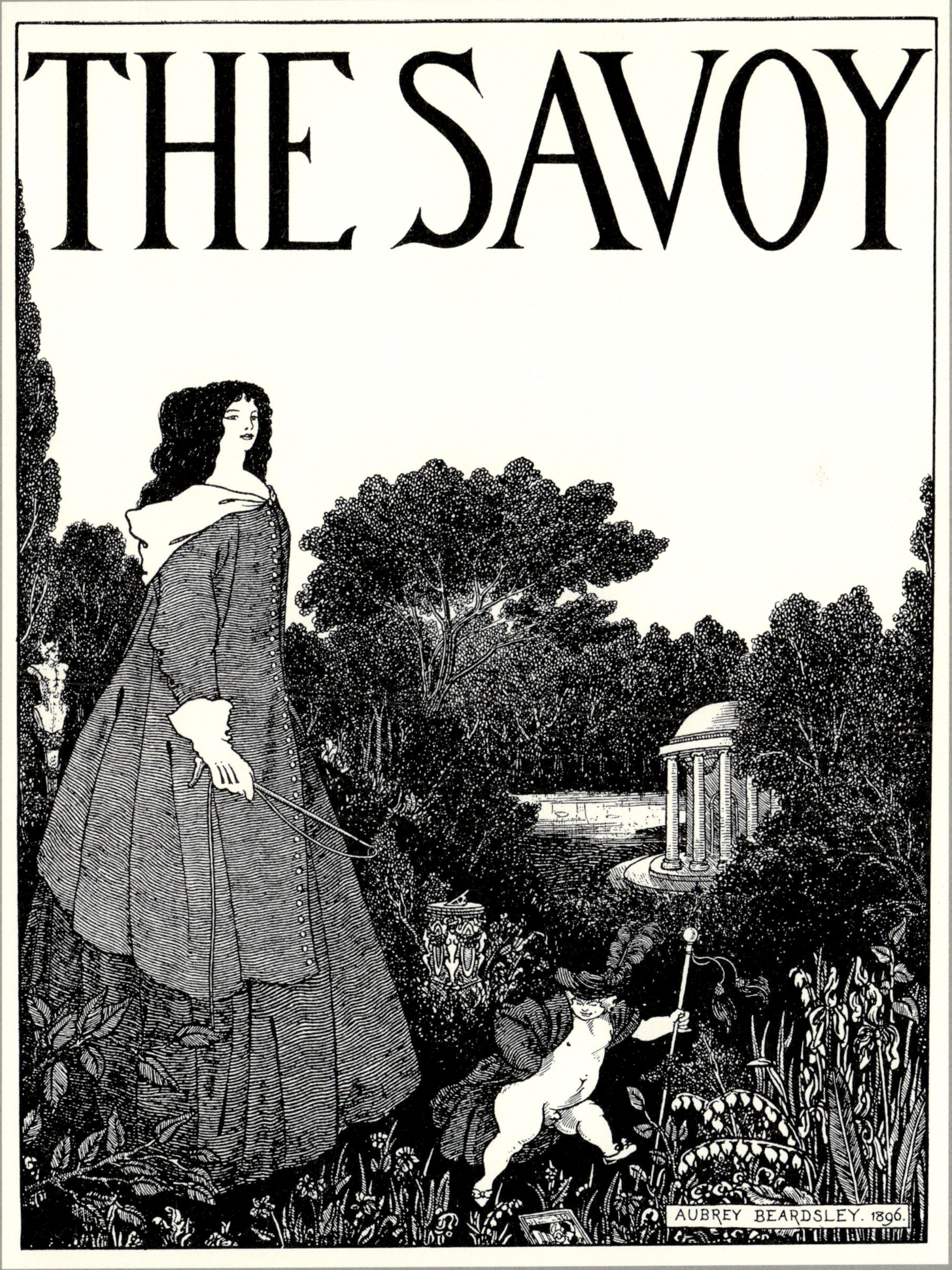

THE SAVOY

Proposed design for the front cover of the first issue of *The Savoy*, featuring a cherubim urinating on a copy of *The Yellow Book*.

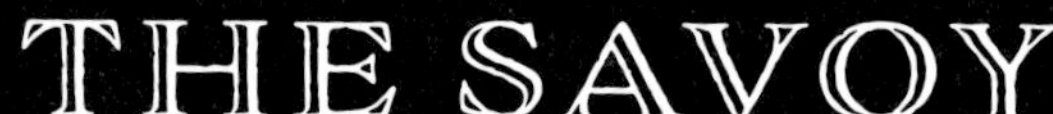

First published in January, 1896
UK (Leonard Smithers, London)

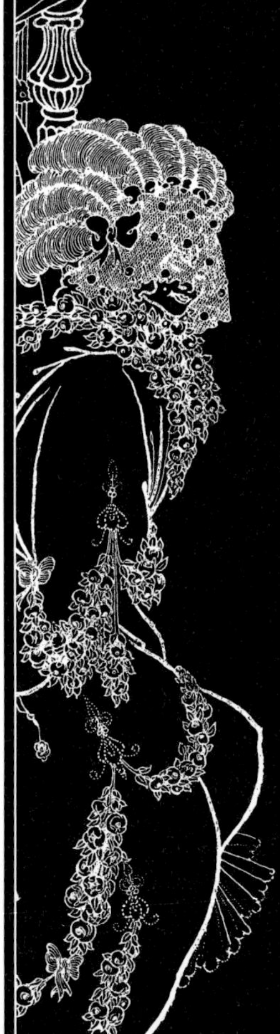

A Fitting Finale to the Nineteenth Century

Beardsley's next project after being expunged from *The Yellow Book* was *The Savoy*, a magazine he created with Edward Smithers, who also published pornographic material. The literary side of the magazine was edited by Arthur Symons, a literary critic who was seen as something of a heretic. The first issue of *The Savoy* was published in January 1896, and its final and eighth issue in December of that year. When Beardsley's condition worsened sufficiently as to make him incapable of producing work, *The Savoy* also folded. Indeed, the periodical was the vessel for Beardsley's final burst of creative light. If we situate his work for *The Yellow Book* as constituting his avant-garde phase, then we can see the work he did for *The Savoy* as belonging to his later, mature phase. Here Beardsley attempted to give everything that he had, also publishing poems and fiction he had penned. Despite the gravity of his illness, the pictures he created at this time were both joyful and precise. We see more open-spirited humour and human intimacy, and the depiction of people's expressions growing increasingly rich, as if Beardsley was feeling affection towards the world he knew he would soon have to part with.

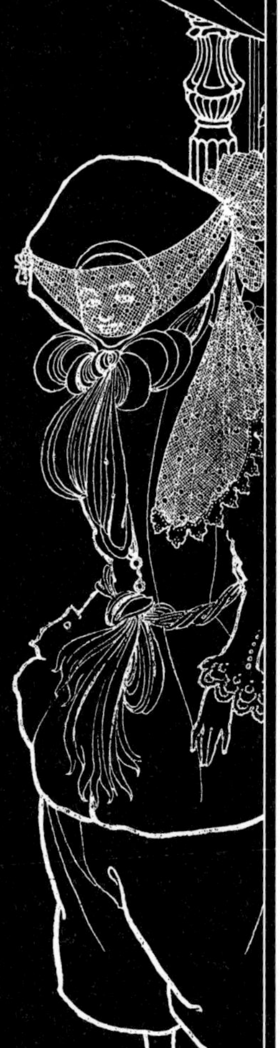

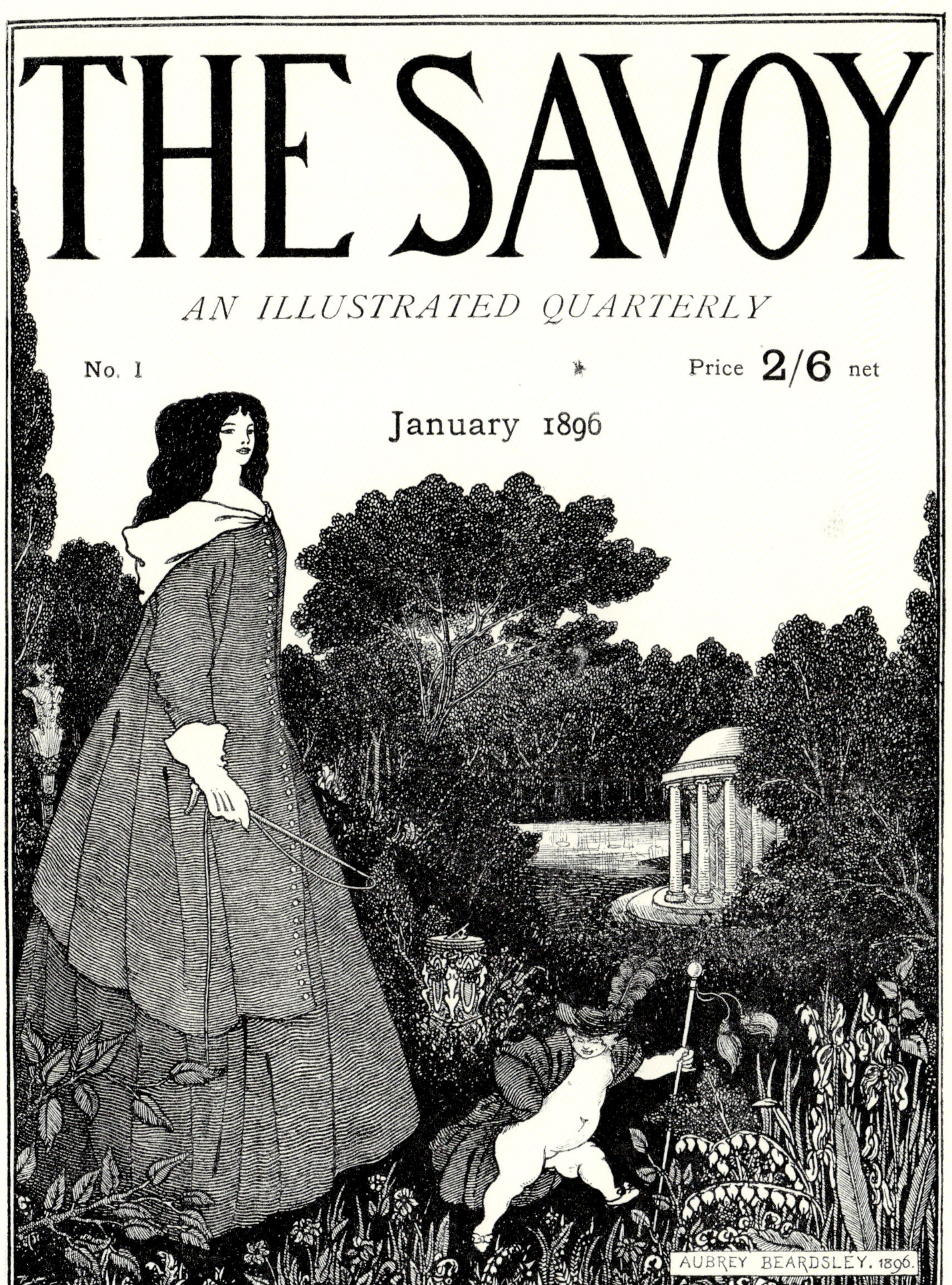

Cover to Volume I

A woman walks with a whip in hand. We can see a circular shrine to love in the centre of a grove of trees, such as is often found in European gardens. A putto is showing the woman the way. In the original drawing there was a small protrusion at the putto's crotch, and he was urinating on a copy of *The Yellow Book* drawn below him (see p.119). George Augustus Moore, who was involved in the editing, objected to this depiction saying that it was too explicit, and thus the protrusion and magazine were deleted. Leaving aside the putto, as a whole the picture has a calm, peaceful feeling to it, as if the pair were strolling through Paradise.

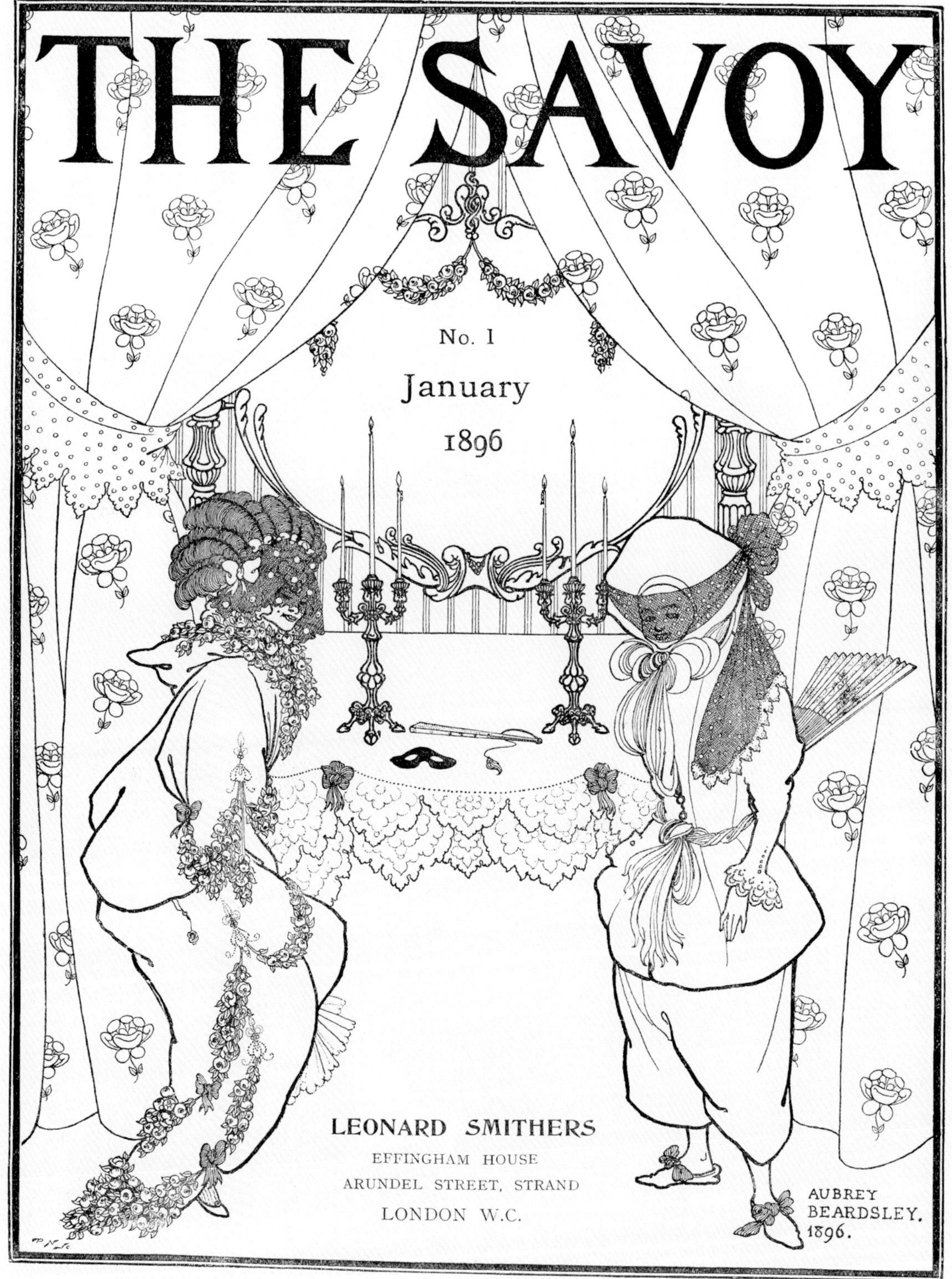

Title Page to Volume I

In this picture festooned with lavish, detailed ornamentation, we see Beardsley's latter-period style in its full glory. In true Beardsley style, the outlines of the two pantalooned figures standing on either side of the grave contain hidden suggestive elements. The knees of the women on the left resemble pair of breasts, and there are other risqué shapes scattered here and there. The shape encased in a baroque-style cartouche also looks like a bottom. In any case, just examining all the details one by one brings the viewer much in the way of entertainment, and elicits many a sigh of admiration at the extent of Beardsley's inventive powers.

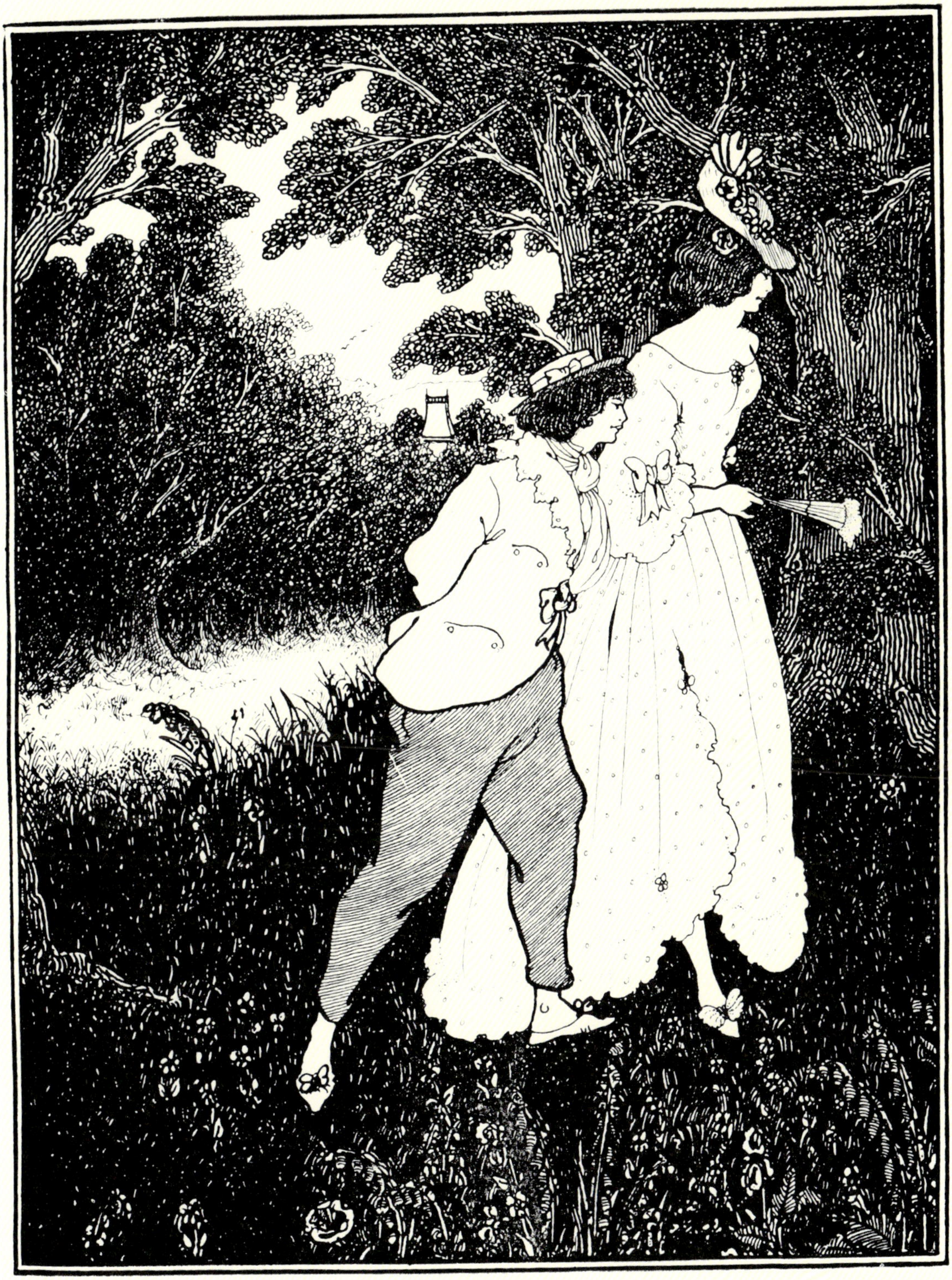

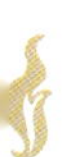

Volume I: 'The Three Musicians'

This drawing was created as an illustration for Beardsley's poem by the same name. The poem tells the story of three musicians are strolling through the forest, with the elderly pianist lagging slightly behind the others. The young composer wishes to confess his love to the young soprano, but hesitates. Here Beardsley draws an image which is a fitting accompaniment to a straightforward love poem. Perhaps he is reminiscing on the days of his adolescence. The detailed depiction of the forest makes one think that his Pre-Raphaelite days have returned. The only woman that Beardsley remained close to throughout his life was his older sister Mabel, so perhaps this picture served as a portrait of Mabel and Aubrey's youth.

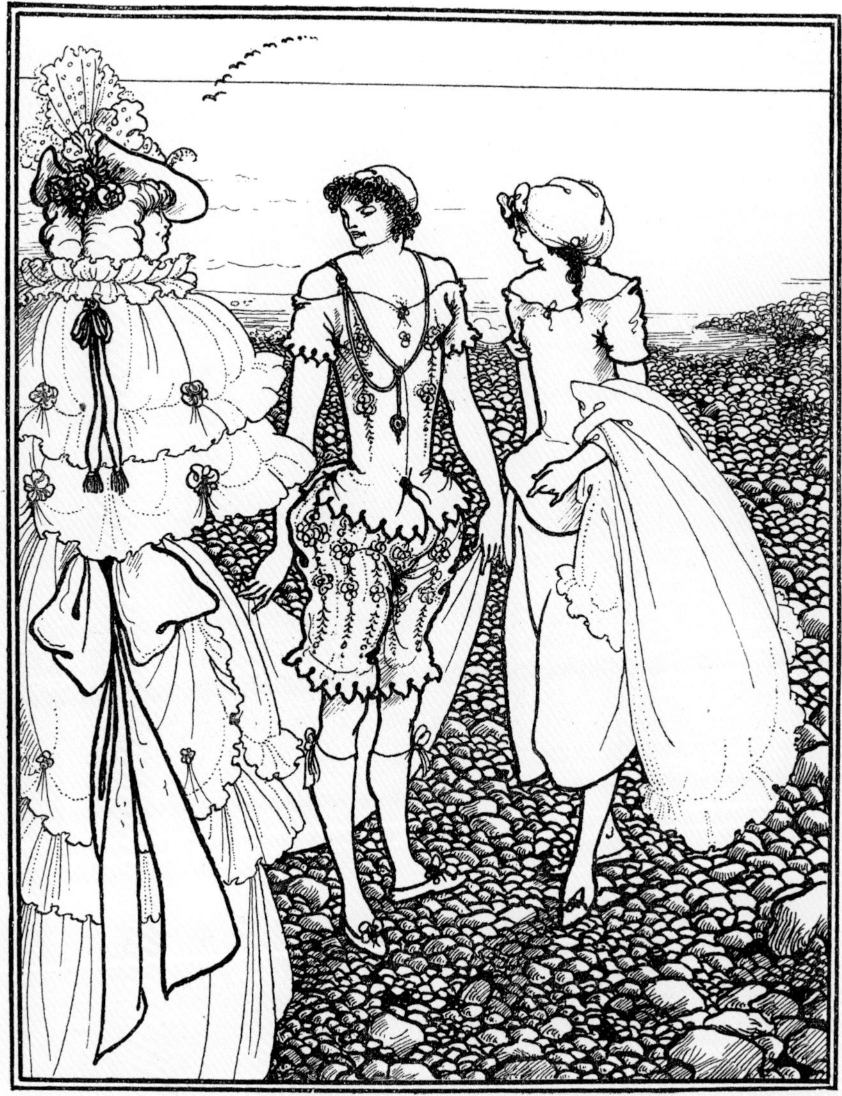

costume, only a grotesque and shapeless image, all in pits and protuberances, for which Nature should be ashamed to accept responsibility. Complete nudity, there is no doubt, has its charm, though of a somewhat primitive kind;

Volume I: 'The Bathers at Dieppe'

This was an illustration for Arthur Symons' essay, 'Dieppe 1895', showing bathers in rather traditional bathing suits. The second half of the twentieth century witnessed the rise of the seaside resort. Brighton was one of the earliest bathing spots to emerge, and so Beardsley would have seen many of these kinds of scenes while growing up. Eventually, the Brits created new resort areas on France's Normandy coastline. One of those was Dieppe, which Beardsley himself had visited. Beardsley was one of the first to record the practice of sea bathing which took off at the end of the century.

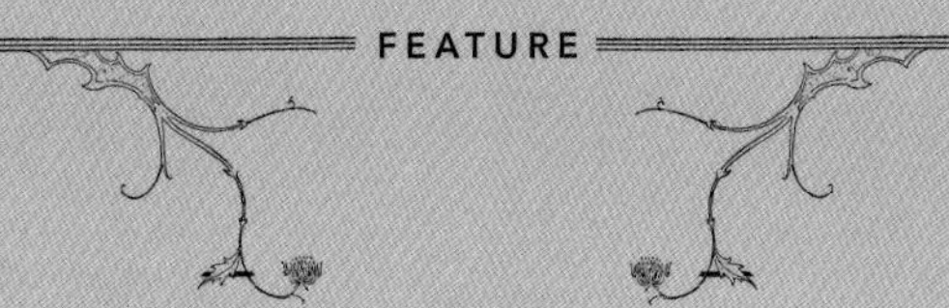

BEARDSLEY'S BEACHES

At the fin de siècle, the seaside was a new cultural hub. Young artists fled the big cities and created artist enclaves by the sea known as 'Bohemia', where they were free to live their lives free from the constraints of Victorian morality.

Into the late nineteenth century, resorts began cropping up on the coastline, to which visitors began to flock. The British were the first to develop these kinds of resorts, and Brighton on England's south coast was one of the lead spots. Such resorts went onto become so popular that the British started crossing the Channel, moving onto France's coastline. Enclaves of British artists appeared on France's coast—first in Normandy, in the north, and then in Brittany. Dieppe, on the west side of the Normandy coast, was one of the first French resorts to be established. It was followed by Trouville-sur-Mer, Deauville, and Cabourg.

Seaside resorts flourished first as spots to recuperate from illnesses such as tuberculosis, and then as tourist destinations where to spend one's free time. Following from Normandy's popularity, seaside resorts on France's Mediterranean coast began to gain favour, with Cannes and Nice attracting many visitors.

Growing up in Brighton, Beardsley had observed the carnival-like atmosphere of a resort town thronging with tourists and those coming for rest and recuperation. Seaside resorts had casinos, and come the season, various shows and circuses would sprout up. Beardsley was based in London, but he had to go to the sea frequently to recuperate from his tuberculosis. As time went on, he spent more of his time coming and going between London and Dieppe or Menton on the Mediterranean.

Resorts on the French coast attracted not only tourists and those recuperating from illness. They also served as a place of respite for those who found it hard to remain in London. Those who couldn't let themselves go publically in the big smoke would escape to the French coast in order to do so; those who had excited a scandal in London took shelter in France. Dieppe became a hideout for homosexual men of letters, including Oscar Wilde and Arthur Symons.

Thinking about the significance of those kinds of beaches, we might recall that Marcel Proust also spent time in Cabourg on the Normandy coast. He was born one year earlier than Beardsley in 1871, making the two exactly the same generation. They probably never met, but perhaps they passed one another by on a Normandy beach.

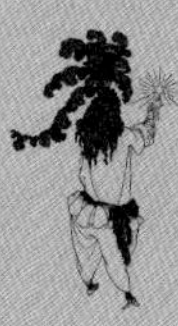

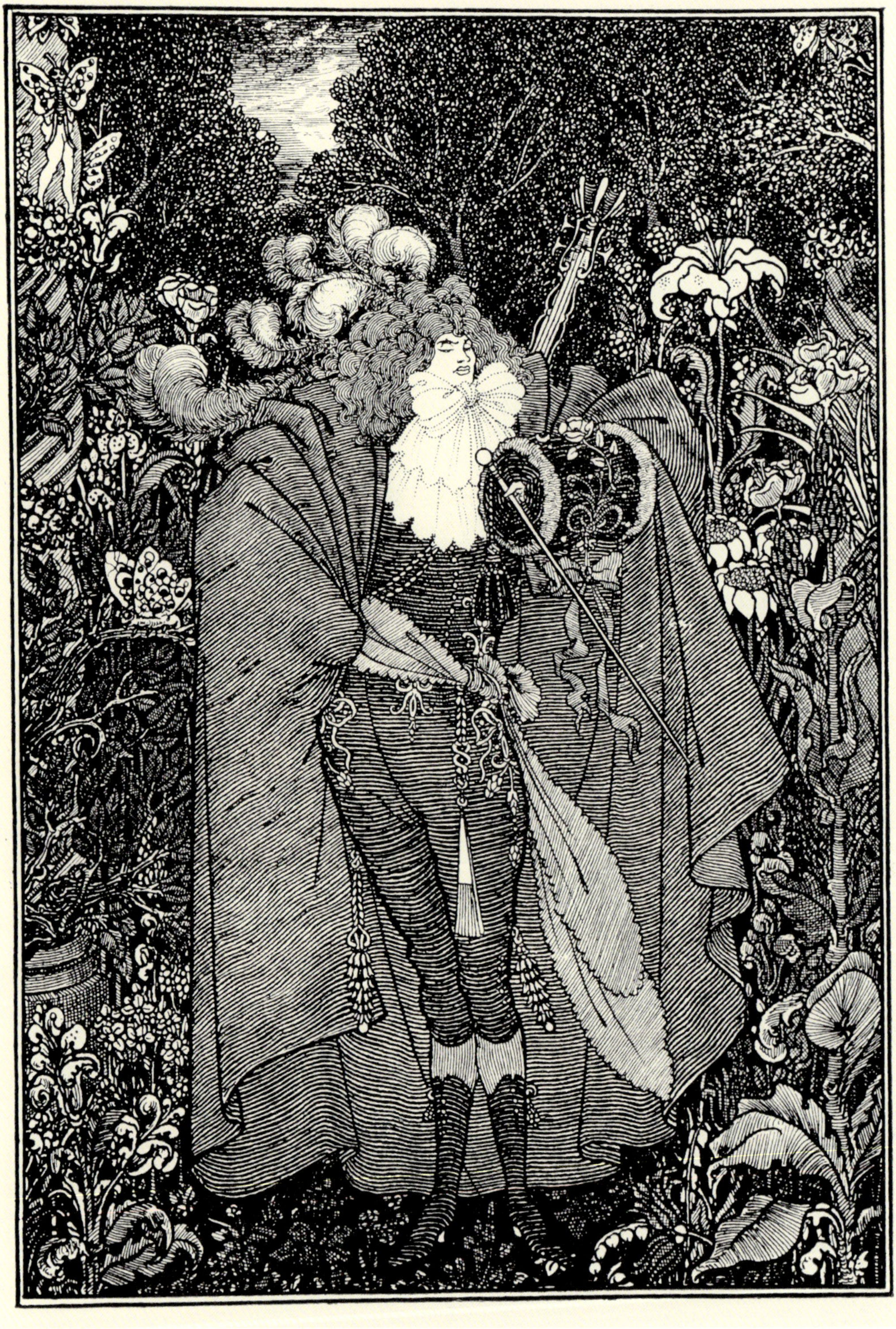

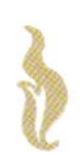

Volume I: 'The Abbé'

Another illustration from Beardsley's work *Under the Hill*, again providing a good example of Beardsley's late style, where every inch of the page is subsumed in lavish detail. The Abbé in the title is a play on Beardsley's initials, AB. Central to the picture stands Abbé Fanfreluche. This story was later reworked into *The Story of Venus and Tannhauser*, and this Abbé transformed into Tannhauser. The upper and lower sections of his body are facing different directions, creating a slightly unnatural look, but Beardsley manages to make such strange anatomical rendering seem permissible.

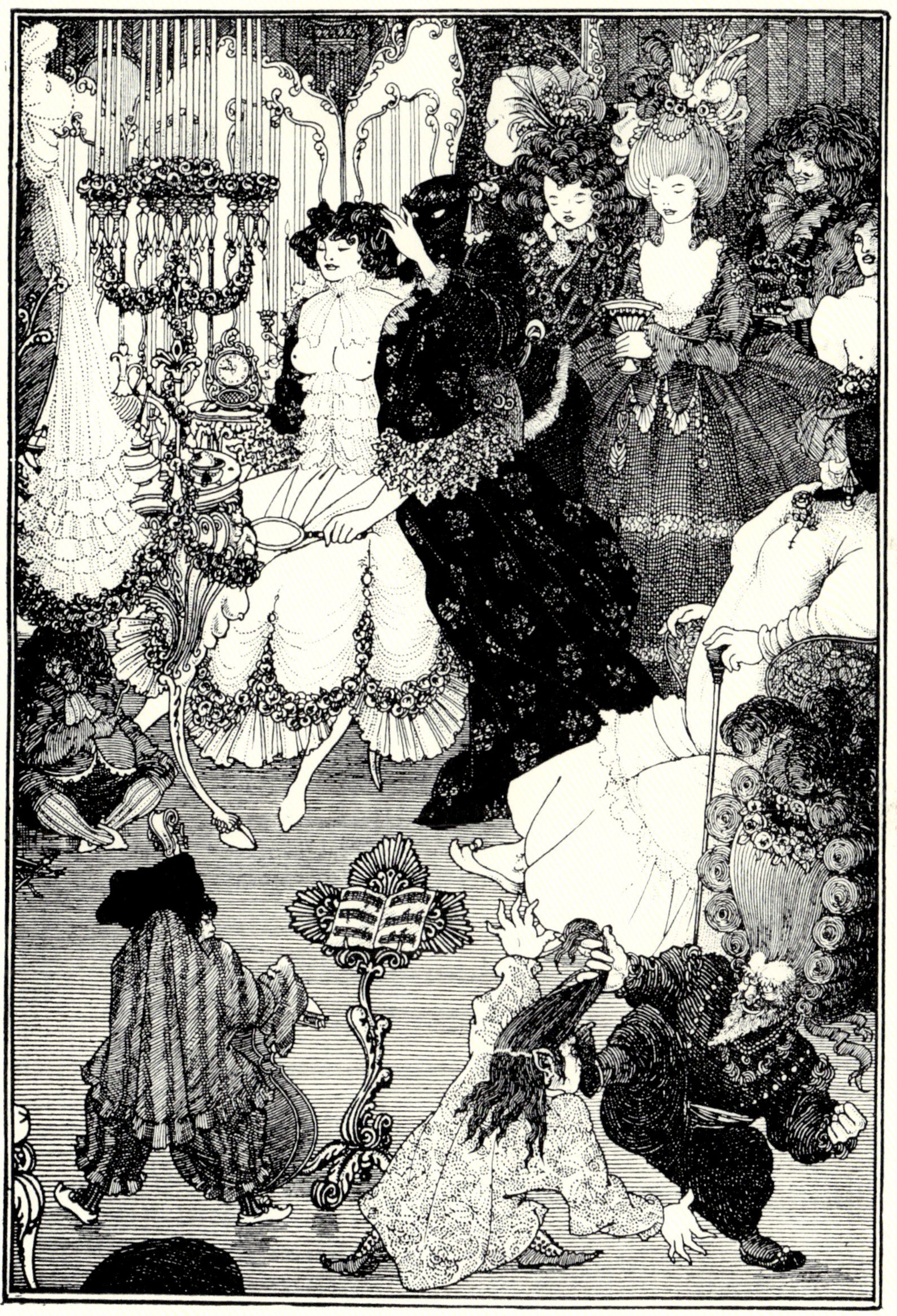

Volume I: 'Venus at her Toilet'

This is an illustration from *Under the Hill*, also known by the alternative title 'The Toilet of Helen'. The heroine of the book, Helen (or Venus). is getting dressed, surrounded by a host of servants. The picture is fearsomely intricate, and full of risqué shapes. The masked hairdresser who is curling Helen's curls is also very mysterious. Four dwarfs are rollicking around on the floor. Moreover, Helen herself cuts a strange figure, with her breasts on display, and the outline of her body suggestive of an erect phallus. Mrs Marsupial, the old woman sitting to her right, is Helen's beloved manicurist. There seems to be no end to this picture's idiosyncrasies.

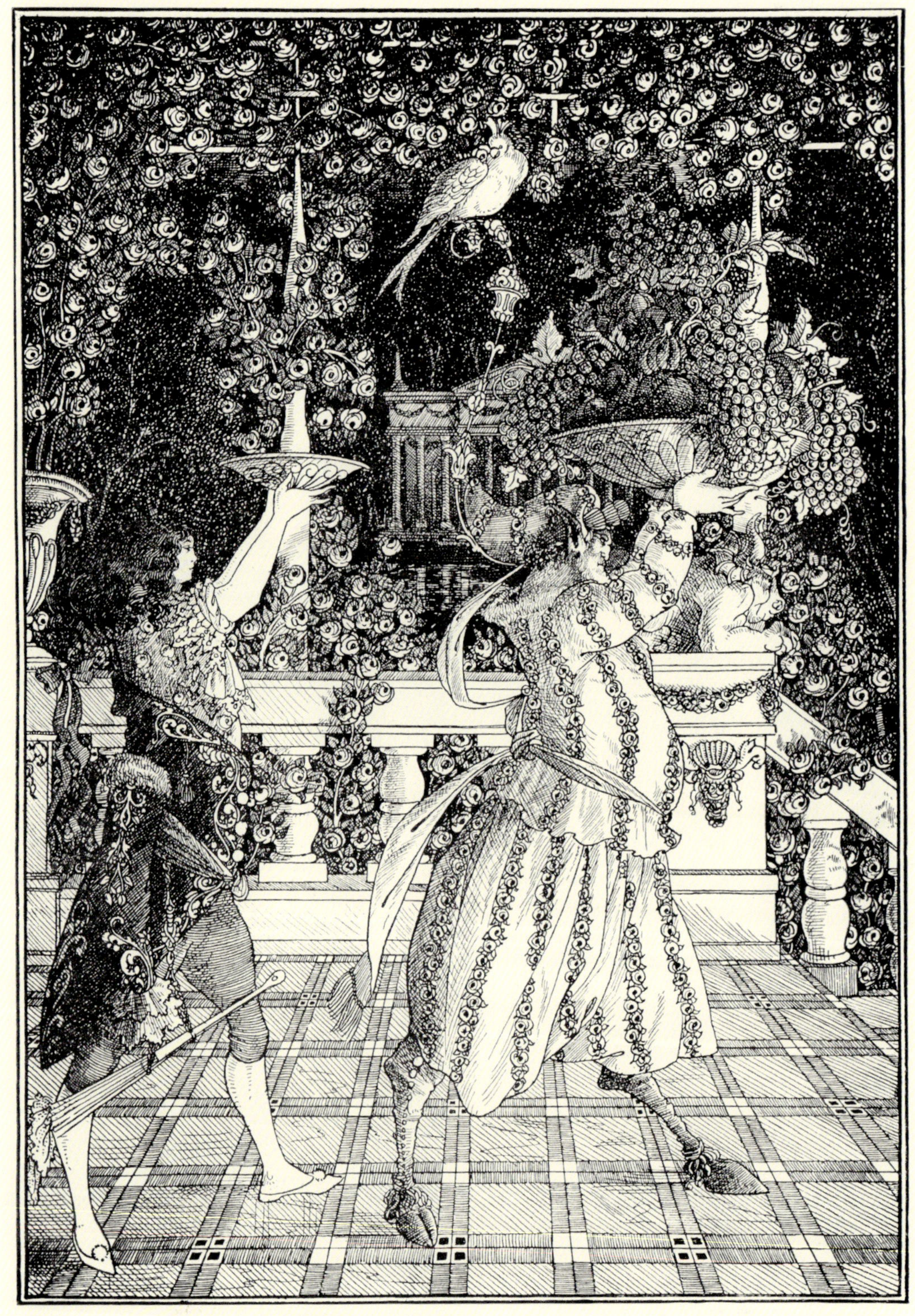

Volume I: 'The Fruit Bearers'

An illustration from *Under the Hill*, rendered in an Arabian Nights-inspired style. A lavish banquet is taking place in Venus' mansion, into which the protagonist has stumbled. In his prose, Beardsley describes in sumptuous detail a banquet prepared by a famous chef called Rambouillet. This illustration depicts a servant carrying a platter heaped with fruit. His legs are those of goats, suggesting that he is either the Greek god Dionysus, or else a satyr. Behind him, a youngster carries something that appears to be a finger bowl.

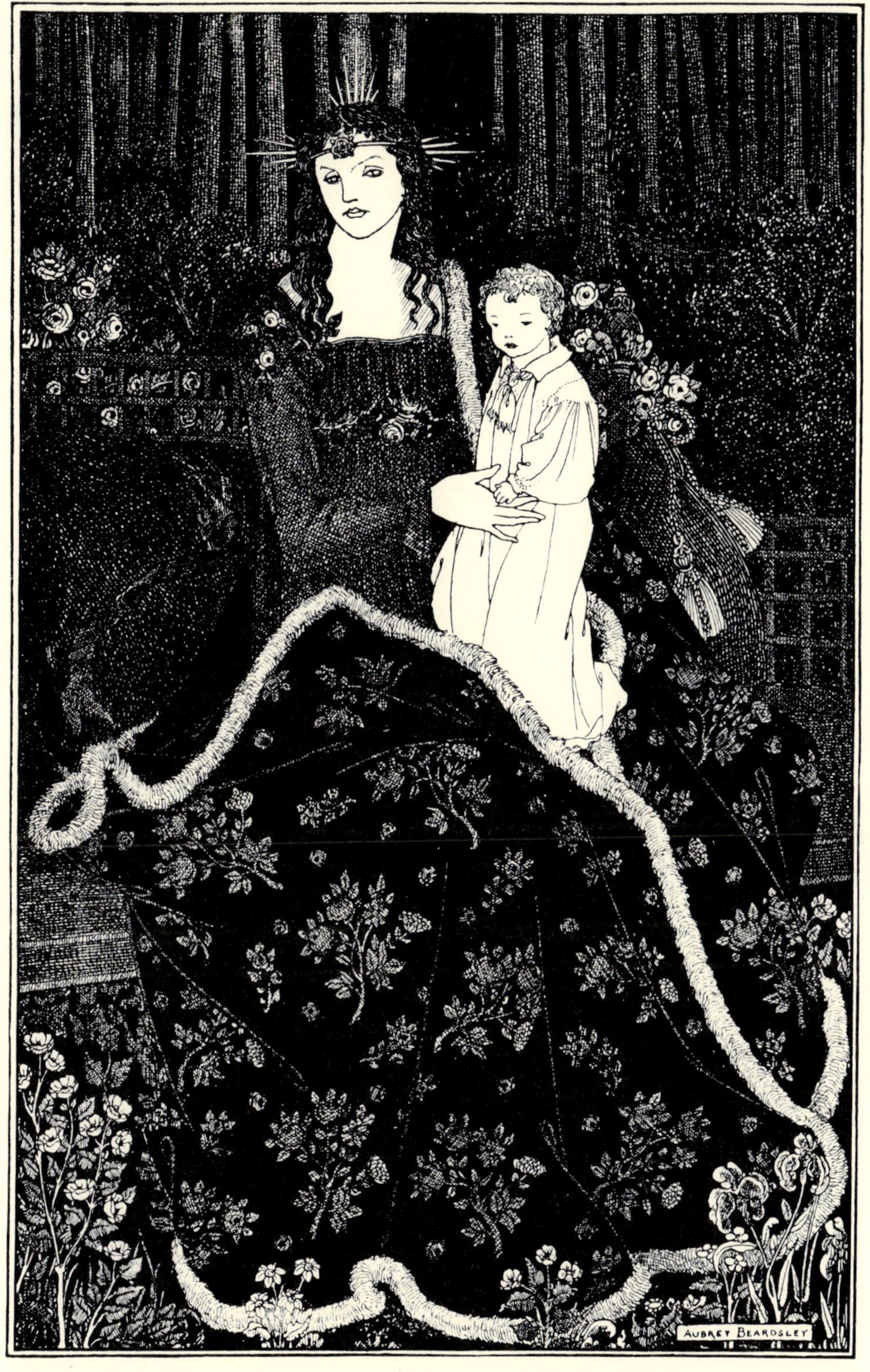

Volume I: 'A Large Christmas Card'

This Christmas card was featured at the back of the first issue, as a free gift. Rather than hinting at any hidden meanings, the picture rather offers a careful study of the Virgin and Child, which makes it a rarity among Beardsley's oeuvre. Yet we could say that the pedestal on which Mary is sat is rather an unusual shape, and features a thick, snakelike border in white that makes it look like a giant skirt. The pattern of leaves and branches owes a debt to William Morris.

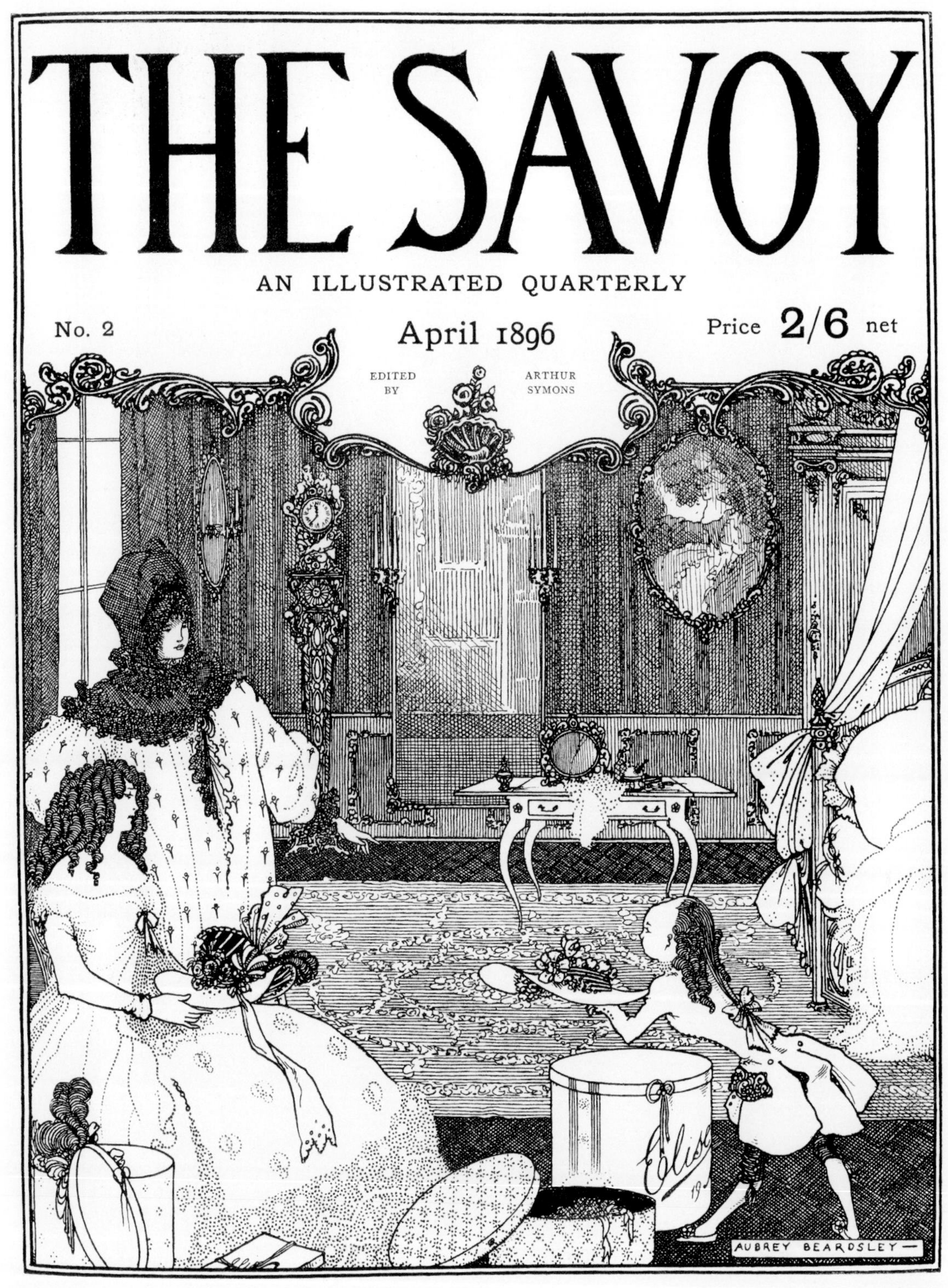

Cover to Volume II

This picture is entitled 'Choosing The New Hat'. The Rococo interior of the hat shop, where the lady is selecting a hat, is portrayed in lush detail. Demonstrating the hats is a milliner with a Chinese-style pigtail. Standing behind the lady in an oversized overall with a hood is her elder attendant. The picture uses fine, dotted lines and dense patches of straight lines, all of which exemplify Beardsley's late style.

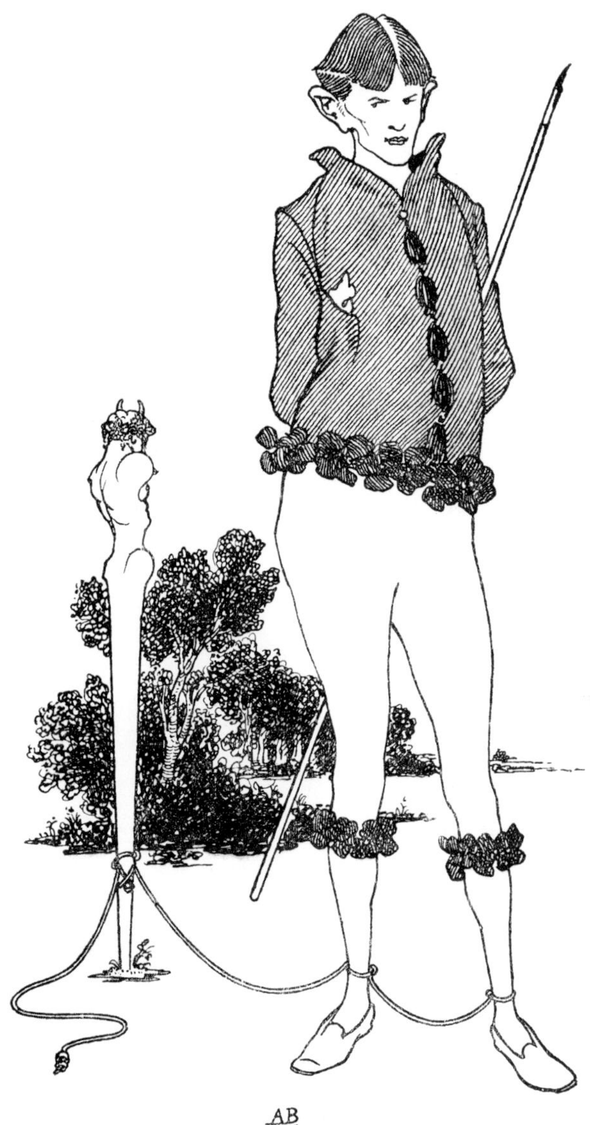

Volume II: 'Self Portrait'

Here Beardsley has pictured himself with a demonic expression. To his right stands a statue of Pan. These kinds of phallic sculptures known as herma were placed by the roadside in ancient Greece, in an analogous way to the *dōsojin*—travellers' guardian deities—found in Japan. Beardsley's feet are tied to Pan's column. In other words, Beardsley is Pan, the deity who frolics around in the forest, and his signature three-lined mark was inspired by Pan's column. In the illustration, he holds a rod like the Staff of Hermes—although in Beardsley's case, this is likely representing a pen. The row of decorations on his breast are also the points of his marks: ink blots, or drips of semen.

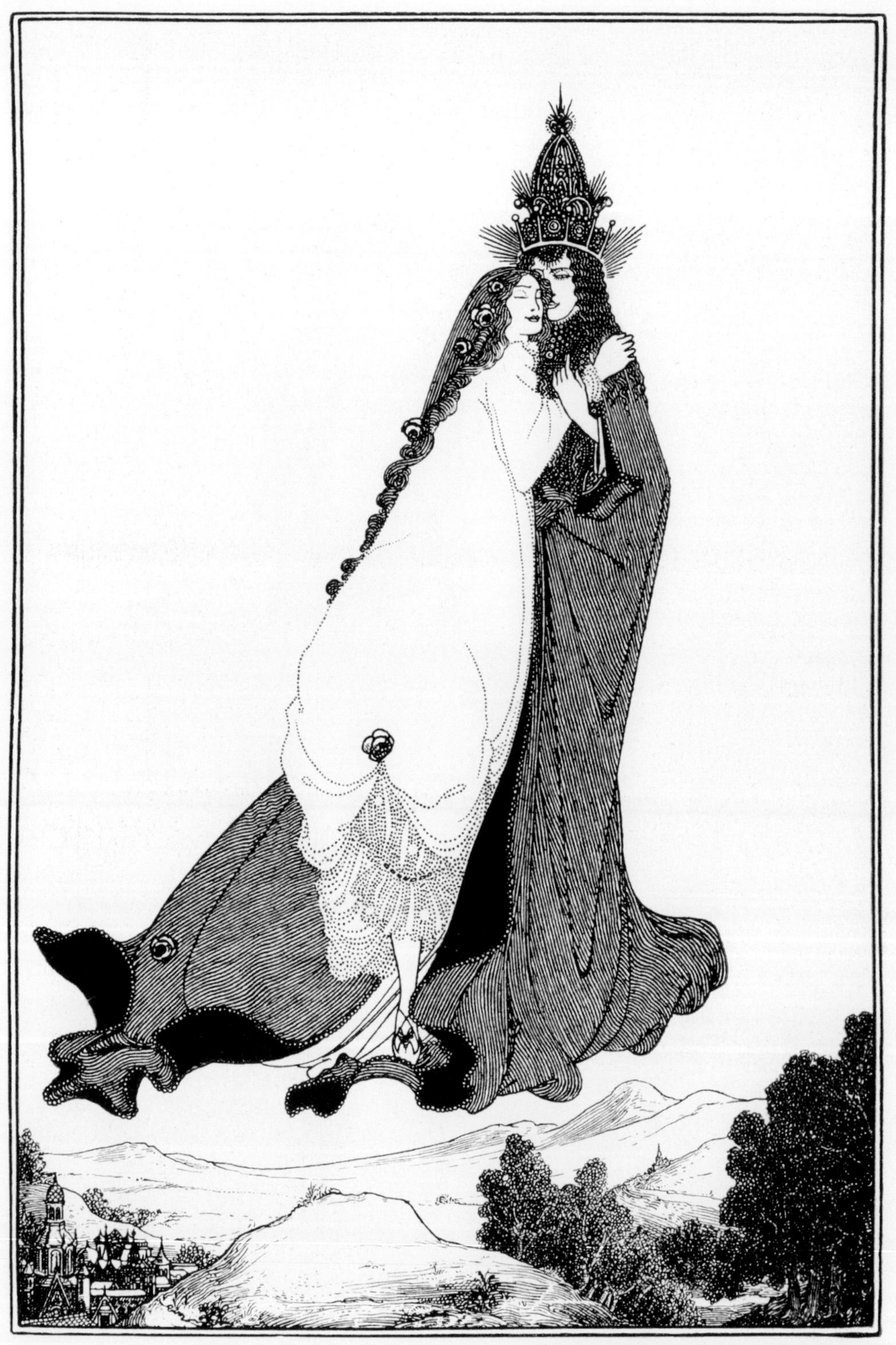

Volume II: 'The Ascension of St. Rose of Lima'

An illustration created for *Under the Hill*. The novel features Fanfreluche musing on the subject of religion, including the story of how a girl of age four in Lima, Peru, swore to remain a virgin eternally. When she came of age and was being pressured to marry, she climbed a mountain and prayed to the Virgin Mary, whereby the Virgin appeared and escorted her to heaven. Yet Beardsley sneaks all kinds of mischief into his depiction of this happy tale. Rose's back is clearly shaped like a penis, a technique which Beardsley appropriated from Japanese woodblock prints. The left section of the hem of the Virgin Mary's skirt resembles a growling beast.

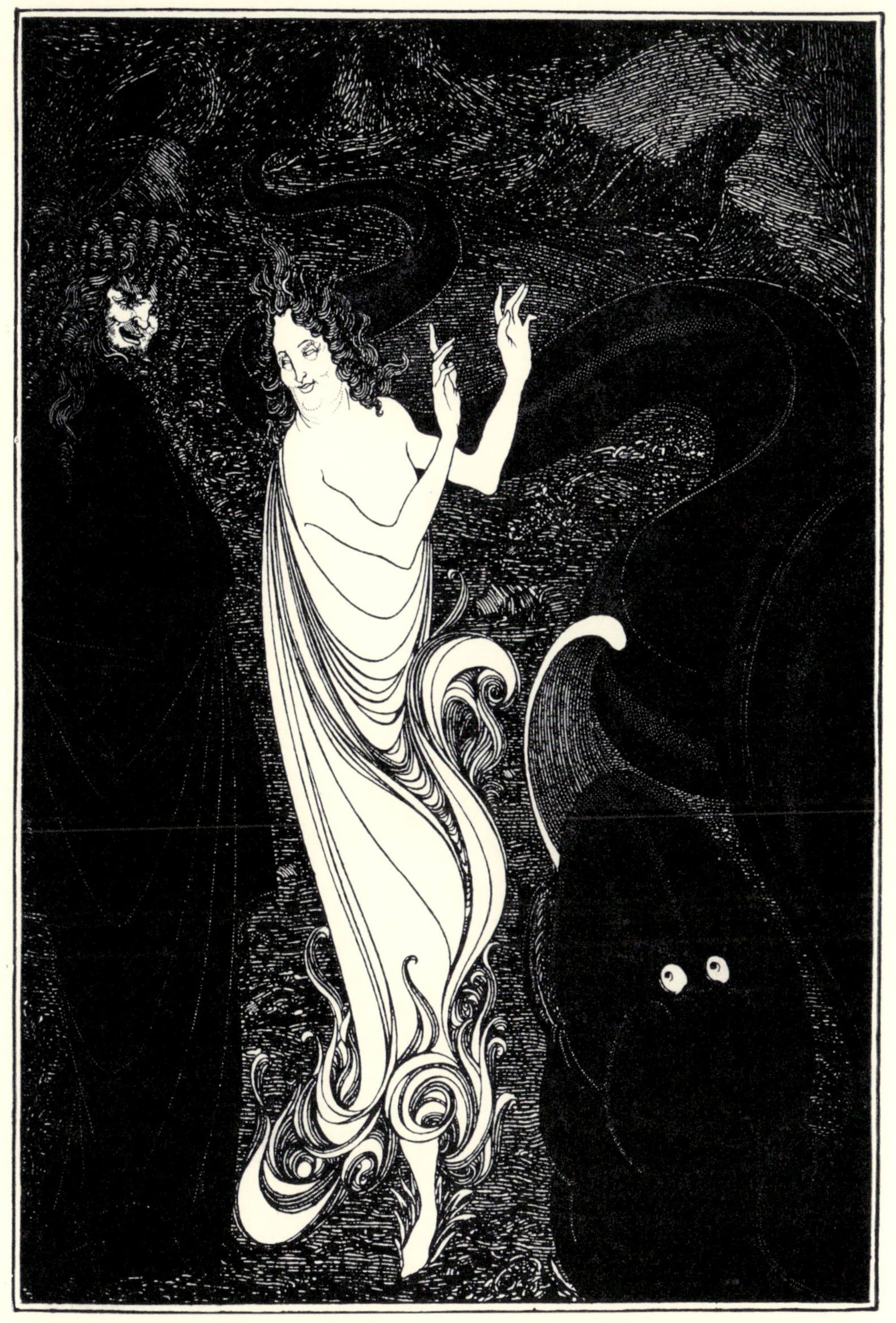

Volume II: 'Das Rheingold'

This is a scene from 'Das Rheingold', the first part of Wagner's Ring Cycle, which runs through the mind of Fanfreluche in *Under the Hill*. On the left is the ruler of the gods from Nordic myth, Wotan; in the centre is the god of fire, Loge; and to the right is the Giant Fafner, who has transformed into a great snake. The entire composition is bathed in darkness, with just Loge in his burst of flames gleaming out in white. Beardsley drew several illustrations for 'Das Rheingold', although I wish he had illustrated the entirety of the Ring Cycle.

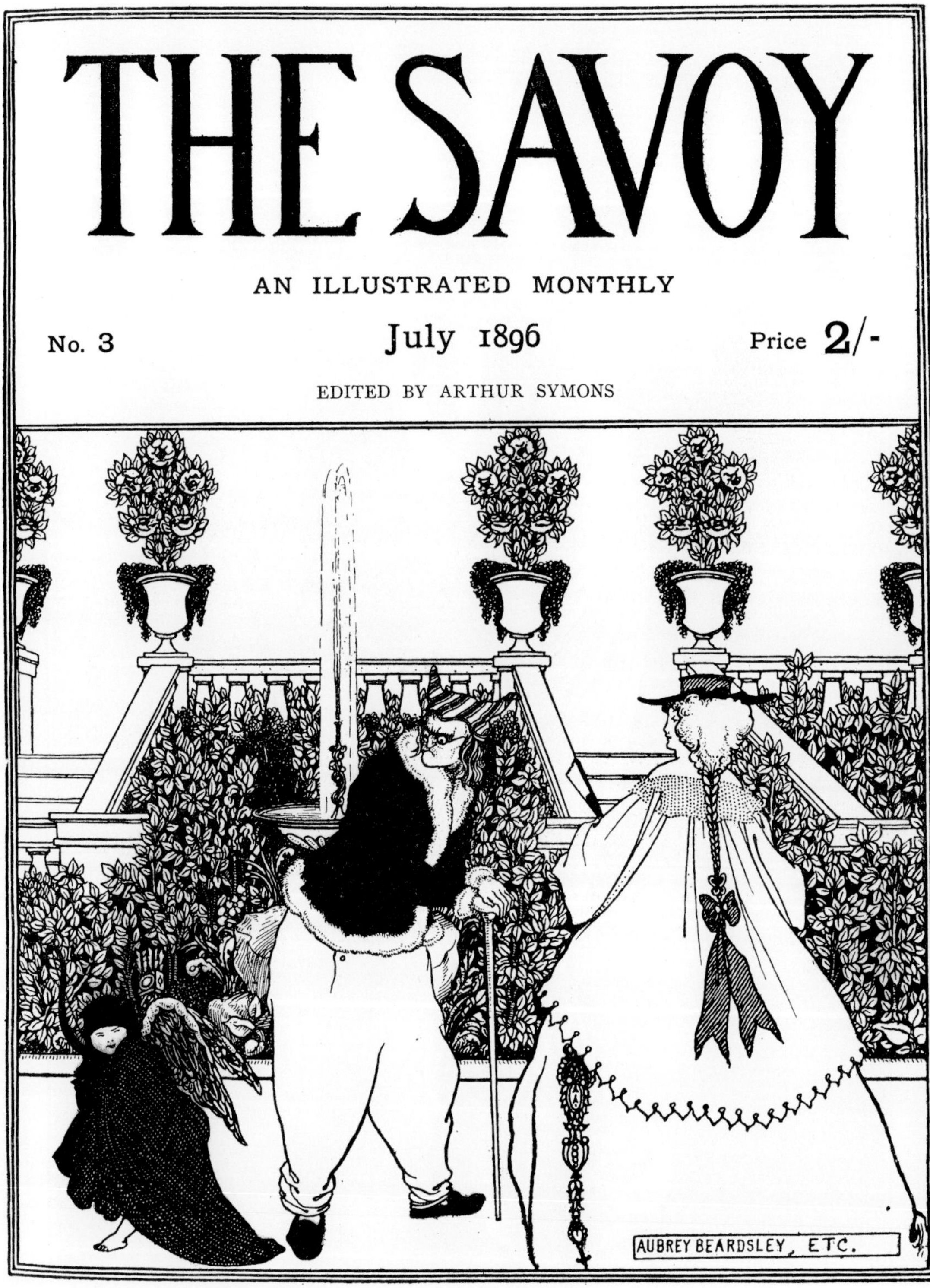

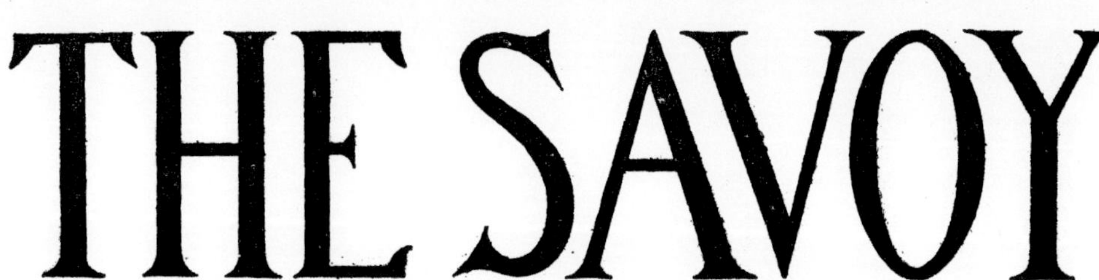

Cover to Volume III

This picture is entitled 'Cupid from the Garden'. An elderly man wearing a peculiar hat is propositioning a young woman. Fed up, Cupid attempts to sneak away from the scene. The old man is angry—why won't Cupid aid their love? Beardsley's name appears in the bottom right. On first sight it seems as though his signature mark is nowhere to be seen, but a closer inspection reveals something of the sort concealed in the ornament hanging down to the left of the woman's skirt. This is a comedic scene unfolding in the elegant surroundings of a French garden.

THE SAVOY

EDITED BY ARTHUR SYMONS

No. 3
July
1896

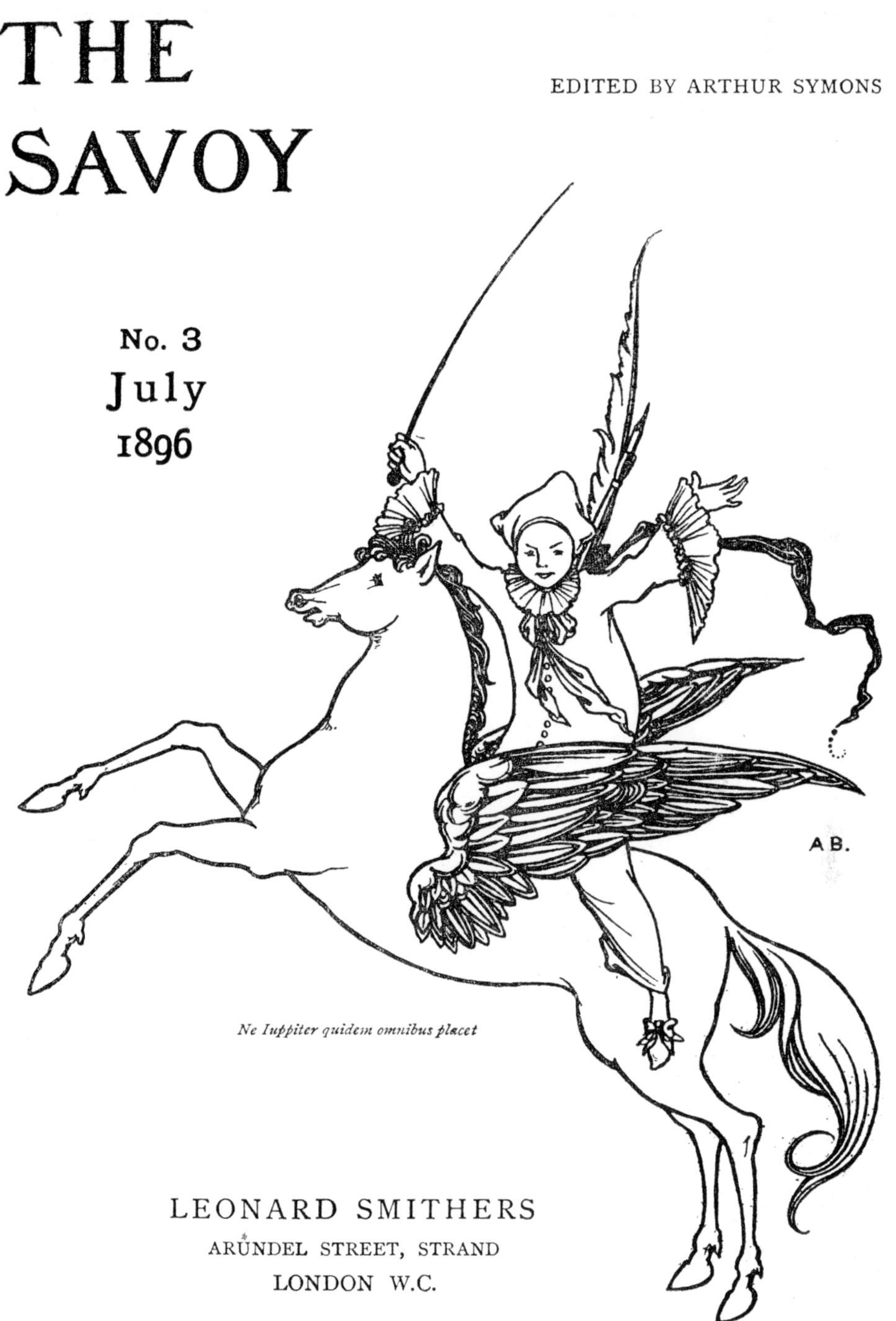

LEONARD SMITHERS
ARUNDEL STREET, STRAND
LONDON W.C.

Title Page to Volume III: 'Puck on Pegasus'

This same design was used from Volume III through to Volume VIII of *The Savoy*. Puck is a mischievous sprite, whose name is used to mean any impish fellow. He also appears in Shakespeare's *Midsummer Night's Dream*. In this picture he is carrying a fountain pen and pencil on his back. Most likely, Beardsley drew Puck here as a self portrait, for he too was an incorrigible lover of mischief. Puck's costume mirrors that of a circus clown.

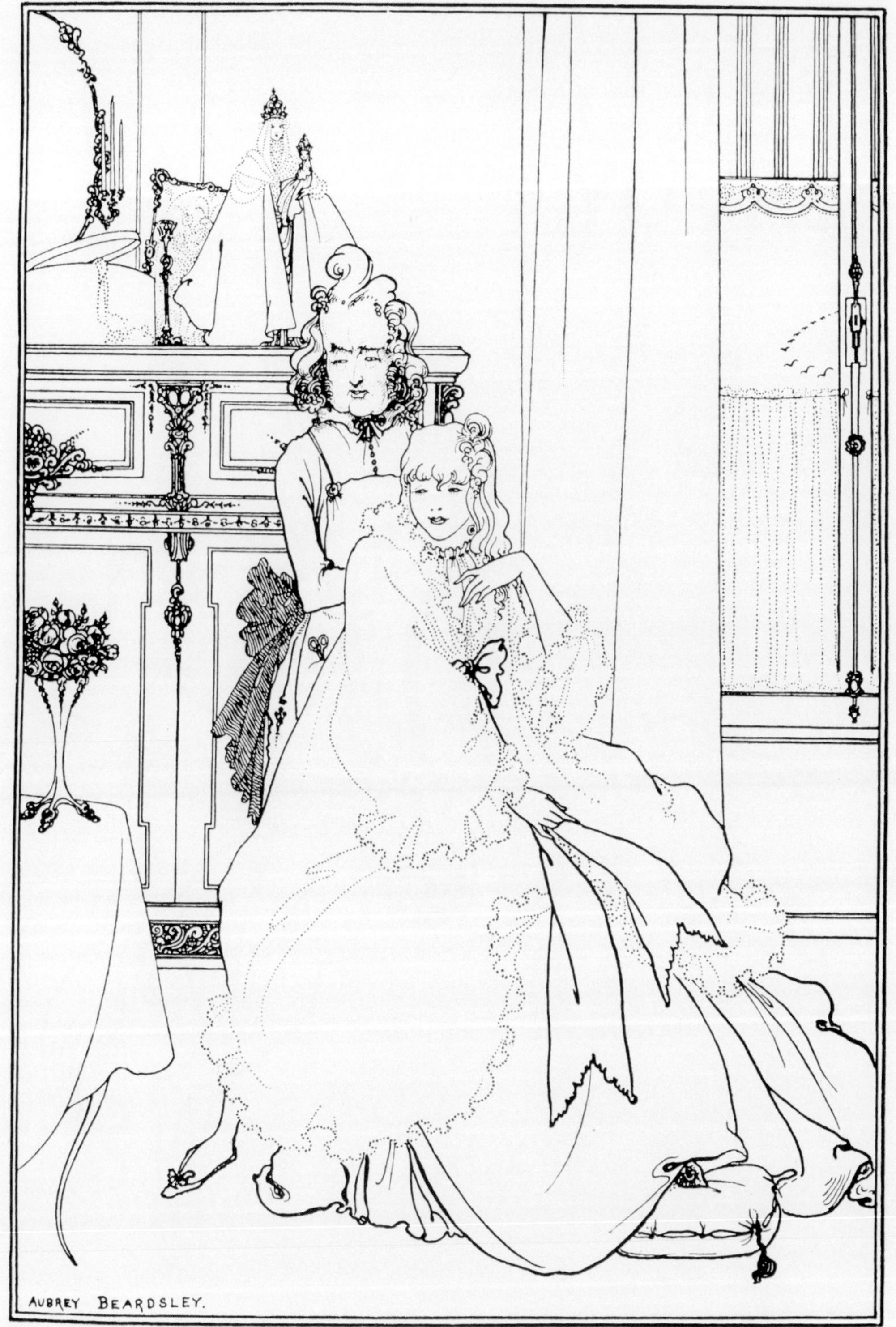

Volume III: 'The Coiffing'

This illustration accompanied Beardsley's poem, 'The Ballad of a Barber'. The picture appears to the uninformed viewer as innocent scene showing a girl having her hair cut. But upon reading the poem, we discover that it is far more sinister than it seems—the girl is a princess of thirteen who the barber plans to do away with. In the poem, he does indeed stab her to death with a broken cologne bottle, and receives the death penalty as a result. According to novelist and critic Brigid Brophy, the face of the barber and the surrounding it hair take the form of an eighteenth century Rococo grandfather clock, indicating that the time of the barber's destiny is drawing close. Above the barber's head is a statue of the Virgin and Child. The time was coming for Beardsley too, and he was deliberating about whether to convert to Catholicism.

Cover to Volume IV

There is no particular narrative behind this picture. Beardsley pursues an interesting balance, with half of the frame taken up by a curtain, and the other half by a woman and fruit mounted on a pedestal. The grapes spilling over from the fruit bowl are a seasonal touch added in view of the issue coming out in August. The curtain has something of a Japanese mosquito net about it, which Beardsley may well have picked up from Japanese woodblock prints. The woman kissing the grapes cuts an elegant figure, but the long thin pedestal has something unmistakably phallic about it which hints towards an altogether more erotic, risqué scene. It seems highly likely that this has been inspired by the world of *ukiyo-e*.

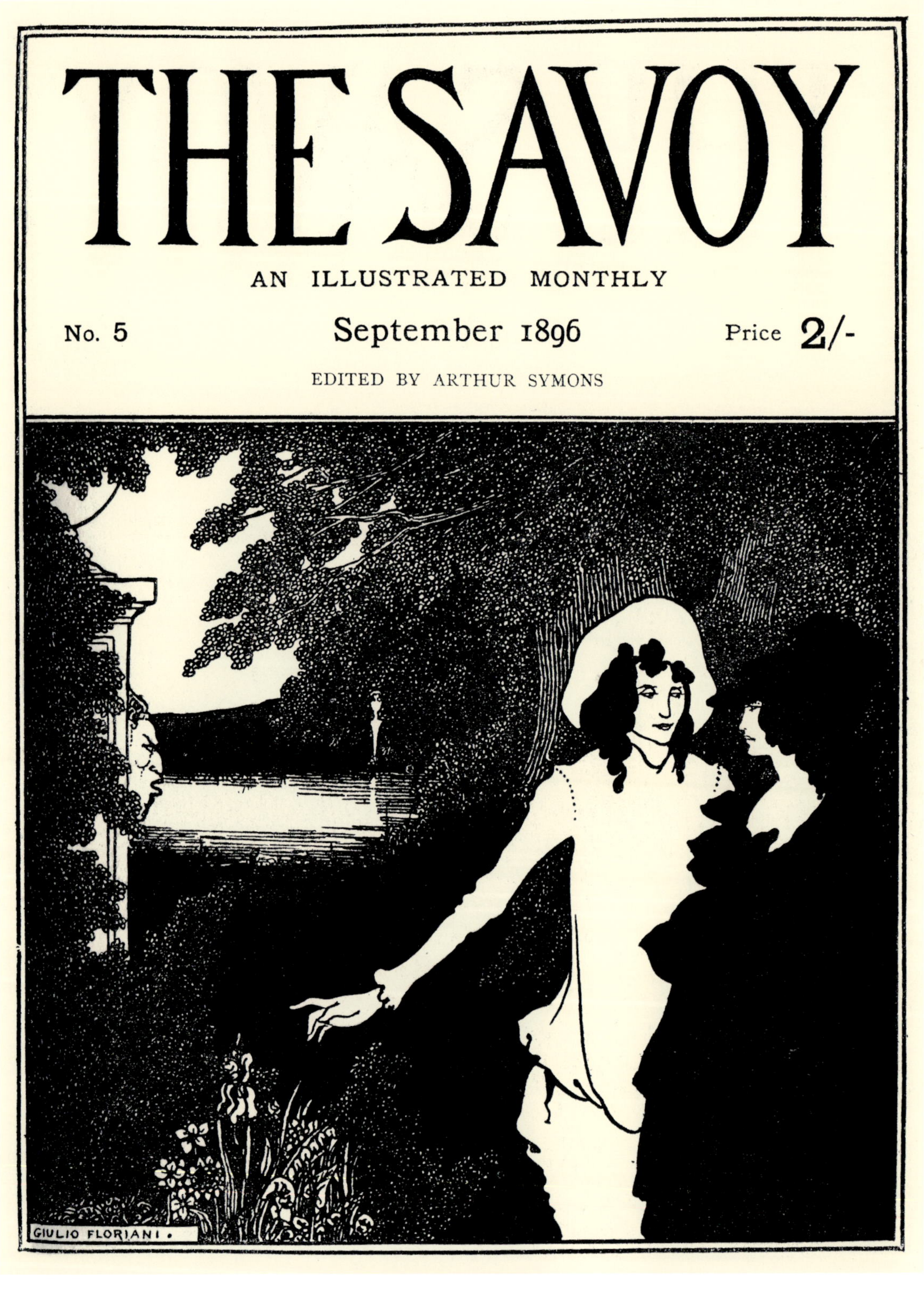

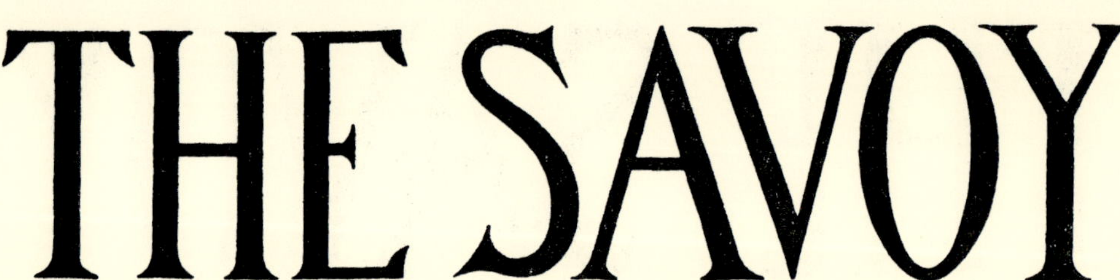

Cover to Volume V

Towards the end of his life, Beardsley's eccentric and unprecedented compositions became increasingly classical in feel, growing quieter and better balanced. In creating the lake scene in this picture, the artist referenced classic scenes from artists such as Antoine Watteau and Claude Rodin. Beardsley had to draw this in the worst of health, when just getting out of bed took everything that he had. On the right hand side of the picture, a young couple are conversing. The man is pointing to the flowers, and the two seem peaceful and in love. However, the grotesque mask affixed to the building on the left is glaring at them. There was still anger left in Beardsley. The signature, Giulio Floriani, is a joke on his part.

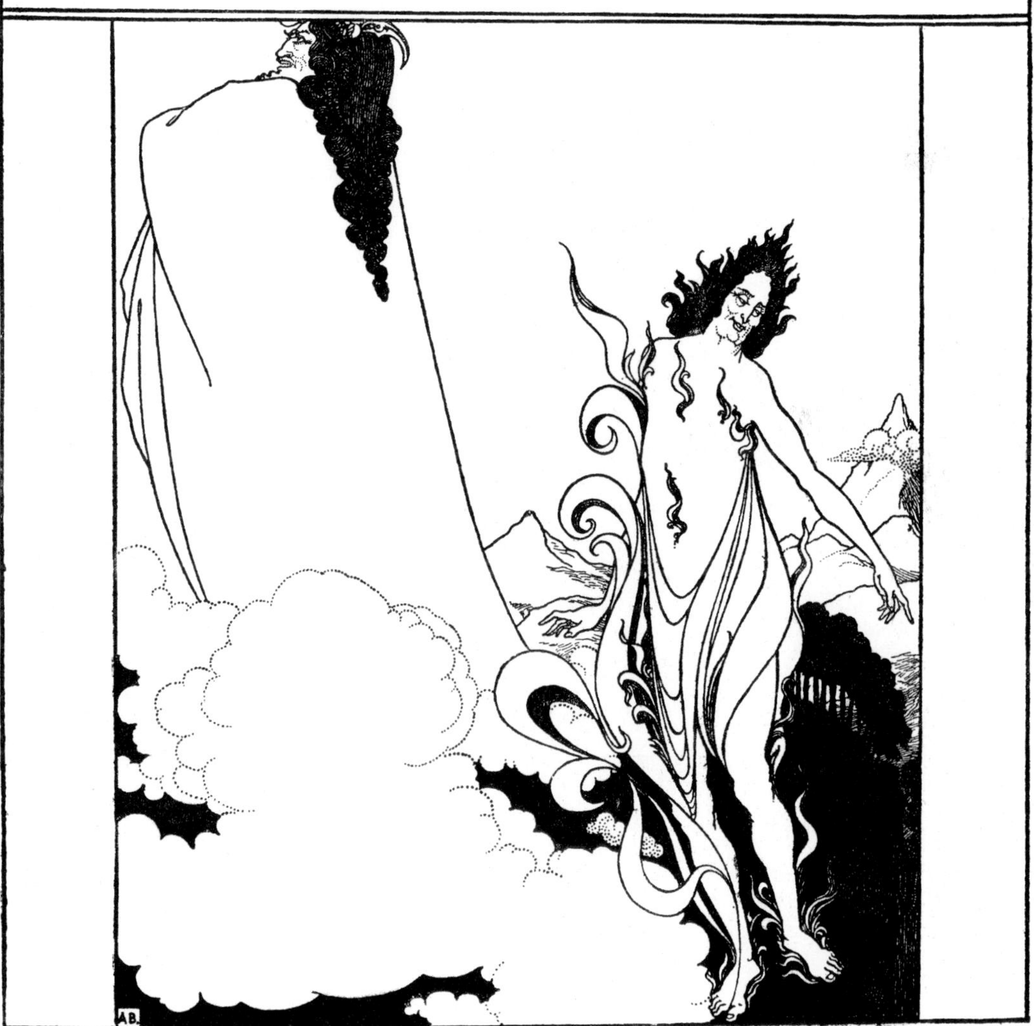

Cover to Volume VI

This Fourth Tableau of *Das Rheingold*, a reworking of the Third Tableau which was featured in Volume II, was used for the front wrapper of Volume VI. On the left is Wotan, on the right is Loge. With Wotan towering as a giant rock-like solid, and Loge changing shape fluidly in the flame, the two are adeptly contrasted with one another. Beardsley embarked on a whole series of illustrations depicting *Das Rheingold*, but was unable to complete it.

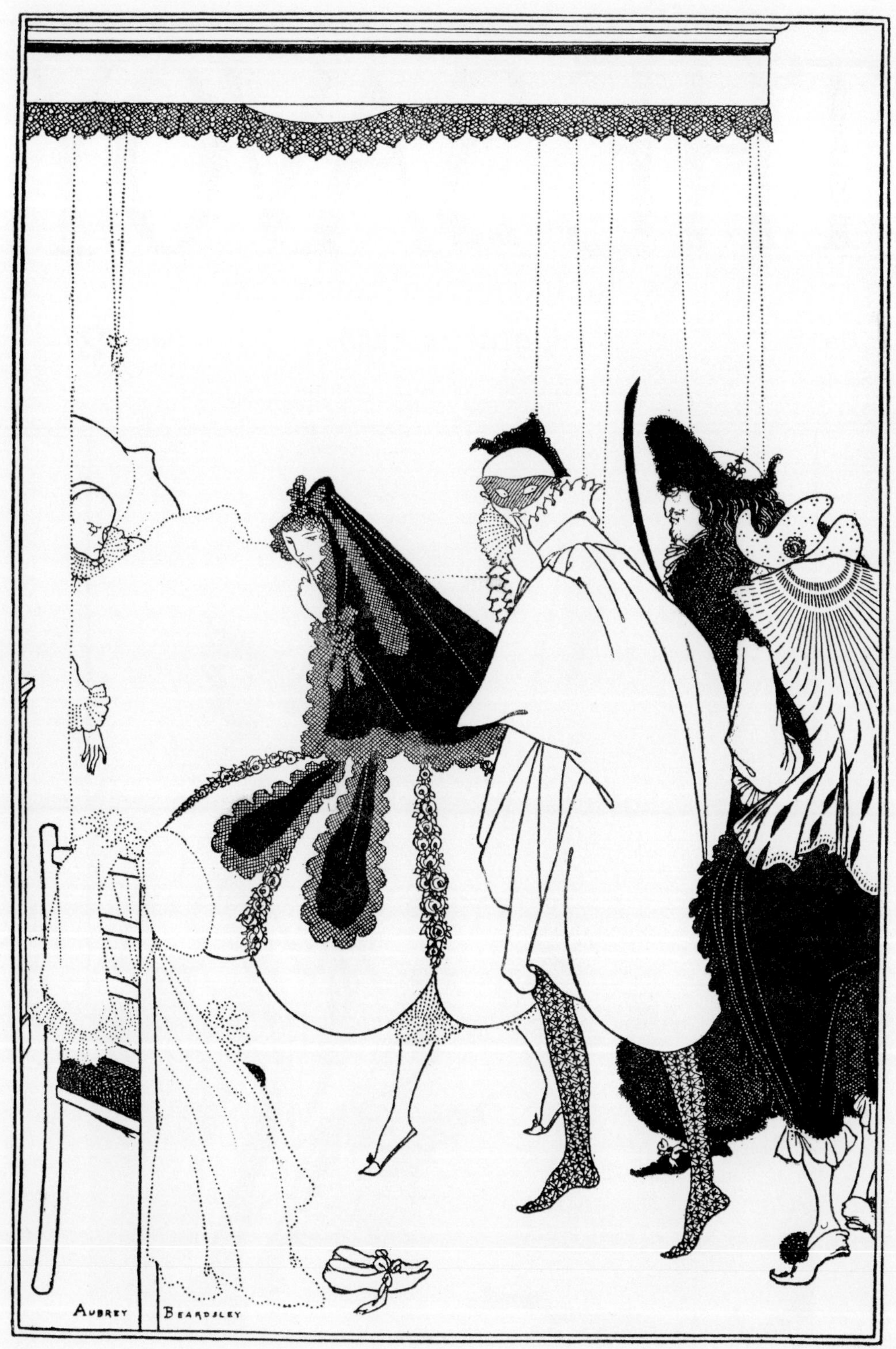

Volume VI: 'The Death of the Pierrot'

Images of the stock characters from the Italian improvisational comedy, commedia dell'arte, were popular in fin-de-siècle art. Pierrot, hailing from the Bergamot region, is on his deathbed. With their fingers to their lips, his friends creep silently into the room: from the left, Colombina, the Harlequin, Il Dottore, and Pantaleone. Quite possibly Beardsley saw himself in the figure of the dying Pierrot. If that was the case, though, he mimics even that feeling, as if inviting people to laugh at him. The shape of Columbina's skirt is rather suggestive.

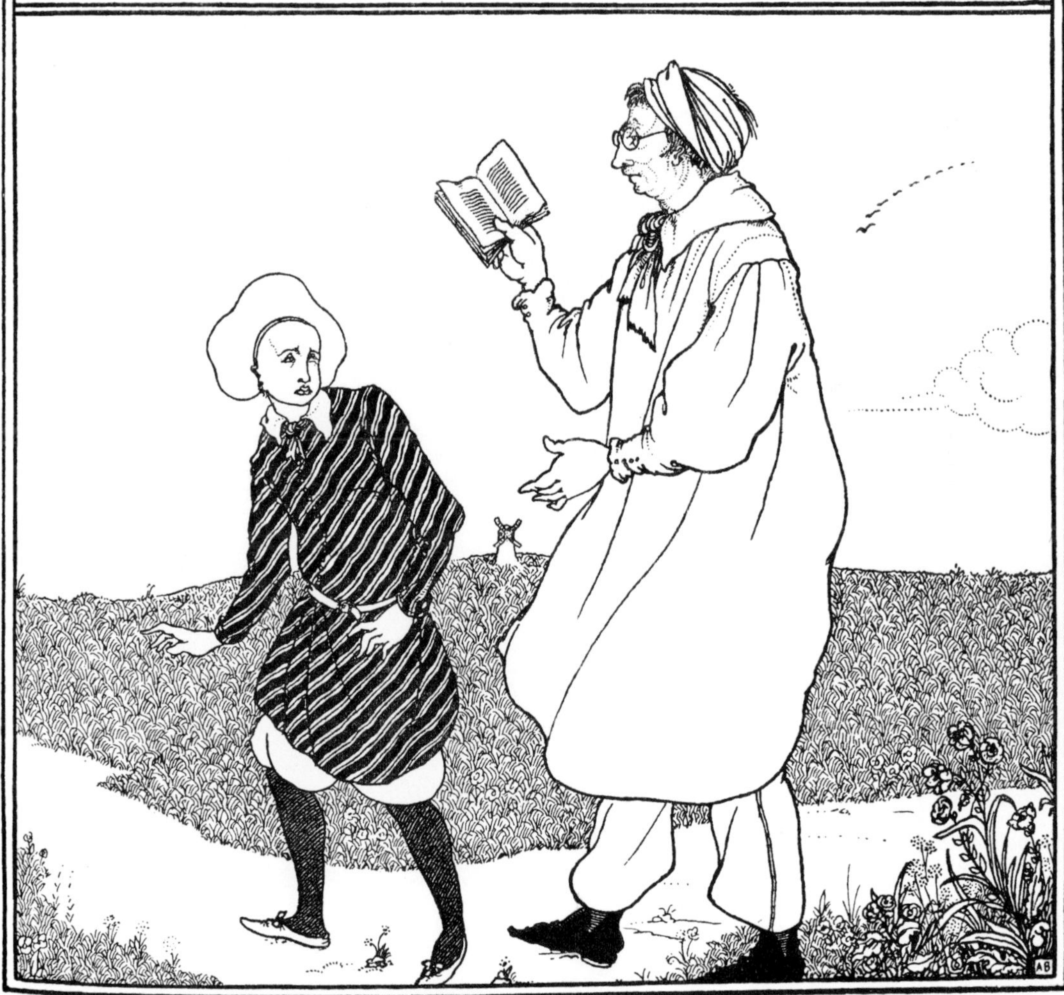

Cover to Volume VII

A scholar and teacher is demonstrating his knowledge, disturbing the child. With his smock and the piece of cloth wound turban-style around his head, the teacher resembles an ancient artist. The child wears a cap like the pierrot in Watteau's famous painting. By Beardsley's standards, this is a comical, relaxed scene. The delicate portrayal of the flowers at their feet and the fields in the background are said to show a Japonist influence. The child with his pierrot's cap could well be Beardsley himself.

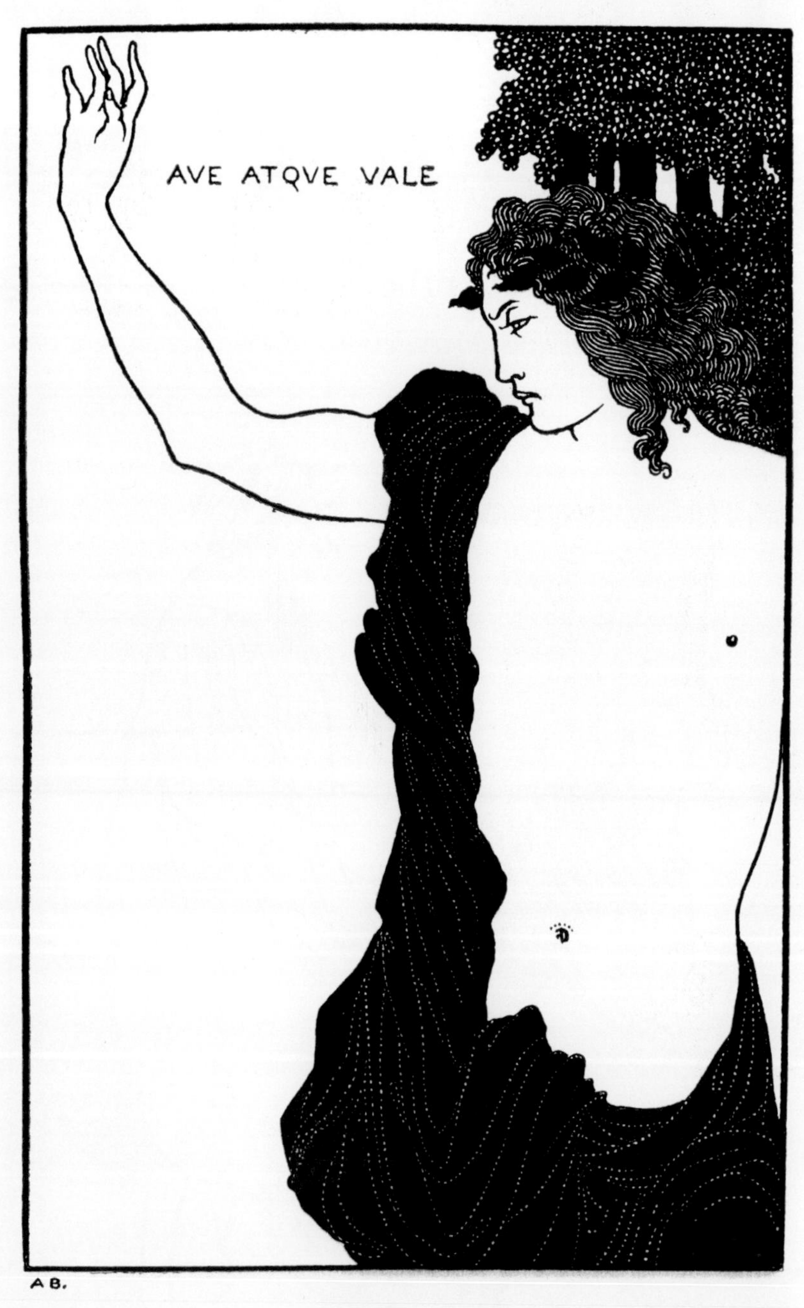

Volume VII: 'Ave Atque Vale'

'Ave Atque Vale' means 'Hail and Farewell' in Latin. This is an illustration produced for the Roman poet Catallus' *Carmen 101*. It is only Beardsley who could produce a composition as formidable as this one in just black and white. With just two dots to mark the nipple and navel, the pure white body of the young man appears positively radiant on the page, forming a wonderful balance with the wooded area above his head and the black cloth hanging from his shoulder. The message of 'hail and farewell' seems to anticipate Beardsley's deep regret at departing the world.

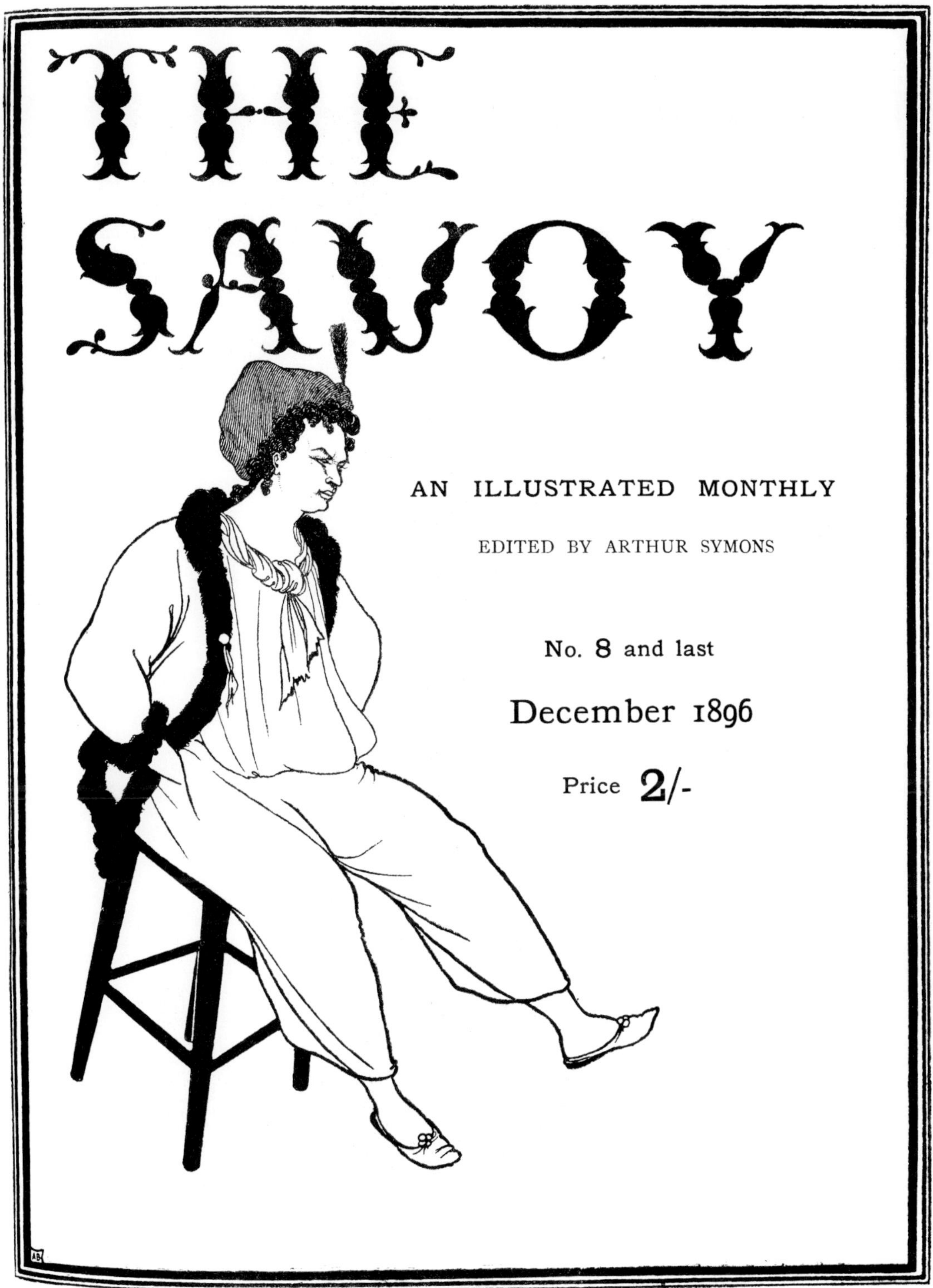

Cover to Volume VIII

This illustration was apparently created for the *Ali Baba* series. Beardsley had always been drawn to the *Arabian Nights* stories, foreshadowing the taste for the oriental, which would later find expression in a love for the Ballet Russes and Paul Poiret's Parisian fashions. The picture shows a slightly cheeky looking boy in baggy pantaloons. Volume VIII was the final issue of *The Savoy* to be published, and it seems that the boy is sulking about the fact. The unbalanced pose, with the chair leaning forward, is typical of Beardsley.

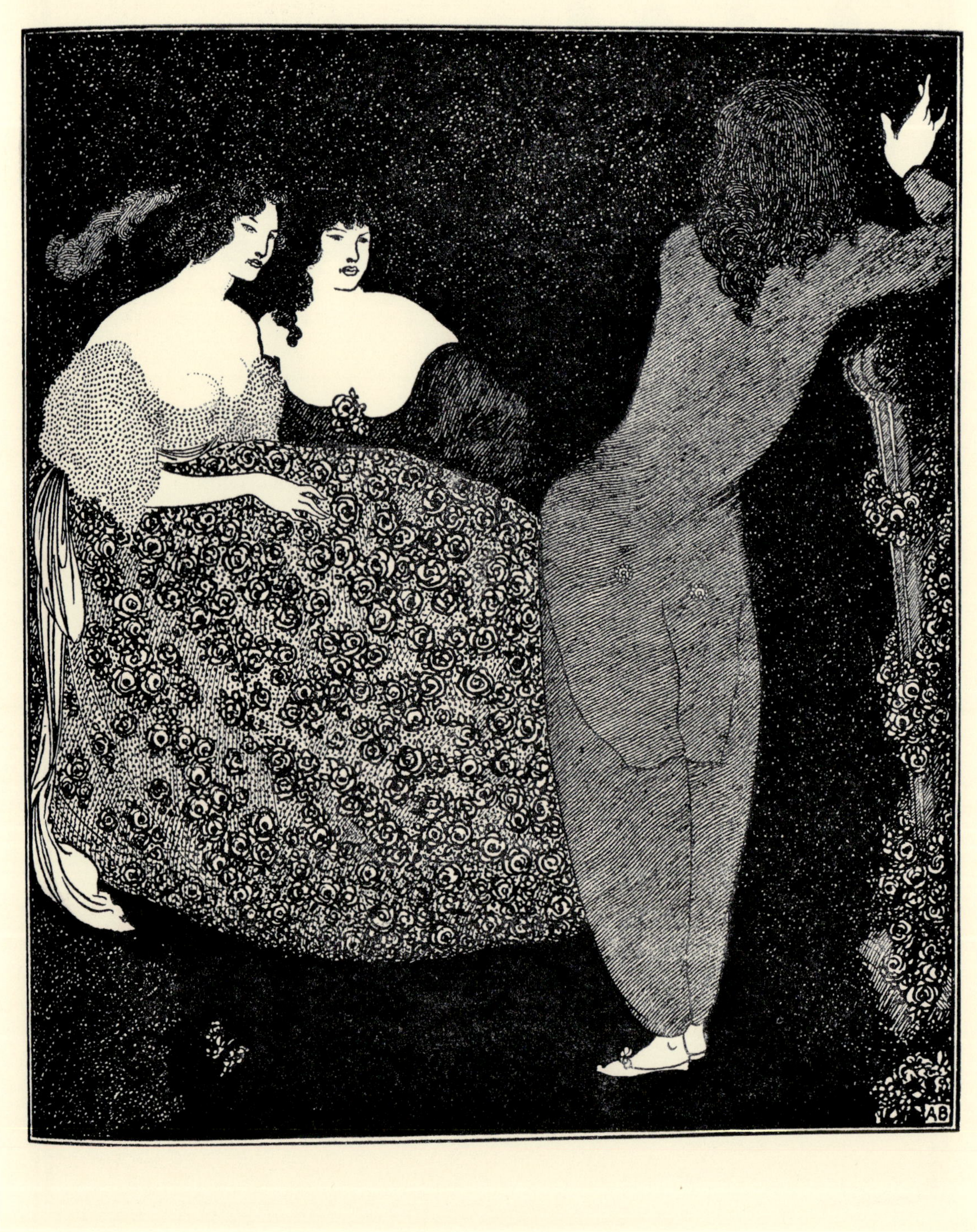

Volume VIII: 'Tristan und Isolde'

Beardsley was a big fan of Wagner's opera, *Tristan und Isolde*. It seems that in this picture, someone is singing the opera to the two women, and making gestures—it could very well be Beardsley himself. In any case, the portrayal of this figure is interesting, with his top and bottom halves seemingly moving independently from one another. In the darkness of the screen, only the women's white faces and shoulders glow out. The kind of textile design, as glimpsed in the elaborate patterning of the women's skirts, is one of the highlights of Beardsley's late-period style.

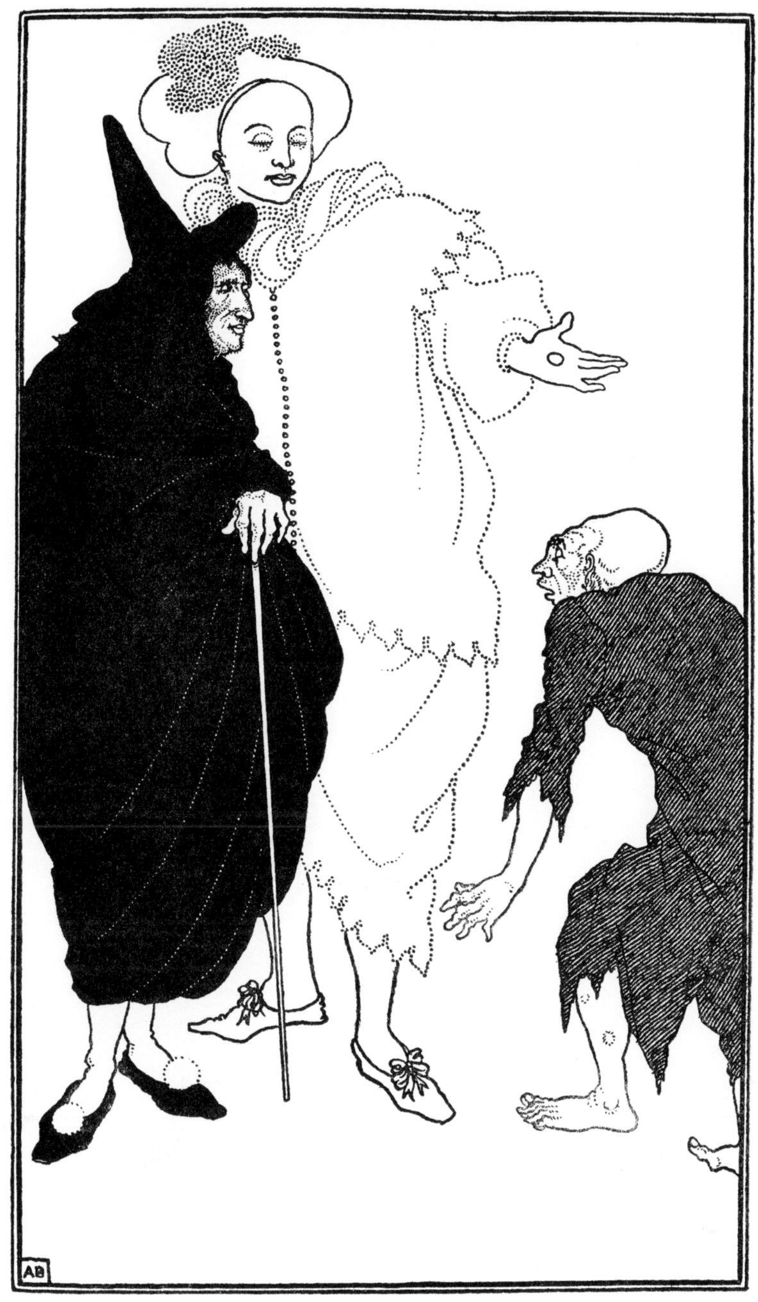

From Volume Eight: 'Don Juan, Sganarelle and the Beggar'

This is an illustration for Molière's *Don Juan*. Sganarelle with his cane and Don Juan in his pierrot outfit are based on Watteau's picture, *The Italian Comedians*. Between the black figure of Sganarelle and the grey of the beggar, the white figure of the pierrot surrounded by dotted lines floats like a mirage. In this figure, Beardsley is projecting his own image onto the pierrot. This diagonal composition, with two figures facing the viewer and one turning his back, is a common device of Beardsley's.

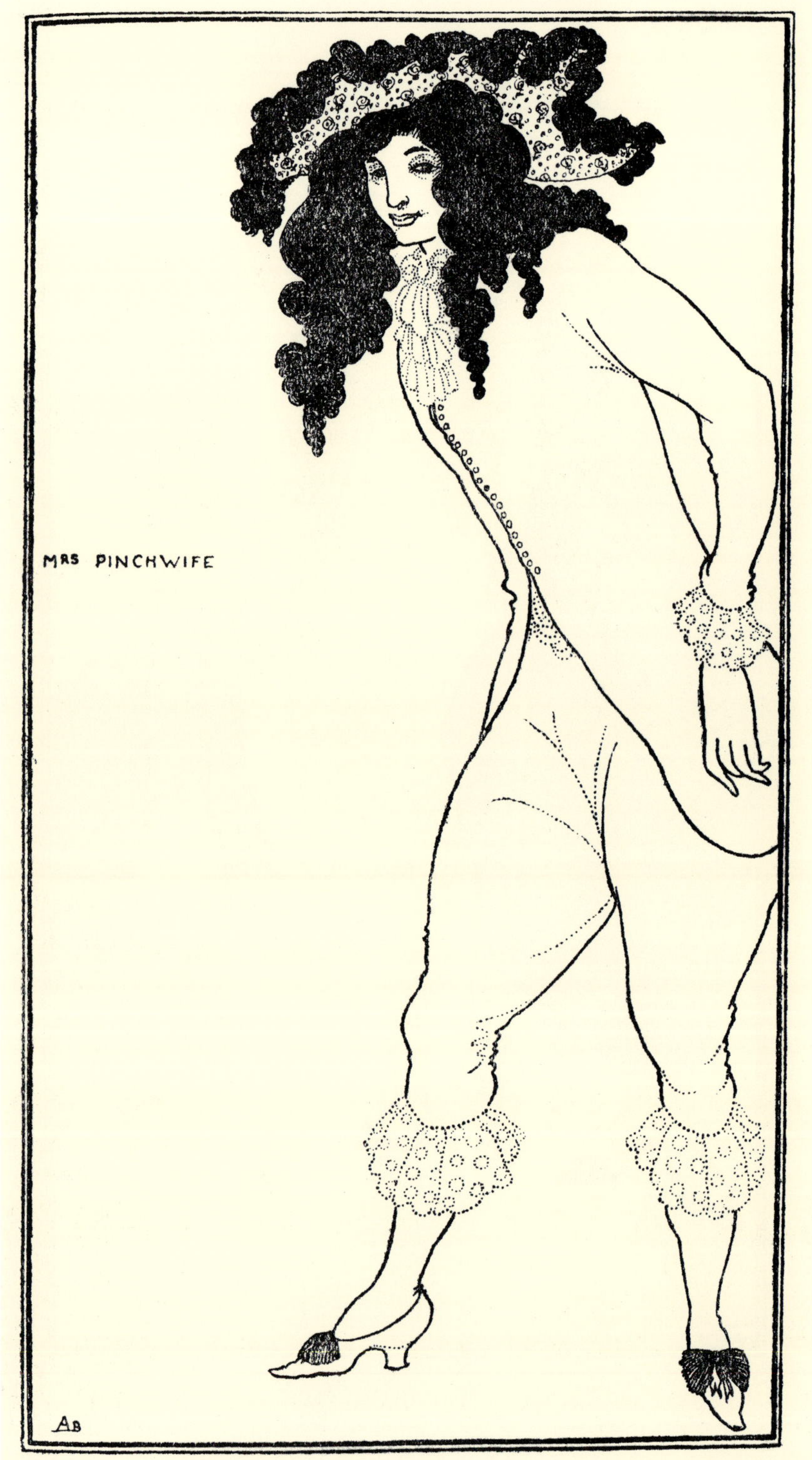

Volume VIII: 'Mrs Pinchwife'

This picture is apparently based on Wycherley's restoration comedy from the seventeenth century, *The Country Wife*, and shows a woman disguised as a man. Beardsley was very interested in people switching genders—a common occurrence in the world of the theatre, where it was used to surprise people and make them laugh. Is Mrs Pinchwife like a 'pinch hitter' in baseball—a woman in man's clothing, who comes in to take over from the man when things get tight? The figure in this picture has an androgynous charm.

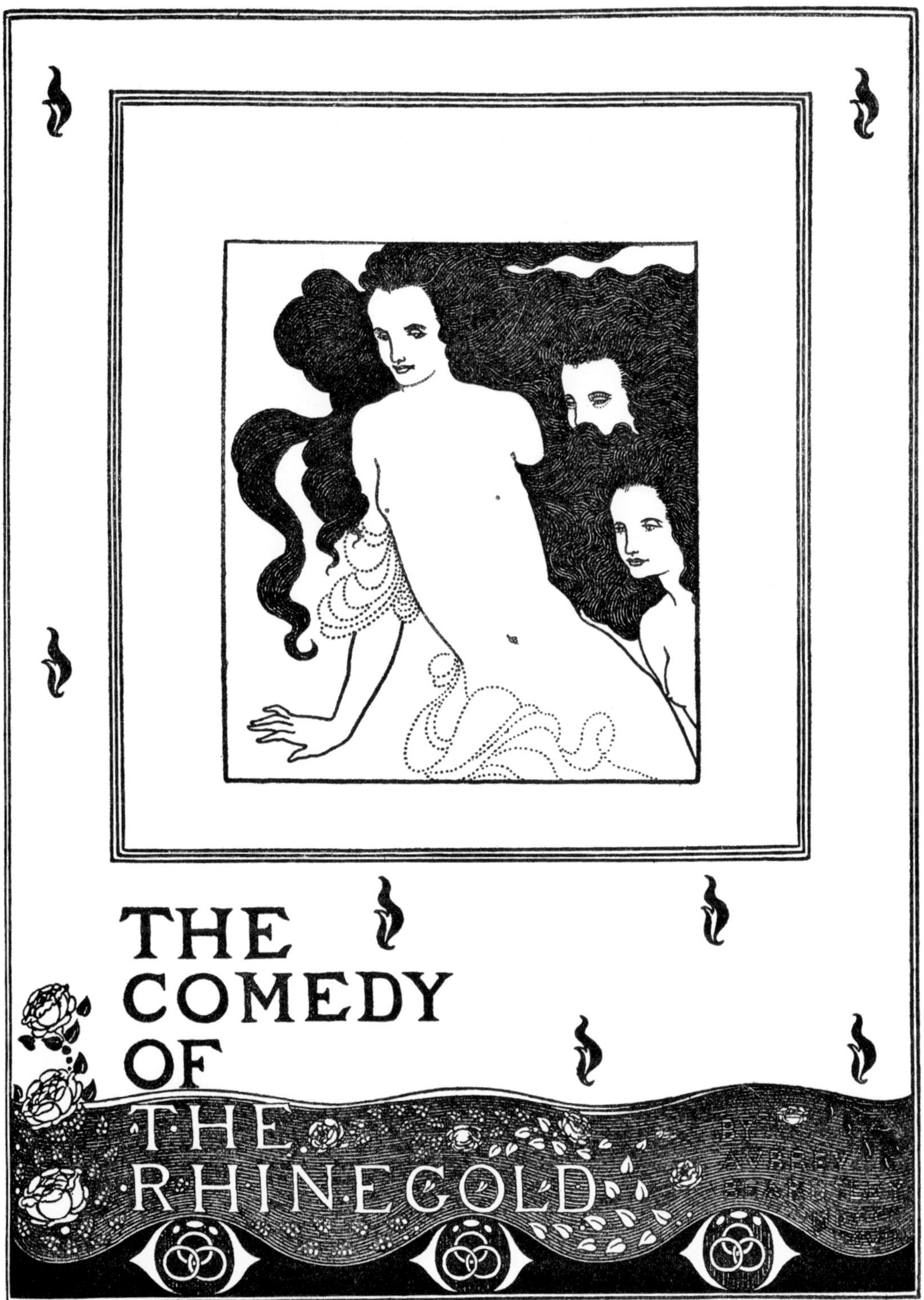

Volume VIII: 'The Comedy of The Rhinegold'

Beardsley intended to publish a selection of his illustrations of 'Das Rheingold', but was unable to finish them. This picture was created as a frontispiece for said book. The picture seems to show three Rhine maidens protecting the Rhinegold—Floßhilde, Woglinde, and Wellgunde—but Beardsley gives them boyish bodies, blurring their genders. The abundance of rich black flowing hair is certainly impressive, and shares the characteristic fluid lines of Art Nouveau, as seen in women's hair cascading like water in pictures by Alphonse Mucha and similar.

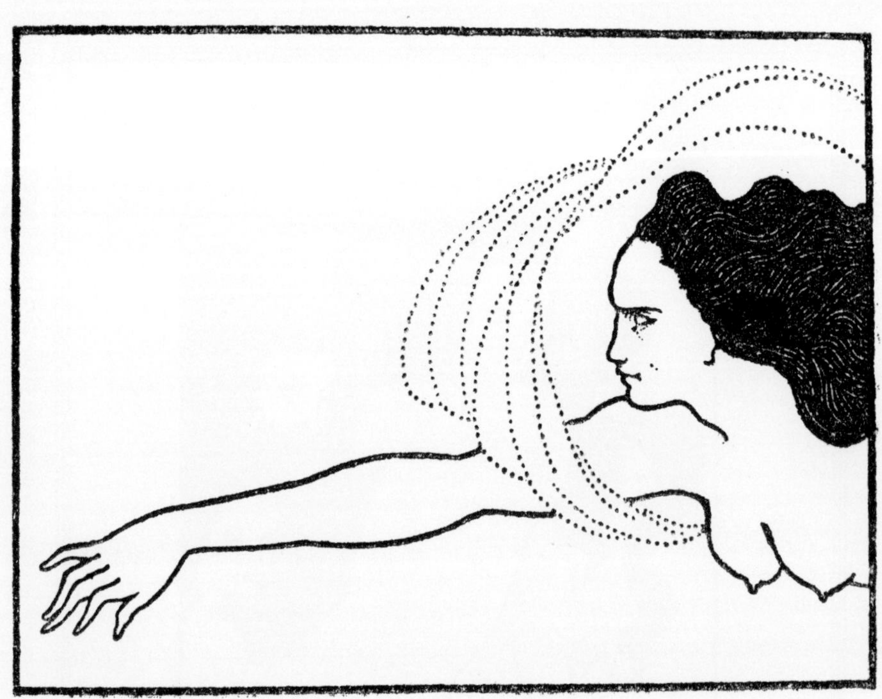

Volume VIII:
(Top) 'Floßhilde'
(Bottom) 'Alberich'

Illustrations II & III from The Rhinegold series.
(Top) In the top illustration, Floßhilde, one of the
Rhine Maidens, extends her arm as if swimming
through water. In the first illustration, her figure
was boyish, but here she has a shapely chest. It's
possible that the picture is referencing scenes of
ama—women divers—from Japanese prints. The
illustration has a wonderfully dynamic composition,
leading the eye from right to left.
(Bottom) Alberich is the leader of the Nibelungen,
the dwarfs who live underground. They are craftsmen
who search out gold that has been buried underground, mining, extracting, and forging it. Alberich
steals the Rhinegold that the three Rhine Maidens
have hidden under the river, and thus the story of
the Nibelungen begins. Beardsley portrays Alberich
as an unsightly, mole-like creature.

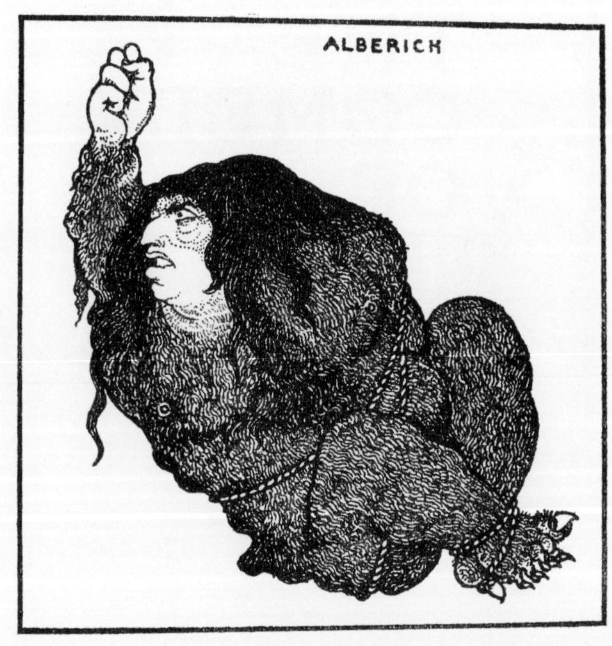

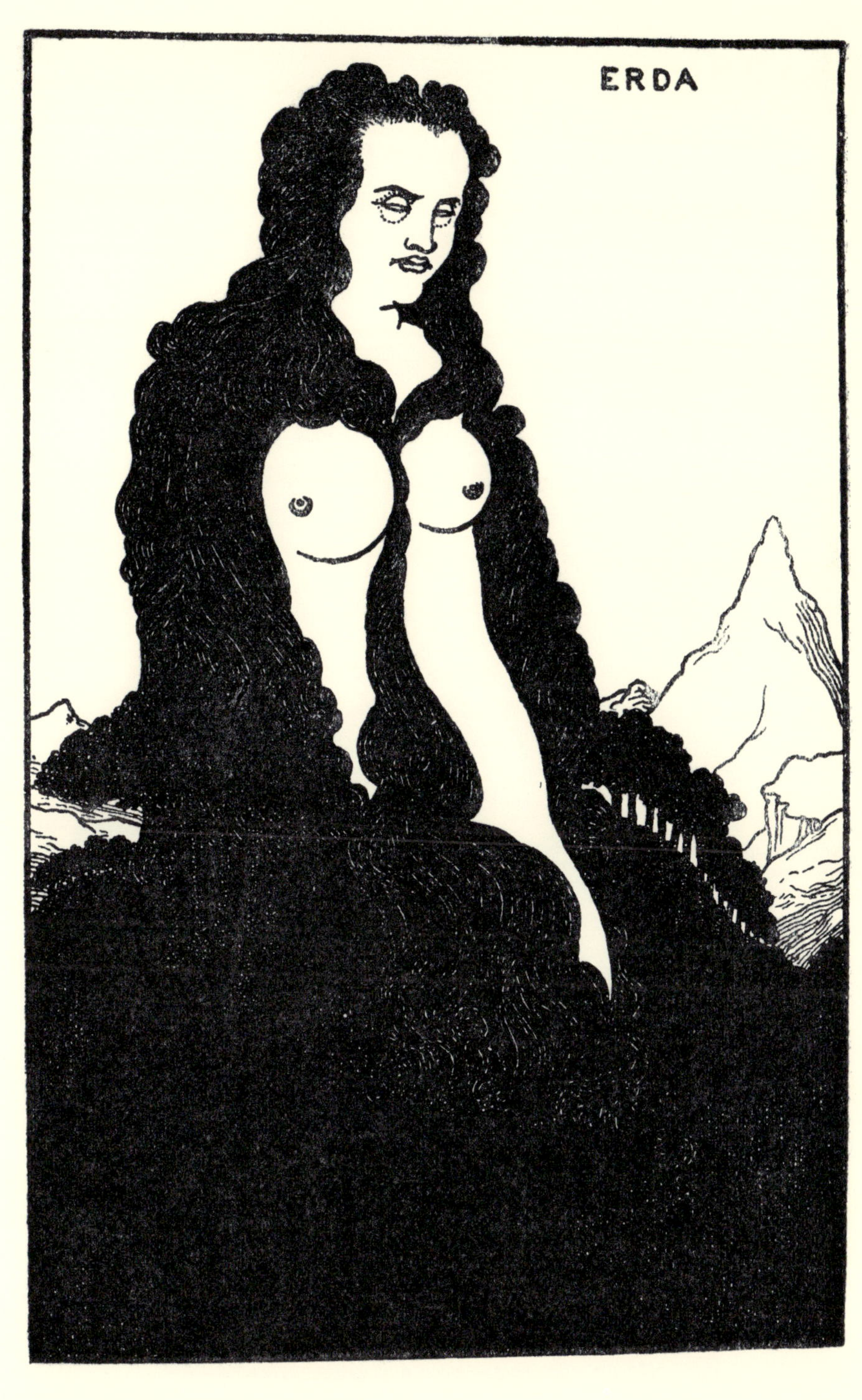

Volume VIII: 'Erda'

The fourth illustration in The Rhinegold series featured in this volume. Erda is the goddess of Mother Earth, and of wisdom, responsible for the creation of Valhalla, the land of the gods where Wotan is. Together, Erda and Wotan have nine children—the nine Valkyries, or goddesses of battle. Beardsley's picture swathes Erda's naked form with its full breasts in her even fuller hair. The peaked mountain to the right could well be Valhalla. Erda looks either exhausted or displeased. Is she grieving the fact that the world she brought into being to will be fought over and destroyed by her own children?

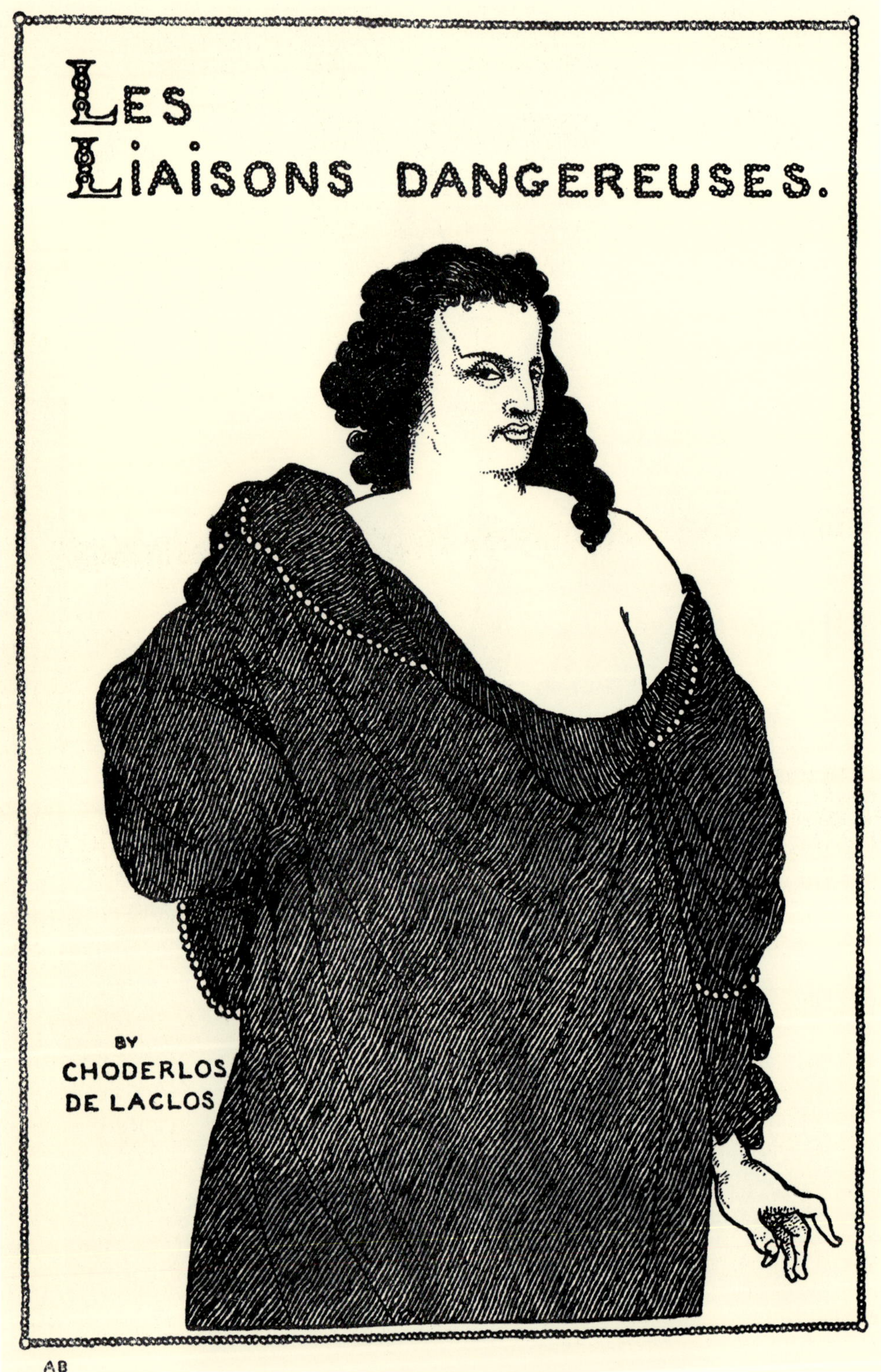

Volume VIII: 'Les Liaisons Dangereux'

This picture depicts Vicomte de Valmont, the protagonist of the eighteenth-century novel by Choderlos de Laclos deemed scandalous and immoral. The portrait of this serial seducer of women is represented by a figure wearing a loose smock over his naked body. His expression is full of confidence, and he makes no attempt to conceal his lasciviousness. The hand visible in the bottom right resembles a snake opening its mouth, apparently ready to grasp something. The other hand is invisible, buried behind his back, but the shape of his sleeve takes an ominous shape, like a huge monster sticking out its tongue.

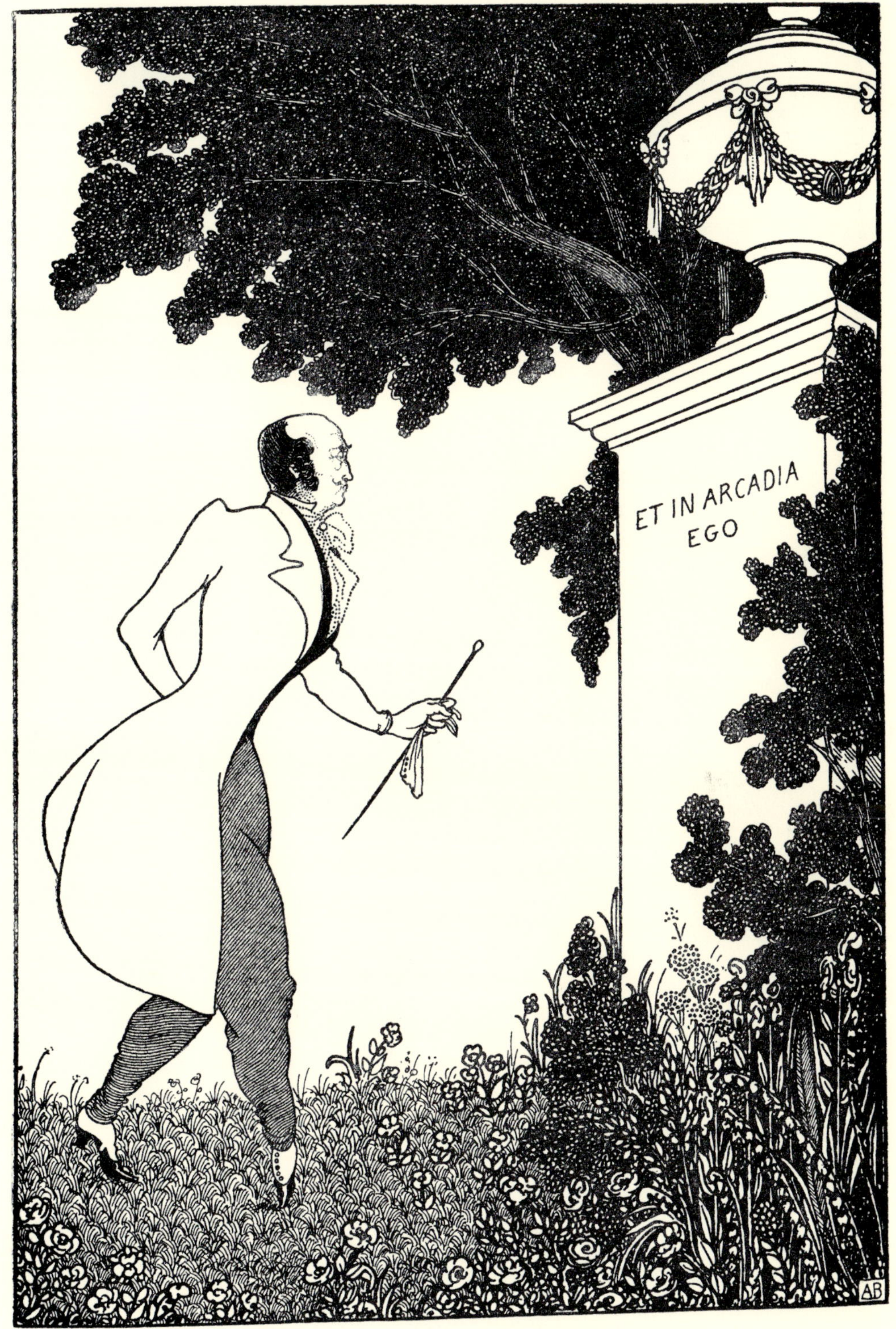

Volume VIII: 'Et in Arcadia Ego'

Arcadia was the ancient Grecians' paradise. In one of Virgil's poems appears the line 'et in arcadia ego' ('Even in Arcadia, there am I'), recording the sadness of being chased out of Paradise. There is a well-known painting of the same name by Nicholas Poussin. In Beardsley's illustration, a middle-aged dandy is looking at the words engraved on an old stone monument. Doubtless he also enjoyed his days in Arcadia, but he is no longer there. Beardsley is getting ready, with a fair amount of sentimentality, to depart this world.

POSTERS AND COLOUR WORKS

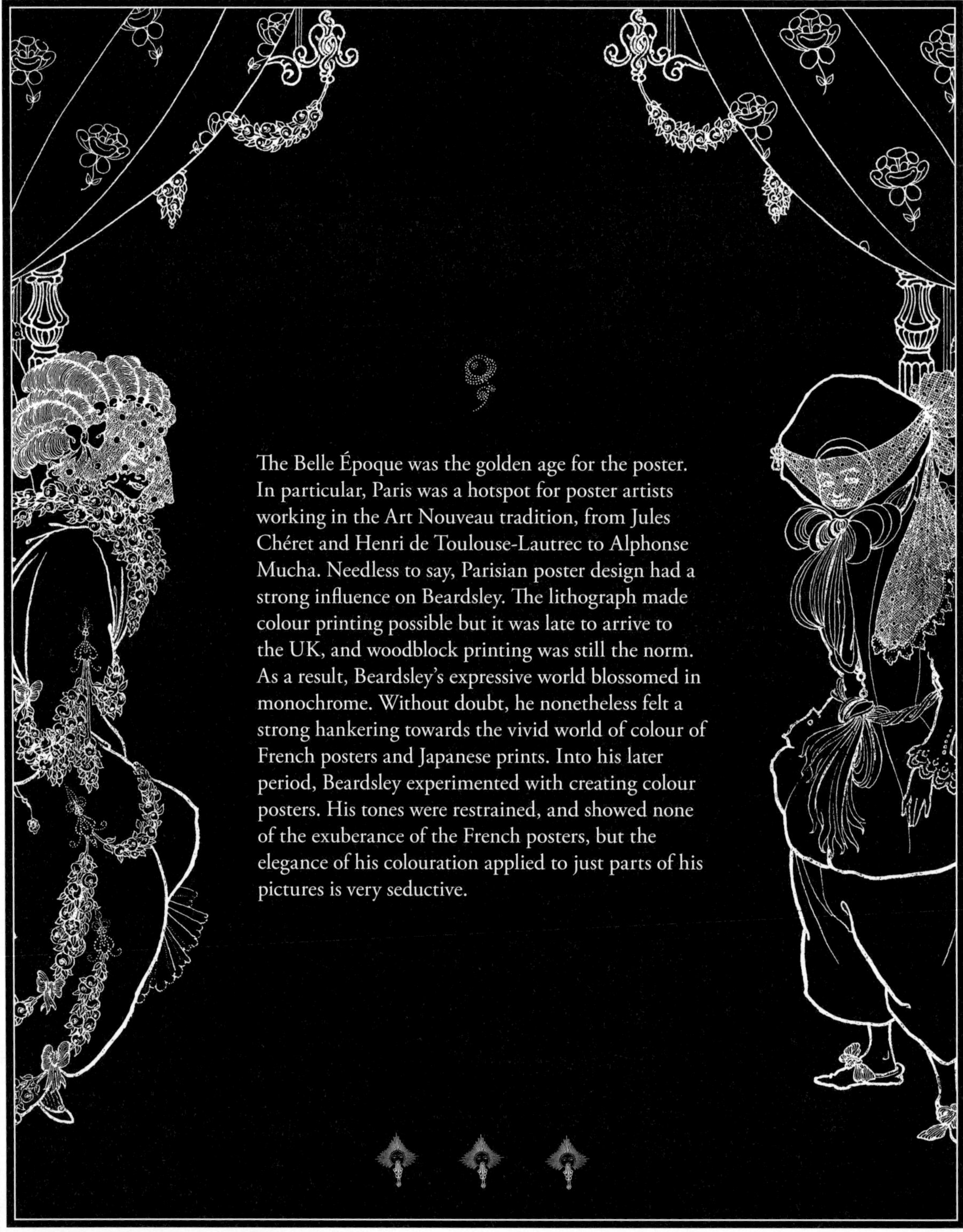

The Belle Époque was the golden age for the poster. In particular, Paris was a hotspot for poster artists working in the Art Nouveau tradition, from Jules Chéret and Henri de Toulouse-Lautrec to Alphonse Mucha. Needless to say, Parisian poster design had a strong influence on Beardsley. The lithograph made colour printing possible but it was late to arrive to the UK, and woodblock printing was still the norm. As a result, Beardsley's expressive world blossomed in monochrome. Without doubt, he nonetheless felt a strong hankering towards the vivid world of colour of French posters and Japanese prints. Into his later period, Beardsley experimented with creating colour posters. His tones were restrained, and showed none of the exuberance of the French posters, but the elegance of his colouration applied to just parts of his pictures is very seductive.

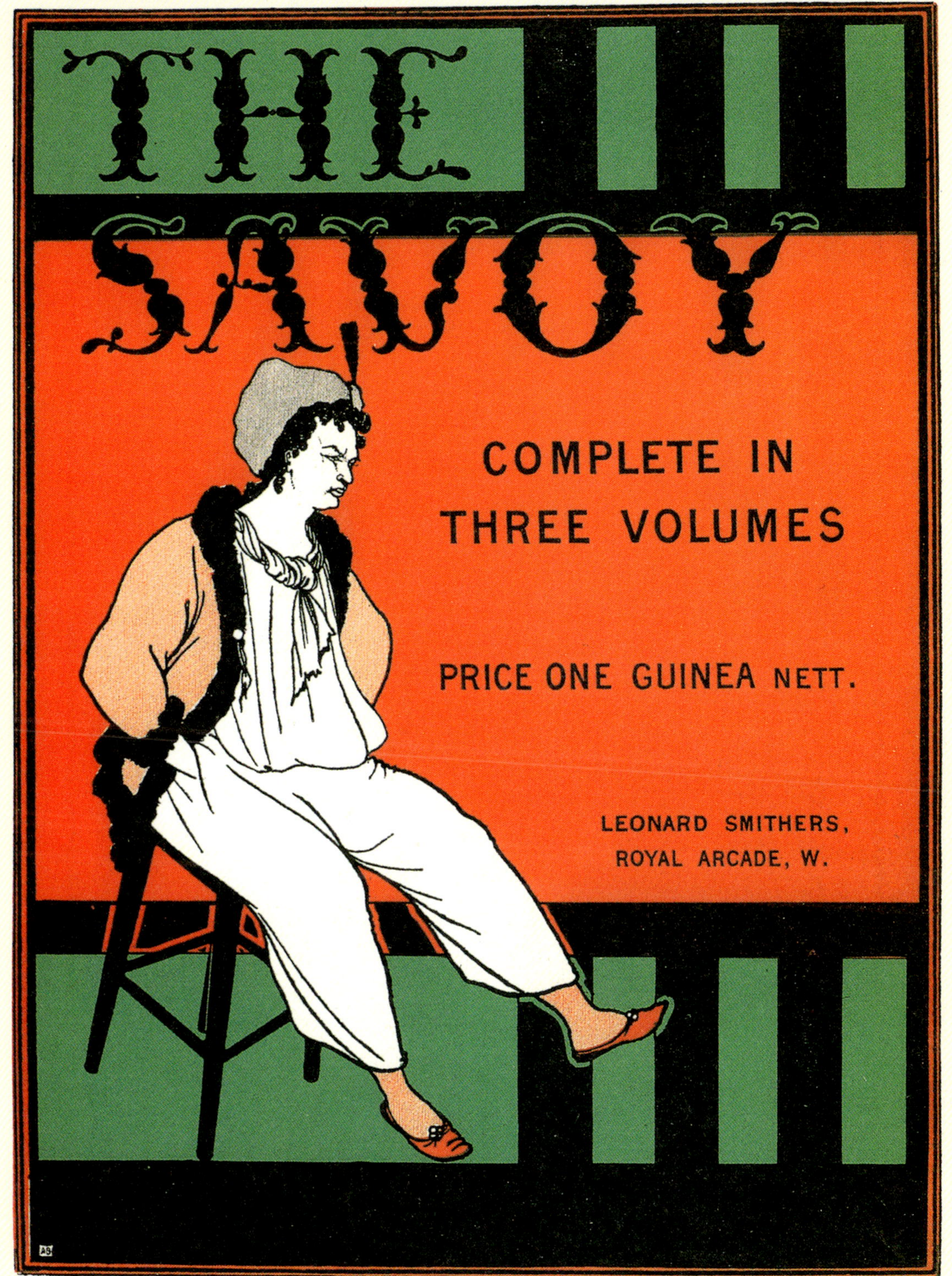

'The Savoy: Complete in Three Volumes' 1896

When *The Savoy* came to an end with Volume VIII, a three-volume compendium of the periodical was produced. This illustration was a small poster for this compendium, with a coloured version of the design of the cover for the final edition. Beardsley had come to think that he wanted to try adding colour to his monochrome works. The design for the cover featured no background, but in this illustration for the poster, the space is divided up by two horizontal and three vertical lines, and brightly coloured. The figure is rendered in a three-dimensional style, while the background is unapologetically flat, and the contrast between these makes for a peculiar impression.

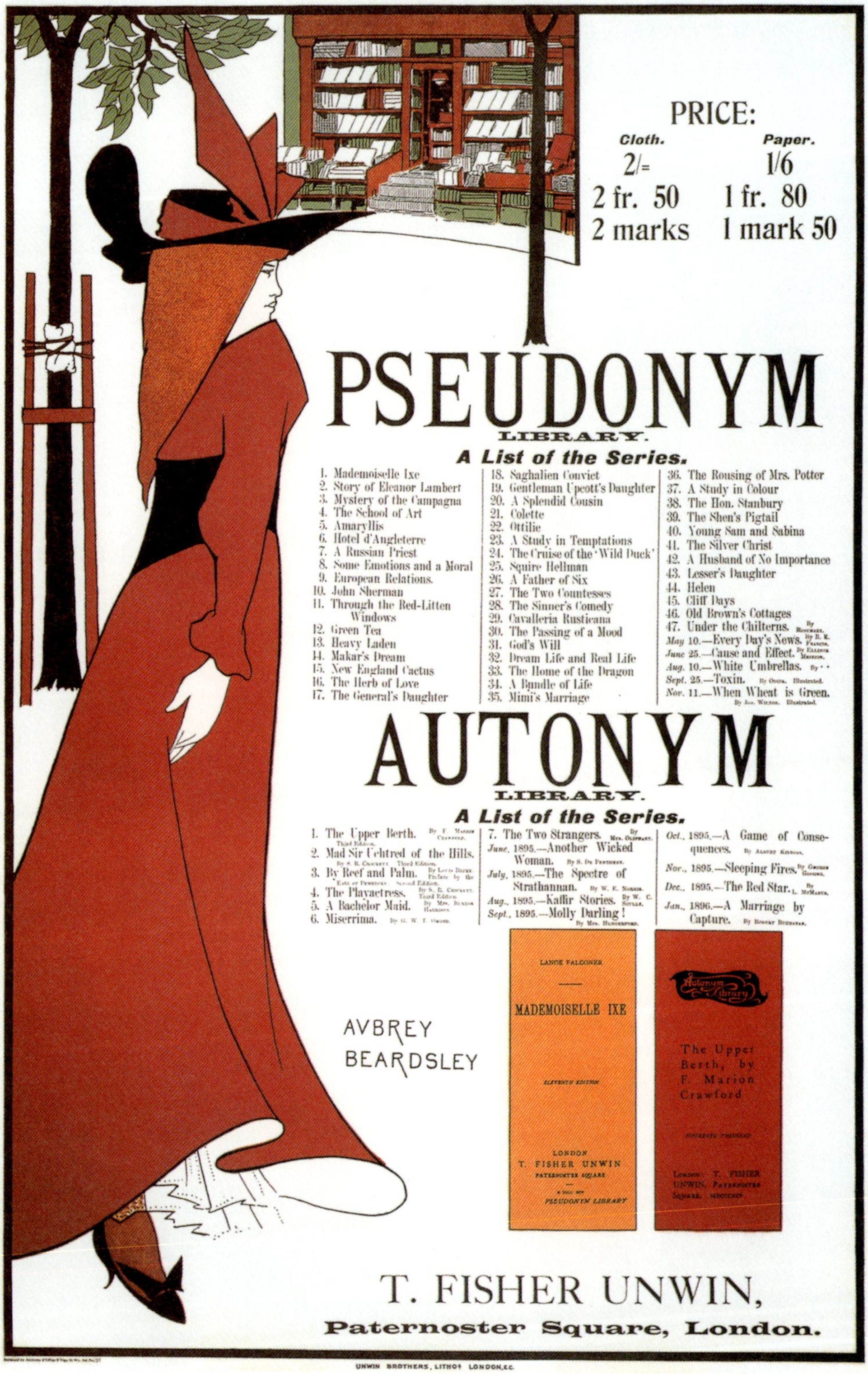

Poster for the T. Fisher Unwin Libraries 1896

This illustration was said to be influenced by French poster design, but the peculiar rendering of the woman's body and clothes makes it unmistakeably Beardsley. The poster was used repeatedly by the publishing company after its first printing in 1894, with the left-hand section remaining the same while the contents of the right-hand side were changed over. Sharp eyed viewers will have noticed that the tree on the left is a modulation of Beardsley's signature mark, confirming the idea that one cannot take one's eyes off him for a moment. Perhaps such a mischievous touch is fitting for a publisher publishing 'Autonym' and 'Pseudonym' series under separate names.

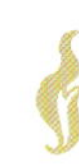

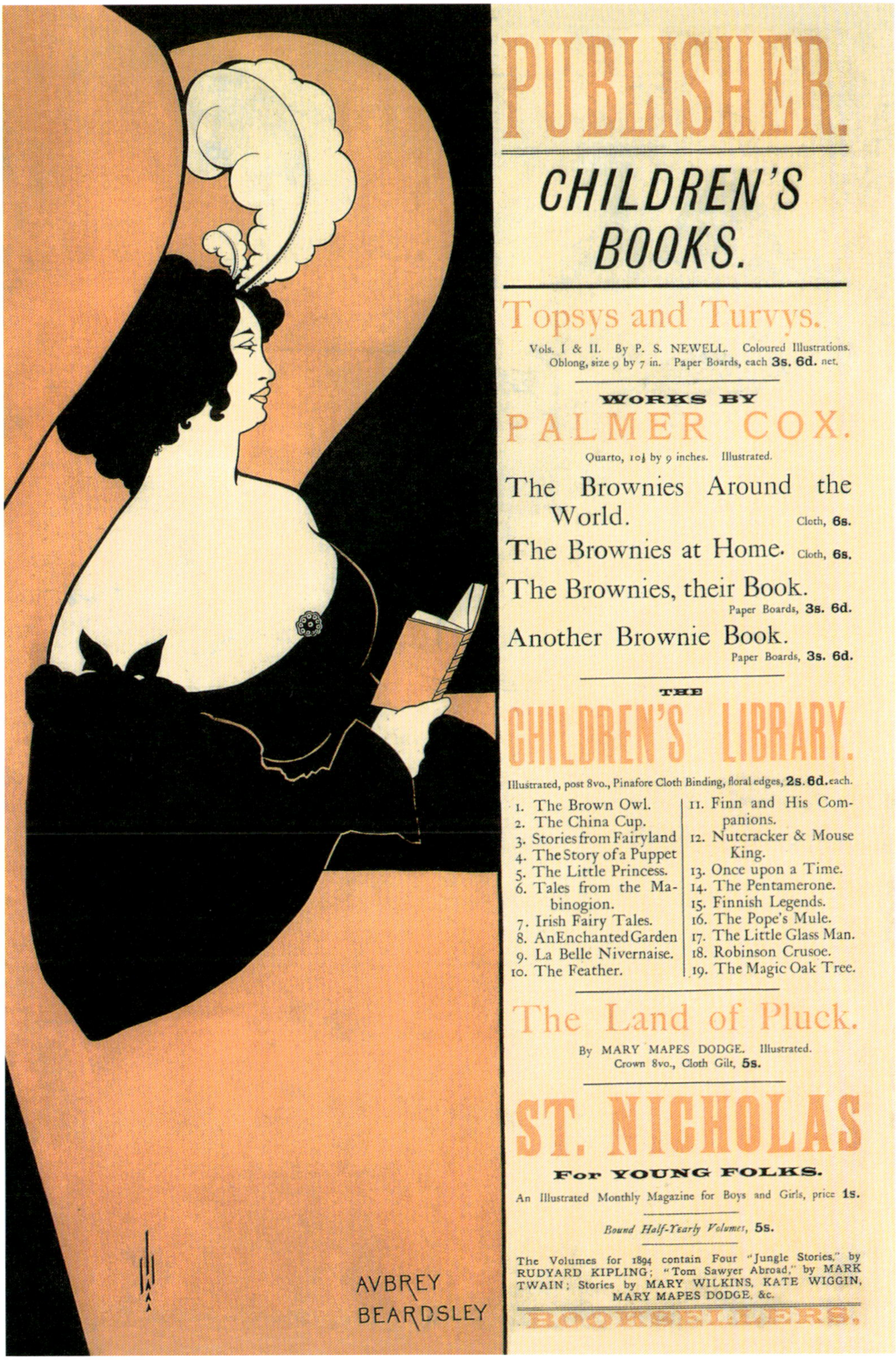

Poster for T. Fisher Unwin Children's Books 1894

Into the latter half of the nineteenth century, picture books and other children's books began to be published more widely. One wonders, though, if this picture of Beardsley's is really helping to advertise children's literature. Into this picture of an alluring lady with a scooped, neckline the artist has smuggled risqué shapes, not to mention his signature mark. If we forget about this mismatch with its purported purpose, we can see that the full, mellow forms are spectacular. Indeed, the picture is nothing short of a masterpiece, showing Beardsley at the zenith of his two-dimensional style. The brooch at the bust is a fine touch.

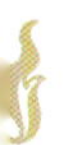
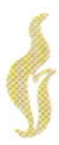

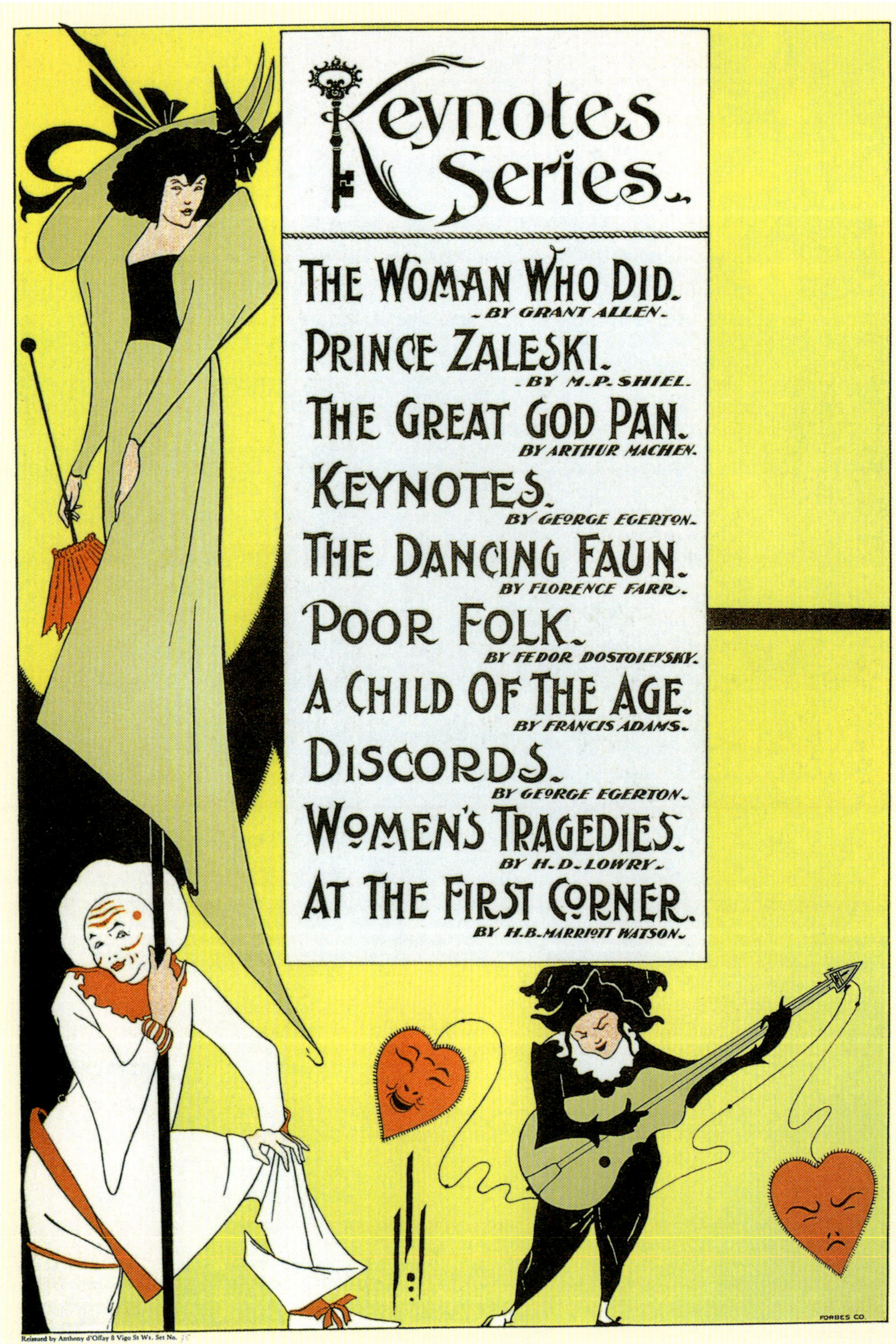

Poster for the Keynotes Series 1896

For this poster, the same picture is used as the cover for the first book in the series: *Keynotes* by George Egerton. The design features a woman, a pierrot and a dwarf. With the flag held by the pierrot vanishing inside the woman's skirt, apparently finishing somewhere between her thighs, the picture has a risqué note. The colour scheme is rather lurid, too, generating a slightly giddy feeling to the thing. With colour lithographs, the lithographer is also involved in the printing process, meaning that the end result is sometimes different from what the artist envisaged. Most likely this was one of the reasons that Beardsley was hesitant about printing his work in colour.

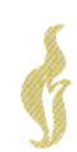

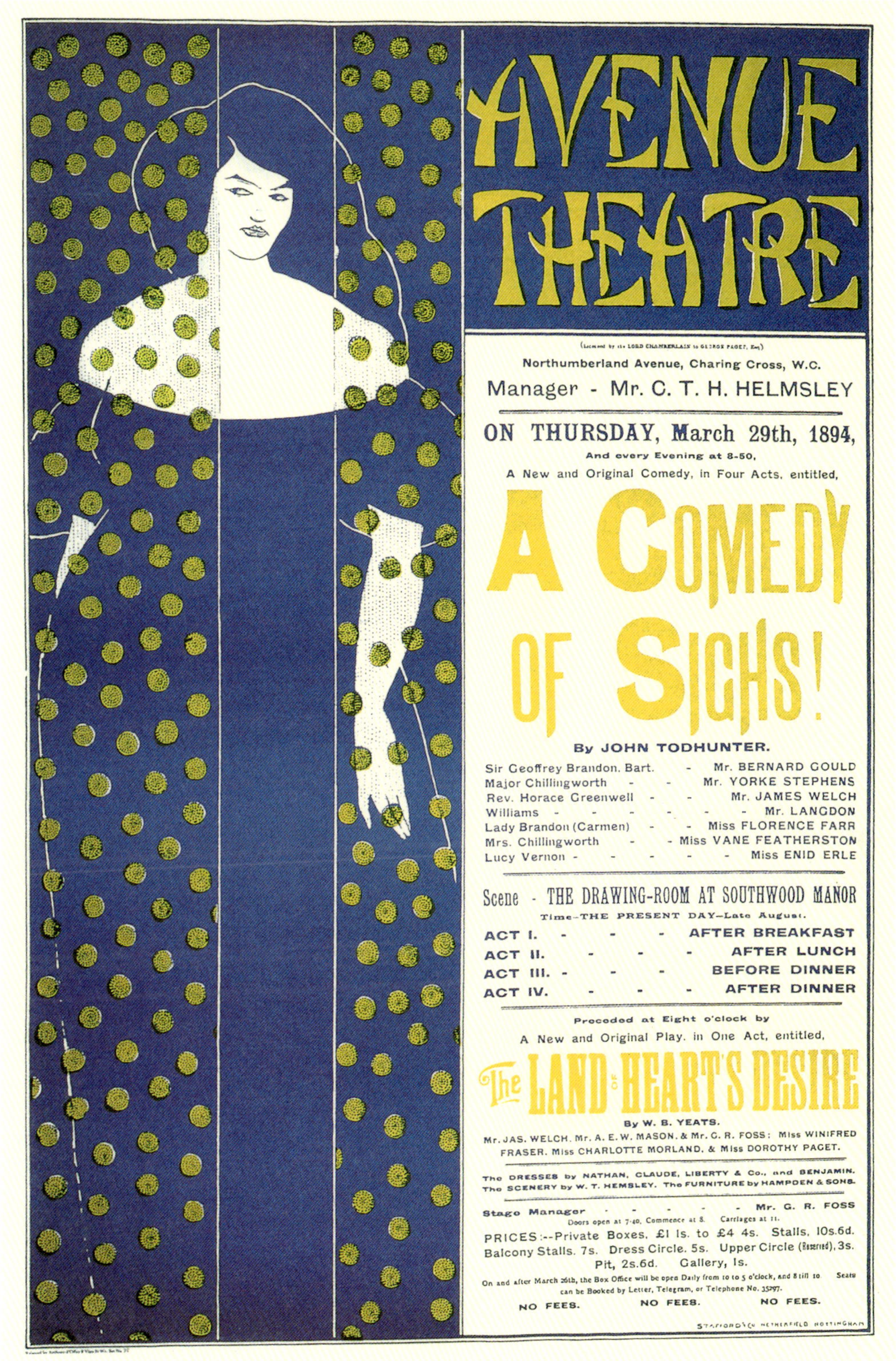

Poster for John Todhunter's 'A Comedy of Sighs' (Avignon Theatre) 1894

The Avignon Theatre was on Northumberland Avenue in London's Charing Cross. In this picture, we see the alluring figure of a woman through a dotted semi-translucent curtain, the shape of her body picked out clearly by the white lines. There are surely not many artists who could succeed in creating such a dramatic image out of such basic shapes and lines—and only using blue and yellow.

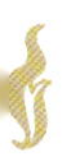

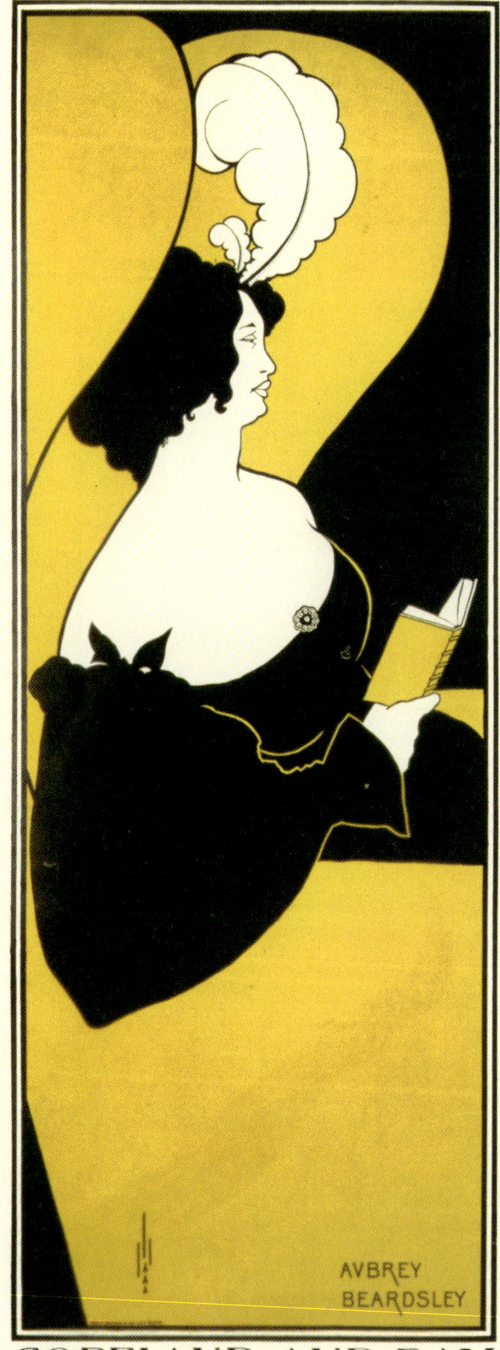

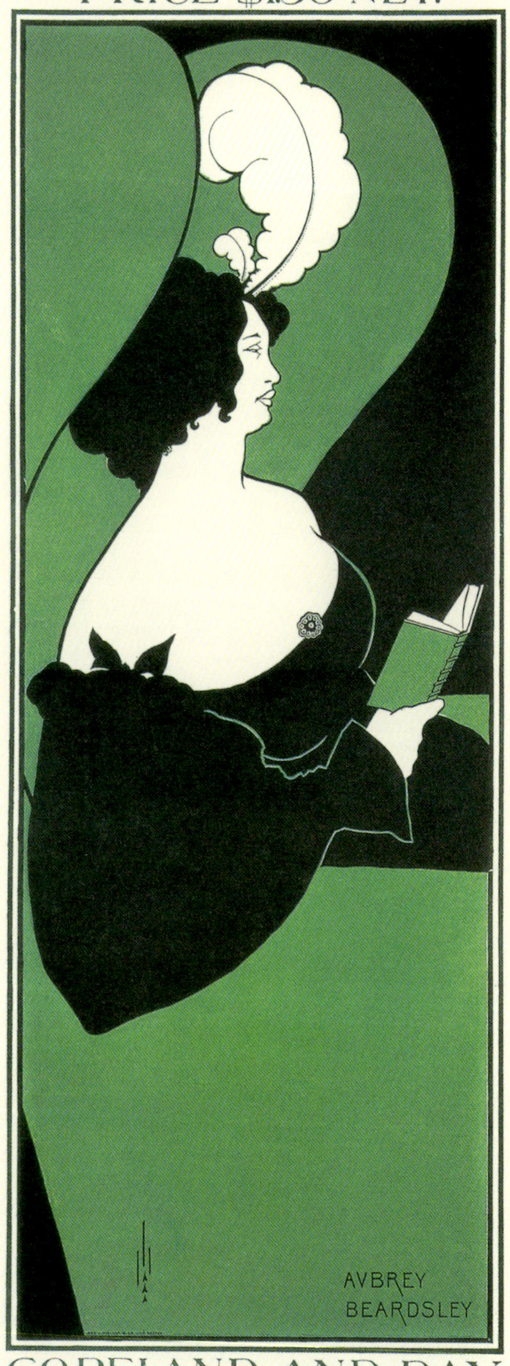

Posters for *The Yellow Book* (Right) 1894 / (Left) 1895

The illustration from the Children's Books poster for T. Fisher Unwin was printed in several colour variations, and was also used as a poster for *The Yellow Book*. In my previous comment, I called this unsuitable for advertising children's books, but one interpretation of this holds that the woman is a grandmother, sitting on a grandfather chair and reading to her grandchild. However, the woman is far too sexy to be a grandmother by my books, and the brooch at her breast looks like a nipple. This version of the poster by American publishers Copeland and Day seems better suited to this picture.

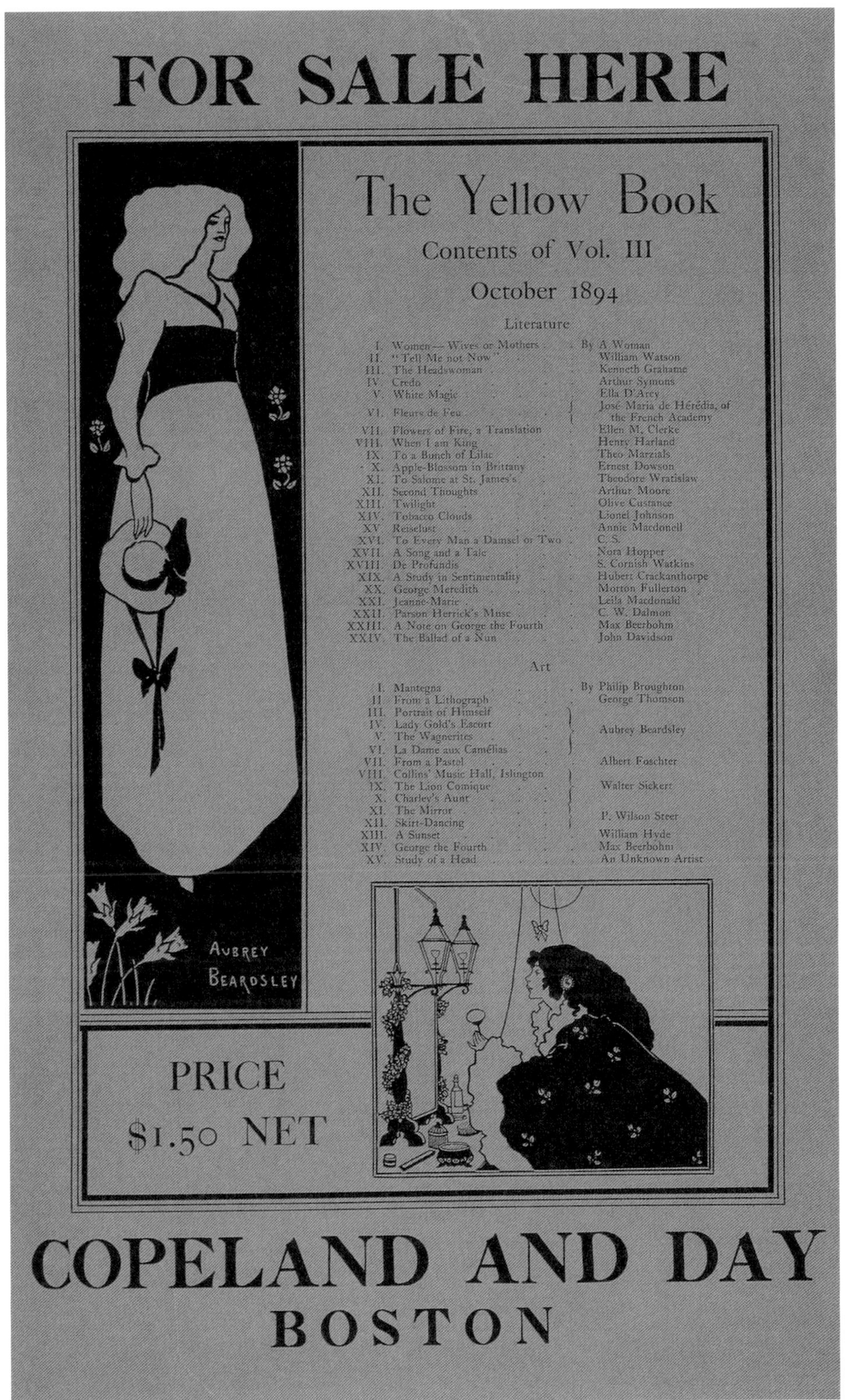

Poster for *The Yellow Book*, Vol. III 1894

The image of the woman to the left was created for this poster, while that at the bottom right is the cover image. It appears that this poster was used repeatedly, with the left-hand side of the poster remaining the same, and the contents and cover design on the right-hand side updated each time. *The Yellow Book* was published by John Lane in Britain, and Boston's Copeland and Day in the USA, with this poster was produced for the American market. The fact that the magazine was published in both the UK and the USA is worthy of note, and is tribute to Beardsley's popularity in America.

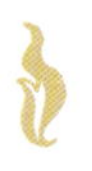

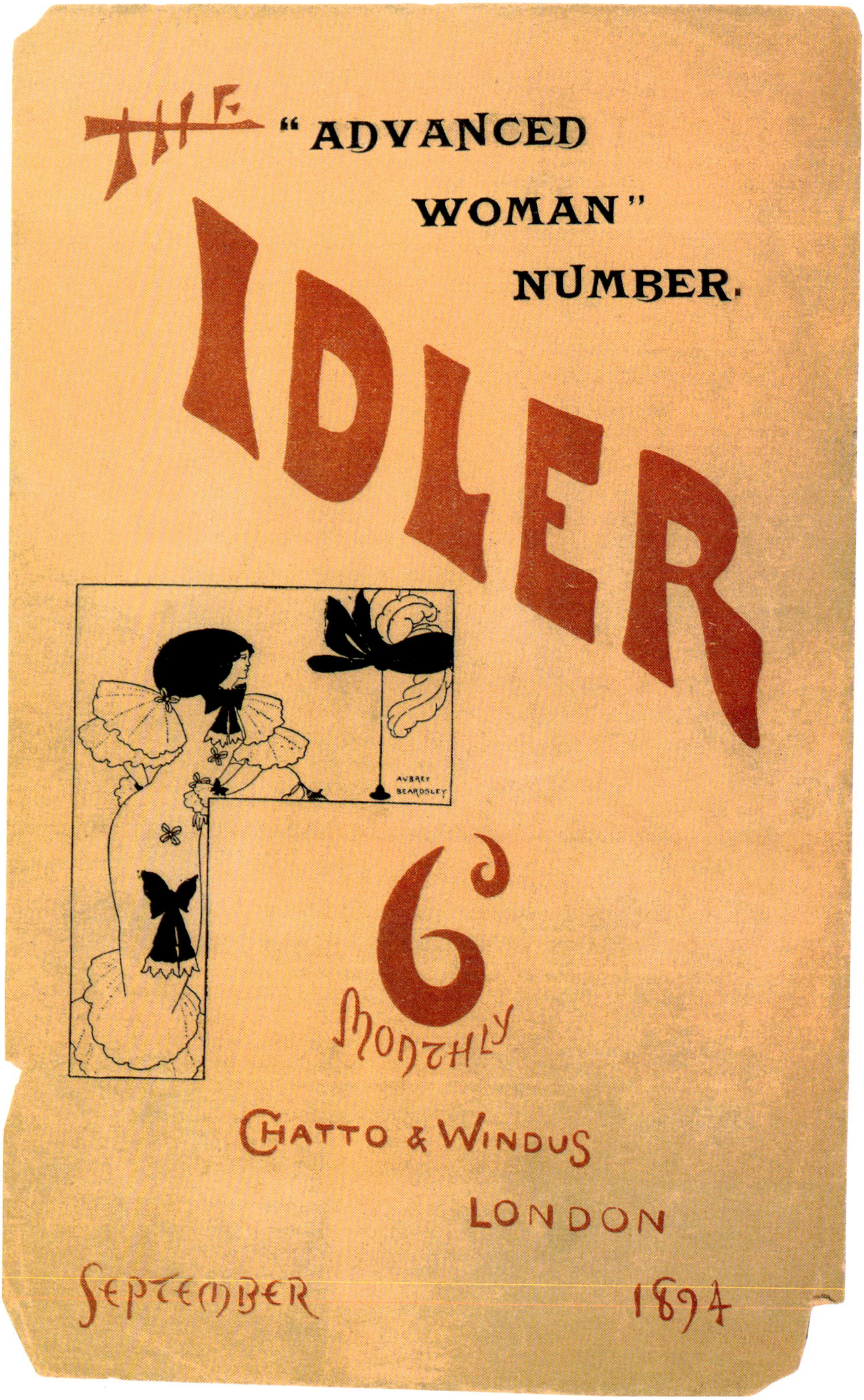

Jacket for *The Idler* 1894

This is a special edition of *The Idler* magazine devoted to 'advanced woman'. The frame for the illustration, like an inverted L, is the same as an illustration used inside the magazine, while the font used to write the magazine title is borrowed from French posters. The magazine contains the article by Angus Evan Abbott, 'How to Court the "Advanced Woman"', for which Beardsley made illustrations. Here we see a mix of the Belle Époque's femme fatale with the modern era girl. The jacket was printed in black and salmon pink.

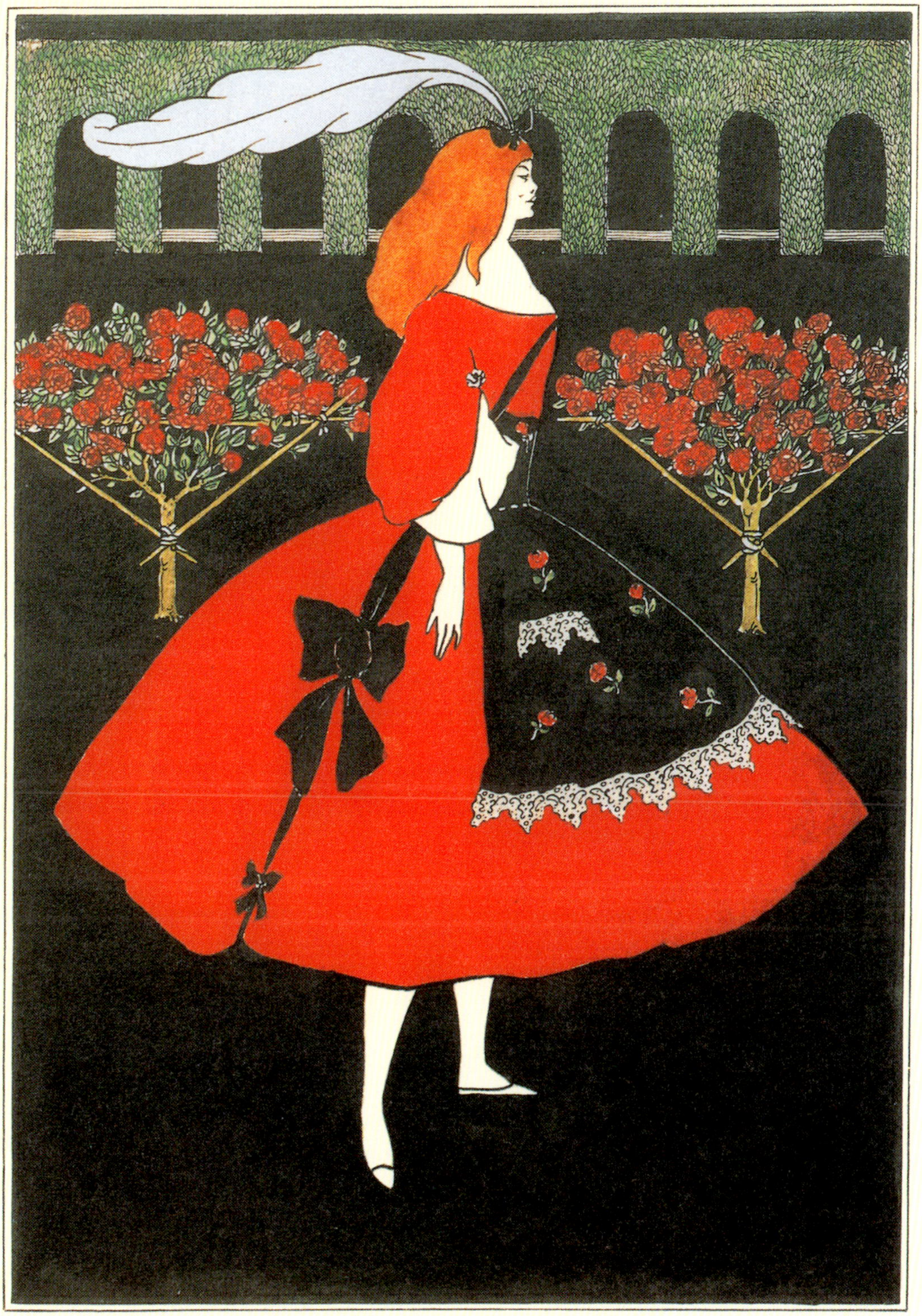

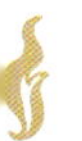
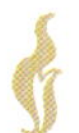

'The Slippers of Cinderella' 1894

This is an illustration that appeared in monochrome in Volume II of *The Yellow Book* (see p.79), which was later coloured in watercolour by Beardsley himself. The mouth-watering red of the skirt and green of the trees gives the illustration a fresh look. It seems that Beardsley was fond of this colour combination, although the red had to be scarlet, and the green emerald. For that reason, he was concerned about how his work was printed. Of course, even in colour, the picture doesn't lose the charm of Beardsley's monochrome original.

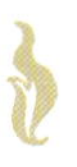

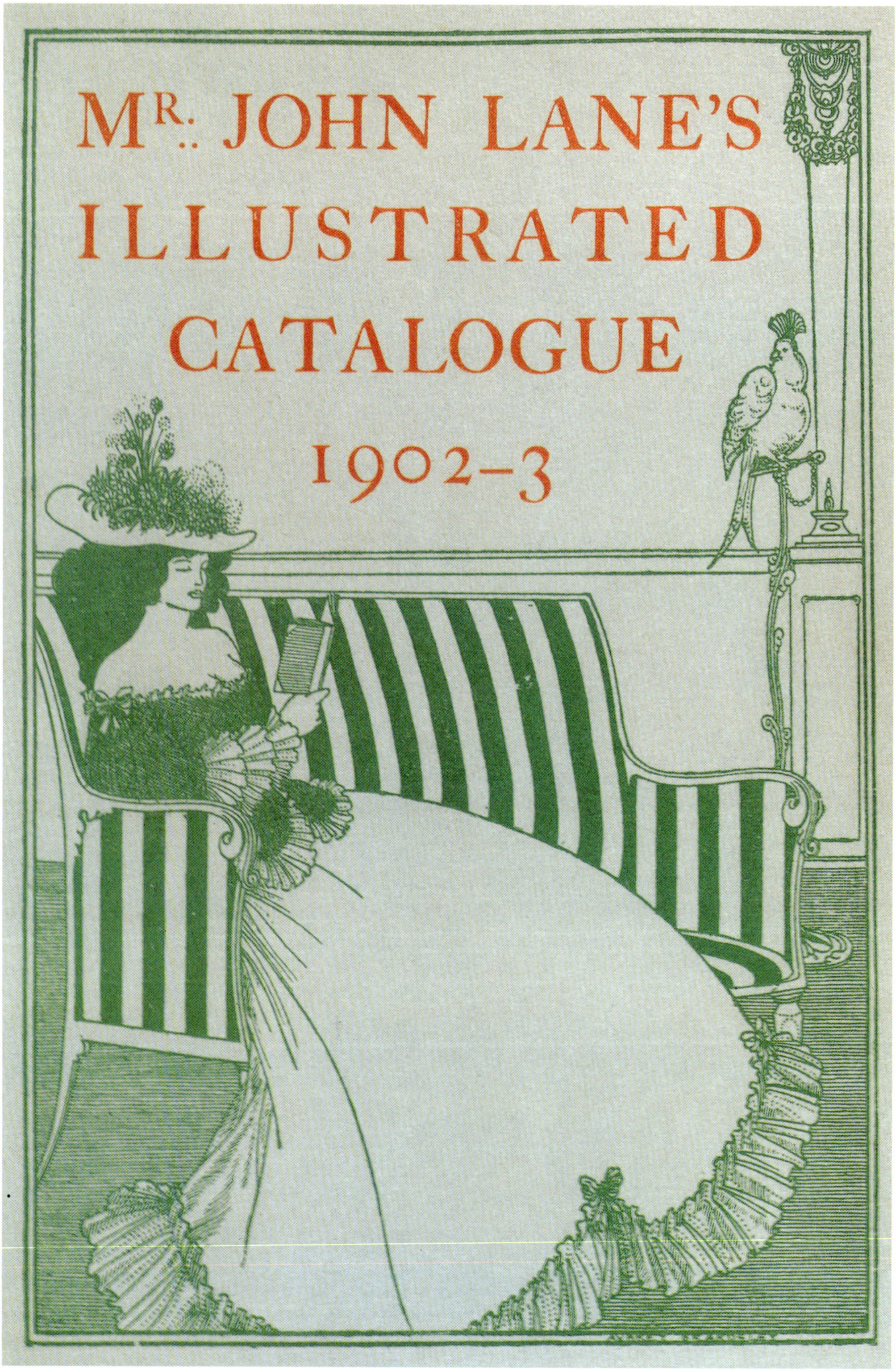

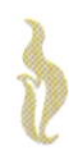

Cover for *Mr John Lane's Illustrated Catalogue* 1902

This same picture was used up until the seventh edition of Leonard Smithers' catalogue of second-hand books, with editions five to seven printed in assorted colour variations. This one is a catalogue of the second-hand John Lane books. The vertical stripes on the sofa are eye-catching. The column at the top right is most likely a permutation of Beardsley's signature mark. Between the framing of the wall and the compositional emphasis to the left where the woman is sitting, the picture shows a sumptuous sense of balance.

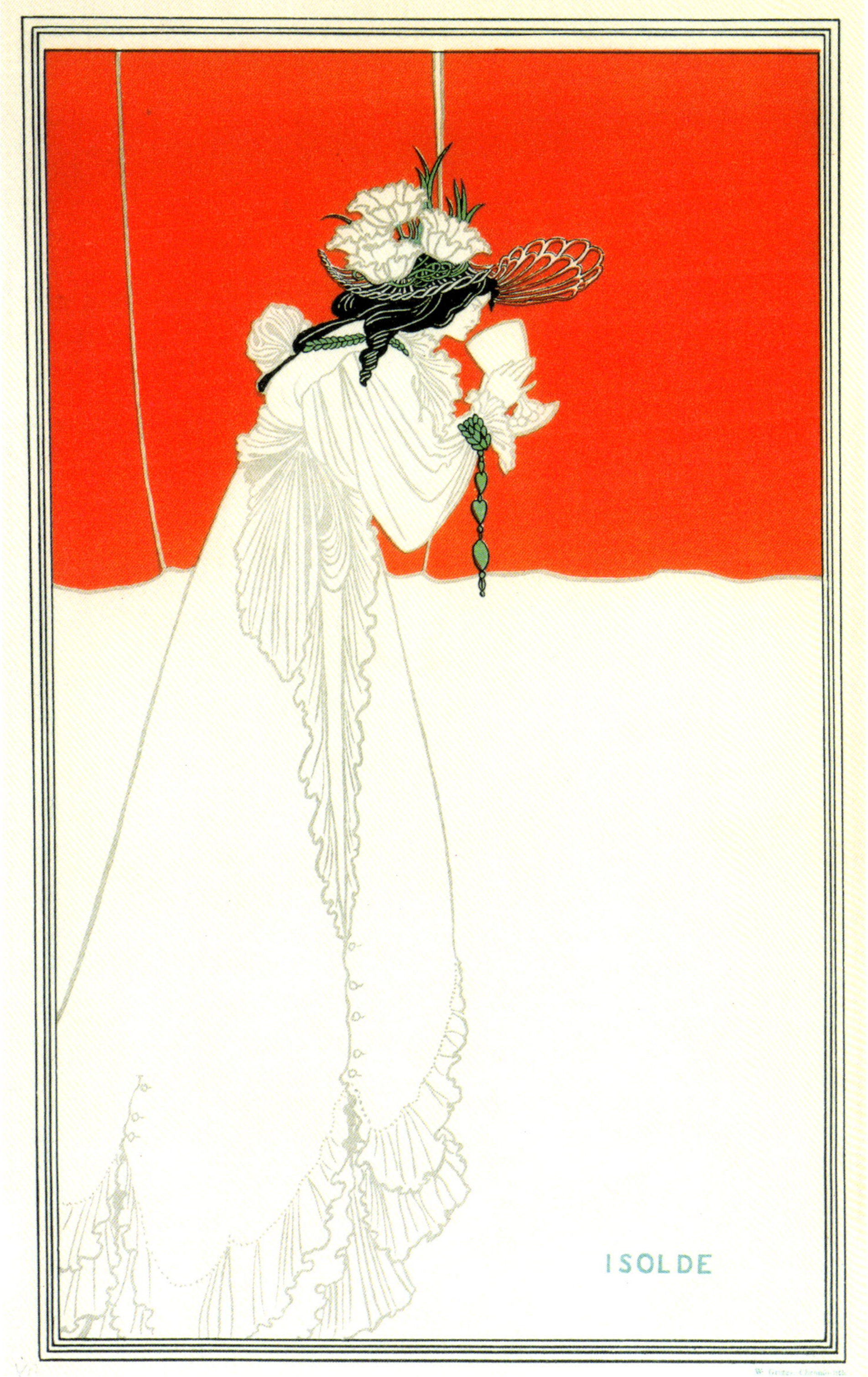

'Isolde' 1898

This is likely the most decorative of all the colour works that Beardsley produced. The contrast between the red and the white is extremely eye-catching. The contour lines are rendered in grey, with the head and bracelet in green and black. The woman's white figure looms large against the impossibly simple background of white floor and red curtain. This is one of Beardsley's colour works where lithograph printing has served him well. Looking at it, one can practically hear the strains of *Tristan und Isolde*, the artist's favourite Wagner opera.

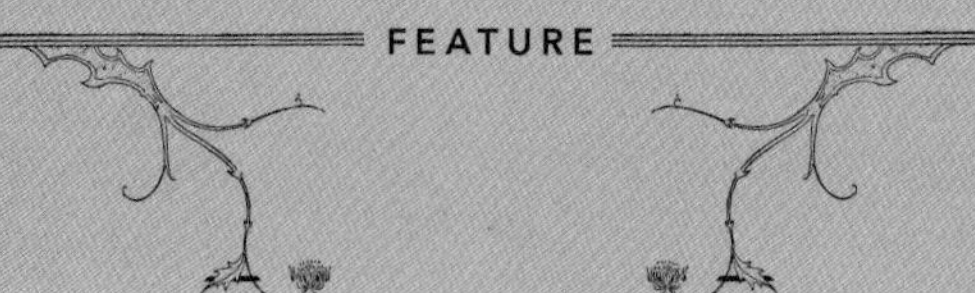

Beardsley and His Colours

Beardsley created his monochrome prints using not the woodcut method that had been used until that point, but a newly developed technique of mechanical printing called the line block, as this meant his works could be printed without necessitating the intervention of a wood-carver. However, when he returned to colour, this once again meant the involvement of another party in the form of a lithographer, which meant the finished product could differ somewhat from his original. With the printing technology of that time, this process did not go so well. Beardsley had a unique sense of colouration, but various circumstantial reasons led him to favour the creation of monochrome prints. One such reason was the fact that he was largely self-taught, and lacked knowledge about oils and other coloured materials. The coloured works he did create were therefore simple watercolour works, where he could unleash his free sensibility with colour that was untethered to academicism in the way that oils were. His brush drew out the charm of the semi-opaque, simple colours.

Another reason for Beardsley's choice of monochrome was a financial one. At the beginning of his career, Beardsley needed to create work whose production costs was minimal.

That period of history was also a transitional stage in terms of the development of colour printing—it was not until into the twentieth century that it really took off. The kind of colour-rich school of illustration that grew up thanks to Beardsley's influence at the hands of Arthur Rackham, Edmund Dulac, Kay Nielsen and others only took shape of after the turn of the century. The age in which Beardsley was working was therefore the period of transition towards colour prints. Very few of his works were initially created as colour works; rather, most of them were first drawn in black and white, with colour added later. Yet there are some of his works that were printed in various different colour variations, all of which have their own unique charms. There is something about Beardsley's pictures which lends them the potential to be created in various colours. Possibly, hidden within Beardsley's monochromes is hidden a secret form of colour. Within our imaginations, we can see them in all kinds of different shades. If that is the case, then we could say his black and white pictures bring the possibility for limitless colouration.

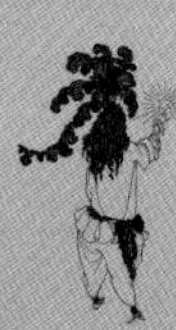

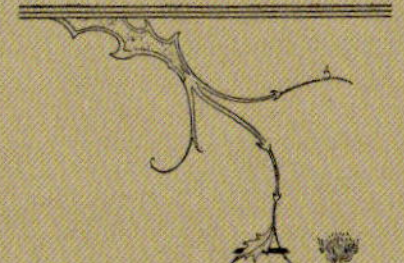
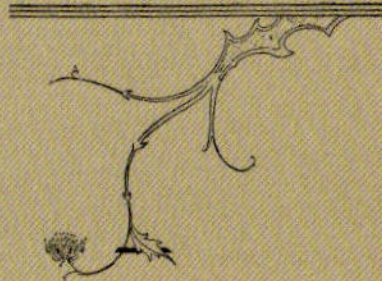

Unlocking Beardsley's Colours:

Black × Single colour

×

At the time Beardsley was making work, colour printing was a new technology that was still rare. For that reason, most of Beardsley's designs are not truly multicolour; rather they use a limited number of colours very effectively. The same design is sometimes printed in several different colour versions. From brights to more subtle shades, even his selection of colours is chic and well-judged.

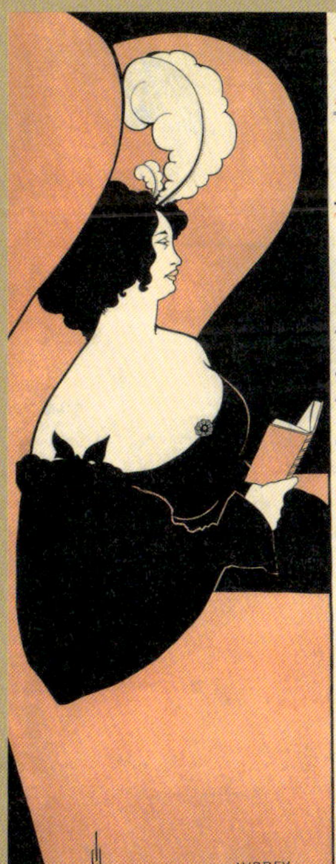

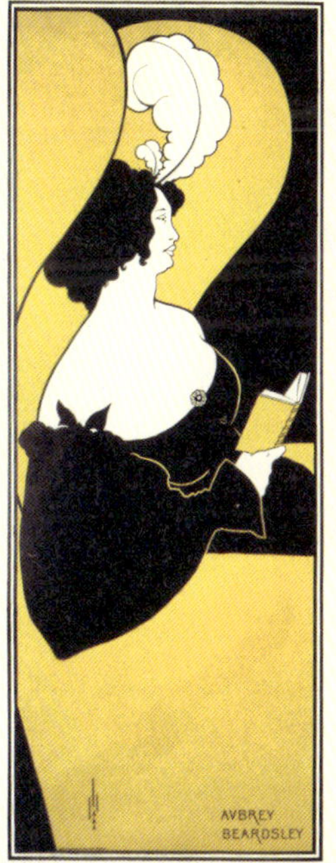

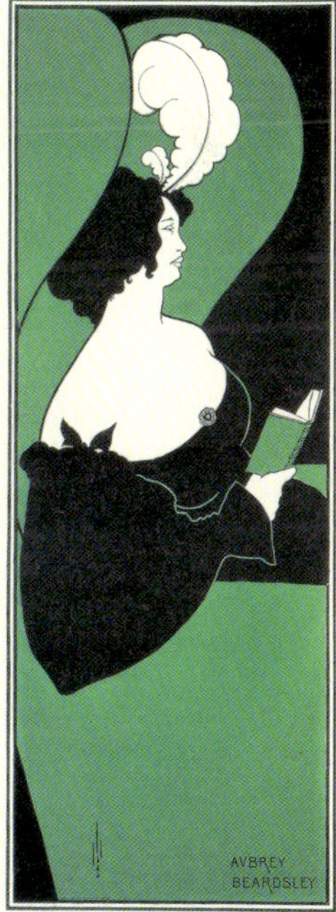

P155   P158   P158

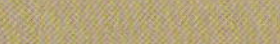
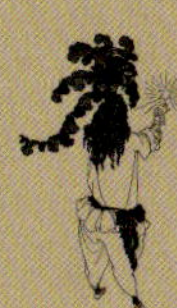

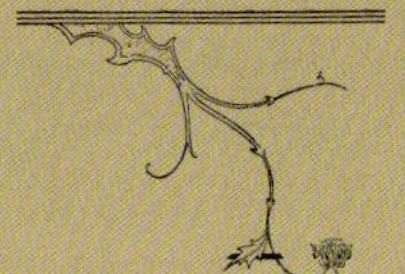
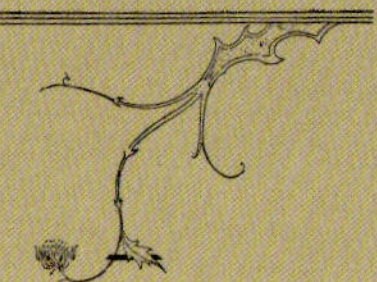

UNLOCKING BEARDSLEY'S COLOURS:

Red × Green

 × 

This is the most common colour combination in Beardsley's work. His red of choice is a scarlet with a yellowish tinge, while his green usually either contains equal parts green or blue or tends towards the bluish end of the spectrum.

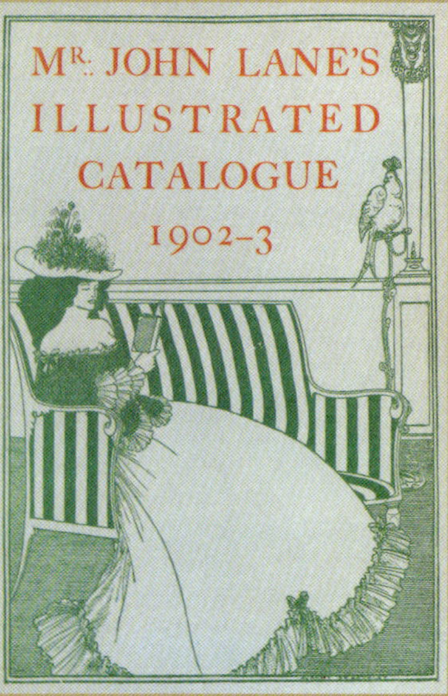

P163

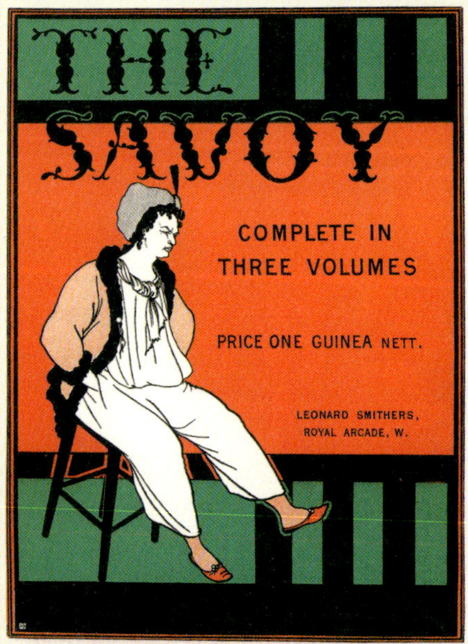

P153

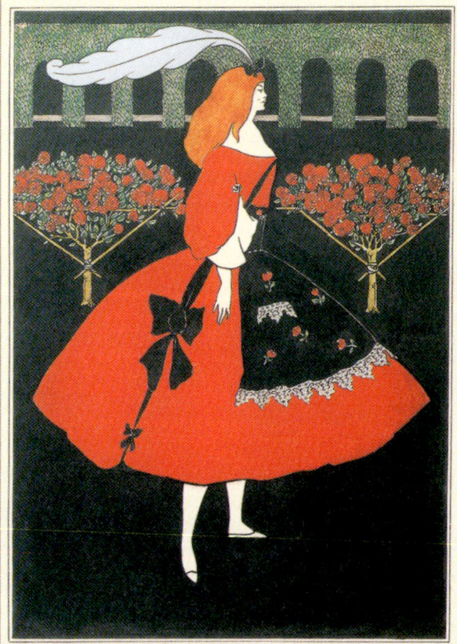

P161

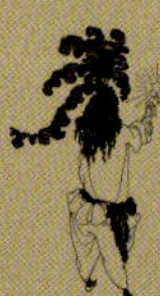

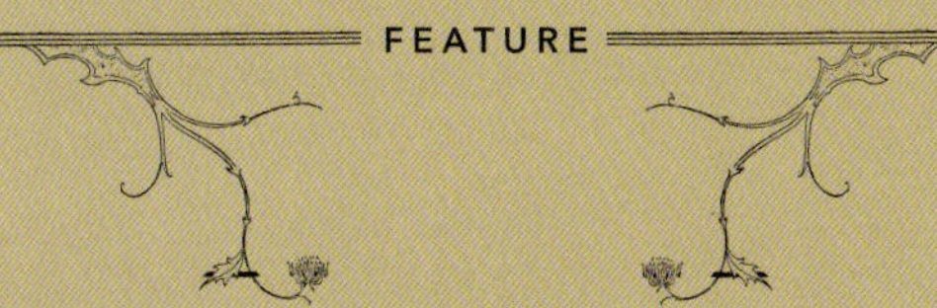

UNLOCKING BEARDSLEY'S COLOURS:

Blue and Yellow

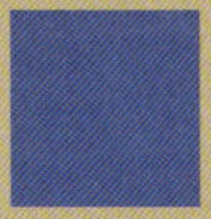 

Blue and yellow were also favourites of Beardsley's. Yellow was the colour of the fin de siècle, used of course for the cover of *The Yellow Book*, and blue used in combination with it supplied a gilded look, so this pair were often chosen for covers.

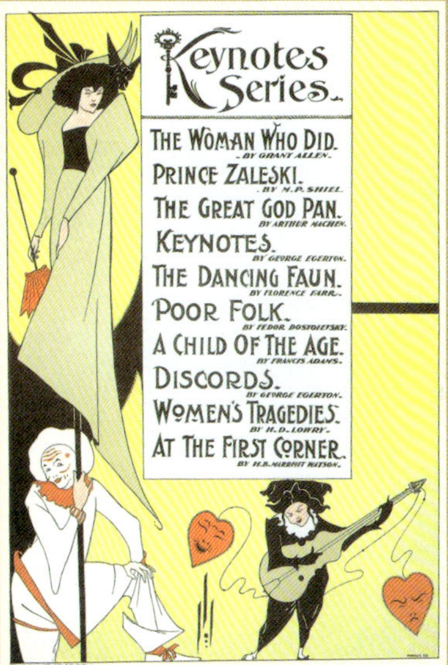

P156

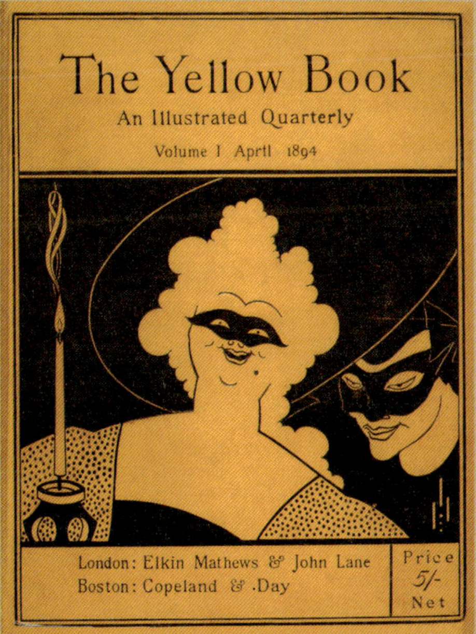

P69

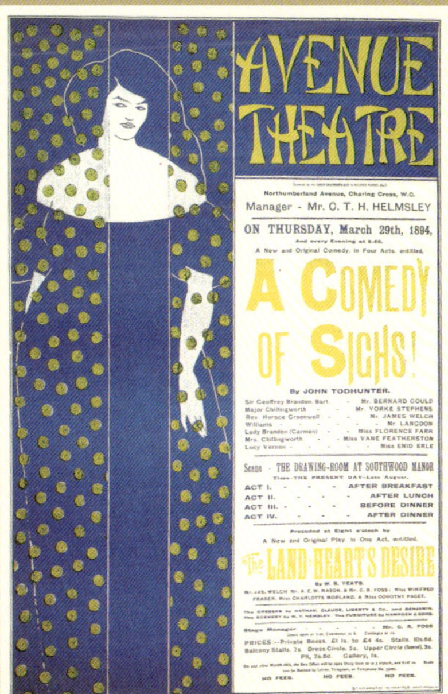

P157

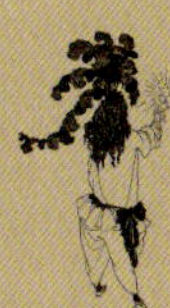

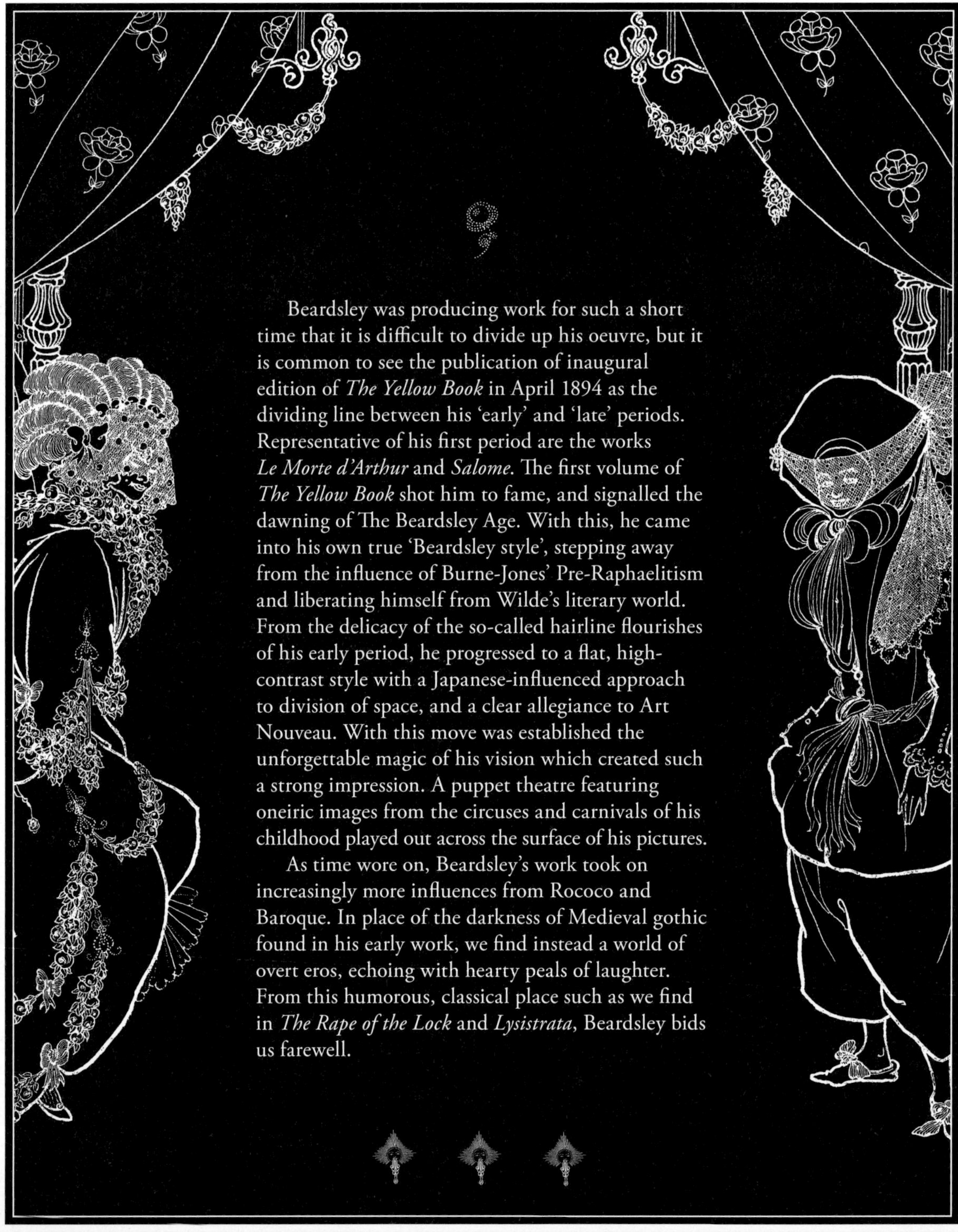

Beardsley was producing work for such a short time that it is difficult to divide up his oeuvre, but it is common to see the publication of inaugural edition of *The Yellow Book* in April 1894 as the dividing line between his 'early' and 'late' periods. Representative of his first period are the works *Le Morte d'Arthur* and *Salome*. The first volume of *The Yellow Book* shot him to fame, and signalled the dawning of The Beardsley Age. With this, he came into his own true 'Beardsley style', stepping away from the influence of Burne-Jones' Pre-Raphaelitism and liberating himself from Wilde's literary world. From the delicacy of the so-called hairline flourishes of his early period, he progressed to a flat, high-contrast style with a Japanese-influenced approach to division of space, and a clear allegiance to Art Nouveau. With this move was established the unforgettable magic of his vision which created such a strong impression. A puppet theatre featuring oneiric images from the circuses and carnivals of his childhood played out across the surface of his pictures.

As time wore on, Beardsley's work took on increasingly more influences from Rococo and Baroque. In place of the darkness of Medieval gothic found in his early work, we find instead a world of overt eros, echoing with hearty peals of laughter. From this humorous, classical place such as we find in *The Rape of the Lock* and *Lysistrata*, Beardsley bids us farewell.

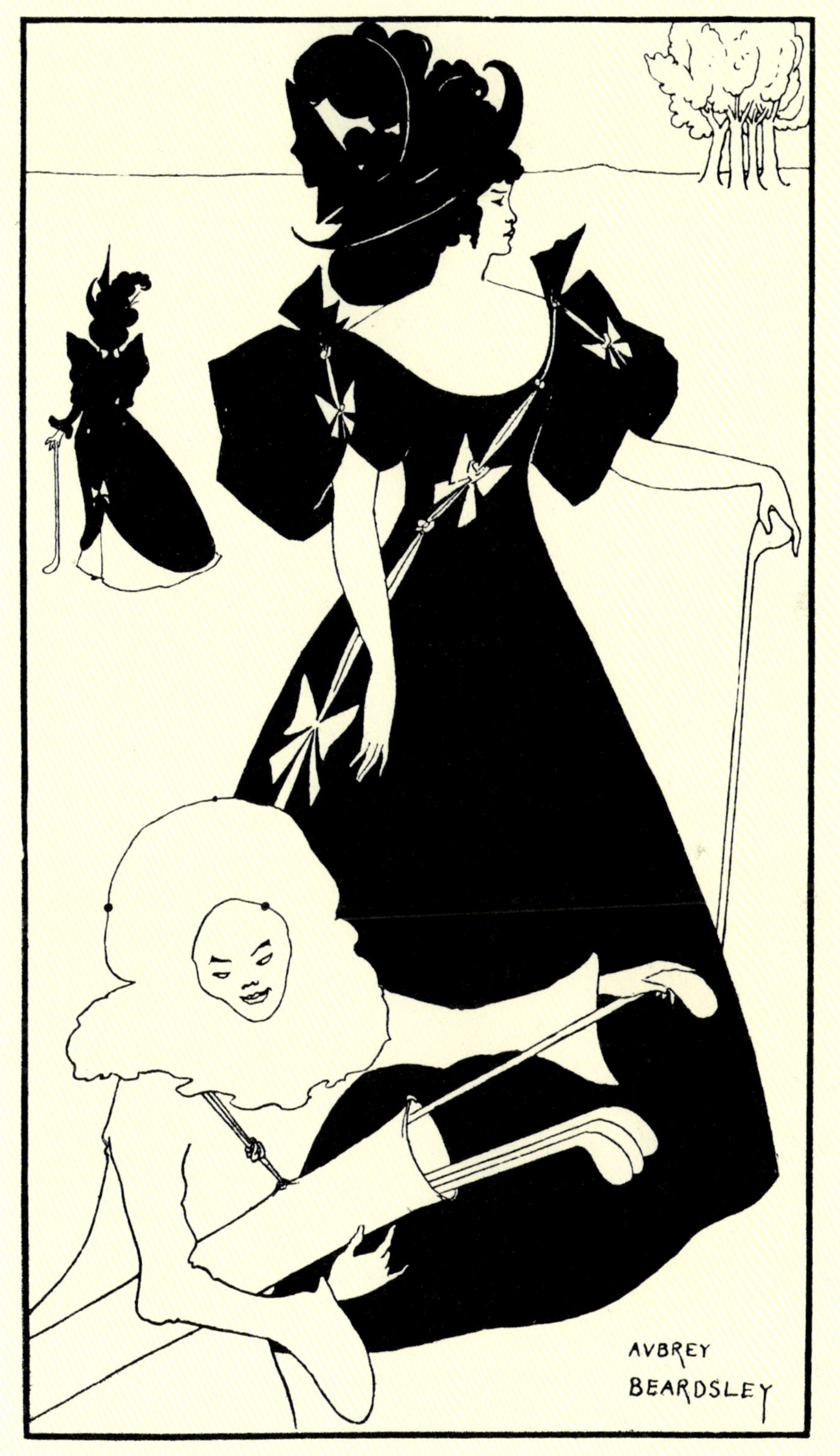

Invitation to the Opening of Prince's Ladies Golf Club
14th July 1894; Mitcham, Surrey

In keeping with the latest fashion trends, a lady in a large-brimmed hat stands holding a golf club, accompanied by a clown serving as her caddy. Golf was a cutting-edge activity for fin-de-siècle women. Of course, this scene was a figment of Beardsley's imagination—in reality nobody would have golfed in outfits such as these. The picture has a simple, eye-catching composition, with the silhouette of a similarly dressed woman in the distance and the trees on the horizon.

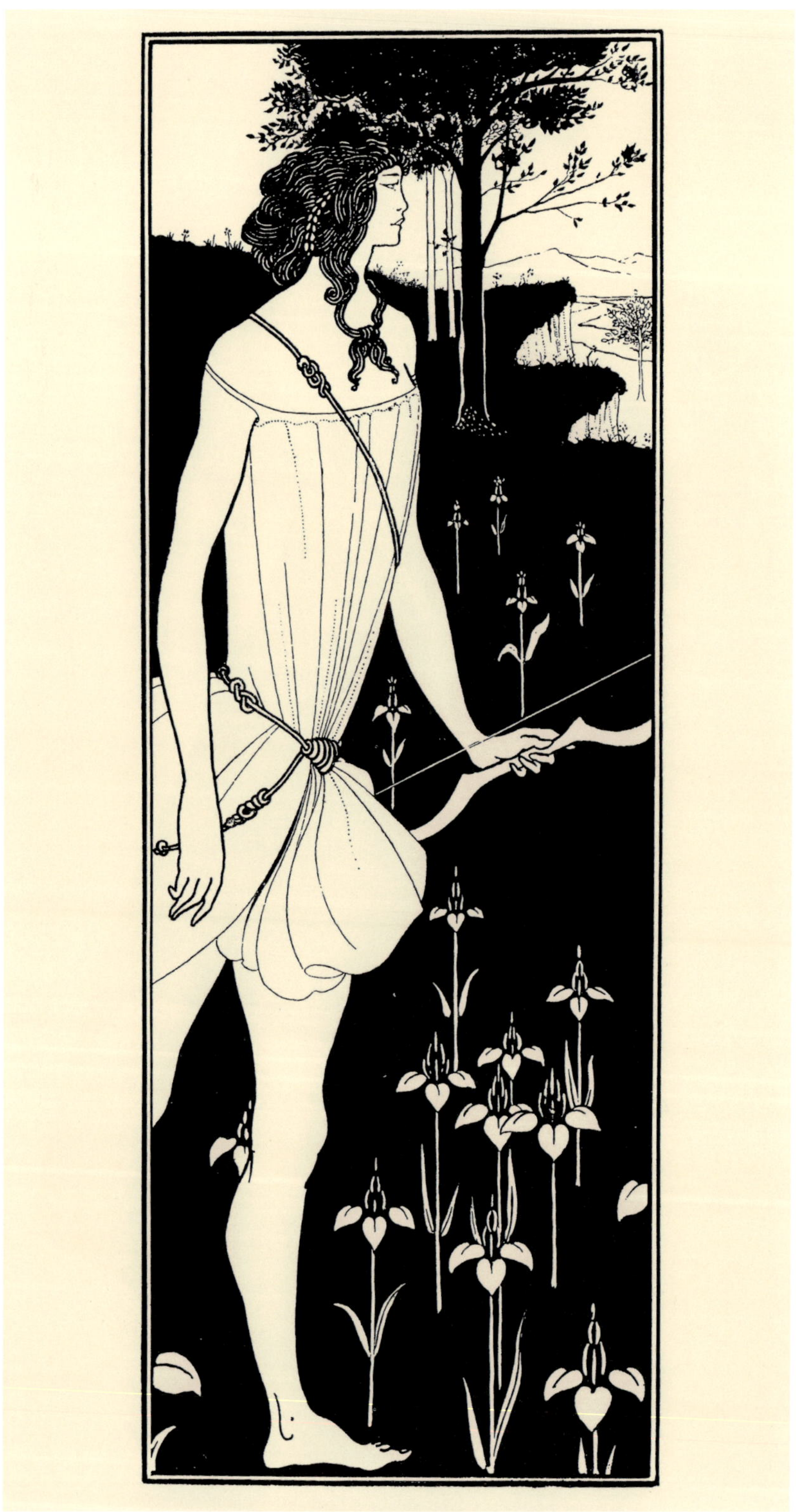

'Atalanta' 1895

This picture shows Atalanta hunting in the wilds of Calydon, but this time sans dog. This picture was due to appear in Volume V of *The Yellow Book*, but was one those Beardsley illustrations that was omitted after Wilde's arrest. In comparison to Atalanta with the dog, this Atalanta appears relatively docile, but if we take her hiked up skirt as two balls, then her lower half traces the shape of a phallus. Beardsley was drawn to women who showed masculine strength.

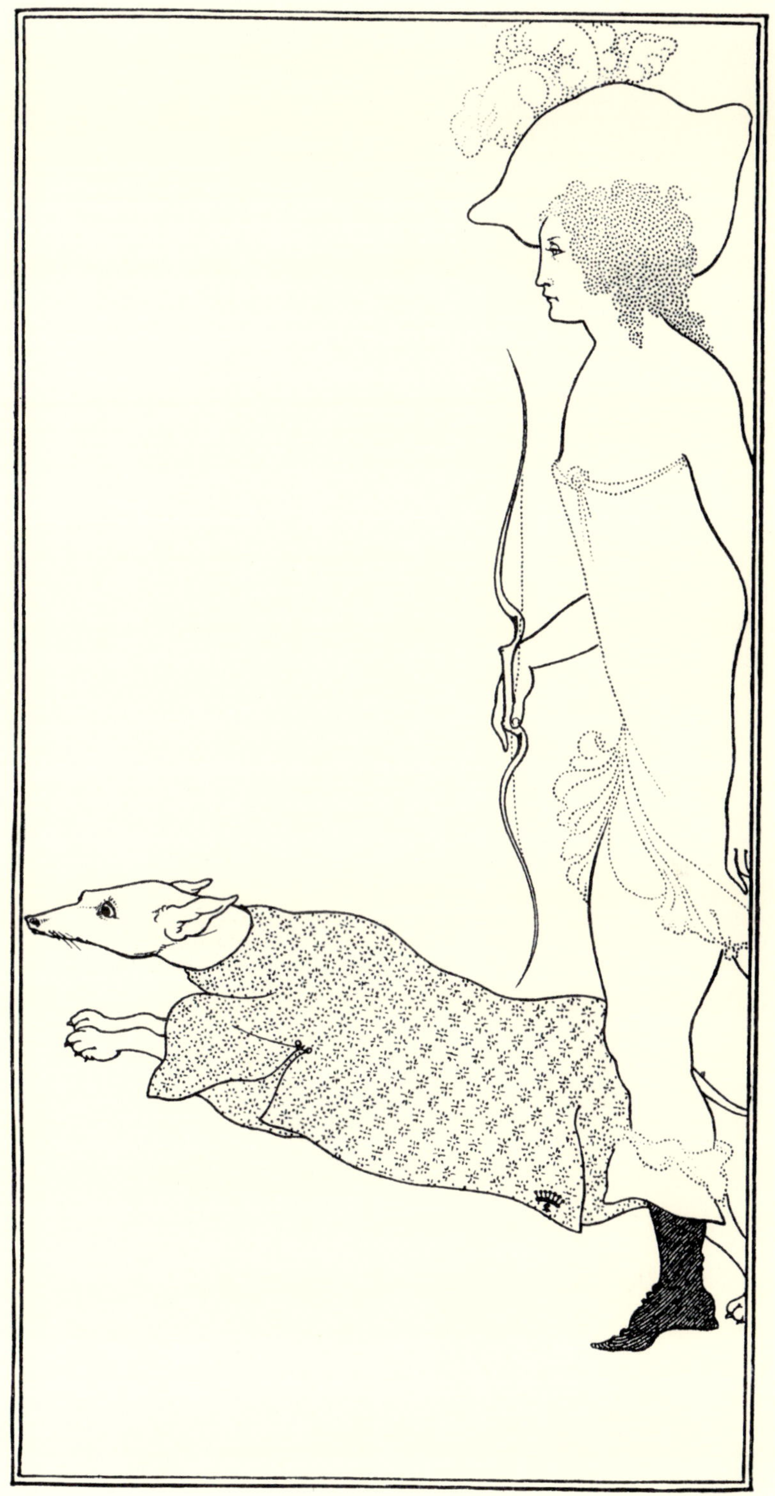

'Atalanta' 1895

In Greek myth, Atalanta is similar to Artemis—a spirited virgin huntress. Beardsley's image is said to derive from A. C. Swinburne's poem, 'Atalanta in Calydon'. The composition, with Atalanta to the right, and the left section left largely blank, has all the hallmarks of a Beardsley, but the content is highly provocative, with Atalanta's body somewhat off, and the hunting dog flying up at her feet perfectly phallic. Why is the dog wearing a coat? Is it not because without, the picture would be deemed obscene? In the place where the dog's genitalia should be, we find a small crown.

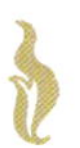

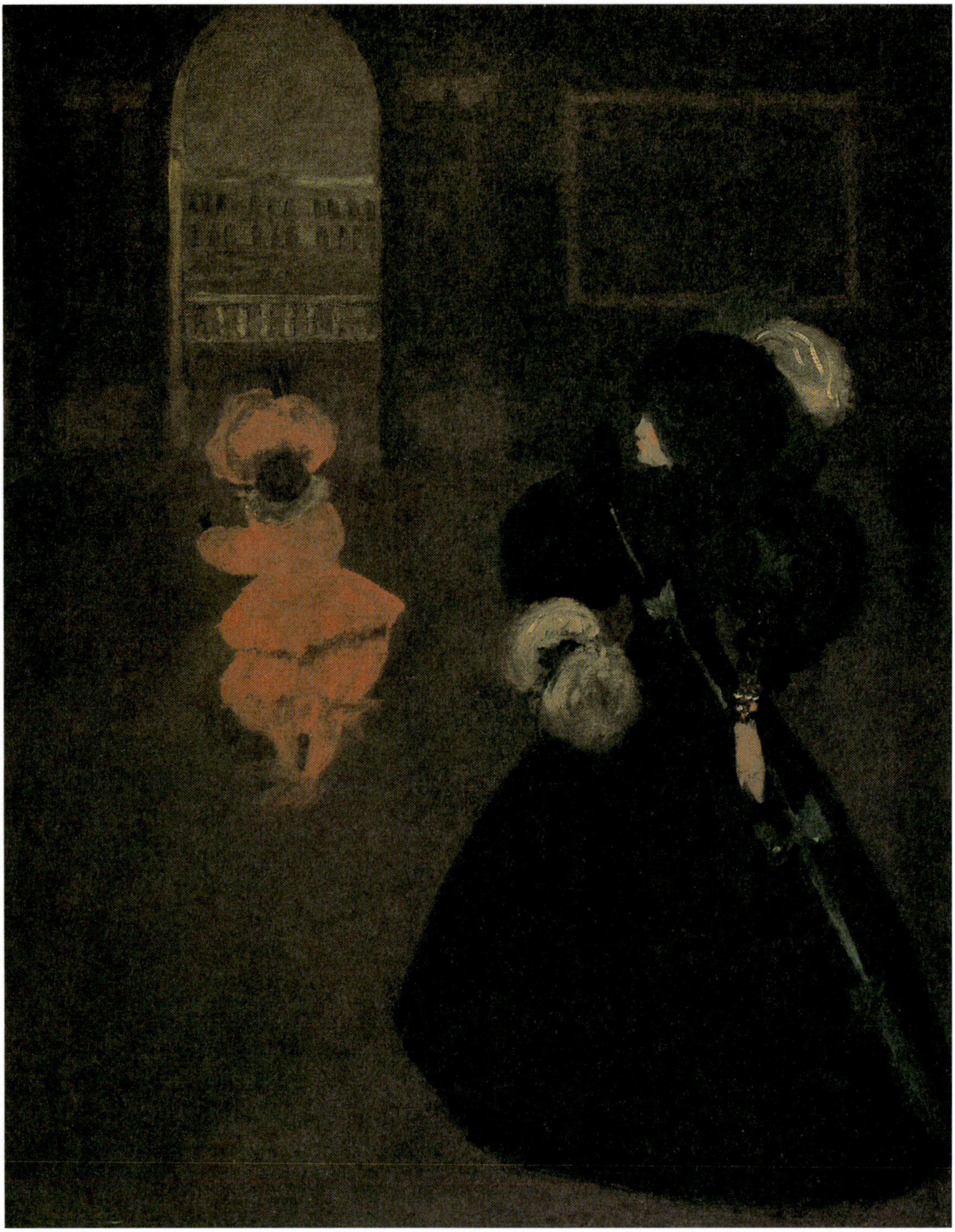

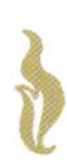

'Caprice' 1894

This and *Masked Woman with a White Mouse* (p.173), both painted on different sides of the same canvas, are the only surviving oil paintings by Beardsley. This is the oil version of 'The Comedy Ballet of Marionettes I' that was featured in *The Yellow Book*. The dwarf is inviting the woman in through the gates of Paradise. The gates are shaped like cannons (phalluses). One interpretation of the picture holds that the woman's hesitation by these masculine gates shows her desire for Sapphic love. Beardsley is seen as a monochrome artist, but his works in colour are also highly distinctive, and one wishes that there were more of them.

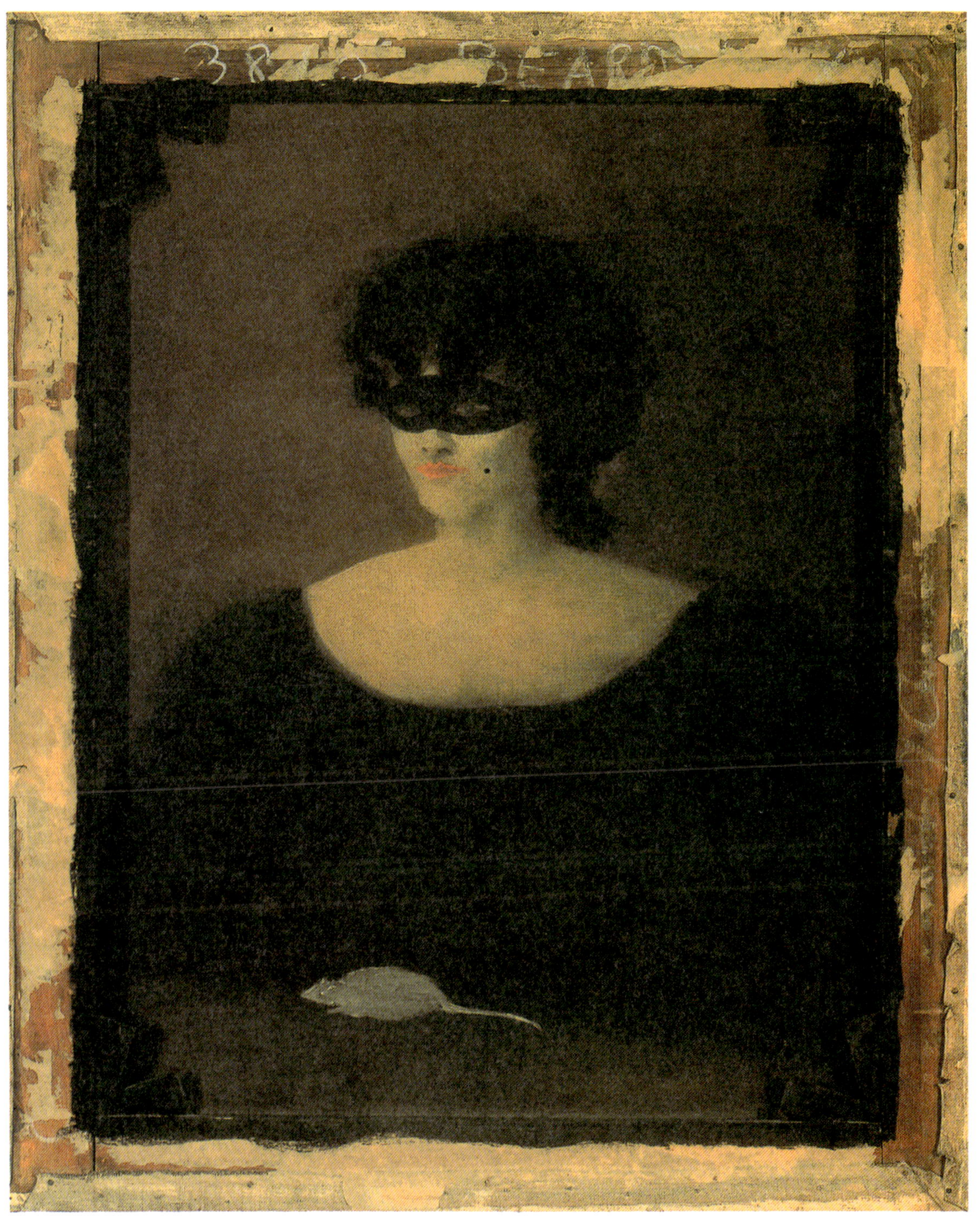

'Masked Woman with a White Mouse' 1894

This is painted on the same canvas as 'Caprice'. The mouse symbolizes sexuality, and also wealth. In Japan, the mouse is seen as the messenger of the god Daikokuten, and associated with prosperity, and it is possible that Beardsley was familiar with Japanese pictures of such mice. The masked woman is a witch who controls the mouse, and is perhaps an incarnation of Daikokuten. The fin de siècle saw many artists portraying mysterious women—this is Beardsley's take on the tradition.

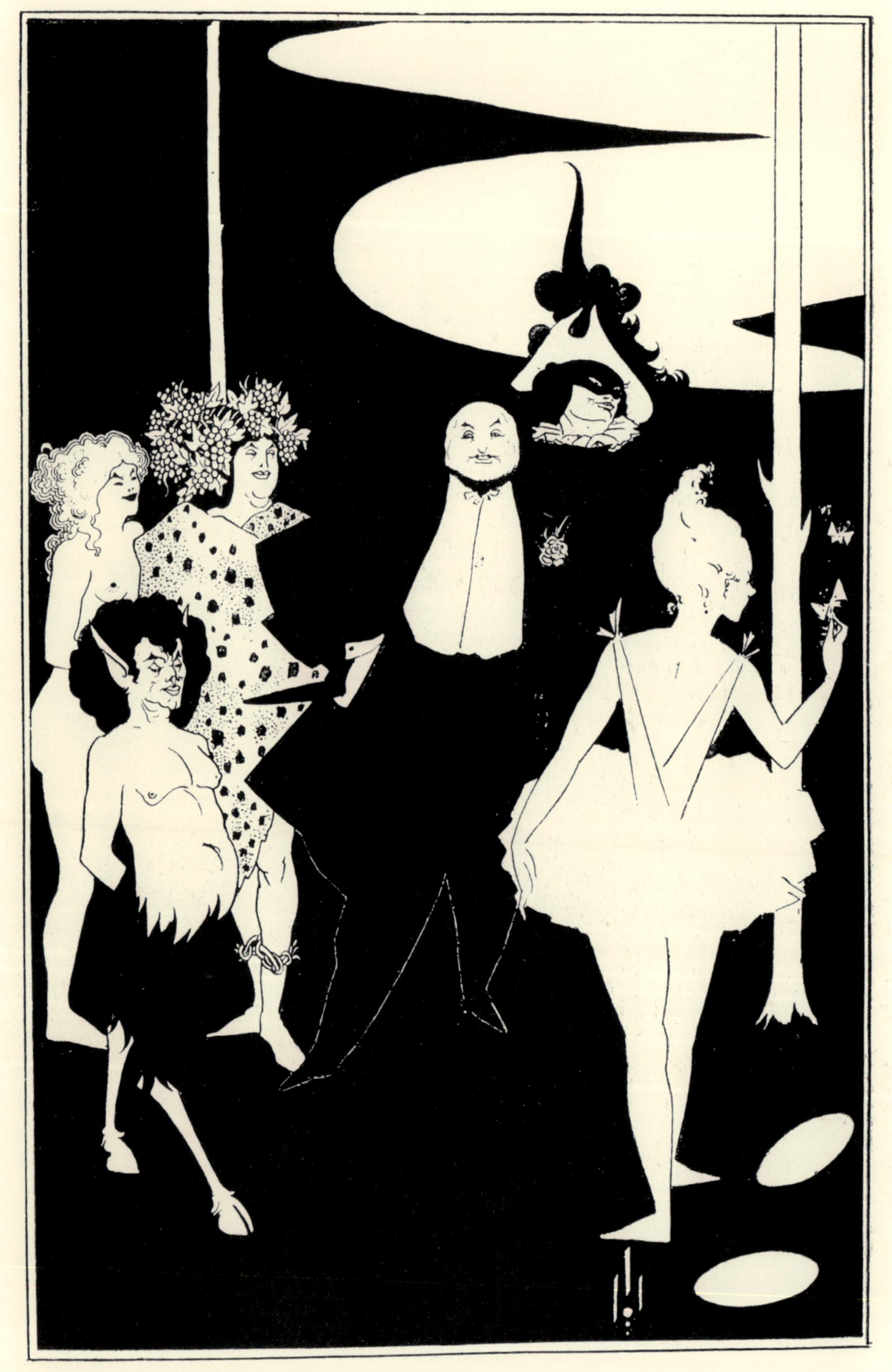

Design for Frontispiece of Plays by John Davidson 1894

This picture is allegedly modelled on the people surrounding Beardsley. The naked woman on the left is his sister Mabel, while the faun is *The Yellow Book* editor, Henry Harland; the man with the grapes on his head is Oscar Wilde, the figure in the centre the theatre manager Augustus Harris, the masked man is the author Richard Le Gallienne, and the dancer is Adeline Genée. None of these likenesses have been verified, however, and the faun could well be Beardsley himself.

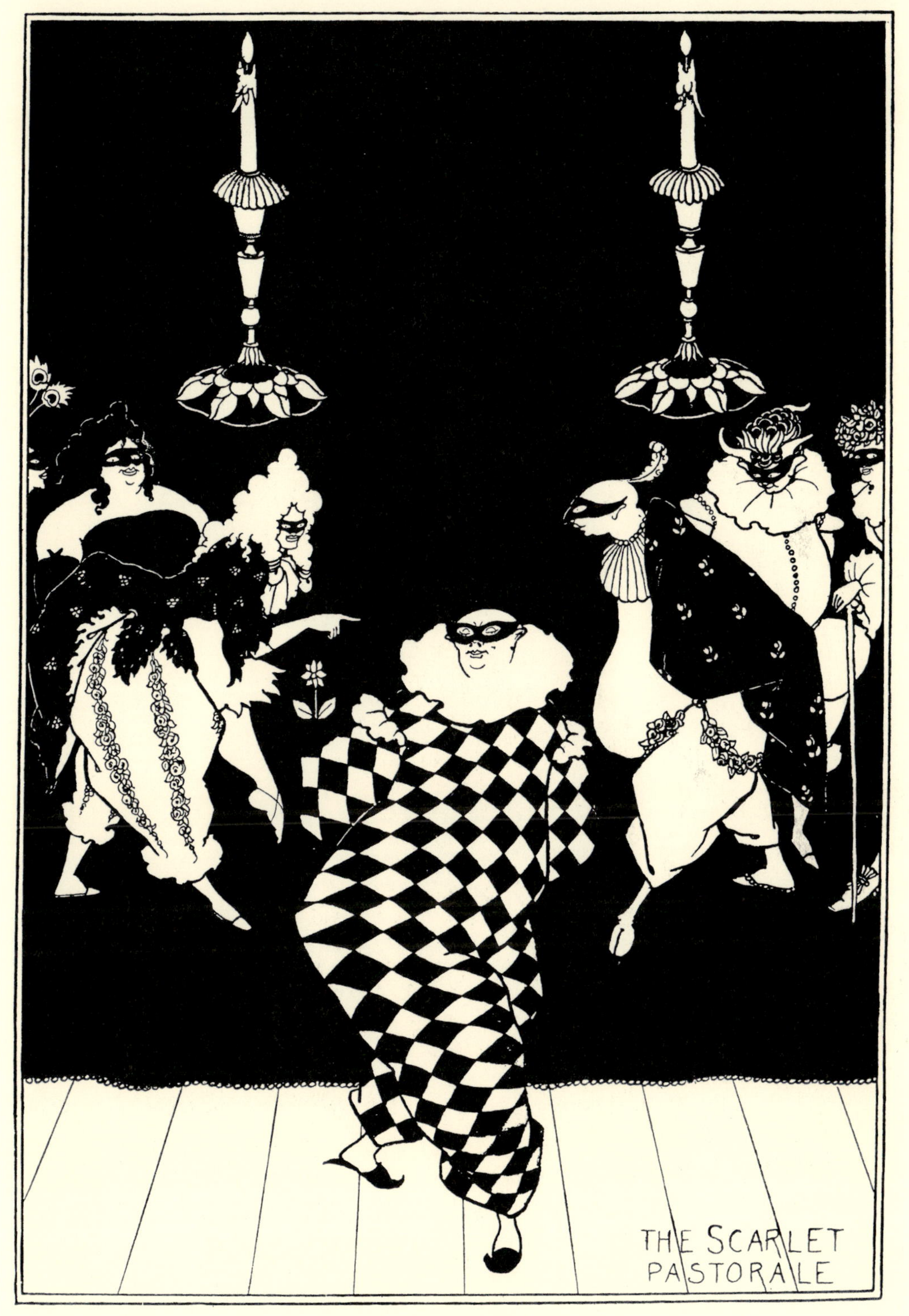

'The Scarlet Pastorale' 1895

This is another of the imaginary theatre scenes Beardsley enjoyed creating. It was drawn in 1895, but first published in 1898 in *The London Year Book* in scarlet ink, as a memorial to Beardsley. On stage is a harlequin in a domino-patterned outfit. Behind him, the woman on the left is pointing and laughing at the man to the right. The men's feet are two-toed animals' feet, and his abdomen juts out strangely, apparently tumescent with desire.

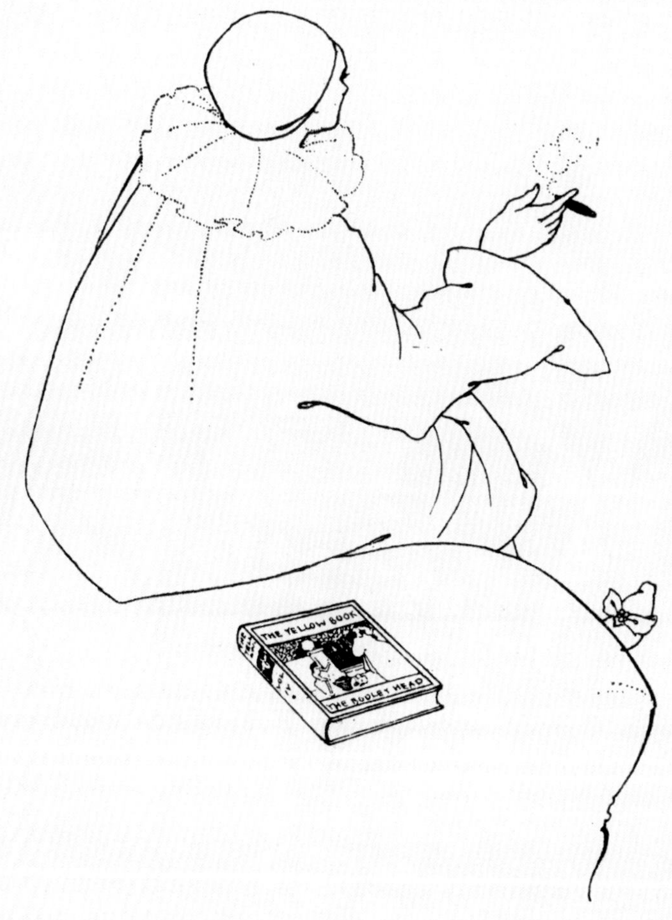

Invitation to John Lane's At Home for the bibliophilic club, The Sette of Odd Volumes 1895

This was a in invitation for an at home held by John Lane to entertain the head of the The Sette of Odd Volumes bibliophilic club, Frances Elgar. A pierrot sits on a sofa, smoking a cigarette. Beside him lies a copy of *The Yellow Book*. There is a glorious quality to the lines in this picture. Beardsley manages to bring pierrots into all kinds of situations. The glimpse of the tip of the pierrot's shoe is a nice touch. The S-shaped line running from the pierrot's head to the bottom of the sofa has a mesmerizing quality to it.

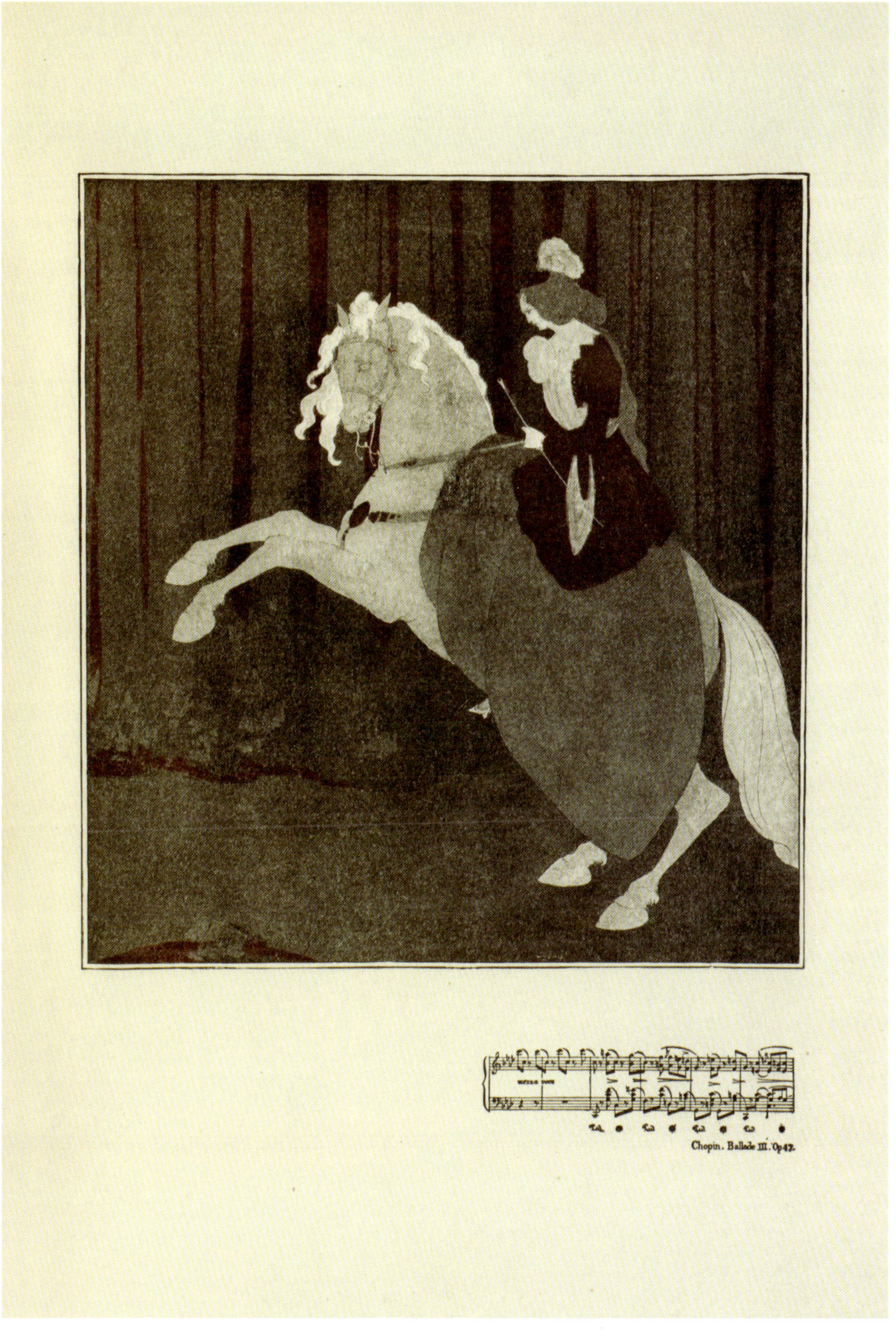

'Chopin, Ballade III'   Frontispiece   1894

This watercolour piece was first published by *The Studio* in 1898. Said to have been created in 1894, the picture is rumoured to be the portrait of a certain marquess related to Chopin's ballade, but this has not been validated. It is believed to be inspired by pictures from the seventeenth or eighteenth century. The horse is rendered in an orthodox style, but in the bulge of the woman's skirt, we sense Beardsley's characteristic approach to form.

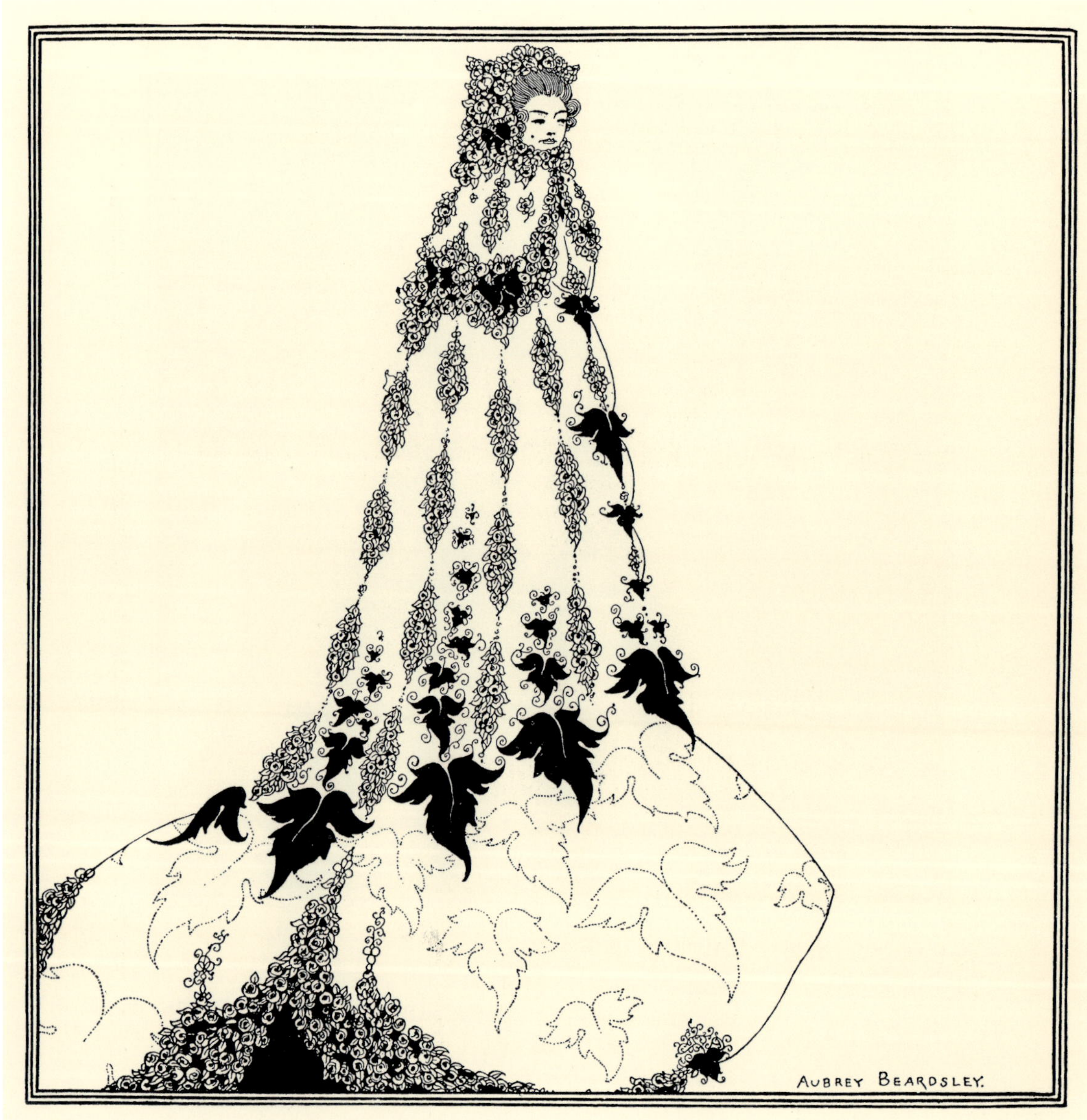

Illustration for Justin Huntly McCarthy's poem, 'At a Distance' 1895

This was rereleased in 1899 under the title 'A Suggested Reform in Ballet Costume'. The figure in the picture takes the form of a towering phallus above two balls, but the decoration of the outfit is quite glorious. Beardsley was heavily influenced by illustrators such as Alastair, and designed new costumes for ballet. Had he only lived a little longer, we think, he would surely have been involved in creating set and costume design for Diaghelev's Ballet Russes.

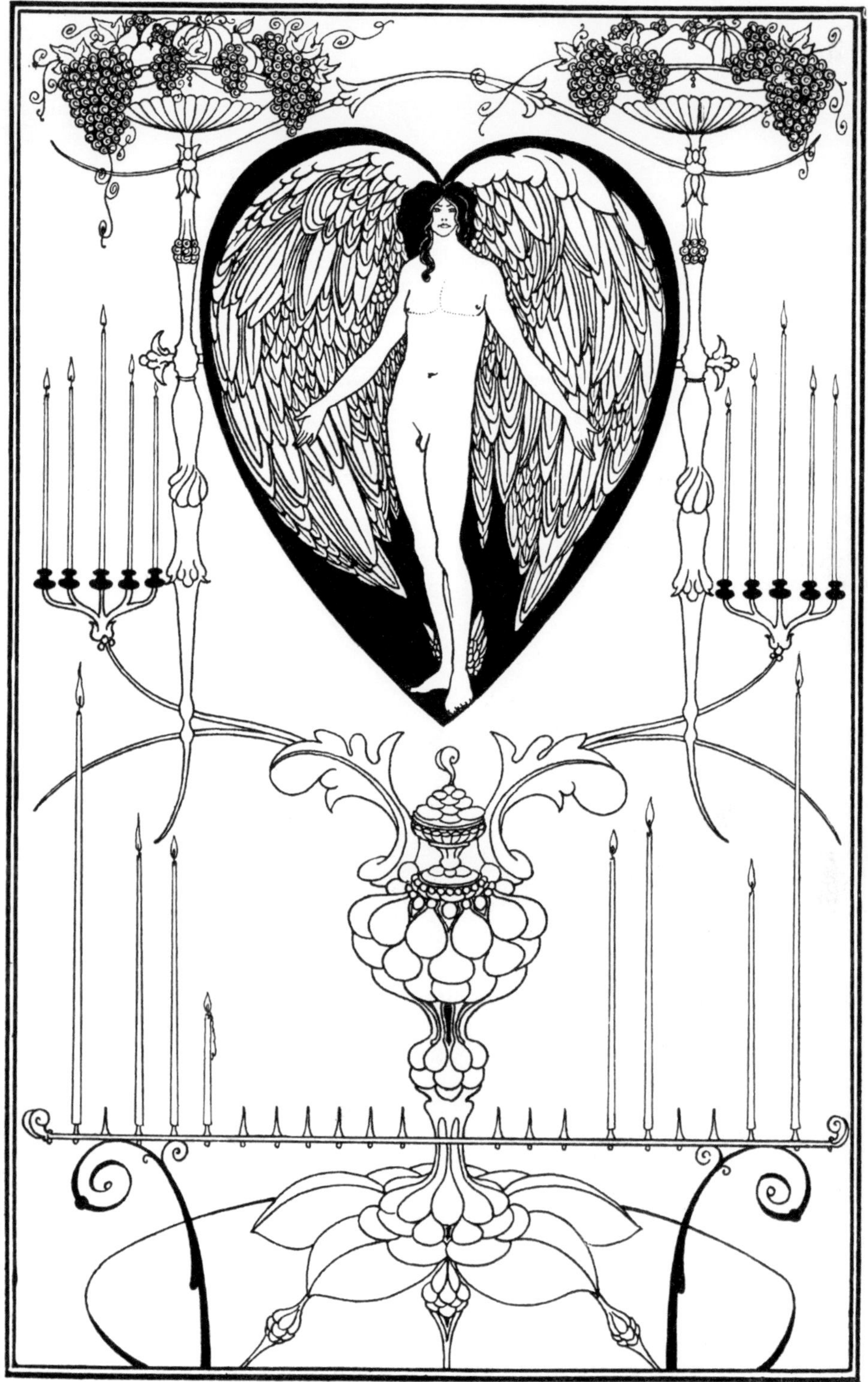

‘The Mirror of Love’; Frontispiece for Marc-André Raffalovich’s poetry collection *The Thread and the Path* 1895

John Gray and Raffalovich, who were part of Wilde's circle, took care of Beardsley towards the end of his life. This illustration was created as an illustration for the line 'Set in the heart as in a frame Love liveth.' Yet finding it far too hermaphrodite in nature, the publisher didn't use the picture. Inside a heart sits a naked angel. Angels are supposedly without sex, but this one has a small penis. The candlestick beneath it has a peculiar, erotic shape.

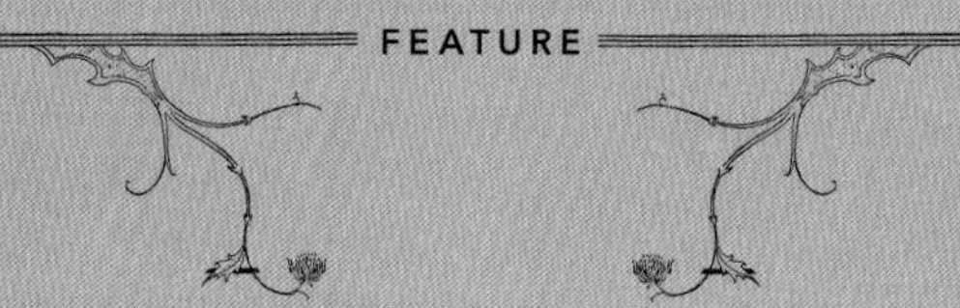

BEARDSLEY AND THE THEATRE

The end of the nineteenth century, when Beardsley was active, was the golden age for British theatre. As many others were, Beardsley was mesmerized and fixated by the theatre. As a child, he would avidly put on plays with his sister Mabel (fig. 1), and into adulthood, leapt headlong into London's theatre boom.

London's theatrical heyday began with the opening of The Savoy Theatre by D'Oyly Carte in 1881 (figs. 2 and 5). Illuminated by hundreds of electrical lights, The Savoy was a brand-new kind of theatre, which dazzled with its brilliance (figs. 3 and 4). These sparkling new venues, which were quite unlike the shabby, dingy theatres of old, began cropping up across London and became the capital's hotspots. D'Oyly Carte scored hit after hit with operettas written by W. S. Gilbert and composed by Arthur Sullivan.

The introduction of electrical lighting changed the performance of the actors. In the forgiving haze of gaslights, the actors' forms were somewhat vague, but with electrical lights, the contours of the face were clearly distinguishable, and the audience could make out subtle changes of expression. In this way, people's individual features stood out better, and a generation of stars began to be born.

In the UK, the laws surrounding theatres were very strict, and there was a limitation on the number of theatres permitted in London. With the amendment of the law, however, new theatres were permitted, and all kinds of performance spaces began to spring up all over London. The addition of electric lights made them a cut above. In addition to regular theatres, but music halls also began to appear, with light plays, operettas and burlesque shows gathering popularity. Rival to The Savoy was The Lyceum on Wellington Street. This was run by the star of the stage, Henry Irving, and produced the famous actress Ellen Terry. In 1885, Irving and Terry's production of *Hamlet* caused a great stir in London.

In the 1890s, Oscar Wilde made a sensational entrance into the theatre world. His play *Salome* was scheduled to be performed, starring French sensation Sarah Bernhardt. The venue was set as the Palace Theatre in London, but just as rehearsals had begun, the performance was prohibited. British law forbade the playing of Biblical characters onstage. It was ironic, then, that *Salome* was published featuring Beardsley's illustrations, and became popular. Beardsley was forever attending shows at London's theatres, and created pictures of actors such as Mrs Patrick Campbell. Not only that, but his illustrations were often plays in and of themselves.

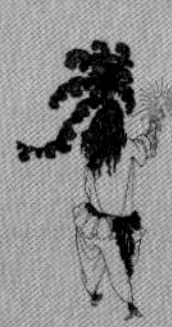

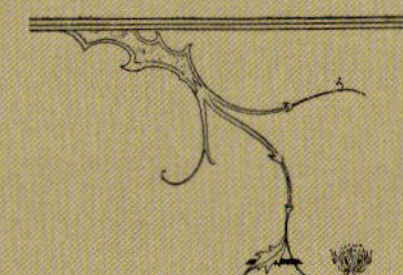

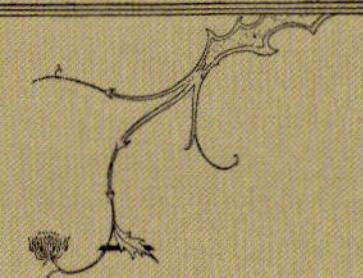

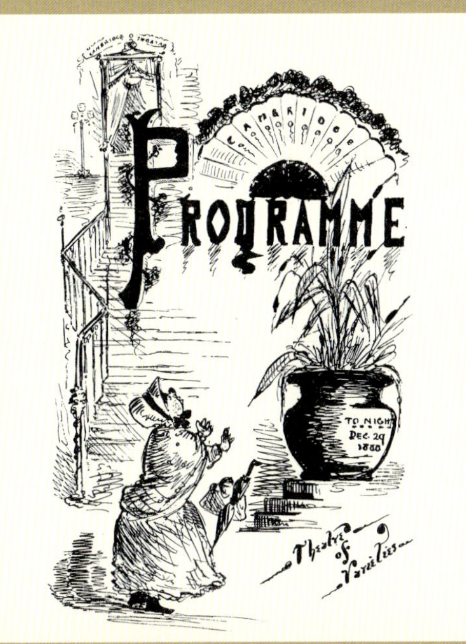

fig.1
An original programme made by Beardsley as a youngster
1884-5

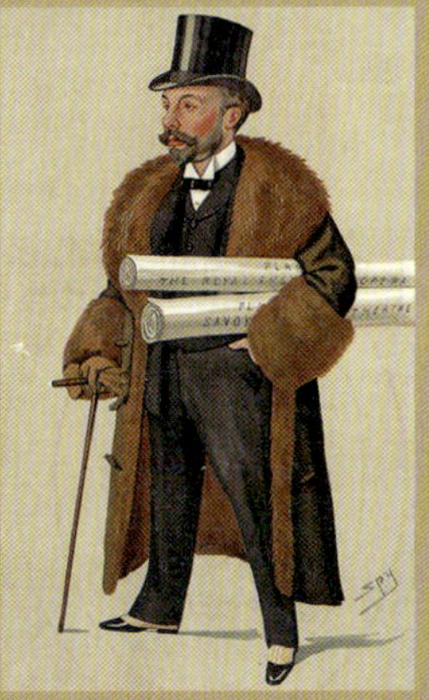

fig.2
Portrait of Richard D'Oyly
Carte by Leslie Matthew
Ward

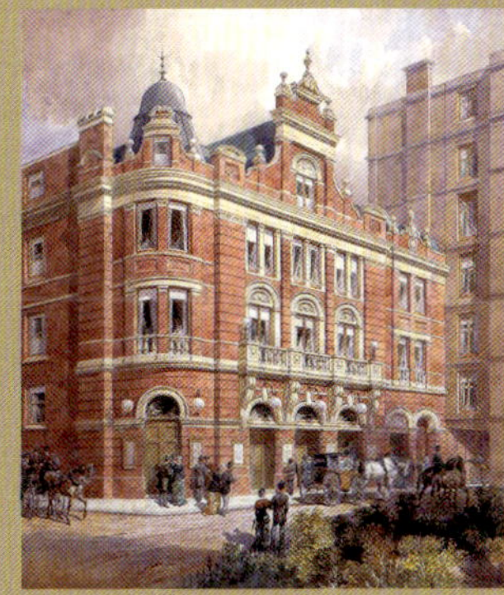

fig.3
The Savoy at the time of opening
(exterior)

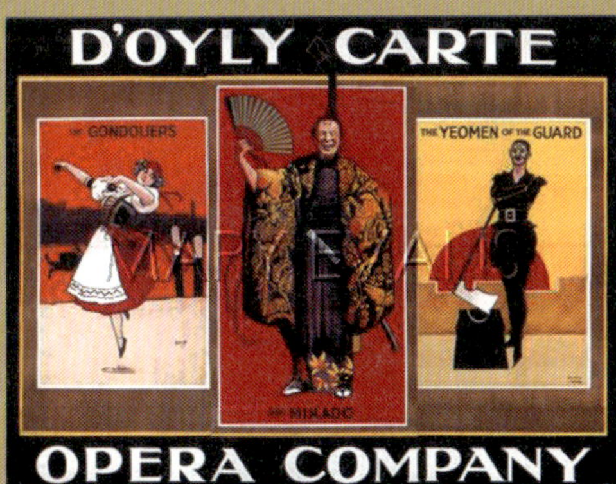

fig.5
An advertisement for the D'Oyly Carte Opera Company

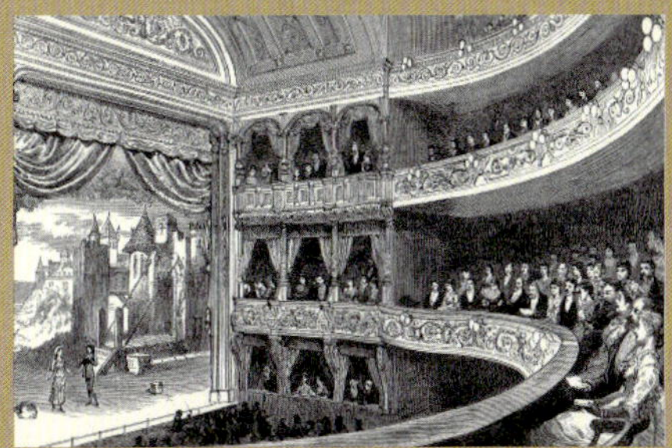

fig.4
The Savoy at the time of opening (interior)

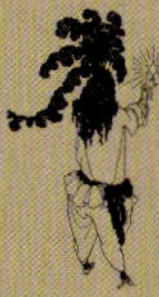

THE STORY OF VENUS AND TANNHAUSER

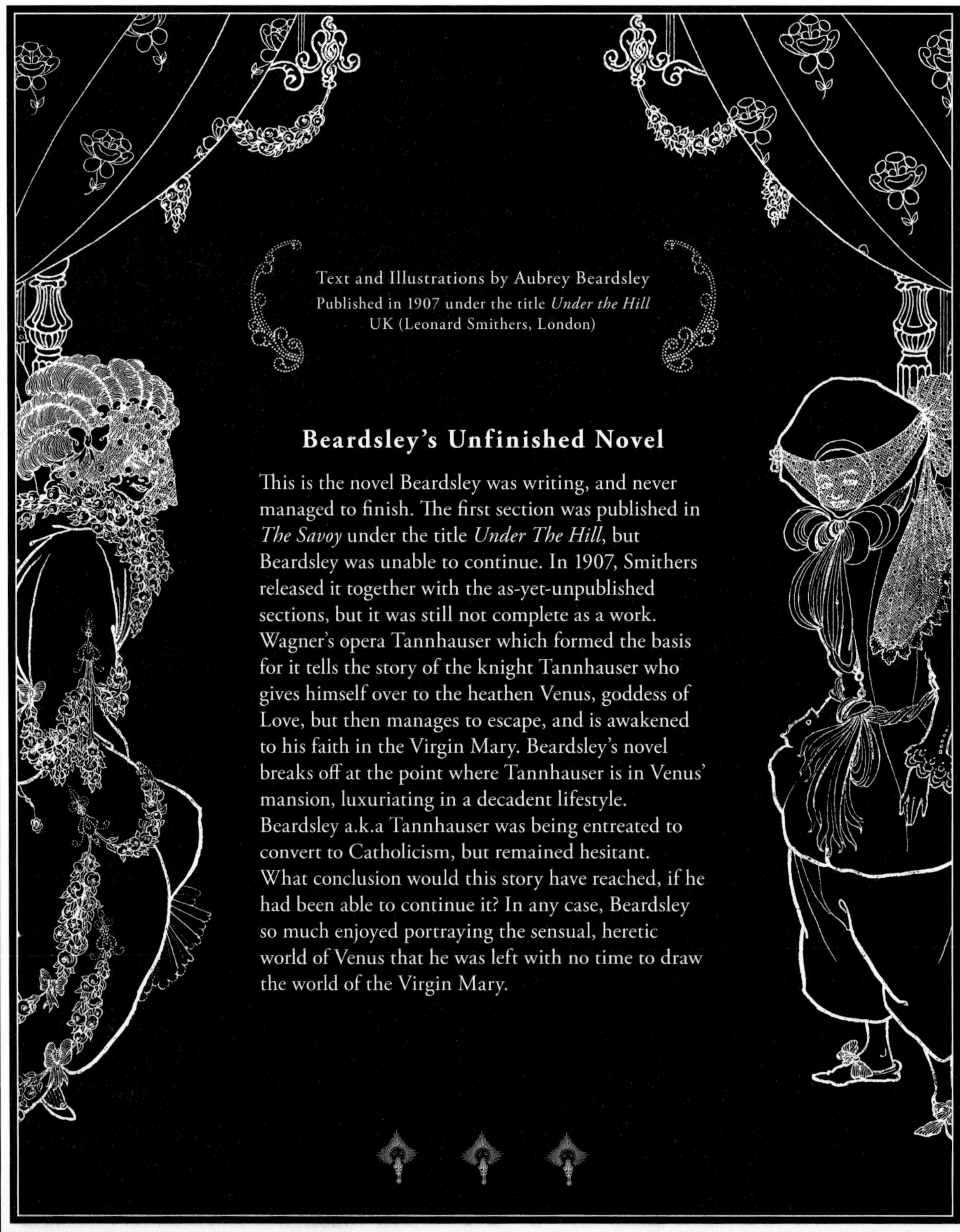

Text and Illustrations by Aubrey Beardsley
Published in 1907 under the title *Under the Hill*
UK (Leonard Smithers, London)

Beardsley's Unfinished Novel

This is the novel Beardsley was writing, and never managed to finish. The first section was published in *The Savoy* under the title *Under The Hill*, but Beardsley was unable to continue. In 1907, Smithers released it together with the as-yet-unpublished sections, but it was still not complete as a work. Wagner's opera Tannhauser which formed the basis for it tells the story of the knight Tannhauser who gives himself over to the heathen Venus, goddess of Love, but then manages to escape, and is awakened to his faith in the Virgin Mary. Beardsley's novel breaks off at the point where Tannhauser is in Venus' mansion, luxuriating in a decadent lifestyle. Beardsley a.k.a Tannhauser was being entreated to convert to Catholicism, but remained hesitant. What conclusion would this story have reached, if he had been able to continue it? In any case, Beardsley so much enjoyed portraying the sensual, heretic world of Venus that he was left with no time to draw the world of the Virgin Mary.

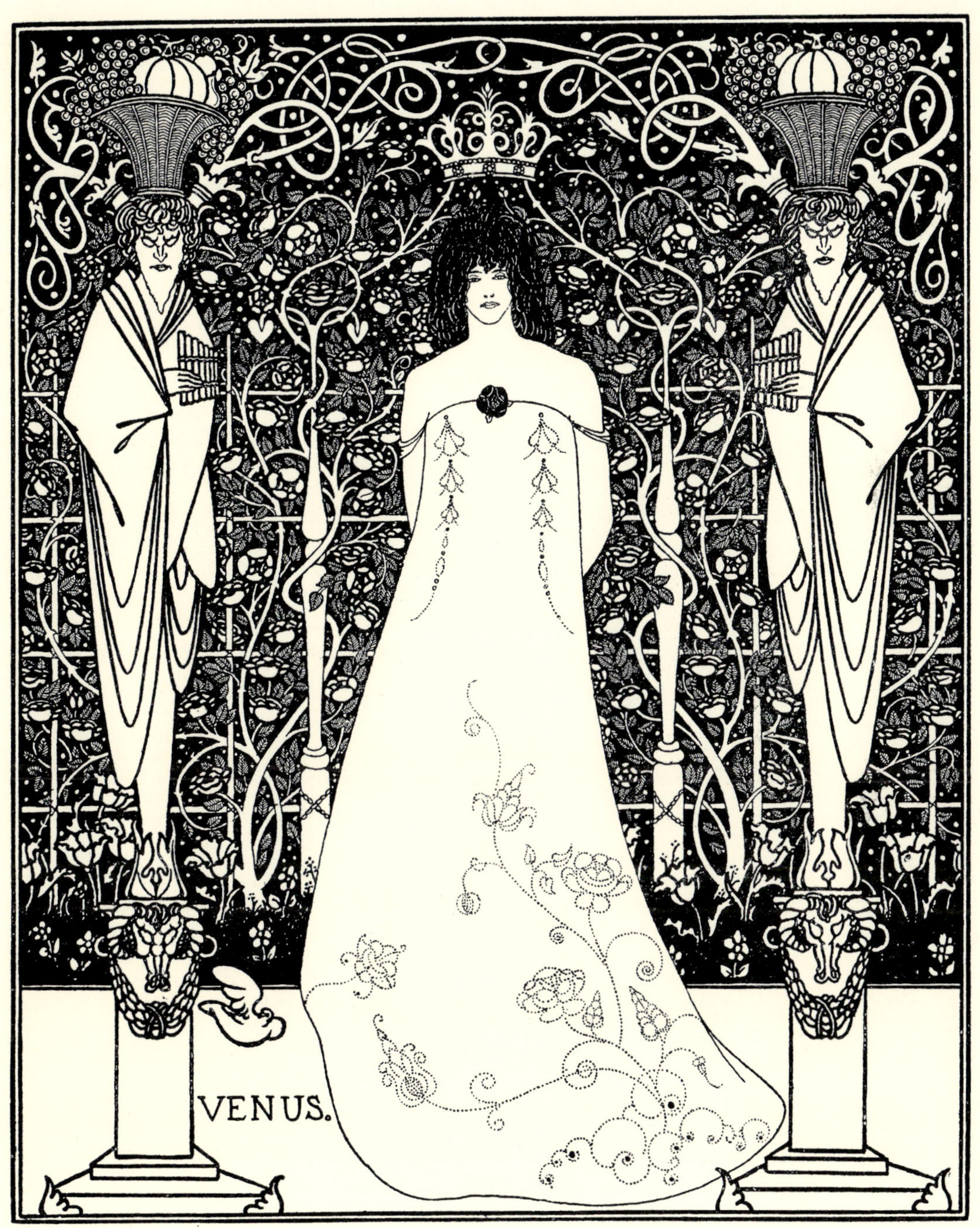

'Venus between Terminal Gods'

This was created as an illustration for the title page of *Under the Hill*, which came out of *The Story Of Venus And Tannhauser*. It was supposed to be published with 24 illustrations, but remained incomplete. The terminal gods seen on either side of Venus were placed along the road as waymarkers to guide travellers. These waymarkers were known in ancient Greece, and took the form of phalluses. The vine growing around the lattice in the background shows the influence of William Morris, while also hinting toward Art Nouveau-style curves. Venus' mansion is a cave under the hill—in other words, a giant vagina.

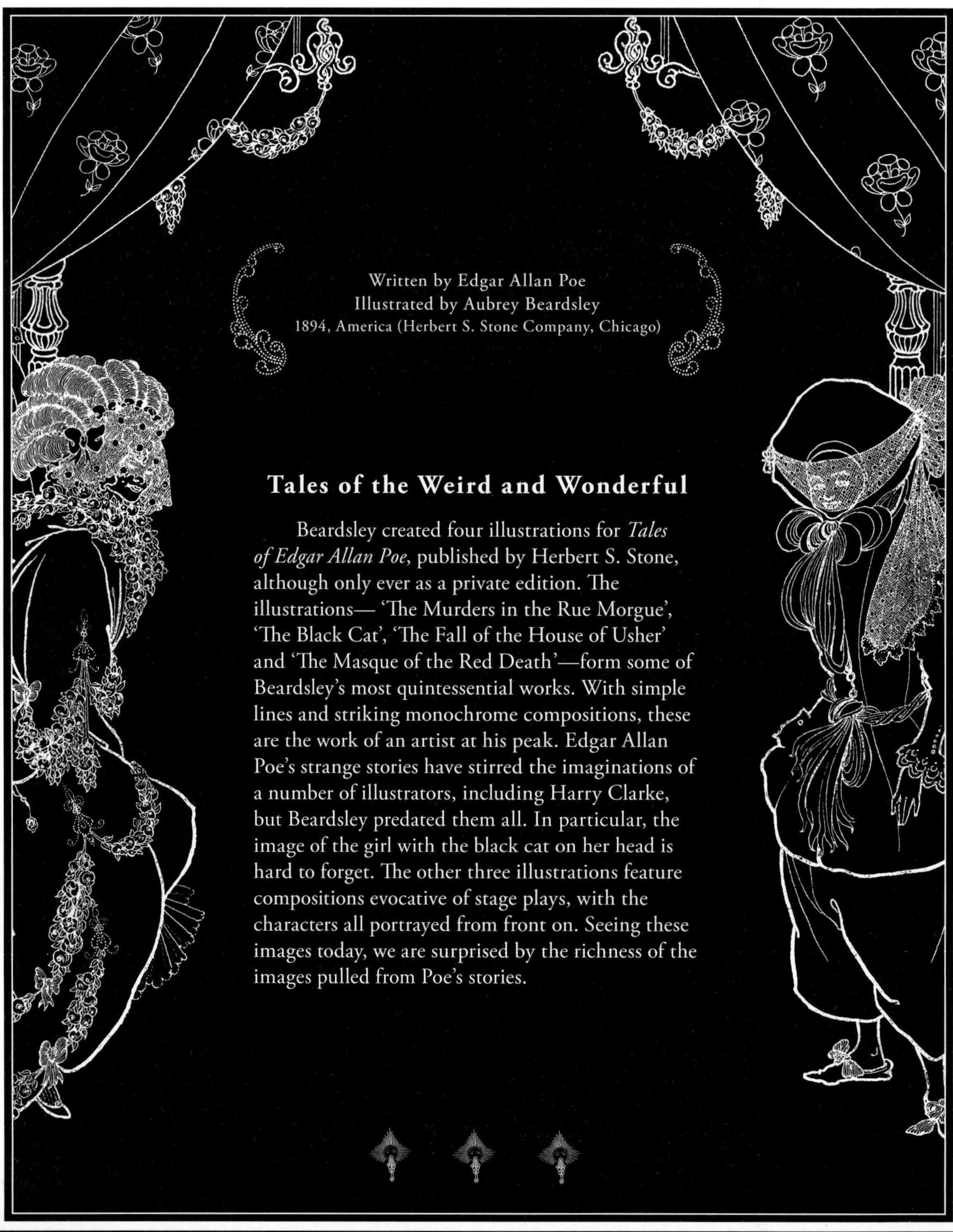

Written by Edgar Allan Poe
Illustrated by Aubrey Beardsley
1894, America (Herbert S. Stone Company, Chicago)

Tales of the Weird and Wonderful

Beardsley created four illustrations for *Tales of Edgar Allan Poe*, published by Herbert S. Stone, although only ever as a private edition. The illustrations— 'The Murders in the Rue Morgue', 'The Black Cat', 'The Fall of the House of Usher' and 'The Masque of the Red Death'—form some of Beardsley's most quintessential works. With simple lines and striking monochrome compositions, these are the work of an artist at his peak. Edgar Allan Poe's strange stories have stirred the imaginations of a number of illustrators, including Harry Clarke, but Beardsley predated them all. In particular, the image of the girl with the black cat on her head is hard to forget. The other three illustrations feature compositions evocative of stage plays, with the characters all portrayed from front on. Seeing these images today, we are surprised by the richness of the images pulled from Poe's stories.

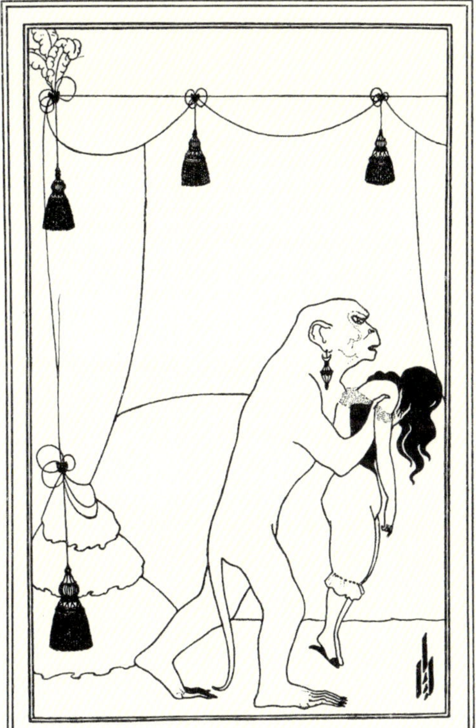

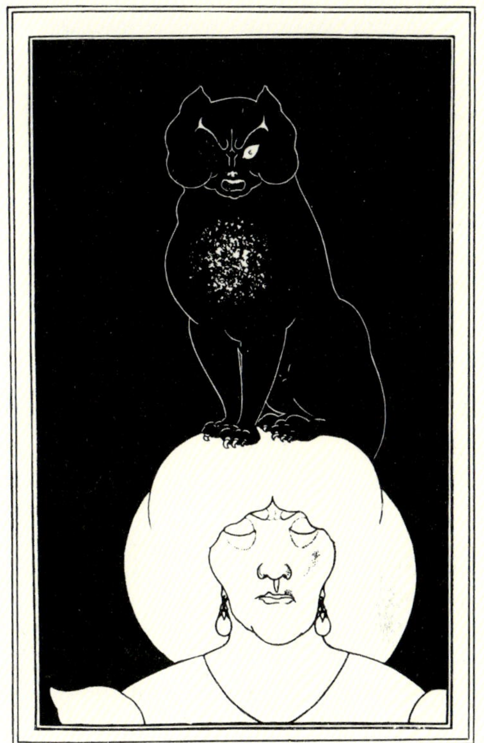

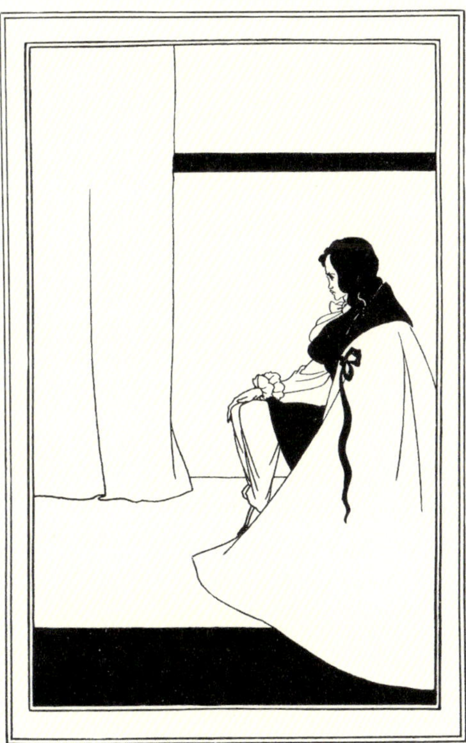

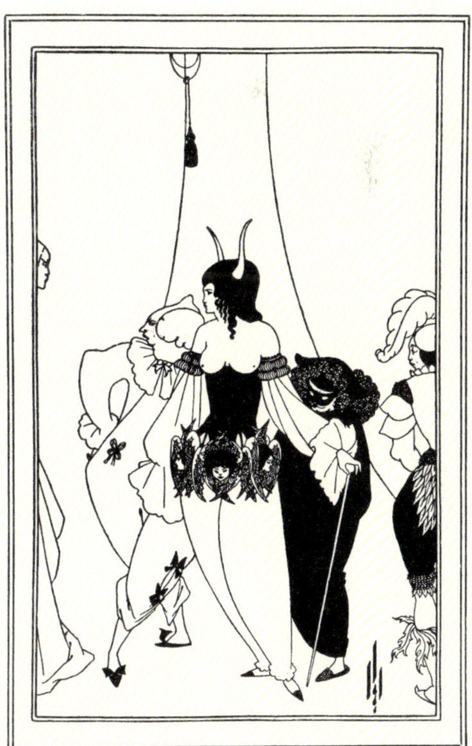

'The Murders in the Rue Morgue', 'The Black Cat',
'The Fall of the House of Usher' and 'The Masque of the Red Death'

In 'The Black Cat' (top right), the clean white outlines ensure the figure of the black cat looms menacingly out of the dark background. The monster carrying off a lifeless woman in 'The Murders in the Rue Morgue' (top left) resembles a person in a costume, giving the scene the look of a stage play. 'The Fall of the House of Usher' (bottom right) recycles a picture of Chopin drawn previously. 'The Masque of the Red Death' (bottom right) shows a scene from a carnivalesque clown show, or else an erotic masked ball, both specialties of Beardsley's.

ALIBABA AND THE FORTY THIEVES

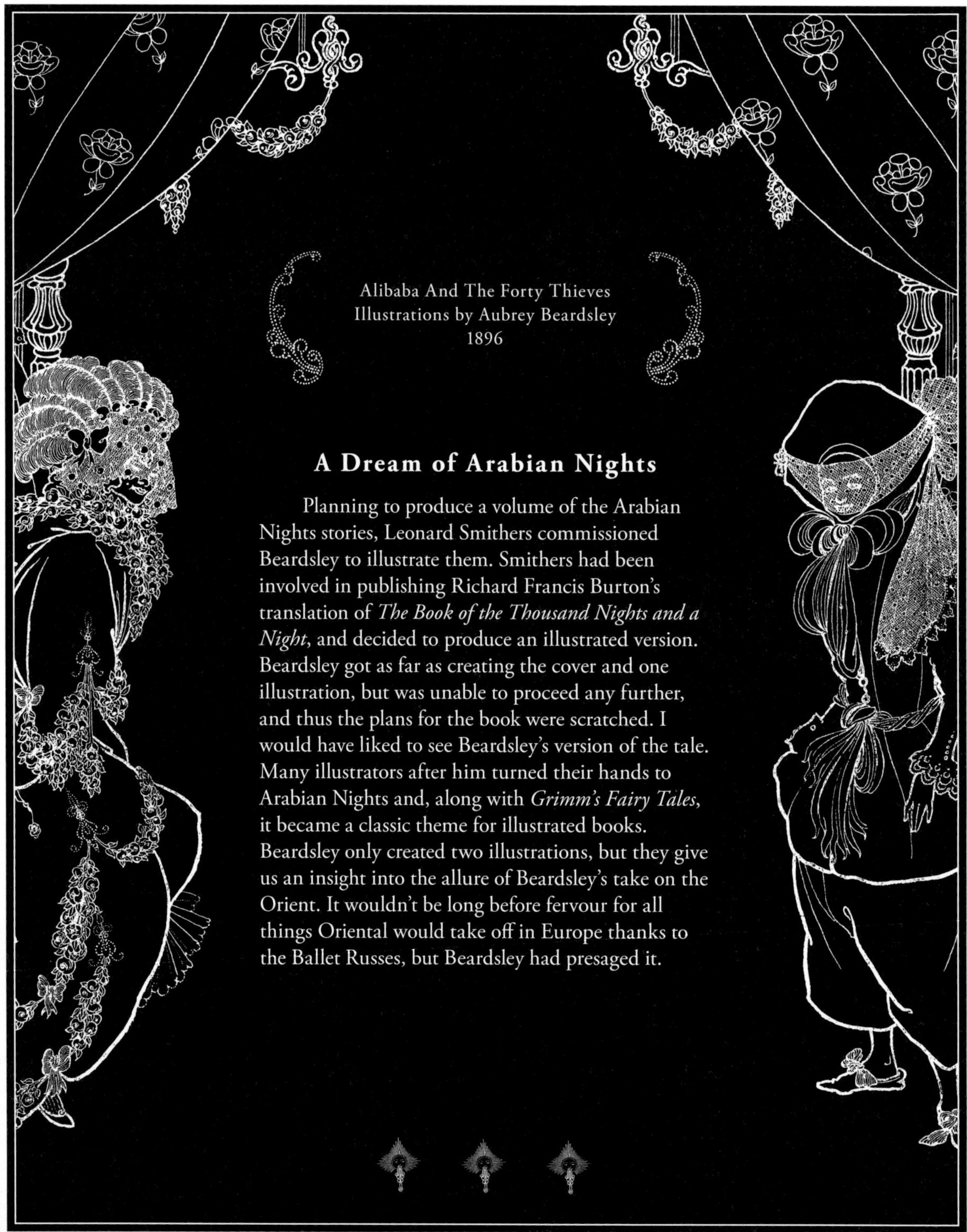

Alibaba And The Forty Thieves
Illustrations by Aubrey Beardsley
1896

A Dream of Arabian Nights

Planning to produce a volume of the Arabian Nights stories, Leonard Smithers commissioned Beardsley to illustrate them. Smithers had been involved in publishing Richard Francis Burton's translation of *The Book of the Thousand Nights and a Night*, and decided to produce an illustrated version. Beardsley got as far as creating the cover and one illustration, but was unable to proceed any further, and thus the plans for the book were scratched. I would have liked to see Beardsley's version of the tale. Many illustrators after him turned their hands to Arabian Nights and, along with *Grimm's Fairy Tales*, it became a classic theme for illustrated books. Beardsley only created two illustrations, but they give us an insight into the allure of Beardsley's take on the Orient. It wouldn't be long before fervour for all things Oriental would take off in Europe thanks to the Ballet Russes, but Beardsley had presaged it.

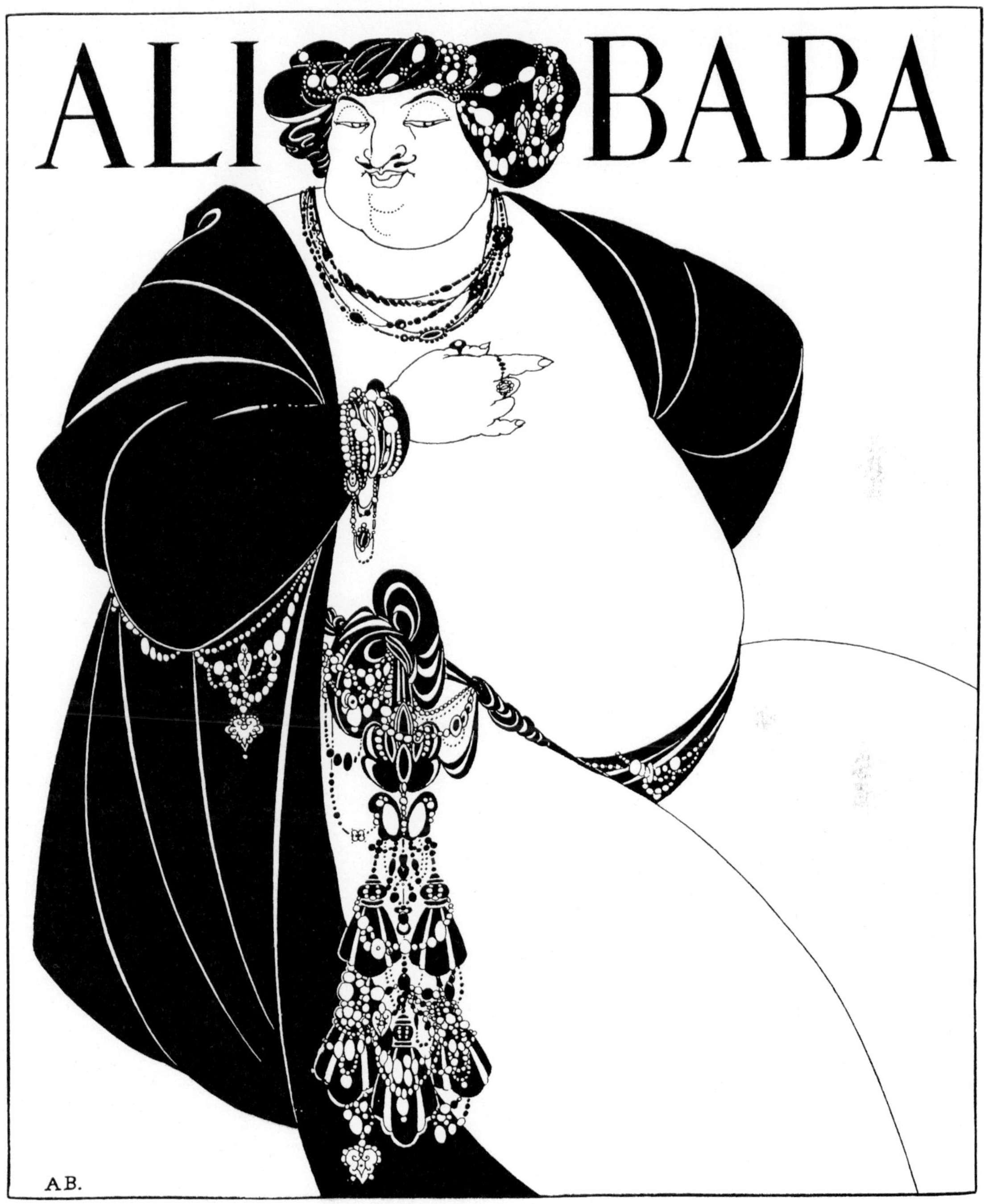

Cover design for *Ali Baba and the Forty Thieves*

The body of Ali Baba, a poor woodcutter who becomes incredibly wealthy, is rendered with loose, flowing lines. The contrast between these simple outlines and the luscious patterning of all the ornate gold jewellery is delightful on the eye. Into his later period, Beardsley took an interest in jewellery, and would supposedly go to look at ancient jewellery in the South Kensington museum. The balance between a simple, abstract composition and complex, ornate sections is characteristic of late Beardsley work.

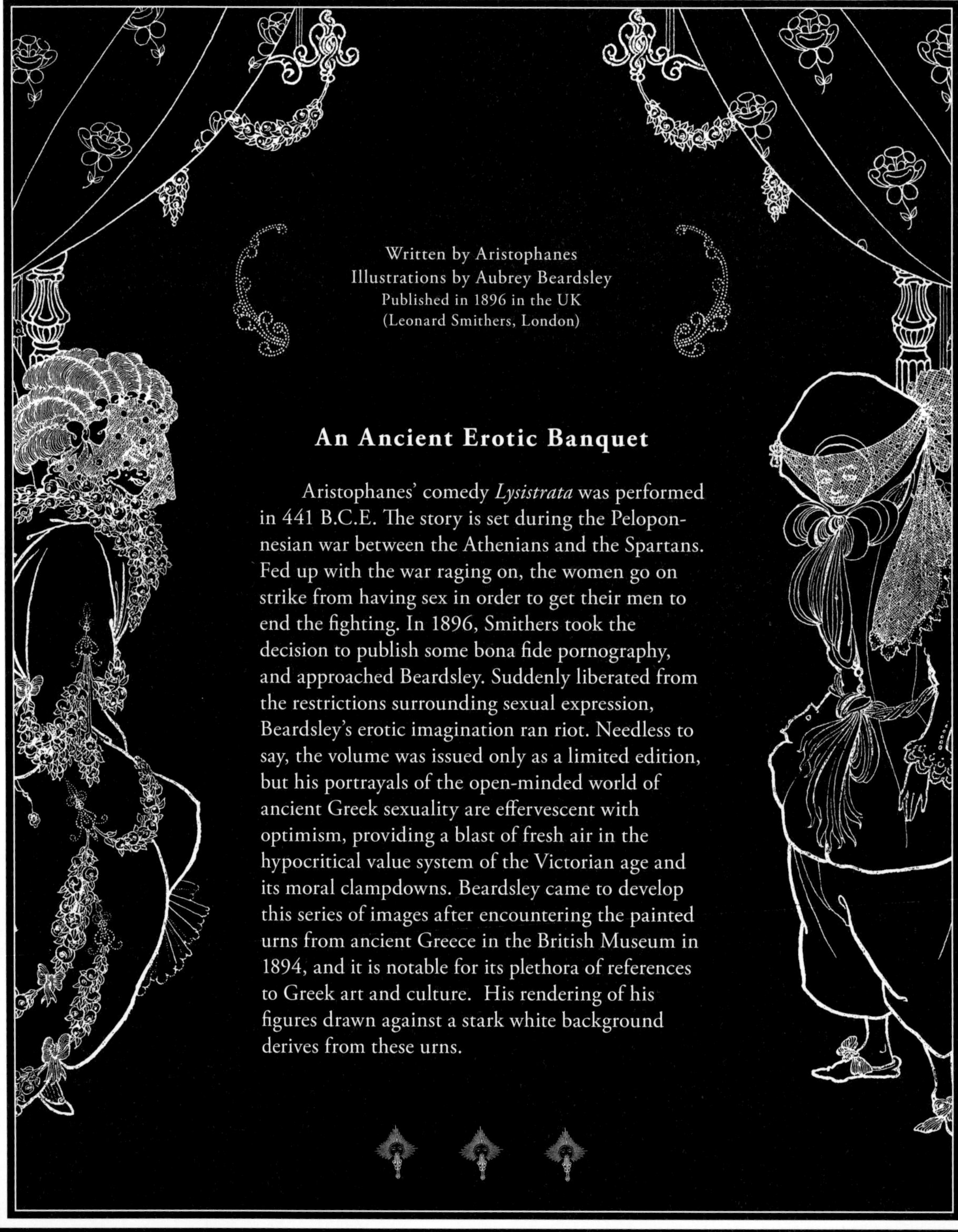

LYSISTRATA

Written by Aristophanes
Illustrations by Aubrey Beardsley
Published in 1896 in the UK
(Leonard Smithers, London)

An Ancient Erotic Banquet

Aristophanes' comedy *Lysistrata* was performed in 441 B.C.E. The story is set during the Peloponnesian war between the Athenians and the Spartans. Fed up with the war raging on, the women go on strike from having sex in order to get their men to end the fighting. In 1896, Smithers took the decision to publish some bona fide pornography, and approached Beardsley. Suddenly liberated from the restrictions surrounding sexual expression, Beardsley's erotic imagination ran riot. Needless to say, the volume was issued only as a limited edition, but his portrayals of the open-minded world of ancient Greek sexuality are effervescent with optimism, providing a blast of fresh air in the hypocritical value system of the Victorian age and its moral clampdowns. Beardsley came to develop this series of images after encountering the painted urns from ancient Greece in the British Museum in 1894, and it is notable for its plethora of references to Greek art and culture. His rendering of his figures drawn against a stark white background derives from these urns.

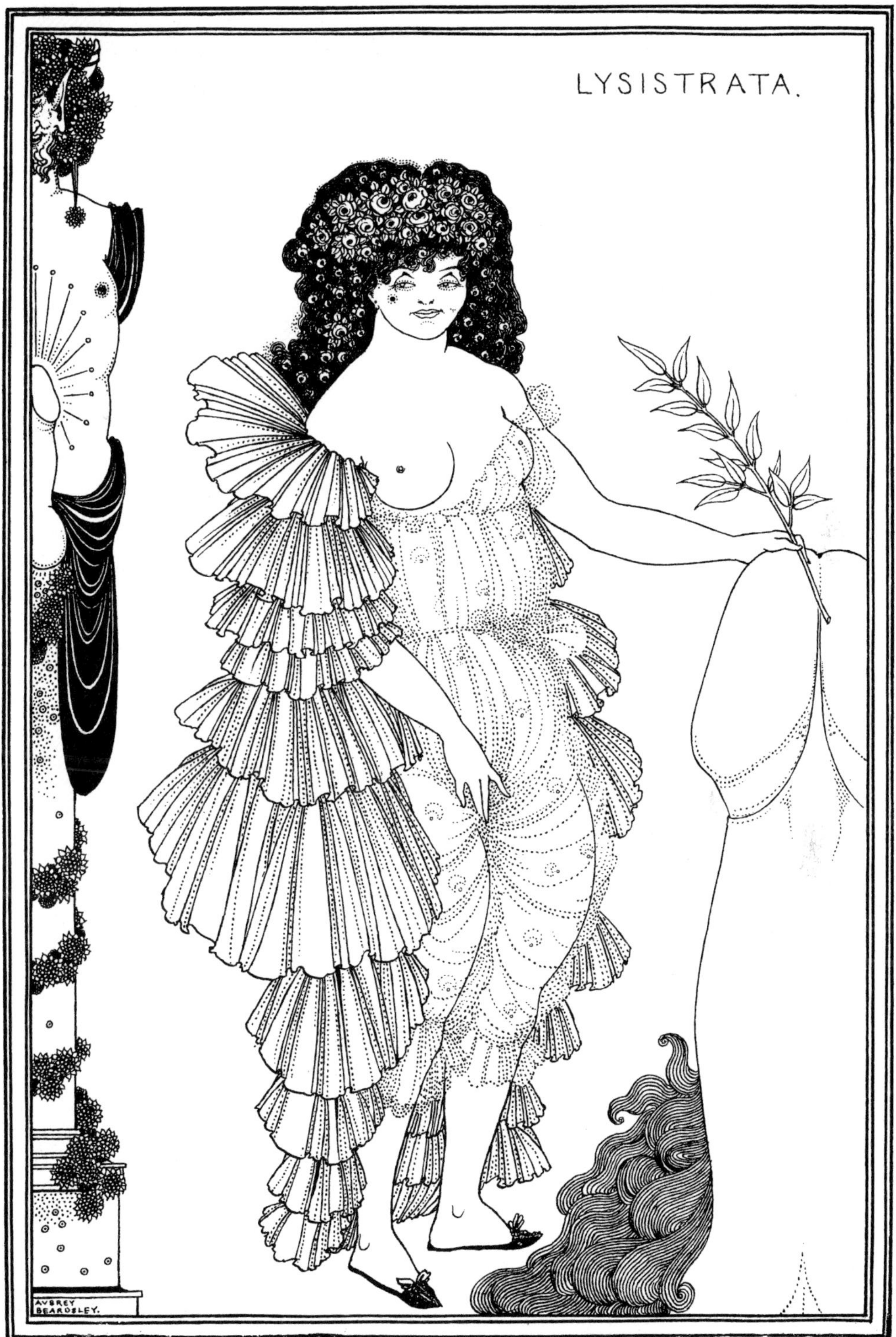

'Lysistrata Shielding her Coynte'

The Athenian Lysistrata is the initiator of the sex strike, calling upon her fellow women to withhold sex from the menfolk until they end their fighting. Here, Lysistrata covers up her sex with a single hand as she attempts to pierce an enormous phallus with an olive branch. At the left-hand side of the picture is a phallic herma statue. The women's fight-back against the lascivious, battle-hungry men is beginning.

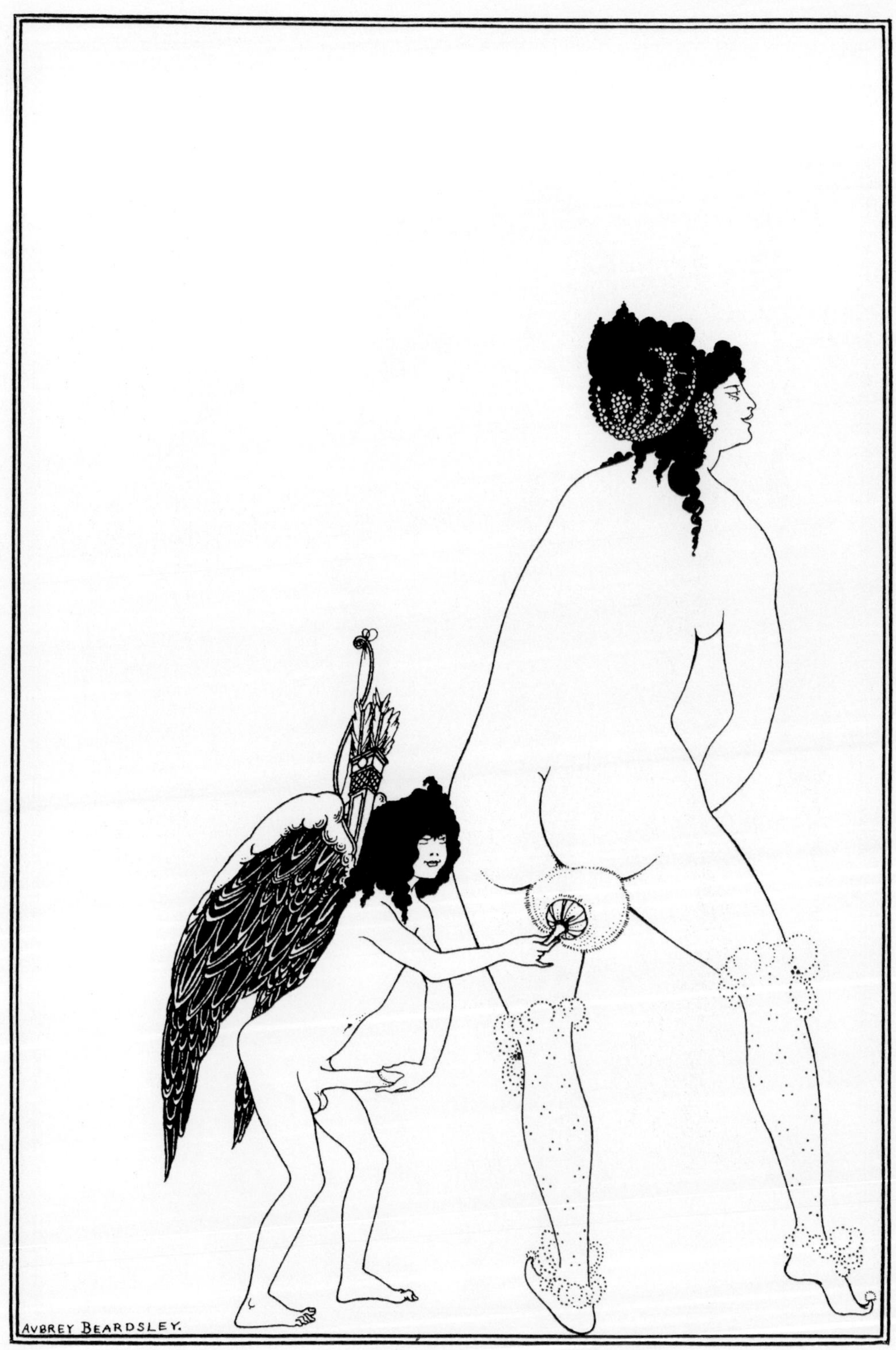

'The Toilet of Lampito'

Lampito was a beauty from Sparta. Spartan women were said to exercise as much as their men, and were known for their attractive muscular physiques. Here Beardsley imagines Lampito's toilet scene, although it doesn't appear in Aristophanes' play. Lampito is scrupulous in her toilet, grooming even her private parts. Eros is masturbating as he dusts her bottom. The scene is full of Beardsley-like roguery.

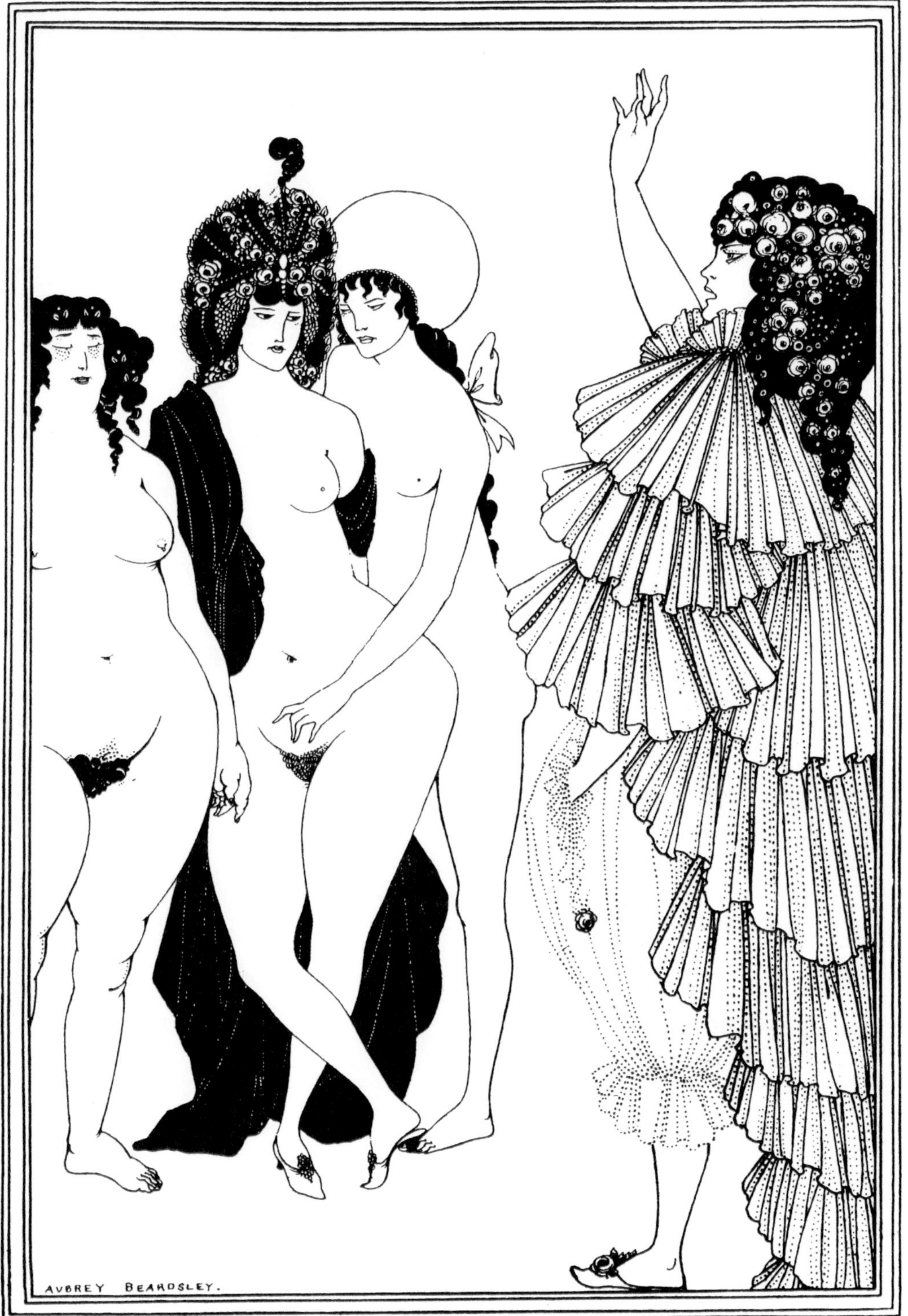

'Lysistrata Haranguing the Athenian Women'

Here Lysistrata entreats her fellow womenfolk to withhold sex from their men until they cease the war. The women are hesitant, as they too enjoy sex. Lysistrata has her hand in her left pocket. As in Japanese prints, pockets and sleeves represent female genitalia. What is Lysistrata doing with her hand in her pocket? Is she masturbating, or rather shielding her sex? One of the women reaches her hand out to another woman's crotch.

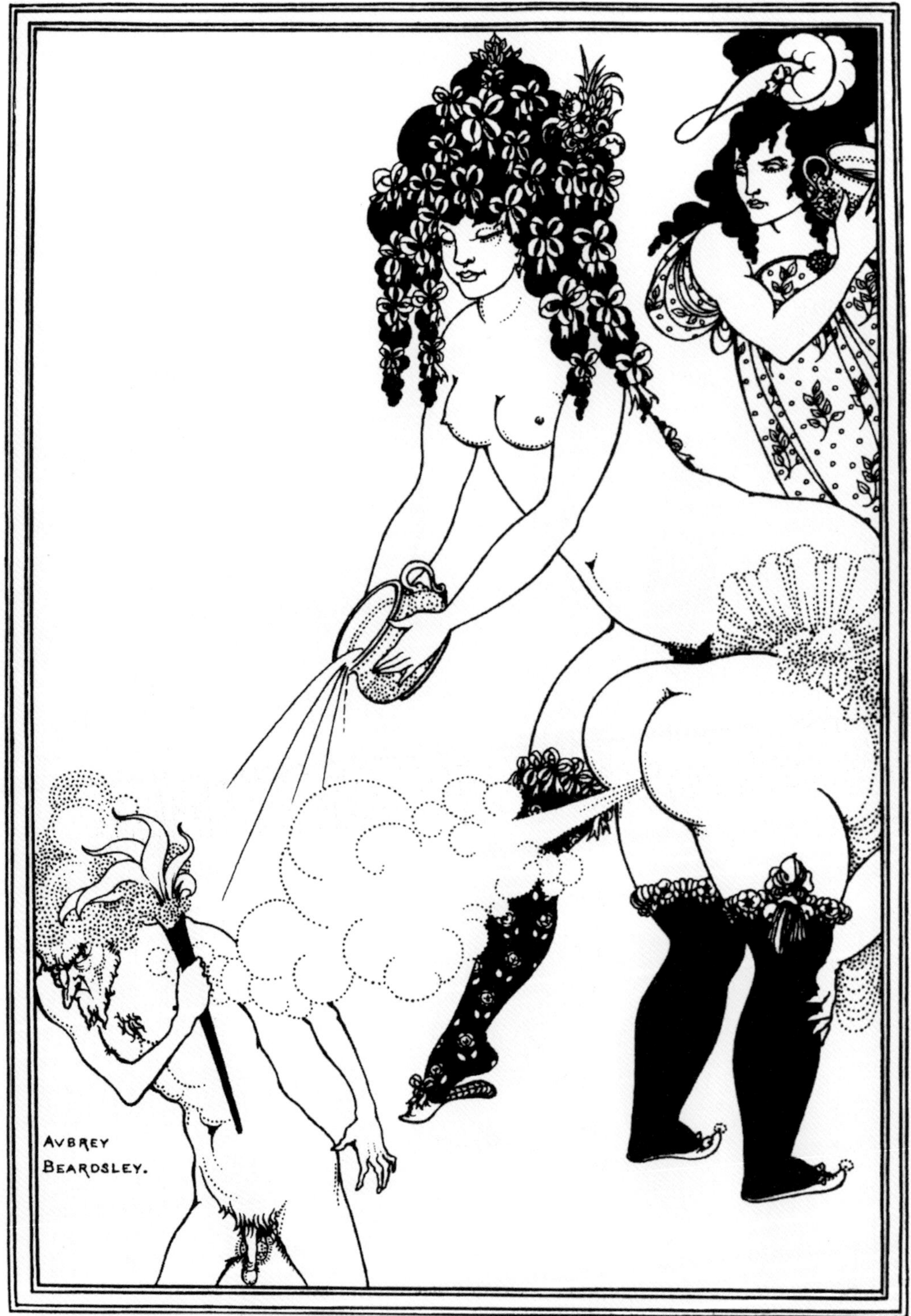

'Lysistrata defending the Acropolis'

The women have occupied the hill of the Acropolis, and are defending it. The male elders are attempting to set the place on fire with torches, while the women throw water to extinguish the fire. Beardsley adds a woman who is attempting to put out the flames by emitting something from her behind, from which the elders flee helplessly. The shape of the gas clouds rendered in dotted lines possibly bear the influence of Japanese illustration. If so, that would make this a fin-de-siècle meeting of Grecian urns and Japanese woodblock prints.

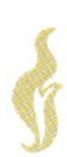

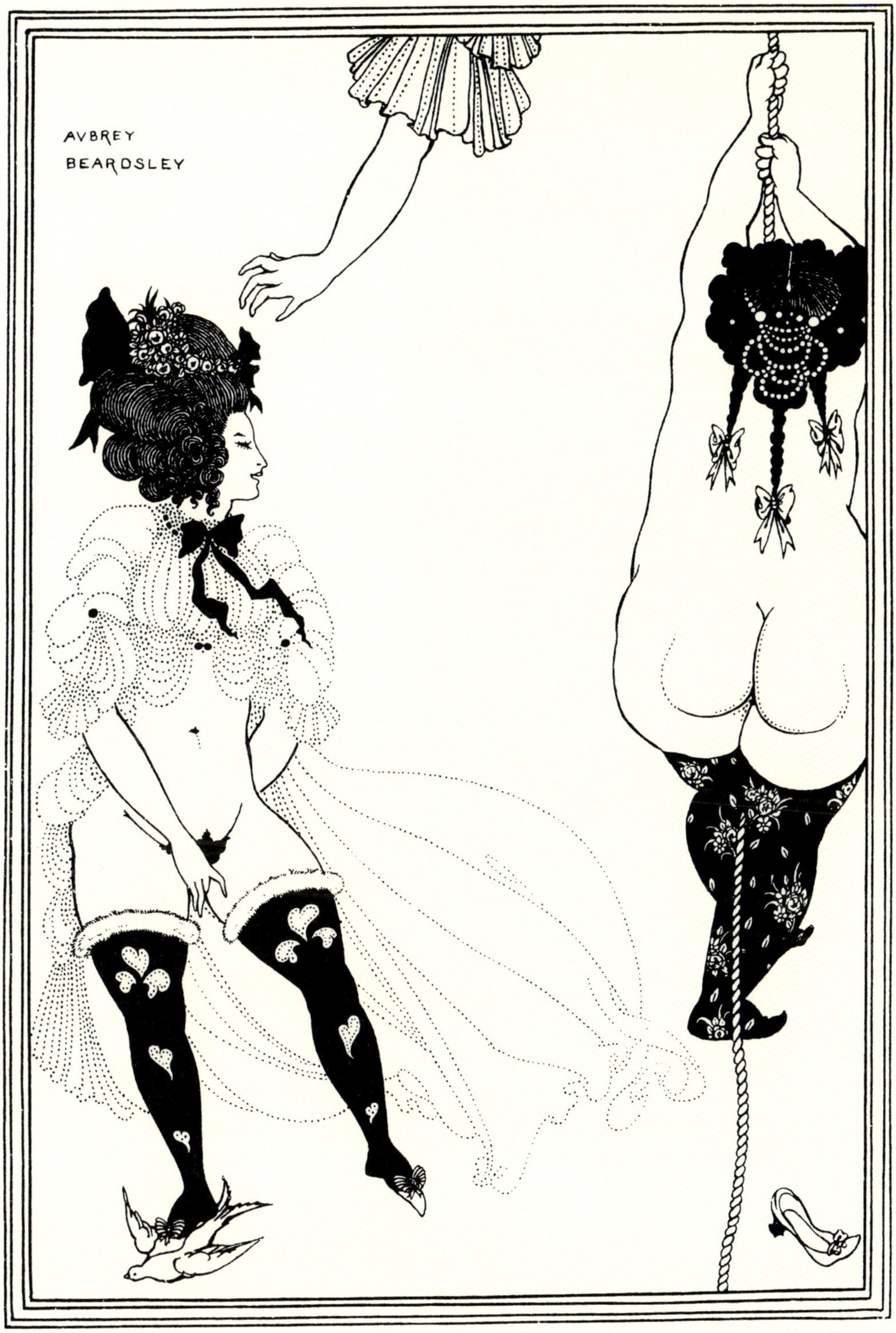

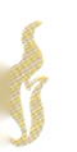

'Two Athenian Women in Distress'

The women's unity is crumbling, and members of the party are fleeing. One woman strings a rope to the pulley of a well and attempts to escape, while they other mounts a sparrow, as a hand from above reaches out and tries to grab her by the hair. There is something very humorous about the big-bottomed woman with the plait descending the rope. The sparrow is seen to be the messenger of the god of love, and the phrase 'with the sparrow' meant to be led by erotic desire. The arm stretching down from above is Lysistrata's. With its mass of open space in the middle, the composition of this frame is intriguing.

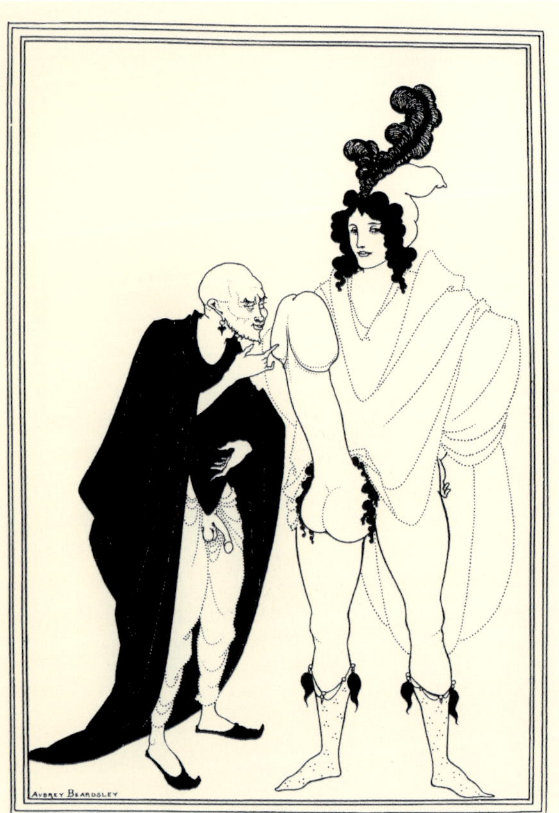

'The Examination of the Herald'

A Spartan herald arrives. Due to his lack of sexual satisfaction, the young herald has a permanent erection. The elder is asking what is going on. In Greece, this section of the play was performed with the actor wearing a giant leather strap-on.

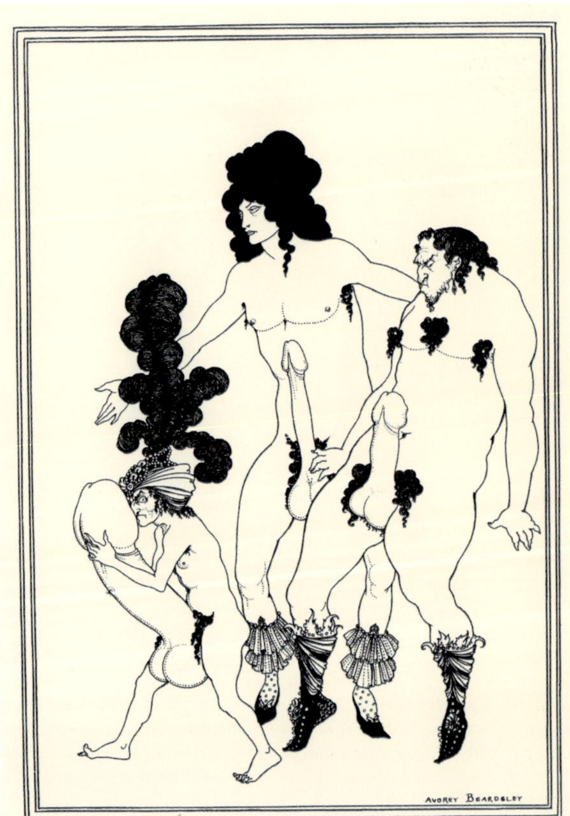

'The Lacedaemonian Ambassadors'

Ambassadors for peace come from Lacedaemon. The depiction of their penises as disproportionately large for their bodies derives from *shunga*, erotic Japanese prints. The man on the right, resembling the hermaphrodite in 'The Mirror of Love', reaches out a hand toward the appendages in a way that hints at his homosexuality.

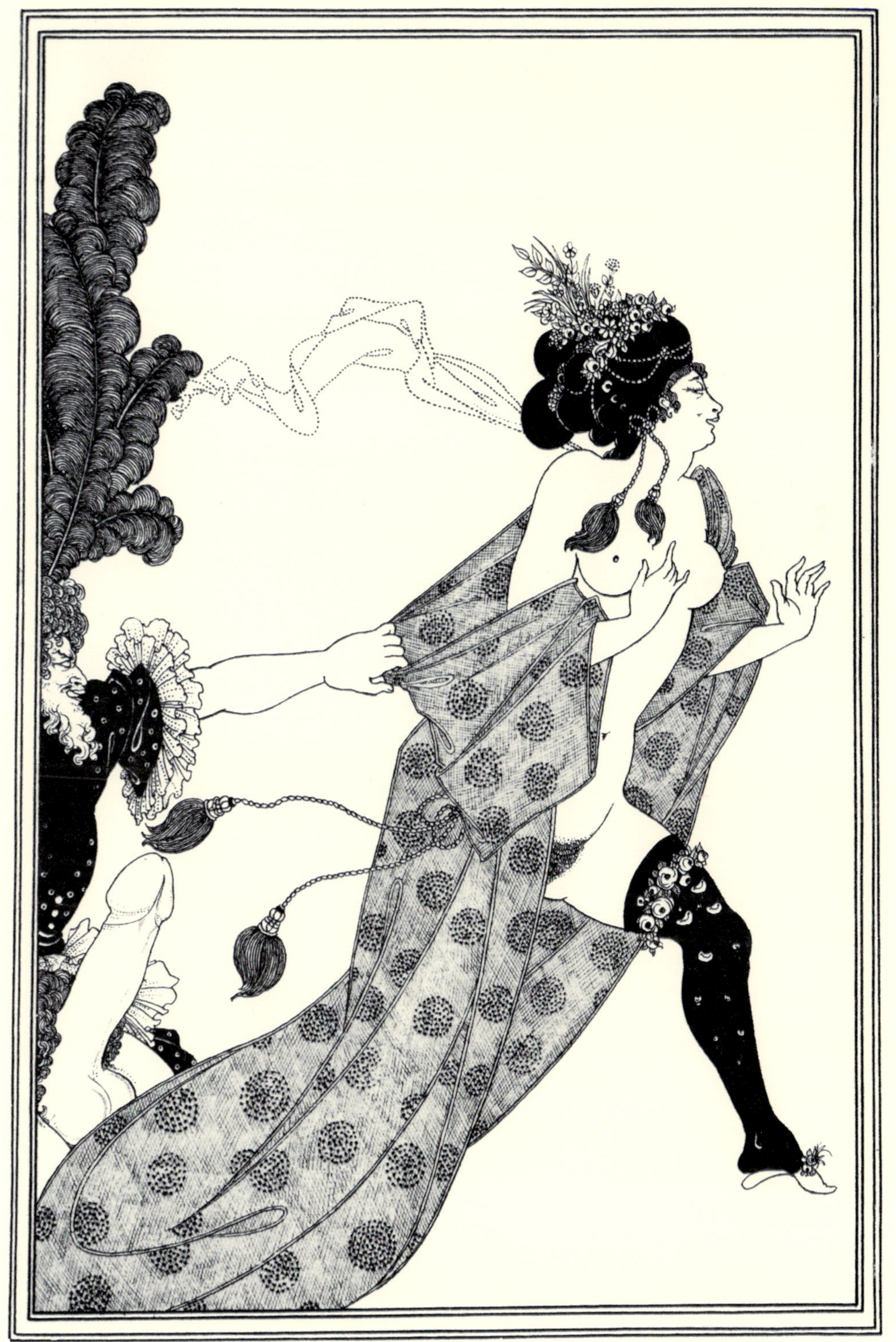

'Kinessia and Mirrina'

Kinesias, Myrrhine's husband, is so desperate for sexual fulfilment that he goes in pursuit of his wife. Myrrhine teases him, stirring up his desire, before escaping. In Beardsley's picture, the aroused man attempts to capture his half-naked wife. The woman's clothes resemble a kimono, and her hair ornament is Japanese-looking also. The picture features a dynamic composition, with the figures dashing from one side to another.

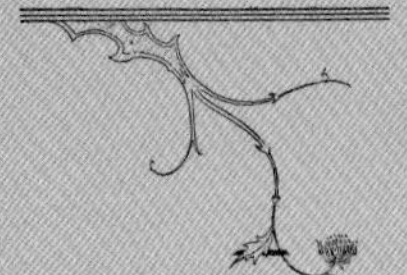

BEARDSLEY AND FIN-DE-SIÈCLE PORNOGRAPHY

Pornography flourished in Victorian society, with its sharp division between the public and the private worlds. Of course, pornography had been in existence since antiquity, with the eighteenth century throwing forth such classics of the genre as *Fanny Hill*, but thanks to late nineteenth century advances in printing technology, it became available to a far wider audience, and thus transformed into a profitable industry.

Leonard Smithers (fig. 2), publisher of *The Savoy* magazine, was also well known for being a publisher of pornography. In 1891, he came to London with printer H. S. Nichols. Nichols had helped print private editions (fig. 3) of Richard Francis Burton's translation of *The Book of the Thousand Nights and a Night* (releasing 15 volumes by 1888). The book contained many erotic scenes, but printing it as a limited edition prevented its being banned. Burton subsequently passed away, leaving behind him a library contained many volumes of Oriental erotica. Nichols and Smithers together set up the publishing company Walpole Press, from which they published pornographic material, including the book *Teleny*, which is often attributed to Oscar Wilde. They also published a twelve-volume illustrated edition of *The Book of the Thousand Nights and a Night* (fig. 4). However, disagreements developed between Nichols whose interest lay squarely with pornography, and Smithers, who also wished to publish books of a more literary bent, and the two eventually parted ways. In 1895, Nichols' publishing house was raided in connection with Wilde's arrest, and Nichols fled to Paris. Meanwhile Smithers, while still continuing to publish literary, artistic pornography, set up *The Savoy*, which resuscitated Beardsley. Smithers commissioned Beardsley to create not only pictures for *The Savoy*, but also erotic illustrations for *Lysistrata*, and on top of that, released a compendium of Beardsley's works. Smithers also extended a helping hand to Wilde, who had fled to France after his release from prison, publishing *The Ballad of Reading Gaol*.

Smithers was himself a collector of erotica, and was drawn to banned literature, apparently deriving a thrill from putting out books that nobody else dared to publish. Wilde allegedly called him 'the most learned erotomaniac in Europe.'

Apparently the crackdown on publication of pornography came in waves. According to H. Montgomery Hyde's book *A History of Pornography*, the Liberal Party was severe, while the Tories were more lenient. It was during the a Liberal government from 1892 to 1895 that Nichols' establishment was raided and Wilde was arrested. Subsequently, the Tories took over and retained power until 1906. This suggests that the government was more lenient during the time of *The Savoy* than it was during that of *The Yellow Book*.

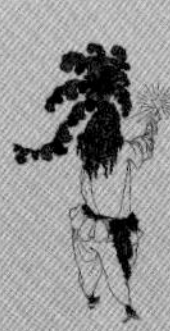

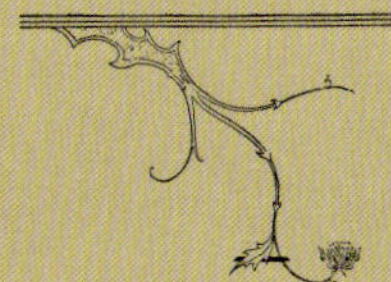

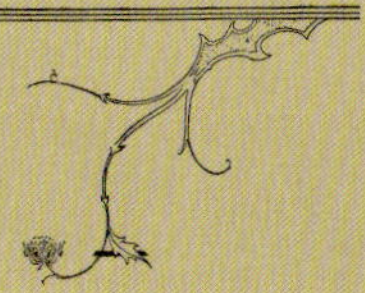

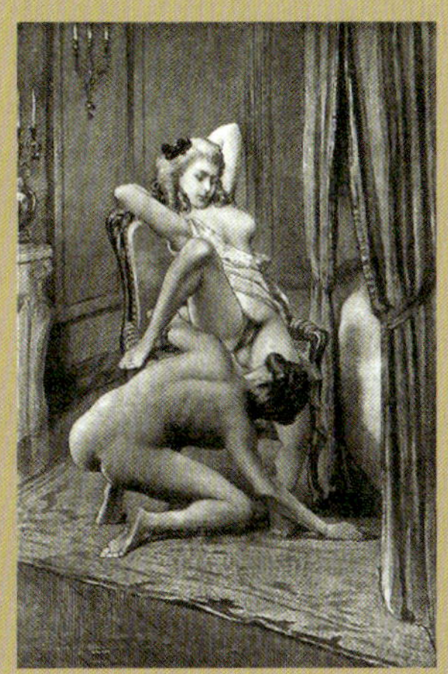

fig.1
Illustration to *Fanny Hill* by Édouard-Henri Avril, 1906

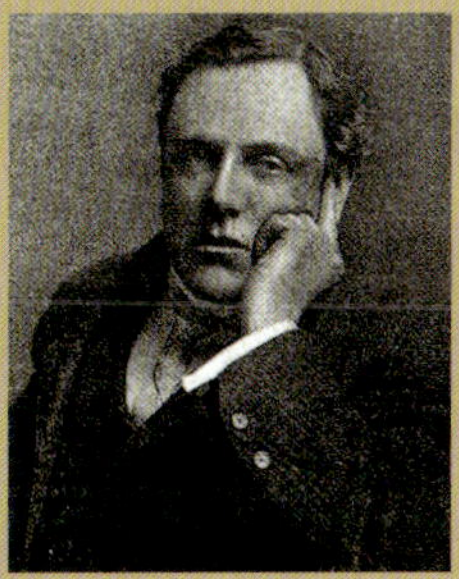

fig.2
Leonard Smithers

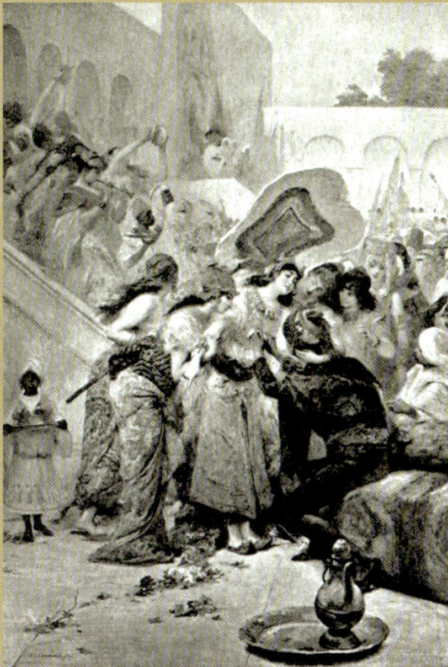

fig.3
Frontispiece for *The Book of the Thousand Nights and a Night* translated by Richard Francis Burton

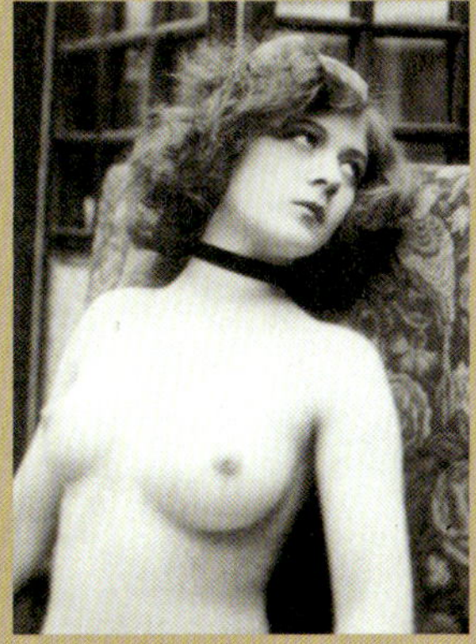

fig.5
A nineteenth-century nude photograph

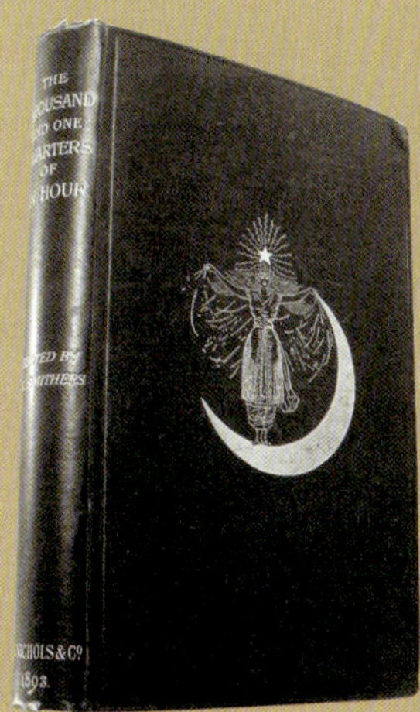

fig.4
Illustrated copy of *The Thousand and One Quarters of an Hour* published by Nichols and Smithers, 1893

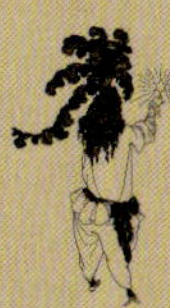

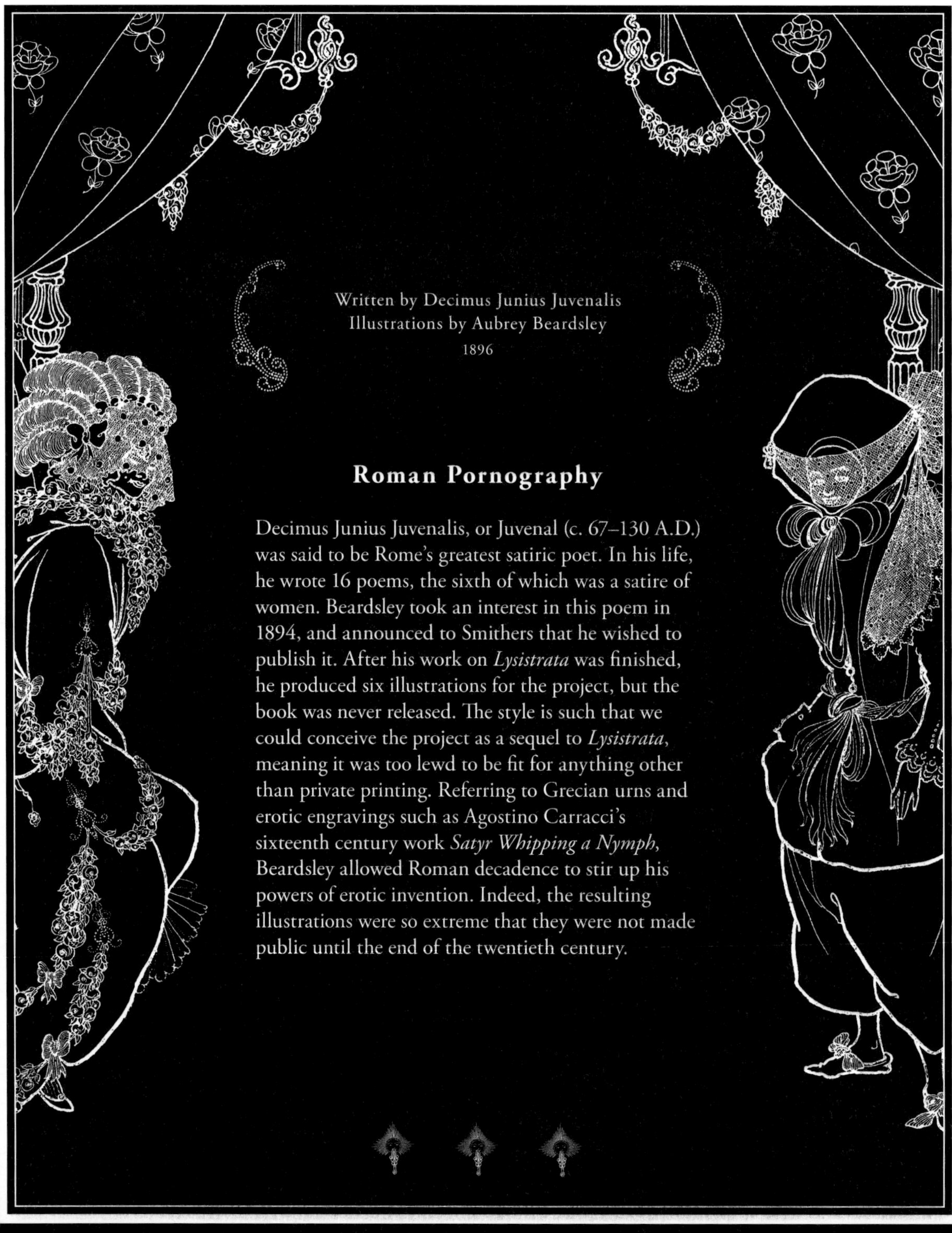

Juvenal's Sixth Satire

Written by Decimus Junius Juvenalis
Illustrations by Aubrey Beardsley
1896

Roman Pornography

Decimus Junius Juvenalis, or Juvenal (c. 67–130 A.D.) was said to be Rome's greatest satiric poet. In his life, he wrote 16 poems, the sixth of which was a satire of women. Beardsley took an interest in this poem in 1894, and announced to Smithers that he wished to publish it. After his work on *Lysistrata* was finished, he produced six illustrations for the project, but the book was never released. The style is such that we could conceive the project as a sequel to *Lysistrata*, meaning it was too lewd to be fit for anything other than private printing. Referring to Grecian urns and erotic engravings such as Agostino Carracci's sixteenth century work *Satyr Whipping a Nymph*, Beardsley allowed Roman decadence to stir up his powers of erotic invention. Indeed, the resulting illustrations were so extreme that they were not made public until the end of the twentieth century.

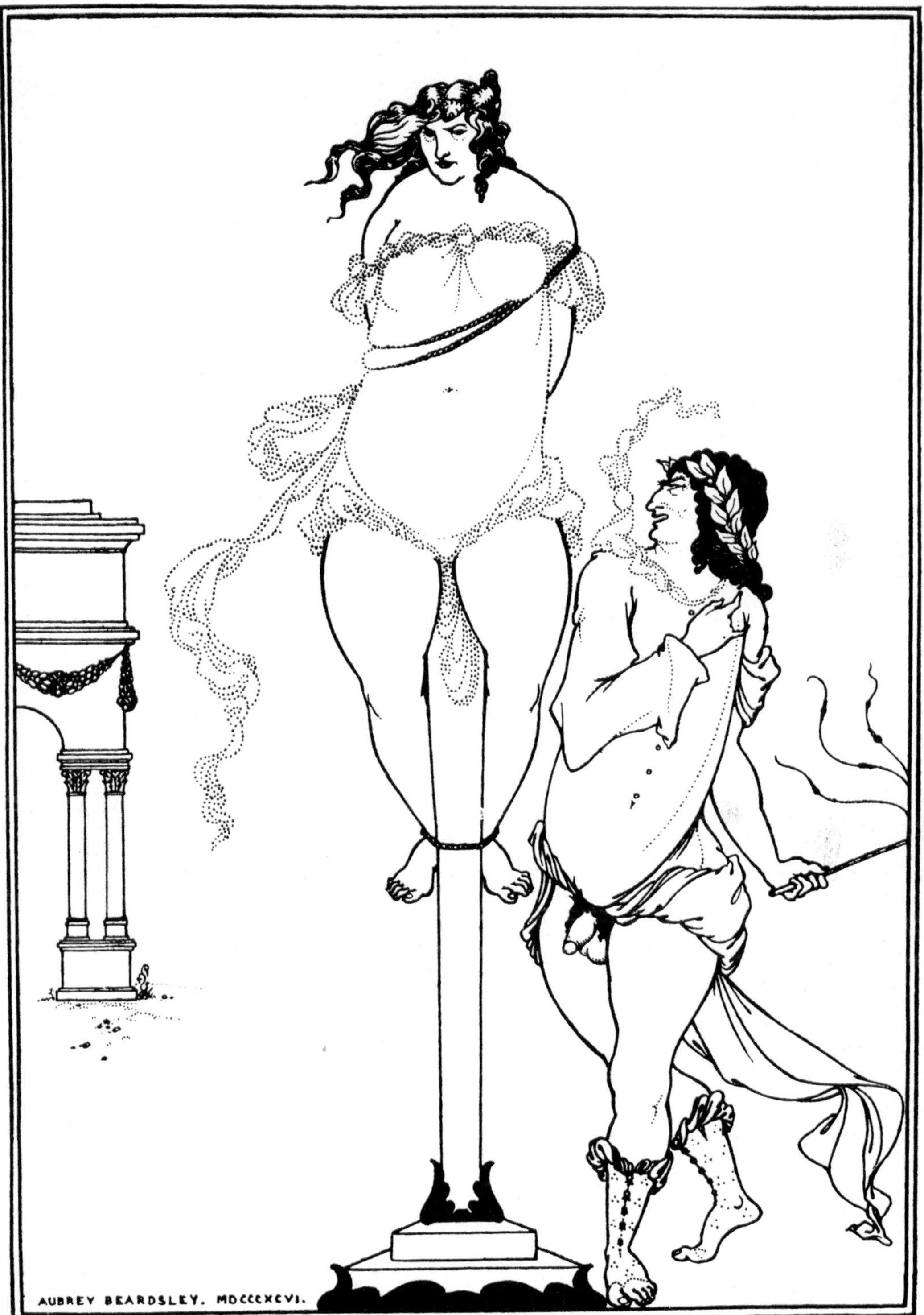

'Juvenal Scourging Woman'

The poet is whipping a woman tied to the top of a column. Here, Beardsley has reimagined Juvenal's biting criticism of women as the sexually arousing pursuit of flagellation. In this plate Juvenal's privates are exposed, although one printed version elided this detail. Scourging is a peculiar sexual activity, but it was an English vice, with specialist brothels existing in London for the activity. The woman on top of the column herself resembles a phallus. Perhaps, as the poet whips the women, he is fact scourging his ego, in the form of his own genitals.

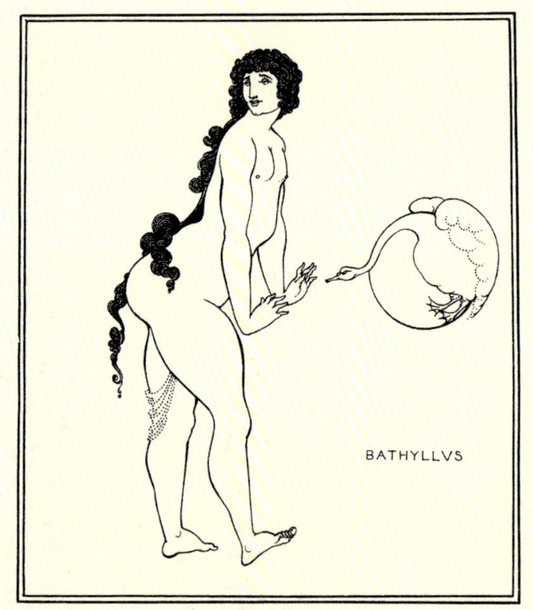

'Bathyllus' Swan Dance'

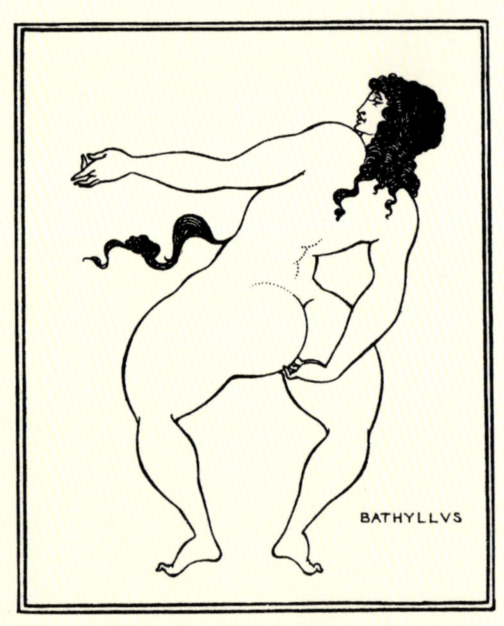

'Bathyllus Posturing'

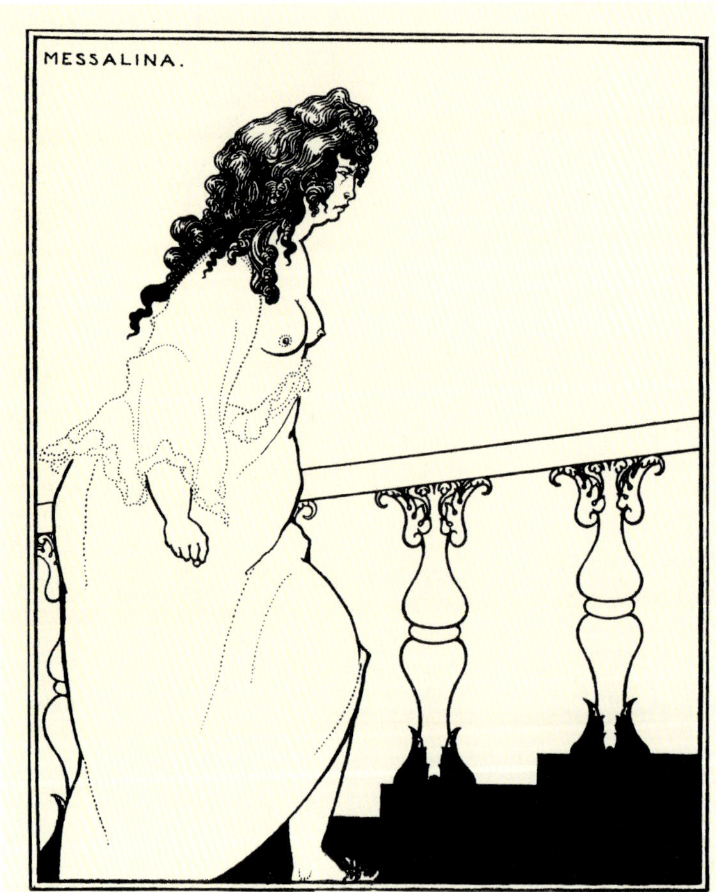

Bathyllus was a Roman cross-dressing dancer, who gave erotic performances. Messalina was the wife of the Roman Emperor Claudius who was known for being rather promiscuous, having sex indiscriminately in the public baths. She would then return home, unsatisfied. Beardsley's portrayal of Messalina clearly records this lack of fulfilment.

'Messalina Returning Home from the Bath'

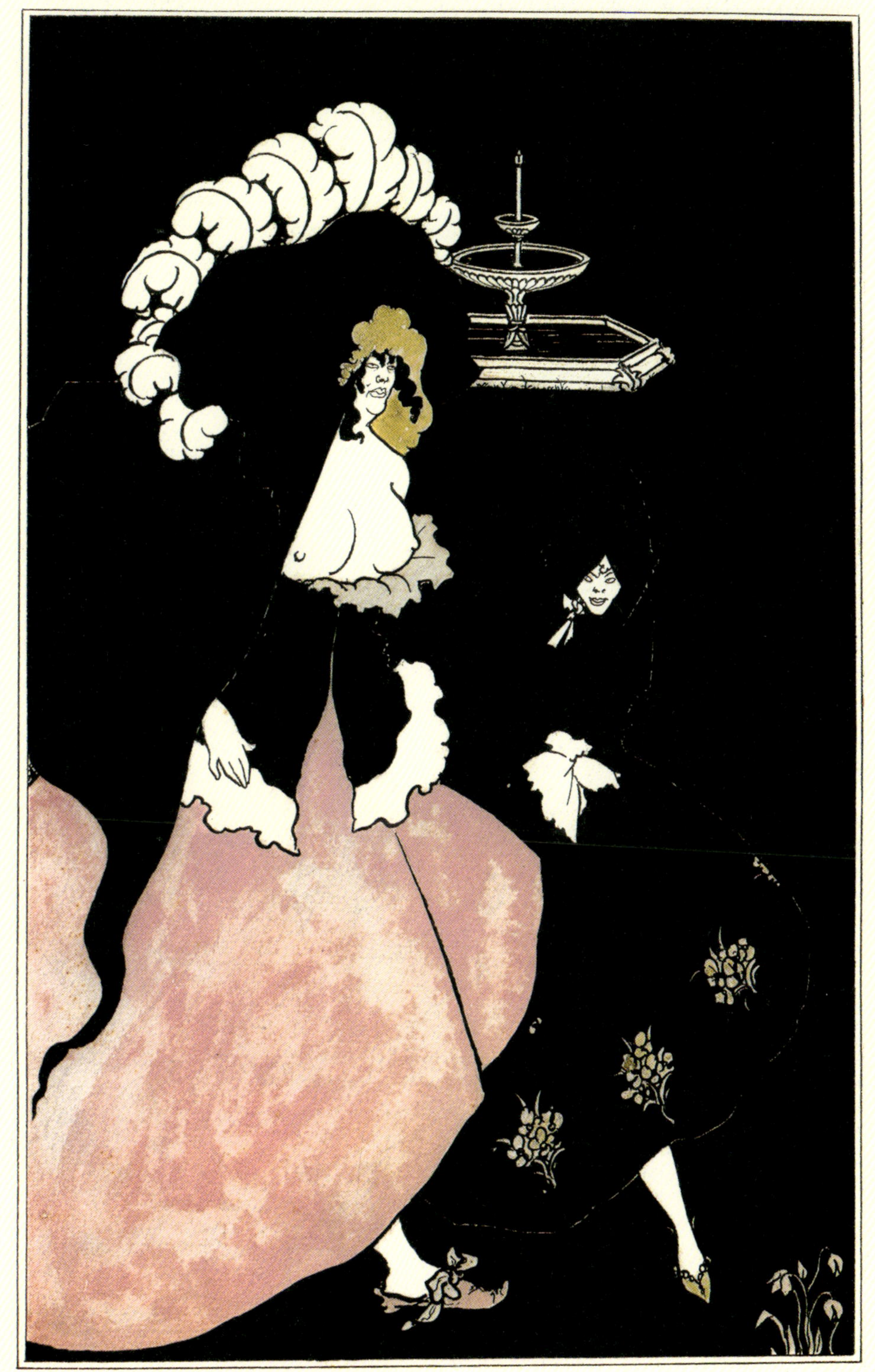

'Messalina and her Companion'

Produced as an illustration for the Sixth Satire, this was later coloured using a peachy purple. It depicts the same scene as 'Messalina Returning Home from the Bath', except here Messaline has a dwarf as a companion, wearing an extravagant hat. Both are on their way home from the orgy, and both wear expressions denoting a lack of satisfaction. As with Salome and other women pictured by Beardsley, Messalina represents the image of the Belle Dame Sans Merci. In Beardsley's rendition, the bold seductive beauty becomes a hermaphrodite monster.

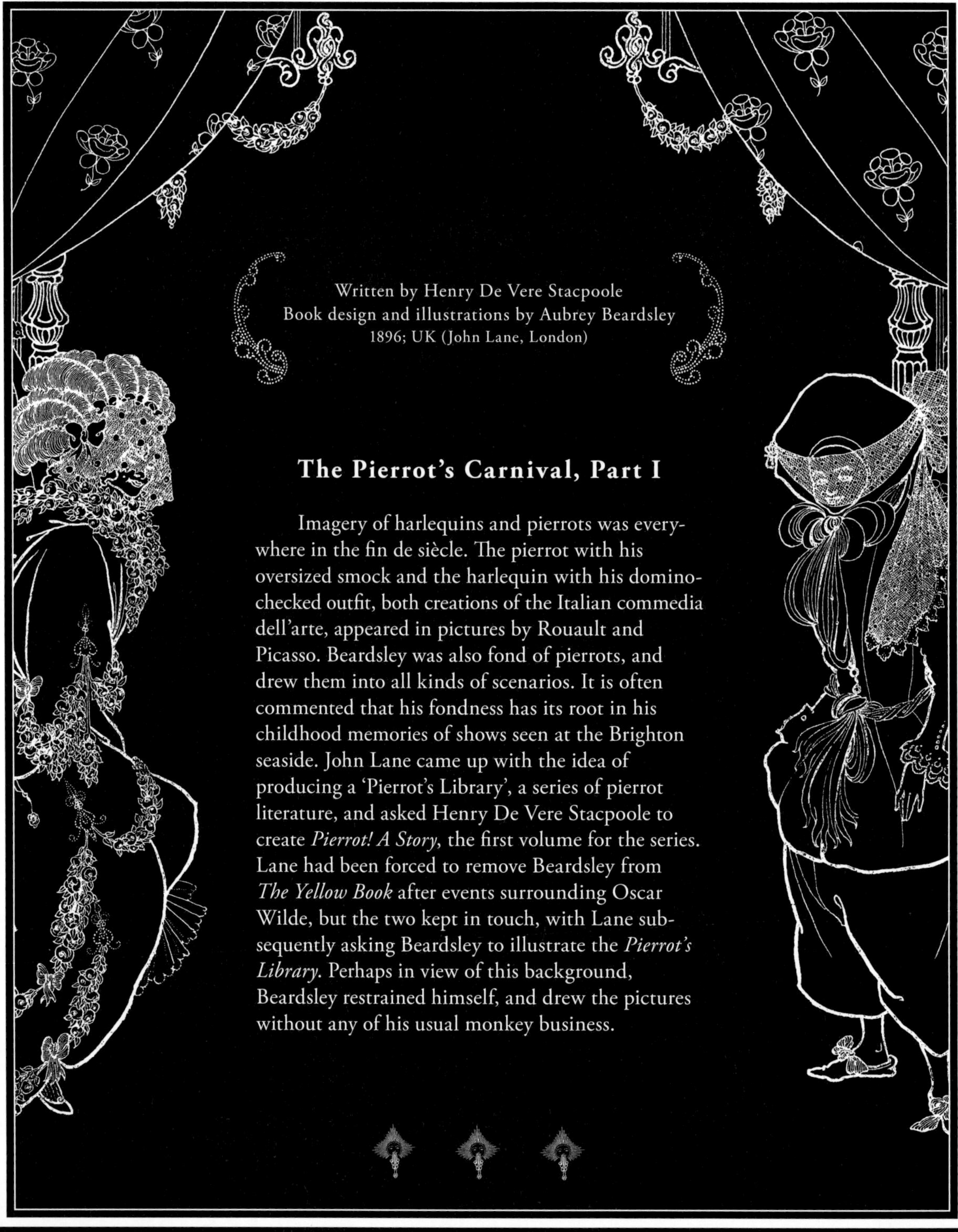

Written by Henry De Vere Stacpoole
Book design and illustrations by Aubrey Beardsley
1896; UK (John Lane, London)

The Pierrot's Carnival, Part I

Imagery of harlequins and pierrots was everywhere in the fin de siècle. The pierrot with his oversized smock and the harlequin with his domino-checked outfit, both creations of the Italian commedia dell'arte, appeared in pictures by Rouault and Picasso. Beardsley was also fond of pierrots, and drew them into all kinds of scenarios. It is often commented that his fondness has its root in his childhood memories of shows seen at the Brighton seaside. John Lane came up with the idea of producing a 'Pierrot's Library', a series of pierrot literature, and asked Henry De Vere Stacpoole to create *Pierrot! A Story*, the first volume for the series. Lane had been forced to remove Beardsley from *The Yellow Book* after events surrounding Oscar Wilde, but the two kept in touch, with Lane subsequently asking Beardsley to illustrate the *Pierrot's Library*. Perhaps in view of this background, Beardsley restrained himself, and drew the pictures without any of his usual monkey business.

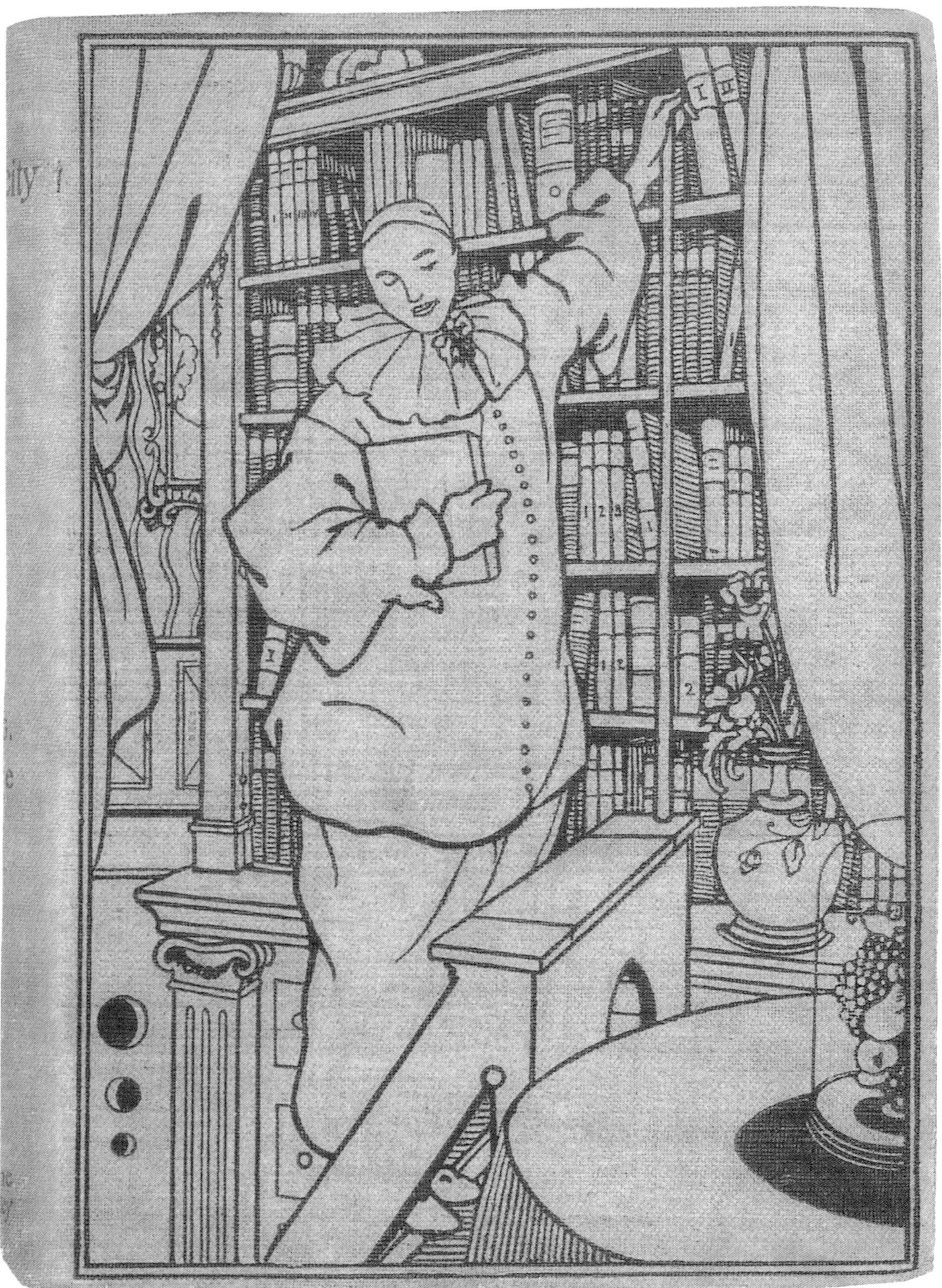

Cover

This design was used as the cover for all the books the Pierrot's Library, in different colour variations. A pierrot is indicating a book on the shelf. If we leave aside his outfit, the interior is a relatively orthodox one, and there are few noticeably risqué elements. It seems that Beardsley kept a check on himself out of consideration for John Lane. If we were looking for roguery, we could perhaps point out the three circles indicating the waxing and waning moon at the bottom left, which is possibly one part of Beardsley's signature mark.

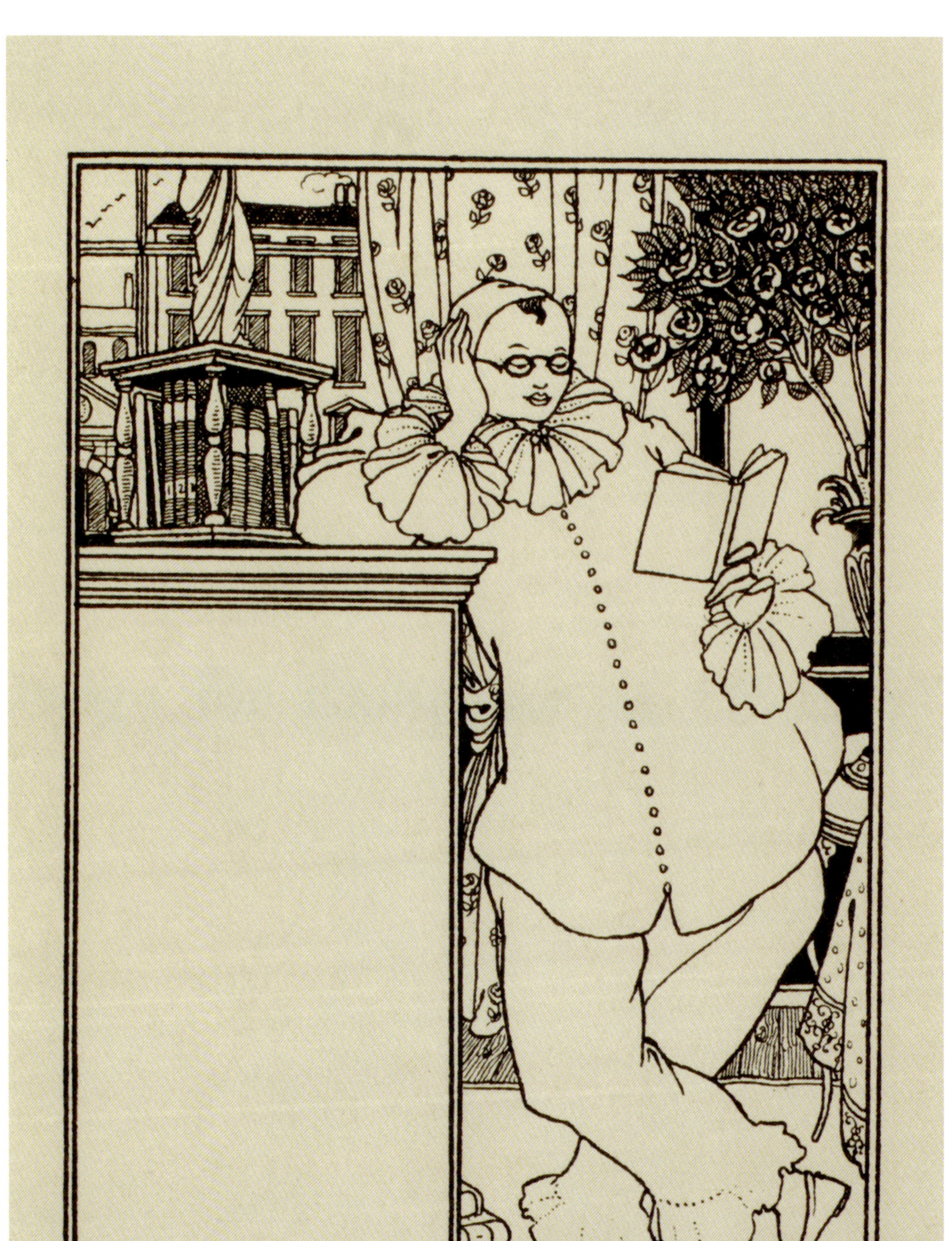

Title Page

This was used throughout as the title page for the Pierrot's Library, with just the title, which went into the space at the bottom left, being switched over. In Beardsley's design, a pierrot wearing glasses is reading a book. He resembles the man who was reading to the boy on the front cover of Volume VII of *The Savoy*. His legs-crossed pose is truly well-rendered, and the picture has a wholesome clarity to it, as if to ensure it wouldn't be met with any complaints.

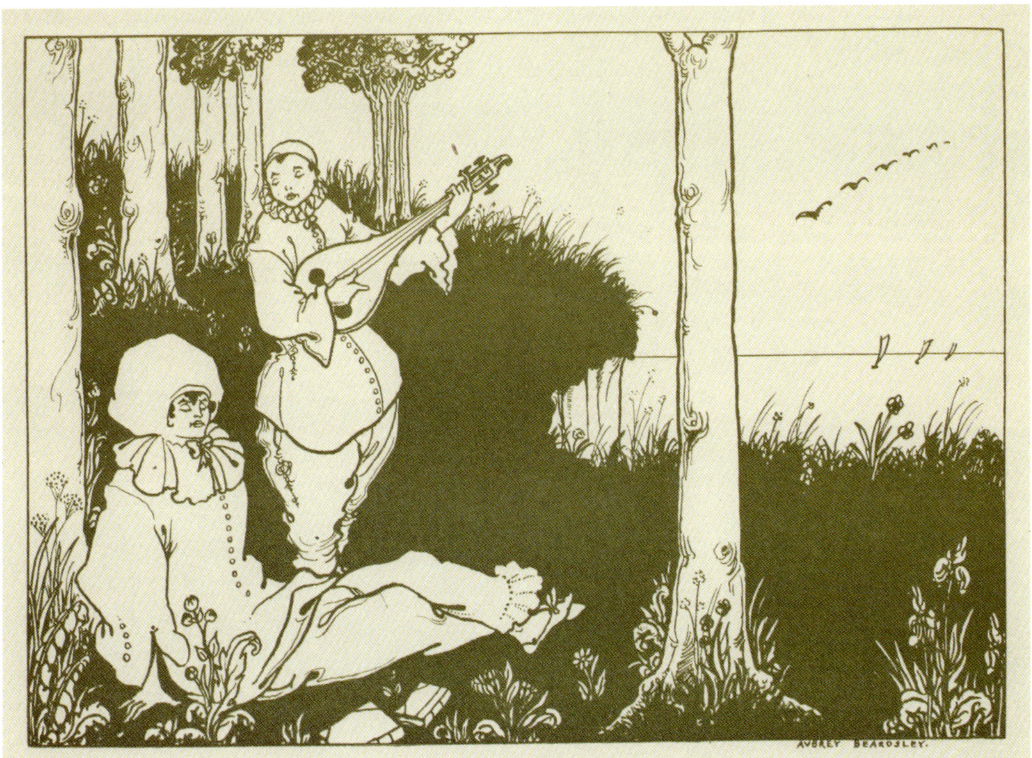

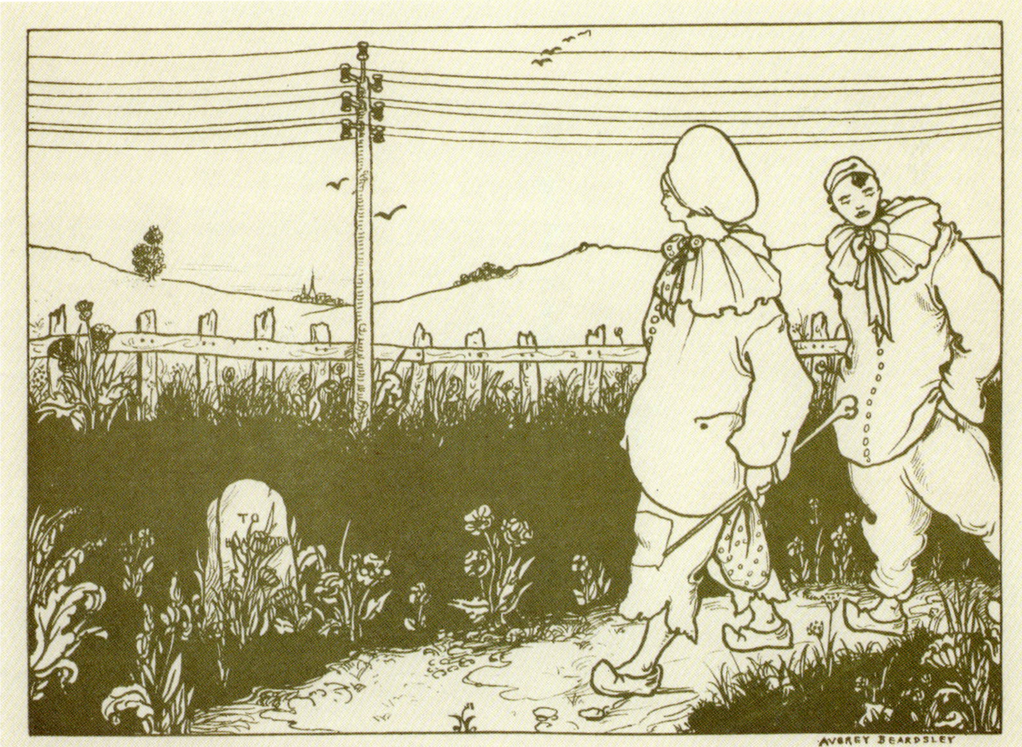

(Top) **Front Endpaper** / (Bottom) **Endpaper**

These two pictures show images of pastoral scenes much like Rococo utopias in the manner of Poussin or Watteau, where pierrots play instruments and stroll through paradise-like scenes. In the front endpaper, two somewhat mature-looking pierrots appear lost in reminiscing, while in the back endpaper, two younger, more mischievous looking pierrots walk alongside a modern railway track. The former shows an eternal paradise, while the latter depicts a modern scene with electricity wires and poles, and where the pierrots themselves seem rather impoverished.

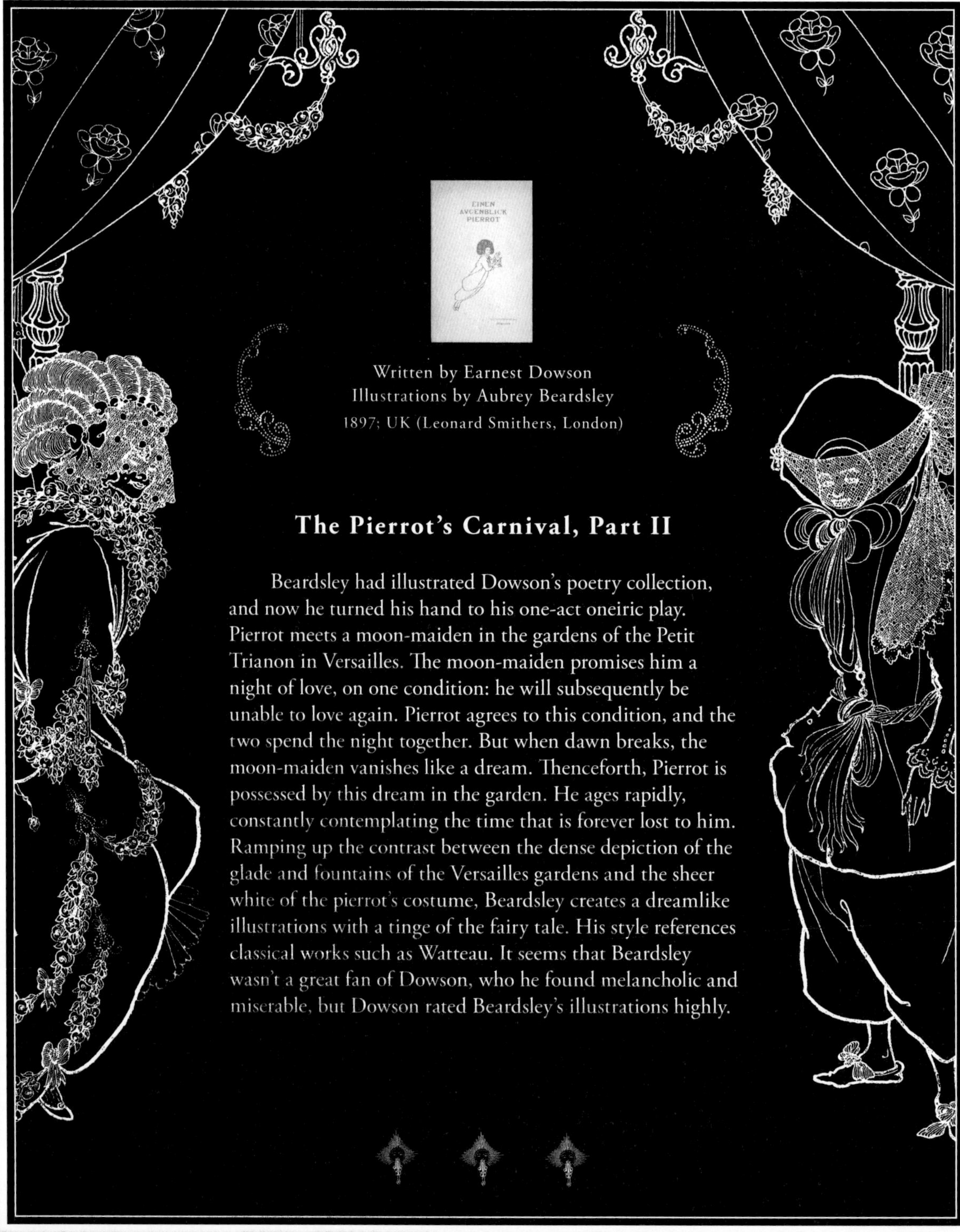

THE PIERROT OF THE MINUTE

Written by Earnest Dowson
Illustrations by Aubrey Beardsley
1897; UK (Leonard Smithers, London)

The Pierrot's Carnival, Part II

Beardsley had illustrated Dowson's poetry collection, and now he turned his hand to his one-act oneiric play. Pierrot meets a moon-maiden in the gardens of the Petit Trianon in Versailles. The moon-maiden promises him a night of love, on one condition: he will subsequently be unable to love again. Pierrot agrees to this condition, and the two spend the night together. But when dawn breaks, the moon-maiden vanishes like a dream. Thenceforth, Pierrot is possessed by this dream in the garden. He ages rapidly, constantly contemplating the time that is forever lost to him. Ramping up the contrast between the dense depiction of the glade and fountains of the Versailles gardens and the sheer white of the pierrot's costume, Beardsley creates a dreamlike illustrations with a tinge of the fairy tale. His style references classical works such as Watteau. It seems that Beardsley wasn't a great fan of Dowson, who he found melancholic and miserable, but Dowson rated Beardsley's illustrations highly.

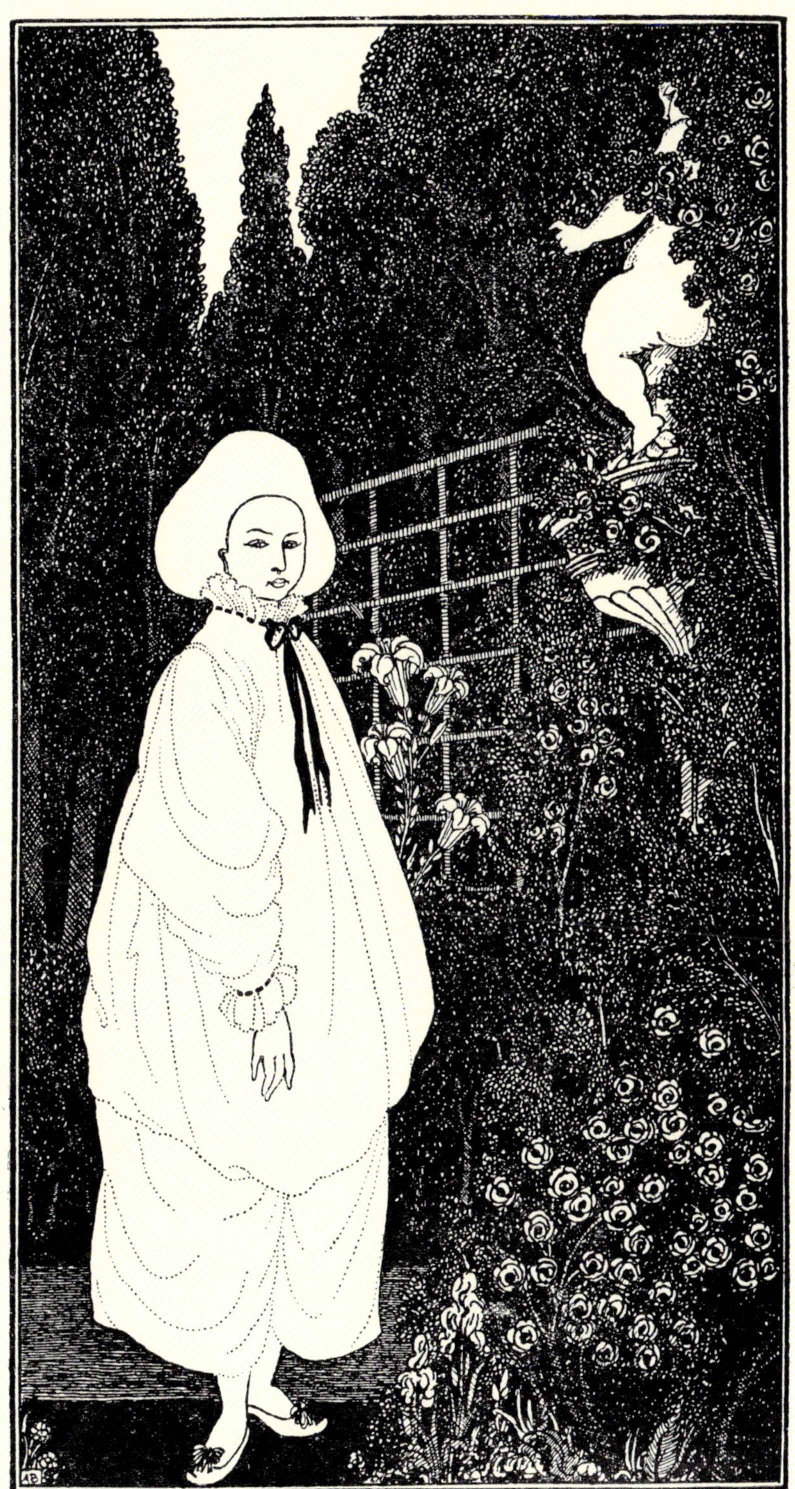

'The Pierrot of the Minute'

Wandering around the Palace of Versailles, Young Pierrot comes upon the Temple of Love, a temple dedicated to Cupid. In its shadows he encounters a moon-maiden, with whom he falls instantly in love. Beardsley's depiction of Pierrot, based upon Antoine Watteau's *Pierrot, formerly known as Gilles*, is rendered with aplomb. Against the background of the dark foliage and blooming lilies, the white Pierrot and the naked Cupid loom out like phantoms. Looked at carefully, the sky visible between the trees looks like the shape of a wolf's mouth, attacking Pierrot from above. Once again, the brilliance of Beardsley's compositional skill astounds.

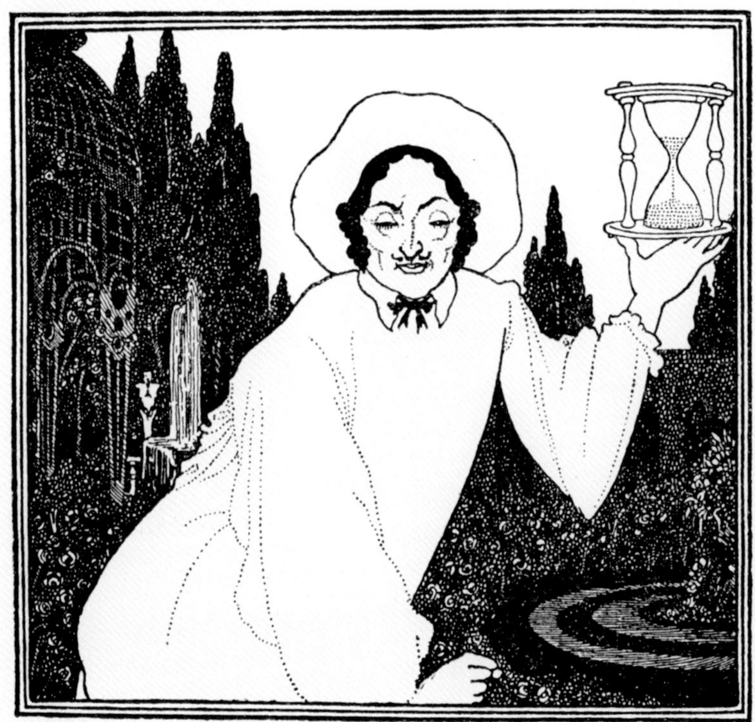

Pierrot tritt auf, seine Hände sind voll von Maiglöckchen. Er trägt einen kleinen Korb. Er bleibt stehen und starrt Tempel und Statue erstaunt an.

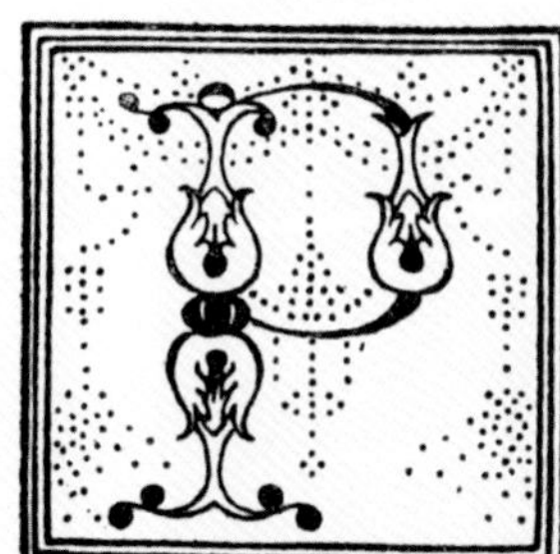

1ERROT

Der Pfad hört auf! Und dies ist auch der
        Hain
Von dem ich las. Mein Eifer war nicht klein:
Maiglöckchenbüschel, hieß es, sollt ich
        finden,
Wo unbekannt sich grüne Gänge winden,

Frontispiece for 'The Pierrot of the Minute'

The picture shows Pierrot in middle age, standing in the gardens. He holds up an hourglass, indicating the passing time. The years have drawn on, and Pierrot is no longer young. And yet he cannot free himself from his recollections of his evening with the moon-maiden. Below the illustration is a decorated 'P', which echoes the shape of the hourglass. The theme of these three illustrations is time, with Pierrot's white clothing representing immutability, while his face alters with the passing hours.

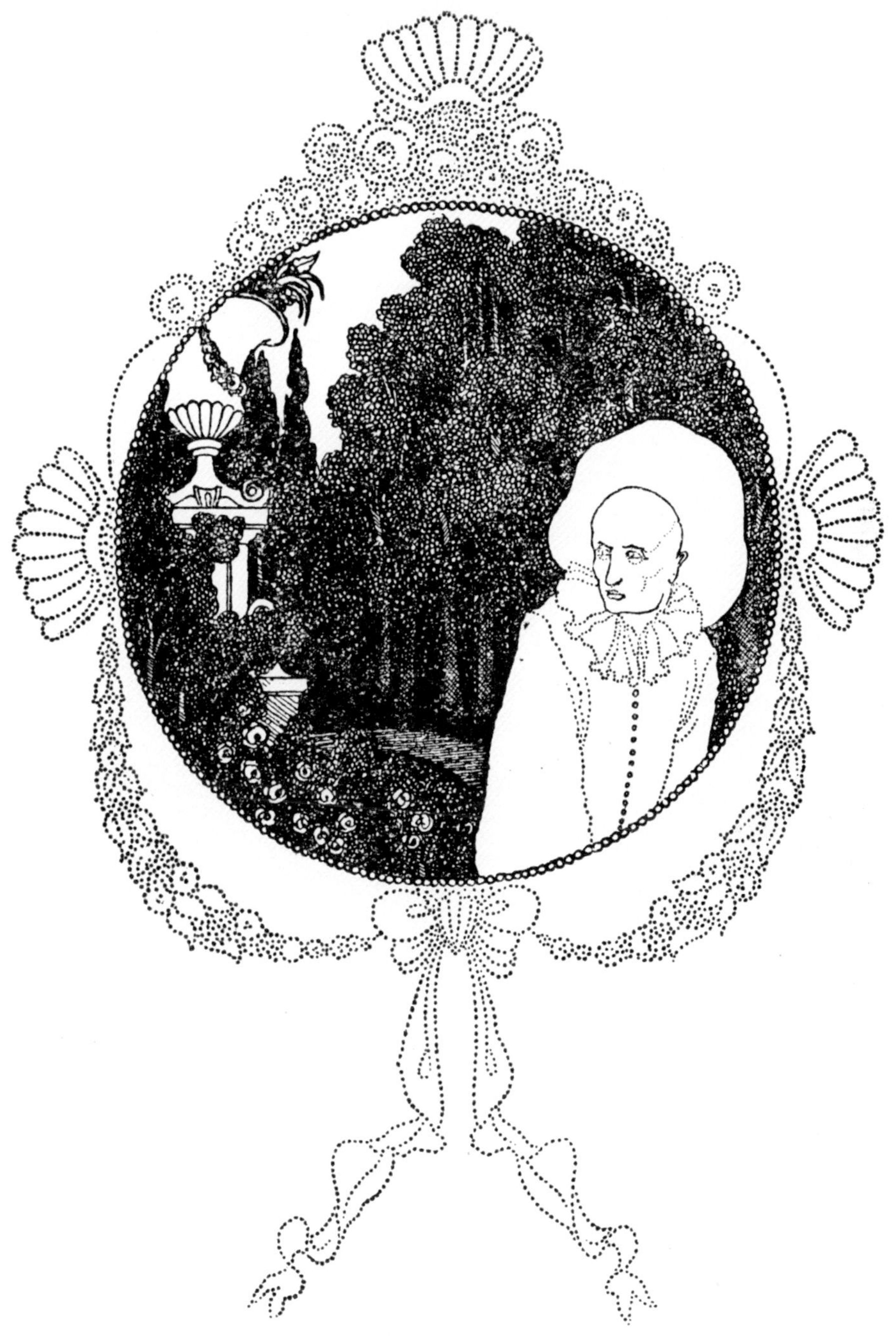

Final illustration for 'The Pierrot of the Minute'

Floral decorations frame a circular Watteau-style scene, showing the gardens of Versailles and an urn on a plinth, which Pierrot gazes at sadly. He is no younger young, and yet, unable to forget the events of that fateful night, he wanders the gardens endlessly. The gardens remain as they were back then, but he cannot reclaim that past time. The Rococo-style frame rendered in tiny points makes the picture seem rather like a mirror. The mirror reflects a passing stream of memories, which go sliding past one after another.

MADEMOISELLE DE MAUPIN

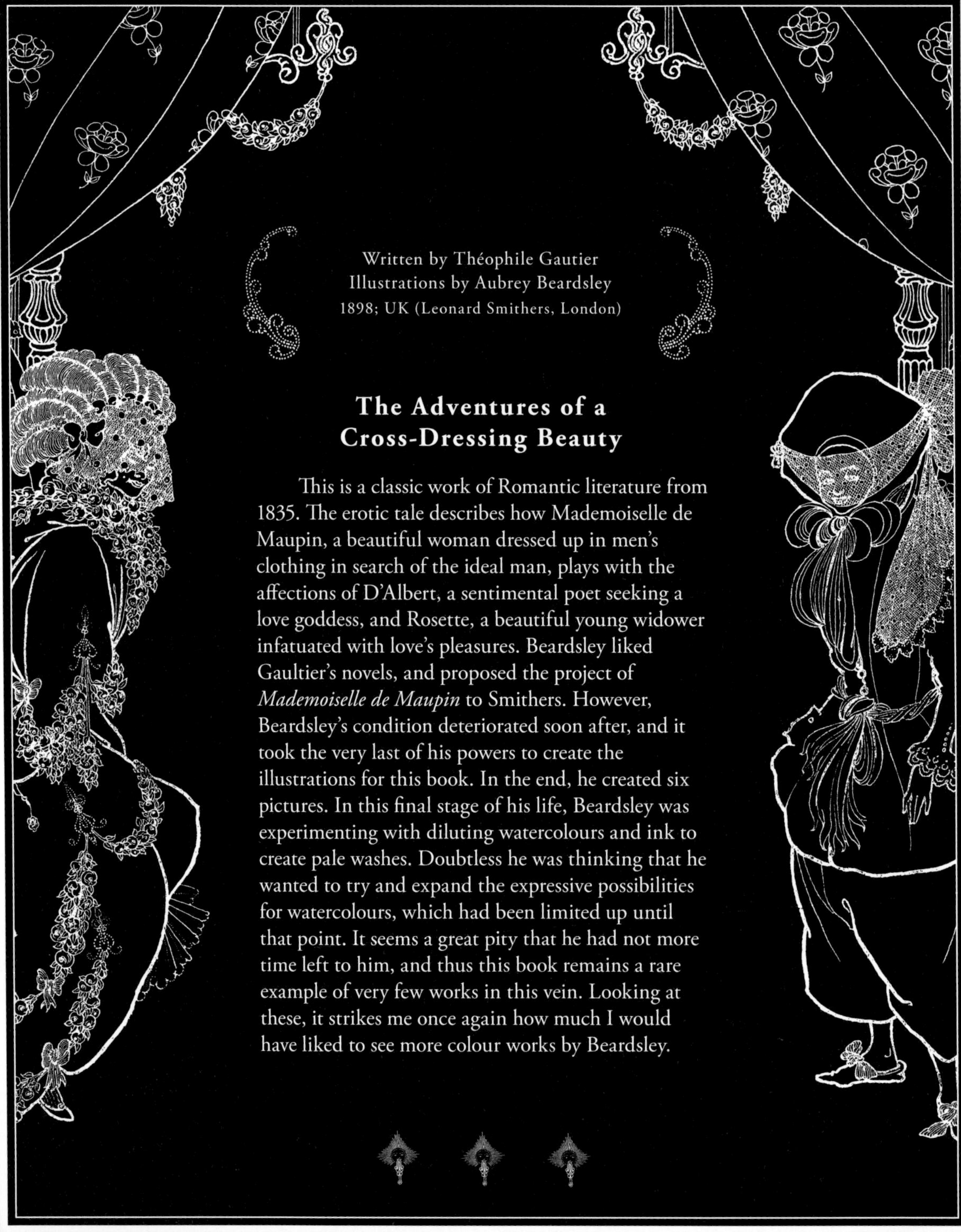

Written by Théophile Gautier
Illustrations by Aubrey Beardsley
1898; UK (Leonard Smithers, London)

The Adventures of a
Cross-Dressing Beauty

This is a classic work of Romantic literature from 1835. The erotic tale describes how Mademoiselle de Maupin, a beautiful woman dressed up in men's clothing in search of the ideal man, plays with the affections of D'Albert, a sentimental poet seeking a love goddess, and Rosette, a beautiful young widower infatuated with love's pleasures. Beardsley liked Gaultier's novels, and proposed the project of *Mademoiselle de Maupin* to Smithers. However, Beardsley's condition deteriorated soon after, and it took the very last of his powers to create the illustrations for this book. In the end, he created six pictures. In this final stage of his life, Beardsley was experimenting with diluting watercolours and ink to create pale washes. Doubtless he was thinking that he wanted to try and expand the expressive possibilities for watercolours, which had been limited up until that point. It seems a great pity that he had not more time left to him, and thus this book remains a rare example of very few works in this vein. Looking at these, it strikes me once again how much I would have liked to see more colour works by Beardsley.

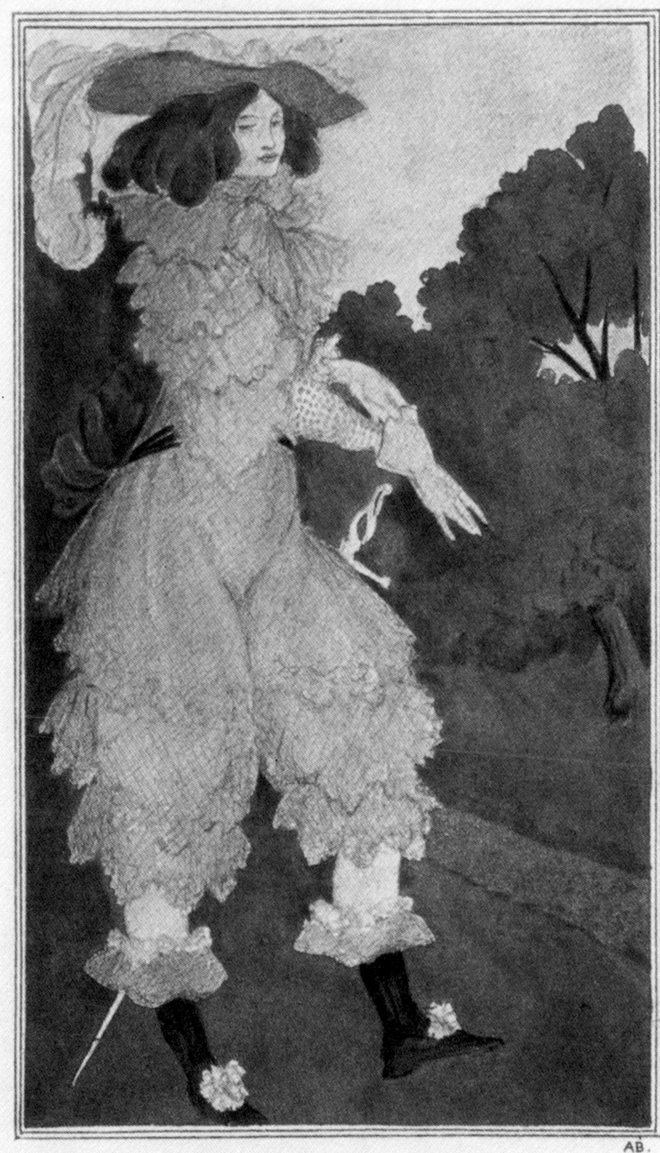

Frontispiece for *Mademoiselle de Maupin*

The novel *Mademoiselle de Maupin* was based on a real person—a cross-dressing woman in the seventeenth century who was a talented fencer. She subsequently moved to Paris and became a successful opera singer. Gaultier portrays her as a virgin swordstress, wandering in search of the ideal man. The idea of drag and other unusual forms of costume always stirred Beardsley's imagination. Here we see a woman dressed as a male fencer, but Beardsley has not yet quite mastered this new technique of applying thin coats of watercolour washes, and the result is slightly unsatisfactory.

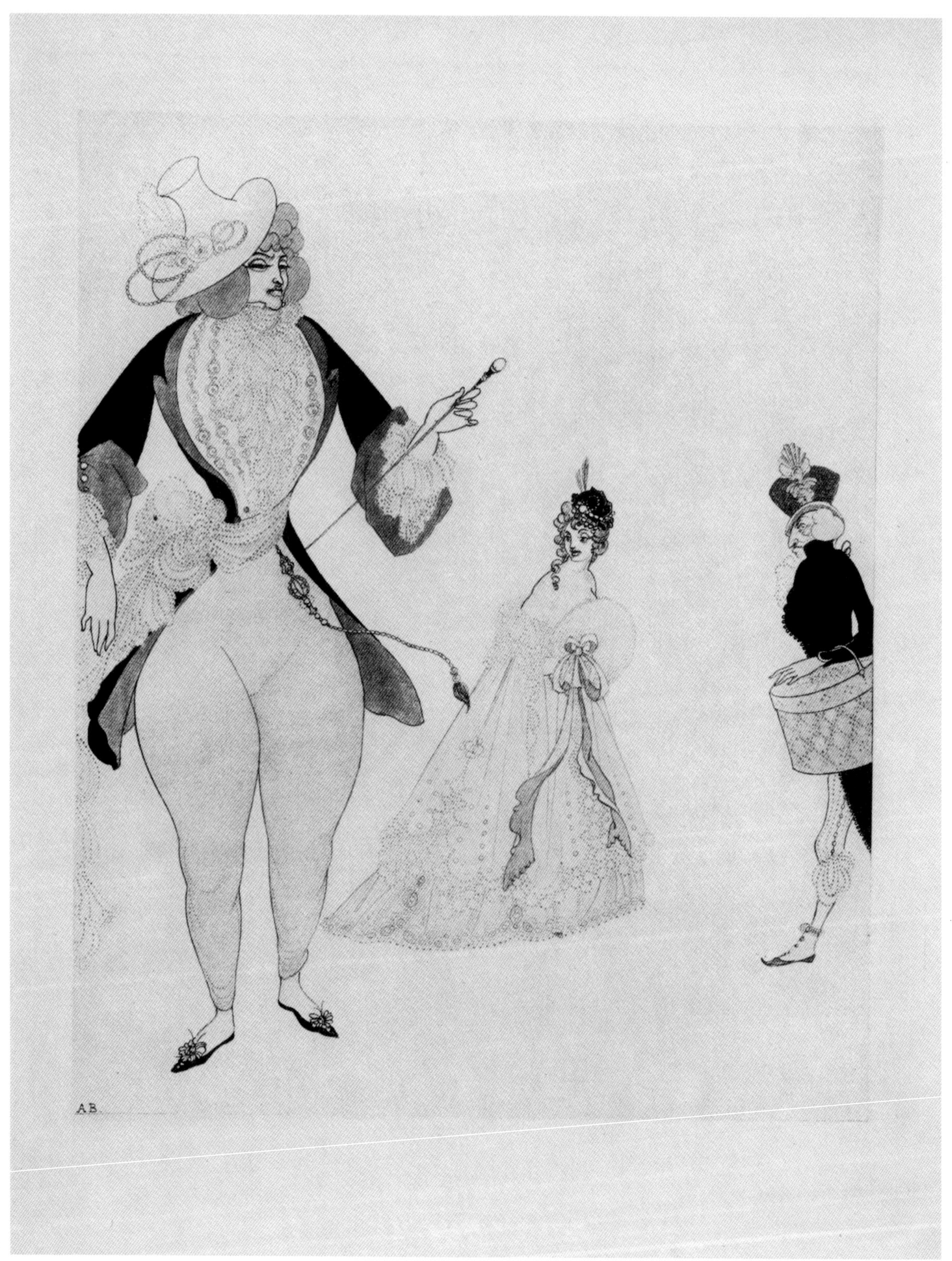

'D'Albert in search of his ideals'

The novel begins with a letter from D'Albert to his friend, where he describes in great detail his ideal woman, from the sort of figure she should have through to her clothes. The modish young man standing to the left of the picture is D'Albert. We can tell from our first glance at him how slavishly devoted he is to fashion, and with his waist sucked in rather unnaturally with a corset, he has a slightly androgynous look. A handsome woman is very taken by the sight of him. At the right of the picture, an older man, apparently the woman's companion, glowers at D'Albert.

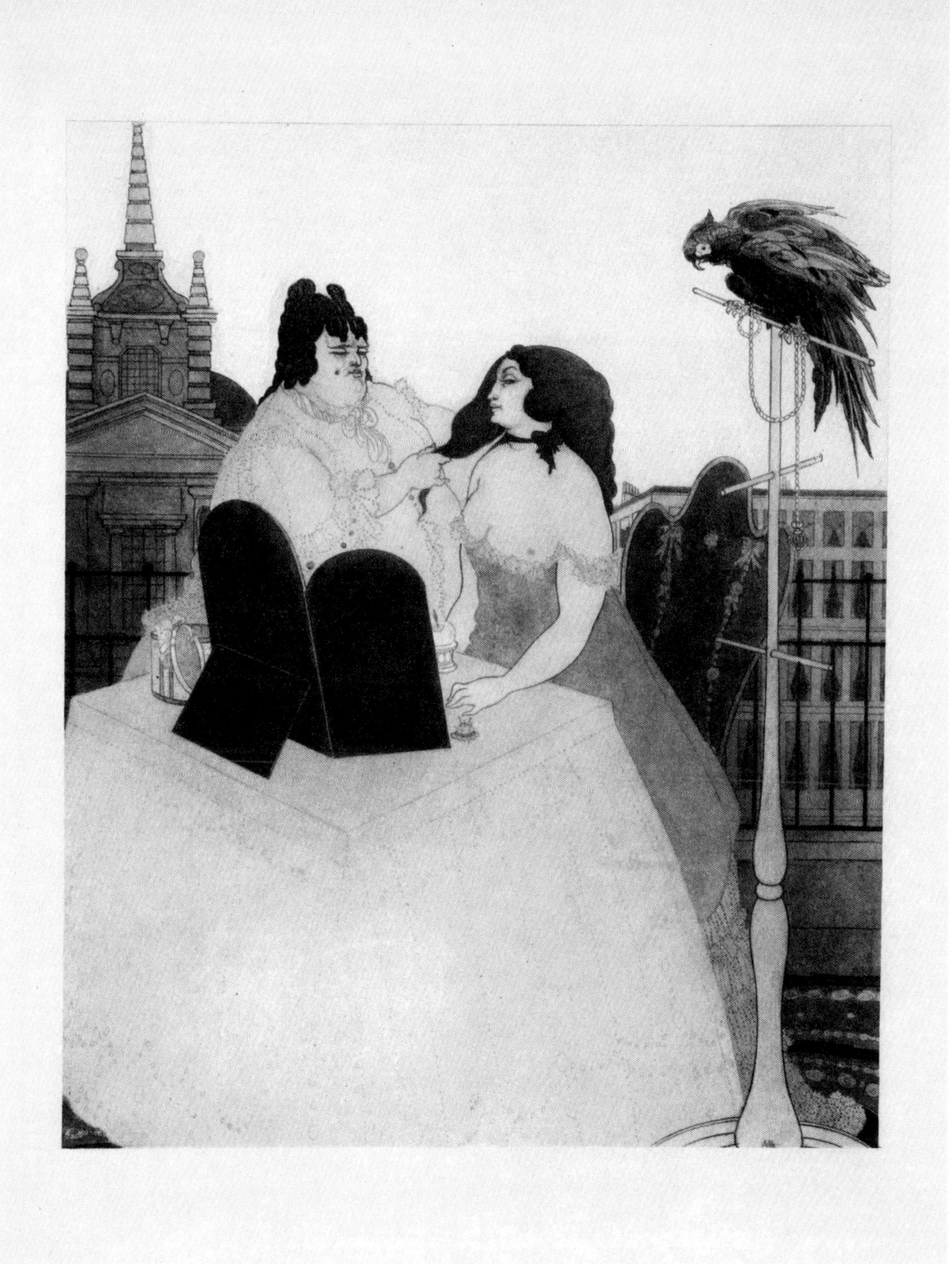

'The Lady at the Dressing Table'

This is another picture delving into one of Beardsley's favourite subjects: the woman at her toilette. Sitting on a balcony backgrounded by Venetian scenery, a lady is having her hair done by a large woman. A parrot is perched close beside. Beardsley's wash technique, whereby the watercolour paint is applied very thinly, has improved considerably. In Venice, D'Albert takes his 'woman in pink', Rosette, as his lover, and the two enjoy themselves greatly. In this picture, Rosette is making herself up to receive him.

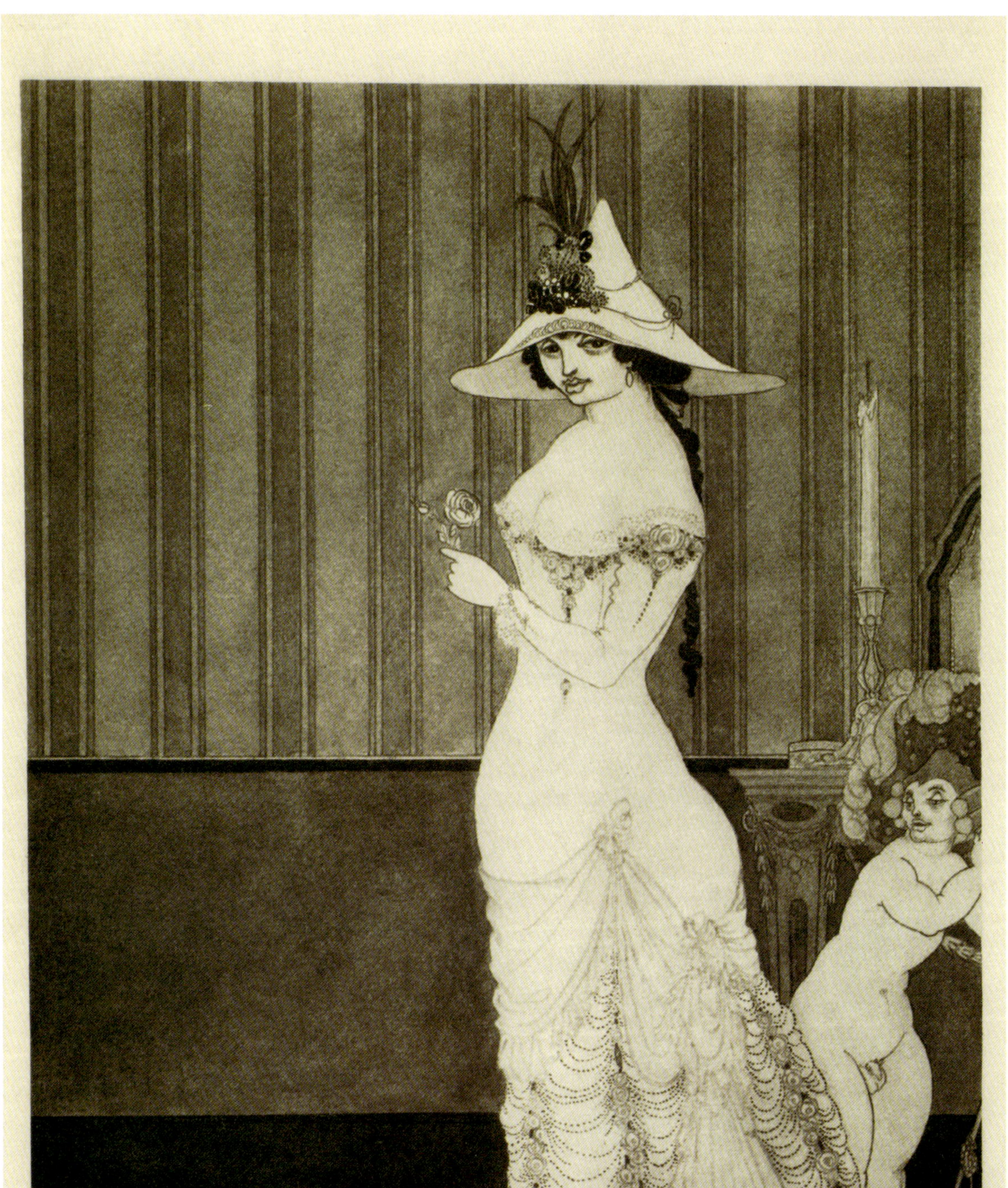

'The Lady with the Rose'

As ever, Beardsley's illustrations stray from the content of the story. This picture features Rosette, the young widow infatuated with love's pleasures. The first time we meet her, she is wearing a pink dress and is introduced as 'the woman in pink'; only later she is referred to by the name Rosette. The nude Eros is Beardsley's addition, and is not in the original. The shape of Rosette's stomach and bottom is extremely erotic, and Eros is fixated by it. Rosette corresponds to Venus, with whom Tannhauser falls in love.

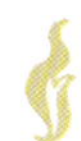

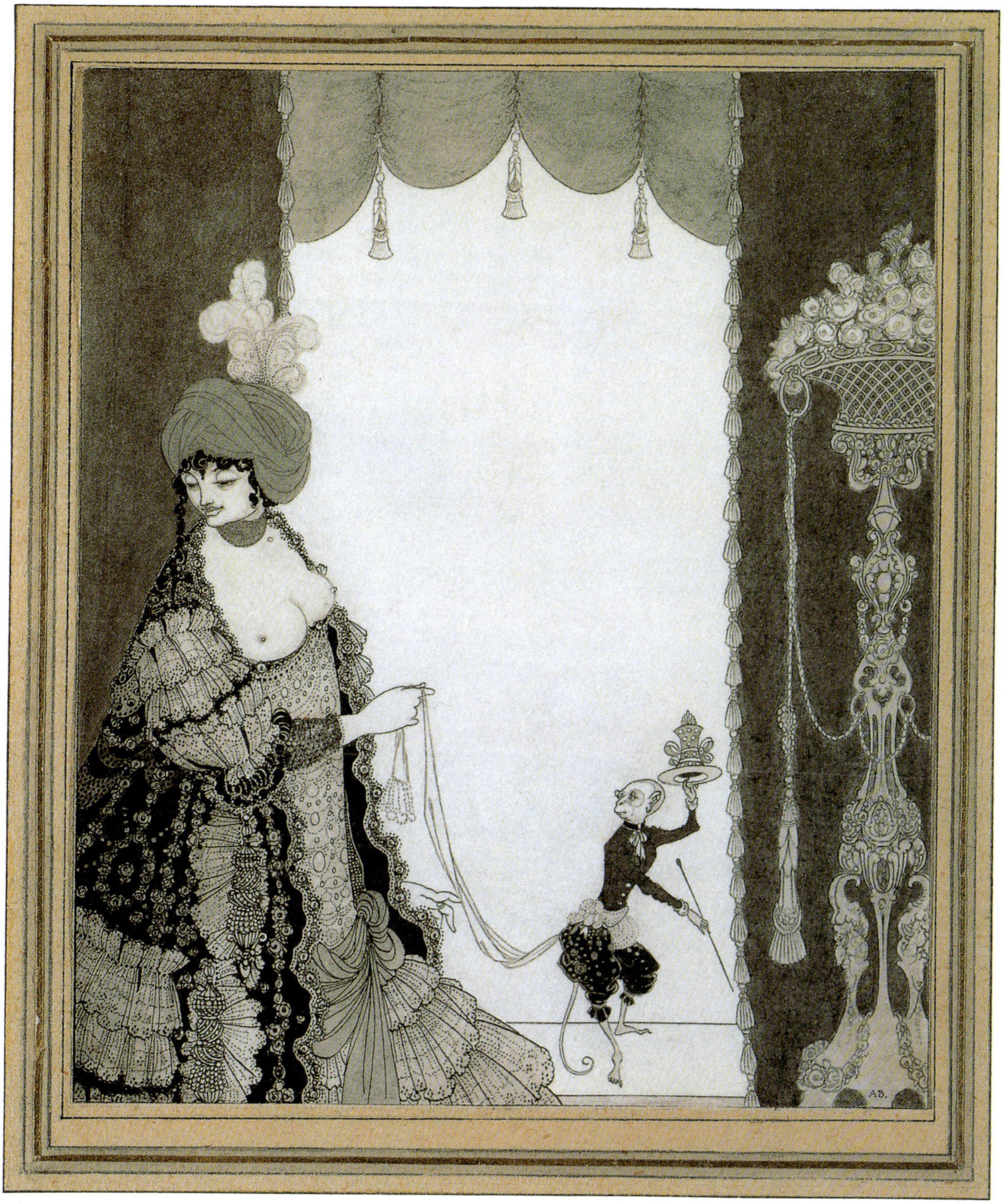

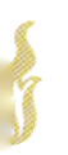

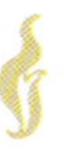

'The Lady with the Monkey'

With this picture, Beardsley departs from Gaultier's novel and enters into his own fantasy world. Here we see a kind of scene that Beardsley had already created several iterations of, with a woman being led through the gates of paradise by dwarfs or monkeys. Guided by a monkey, the woman in a turban looks to her left, beckoning to someone. This is Rosette, the woman in pink, and she is gesturing to an invisible D'Albert. D'Albert hesitates about whether to follow her. Beardsley casts an ironic eye on the play.

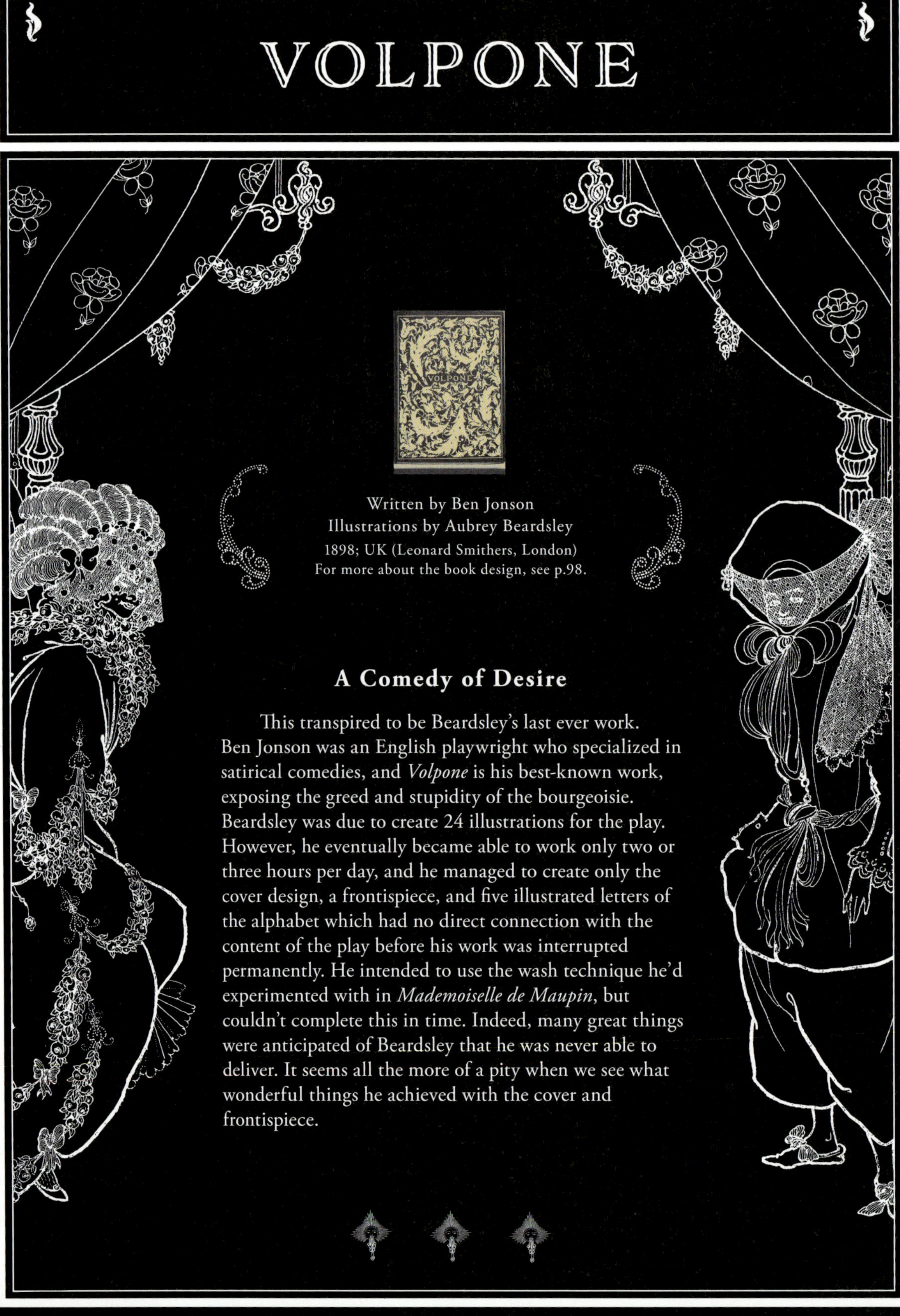

VOLPONE

Written by Ben Jonson
Illustrations by Aubrey Beardsley
1898; UK (Leonard Smithers, London)
For more about the book design, see p.98.

A Comedy of Desire

This transpired to be Beardsley's last ever work. Ben Jonson was an English playwright who specialized in satirical comedies, and *Volpone* is his best-known work, exposing the greed and stupidity of the bourgeoisie. Beardsley was due to create 24 illustrations for the play. However, he eventually became able to work only two or three hours per day, and he managed to create only the cover design, a frontispiece, and five illustrated letters of the alphabet which had no direct connection with the content of the play before his work was interrupted permanently. He intended to use the wash technique he'd experimented with in *Mademoiselle de Maupin*, but couldn't complete this in time. Indeed, many great things were anticipated of Beardsley that he was never able to deliver. It seems all the more of a pity when we see what wonderful things he achieved with the cover and frontispiece.

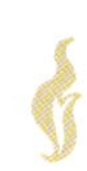

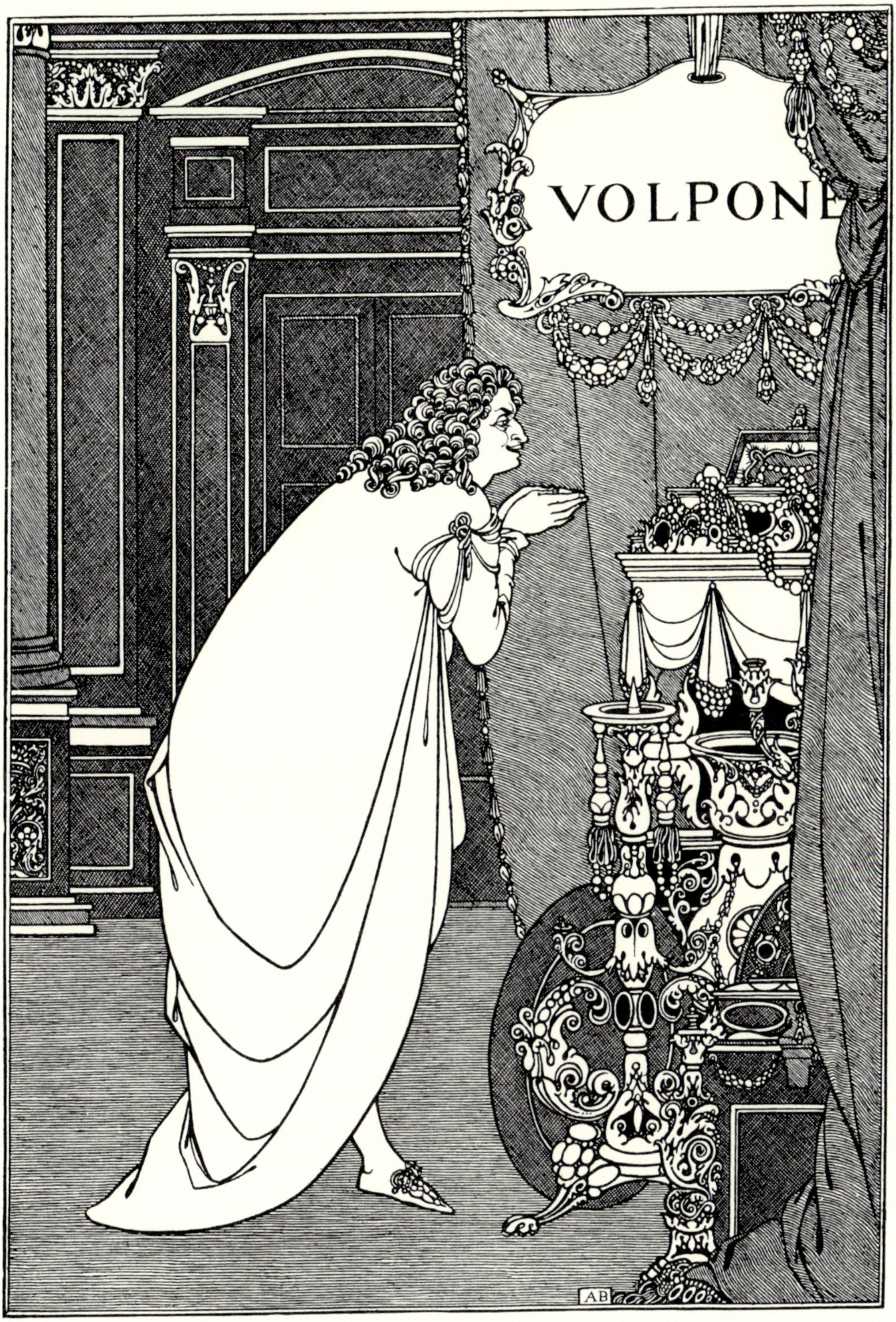

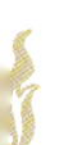

'Volpone Adoring his Treasures'

This was the only illustration that Beardsley created for *Volpone*: a caricature of the figure of the avaricious bourgeoisie who emerged during the seventeenth century. The mass of clothing rendered in the traditional Beardsley style forms the centrepiece of the picture, forming a contrast with the fine, ornate depiction of the 'treasures'. Volpone is drawn from the side, while the treasures are pictured from front on. The walls, floor, curtain and so on are covered in striped or checked lines, creating a grey background tone that enables the white contours to stand out.

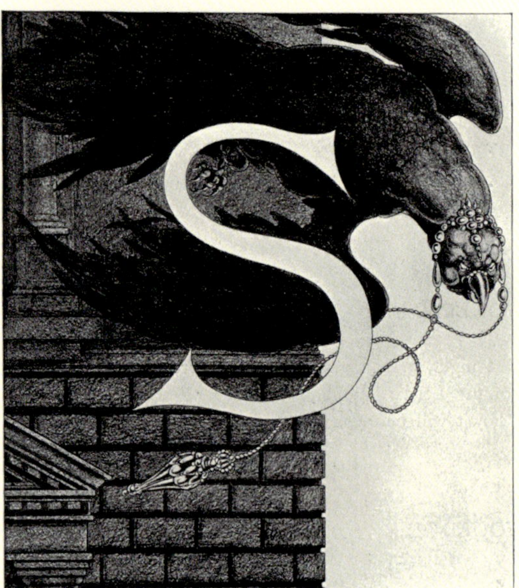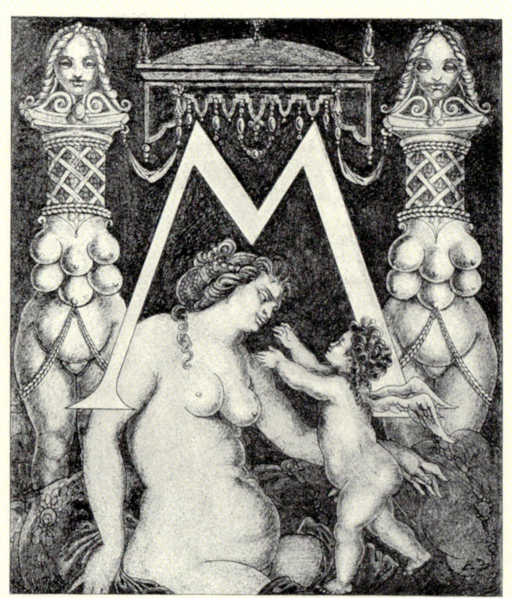

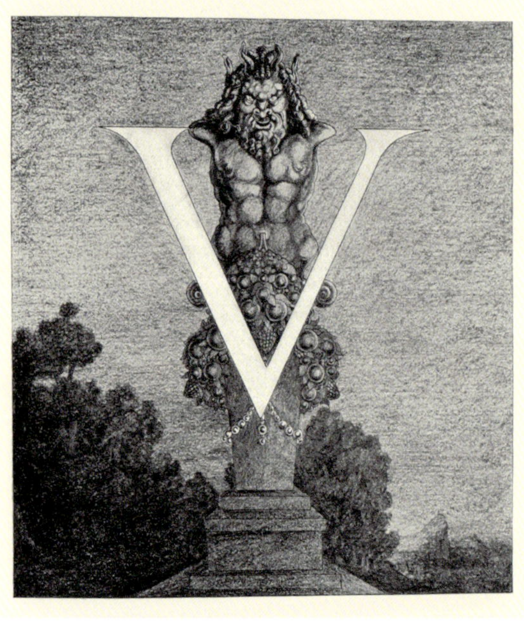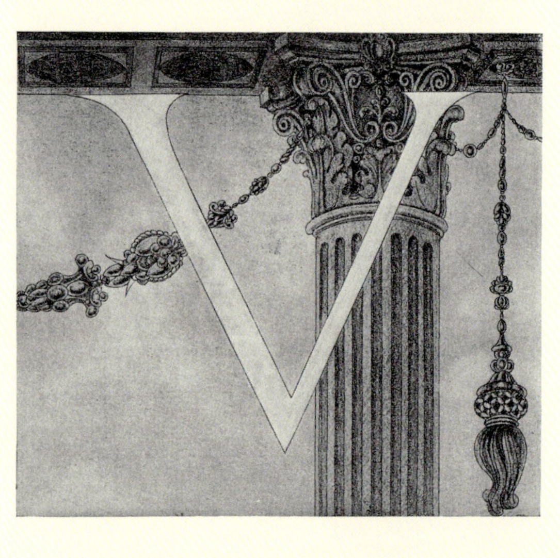

Letter Designs for Volpone

Beardsley produced Baroque-style decorated plates of the letters M, S, and V, which had no connection with the content of the play. Perhaps the trajectory of his style could be fairly described as moving from gothic to Baroque. His 'M' is dotted with naked mother and children and many-breasted mother goddesses. His S contained a giant bird, and his V a great elephant. His shading for these was rendered in pencil, so they were printed in half-tones.

VOLPONE. MOSCA.

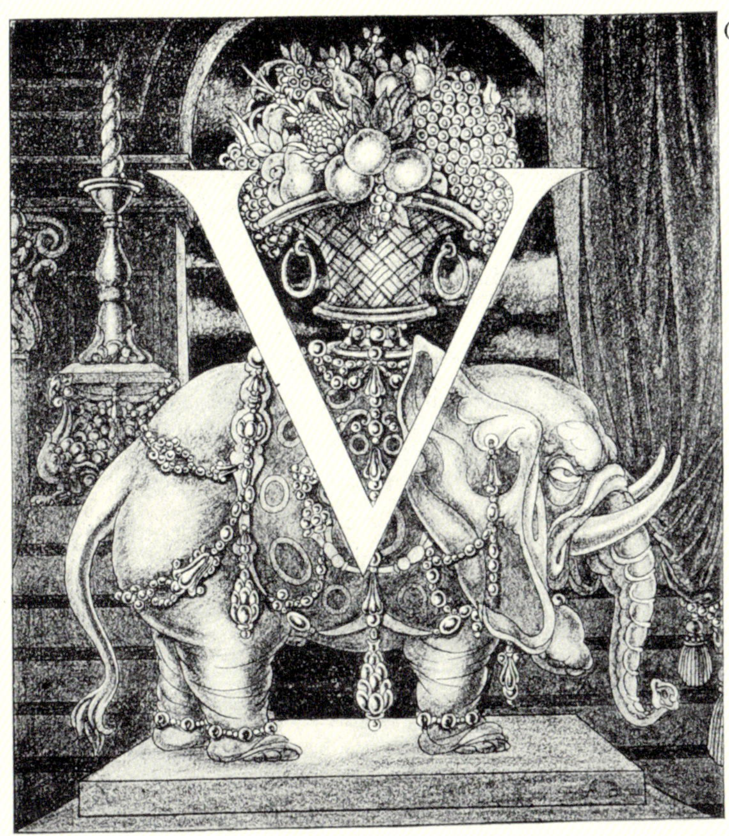

OLPONE.

Good morning to the Day; and next, my Gold :
Open the shrine, that I may see my *Saint*,
Hayle the worlds soule, and mine. More glad then is
The teeming earth, to see the longd-for *Sunne*
Peepe through the horns of the *Coelestiall Ram*,
Am I, to view thy splendor, dark-ening his :
That lying here, amongst my other hoordes,

Shew'st like a flame, by night ; or like the Day
Strooke out of *Chaos*, when all darkenes fled
Unto the center. O thou Sonne of *Sol*,
(But brighter than thy father) let me kisse,
With adoration, thee, and every relique
Of sacred treasure, in this blessed roome.

21

7. THE FINALE

1897 arrived. John Gray and Raffalovich frequently visited Bournemouth to see Beardsley, who continued to work on the jobs Smithers had given him. People joked that Smithers owned him, and indeed he did continue to draw for Smithers right up until his death. Most likely, though, this was because for Beardsley, drawing was life itself.

In April, a doctor advised him to move to a warm seaside spot in the south of France. Before leaving the UK, Beardsley converted to Catholicism. Death was already drawing nigh. Raffalovich saw to organizing everything, from his conversion to the arrangements for his journey to France.

On his way to France, Beardsley stopped by London and bade farewell to Smithers. The strange friendship of those two men remains something of a mystery. Many authors hated Smithers, calling him avaricious, lecherous and coarse. He treated Beardsley like an object, they said, squeezing work out of him. What was more, he forced Beardsley to create pornography, sacrificing his artistic talent. However, Beardsley kept creating work faithfully for Smithers, right up to the end of his life. Even if Smithers did use Beardsley, without him, Beardsley's work could likely not have made it into the world. It seems that the two of them had a brotherly friendship, based upon their joint venture to wage war on the pristine, morally upstanding world of the Victorian era.

Having said his goodbyes to Smithers and to London, Beardsley set off, with his mother and attendant doctor for company. In Paris, he visited print shops, before moving to Dieppe in July. On the beach there, he met with Oscar Wilde, who had fled to France after his release from jail. Yet Beardsley had no intention of creating work for Wilde.

Into autumn, Beardsley moved back to Paris, before heading to Menton by the warm Mediterranean for winter. Here Beardsley created the illustrations for *Volpone*.

New year ended, and 1898 dawned. Beardsley was looking forward to the release of *Volpone*, but come February, he became unable to leave the house. On the 16th March, Beardsley drew his last breath, his mother and Mabel by his side.

Smithers published *Volpone* at the end of 1898. The cover, frontispiece, and five letters were those that Beardsley had drawn. The twenty-five year old had shot across the sky like a shooting star, leaving in his trail a scattering of stardust that glittered as entrancingly as a jewel.

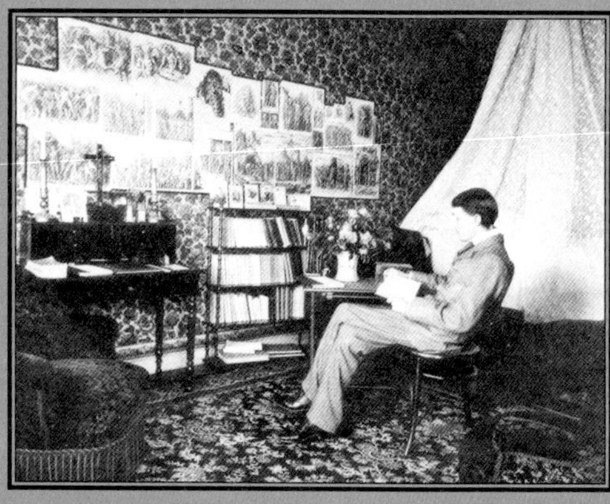

The last photo of Aubrey Beardsley at the Hotel Cosmopolitan in Menton where he passed away.

8. Beardsley Again

Beardsley was the genius of mischief. He was able to draw endless different images from a single shape, which he wielded like a dexterous magician, surprising all that encountered his work. Things of no particular significance suddenly transformed before their eyes into bizarre, funny, or else erotic and obscene sights.

Those living through the fin-de-siècle were accustomed to this, and were on the look out for things transforming into other more suspicious ones, but nonetheless felt unease to have their world shaken up in this way. They hunted down Wilde, and silenced Beardsley.

A lover of literature, Beardsley initially intended to become an author. Yet his imaginative powers extended to both words and images, and it was the visions he had which sparked off his words and made them fly—it was imagery that filled his dreams. In his illustrations he journeyed through these dreams, and the stage on which he performed the book that combined words and image.

The sources of Beardsley's images were various, and included scenes from his native Brighton such as sea bathers, funfairs, side-shows, circuses, as well as London cafes, music halls, secret clubs and prostitutes in the back streets. He used his art to depict all those things that had not found a place in art before—the fin-de-siècle street scenes, with all their underground and squalid characters.

Subsequently, owing to their extreme, underground nature, as well as to the fact that they were illustrations, which made them a 'lesser' art form, Beardsley's pictures were left out of the canon of contemporary expression.

However, Beardsley's world where a single shape undergoes endless contortions, and where underground, lost objects are revived made to cavort with one another, hold a charm that feels fresh and modern even now.

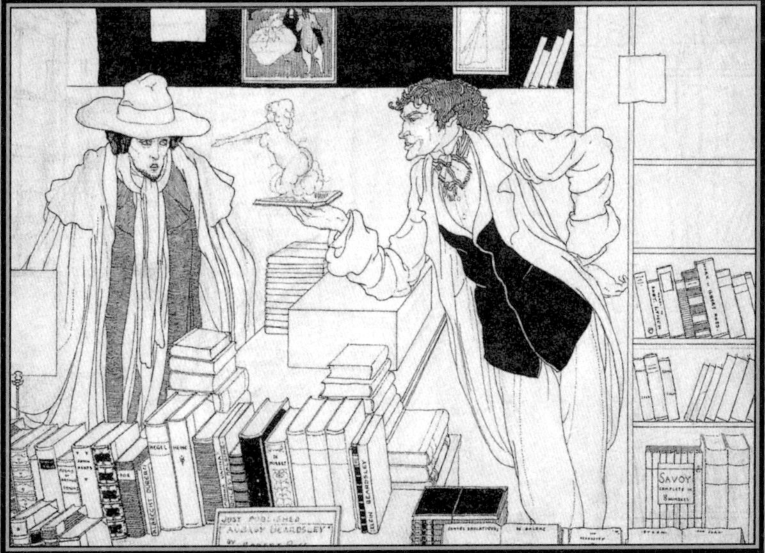

Illustration by Ilbery Lynch for an advertisement for Robert Ross's biography, *Aubrey Beardsley*. The picture shows a bookshop stocking many Beardsley books, with the author's picture hung on the wall.

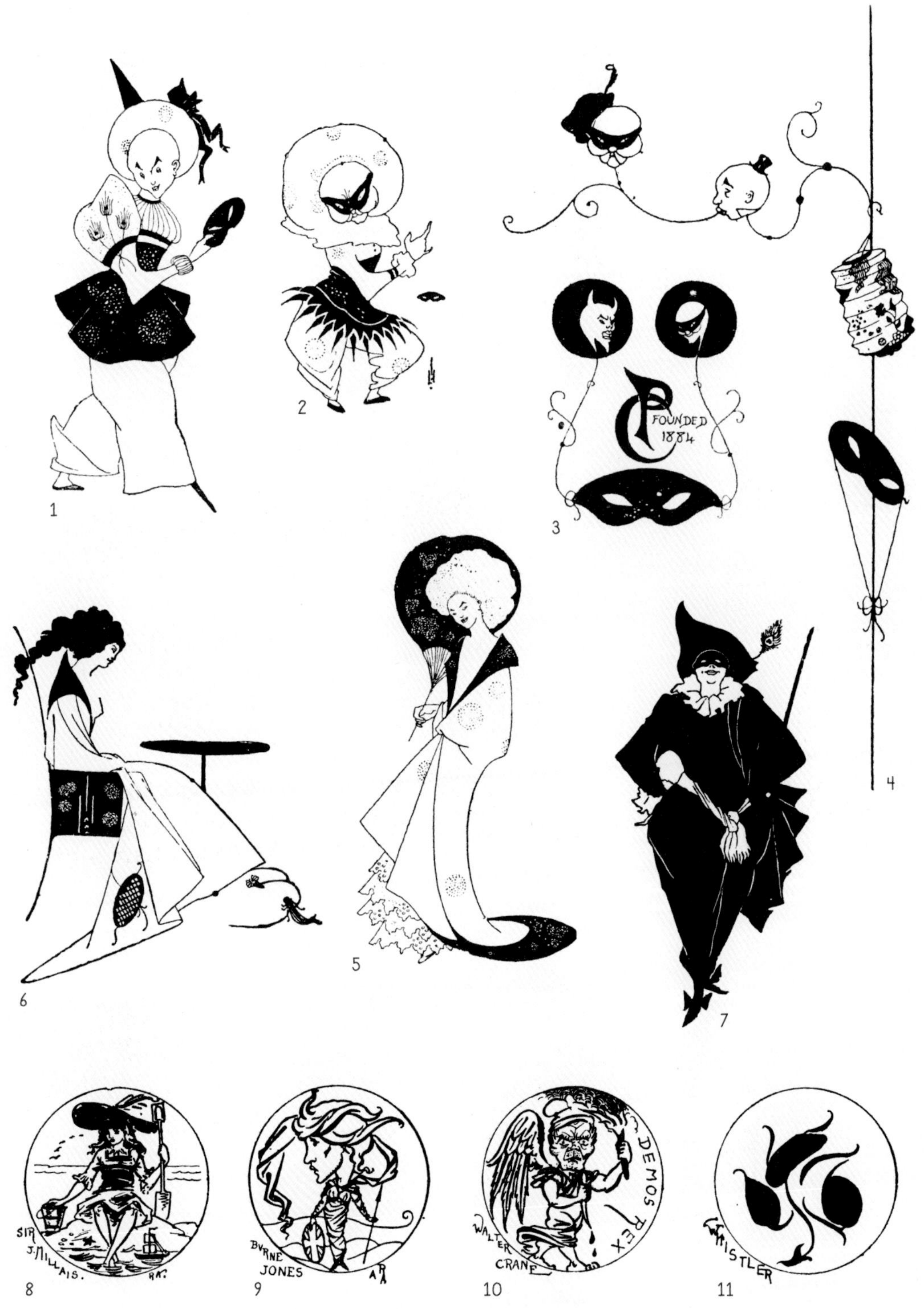

Small Illustrations I

1–5. Designs for the Playgoers' Club Menu (1894). 6. *Chapter Heading* (From *Saint Paul* magazine, 1894). 7. For John Davidson's poetry collection (1894). 8–11. Caricatures of Sir John Millais, Walter Klein, Edward Burne-Jones, and Whistler (*The Pall Mall Magazine*, 1893).

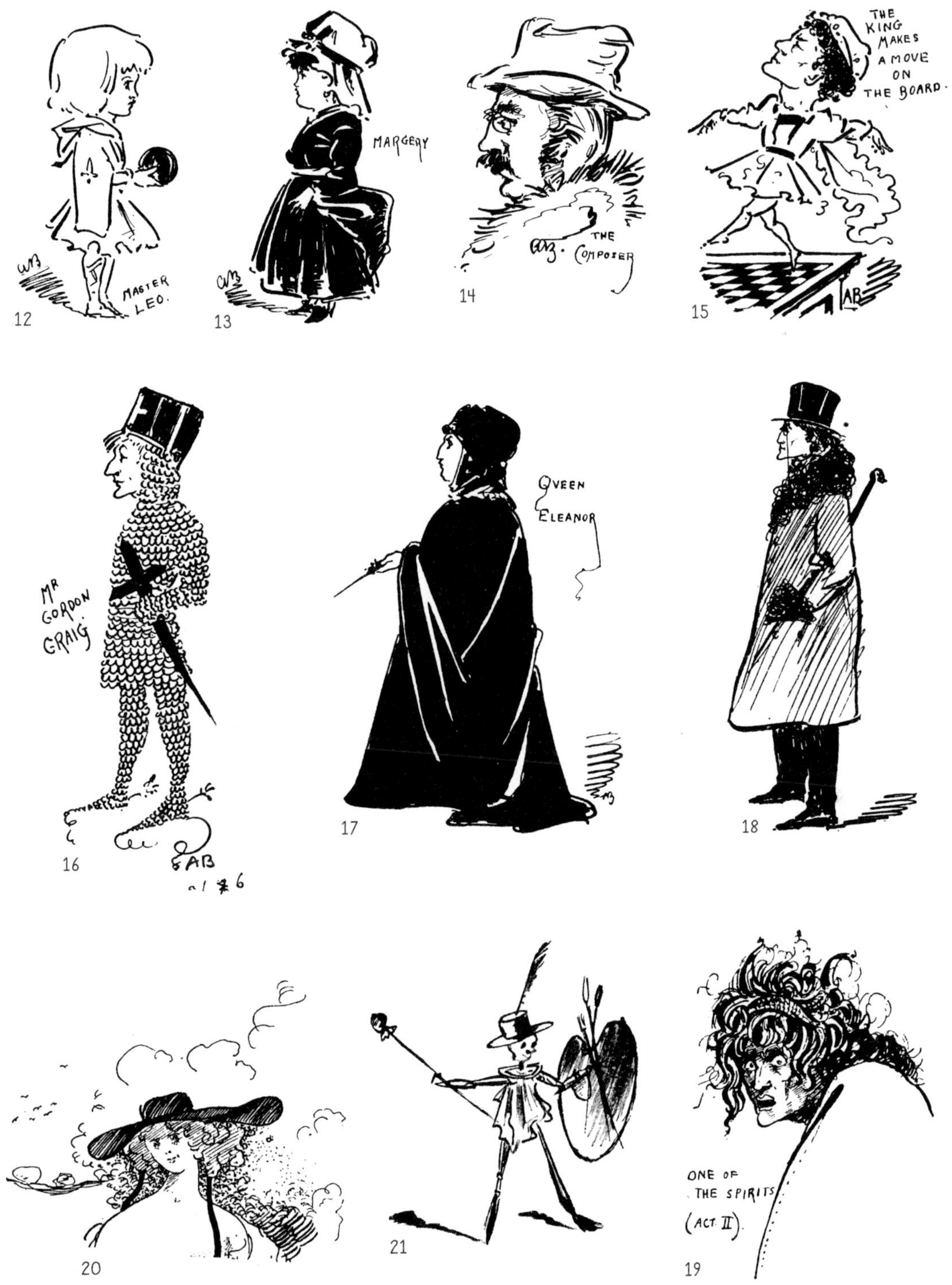

Small Illustrations II

12–17. Sketches from the play 'Becket,' in which Beardsley performed as a student. 18–19. Sketches from the play 'Orpheus' in which he performed as a student (from *The Pall Mall Magazine*, 1893). 20. Girl's face (from the artist's sketchbook.) 21. A small sketch in a letter to Frederick Scotson Clark (1891).

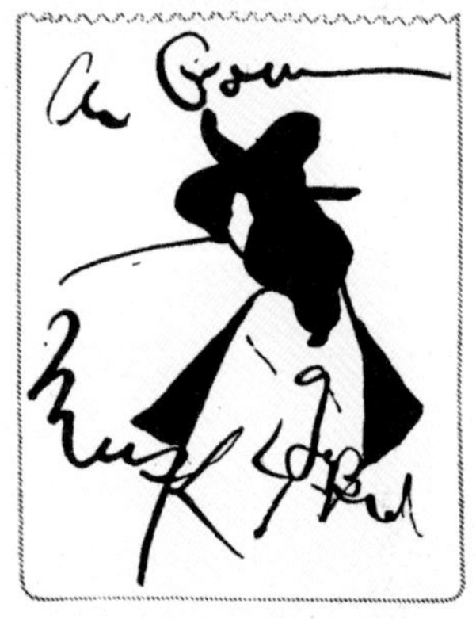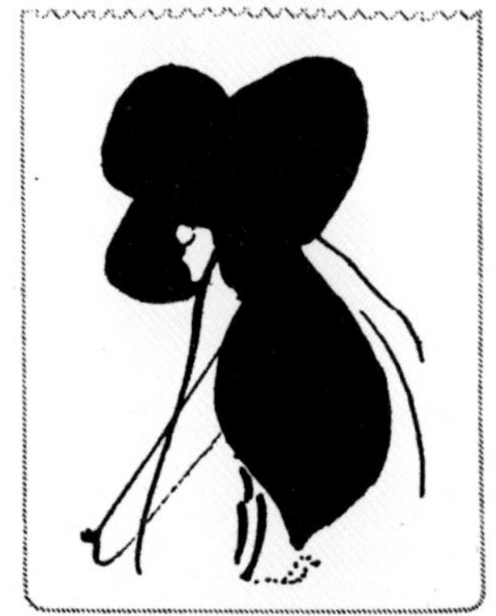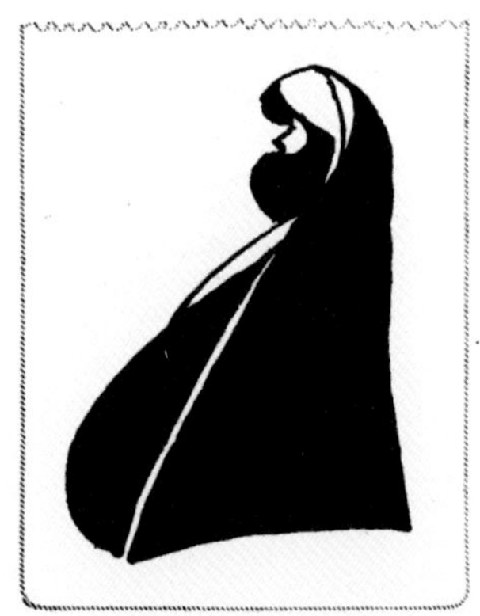
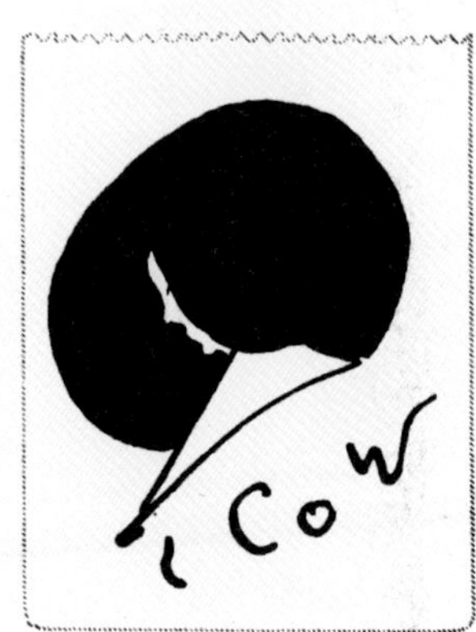

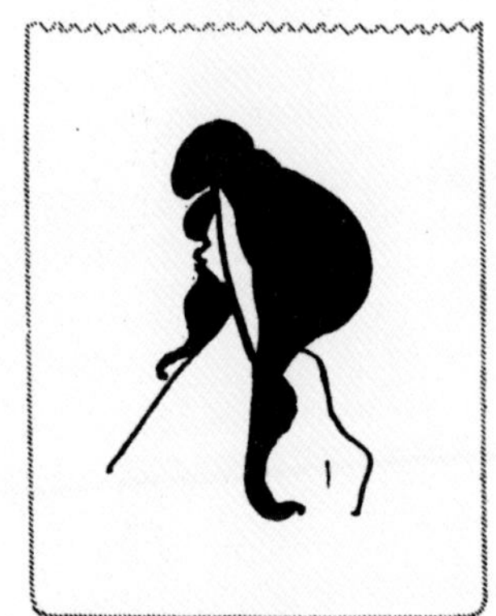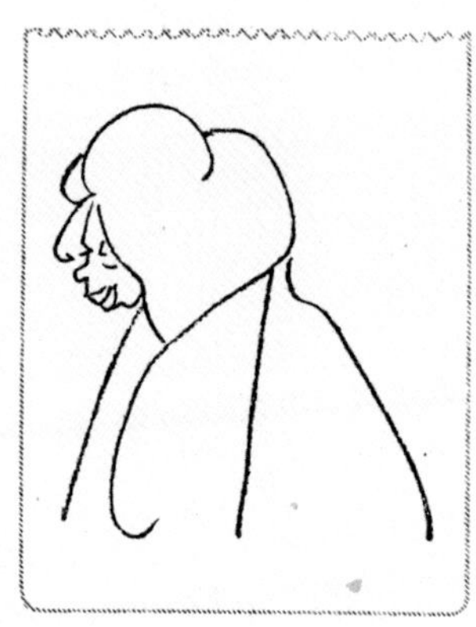
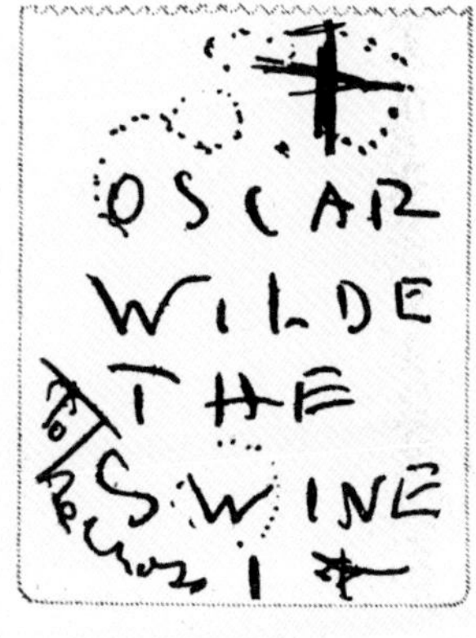

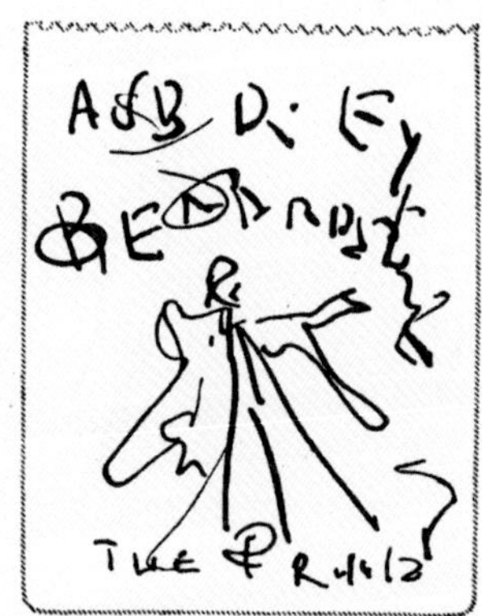

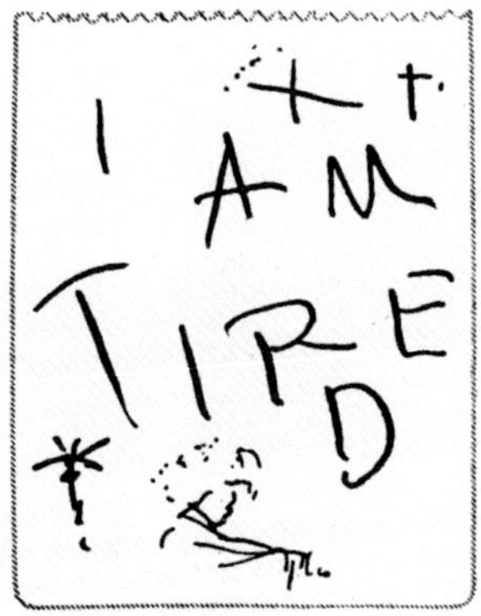

Small Illustrations III

From Beardsley's pocketbook (the ruled lines surrounding the pictures denote the size of the notebook).

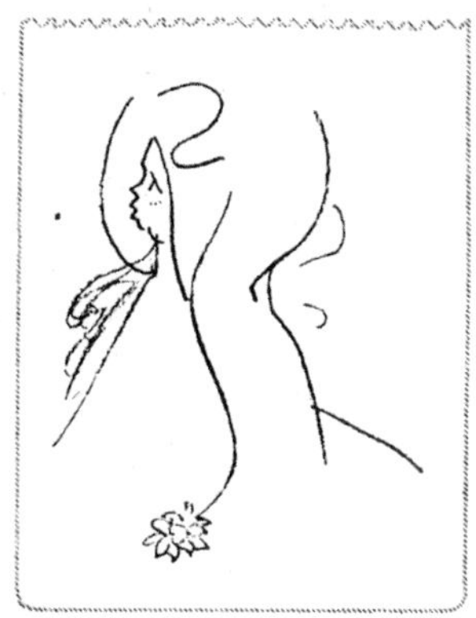

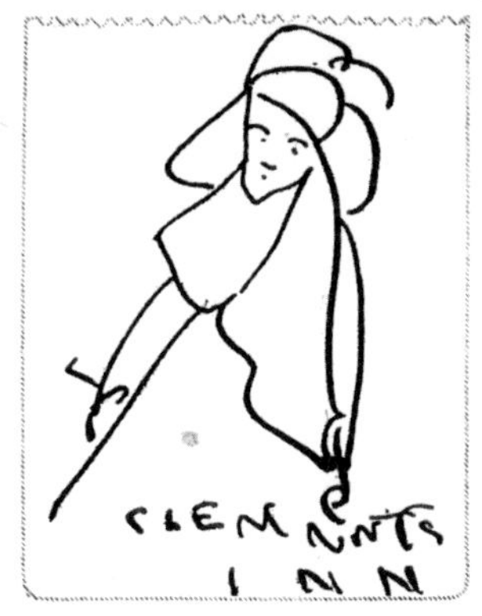

CLEMENTS
INN

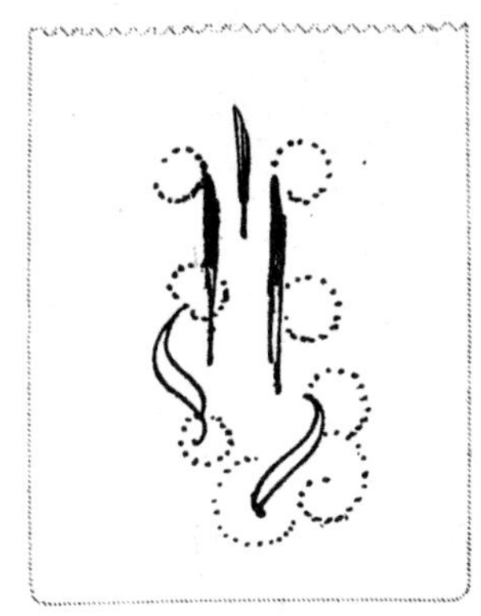

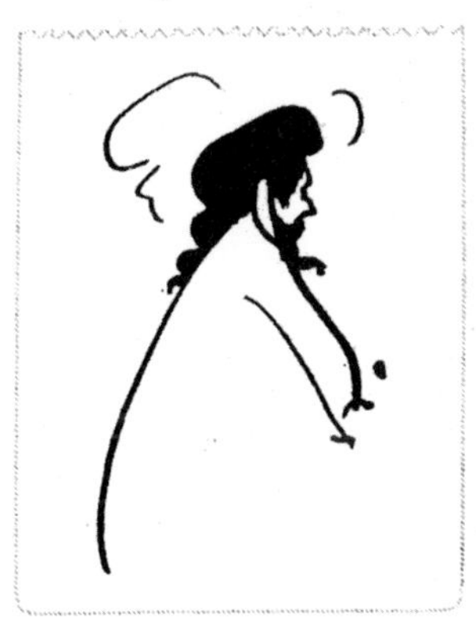

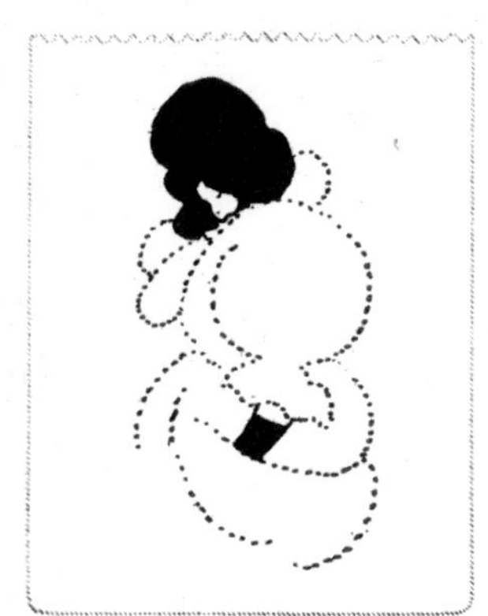

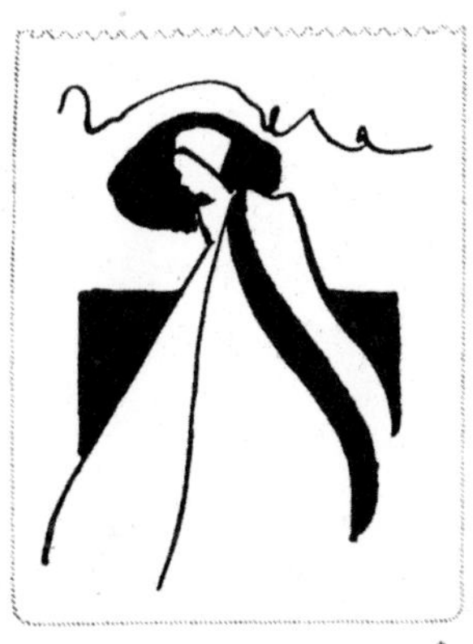

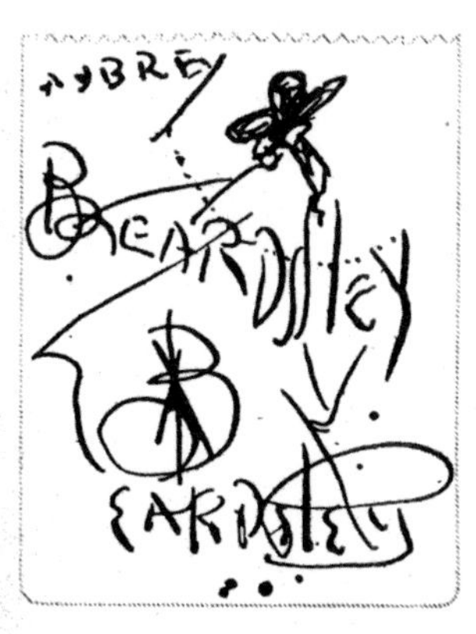

AVBREY
BEARDSLEY
BEARDSLEY

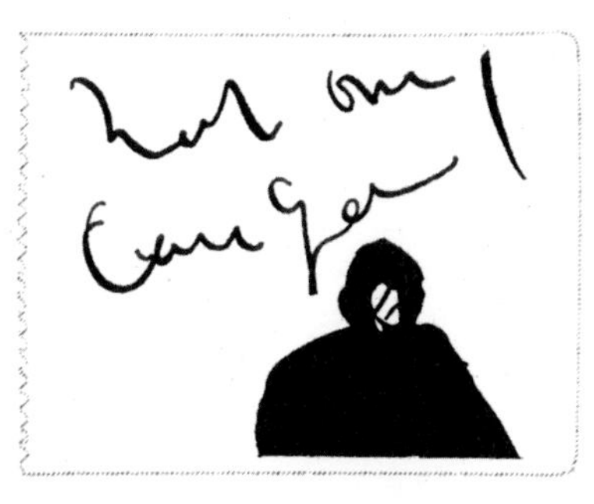

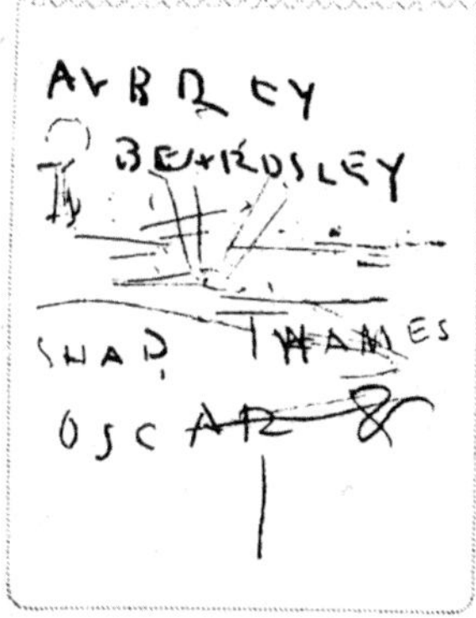

AVBREY
BEARDSLEY
SHAD THAMES
OSCAR

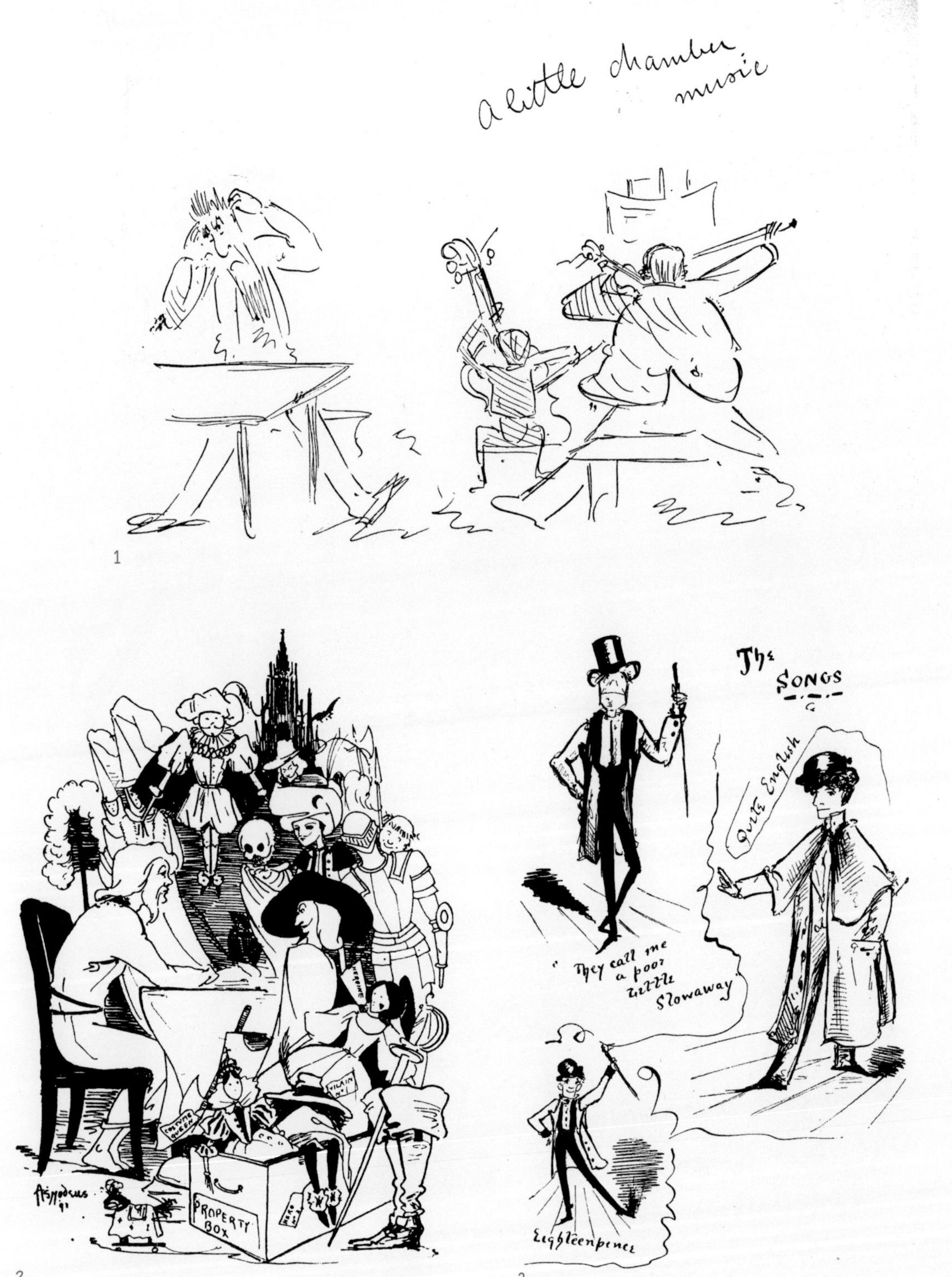

Beardsley's Sketches

1. 'A little chamber music', circa 1888. 2. 'Mr. Harrison's "Ideal Novelist"' (from *The Pall Mall Magazine*, 1893). 3–7. Programme designs Beardsley produced as a youngster 1884-85.

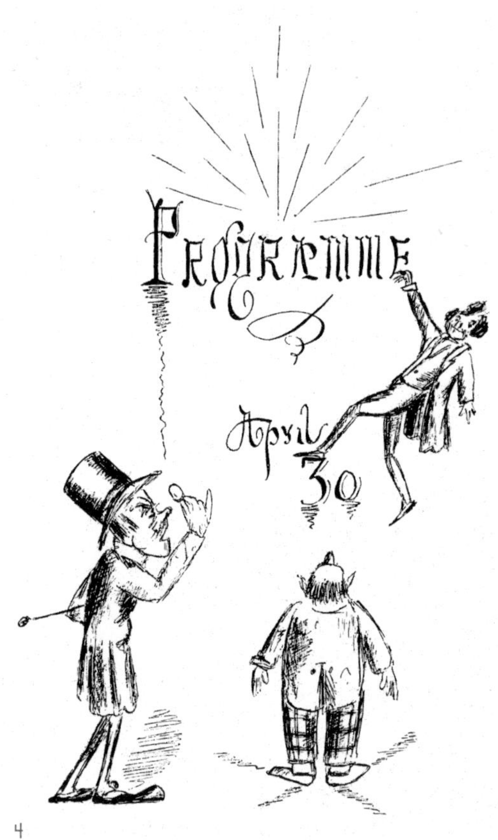

PROGRAMME
of
April 30

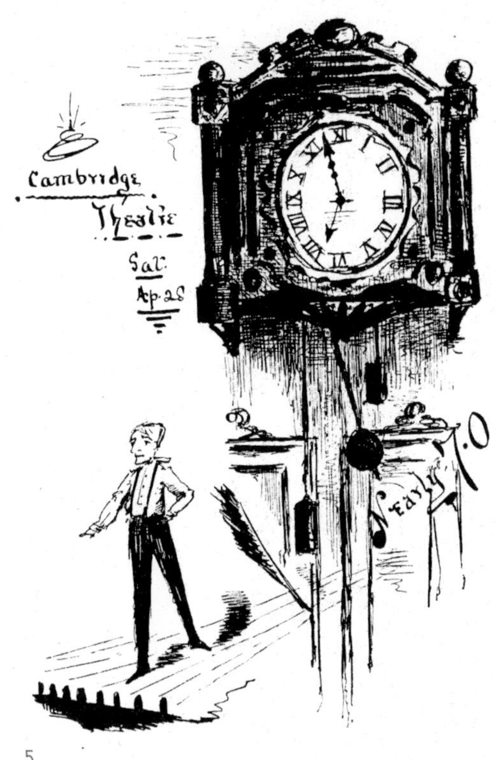

Cambridge
Theatre
Sat.
Ap. 28
Nearly 7.0

4

5

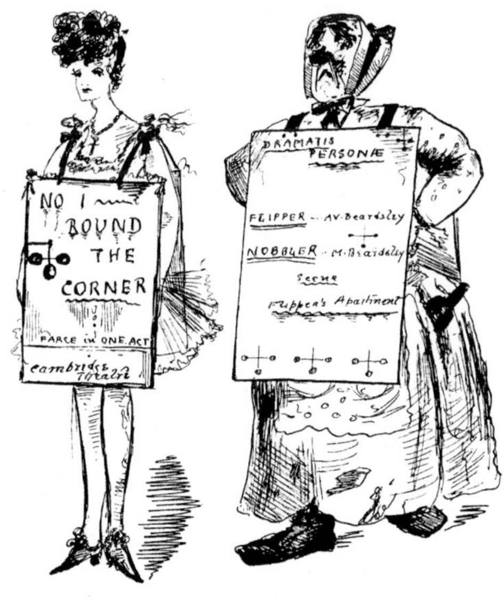

NO 1
BOUND
THE
CORNER
FARCE IN ONE ACT
Cambridge
Theatre
DRAMATIS
PERSONÆ
FLIPPER - A.V. Beardsley
NOBBLER - M. Beardsley
Scene
Flipper's Apartment
OPINIONS
OF THE PRESS
ON THE CAM. THEATRE
I prefer it to any other " (Ally Sloper)
How superior is the tone of this Theatre (Pink-un)
Modest Mabelle & vivacious Vincent
are truly unique (Referee)

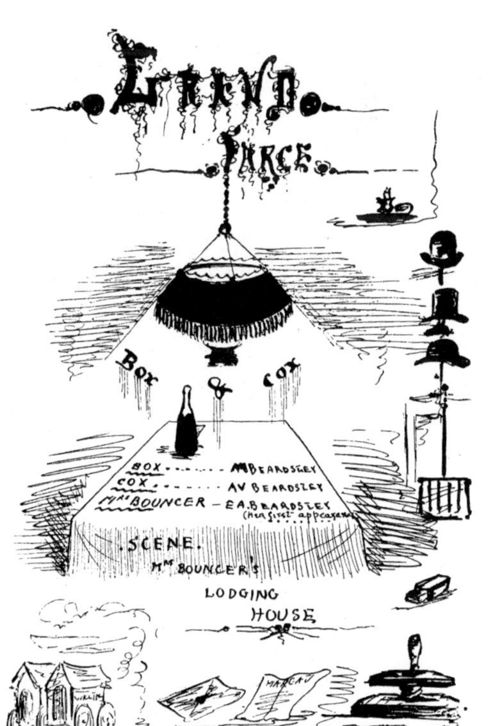

GRAND
FARCE
Box & Cox
BOX .... M. Beardsley
COX .... A.V. Beardsley
Mrs BOUNCER - E.A. Beardsley
(her first appearance)
SCENE.
Mrs BOUNCER'S
LODGING
HOUSE

6

7

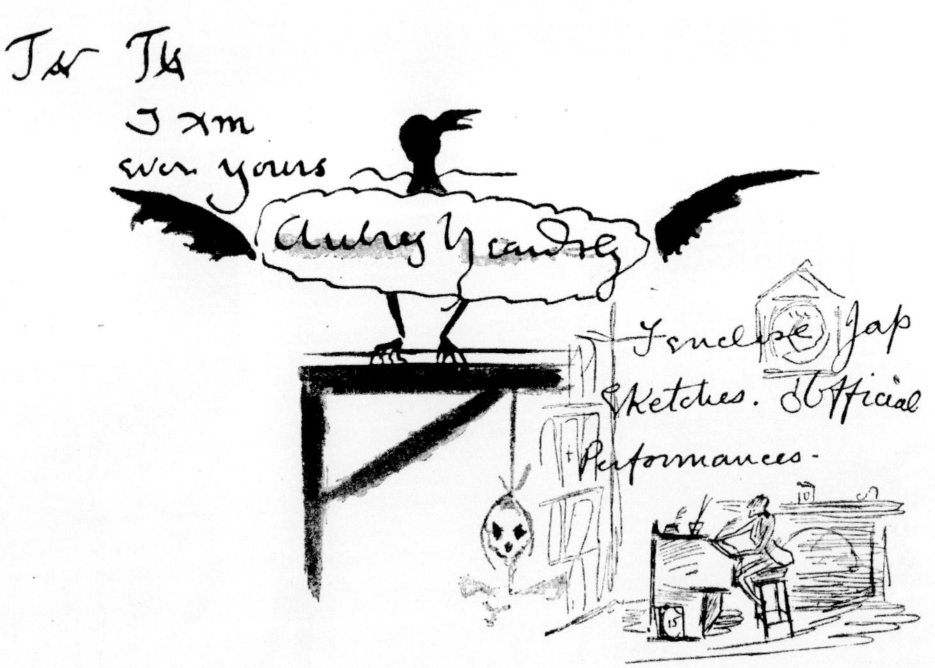

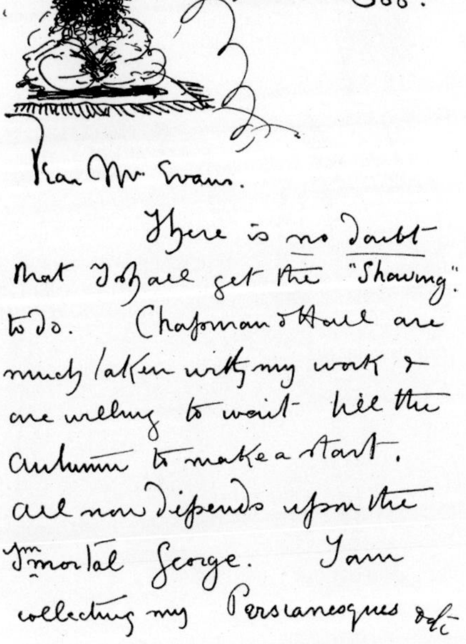

Beardsley's Letters

Top: Letter written to his friend Frederick Scotson Clark in his student days (1891). Beardsley writes of his excitement at having seen Whistler's Peacock Room.

Bottom left: Letter to Frederick Scotson Clark (1893). He recommends that Scotson-Clark returns from London, writing that 'England after all is the place for oof and fame.'

Bottom right: Letter to Frederick H. Evans (ca 1893). He writes that he is focusing on producing work to show George (Bernard-Shaw).

Right-hand page: Letter to his benefactor, Arthur King (1893). He tells him of his news since moving to London, writing that his job 'is not hard'.

I am very glad the new Matron
is pleasant. I suppose that means
some respectable suppers for you

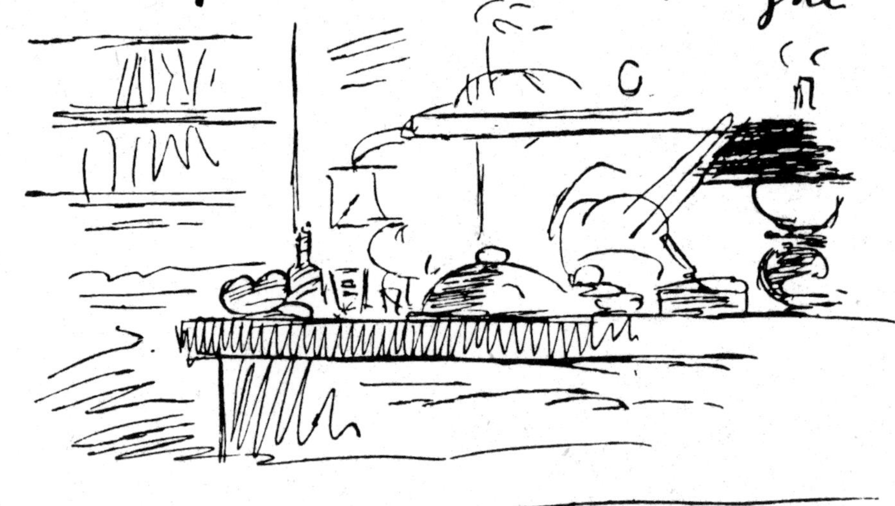

who is in your room this term?

I have been "In Business" since new
years day I dont exactly dislike but
am not (as yet) frantically attached
to it. My work however is but hard.

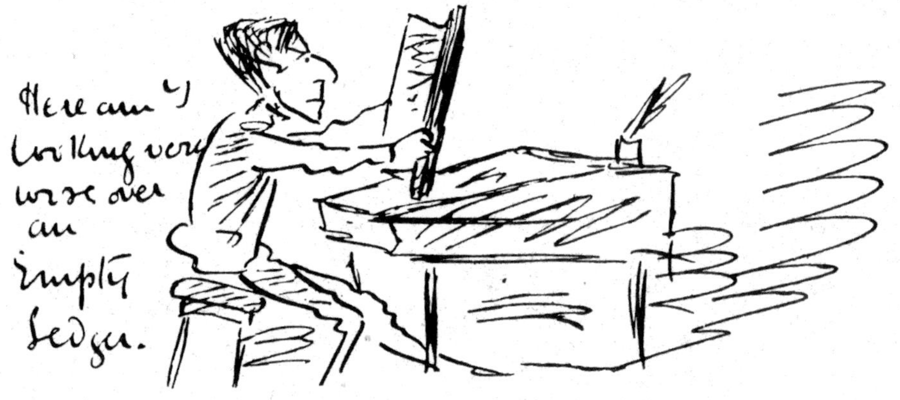

KEY BEARDSLEY FEATURES I

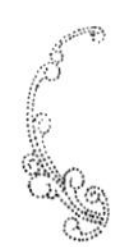

BEARDSLEY'S SIGNATURE

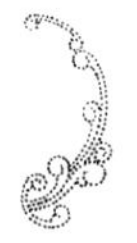

The mark that Beardsley used in place of a signature featured a longer line, signifying a phallus, sandwiched between two lines, with semen dripping from the end. This Beardsley would secrete somewhere within his pictures, and is particularly often seen in works around the *Salome* era.

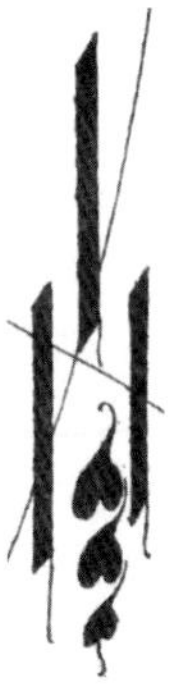

p.29

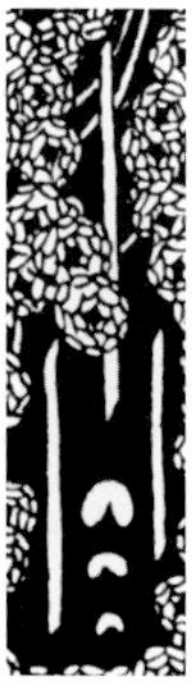

p.30

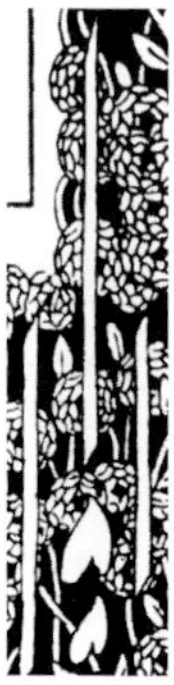

p.31

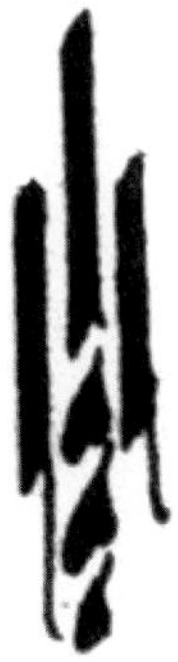

p.32

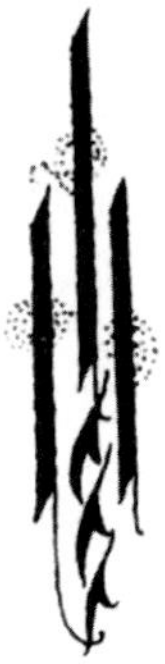

p.33

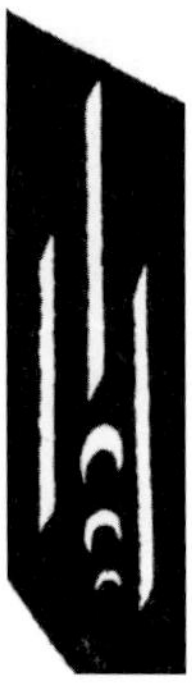

p.34

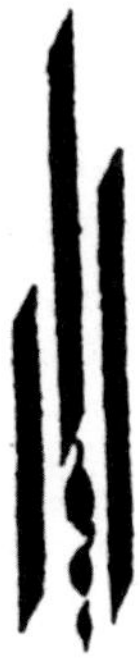

p.35

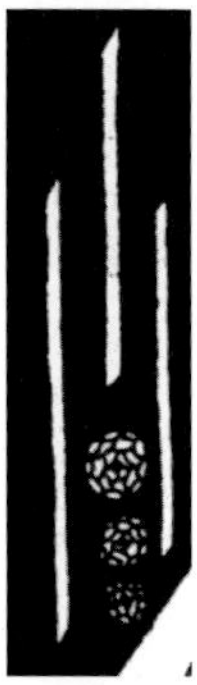

p.36-37

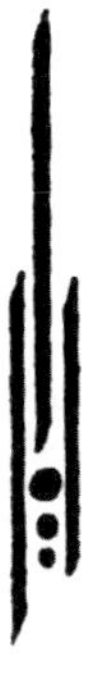

p.38

p.39

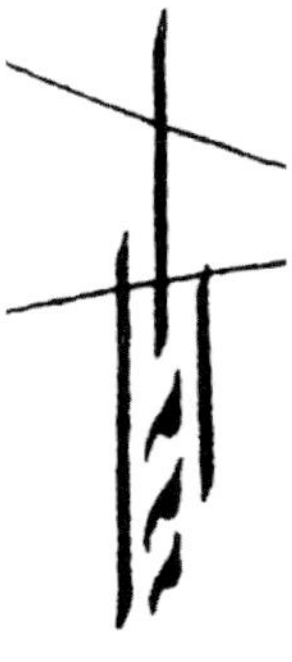

p.40

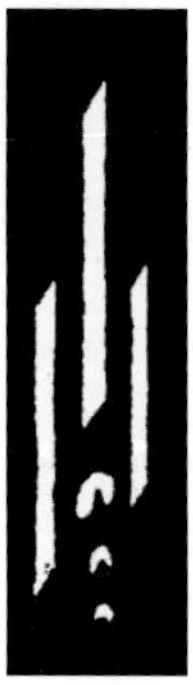

p.41

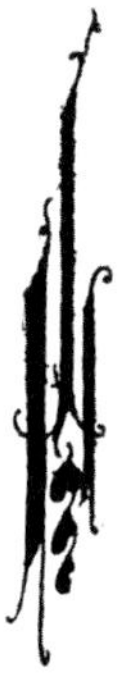

p.42
p.43 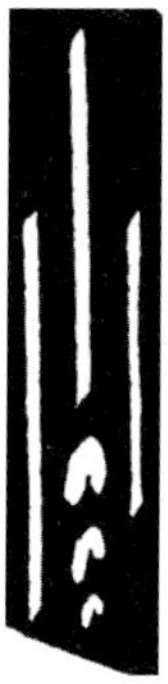
p.44 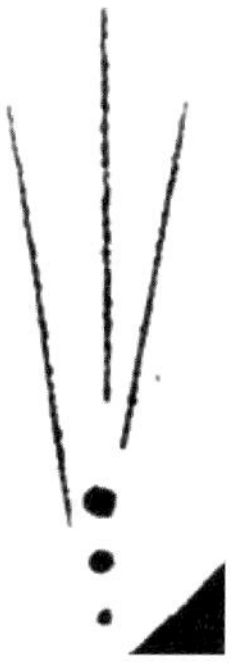
p.45
p.47
p.51 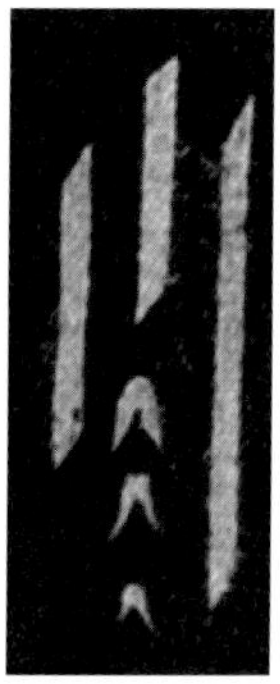
p.54 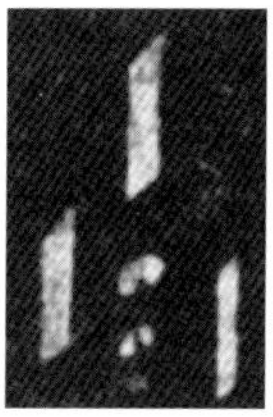
p.60 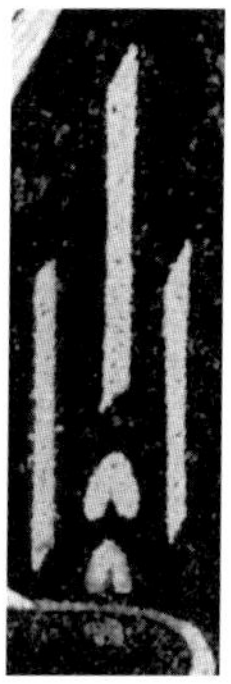
p.63 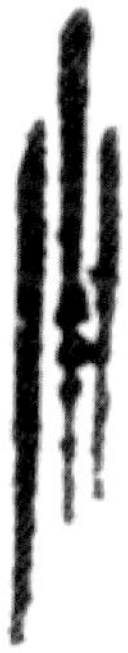
p.69 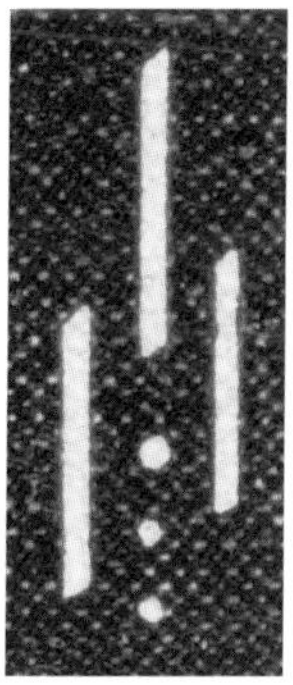
p.71 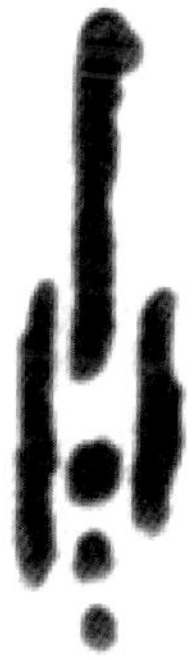
p.72 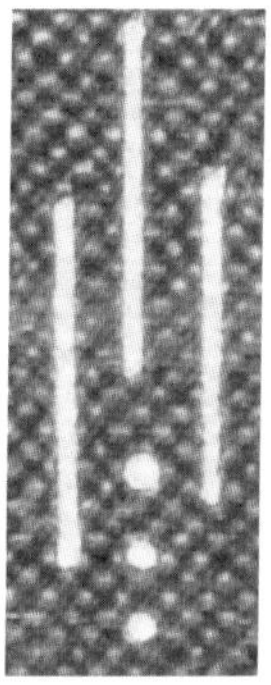
p.73 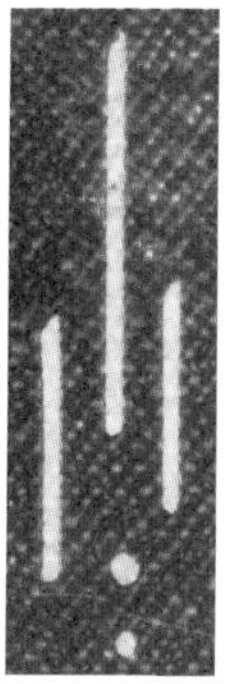
p.74 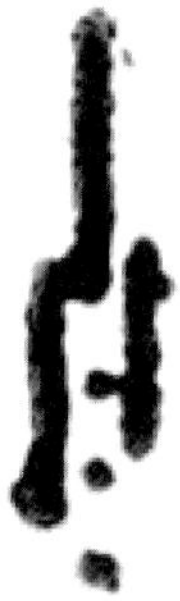
p.92 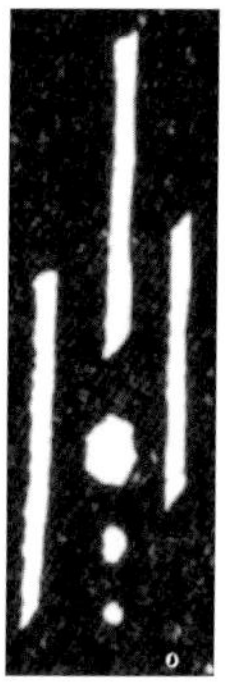
p.96

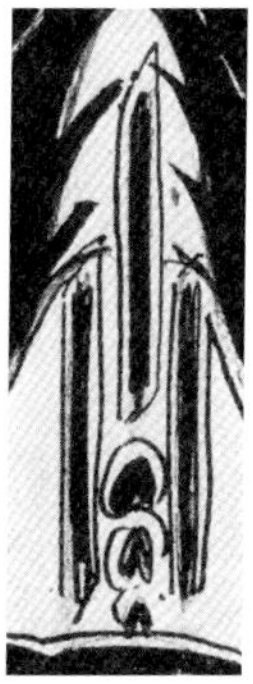

KEY BEARDSLEY FEATURES II

BEARDSLEY'S EXPRESSIVE RANGE

Beardsley's facial expressions were somewhat distinctive. In these we can see the movings of his very human heart, glimpsing his sense of mischief towards those to whom he felt antipathy, as well as his ironic take on the world.

Scorn and sneers

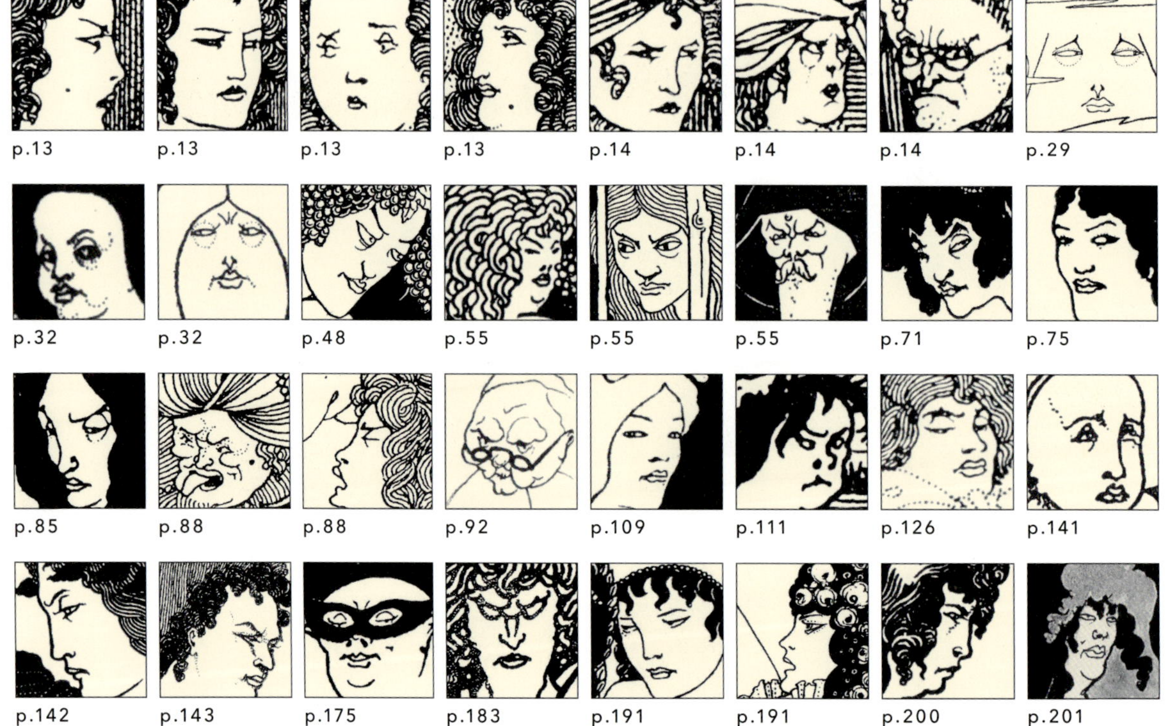

p.13   p.13   p.13   p.13   p.14   p.14   p.14   p.29

p.32   p.32   p.48   p.55   p.55   p.55   p.71   p.75

p.85   p.88   p.88   p.92   p.109   p.111   p.126   p.141

p.142   p.143   p.175   p.183   p.191   p.191   p.200   p.201

Blank faces

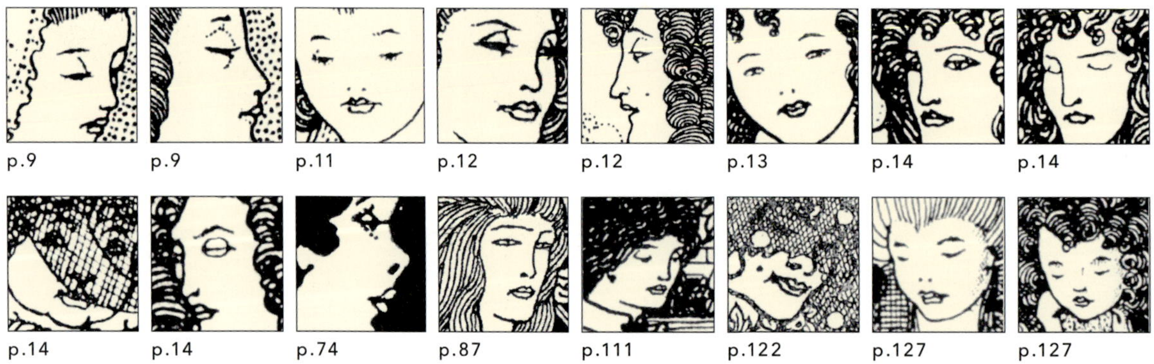

p.9   p.9   p.11   p.12   p.12   p.13   p.14   p.14

p.14   p.14   p.74   p.87   p.111   p.122   p.127   p.127

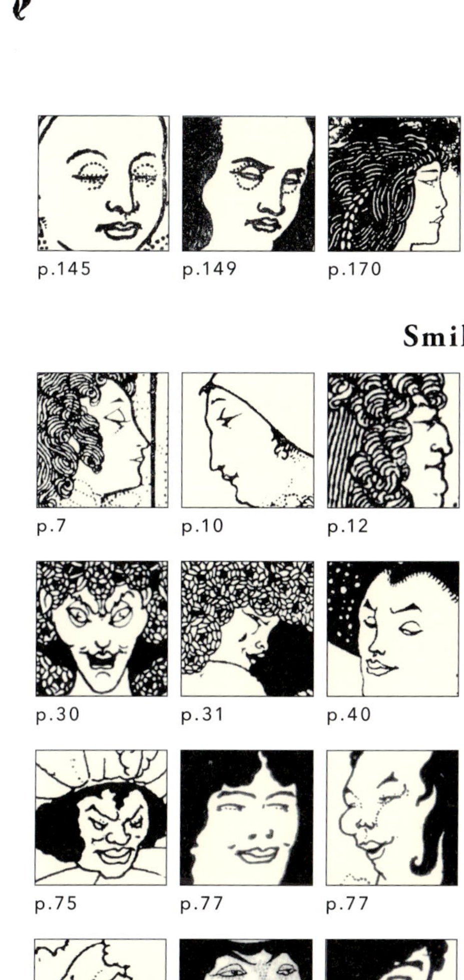

p.145　　p.149　　p.170　　p.171　　p.178　　p.183　　p.199　　p.212

Smiles and strange laughter

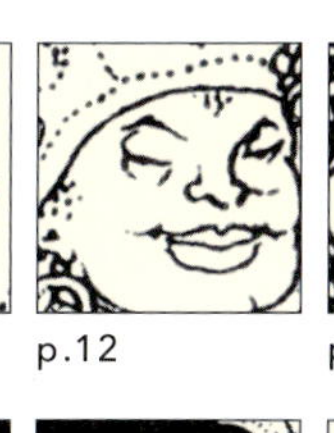 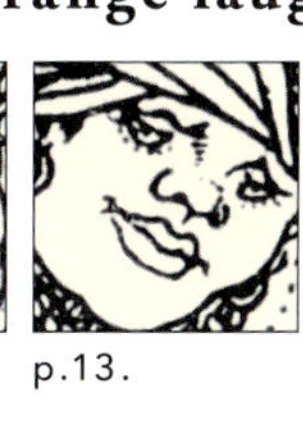 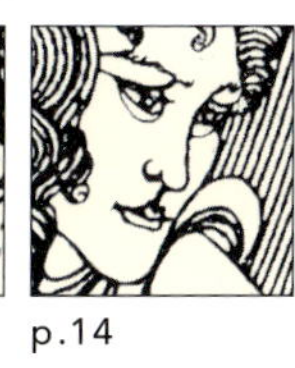 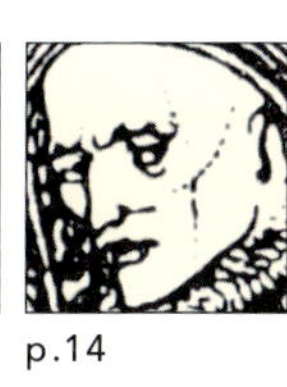 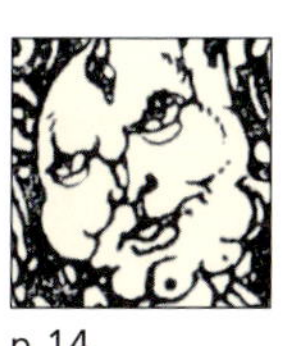

p.7　　p.10　　p.12　　p.12　　p.13.　　p.14　　p.14　　p.14

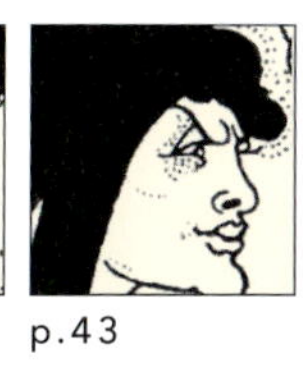 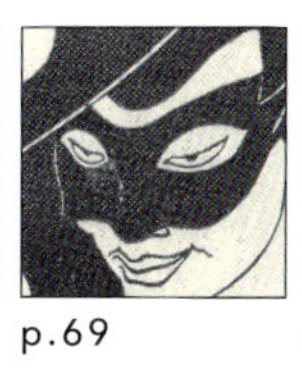 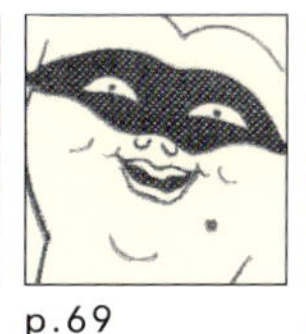 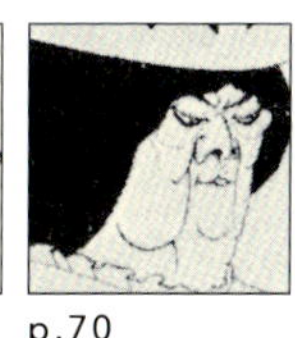 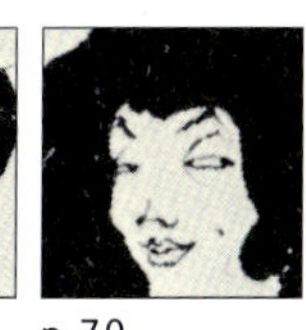

p.30　　p.31　　p.40　　p.43　　p.69　　p.69　　p.70　　p.70

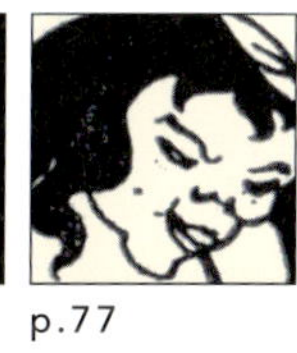 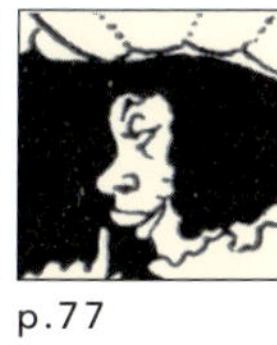 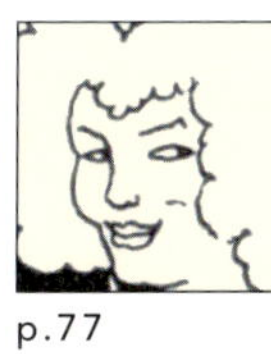 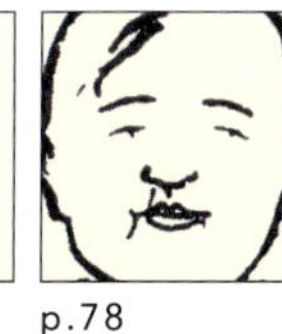 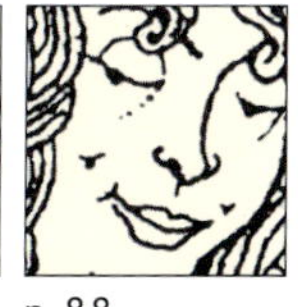

p.75　　p.77　　p.77　　p.77　　p.77　　p.77　　p.78　　p.88

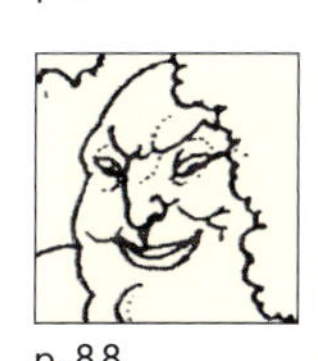 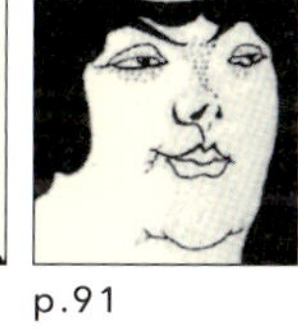 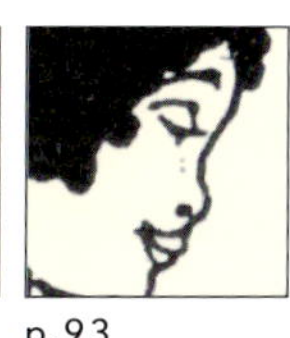 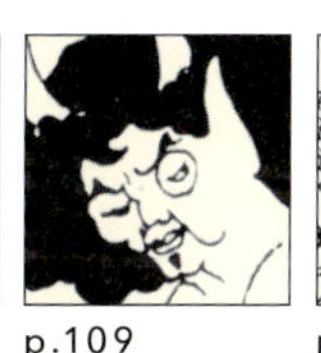 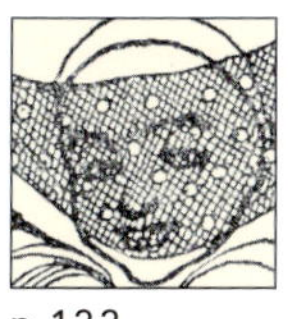 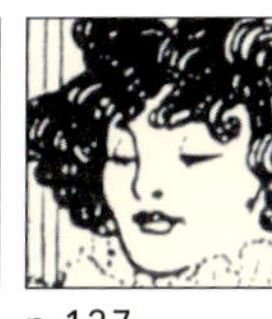 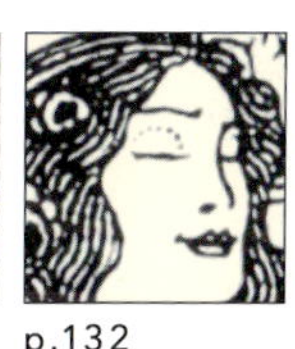 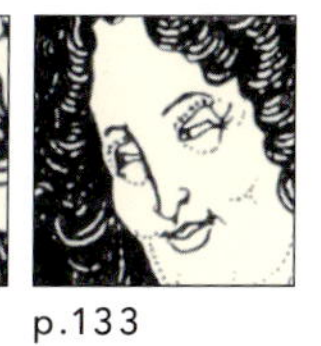

p.88　　p.91　　p.93　　p.109　　p.122　　p.127　　p.132　　p.133

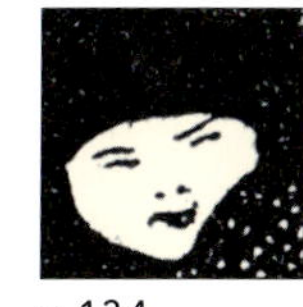 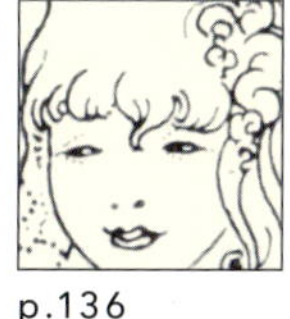 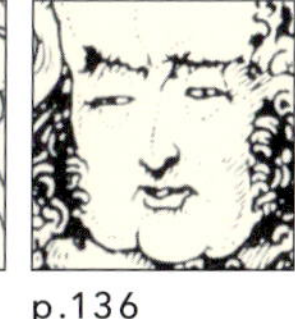 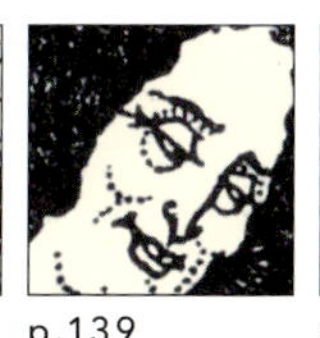 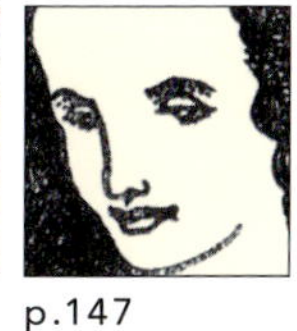 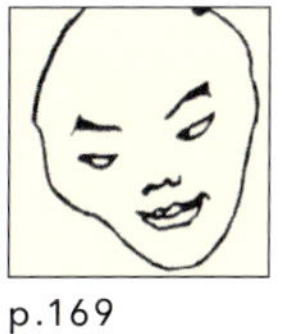 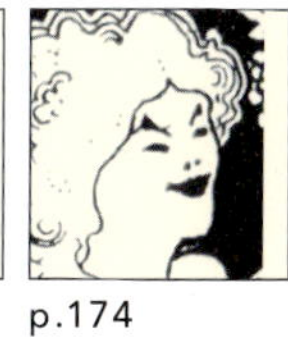 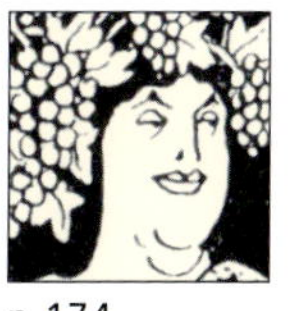

p.134　　p.136　　p.136　　p.139　　p.147　　p.169　　p.174　　p.174

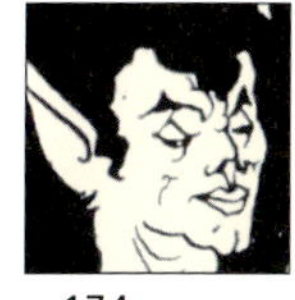 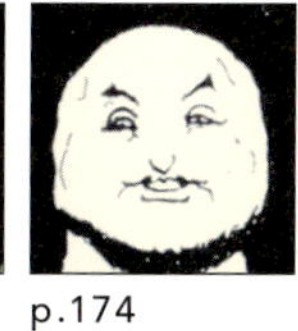 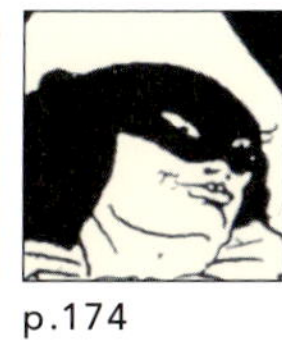 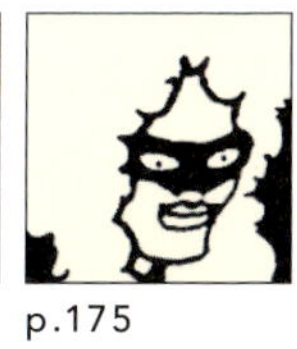 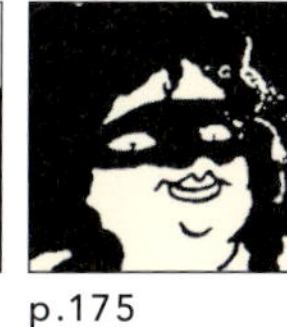 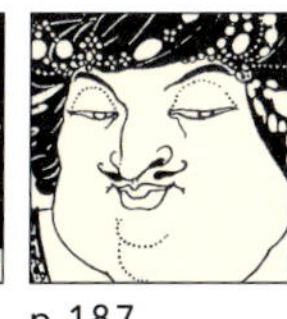 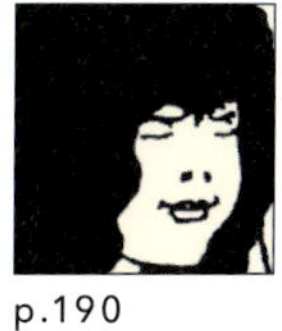 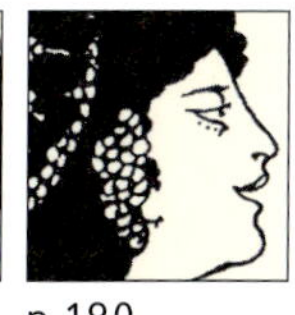

p.174　　p.174　　p.174　　p.175　　p.175　　p.187　　p.190　　p.190

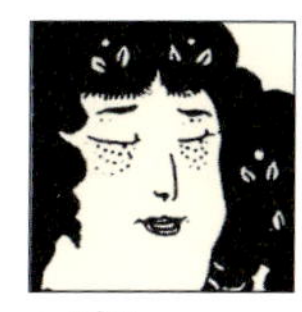 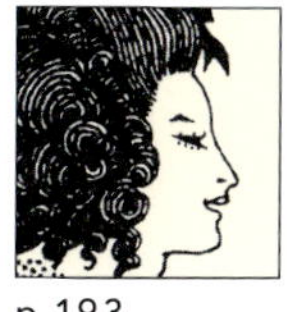 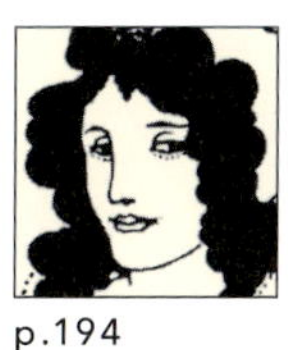 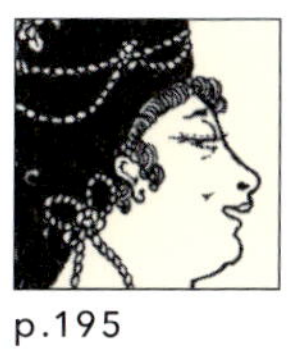 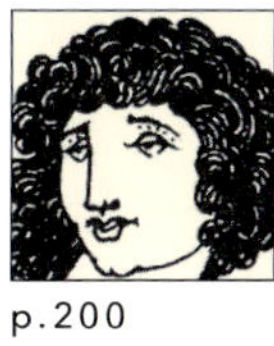 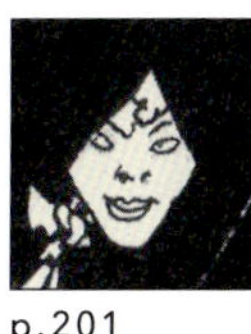 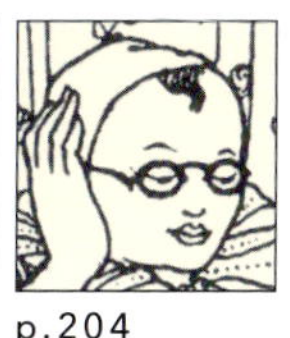 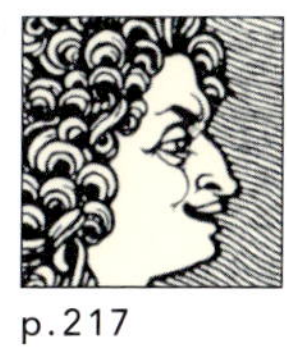

p.191　　p.193　　p.194　　p.195　　p.200　　p.201　　p.204　　p.217

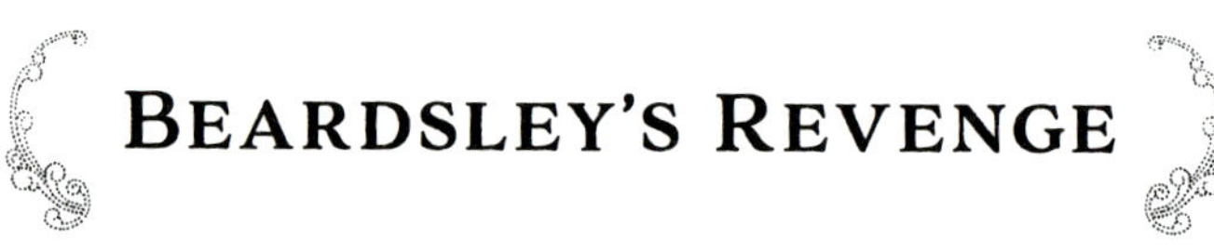

KEY BEARDSLEY FEATURES III

BEARDSLEY'S REVENGE

When Beardsley was angry with someone, he would frequently insert a cruelly rendered portrait of them into his pictures as a form of revenge. It was a childish tactic to be sure, but looking at the caricatures of Oscar Wilde in *Salome*, we find a touch of genius even in their cruelty.

Revenge on *The Yellow Book*

To get back at *The Yellow Book*, where he had worked as editor but been kicked out, Beardsley created a cover for the first volume of *The Savoy* magazine where he was now working featuring a cherub urinating on a copy of *The Yellow Book* (although *The Savoy*'s editor Smithers immediately ordered he revise it).

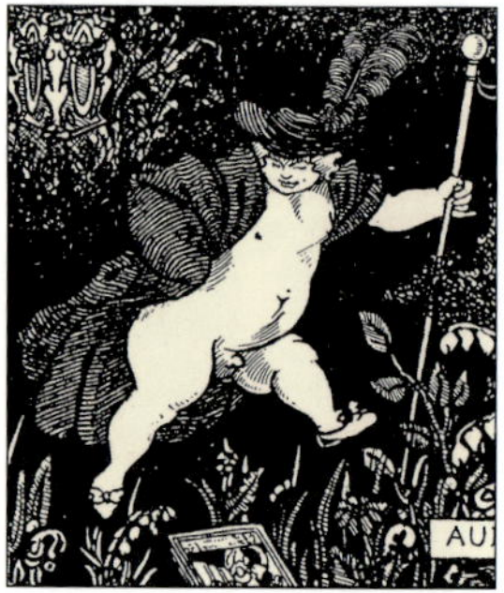

Revenge on Whistler

Initially, Beardsley had felt admiration towards Whistler, but after the artist termed his pictures in bad taste, Beardsley began drawing caricatures not only of Whistler himself but of his wife too, which succeeded in angering Whistler (although later, seeing his illustrations for *The Rape of the Lock*, Whistler recognized Beardsley's talent, and the two were reconciled).

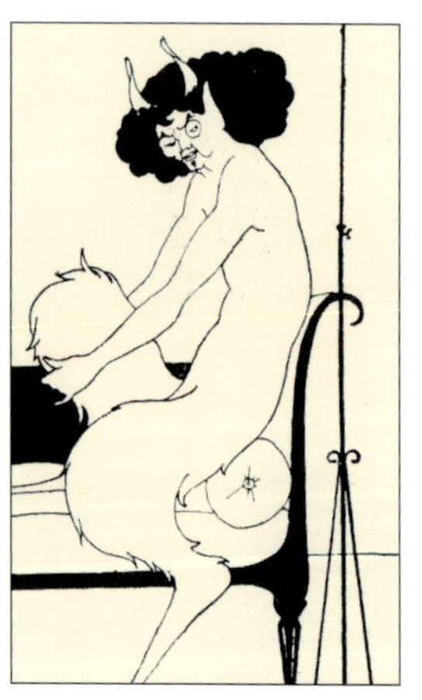

p.109

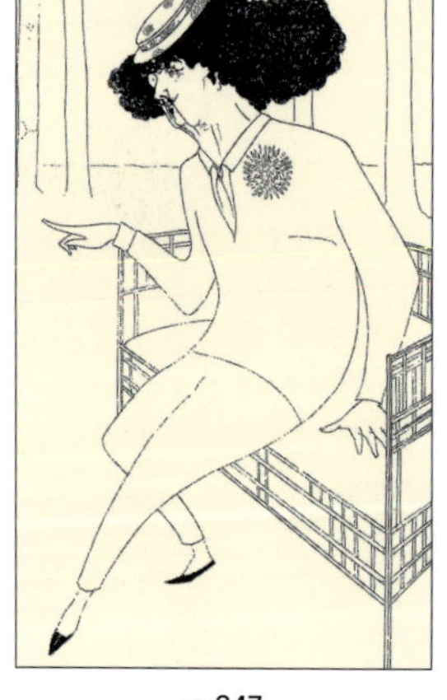

p.247

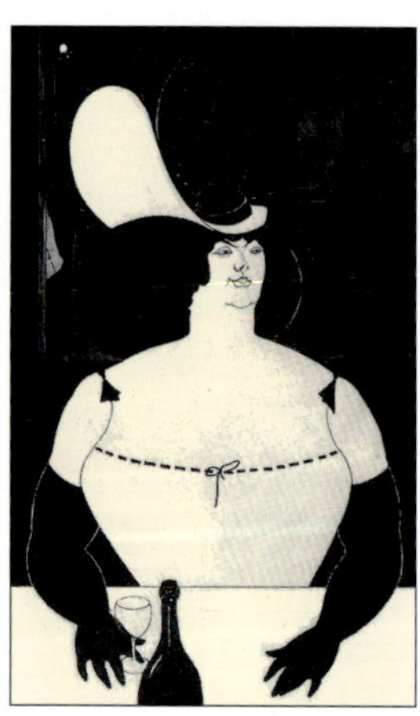

p.91

Revenge on Wilde

Beardsley had first admired Oscar Wilde, and felt honoured to work with him, but he grew progressively tired of the hedonistic and egotistical Wilde, and began to find Wilde's attempts to act as guardian tiresome.

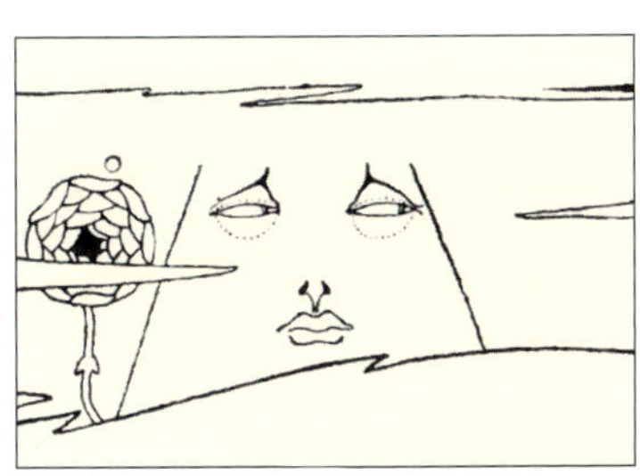

p.29

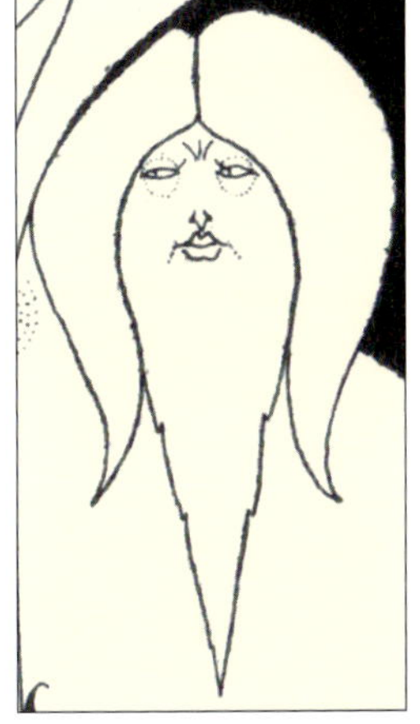

p.32

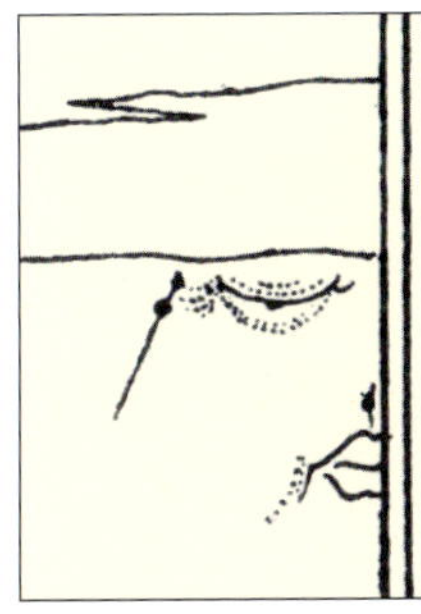

p.35

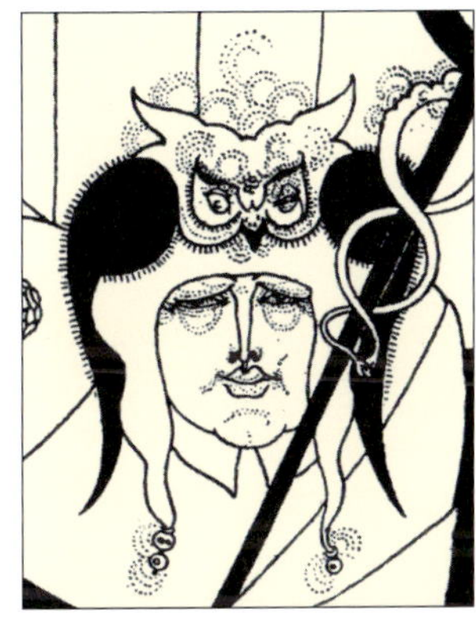

p.37

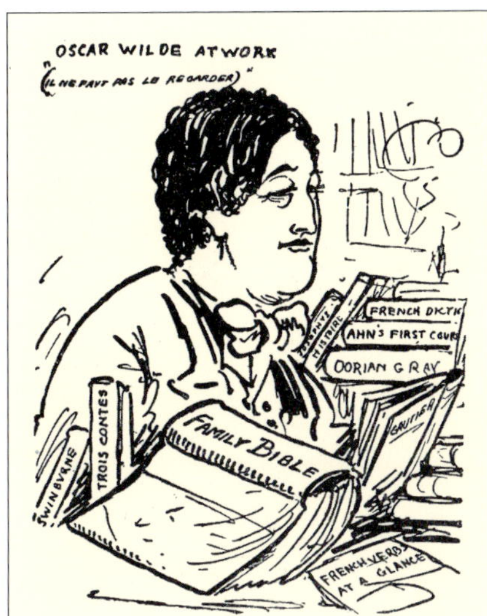

p.26

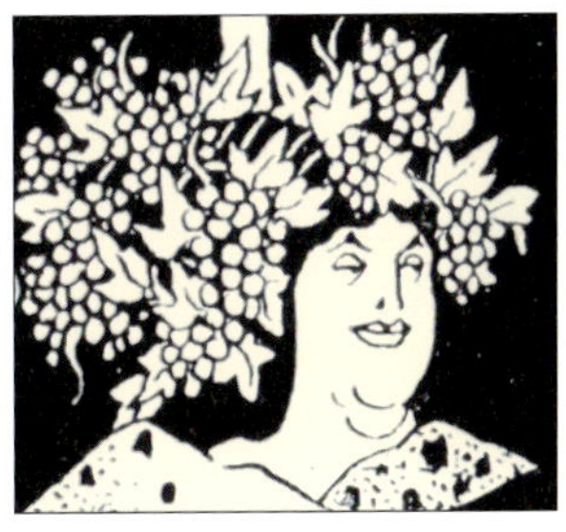

p.174

Caricatures of Wilde. As a dig at Wilde, who liked to boast that he had written *Salomé* in French without consulting any reference materials, Beardsley included books called *Grammar*, *French Verbs a Glance*, and *Ann's First Course* in the piles of books by which surrounding him.

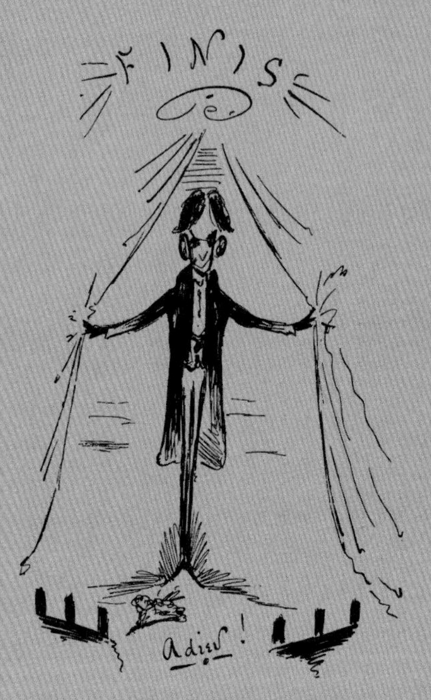
FINIS
Adiù!

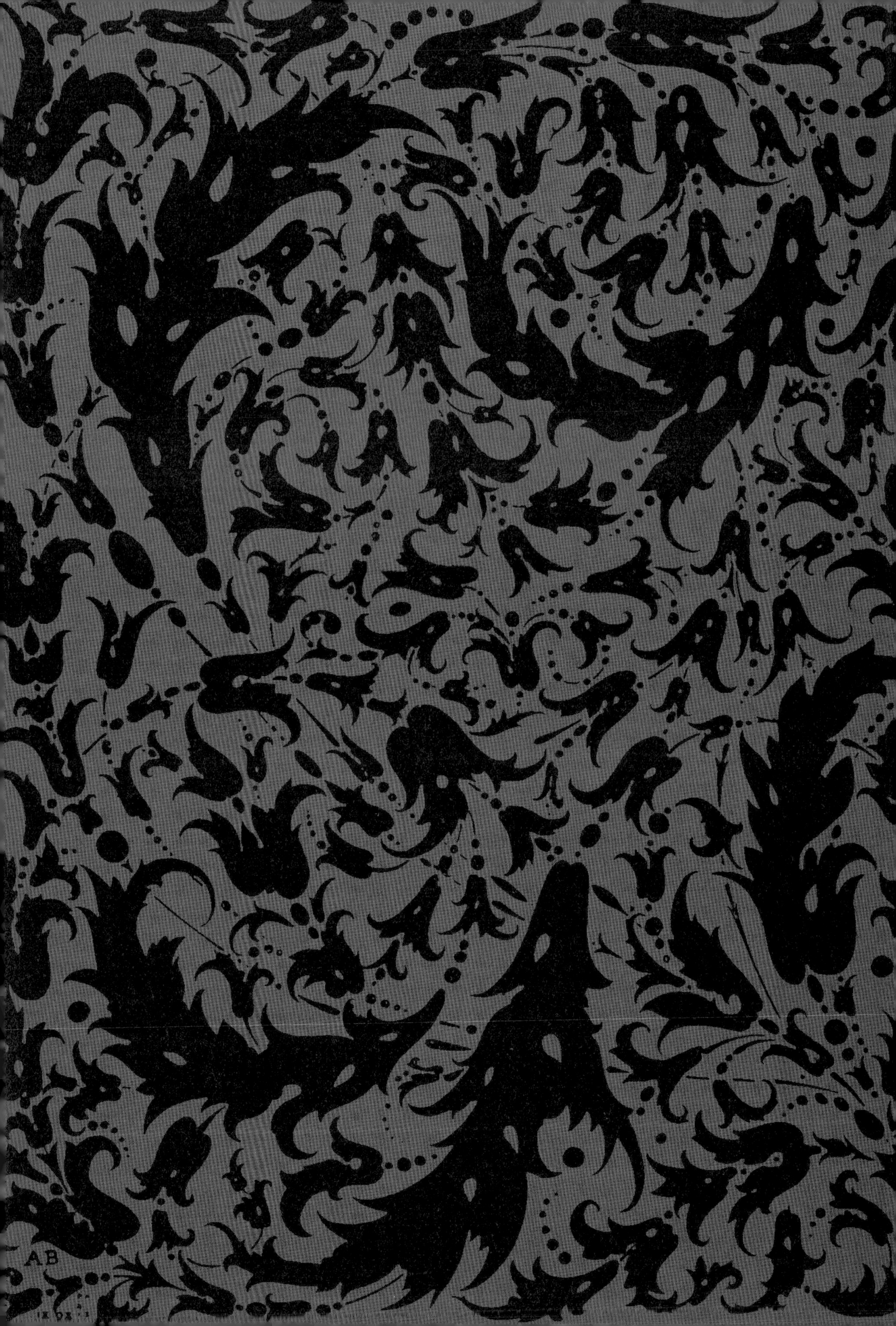

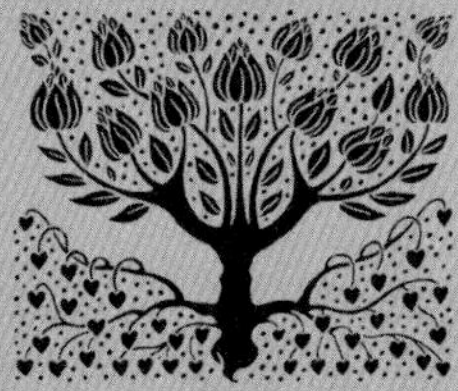

HIROSHI UNNO

Born in Tokyo, 1939. Hiroshi Unno is a critic and writer who has contributed to many books on fin-de-siècle arts. He wrote his first book on art nouveau in the 1960s focusing on this movement when nobody was paying attention to it at that time. After working as an editor he became a freelance writer and critic, contributing to a wide range of fields, from the reassessment of Art Deco, City Theory to Music, Cinema and Fashion. He is one of the most popular contributors at PIE International. His western art collection series, which was first published in 2011, now has 23 titles in the series and many of the titles are distributed worldwide. His book, *The Art of Fantasy, Sci-Fi and Steampunk* has won Foreword Indies 2018 Book Gold Award for Art.

RELATED TITLES BY THE AUTHOR

Fantastical Illustrations of Fairy Tales (2011)
George Barbier (2011)
Art Deco Fashion Illustrations (2012)
The World Flower Book (2012)
Fairy Tales in Old Books (2012)
Russian Children's Book Illustrations and Fairy Tales (2012)
William Morris (2013)
The History of French Ornaments and Motifs (2013)
Aubrey Beardsley (2013)
Icon of Europe: Mythology, Legend, Fairy Tales (2013)
Harry Clarke (2014)
Czech Children's Book Illustrations (2014)
Avant-Garde Graphics in Russia (2015)
Northern European Folk Tale and Mythological Illustration (2015)
The World of Matisse's Cut-outs and Illustrations (2016)
Beautiful Book Designs (2016)
The World of Mucha (2016)
A Thousand and One Nights (2016)
The Art of Decadence (2017)
Icons of Europe: The Story of Flower Art (2017)
The Art of Fantasy, Sci-fi and Steampunk (2017)
The World of Gustav Klimt (2018)
The Art of Fairy Tale Illustrations in Black and White (2018)

*All of them above were published by PIE International Inc.

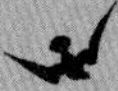

AUBREY BEARDSLEY
THE FIN-DE-SIÈCLE MAGICIAN OF LIGHT AND DARKNESS

AUTHOR: HIROSHI UNNO

First English edition published in March 2020 by PIE International Inc.,
2–32–4 Minami-Otsuka, Toshima-ku, Tokyo, Japan 170–0005

www.pie.co.jp/english
international@pie.co.jp

Art direction and cover design: Reiko Harajo
Design: Sayuri Seria Takamatsu (PIE Graphics)
Editor: Kayako Nezu (PIE International)

Photography: Kuniharu Fujimoto and Jin Hongo
Additional images provided by Art Harvest, Wayo Women's University,
Media Center, and Pacific Press Service

English edition
English translation: Polly Barton
Typesetting and design (English edition): Bonnie Pong-Wai Ma
Copyediting and production: Kyoko Wada (Goliga Books)

ISBN: 978-4-7562-5288-3

First Printing in March 2020

Printed and bound in Singapore